A Sailor's Guide
to Production Sailboats

D1614339

A Sailor's Guide to Production Sailboats

Roger Marshall

Hearst Marine Books
New York

Library of Congress Cataloging-in-Publication Data

Marshall, Roger.
   A sailor's guide to production sailboats.

   Includes index.
   1. Sailboats. I. Title.
VM351.M365 1986   623.8′223   86-224
   ISBN 0-688-05842-6 (pbk.)

Printed in the United States of America

First Edition

1 2 3 4 5 6 7 8 9 10

PREFACE

This book evolved from the reports I write each month for *Motor Boating & Sailing* magazine. In these reports I review two or three new boats after actually sailing on them. This enables me to try out and compare many boats during the course of a year. As a result, I get many inquiries about which boat is best or which boat is most suited for a particular budget and purpose. It soon became apparent to me that there is no standard reference to help boat buyers make their selections wisely. This book is intended to fill that information gap.

The data sheets at the end of this book were originally produced from manufacturers' brochures. Each sheet was then sent to the manufacturer to give its staff the opportunity to correct any errors or out-of-date material and to fill in omissions. At the same time, the manufacturer was also given the chance to provide both pictures of its products and brief descriptions of them. However, even with all these efforts to make our data sheets as accurate as possible, mistakes may exist. At the very least, some details about particular boats may have changed since the time of our writing, in August 1985. To find out the very latest information, especially about price, there is no substitute for contacting the manufacturer. Nevertheless, the data sheets in this book should prove invaluable in conducting your initial search for a new boat.

Chapter 5 is a discussion of the boat builders that I think are among the very best in the world. Many of the boats I have inspected and sailed firsthand, and in my opinion they represent good value for the money. Note that I cannot say that these are the *best* production boats available. For one thing, what is "best" depends so much on individual preferences. For another, my choice for this chapter was limited to boats that I had personally seen and sailed. This excluded many of the more than four hundred boats for which we include data sheets. Some of these other boats may be equally as good, perhaps even better. All I can say is that of the boats of which I have firsthand knowledge, those constructed by the builders listed in Chapter 5 are good choices if they suit the type of sailing you do.

Like all books that include vast amounts of data, this one required the efforts of many different people. I owe a debt of thanks to all the sales managers who answered my letters and telephone calls. I am also very grateful to my wife, Mary, who supervised a team of helpers who sifted through hundreds of brochures and entered the data on computer. These helpers are Angela Stringer, Karen Vinbury, Sue Pease, and Jeanne Chappel. My thanks to them all.

—RJM

Your Ideal Boat

STATISTICS

LOA: _____

LWL: _____

Beam: _____

Displacement: _____

Maximum Draft: _____

Sail Area: _____

Fresh Water: _____

Fuel Capacity: _____

COSTS

Maximum total: _____

RATIOS

Sail Area/Disp.: _____

Disp./Length: _____

Ballast ratio: _____

Fuel/Disp.: _____

Water/Disp.: _____

INTERIOR

BERTHS: number of single berths _____ number of double berths _____

TABLE: fixed _____ dropleaf _____ bulkhead-mounted _____

hi-lo _____ other _____

HEAD: number of heads _____ number of showers _____

number of sump pumps _____ number of holding tanks _____

COLD STORAGE: portable ice chest _____ built-in icebox _____

refrigerator/freezer _____

cold storage volume _____

STOVE: number of burners _____ oven desired? _____

type of stove fuel _____

MAX. HEADROOM: _____

MACHINERY

ENGINE: preferred engine manufacturer _____

horsepower _____

PROPELLER: fixed _____ folding _____ feathering _____

GENERATOR: _____

DECK

STEERING: wheel _____ tiller _____

WINCHES: minimum number of winches _____

preferred winch manufacturer _____

SAFETY: bow pulpit _____ stern pulpit _____

single lifelines _____ double lifelines _____

ANCHOR: desired anchor type and size _____

anchor well or locker desired? _____

NAV LIGHTS: bow light _____ stern light _____ masthead light _____

RIG

TYPE: _____

preferred mast manufacturer _____

RIGGING: rod _____ wire _____

MAINSHEET: mid-boom sheeting _____ boom-end sheeting _____

SAILS: mainsail _____ 150% genoa _____ 130% genoa _____

110% genoa _____ working jib _____ spinnaker _____

MPS _____ other _____

preferred sailmaker _____

COMMENTS: _____

_____

_____

_____

Note: Make a star beside the factors that you consider are absolutely essential in your new boat.

CONTENTS

Part I

Buying a New Boat

CHAPTER 1

PICKING THE BOAT THAT'S RIGHT FOR YOU

The moment comes when you decide you want to buy a new boat. Where do you begin? If you are like many people, you begin with a preconceived idea that you need a boat X feet in length with X number of berths, at a cost that cannot exceed X dollars. With this in mind, you go to a boat show, find a craft that fits your general description, and plunk down your hard-earned cash. Only later may you discover that the boat you bought is totally unsuited to the type of sailing you do. This book is intended to help you avoid making such costly and disappointing mistakes. In this chapter we guide you through some preliminary steps in picking the boat that's right for you.

STEP 1: ANALYZE WHERE YOU WILL BE SAILING

Suppose your family of four enjoys sailing together and you think you can afford to spend $60,000 on a new boat. Your first step is to list the areas where you'll be using the boat. In the Northeast, the list might look like this:

- The boat will be moored in New-port harbor.
- Weekends we will sail around Narragansett Bay, to Block Island, to Martha's Vineyard, and occasionally to Nantucket.
- We plan to race Tuesday and Thursday nights in the local club-level fleets.
- On a two-week vacation cruise we might go to Maine or to Long Island Sound.
- There is a good chance we could get away for a four-week cruise, in

which case we would explore the Chesapeake Bay. This would entail sailing from Newport to Annapolis and going offshore along the coast of New Jersey.
- We never plan to go offshore as far as, say, Bermuda.

With this list completed you can begin to analyze the implications of each item you've written down. For instance:

- The boat will be moored in a harbor. This means that we should carefully check the chocks and cleats on any boat we consider buying in order to ensure that the mooring lines aren't likely to chafe through.
- We plan to do club-level racing on a regular basis. This means that we want a boat with some speed. However, we don't want to sacrifice interior comfort for the sake of speed.
- Our plans include a possible trip to the Chesapeake, which would entail a day or so offshore in order to avoid some of the tricky inlets on the New Jersey coast. This means we should look for a boat with good structural integrity and a reasonably good navigation area.

Clearly, the more thorough you make your initial list, the more suited to your sailing plans your new boat will be.

STEP 2: ANALYZE YOUR STYLE OF SAILING

With Step 1 completed, you can now proceed to make a second list—this one of your particular style of sailing and maintaining a

boat. Here you might note the following:

- On weekend or vacation cruises, we always moor up in a marina or anchor at night.
- We almost always eat onboard when we are sailing.
- Generally, the entire family sails together, including both children.
- We seldom have additional crew onboard who can help with sail handling.
- Although we will have a yard do major repairs, we plan to do our own routine maintenance.

Having finished this list, you should once again draw out the implications. For instance:

- At night, we always moor in a marina or anchor. This means that we can accept bunks in slightly unusual positions, such as a transverse aft double.
- We almost always eat onboard while cruising. This means the galley must be capable of storing a week's worth of food. The icebox or refrigerator should be of a good size, the stove should have at least three burners and an oven, and we will need a large sink.
- Generally, the entire family sails together. This means that we will need a fairly large amount of fresh water, including hot water. While we could live with hand pumps, pressure water would be nice. The two children will need separate bunks.
- We seldom have additional crew onboard. This means that certain sail-handling gear is desirable, such as self-tailing primary winches and a roller furling head-

stay. A masthead sloop is also preferable.

- We plan to do our own routine maintenance. This means, for one thing, that exterior bright work should be kept to a minimum.

STEP 3: DETAILING YOUR IDEAL BOAT

By now you are forming a list of items you want on your new boat. In order to establish a comprehensive list of this kind, you can fill out the blank "ideal boat" sheet at the end of this chapter. (Consult Chapter 2 if you are uncertain about the "ratios" section.) It is a good idea to star all the factors on this sheet that you consider absolutely essential. This will help you to see at a glance which things you can and cannot compromise on. Figure 1–1 shows an "ideal boat" sheet as filled out by the boat buyer in the hypothetical example above.

STEP 4: MATCHING YOUR IDEAL TO WHAT'S AVAILABLE

Armed with the description of your ideal boat, you can now turn to the information at the back of this book. Here we describe over 400 production boats, 20 feet in length and over, that are currently on the market. The boats appear in order of size, from smallest to largest. Very likely some of them will seem suited to your needs and budget. You can make a list of these possibilities and send for the brochures. (Manufacturers' addresses and phone numbers are given at the back of this book.) By looking through the brochures and talking with the sales repre- sentatives, you can fill in any information that might be missing on our data sheets.

Of course, you may locate other boats not included in this book that are also of interest to you. If so, you may want to fill out one of our data sheets for them. Doing so can make comparisons a great deal easier. For this purpose we have provided blank data sheets at the back of this book.

Once you have narrowed your list of possibilities down to a manageable size, it is time to inspect them firsthand. To do this, you can either arrange with each manufacturer for an inspection or attend a boat show in your area. Boat shows are often better places to shop, because comparisons can be made quickly and easily. Still, it requires a little know-how to evaluate a boat carefully. Chapter 3 of this book gives you some tips for this task.

Figure 1—1
Your Ideal Boat

STATISTICS
LOA: _30—34 ft._
LWL: _____
Beam: _about 10 ft._
Displacement: _medium_
Maximum Draft: _5—6 ft. (prefer 4'6")_
Sail Area: _____
★ Fresh Water: _50 gals._
Fuel Capacity: _25 gals._

COSTS
★★ Maximum total: _$60,000_

RATIOS
Sail Area/Disp.: _____
Disp./Length: _____
Ballast ratio: _____
Fuel/Disp.: _____
Water/Disp.: _____

INTERIOR
★ BERTHS: number of single berths _3_   number of double berths _1_
TABLE: fixed _____ dropleaf _X_   bulkhead-mounted _____
hi-lo _____   other _____
HEAD: number of heads _1_   number of showers _1_
number of sump pumps _1_   number of holding tanks _1_
COLD STORAGE: portable ice chest _____   built-in icebox _X_
refrigerator/freezer _____
cold storage volume _as much as possible_
STOVE: number of burners _3_   oven desired? _yes_
type of stove fuel _propane_
MAX. HEADROOM: _6'2"_

MACHINERY
ENGINE: preferred engine manufacturer _Westerbeke_
horsepower _18—25_
PROPELLER: fixed _____   folding _2nd_   feathering _1st_
GENERATOR:

DECK
STEERING: wheel _X_   tiller _____
WINCHES: minimum number of winches _4_
preferred winch manufacturer _Barient_
SAFETY: bow pulpit _X_   stern pulpit _X_
single lifelines _____   double lifelines _X_
ANCHOR: desired anchor type and size _35 lb._
anchor well or locker desired? _yes_
NAV LIGHTS: bow light _X_   stern light _X_   masthead light _X_

RIG
★ TYPE: _double-spreader masthead sloop_
preferred mast manufacturer _Hall Spars_
RIGGING: rod _X_   wire _____
MAINSHEET: mid-boom sheeting _X_   boom-end sheeting _____
SAILS: mainsail _X_   150% genoa _X_   130% genoa _____
110% genoa _X_   working jib _X_   spinnaker _____
MPS _____   other _____
preferred sailmaker
COMMENTS: _headfoil required; perforated toe rail required; also want jiffy reefing._

★Note: Make a star beside the factors that you consider are absolutely essential in your new boat.

CHAPTER 2

WHAT OUR DATA SHEETS COVER

There is often a confusing mass of information in a boat brochure. First-time buyers in particular may have trouble sorting out important facts from sales hype. Even more confusing is comparing boats from different companies. Each manufacturer organizes its brochures in its own unique way and many do not even include the same information. Buyers may begin to feel as if they are comparing apples and oak trees.

In this book we try to solve the problem of comparisons by listing in a standard format all the basic data about a large number of production boats currently on the market. Whatever comparisons you wish to make—number of berths, sails supplied, galley equipment, or performance ratios—this book allows you to make them at a glance. In this chapter we familiarize you with our data sheets by summarizing what they include.

STATISTICS

Basic statistics such as LOA, LWL, beam, displacement, ballast, and draft may seem straightforward, but there are tricks to making sure you are not misled. Here are the "numbers" we include and some tips on reading them.

LOA

When looking at LOA, make sure that the measurement is taken from the stern to the bow and not to the forward end of the bowsprit or to the anchor platform. Measuring to the end of the bowsprit is an easy way to make a boat seem larger than it really is.

LWL

LWL is the distance from the intersection of the bow and the waterline to any one of three points. Usually, that point is the centerline of the rudderstock. However, occasionally the measurement will be taken either to the fairbody line of the hull or to the end of the rudder blade.

Beam

When the beam of a boat is measured, make sure it does not include any rubrails or fairing strips, which will artificially increase the figure. In general, the beamier the boat, the more volume there is inside. However, too much beam can have a detrimental effect on performance.

Displacement

Displacement may be given in "sailing condition" or in "light ship condition." Light ship condition is the one you are looking for. Sailing condition means that the boat is loaded down with stores, clothes, and crew. This will make it appear much heavier than it actually is.

Ballast

Part of the displacement of a boat is in the ballast. When looking at the cost of a boat, you should subtract the ballast in order to obtain a more accurate cost for the construction.

Draft

Draft will vary according to the type of keel used. When comparing boats, try to be consistent in keel type. Compare only deep keels with deep keels, shoal keels with shoal keels, and centerboarders with other centerboarders. This is because displacement, ballast, and key performance ratios may vary depending on the type of keel.

Sail Area

Sail area is sometimes calculated as a mainsail + a topsail + a staysail. This arrangement is shown in Figure 2–1a. Notice that these sails overlap so the resulting sail area is quite large. In Figure 2–1b, you see how a change in sail shapes can increase sail area without increasing rig size. Clearly, the mainsail + topsail + staysail formula can often be misleading.

A better and more accurate way of specifying sail area is to use 100% of the mainsail area plus 100% of the fore triangle area, as shown in Figure 2–2. If the boat is a ketch or a yawl, then 50% of the mizzen area should be added on the theory that the mizzen is used 50% of the time. The letters I and J refer to the height and the base of the foretriangle. P is the mainsail luff length and E is the mainsail foot length. To calculate the total sail area, the following formula is used:

$$\frac{(P \times E)}{2} + \frac{(I \times J)}{2} = \text{sail area}$$

If a mizzen is used, add to that:

$$\frac{(IY \times PY)}{4}$$

Fresh Water

Our data sheets include a boat's fresh water tankage. When looking through a brochure, this figure is sometimes hard to find. It may be listed under "plumbing" or even under "galley," depending on the manufacturer.

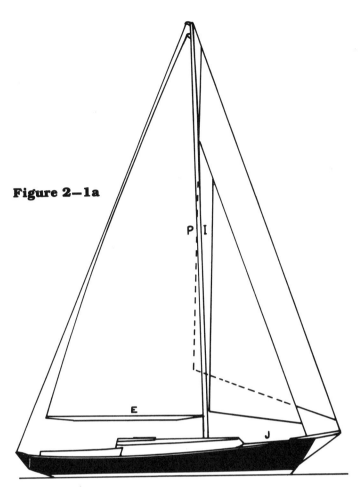

Figure 2—1a

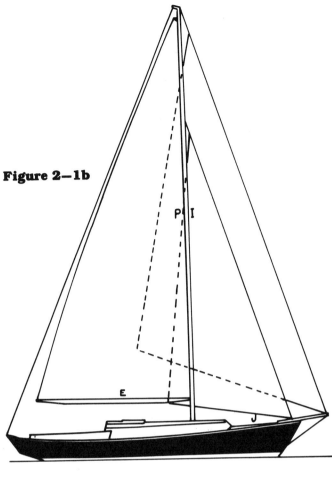

Figure 2—1b

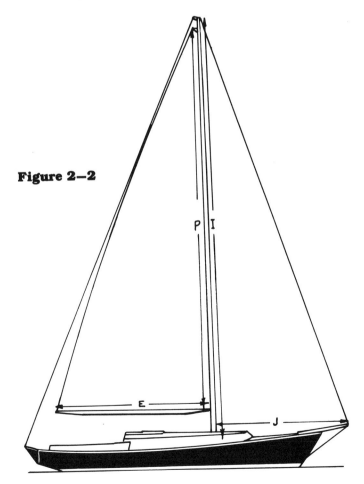

Figure 2—2

Fuel Capacity

A similar search will often have to be made for a boat's fuel capacity. It may be listed under "engine" or possibly under "tankage." On boats smaller than 30 feet LOA, the engine is often an extra and no fuel capacity is given. The best way to find out what is *not* included on a boat is to read the list of options. Anything on that list is not part of the base boat package.

Costs

Our data sheets give the latest base boat price available at the time of writing. Prices, however, do change, often at the end of the year. Only by contacting the manufacturer can you verify the current price of any boat.

On our sheets, we have also tried to include the estimated cost of a boat on the water. These estimates were made by each boat's manufacturer. When no such estimate appears, it means either that the manufacturer did not provide this information or that the base boat price is also the "sail-away" price. Tips on how to estimate the cost-on-the-water yourself are covered in Chapter 4.

RATIOS

When designing a new boat in my design office, we figure out all the design characteristics and then work up a set of lines from which we derive a computerized performance estimate. This provides a thorough picture of how the boat is likely to perform under various conditions. If we need to evaluate designs by others, we work up over 20 simple ratios. These ratios, when compared to our own figures, give us a feel for how competitors' boats stack up against ours. Unfortunately, most production boat manufacturers do not supply enough statistics in their brochures to allow a potential buyer to work up this many ratios. There are, however, a few performance ratios that can usually be calculated from a standard boat brochure. These are the sail area/displacement ratio, the displacement/length ratio, the ballast

ratio, the fuel/displacement ratio, and the fresh water/displacement ratio. All are included on our data sheets.

Sail Area/Displacement and Displacement/Length Ratios

The sail area/displacement ratio is calculated with the following formula:

$$\frac{\text{Sail Area}}{\left(\dfrac{\text{Disp}}{64}\right)^{\frac{2}{3}}}$$

This ratio gives a good indication of the amount of sail area a boat has to push its displacement through the water. The higher the number, the faster the boat will reach its maximum speed and the longer the boat will stay at that speed.

The displacement/length ratio serves as an indication of a boat's potential speed. It is found using the formula:

$$\frac{\text{Disp}/2240}{(0.01 \times \text{LWL})^3}$$

In very rough terms, a low displacement/length ratio says that the boat will accelerate quickly and be fast in light airs, while a high ratio says the opposite.

The best way to find out about a boat's speed potential, however, is

to use the displacement/length ratio in conjunction with the sail area/displacement ratio. By using both ratios together, you can obtain a much more complete picture of performance. For instance, let's look at two boats, both with an LWL of 30 feet. Boat A has a displacement of 25,000 lbs., while boat B has a displacement of 12,000 lbs. The displacement/length ratio of boat A is 413, while that of boat B is 198. If both boats have a sail area of 700 square feet, then the sail area/displacement ratio of boat A is 13.1 and that of boat B is 21.4. As you can see, boat B has a low displacement/length ratio and a high sail area/displacement ratio. Since displacement/length bears a direct relationship to wetted surface, we can say that B has a low wetted surface and a high sail area, which will make it fast in light airs. Boat B will also accelerate quicker than A. With its high displacement/length ratio and low sail area, boat A will probably be quite slow in light winds.

What sail area/displacement and displacement/length ratios should you look for in the boat you buy? That depends on the type of boat and what kind of sailing you plan to do. The graphs in Figure 2—3 show typical sail area/displacement

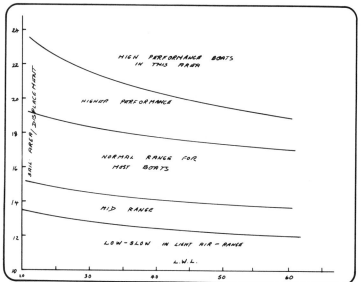
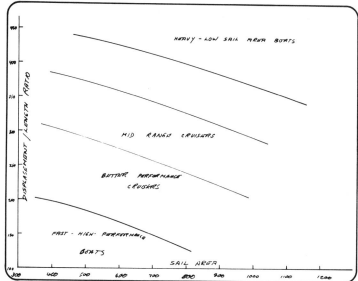

Figure 2—3

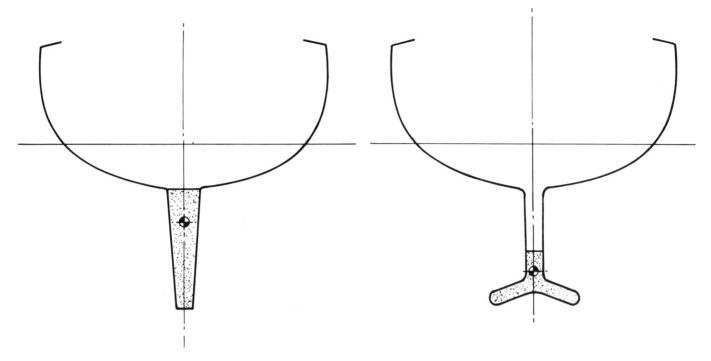

Figure 2—4a   **Figure 2—4b**

and displacement/length ratios for cruising, racing, and lightweights or ULDBs.

Ballast Ratio

I am not a great believer in the value of the ballast ratio. But for those who are, it is calculated with the formula:

$$\frac{\text{Ballast} \times 100}{\text{Displacement}}$$

As a measure of stability, which it is widely believed to be, the ballast ratio fares rather badly. For instance, taking our boat A and boat B in the above example and looking at Figure 2-4, you can see that boat A, which has 25,000 lbs. of displacement and 10,000 lbs. of ballast, has a ballast ratio of 40%, while boat B, with only 5,000 lbs. of ballast, has a ballast ratio of 20%. But look at the distribution of the lead in A; it is very high. In boat B, in contrast, the center of the lead is very low. This means that while B has a much lower ballast ratio, it has much more stability.

Fuel/Displacement Ratio

How much fuel should you carry? Once again, this is a difficult question to answer. You can figure out how much fuel your engine will use over a given period and how far you can motor in that time. But that won't tell you how much fuel you should have onboard. One rule of thumb is to check a simple ratio:

$$\frac{\text{Fuel} \times 100}{\text{Displacement}}$$

Cruising boats have a high ratio, over 5%, while racing boats are often under 1%. Most production cruisers are in the 1% to 3% range.

Fresh Water/Displacement Ratio

Imagine yourself sitting behind the wheel of your new boat. It is Saturday afternoon and you are on the first leg of your two-week vacation cruise. You have been aboard one day and everything has been perfect. Now your wife is getting dressed for dinner ashore. Suddenly she appears in the companionway dressed in a robe, her hair soapy and wet. "We're out of water," she says.

"You must have had a long shower," you mutter as you struggle to get the hose out of the lazarette and connected to the boat. Within twenty-four hours of con-

tinuing your cruise you are out of water again, this time in a secluded cove. You must motor three hours to the nearest marina for water, wrecking your plans for that day. In exasperation, you check for leaks only to find nothing wrong. Finally, you look up the specifications on your new boat and discover that the fresh water tank holds only twenty gallons. You have just found the Achilles heel of many cruising boats.

How much water do you need? Even the best experts do not always agree. Many suggest two gallons per day for drinking and cooking. But that figure seems to be a holdover from the days when people actually drank mostly water on a boat. If you usually drink juices, sodas, beer, and so forth, you may get by with less than two gallons for drinking and cooking. However, if you intend to shower on your boat, your water supply must be increased substantially. Allow 3 to 5 gallons per shower. Now you are better able to estimate just how much fresh water you and your crew will use each day. But note that the amount will vary depending on temperature and activities.

Another way to get an idea of the

adequacy of water onboard a boat is to calculate the ratio of fresh water to displacement. The formula is quite simple:

$$\frac{\text{Fresh water} \times 100}{\text{Displacement}}$$

Experience shows that a true cruising boat has a ratio of over 5%, while a racing boat rarely exceeds 2% and is often around 1%. If your boat is somewhere in the middle of this range, say 3 or 4%, then you will have sufficient water for most of your needs, but you should carry a few gallons of emergency supply. The only exceptions to this rule are boats that carry a watermaker and they are generally over 40 feet LOA.

THE INTERIOR

What features of the interior do most people want to know about when they consider buying a new boat? When we were organizing this guide, we asked ourselves this question. Our answers were number and type of berths, type of table, number of heads and their fixtures, type and size of cold storage, kind of cooking facilities, and the maximum headroom.

Berths

How many bunks does the boat have and how are they laid out? In our analysis, we looked at the layout of the boat and at the brochure description to determine the number of berths and their type.

We found that many sales managers think their bunks are larger than they really are. For instance, I once stepped on a boat where the bunk in the aft cabin was described in the brochure as king-size, but when I measured it, the width was only 4 feet 8 inches. (A standard king-size bed is 6 feet by 6 feet.) Unfortunately, we were not able to measure all the berths for this book. We had to rely on pictures and the manufacturer's judgment as to what is an adequate single and what is an adequate double.

When you actually go to inspect a boat, however, you can bring along a pocket measuring tape and find out more. In my view, the minimum width for a good seaworthy single berth is 27 inches at the shoulders. It can taper to 14 inches at the feet, but no less. The minimum width for a double berth is 54 inches, and that is a fairly snug double. If you are in doubt as to how comfortable a bunk will be, measure it, mark out its width on your bed at home, and try sleeping in that area for the night. This simple exercise will soon give you some experience in checking out bunk sizes. As for bunk lengths, 6 feet 6 inches is a comfortable length for me (I'm 6'1"). If you are taller and require a longer bunk, don't be afraid to ask if it can be built to suit you. Many manufacturers will accommodate a reasonable request.

As for types of berths, there are many. In our data sheets we have included eight different kinds. Here's how we define each one:

V berths: These are the bunks in the forepeak of the boat, which are usually over six feet long. If you are intending to use the V berth as a sleeping area for two adults, make sure that you and another person climb into them and check to see if there is enough room for both pairs of feet.

Forward berths: On larger boats, there is often a cabin or two between the forepeak and the main salon. We call the berths in these cabins simply forward berths. They can be either single or double, upper or lower.

Settee berths: A settee berth is any berth that is used during the daytime as a settee. It is relatively easy to evaluate. Just sit on it to see if it is comfortable and then lie down to see if it provides adequate sleeping room. Usually, if the berth is very comfortable for sitting, it will be too narrow for use as a berth. In this case, look for an extension transom that will slide out to make the bunk wider (in our data sheets, we call this subtype of settee berth an *extension berth*). Often, however, a manufacturer will avoid the expense of making an extension transom by making the back cushions of the settee very wide and removable. This is fine as long as the bunk is wide enough when you lie on it in your normal sleeping position.

Convertible dinette berths: These are another way of making a single item do the work of two. In most cases the dinette seats are situated transversely across the boat with the table between them. The table drops down to form a platform for the seatback cushions, which become the mattress. These bunks are usually adequate as double berths unless they are very small.

Quarterberths: I have often heard it said that a quarterberth (any berth in one of the aft quarters) is the most comfortable bunk on a boat. Usually this is true, but be wary of the quarterberth that fits snugly against the side of the hull. It will be perfectly comfortable while the boat is upright, but if you intend to do any nighttime sailing, you will find that the bunk on the lee side slopes outboard as the boat heels. This means that the person sleeping in that bunk will assume an uncomfortable head-down position. The problem is even worse if the boat is fine-ended or has a round stern with the bunks in the end of the hull.

Pilot berths: In recent years the humble pilot berth has moved all around the boat. Originally, a pilot berth was in the wheelhouse next to the chart table, used by the navigator or pilot while the boat was under way. Nowadays, it seems that whenever a salesman cannot think of a suitable name for a bunk, it becomes a pilot berth. In this book we use the term *pilot berth* for bunks outboard of the main cabin or dining area.

Pipe berths: The lengthwise edges of a pipe berth are usually framed of ¾-or 1-inch diameter aluminum pipe. The sleeping surface generally is made of canvas, sewn around the pipes. Typically, a pipe berth, when not in use, can be removed and stored.

Center aft berths: One modern trend is a large double berth in an aft cabin. Although this type of berth is somewhat unseaworthy, it has become very popular because of its space and privacy. As we mentioned earlier, however, beware of aft doubles called king- or queen-size; they rarely are. Also something to be cautious about if you are going to do offshore sailing is the transverse aft double. On one tack your head will be down, while on the other your head will be up. This arrangement is quite all right if you are sleeping in a marina, however.

Tables

Manufacturers have many ways of describing the tables they install in their boats. On our data sheets we have tried to group these into a few basic categories. One is the *fixed table*, which is fixed in both position and size. Another is the *dropleaf*, which has one or more leaves that can be folded down to make the table smaller. A third category is the *bulkhead-mounted table*, which stores flat against a bulkhead. A fourth is the *hi-lo table*, which can be raised or lowered to two different heights. We have not specified the size of tables on our data sheets, because this information is seldom listed in brochures. When buying a boat, I recommend that you sit your family or crew down at the table provided and make sure everyone fits.

Heads

In old-time sailing ships, the crews' toilet was performed in areas to either side of the bowsprit, called the heads. This term has carried over into modern usage, where it applies to the entire bathroom, not simply the WC.

When evaluating head facilities on a new boat, most people want to know how many showers, holding tanks, and sump pumps are provided, so we have included these items on our data sheets. The number of showers is a matter of personal preference, but remember that holding tanks should be large enough so that you don't have to stop showering to pump the tank out. This generally means that the tank needs to hold a minimum of about 15 gallons. Often it should be larger, especially if people want to wash their hair frequently. Another small point is that the sump tank should be pumpable from onboard rather than having to wait to get to a pump-out station.

Cold Storage

Most sailing is done in warm weather and nothing is quite so enjoyable after a long day on the water than a cool thirst quencher. Consequently, even the smallest boats carry some form of icebox. The smallest craft generally use a portable ice chest, which has the advantage of allowing you to pack it at home. Larger boats tend to have built-in units and, depending on the size and displacement of the boat, they may have a refrigerator or freezer fitted.

The size of the icebox or refrigerator you need depends on the number of people you intend to have onboard, the amount of time you spend sailing, and the type of food or drink you prefer. In general, most manufacturers have predetermined the size of their cold storage and will change it only as a special order.

Stoves

The food you eat and your style of cooking affects the type of stove you look for. For instance, the sailor who wants only sandwiches and beer doesn't need much in the way of cooking equipment but will probably need a large icebox. The family man, in contrast, who cruises often with his wife and two children, will probably require two burners and an oven.

What kind of fuel a stove should use is a contentious subject. There are sailors who will never have a propane (LPG) stove onboard, others who prefer one. There are also those who prefer alcohol or compressed natural gas (CNG). Almost all boatbuilders have options regarding stoves so all you need do is ask for the type you want.

Headroom

Wherever possible on our data sheets, we have tried to give the maximum headroom in the boat. If this maximum headroom requires that a pop top be up, we have also tried to give the headroom with the pop top down. In general, expect to get over 6 feet of headroom in boats that are over 30 feet long. If you have 6 feet of headroom in smaller boats, it is because the boat has a very heavy displacement or a very high freeboard and cabin top.

MACHINERY

In the excitement of getting a new sailboat, many buyers often overlook the machinery. In our data sheets, we have considered the three most important pieces of mechanical equipment on a boat: the engine, the propeller, and the generator, if one is supplied.

Engines

When evaluating the engine of a new boat, you should compare its horsepower with that of other boats of similar displacement. Occasionally, you will find that a manufacturer has used a smaller engine than everyone else in an effort to save money. The sales representative for that manufacturer will probably tell you that the size is perfectly adequate, and it probably will be as long as you are using the engine to get you home during calm periods. However, when you have to power home against a headwind and rough sea, you may find that your speed is very much reduced. For instance, a few years ago a very well known manufacturer put a 23-horsepower engine in a 40-footer with 18,000 lbs. displacement. Under power in flat water, the speed was a good 6 knots, but as soon as the seas got up, boat speed fell off. In a 25-knot headwind with its accompanying high seas, the boat would power at about 1 knot. Imagine trying to get home in a hurry against a rising gale with this engine! Subsequently, the boat was repowered with a 45-horsepower motor that would comfortably move it along at 6 knots in 20 knots plus of headwind.

Another fact to note about an engine is the reduction gear ratio. It affects the propeller size, in that usually a higher reduction gear ratio means that the propeller will turn more slowly and will be slightly larger. The reduction gear ratio and the propeller diameter and pitch are all carefully calculated at the design stage and are best left alone unless severe powering problems arise.

Propellers

Certain types of propellers have certain characteristics. For instance, folding props occasionally have problems backing down, although the sailing performance with them is greatly enhanced. Fixed props, on the other hand, have appreciable drag under sail but power equally as well both forward and aft. The best compromise performance-wise seems to be the feathering type of propeller, but because of the gearing inside the hub, it is generally more expensive. In addition to propeller type, our data sheets may include the diameter and pitch of the propeller, the number of blades, and the shaft diameter.

Generators

On our data sheets we have listed generators when they are part of the base boat inventory. Note that this is not the generator

that comes bolted on to the engine to charge batteries, but rather a separate unit. If you intend to have air-conditioning, you will need a fairly large generator. With most generators it is often wise to include the sound shield, which usually comes as an extra. This will help keep the noise level down, something that a well-insulated engine compartment cannot always do alone.

DECK GEAR

When looking at the equipment on deck, you can often get a quick feel for the quality of a boat and whether the people who built it are sailors. In general, higher quality boats use deck gear from more well known manufacturers, and when the gear is installed, it is done in such a way that everything works efficiently without having leads crossing or binding. The following pages give you some idea of what to look for when assessing the various pieces of deck gear listed on our data sheets.

Steering

Most people prefer wheel steering, but on a small boat a wheel is often ludicrous. My own feeling is that a wheel should be reserved for boats over 32 feet long, except on center cockpit versions, where a tiller is not feasible. If the boat you are considering has a tiller instead of a wheel, you should try to determine how much of the cockpit the tiller sweeps on every tack. Will it displace crew?

On boats with wheel steering, we have tried to include on our data sheets the wheel diameter. Wheel size is something you should always check when assessing a new boat. Can you get past the wheel easily? Can you see the sails while steering? Check also to see that the wheel turns easily and is fairly loose, but without any slop.

Whenever a wheel is fitted, there should be an emergency tiller. If

you have a chance, try to fit the emergency tiller. You may need it to get you home one day.

Winches

You should carefully check the number and size of the winches that come with a boat. Quite often you will find that only a few winches are supplied and that you will have to purchase more before you can go sailing. In most cases you will have to buy secondary winches if you intend to fly a spinnaker, although some boats (especially the racier or more expensive ones) do provide them with the base boat. Quite often, too, you will find that a boat's standard winches are too small to do a really good job; larger ones may be needed, at extra expense to you. Also check to see that the winches supplied are from a reputable manufacturer and that spare parts are easily available. On our data sheets we indicate the type, size, and manufacturer of the winches whenever possible.

Safety

Under safety, we have indicated only if a bow or stern pulpit is supplied together with lifelines and stanchions. If you inspect the pulpits and stanchions on a boat you are considering buying, make sure that they are all through-bolted and have a backing plate in accordance with best yacht practice. Other safety equipment is usually owner-supplied and should be, at a minimum, in accordance with Coast Guard standards.

Anchors

Our data sheets indicate whether an anchor is supplied and, if so, what size and type. Note, however, that the kind of anchor you use greatly depends on the kind of bottom where you anchor. For this reason, the majority of builders let owners supply their own anchors. I think this is a reasonable policy in that it allows you to select the type that best suits your area. But remember that the extra cost of a pair of anchors and anchor rodes should be figured into your budget.

An anchor roller is a very handy item on many cruising boats, and our data sheets indicate whether one is provided. In checking out an anchor roller, make sure that it is large enough to hold the anchor and, more importantly, that it is strong enough to bear the heave and pitch of the boat if the line is permanently led over the roller.

Another item our data sheets include is a built-in anchor well (or alternatively, an anchor locker). Make sure there is a place in an anchor well to tie the other end of the anchor line. Many anchor lines have vanished over the side because the inboard end was left unsecured! Also check to see that the well is large enough to hold the anchor you intend to use.

Navigation Lights

Internationally approved navigation lights are required on all boats except a vessel under oars (the latter must have a lantern or flashlight that can be exhibited in time to prevent a collision). Sailing craft must show a red and green bow light and a white stern light. Almost all manufacturers include these lights in their base boat package; it is the extra lights that cause confusion. No sailboat is required to have a masthead light while under sail, but when a sailboat is under engine power, it becomes a powerboat and should display a white light at least 1 meter (3.3 feet) above the colored side lights. This white light on the mast should be visible only through an arc of 20 points, not all around. In addition to these lights, a sailboat under 20 meters (66 feet) can display an optional red, white, and green light at the masthead or a red over green masthead light.

In our data sheets, we have limited our listing to bow and stern lights (collectively called running lights) and to the general category of masthead light. Note, however, that different manufacturers may mean different things by the term *masthead light.* Check to find out exactly what is supplied. Note also that in inland waters required navigation lights may vary, so check with your local Coast Guard to make sure your new boat is legal.

THE RIG

The rig can be thought of as the engine of a sailboat. Of all the things we could consider about rigs, the most important for the buyer are probably the rig type, the rigging material and diameter, and how easy it is to trim the mainsheet.

Rig Type

Although most production sailboats are sloops, there are a number of variations such as a fractional rig or a masthead sloop, a cat rig, a ketch, or a yawl. The simplest rig to handle is probably the masthead sloop, especially if it has a roller furling headsail and main. While a cat rig is even simpler than a sloop, cat boats are generally limited in size (they are usually under 24 feet LOA) and they are sometimes a bit of a handful to steer in heavier winds. Many people used to think that ketches and yawls had an advantage over single-masted boats because their more divided sail area made sail handling easier. With modern sail handling gear, however, this traditional advantage has almost disappeared. While the sails for a fractional rig are up to 30 percent less expensive than those for a similar size masthead rig, a fractional rig requires a lot of mainsail trimming to get optimum performance. The masthead rig is not as sensitive to mainsail trim and is therefore a good option for the less experienced sailor.

In our data sheets we have indicated not only rig type but also, whenever possible, the mast maker. This will enable you to get a feel for the quality of the spars.

Rigging

Where rigging is given, we have shown the material and diameter of the standing rigging. A reasonable method of comparing stability between two boats is to compare the standing rigging size. Usually, the boat with the larger rigging has more stability.

Mainsheet

Many sailors prefer to have the mainsheet in the cockpit while others like to have it on the cabin-top, where it is out of the way. We have therefore indicated the position of the mainsheet on our data sheets. We have also indicated the number of parts on the mainsheet to enable you to see if it needs a winch or can be handled by the person in the cockpit.

SAILS

Under this heading, we have listed only the sails supplied with the base boat. If no sails are provided, you will have to buy them and their cost should be added in your budget. At a minimum, you will need a mainsail and a working jib. A larger inventory will include an overlapping genoa, often 150% of J, a storm jib, and a spinnaker or two. A cruising poleless spinnaker may be more suitable, depending on the type of sailing you intend to do. When the sails are supplied, you should make sure they are of reputable quality. You may even want to take an expert along to check out the sails on your trial sail.

BUILDERS' COMMENTS

Finally, we come to the builders' comments. All the manufacturers of the boats listed in this book were given the chance to briefly describe their product. These comments allow you to see how the builders view their own boats. They also give you an overall feel for the kind of boat that is being offered.

CHAPTER 3

HOW TO INSPECT A NEW BOAT

You have looked through this book, sent for brochures, and narrowed your choices down. Now you are ready to look firsthand at boats that seem to fit your needs. But when you go to inspect a boat you are thinking about buying, do you know exactly what to look for? Can you evaluate the boat both at the dock and out on sailing trials? In this chapter we give you some tips on conducting these all-important final steps in selecting a new boat. A thorough inspection before you buy can spare you much disappointment later. It can also help you get the best quality possible for the dollars you spend.

INSPECTING THE INTERIOR

"Step aboard," says the sales representative. But when you do, where do you begin your inspection? If you are like many people, you begin with the interior. What are the steps involved in giving an interior your stamp of approval?

First consider the type of sailing you do, as we described in Chapter 1. Are you an offshore cruiser, or do you rarely leave the dock? Do you always try to moor up for the night, or do you keep on sailing? These questions and others must be answered if you are going to get the interior that is right for you.

Suppose you are an offshore sailor who sails all night, does an occasional overnight race, and cruises for two weeks every year. In this case, the interior layout that you would probably find best is one with comfortable single berths, a good navigation area, a moderate dining area, reasonable

sail stowage, and a fairly large fresh water capacity. On the other hand, if you are a sailor who uses his boat only during the day and moors up in a marina overnight, you probably want most of the comforts of home: air-conditioning, ample hot water, double berths (even a transverse double is acceptable here), minimal navigation facilities, a large dining-cum-entertainment area, and large separate showers or even a tub (larger boats may even have a Jacuzzi or sauna). For those who hope to charter their boat, still other features should be looked for: separate staterooms, for example, or perhaps a fresh water maker.

Having found an interior you think may be right for you at a price you can afford, the next step is to consider how that interior will perform at sea. Stand inside the boat and try walking through it. Imagine it heeled and reach out for handholds. Do they come to hand naturally or are they awkward to grasp? Next, look at each individual area of the boat. Start in the aft cabin. Are the bunks long enough? Are they wide enough? If you have to sleep when the boat is heeled, can a leecloth be fitted? Find out how much the leecloths will cost, because they'll have to be included in your budget. If the bunk in the aft cabin is a double, is there any provision for sleeping when the boat is heeled or will you simply roll from side to side?

Next, look over the aft head. Is it large enough for a comfortable shower? Even more important, do you have enough fresh water for a comfortable shower? If in doubt, check the fresh water/displace-

ment ratio, described in Chapter 2. For a cruising boat, look for a ratio over 4%. For a racing boat or a boat with a water maker, a ratio below 2% is often adequate.

The watertightness of the shower is another important factor. Ideally, the shower unit should be separate from the head compartment, but if it isn't, you should check to see that everything in the head can take constant soakings. Unsealed wood may suit the decor but could rot out in a few years unless it is teak. Look also for potential sources of water seepage. You may find that water will flow into the lockers or into an adjacent cabin.

Next, look through the galley. Will your wife be able to reach the bottom of the icebox? Think about access to the icebox when the boat is heeled. Check also the size of the icebox. If you usually cruise for a week at a time, make sure it will hold enough ice and provisions. Can you get a full bag of ice or a large piece of solid ice into the box easily? If uncertain, check with your local marina to see what size their ice bags or ice blocks are.

After examining the icebox, consider work space and stowage in the galley. Are the countertops at a comfortable height? Are all the lockers reachable? Are the locker door catches secure? Magnetic catches can fly open if a can or jar rolls against them, depositing the entire contents of the locker on the cabin sole. Stoves are another important aspect of the galley. The Offshore Racing Council currently recommends that all stoves be securely installed against capsize. So take a look at the stove if you intend to race the boat, and make sure it will not jump out of its moorings.

If your sailing takes you off-shore, the navigation area will also be an important place to check. Is the table large enough for the type of charts you use? Is there enough room for all the electronics that you intend to buy? Will the power supply support all those electronics, or will you have to buy larger batteries? Is the seat comfortable? You may spend a lot of time using it. Check to see if you press against the lighting panel when you lean outboard (as most navigators do when the boat is heeled). This can be a source of constant irritation if you cannot get comfortable or if you accidentally turn off breakers when using the nav seat. Check also to see if there is storage available for flags, foghorn, sextant (if you use one), radar reflector, rules, pencils, books, and all the other paraphernalia of the competent navigator.

The next step is the dining area. Is the table large enough? For a racing crew, a table will probably just be in the way, but for someone who entertains in a marina, a large table will be needed. Check access around the table. People may want to get up or move around to get more comfortable. Also take a look at the seating. If the settees are to be used as bunks, they must be wide enough, but settees that are too wide are not comfortable to sit on. One solution is a wide, removable seat-back cushion to decrease the depth of a wide settee; another is a relatively narrow settee with an extension transom for sleeping. If the table lowers and converts to a bunk, you should carefully check the conversion mechanism. Occasionally you will find a convertible table that collapses on the cabin sole at the wrong moment.

Lockers are also of critical importance on a boat that will be used for cruising. Hanging lockers should be large enough to hold most garments without folding or creasing them. How big a hanging locker should you look for? It depends on the type of sailing you do. In my office, we allow 6 inches

of hanging space per crew member. This means that a boat with a crew of four should have a locker with at least 24 inches of storage space. A wet locker is always a good idea to keep wet clothes away from dry gear. If you keep a lot of clothes onboard, you should also check for drawers or shelves to stow them. The galley always seems to be an area that is short of stowage space. If this is so on a boat you are considering, check around to see if there are other places where you can stow foodstuffs. For instance, cans and plastic bottles can be placed in the bilge under the cabin soleboards. If you intend to keep good stemware onboard, it should have its own locker and built-in racks to ensure it doesn't get broken under way. Books, too, should have a particular storage area. A book that falls in the bilge is quickly ruined and can clog up bilge pumps extremely well.

Finally, you will want to check out the fore cabin. Almost all the boats I have looked at have a V berth here, usually intended as a double. One common problem is insufficient footroom when two people are sharing the bunk; another common problem here is bunks that are too short. Both these potential drawbacks can easily be spotted just by trying the bunk out. While you are in the fore cabin also check for headroom, especially if you are going to use this bunk as the main double.

Although you may tend to overlook them when examining a new boat, the colors used throughout a boat are also very important. Will that puce green cushion cover induce seasickness when the boat is under way? Remember that light colors make an interior look larger, while dark colors tend to make a boat look like a cave. Throw in some dampness and a little fog and you will have all the makings of a horror show. Patterns are something to consider as well. For instance, stripes tend to make things look longer along the stripe and shorter across it.

So how can we sum up what you should look for when you inspect the interior of a boat? First, take the macro view. Look at the interior from the perspective of how it suits your type of sailing and your budget. If the boat is not appropriate for you, don't waste the sales representative's and your own time by continuing with an exhaustive inspection. Only if the design really suits your needs should you move on to a micro look at how well the boat is built and how each component is integrated into the whole.

CONDUCTING SAILING TRIALS

Buying a boat without sailing it first is like buying a stereo without turning it on. You really don't know what you're getting. After years of evaluating new boats for *Motor Boating & Sailing* magazine, I have evolved procedures for getting the maximum amount of information out of a relatively short sailing trial. Here is a brief description of what those procedures are.

The first step is to fire up the engine in preparation for leaving the dock. While the engine is running, you should go below and check out the noise level. It should not be so loud that you can't carry on a normal conversation. Now it is time to leave the dock. Helping with this task will give you a chance to see whether the sidedecks are easily accessible. Sometimes the shroud chainplates are positioned right in the middle of the sidedecks, making movement fore and aft difficult. Also check to see where the fenders are positioned. Ideally, they should be alongside the widest part of the hull.

Having left the dock, power out to a reasonably clear area. Along the way, I like to compare engine rpms against boat speed to get a feel for how well the engine is pushing the boat along. Once clear of the harbor, you can conduct a few tests. First, try going hard astern. (Remember to shut the engine revs down before changing gear and then build the revs back up. Going from full ahead to full astern without lowering the revs is a good way to ensure that you will own that engine transmission!) See how long it takes for the boat to get a grip of the water and how the boat steers going astern. You will probably find it is hard to steer, the rudder tending to want to go to one side or the other. This is natural. Rudders are made to work most efficiently when the boat is moving forward. Check also to see if the propeller wants to pull the boat off to one side. This, too, is natural and will have to be compensated for when you are coming into a dock. As a final test, I like to spin the boat around in a circle to see what kind of turning radius it has. But don't try to compare the turning radii of long keeled boats and fin keeled ones; they will be very different. If you try this maneuver, be sure to warn everyone onboard beforehand or you could end up throwing someone over the side.

Now it is time to put the sails up. Again, offer to help. Helping will give you insight into any potential problems, and if you get on the winching end of the deal, you will learn if the winches are large enough. When hoisting the mainsail, look to see if the usual sail adjustments are provided. For instance, you may want an outhaul or a topping lift and these could be optional items. If so, you will have to add in the extra cost. You may want other gear that perhaps is optional, so make sure you know exactly what comes with the base boat package. Just because something is found on the boat you are sailing does not necessarily mean it is standard equipment. When in doubt, ask and avoid surprises later.

When putting up the headsail, check to see what if any headfoil is included and how easy it is to use. Check also the tack fitting. Often, just two hooks are used and they may need some adjustment to keep the sail on them during hoisting. Look to see how the halyard exits from the mast. It should be high enough for a person to catch hold of in order to help raise the sail (6 to 8 feet is customary). Again, make sure the winch is large enough.

Under sail, you can find out a great deal. First, try the boat on the wind. Look for how much it heels, how close it sails, and how fast it goes. You can also get a feel for the boat's motion through the water—whether it pitches or moves smoothly and easily. When you are on the helm, you should try to note any tendency toward weather or lee helm. All this data can easily be recorded for later comparisons with other boats. When making such comparisons, however, make sure that key factors—wind strength, sea state, and apparent wind angle—are held constant.

Another thing you should be checking while under sail is how comfortable the seating is. Check the helmsman's seat from several different positions even though you usually sit in only one place. Also note how easy it is to sit in the other cockpit seats while under way. Now is the time to check the sheetleads for fairness and to see that all the lines are accessible and easy to operate. You might also see whether you can move easily up and down the companionway ladder. While momentarily belowdeck, try walking through the cabin to see how well the handholds are positioned.

When you get back on deck, it is time to try a few tacks. While tacking, see how the lines run,

whether they bind up or snag anywhere. Look to see how easy it is to cast the line off and get the headsail in on the other side. This may be a point at which you decide that the primary winches are too small or that they are situated in an awkward position. Also look to see how the mainsheet operates. You may want to order taglines to ensure that the mainsheet can be moved easily during a tack. Check, too, the height of the main boom to make sure it clears everyone easily.

Having sailed on the wind for a while, come off onto a reach. Ease the sheets out, and check to see that they run easily without binding or fouling another piece of gear. Now try a reach-to-reach gybe and make sure that everything works as it is supposed to. Again, note your boat speeds if you want to compare details later with other boats.

Finally, run downwind and check that everything works well. If you normally set a spinnaker on downwind legs, you may want to try that now. Most sales reps will let you set a spinnaker if you are a competent sailor. Check all the sheet leads, try a gybe or two, and record any changes that you may want on your boat. If your requests are reasonable, most builders will accommodate them.

After trying all these performance tests, the next one is equally important. When you are powering or sailing back to the marina, relax and enjoy the cockpit and the sailing. If any overlooked problems exist, you may very well spot them now. If you and the sales representative agree on certain changes to rectify problems, make sure that all those changes are specified in the contract before you buy.

CHAPTER 4

ADDING UP THE COSTS

The way some boat manufacturers operate is almost a scam. They show you pictures of a well fitted-out boat, the crew of which is happily sailing off into the sunset. Then, in tiny type tucked away in a remote corner of the brochure, a note says "Many of the items pictured here are optional." Just how do you tell what is optional equipment and what is standard? Many builders provide a standard equipment list on the back of their brochures. You should go through this list very carefully to find out exactly what you get for the price of the base boat. Also carefully check the options list; it is another way of telling what is standard and what is not.

KNOWING WHAT EXTRAS YOU NEED

Even when a manufacturer lists its standard equipment, it sometimes takes a little experience to read this list knowledgeably. Below are some typical listings that you might find, along with what each can mean in terms of extra cost. At the far right, spaces are provided for you to write in the estimated additional dollars needed to buy the options you want your boat to have.

STANDARD EQUIPMENT	COST OF EXTRAS
Hull and Deck	
* White hand-laminated hull	* Other colors are optional and cost more. _____
* White hand-laminated balsa-cored deck	* Again, any other color costs more. _____

STANDARD EQUIPMENT	COST OF EXTRAS
* External keel	* A shallow draft keel or centerboard is an option and may cost more. _____
* Extruded aluminum toerail with stanchion bases	* Check to see if stanchions are included. If not, they mean an extra cost. _____
* Bow and stern pulpits	* Are lifelines supplied? If not, how much do they cost? _____
* 2 Barlow primary winches	* Check to see if the winch size is adequate. Bigger winches cost more. _____
* 1 Barlow mainsheet winch	* Once again, include the cost of larger winches if they are needed. If you want to use a spinnaker, you will probably need two secondary winches, two or more extra blocks, sheets, and guys, a spinnaker pole, a foreguy, and a topping lift. Calculate the extra costs involved. _____
* Genoa tracks and blocks	* You may need extra blocks. If so, check their size and cost. _____
* Mainsheet traveler and track	* Look to see if taglines are included. If not, add in the extra cost if you want them. _____

STANDARD EQUIPMENT	COST OF EXTRAS
* Pedestal steering	* Does a compass come with the steering system? _____
* Anchor well	* Anchors, cable, and bow roller are extras. _____
Mechanical and Electrical	
* Yanmar 3HM35F Diesel	* Check to make sure that the engine instruments are included. If not, add in the extras. _____ Is the engine compartment insulated? _____ Are fuel and water filters supplied? _____
* Two-bladed propeller	* A folding or feathering propeller will enhance sailing performance, but it will cost more. _____
* Electrical panel with 12-volt system	* If you want a 110-volt system, it will cost extra. _____
* Running lights	* Check to see if a masthead and foredeck light are included. If not, add in their cost. _____
Spars and Rigging	
* 1x19 wire shrouds	* Rod rigging is extra. _____
* Turnbuckles on all shrouds	* A hydraulic backstay is extra. _____ Check also for toggles on the headstay and backstay. If they are not fitted, they entail extra cost. _____

STANDARD EQUIPMENT	COST OF EXTRAS
* 2 Barlow halyard winches	* Check size and cost if larger units are needed. _____
* Internal genoa halyards	* Spinnaker halyards are extra and will cost more. _____
* One reefing line on boom	* A second reefing line will cost extra. _____

Interior Fittings

STANDARD EQUIPMENT	COST OF EXTRAS
* Molded base for marine head with 18-gallon holding tank and deck discharge	* A WC unit is extra. Add in its cost and the cost of installation. _____
* Two settee berths with 4-inch cushions	* Leecloths are extra. _____
* Stainless steel around stove bay	* A stove is extra and its cost must be added in. _____
* 2 hanging lockers with fabric fronts	* Louvred doors are extra. _____
* 5 interior lights	* Additional cost for bunk lights. _____

Remember that the examples above are purely hypothetical. Some production boats come loaded with equipment; others provide the bare minimum. The problem comes in finding out what is standard and what is optional on the particular boat you want. We are not saying that most manufacturers are out to deceive the boat-buying public. We are merely saying that as a consumer, you need to read equipment lists very carefully. In addition to the possible options we have just mentioned, here are some other items you should look for when you read a brochure.

* Sails (at a minimum a mainsail and jib are required) _____
* A sail luff groove or sail hanks _____
* Extra cleats _____
* Winch handles _____
* Dock lines _____
* Fenders _____
* Fire extinguishers _____
* An emergency tiller _____
* A signal horn _____
* A liferaft and life preservers _____

ADDING IN THE NONESSENTIALS

Then there are the nonessential items you would *like* to have on-board. Although many people try to convince themselves they can live without these, in the end they often tend to be added. Among those you might consider are the following:

* Cockpit cushions _____
* A cockpit table _____
* A depth sounder _____
* A wind direction indicator _____
* A loran _____

* A single sideband radio _____
* A VHF radio _____
* A stereo _____
* A Windex _____
* Charts _____
* Extra sails _____

THE COST OF GETTING A BOAT ON THE WATER

If you want to get an even more accurate picture of the cost of buying a new boat, you should add on the expenses of actually getting the boat on the water. These include the cost of:

* Commissioning _____
* Delivery _____
* Launching and rigging _____
* Rating the boat if you want to race _____
* Mooring and dockage _____
* Insurance _____
* Documentation _____

Our intention here is not to frighten you out of buying a new boat. We simply want to encourage you to consider beforehand all the expenses involved. If the total is spiraling far beyond your budget, you can always adjust your thinking and look for a smaller boat. The buyer who gets the best deal is the one who encounters no surprises. Add up all the costs, shop around, and buy the boat that you can afford.

CHAPTER 5

*T*HE PICK OF THE PACK

As you can see from the list at the back of this book there are hundreds of boats on the market. Often I am asked which ones are best. That is a hard question to answer because it depends so much on what you want a boat to do and what particular features are most important to you. In short, you must first define your own needs and objectives before anyone can say which boat is best for you.

Despite the fact that no one boat is best for everyone, I am going to describe a few boats that I think are especially good choices. This list does not include *all* my personal favorites, because space permitted room for only eight. Thus, if a particular boat you like is not mentioned here, that boat may still be an excellent value. With this in mind, here is my personal "pick of the pack."

*H*ENRY R. HINCKLEY

Top of the line for quality has to be the boats from Henry R. Hinckley. They are superbly crafted and can be sailed anywhere, any time. If you own one you can be secure in the knowledge that it is not likely to be a boat failure that keeps you from reaching your destination. The old-time craftsmen at the Hinckley yard in Maine know how to put a boat together extremely well when they are given the time to do so.

Some might argue that Hinckleys are expensive boats. They are, but you are certainly getting something for your money. It takes a lot of time to select quality wood and shape it to conform exactly to the contours of the interior. It takes even more time to sand, polish, and varnish that wood to obtain a dust-free mirror finish. This is what you are paying for when you buy a Hinckley.

In doing reviews for *Motor Boating & Sailing* magazine, I have sailed a number of Hinckleys and have found that Jim McCurdy's designs sail well on all points of sail. The Hinckley deck plans are also a strong point. There are obviously some good sailors at Hinckley, such as Hank Halsted and John Marshall, who have had some say in how the decks are laid out. Everything on deck comes readily to hand and is easy to operate.

The only negative point I could find on the Sou'wester 51 is partly a matter of personal opinion. Hinckley likes to make all the door frames with mitered corners, but I feel that on a boat mitered corners almost always work and crack. I think that a stronger joint is obtained by making the doors with radiused corners. As I said, however, this is largely a matter of personal opinion. The Hinckley is an all-around quality boat.

*C*AMPER AND NICHOLSONS

Years ago I looked after a large Camper and Nicholson boat, and to this day I am impressed with the quality of the craftsmanship that went into it. I recently sailed the Nicholson 58 and can say that the quality is still there. These boats are exquisite in every sense of the word. The company will virtually design and build the interior that you want. "Campers," as they are known, are based in Gosport, England, and went through some rough times in the late seventies when they tried to move into the mass production end of the mar-

ket. From the rumors I heard, this was not a successful venture and now they are back doing what they do best: building large, high-quality sailing yachts that have the ability to go anywhere and do anything. The price of a Nicholson depends partly on the relationship between the pound and the dollar. At the time of this writing they are well worth a long, hard look.

*N*AUTOR SWAN

Another import worth a look is the Nautor line of boats from Finland. Nautor has been in business building boats since the late sixties and has had a range from thirty-six to seventy-six feet. Currently, they build boats from thirty-nine feet LOA up. The company became renowned for quality during the days when S&S designed the boats and Rod Stephens rode herd over quality control. In those days several virtually unmodified Swans competed in the Whitbread round-the-world race. Today the emphasis appears to be on getting more speed out of the boats. Nautor uses well-known designers and markets their product aggressively. Because it is imported, a new Swan should be a good value in terms of price.

*S*HANNON BOAT COMPANY

Probably the best-kept secret in the marine industry is a small company working out of Bristol, R.I.: the Shannon Boat Company. They are very understated but very good. I would have no qualms about sailing transatlantic in one of their boats straight out of the factory. These boats are solidly built, well crafted, and, for what you get, not overly expensive.

Their craftsmanship is on a par with Hinckley but their finish work needs a little more attention to detail to be up to Hinckley standards. This costs more money, however, so it becomes a trade-off between finish and cost.

I sailed the Shannon 43 most recently and found it to be a comfortable, easy-to-sail cruising boat. Initially it seemed a little tender, but as soon as we heeled to perhaps fifteen degrees the boat stiffened right up and drove to windward very comfortably. I especially liked the massive stemhead/roller furling fitting, the double headsail rig, and the care that has gone into making the deck layout work well.

Shannon makes a line of boats ranging from twenty-eight to fifty-one feet LOA. All of them are crafted with the same meticulous care. Almost all can be modified to suit the owner's requirements. For instance, if you want a cutter, sloop, or ketch rig, it can be built for you. Some boats have a centerboard option; most have a pilot house option; many have various interior arrangements. Everything about these boats seems right. They should be good for long-distance cruising in almost hedonistic comfort. For a weekend jaunt around Narragansett Bay or the Chesapeake, you can hardly go wrong with a Shannon.

CARROLL MARINE, LIMITED

Next on my list is another small company in Rhode Island that makes only two boats but is about to start tooling on a thirty-three-footer. One boat is the Frers 36 and the other is the Block Island 40. On both Carroll Marine does an excellent job. The 36 is a performance cruiser/club-level racer that is fitted out extremely well. Of all the boats I have mentioned so far, this is probably the most performance-oriented. Even so, the quality is there. The Block Island 40 is well known to some for its good

looks. Now the quality of the product has been enhanced since Carroll Marine took over its manufacture.

Carroll Marine is one of the few builders I know that sends its workmen to boat shows and out sailing to make sure they know how their boats perform and how buyers perceive them. This can only result in more feedback to the shop floor and in the end, a better product. Look for more good things from this company in the future.

BRISTOL YACHTS

Yet another Rhode Island firm that produces a superb yacht and keeps its skills fairly quiet is the Bristol Yachts Company located in Bristol. These boats come remarkably well fitted-out and extremely well finished. A friend of mine describes them as a boat in which you can put your hand out expecting to find a handhold, and there it is just where you thought it should be. Everything is in the right place and everything works efficiently. This is one of the few lines of boats that I have not sailed personally. However, all the reports I get from those who have say that Bristols sail extremely well without any crankiness or unexpected glitches. Most of the line has been designed by Ted Hood. It ranges from a thirty-one-footer to a seventy-two-footer that is under construction at the time of this writing.

CAPE DORY YACHTS

Last year I happened to be passing the Newport Yachting Center during the time the Cape Dory rendezvous was being held. I remember being amazed by the number of brown sail covers and dodgers that were in the marina. That color turned out to be a Cape Dory trademark. But that is not all Cape Dory is known for. While its boats are oriented more toward production and the demands of

the production market, Cape Dory produces a solid, comfortable cruiser that will be around for a long time. The designs come from a number of different designers, all of whom have done a good job. The Cape Dory line starts with the eighteen-foot six-inch Typhoon and goes in three or four foot jumps all the way up to the Cape Dory 45.

Cape Dory also has a line of power boats, as well as the Intrepid line of slightly more performance-oriented sailing yachts. To get good value for your money you should look at Cape Dory.

NONSUCH

Some people call them unpretentious, others downright ugly. But every Nonsuch owner I know extols their comfort and performance. These Mark Ellis-designed boats are functional, well built, roomy, and easy to sail thanks to their unstayed cat rigs. In spite of many comments to the contrary, they will outpoint a conventional sloop to windward. I know, because I've done it! The large, deep cockpit is comfortable for single-handing, and safe for taking even very young children sailing. Belowdeck, you get just about all that you could ask for. How many other twenty-six-footers have full standing headroom, two bunks in the main cabin and two forward, a full-size enclosed head, a large dining table, plus an inboard engine? The joinerwork on the Nonsuch line is good by production standards, and the deck layouts are very well thought-out.

Nonsuch is fortunate that these boats are marketed by enthusiasts like Jim Eastland in Essex, Connecticut. Dealers like Eastland have sailed the boats a lot and the suggestions they make to the builder usually get listened to. This attention to practical experience shows in the end result. The Nonsuch may be the ugly duckling of the industry, but many think it sails like a swan.

Part II

Production Boat
Data Sheets

A blank space usually means that the item is not supplied with the boat, but in some places the information furnished by the manufacturer is inadequate to complete the data. Where a 0 is shown the item is definitely not included.

GLOUCESTER 20

DESIGNER: Stu Winbley
BUILDER: Gloucester Yachts, Inc.

STATISTICS

LOA: 19 ft. 6 ins
LWL: 16 ft. 6 ins.
BEAM: 7 ft. 6 ins.
DISPLACEMENT
deep keel: 1,560 lbs.
shoal keel:
c/board:
BALLAST
deep keel: 550 lbs.
shoal keel:
c/board:
DRAFT
deep keel: 2 ft. 3 ins.
shoal keel:
c/board up: 1 ft. 0 ins.
c/board down: 4 ft. 6 ins.

SAIL AREA: 174 sq. ft
FRESH WATER: 0
FUEL CAPACITY: 0

COSTS

BASE BOAT: $7,250
DATE: 02/01/85
EST. ON WATER: $8,500
DATE: 02/01/85

RATIOS

SAIL AREA/DISP:20.67
DISP/LENGTH: 155
BALLAST RATIO: 35.25
FUEL/DISP: 0.0
FRESH WATER/DISP: 0.0

INTERIOR

BERTHS: 4 berths: 1 double V, 2 single settees
TABLE:
HEAD(S):
COLD STORAGE: cooler
STOVE:
MAX. HEADROOM: sitting

MACHINERY

ENGINE:
PROPELLER:
GENERATOR:

DECK

STEERING: tiller
WINCHES:
SAFETY:
ANCHOR:
NAV LIGHTS:

RIG

TYPE: fractional rig sloop
RIGGING: wire (1/8")
MAINSHEET: boom-end sheeting

SAILS

SUPPLIED WITH BASE BOAT: main, jib

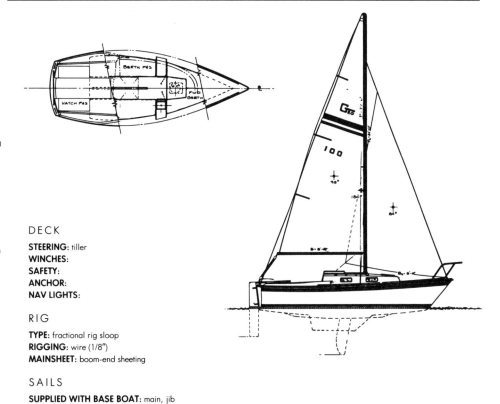

FLICKA 20

DESIGNER: Bruce Bingham
BUILDER: Pacific Seacraft Corp.

STATISTICS

LOA: 20 ft. 0 ins.
LWL: 18 ft. 2 ins.
BEAM: 8 ft. 0 ins.
DISPLACEMENT
deep keel: 6,000 lbs.
shoal keel:
c/board:
BALLAST
deep keel: 1,750 lbs.
shoal keel:
c/board:
DRAFT
deep keel: 3 ft. 3 ins.
shoal keel:
c/board up:
c/board down:

SAIL AREA: 250 sq. ft.
FRESH WATER: 20 gals.
FUEL CAPACITY: 0 gals.

COSTS

BASE BOAT: $25,600
DATE: 06/85
EST. ON WATER: $29,000
DATE: 06/85

RATIOS

SAIL AREA/DISP: 12.11
DISP/LENGTH: 446
BALLAST RATIO: 29.16
FUEL/DISP: 0.0
FRESH WATER/DISP: 2.66

DECK

STEERING: tiller
WINCHES: 2 Lewmar sheet winches (#8)
SAFETY: bow and stern pulpits
ANCHOR:
NAV LIGHTS: running

RIG

TYPE: masthead sloop
RIGGING: 1x19 SS wire
MAINSHEET: main (2 reefs), 100% working jib

SAILS

SUPPLIED WITH BASE BOAT:

INTERIOR

BERTHS: 4 berths: 1 double V, 1 single settee, 1 single quarterberth
TABLE:
HEAD(S):
COLD STORAGE: built-in icebox
STOVE: 2-burner kerosene
MAX. HEADROOM: 6 ft. 0 ins.

MACHINERY

ENGINE:
PROPELLER:
GENERATOR:

BUILDER'S COMMENTS Designed by Bruce Bingham, Flicka is one of the most remarkable boats ever built. Primarily built for safe, simple and comfortable family cruising, she has also been chosen by many experienced sailors for countless offshore passages and ocean crossings. Her seaworthy design and sturdy construction have been proven in nearly every ocean of the world.

MISTRAL T-21

DESIGNER: Mistral Sailboats Inc.
BUILDER: Mistral Sailboats Inc.

STATISTICS

LOA: 21 ft. 0 ins.
LWL: 18 ft. 8 ins.
BEAM: 8 ft. 2 ins.
DISPLACEMENT
deep keel:
shoal keel:
c/board: 2,400 lbs.
BALLAST
deep keel:
shoal keel:
c/board: 770 lbs
DRAFT
deep keel:
shoal keel:
c/board up: 1 ft. 2 ins.
c/board down: 5 ft. 11 ins.

SAIL AREA: 237 sq. ft.
FRESH WATER: 12 gals.
FUEL CAPACITY: 0 gals.

COSTS

BASE BOAT: $14,374
DATE: 05/30/85
EST. ON WATER:
DATE:

RATIOS

SAIL AREA/DISP: 21.16
DISP/LENGTH: 164.90
BALLAST RATIO: 32.08
FUEL/DISP: 0.0
FRESH WATER/DISP: 4.0

DECK

STEERING: tiller
WINCHES: 3 winches
SAFETY: bow pulpit with single lifelines
ANCHOR: anchor well
NAV LIGHTS: running

RIG

TYPE: fractional rig sloop
RIGGING: 1x19 SS wire
MAINSHEET: 3-part with boom-end sheeting

SAILS

SUPPLIED WITH BASE BOAT: main, jib, genoa

INTERIOR

BERTHS: 5 berths: 1 double convertible V, 1 double convertible dinette, 1 single quarterberth
TABLE: convertible dinette
HEAD(S): portable with pump-out attachments
COLD STORAGE: cooler
STOVE: 2-burner alcohol
MAX. HEADROOM: 4 ft. 7 ins.

MACHINERY

ENGINE:
PROPELLER:
GENERATOR:

BUILDER'S COMMENTS Roomy, sporty, with accommodations for easy living, the Mistral T-21 is THE craft for weekend cruises. Equipped for long trips, it can sleep five comfortably. It is spacious enough for cooking standing up and there's ample storage space, including a closet. Since 1979, the T-21 has participated in the "Mini Transat" trials where it has distinguished itself by its great speed attributed to its special, patented hull. Because its ballasted retractable keel can be completely raised, the T-21 is easier to transport.

MACGREGOR 21

DESIGNER:
BUILDER: MacGregor Yacht Corporation

STATISTICS

LOA: 21 ft. 0 ins.
LWL:
BEAM: 6 ft. 10 ins.
DISPLACEMENT
deep keel: 1,175 lbs.
shoal keel:
c/board:
BALLAST
deep keel: 400 lbs.
shoal keel:
c/board:
DRAFT
deep keel:
shoal keel:
c/board up: 1 ft. 0 ins.
c/board down: 5 ft. 6 ins.

SAIL AREA: 175 sq ft.
FRESH WATER: 0
FUEL CAPACITY: 0

COSTS

BASE BOAT: $5,495
DATE: 04/01/85
EST. ON WATER:
DATE:

RATIOS

SAIL AREA/DISP: 25.15
DISP/LENGTH:
BALLAST RATIO: 34.04
FUEL/DISP: 0.0
FRESH WATER/DISP: 0.0

INTERIOR

BERTHS: 4 berths: 1 double V, 2 single settees
TABLE:
HEAD(S):
COLD STORAGE:
STOVE:
MAX. HEADROOM:

MACHINERY

ENGINE:
PROPELLER:
GENERATOR:

DECK

STEERING: tiller
WINCHES: N/A
SAFETY: bow and stern pulpits with single lifelines
ANCHOR:
NAV LIGHTS: running and masthead

RIG

TYPE: masthead sloop
RIGGING: wire
MAINSHEET: boom-end sheeting

SAILS

SUPPLIED WITH BASE BOAT: main, working jib

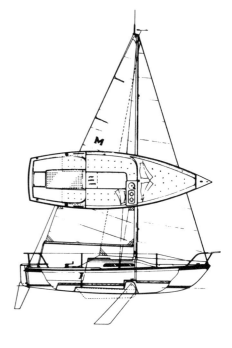

SEA PEARL 21

DESIGNER: Marine Concepts
BUILDER: Marine Concepts

STATISTICS

LOA: 21 ft. 0 ins.
LWL: 19 ft. 0 ins.
BEAM: 5 ft. 6 ins.
DISPLACEMENT
deep keel:
shoal keel:
c/board: 550 lbs.
BALLAST
deep keel:
shoal keel:
c/board: 15 lbs.
DRAFT
deep keel:
shoal keel:
c/board up: ft. 6 ins.
c/board down: 3 ft. 6 ins.

SAIL AREA: 136 sq. ft.
FRESH WATER: 0
FUEL CAPACITY: 0

COSTS

BASE BOAT: $4,800
DATE: 12/01/84
EST. ON WATER:
DATE:

RATIOS

SAIL AREA/DISP: 32.42
DISP/LENGTH: 35.80
BALLAST RATIO: 2.73
FUEL/DISP: 0.0
FRESH WATER/DISP: 0.0

INTERIOR

BERTHS: 2 berths: 1 double V (on sole)
TABLE:
HEAD(S):
COLD STORAGE:
STOVE:
MAX. HEADROOM:

MACHINERY

ENGINE:
PROPELLER:
GENERATOR:

DECK

STEERING: tiller
WINCHES:
SAFETY:
ANCHOR:
NAV LIGHTS:

RIG

TYPE: cat ketch with A & D Mast, Inc. spars
RIGGING: unstayed
MAINSHEET: 1-part with boom-end sheeting

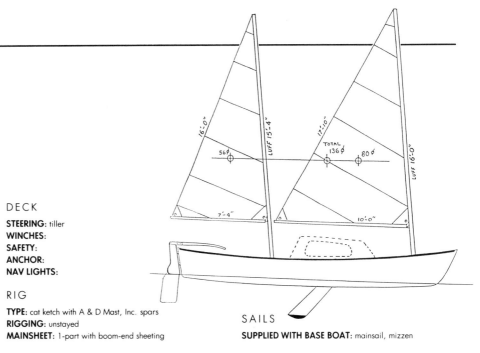

SAILS

SUPPLIED WITH BASE BOAT: mainsail, mizzen

BUILDER'S COMMENTS The Sea Pearl 21 is America's most versatile boat. She can be sailed, rowed, poled or motored. Launch her at the beach or on a ramp. Let her ghost along in the lightest of airs or reef her down in record time for a comfortable margin of safety during summer squalls. There is plenty of room for day sailing with six or more aboard and with the optional dodger there is room for two and all their gear to overnight in protected comfort. Her hull shape is an expanded version of the Herreshoff Carpenter, made to handle surf. Practicality is a bonus with the Sea Pearl. She is light enough to tow behind the smallest of vehicles. You will be amazed at the ease of operation and carefree aspect of this unique boat.

BAVARIA 606

DESIGNER: Axel Mohnhaupt
BUILDER: Bavaria Yachtbau GmbH

STATISTICS

LOA: 21 ft. 4 ins.
LWL: 17 ft. 0 ins.
BEAM: 8 ft. 0 ins.
DISPLACEMENT
deep keel: 1,980 lbs.
shoal keel:
c/board:
BALLAST
deep keel: 840 lbs.
shoal keel:
c/board:
DRAFT
deep keel: 4 ft. 2 ins.
shoal keel:
c/board up: 1 ft. 7 ins.
c/board down: 3 ft. 7 ins.

SAIL AREA: 218 sq. ft.
FRESH WATER: 0 gals.
FUEL CAPACITY: 0 gals.

COSTS

BASE BOAT:
DATE:
EST. ON WATER:
DATE:

RATIOS

SAIL AREA/DISP: 22.12
DISP/LENGTH: 179
BALLAST RATIO: 42.42
FUEL/DISP: 0.0
FRESH WATER/DISP: 0.0

INTERIOR

BERTHS: 4 berths: 1 double V, 2 single settees
TABLE: dropleaf
HEAD(S):
COLD STORAGE:
STOVE:
MAX. HEADROOM: 6 ft. 3 ins.

MACHINERY

ENGINE:
PROPELLER:
GENERATOR:

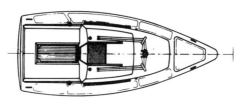

DECK

STEERING: tiller
WINCHES: 4 Enkes or Lewmar winches: 2 primary, 2 halyard
SAFETY: bow and stern pulpits with lifelines
ANCHOR: anchor well
NAV LIGHTS:

RIG

TYPE: fractional rig sloop
RIGGING: 1x19 wire
MAINSHEET: 4-part with boom-end sheeting

SAILS

SUPPLIED WITH BASE BOAT: main (2 reefs), working jib

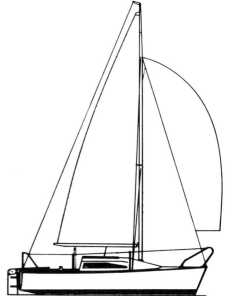

BUILDER'S COMMENTS The Bavaria 606's designer, Axel Mohnhaupt, has given this boat every enviable sailing characteristic that her larger sisters have. She accelerates in the lightest of airs. She's easy on the helm and her full lines have been given much innovative thought to reduce drag.

CATALINA 22

DESIGNER:
BUILDER: Catalina Yachts

STATISTICS

LOA: 21 ft. 6 ins.
LWL: 19 ft. 4 ins.
BEAM: 7 ft. 8 ins.
DISPLACEMENT
deep keel: 2,490 lbs.
shoal keel:
c/board: 2,250 lbs.
BALLAST
deep keel: 800 lbs.
shoal keel:
c/board: 550 lbs.
DRAFT
deep keel: 3 ft. 6 ins.
shoal keel:
c/board up: 2 ft. 0 ins.
c/board down: 5 ft. 0 ins.

SAIL AREA: 212 sq. ft.
FRESH WATER: 5 gals.
FUEL CAPACITY: 0

COSTS

BASE BOAT: $6,595
DATE: 02/01/85
EST. ON WATER:
DATE:

RATIOS

SAIL AREA/DISP: 18.46
DISP/LENGTH: 153.9
BALLAST RATIO: 32.1
FUEL/DISP: 0.0
FRESH WATER/DISP: 1.6

DECK

STEERING: tiller
WINCHES: 2 primary winches
SAFETY: bow pulpit
ANCHOR:
NAV LIGHTS: running

RIG

TYPE: masthead sloop
RIGGING: wire
MAINSHEET: 4-part with boom-end sheeting

SAILS

SUPPLIED WITH BASE BOAT: main, 110% jib

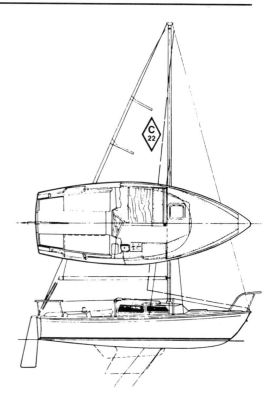

INTERIOR

BERTHS: 5 berths: 1 double V, 1 double convertible dinette, 1 single quarterberth
TABLE: fixed dinette
HEAD(S):
COLD STORAGE:
STOVE:
MAX. HEADROOM: 5 ft. 7 ins. with pop top up (4'4" with pop top down)

MACHINERY

ENGINE:
PROPELLER:
GENERATOR:

LAGUNA 22

DESIGNER: W. Shad Turner
BUILDER: Laguna Yachts, Inc.

STATISTICS

LOA: 21 ft. 7 ins.
LWL: 19 ft. 0 ins.
BEAM: 8 ft. 0 ins.
DISPLACEMENT
deep keel: 2,280 lbs.
shoal keel:
c/board:
BALLAST
deep keel: 900 lbs.
shoal keel:
c/board:
DRAFT
deep keel: 2 ft. 11 ins.
shoal keel:
c/board up:
c/board down:

SAIL AREA: 206 sq. ft.
FRESH WATER: 0 gals.
FUEL CAPACITY: 0 gals.

COSTS

BASE BOAT:
DATE:
EST. ON WATER:
DATE:

RATIOS

SAIL AREA/DISP: 19.02
DISP/LENGTH: 148
BALLAST RATIO: 39.47
FUEL/DISP: 0.0
FRESH WATER/DISP: 0.0

DECK

STEERING: tiller
WINCHES: genoa sheet
SAFETY: bow and stern pulpits with lifelines
ANCHOR: anchor well
NAV LIGHTS: running and masthead

RIG

TYPE: fractional sloop
RIGGING:
MAINSHEET: boom-end sheeting

SAILS

SUPPLIED WITH BASE BOAT: reefable main, working jib

INTERIOR

BERTHS: 5 berths: 1 double V, 1 double convertible dinette, 1 single quarterberth
TABLE: dinette
HEAD(S):
COLD STORAGE: portable ice chest
STOVE: 2-burner alcohol
MAX. HEADROOM: 5 ft. 8 ins. with pop top up (4'5" with pop top down)

MACHINERY

ENGINE:
PROPELLER:
GENERATOR:

FREEDOM 21

DESIGNER: Gary Hoyt
BUILDER: Freedom Yachts International, Inc.

STATISTICS

LOA: 21 ft. 8 ins.
LWL: 17 ft. 8 ins.
BEAM: 8 ft. 0 ins.
DISPLACEMENT
deep keel: 1,800 lbs.
shoal keel: 2,050 lbs.
c/board:
BALLAST
deep keel: 500 lbs.
shoal keel: 750 lbs.
c/board:
DRAFT
deep keel: 3 ft. 9 ins.
shoal keel: 2 ft. 0 ins.
c/board up:
c/board down:

SAIL AREA: 200 sq. ft.
FRESH WATER:
FUEL CAPACITY:

COSTS

BASE BOAT: $12,850
DATE:
EST. ON WATER:
DATE:

RATIOS

SAIL AREA/DISP: 21.6
DISP/LENGTH: 145.9
BALLAST RATIO: 27.8
FUEL/DISP:
FRESH WATER/DISP:

DECK

STEERING: tiller
WINCHES:
SAFETY: bow and stern pulpits with single lifelines
ANCHOR:
NAV LIGHTS:

RIG

TYPE: cat rig
RIGGING: unstayed
MAINSHEET: mid-boom sheeting

SAILS

SUPPLIED WITH BASE BOAT:

INTERIOR

BERTHS: 4 berths: 1 double V, 2 single settees
TABLE: removable
HEAD(S): 1 head
COLD STORAGE: built-in icebox
STOVE:
MAX. HEADROOM: ft. ins.

MACHINERY

ENGINE:
PROPELLER:
GENERATOR:

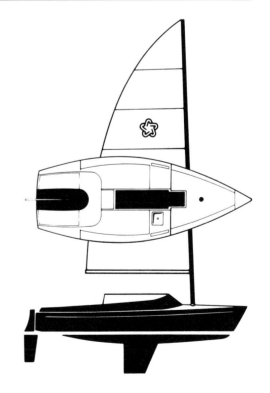

GLOUCESTER 22

DESIGNER: Stu Windley
BUILDER: Gloucester Yachts, Inc.

STATISTICS

LOA: 21 ft. 8 ins.
LWL: 18 ft. 8 ins.
BEAM: 8 ft. 3 ins.
DISPLACEMENT
deep keel: 2,400 lbs.
shoal keel:
c/board:
BALLAST
deep keel: 800 lbs.
shoal keel:
c/board:
DRAFT
deep keel:
shoal keel:
c/board up: 1 ft. 8 ins.
c/board down: 4 ft. 11 ins.

SAIL AREA: 216 sq. ft.
FRESH WATER: 0 gals.
FUEL CAPACITY: 0 gals.

COSTS

BASE BOAT: $10,450
DATE: 02/01/85
EST. ON WATER: $12,000
DATE: 02/01/85

RATIOS

SAIL AREA/DISP: 19.28
DISP/LENGTH: 164
BALLAST RATIO: 33.33
FUEL/DISP: 0.0
FRESH WATER/DISP: 0.0

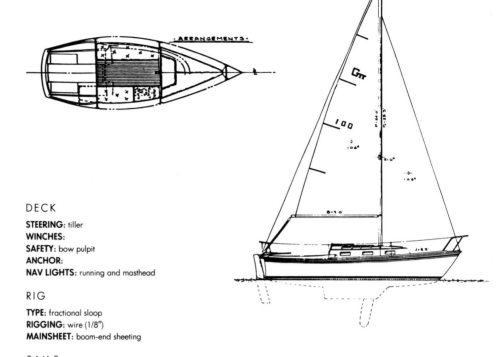

INTERIOR

BERTHS: 4 berths: 1 double V, 2 single settees
TABLE:
HEAD(S):
COLD STORAGE: 2 coolers (48 qt.)
STOVE:
MAX. HEADROOM: sitting

MACHINERY

ENGINE:
PROPELLER:
GENERATOR:

DECK

STEERING: tiller
WINCHES:
SAFETY: bow pulpit
ANCHOR:
NAV LIGHTS: running and masthead

RIG

TYPE: fractional sloop
RIGGING: wire (1/8")
MAINSHEET: boom-end sheeting

SAILS

SUPPLIED WITH BASE BOAT: main, jib

O'DAY 222

DESIGNER: C. Raymond Hunt Associates
BUILDER: Lear Siegler Marine

STATISTICS

LOA: 21 ft. 9 ins.
LWL: 19 ft. 7 ins.
BEAM: 7 ft. 11 ins.
DISPLACEMENT
deep keel: 2,200 lbs.
shoal keel:
c/board:
BALLAST
deep keel: 800 lbs.
shoal keel:
c/board:
DRAFT
deep keel:
shoal keel:
c/board up: 1 ft. 8 ins.
c/board down: 4 ft. 8 ins.

SAIL AREA: 207 sq. ft.
FRESH WATER: 0 gals.
FUEL CAPACITY: 0 gals.

COSTS

BASE BOAT: $11,500
DATE: 11/85
EST. ON WATER:
DATE:

RATIOS

SAIL AREA/DISP: 19.57
DISP/LENGTH: 130
BALLAST RATIO: 36.36
FUEL/DISP: 0.0
FRESH WATER/DISP: 0.0

DECK

STEERING: tiller
WINCHES: 2 Barlow winches (#16)
SAFETY:
ANCHOR:
NAV LIGHTS: running and masthead

RIG

TYPE: fractional rig sloop
RIGGING: 1 × 19 SS wire
MAINSHEET: 3-part with boom-end sheeting

SAILS

SUPPLIED WITH BASE BOAT: main (1 reef), jib (roller furling)

INTERIOR

BERTHS: 4 berths: 1 double V, 2 single settees
TABLE:
HEAD(S):
COLD STORAGE:
STOVE:
MAX. HEADROOM:

MACHINERY

ENGINE:
PROPELLER:
GENERATOR:

BUILDER'S COMMENTS An ideal trailable boat for the 1980s, the O'Day 222 offers an inexpensive, easy to sail and trail package while delivering the "big boat" feel of her larger sisters.

CAL 22

DESIGNER: C. Raymond Hunt Associates
BUILDER: Lear Siegler Marine

STATISTICS

LOA: 22 ft. 0 ins.
LWL: 19 ft. 7 ins.
BEAM: 7 ft. 9 ins.
DISPLACEMENT
deep keel: 2,100 lbs.
shoal keel:
c/board:
BALLAST
deep keel: 775 lbs.
shoal keel:
c/board:
DRAFT
deep keel: 3 ft. 6 ins.
shoal keel: 2 ft. 10 ins.
c/board up:
c/board down:

INTERIOR

BERTHS: 4 berths: 1 double V, 2 single settees
TABLE: fold-down
HEAD(S):
COLD STORAGE:
STOVE:
MAX. HEADROOM:

MACHINERY

ENGINE:
PROPELLER:
GENERATOR:

SAIL AREA: 277 sq. ft.
FRESH WATER: 0 gals.
FUEL CAPACITY: 0 gals.

COSTS

BASE BOAT: $12,500
DATE: 1/1/86
EST. ON WATER:
DATE:

RATIOS

SAIL AREA/DISP: 27.02
DISP/LENGTH: 124
BALLAST RATIO: 36.90
FUEL/DISP: 0.0
FRESH WATER/DISP: 0.0

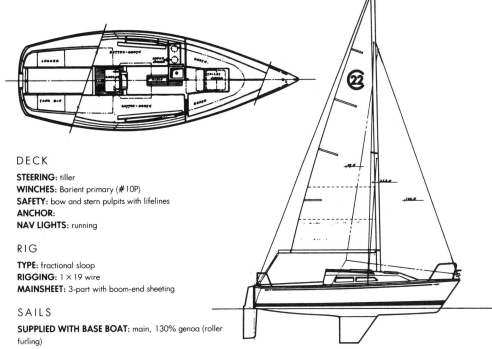

DECK

STEERING: tiller
WINCHES: Barient primary (#10P)
SAFETY: bow and stern pulpits with lifelines
ANCHOR:
NAV LIGHTS: running

RIG

TYPE: fractional sloop
RIGGING: 1 × 19 wire
MAINSHEET: 3-part with boom-end sheeting

SAILS

SUPPLIED WITH BASE BOAT: main, 130% genoa (roller furling)

BUILDER'S COMMENTS When you're ready to move up to the stability and safety of a keel boat, the Cal 22 is the most logical step. Standard roller furling, 130% genoa, and aft-led halyard and reef line contributes to ease of handling and safety. Attention to detail sets Cal apart.

MACGREGOR 22

DESIGNER:
BUILDER: MacGregor Yacht Corporation

STATISTICS

LOA: 22 ft. 0 ins.
LWL:
BEAM: 7 ft. 4 ins.
DISPLACEMENT
deep keel: 1,800 lbs.
shoal keel:
c/board:
BALLAST
deep keel: 500 lbs.
shoal keel:
c/board:
DRAFT
deep keel:
shoal keel:
c/board up: 1 ft. 0 ins.
c/board down: 5 ft. 6 ins.

INTERIOR

BERTHS: 5 berths: 1 double V, 1 single settee, 1 double convertible dinette
TABLE: dinette converting to bunk
HEAD(S): 1 head
COLD STORAGE:
STOVE:
MAX. HEADROOM:

MACHINERY

ENGINE:
PROPELLER:
GENERATOR:

SAIL AREA: 177 sq. ft.
FRESH WATER:
FUEL CAPACITY:

COSTS

BASE BOAT: $6,580
DATE: 04/01/85
EST. ON WATER:
DATE:

RATIOS

SAIL AREA/DISP: 19.18
DISP/LENGTH:
BALLAST RATIO: 27.78
FUEL/DISP:
FRESH WATER/DISP:

DECK

STEERING: tiller
WINCHES:
SAFETY: bow and stern pulpits with single lifelines
ANCHOR:
NAV LIGHTS: running and masthead

RIG

TYPE: masthead sloop
RIGGING:
MAINSHEET: boom-end sheeting

SAILS

SUPPLIED WITH BASE BOAT: main, working jib

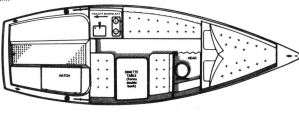

NONSUCH 22

DESIGNER: Mark Ellis Design, Ltd.
BUILDER: Hinterhoeller Yachts

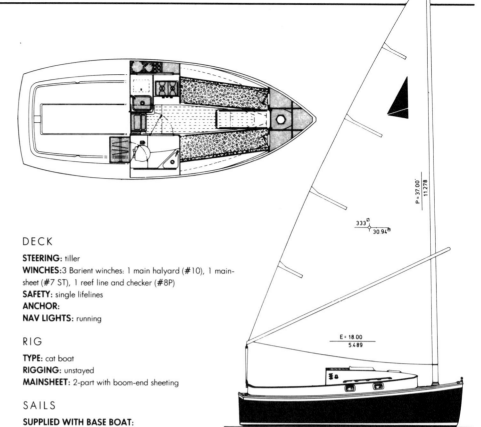

STATISTICS

LOA: 22 ft. 0.0 ins.
LWL: 20 ft. 6.5 ins.
BEAM: 8 ft. 6.0 ins.
DISPLACEMENT
deep keel: 5,000 lbs.
shoal keel:
c/board:
BALLAST
deep keel: 1,800 lbs.
shoal keel:
c/board:
DRAFT
deep keel: 3 ft. 8 ins.
shoal keel:
c/board up:
c/board down:

SAIL AREA: 333 sq. ft.
FRESH WATER: 23 gals.
FUEL CAPACITY: 15 gals.

COSTS

BASE BOAT:
DATE:
EST. ON WATER:
DATE:

RATIOS

SAIL AREA/DISP: 18.27
DISP/LENGTH: 257.59
BALLAST RATIO: 36
FUEL/DISP: 2.25
FRESH WATER/DISP: 3.68

INTERIOR

BERTHS: 3 berths: 1 single settee, 1 double extension settee
TABLE: bulkhead-mounted stowaway
HEAD(S): 1 head with holding tank (23 gal.)
COLD STORAGE: built-in icebox
STOVE:
MAX. HEADROOM: 6 ft. 0 ins.

MACHINERY

ENGINE: 8 HP Westerbeke #2-10 diesel with 2:1 reduction gear
PROPELLER: 2-blade
GENERATOR:

DECK

STEERING: tiller
WINCHES: 3 Barient winches: 1 main halyard (#10), 1 mainsheet (#7 ST), 1 reef line and checker (#8P)
SAFETY: single lifelines
ANCHOR:
NAV LIGHTS: running

RIG

TYPE: cat boat
RIGGING: unstayed
MAINSHEET: 2-part with boom-end sheeting

SAILS

SUPPLIED WITH BASE BOAT:

DEHLER 22

DESIGNER: Van de Stadt
DISTRIBUTOR: Southwest Marine Sales, Inc. (built in Germany by Dehler Yachts)

STATISTICS

LOA: 22 ft. 0 ins.
LWL:
BEAM: 8 ft. 0 ins.
DISPLACEMENT
deep keel: 1,980 lbs.
shoal keel:
c/board:
BALLAST
deep keel: 440 lbs.
shoal keel:
c/board:
DRAFT
deep keel: 4 ft. 0 ins.
shoal keel:
c/board up:
c/board down:

SAIL AREA: 247 sq. ft.
FRESH WATER:
FUEL CAPACITY:

COSTS

BASE BOAT:
DATE:
EST. ON WATER:
DATE:

RATIOS

SAIL AREA/DISP:
DISP/LENGTH: 229
BALLAST RATIO: 22.2
FUEL/DISP:
FRESH WATER/DISP:

DECK

STEERING: tiller
WINCHES:
SAFETY:
ANCHOR:
NAV LIGHTS:

RIG

TYPE:
RIGGING:
MAINSHEET:

SAILS

SUPPLIED WITH BASE BOAT: main, working jib

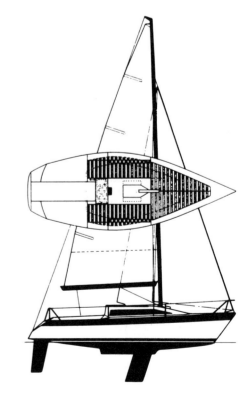

INTERIOR

BERTHS: 4 berths: 1 double V, 2 single settees
TABLE: centerline
HEAD(S):
COLD STORAGE:
STOVE: 2-burner
MAX. HEADROOM:

MACHINERY

ENGINE: 6 HP BMW diesel
PROPELLER:
GENERATOR:

S2 6.9/22'

DESIGNER: S2 Yachts
BUILDER: S2 Yachts, Inc.

STATISTICS

LOA: 22 ft. 0 ins.
LWL: 18 ft. 9 ins.
BEAM: 8 ft. 0 ins.
DISPLACEMENT
deep keel: 2,200 lbs.
shoal keel:
c/board:
BALLAST
deep keel: 770 lbs.
shoal keel:
c/board:
DRAFT
deep keel:
shoal keel:
c/board up: 0 ft. 10 ins.
c/board down: 4 ft. 6 ins.

INTERIOR

BERTHS: 4 berths: 1 double V, 2 single settees
TABLE:
HEAD(S):
COLD STORAGE: built-in icebox
STOVE:
MAX. HEADROOM: 4 ft. 6 ins.

MACHINERY

ENGINE:
PROPELLER:
GENERATOR:

SAIL AREA: 229 sq. ft.
FRESH WATER: 0 gals.
FUEL CAPACITY: 0 gals.

COSTS

BASE BOAT:
DATE:
EST. ON WATER:
DATE:

RATIOS

SAIL AREA/DISP: 22.18
DISP/LENGTH: 148
BALLAST RATIO: 35.0
FUEL/DISP: 0.0
FRESH WATER/DISP: 0.0

DECK

STEERING: tiller
WINCHES: 4 Lewmar winches: 2 primary (#46 2sp), 2 halyard (#8)
SAFETY: bow pulpit with lifelines
ANCHOR:
NAV LIGHTS: running

RIG

TYPE: fractional rig sloop
RIGGING: 1 × 19 wire
MAINSHEET: 4-part with boom-end sheeting

SAILS

SUPPLIED WITH BASE BOAT:

BUILDER'S COMMENTS The "pocket" version of the formidable 7.9M, designed to match performance aspects in a reduced size. The S2 6.9M is a good all-around club racer/daysailer, with accommodations that make her a weekend cruiser. The assurance of S2 quality is evident in engineering, performance craftmanship, and attention to detail throughout.

SIRIUS 22

DESIGNER: Vandestadt & McGruer
BUILDER: Vandestadt & McGruer, Ltd.

STATISTICS

LOA: 22 ft. 1 ins.
LWL: 19 ft. 9 ins.
BEAM: 7 ft. 11 ins.
DISPLACEMENT
deep keel: 2,000 lbs.
shoal keel:
c/board:
BALLAST
swing keel: 525 lbs.
fixed keel: 750 lbs.
c/board:
DRAFT
swing keel: 16 ins. to 5 ft.
fixed keel: 3 ft. 6 ins.
c/board up:
c/board down:

INTERIOR

BERTHS: 5 berths: 1 double V, 2 double settees, 1 single quarterberth
TABLE: dropleaf
HEAD(S): recirculating portable
COLD STORAGE:
STOVE:
MAX. HEADROOM: 6 ft. 0 ins. with pop top up (4 ft. 9 ins. with pop top down)

MACHINERY

ENGINE: 9 HP Yanmar #1 GM10 diesel outboard
PROPELLER: 2-blade
GENERATOR:

SAIL AREA: 203 sq. ft.
FRESH WATER: 5 gals.
FUEL CAPACITY:

COSTS

BASE BOAT: $10,950
DATE: 06/24/85
EST. ON WATER: $10,950
DATE: 06/24/85

RATIOS

SAIL AREA/DISP: 20.51
DISP/LENGTH: 117.5
BALLAST RATIO: 39
FUEL/DISP:
FRESH WATER/DISP: 2.00

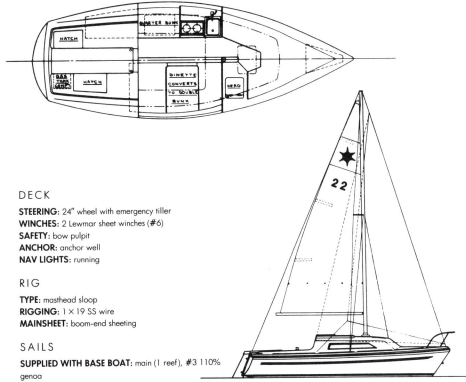

DECK

STEERING: 24" wheel with emergency tiller
WINCHES: 2 Lewmar sheet winches (#6)
SAFETY: bow pulpit
ANCHOR: anchor well
NAV LIGHTS: running

RIG

TYPE: masthead sloop
RIGGING: 1 × 19 SS wire
MAINSHEET: boom-end sheeting

SAILS

SUPPLIED WITH BASE BOAT: main (1 reef), #3 110% genoa

MARSHALL 22

DESIGNER: Breck Marshall
BUILDER: Marshall Marine Corporation

STATISTICS

LOA: 22 ft. 2 ins.
LWL: 21 ft. 4 ins.
BEAM: 10 ft. 2 ins.
DISPLACEMENT
deep keel: 5,660 lbs.
shoal keel:
c/board:
BALLAST
deep keel: 850 lbs.
shoal keel:
c/board:
DRAFT
deep keel:
shoal keel:
c/board up: 2 ft. 0 ins.
c/board down: 5 ft. 6 ins.

SAIL AREA: 388 sq. ft.
FRESH WATER: 20 gals.
FUEL CAPACITY: 19 gals.

COSTS

BASE BOAT: $29,500
DATE: 04/01/85
EST. ON WATER: $32,000
DATE: 04/01/85

RATIOS

SAIL AREA/DISP: 19.54
DISP/LENGTH: 260
BALLAST RATIO: 15.02
FUEL/DISP: 2.52
FRESH WATER/DISP: 2.83

DECK

STEERING: wheel
WINCHES:
SAFETY:
ANCHOR: Danforth 135 anchor with 120' nylon line
NAV LIGHTS: running

RIG

TYPE: cat boat
RIGGING: SS headstay
MAINSHEET: 5-part

SAILS

SUPPLIED WITH BASE BOAT: reefable main

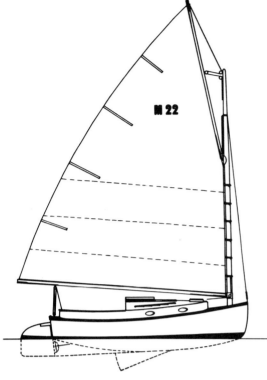

INTERIOR

BERTHS: 4 berths: 2 single settees, 2 single quarterberths
TABLE: dropleaf on centerboard trunk
HEAD(S): 1 head
COLD STORAGE: icebox in cockpit (2.5. cu. ft.)
STOVE:
MAX. HEADROOM: 4 ft. 7 ins.

MACHINERY

ENGINE: 18 HP Yanmar #26m diesel
PROPELLER: 2-blade 13" × 14" on 1" shaft
GENERATOR:

CAPE DORY 22 & 22D

DESIGNER:
BUILDER: Cape Dory Yachts

STATISTICS

LOA: 22 ft. 4 ins.
LWL: 16 ft. 3 ins.
BEAM: 7 ft. 4 ins.
DISPLACEMENT
deep keel: 3,200 lbs.
shoal keel:
c/board:
BALLAST
deep keel: 1,400 lbs.
shoal keel:
c/board:
DRAFT
deep keel: 3 ft. 0 ins.
shoal keel:
c/board up:
c/board down:

SAIL AREA: 240 sq. ft.
FRESH WATER: 24 gals.
FUEL CAPACITY:
13 gals. (22D only)

COSTS

BASE BOAT:
DATE:
EST. ON WATER:
DATE:

RATIOS

SAIL AREA/DISP: 17.68
DISP/LENGTH: 332.92
BALLAST RATIO: 43.75
FUEL/DISP: 3.05
FRESH WATER/DISP: 6.00

DECK

STEERING: tiller
WINCHES: 3 winches: 2 primary, 1 halyard
SAFETY: bow pulpit
ANCHOR: anchor roller
NAV LIGHTS: running

RIG

TYPE: masthead sloop
RIGGING: 1 × 19 wire
MAINSHEET: 3-part with boom-end sheeting

SAILS

SUPPLIED WITH BASE BOAT:

INTERIOR

BERTHS: 3 berths: 1 double V, 1 single settee
TABLE:
HEAD(S):
COLD STORAGE: portable ice chest in 22, built-in icebox in 22D
STOVE:
MAX. HEADROOM:

MACHINERY

ENGINE: 7.5 HP Yanmar diesel (22D only)
PROPELLER: fixed on 1" shaft (22D only)
GENERATOR:

CAPE DORY TYPHOON SENIOR

DESIGNER: Carl Alberg
BUILDER: Cape Dory Yachts

STATISTICS

LOA: 22 ft. 5 ins.
LWL: 16 ft. 6 ins.
BEAM: 7 ft. 5 ins.
DISPLACEMENT
deep keel: 3,300 lbs.
shoal keel:
c/board:
BALLAST
deep keel: 1,700 lbs.
shoal keel:
c/board:
DRAFT
deep keel: 3 ft. 1 ins.
shoal keel:
c/board up:
c/board down:

SAIL AREA: 245 sq. ft.
FRESH WATER: 0 gals.
FUEL CAPACITY: 0 gals.

COSTS

BASE BOAT:
DATE:
EST. ON WATER:
DATE:

RATIOS

SAIL AREA/DISP: 17.68
DISP/LENGTH: 327.95
BALLAST RATIO: 51.51
FUEL/DISP: 0.0
FRESH WATER/DISP: 0.0

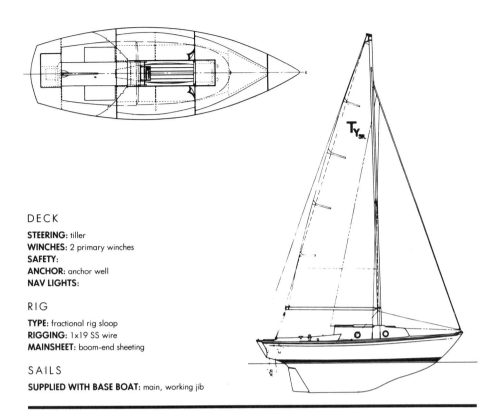

INTERIOR

BERTHS: 4 berths: 1 double V, 2 single settees
TABLE:
HEAD(S):
COLD STORAGE:
STOVE:
MAX. HEADROOM:

MACHINERY

ENGINE:
PROPELLER:
GENERATOR:

DECK

STEERING: tiller
WINCHES: 2 primary winches
SAFETY:
ANCHOR: anchor well
NAV LIGHTS:

RIG

TYPE: fractional rig sloop
RIGGING: 1x19 SS wire
MAINSHEET: boom-end sheeting

SAILS

SUPPLIED WITH BASE BOAT: main, working jib

J-22

DESIGNER: Rod Johnstone
BUILDER: J Boats, Inc.

STATISTICS

LOA: 22 ft. 5 ins.
LWL: 19 ft. 0 ins.
BEAM: 8 ft. 0 ins.
DISPLACEMENT
deep keel: 1,750 lbs.
shoal keel:
c/board:
BALLAST
deep keel: 700 lbs.
shoal keel:
c/board:
DRAFT
deep keel: 3 ft. 7 ins.
shoal keel:
c/board up:
c/board down:

SAIL AREA: 223 sq. ft.
FRESH WATER: 0 gals.
FUEL CAPACITY: 0 gals.

COSTS

BASE BOAT: $9,650
DATE: 04/01/85
EST. ON WATER:
DATE:

RATIOS

SAIL AREA/DISP: 24.57
DISP/LENGTH: 113.9
BALLAST RATIO: 40.00
FUEL/DISP: 0.0
FRESH WATER/DISP: 0.0

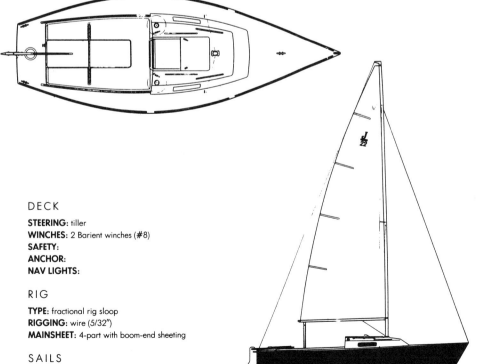

INTERIOR

BERTHS: 2 berths: 1 double V
TABLE:
HEAD(S):
COLD STORAGE:
STOVE:
MAX. HEADROOM:

MACHINERY

ENGINE:
PROPELLER:
GENERATOR:

DECK

STEERING: tiller
WINCHES: 2 Barient winches (#8)
SAFETY:
ANCHOR:
NAV LIGHTS:

RIG

TYPE: fractional rig sloop
RIGGING: wire (5/32")
MAINSHEET: 4-part with boom-end sheeting

SAILS

SUPPLIED WITH BASE BOAT:

TANZER 22

DESIGNER: J. Tanzer
BUILDER: Tanzer industries, Inc.

STATISTICS

LOA: 22 ft. 6 ins.
LWL: 19 ft. 9 ins.
BEAM: 7 ft. 10 ins.
DISPLACEMENT
deep keel: 2,900 lbs.
shoal keel:
c/board: 3,100 lbs.
BALLAST
deep keel: 1,250 lbs.
shoal keel:
c/board: 1,500 lbs.
DRAFT
deep keel: 3 ft. 5 ins.
shoal keel:
c/board up: 2 ft. 0 ins.
c/board down: 4 ft. 0 ins.

SAIL AREA: 222 sq. ft.
FRESH WATER: 15 gals.
FUEL CAPACITY: 0 gals.

COSTS

BASE BOAT: $12,585
DATE: 02/01/85
EST. ON WATER: $13,000
DATE: 02/01/85

RATIOS

SAIL AREA/DISP:
DISP/LENGTH: 168
BALLAST RATIO: 43.10
FUEL/DISP: 0.0
FRESH WATER/DISP: 4.13

INTERIOR

BERTHS: 5 berths: 1 double V, 1 double convertible settee, 1 single quarterberth
TABLE: dinette
HEAD(S): 1 portable Porta-Potti
COLD STORAGE: built-in icebox
STOVE: 2-burner alcohol
MAX. HEADROOM: 6 ft. 2 ins. (with optional pop top)

MACHINERY

ENGINE:
PROPELLER:
GENERATOR:

DECK

STEERING: tiller
WINCHES: 3 winches:
2 primary, 1 halyard
SAFETY: bow pulpit
ANCHOR: anchor well
NAV LIGHTS: running

RIG

TYPE: masthead sloop
RIGGING: wire (5/32")
MAINSHEET: boom-end sheeting

SAILS

SUPPLIED WITH BASE BOAT:
main (1 reef), working jib or lapper

BUILDER'S COMMENTS First introduced in 1970, over 2,200 Tanzer 22s can now be found sailing in Canada and the U.S.A., from Newfoundland to Florida, Alaska to California. A true cruiser/racer with particular emphasis on performance. A strong Class/Owners' Association sponsors international and local racing, fleet rendezvous, seminars, and other activities of interest to Tanzer 22 owners.

ROB ROY 23

DESIGNER: Ted Brewer
BUILDER: Marine Concepts

STATISTICS

LOA: 22 ft. 8 ins.
LWL: 20 ft. 10 ins.
BEAM: 6 ft. 11 ins.
DISPLACEMENT
deep keel: 2,800 lbs.
shoal keel:
c/board:
BALLAST
deep keel: 900 lbs.
shoal keel:
c/board:
DRAFT
deep keel:
shoal keel:
c/board up: 1 ft. 7 ins.
c/board down: 4 ft. 8 ins.

SAIL AREA: 264.0 sq. ft.
FRESH WATER: 14.5 gals.
FUEL CAPACITY: 0 gals.

COSTS

BASE BOAT: $18,000
DATE: 04/85
EST. ON WATER:
DATE:

RATIOS

SAIL AREA/DISP: 20.8
DISP/LENGTH: 132.6
BALLAST RATIO: 32.14
FUEL/DISP: 0.0
FRESH WATER/DISP: 4.14

INTERIOR

BERTHS: 2 berths: 2 single settees converting to 1 double
TABLE: 2 bulkhead-mounted
HEAD(S): 1 Porta Potti
COLD STORAGE:
STOVE: 1- or 2-burner alcohol
MAX. HEADROOM: 4 ft. 4 ins.

MACHINERY

ENGINE:
PROPELLER:
GENERATOR:

DECK

STEERING: tiller
WINCHES:
SAFETY:
ANCHOR:
NAV LIGHTS: running and masthead

RIG

TYPE: fractional rig canoe yawl with A & D Mast, Inc. spars
RIGGING: 1x19 wire (1/8")
MAINSHEET: 3-part with mid-boom sheeting

SAILS

SUPPLIED WITH BASE BOAT: main, working jib, mizzen

BUILDER'S COMMENTS The Rob Roy 23 is a classic canoe yawl, a true pocket cruiser designed by Ted Brewer. She opens up a new world of sailing. Her light displacement and shallow draft offer the trailering ability associated with much smaller boats. The ease of launching and short set-up time guarantee you will use your boat often. She has sail enough for light air cruising with the ability to stand up to a breeze. Her easy reefing system makes this possible. The yawl rig allows you to reef easily from the cockpit and maintain balance while lowering the center of effort quickly. In 18 knot winds, she will cruise comfortably to windward at 4.5 knots under jib and jigger alone.

JEANNEAU BAHIA

DESIGNER: Philippe Harle
DISTRIBUTOR: Nautique International (built in France by Jeanneau, S.A.)

STATISTICS

LOA: 22 ft. 9 ins.
LWL: 18 ft. 1 ins.
BEAM: 7 ft. 11 ins.
DISPLACEMENT
deep keel:
shoal keel:
c/board: 1,850 lbs.
BALLAST
deep keel:
shoal keel:
c/board: 620 lbs.
DRAFT
deep keel:
shoal keel:
c/board up: 1 ft. 5 ins.
c/board down: 4 ft. 9 ins.

INTERIOR

BERTHS: 4 berths: 1 double V, 2 single settees
TABLE: bulkhead-mounted folding
HEAD(S):
COLD STORAGE:
STOVE:
MAX. HEADROOM:

MACHINERY

ENGINE:
PROPELLER:
GENERATOR:

SAIL AREA: 240 sq. ft.
FRESH WATER:
FUEL CAPACITY:

COSTS

BASE BOAT:
DATE:
EST. ON WATER:
DATE:

RATIOS

SAIL AREA/DISP: 25.48
DISP/LENGTH: 139.74
BALLAST RATIO: 33.51
FUEL/DISP:
FRESH WATER/DISP:

DECK

STEERING: tiller
WINCHES: 3 winches: 2 primary, 1 halyard
SAFETY: bow pulpit with lifelines
ANCHOR: anchor locker
NAV LIGHTS:

RIG

TYPE: fractional rig sloop
RIGGING:
MAINSHEET: mid-boom sheeting

SAILS

SUPPLIED WITH BASE BOAT: main, genoa

PEARSON 23

DESIGNER: Bill Shaw
BUILDER: Pearson Yachts

STATISTICS

LOA: 23 ft. 0 ins.
LWL: 20 ft. 0 ins.
BEAM: 8 ft. 0 ins.
DISPLACEMENT
deep keel: 3,500 lbs.
shoal keel:
c/board:
BALLAST
deep keel: 1,200 lbs.
shoal keel:
c/board:
DRAFT
deep keel:
shoal keel:
c/board up: 2 ft. 4 ins.
c/board down: 5 ft. 2 ins.

INTERIOR

BERTHS: 4 berths: 1 double V, 1 double convertible
TABLE:
HEAD(S):
COLD STORAGE:
STOVE:
MAX. HEADROOM:

MACHINERY

ENGINE:
PROPELLER:
GENERATOR:

SAIL AREA: 232 sq. ft.
FRESH WATER: 5 gals.
FUEL CAPACITY: 0 gals.

COSTS

BASE BOAT:
DATE:
EST. ON WATER:
DATE:

RATIOS

SAIL AREA/DISP: 16.15
DISP/LENGTH: 167
BALLAST RATIO: 40.00
FUEL/DISP: 0.0
FRESH WATER/DISP: 1.14

DECK

STEERING: tiller
WINCHES:
SAFETY: bow pulpit with single lifelines
ANCHOR:
NAV LIGHTS:

RIG

TYPE: sloop
RIGGING:
MAINSHEET: mid-boom sheeting

SAILS

SUPPLIED WITH BASE BOAT: main

SOVEREIGN 23

DESIGNER: Sovereign Design Group
BUILDER: Sovereign Yacht Co., Inc.

STATISTICS

LOA: 23 ft. 0 ins.
LWL: 18 ft. 6 ins.
BEAM: 8 ft. 0 ins.
DISPLACEMENT
deep keel: 3,250 lbs.
shoal keel:
c/board:
BALLAST
deep keel: 1,350 lbs.
shoal keel:
c/board:
DRAFT
deep keel: 3 ft. 8 ins.
shoal keel:
c/board up: 2 ft. 4 ins.
c/board down: 5 ft. 10 ins.

SAIL AREA: 240 sq. ft.
FRESH WATER: 20 gals.
FUEL CAPACITY: 0 gals.

COSTS

BASE BOAT: $13,495
DATE: 05/01/85
EST. ON WATER: $15,500
DATE: 05/01/85

RATIOS

SAIL AREA/DISP: 17.50
DISP/LENGTH: 229
BALLAST RATIO: 41.53
FUEL/DISP: 0.0
FRESH WATER/DISP: 4.92

DECK

STEERING: tiller
WINCHES: 2 genoa winches
SAFETY: bow pulpit with single lifelines
ANCHOR: anchor well
NAV LIGHTS: running

RIG

TYPE: masthead sloop
RIGGING: 1x19 SS wire
MAINSHEET: mid-boom sheeting

SAILS

SUPPLIED WITH BASE BOAT: main, genoa

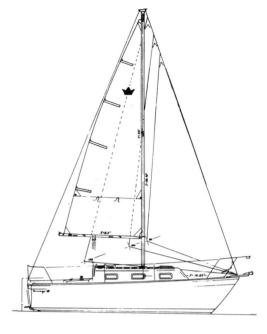

INTERIOR

BERTHS: 4 berths: 1 double V, 2 single settees
TABLE: dinette
HEAD(S):
COLD STORAGE: 3 cu. ft.
STOVE:
MAX. HEADROOM: 5 ft. 7 ins.

MACHINERY

ENGINE:
PROPELLER:
GENERATOR:

BAVARIA 707

DESIGNER: K. W. Schroeder
BUILDER: Bavaria Yachtbau GmbH

STATISTICS

LOA: 23 ft. 3 ins.
LWL: 20 ft. 0 ins.
BEAM: 8 ft. 0 ins.
DISPLACEMENT
deep keel: 3,085
shoal keel:
c/board:
BALLAST
deep keel: 1,230 lbs.
shoal keel:
c/board:
DRAFT
deep keel: 4 ft. 1 ins.
shoal keel:
c/board up: 2 ft. 3 ins.
c/board down: 4 ft. 1 ins.

SAIL AREA: 257 sq. ft.
FRESH WATER: 28 gals.
FUEL CAPACITY: 0 gals.

COSTS

BASE BOAT:
DATE:
EST. ON WATER:
DATE:

RATIOS

SAIL AREA/DISP: 19.40
DISP/LENGTH: 172
BALLAST RATIO: 39.87
FUEL/DISP: 0.0
FRESH WATER/DISP: 7.26

DECK

STEERING: tiller
WINCHES: 4 winches: 2 primary, 2 halyard
SAFETY: bow and stern pulpits with double lifelines
ANCHOR: anchor roller and locker
NAV LIGHTS: running and masthead

RIG

TYPE: masthead sloop
RIGGING: 1x19 wire
MAINSHEET: mid-boom sheeting

SAILS

SUPPLIED WITH BASE BOAT: main (2 reefs), working jib

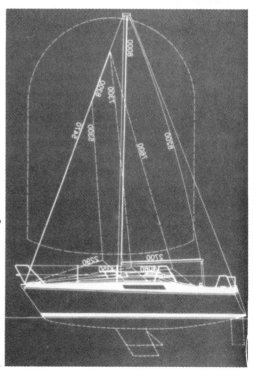

INTERIOR

BERTHS: 5 berths: 1 double V, 1 double convertible dinette, 1 single settee
TABLE: dinette
HEAD(S):
COLD STORAGE: built-in icebox (5 gal.)
STOVE: two-burner alcohol
MAX. HEADROOM: 5 ft. 6 ins.

MACHINERY

ENGINE:
PROPELLER:
GENERATOR:

BUILDER'S COMMENTS The Bavaria 707 is the yacht that has been built the longest by Bavaria Yachtbau GmbH. With her pleasant lines and functional, safe deck fittings and equipment, she is in a class by herself.

HUNTER 23

DESIGNER: Hunter Design Group
BUILDER: Hunter Marine

STATISTICS

LOA: 23 ft. 3 ins.
LWL: 19 ft. 7 ins.
BEAM: 8 ft. 0 ins.
DISPLACEMENT
deep keel: 2,300 lbs.
shoal keel:
c/board:
BALLAST
deep keel: 820 lbs.
shoal keel:
c/board:
DRAFT
deep keel:
shoal keel:
c/board up: 2 ft. 2 ins.
c/board down:

SAIL AREA: 235 sq. ft.
FRESH WATER: 5 gals.
FUEL CAPACITY: 0 gals.

COSTS

BASE BOAT:
DATE:
EST. ON WATER: $11,000
DATE: 11/85

RATIOS

SAIL AREA/DISP: 21.62
DISP/LENGTH: 136
BALLAST RATIO: 35.65
FUEL/DISP: 0.0
FRESH WATER/DISP: 1.74

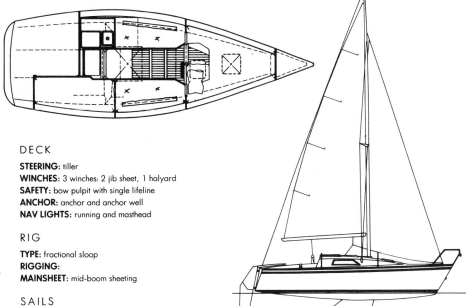

INTERIOR

BERTHS: 5 berths: 1 double V, 2 single settees, 1 single quarterberth
TABLE: dinette
HEAD(S): portable
COLD STORAGE:
STOVE: 1-burner alcohol
MAX. HEADROOM:

MACHINERY

ENGINE: outboard
PROPELLER:
GENERATOR:

DECK

STEERING: tiller
WINCHES: 3 winches: 2 jib sheet, 1 halyard
SAFETY: bow pulpit with single lifeline
ANCHOR: anchor and anchor well
NAV LIGHTS: running and masthead

RIG

TYPE: fractional sloop
RIGGING:
MAINSHEET: mid-boom sheeting

SAILS

SUPPLIED WITH BASE BOAT: main, jib

BUILDER'S COMMENTS The Hunter 23 comes complete with boat, motor, and trailer. Combined with Cruise Pac (TM), you have everything you need to set sail the day of your purchase. The Hunter 23 has been built with our "Commitment to Better Engineering." Proof is shown in the spacious cabin area for a 23 and the new "Winged Keel" design for better performance. The only complete trailerable sailboat available at a price you won't believe.

LAGUNA 24

DESIGNER: W. Shad Turner
BUILDER: Laguna Yachts, Inc.

STATISTICS

LOA: 23 ft. 7 ins.
LWL: 20 ft. 0 ins.
BEAM: 8 ft. 4 ins.
DISPLACEMENT
deep keel: 2,600 lbs.
shoal keel:
c/board:
BALLAST
deep keel: 900 lbs.
shoal keel:
c/board:
DRAFT
deep keel: 2 ft. 11 ins.
shoal keel:
c/board up:
c/board down:

SAIL AREA: 251 sq. ft.
FRESH WATER: 0 gals.
FUEL CAPACITY: 0 gals.

COSTS

BASE BOAT:
DATE:
EST. ON WATER:
DATE:

RATIOS

SAIL AREA/DISP: 21.23
DISP/LENGTH: 145
BALLAST RATIO: 34.61
FUEL/DISP: 0.0
FRESH WATER/DISP: 0.0

DECK

STEERING: tiller
WINCHES: genoa sheet
SAFETY: bow and stern pulpits with lifelines
ANCHOR: anchor well
NAV LIGHTS: running and masthead

RIG

TYPE: masthead sloop
RIGGING:
MAINSHEET: boom-end sheeting

SAILS

SUPPLIED WITH BASE BOAT: main, working jib

INTERIOR

BERTHS: 5 berths: 1 double V, 1 double convertible dinette, 1 single quarterberth
TABLE: dinette
HEAD(S):
COLD STORAGE: portable ice chest
STOVE: 2-burner alcohol
MAX. HEADROOM: 6 ft. 0 ins. with pop top up (4'6" with pop top down)

MACHINERY

ENGINE:
PROPELLER:
GENERATOR:

S2 7.3/24'

DESIGNER: S2 Yachts
BUILDER: S2 Yachts, Inc.

STATISTICS

LOA: 23 ft. 10 ins.
LWL: 18 ft. 6 ins.
BEAM: 8 ft. 0 ins.
DISPLACEMENT
deep keel: 3,250 lbs/
shoal keel:
c/board:
BALLAST
deep keel: 255 lbs.
shoal keel:
c/board:
DRAFT
deep keel: 4 ft. 0 ins.
shoal keel:
c/board up:
c/board down:

INTERIOR

BERTHS: 4 berths: 1 double V, 2 single settees
TABLE: bulkhead-mounted
HEAD(S):
COLD STORAGE:
STOVE: stowaway alcohol
MAX. HEADROOM: 5 ft. 0 ins.

MACHINERY

ENGINE:
PROPELLER:
GENERATOR:

SAIL AREA: 255 sq. ft.
FRESH WATER: 12 gals.
FUEL CAPACITY: 0 gals.

COSTS

BASE BOAT:
DATE:
EST. ON WATER:
DATE:

RATIOS

SAIL AREA/DISP: 18.59
DISP/LENGTH: 229
BALLAST RATIO: 40.00
FUEL/DISP: 0.0
FRESH WATER/DISP: 2.95

DECK

STEERING: tiller
WINCHES: 2 Lewmar primary winches (#7)
SAFETY: bow pulpit with lifelines
ANCHOR:
NAV LIGHTS: running

RIG

TYPE: masthead sloop
RIGGING: 1x19 wire
MAINSHEET: 4-part with mid-boom sheeting

SAILS

SUPPLIED WITH BASE BOAT:

BUILDER'S COMMENTS Proof that performance engineering isn't proportionate to size. A trim capable 24' cruiser/daysailer that offers the perfect invitation into the S2 cruising line. With the classic S2 lines and the engineering features of a substantial cruising sailboat, the S2 7.3M is pure S2 quality.

JEANNEAU TONIC

DESIGNER: Doug Peterson
DISTRIBUTOR: Nautique International, Inc. (built in France by Jeanneau, S.A.)

STATISTICS

LOA: 23 ft. 11 ins.
LWL: 20 ft. 4 ins.
BEAM: 8 ft. 2 ins.
DISPLACEMENT
deep keel: 2,860 lbs.
shoal keel:
c/board: 2,926 lbs.
BALLAST
deep keel: 990 lbs.
shoal keel:
c/board: 1,086 lbs.
DRAFT
deep keel: 3 ft. 7 ins.
shoal keel:
c/board up: 2 ft. 3 ins.
c/board down: 4 ft. 6 ins.

INTERIOR

BERTHS: 4 berths: 1 double V, 1 double quarterberth
TABLE: fold-down
HEAD(S): 1 head
COLD STORAGE: portable ice chest
STOVE: 1-burner
MAX. HEADROOM.

MACHINERY

ENGINE: outboard well
PROPELLER:
GENERATOR:

SAIL AREA: 243.0 sq. ft.
FRESH WATER: 4.4 gals.
FUEL CAPACITY:

COSTS

BASE BOAT: keel $16,900
DATE: 02/01/85
c/board: $17,400
DATE: 02/01/85
EST. ON WATER:
DATE:

RATIOS

SAIL AREA/DISP: 19.35
DISP/LENGTH: 151.95
BALLAST RATIO: 34.62
FUEL/DISP:
FRESH WATER/DISP: 1.23

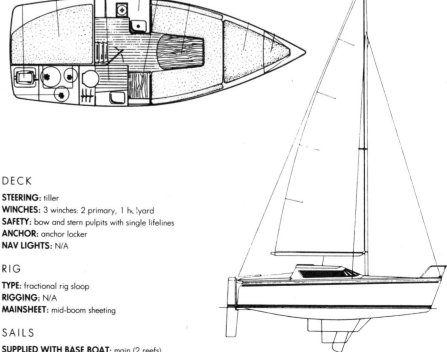

DECK

STEERING: tiller
WINCHES: 3 winches: 2 primary, 1 halyard
SAFETY: bow and stern pulpits with single lifelines
ANCHOR: anchor locker
NAV LIGHTS: N/A

RIG

TYPE: fractional rig sloop
RIGGING: N/A
MAINSHEET: mid-boom sheeting

SAILS

SUPPLIED WITH BASE BOAT: main (2 reefs)

J-24

DESIGNER: Rod Johnstone
BUILDER: J Boats, Inc.

STATISTICS

LOA: 24 ft. 0 ins.
LWL: 20 ft. 0 ins.
BEAM: 8 ft. 11 ins.
DISPLACEMENT
deep keel: 3,100 lbs.
shoal keel:
c/board:
BALLAST
deep keel: 935 lbs.
shoal keel:
c/board:
DRAFT
deep keel: 4 ft. 0 ins.
shoal keel:
c/board up:
c/board down:

INTERIOR

BERTHS: 4 berths: 1 double V, 2 single quarterberths
TABLE:
HEAD(S):
COLD STORAGE: cooler (48 qt.)
STOVE:
MAX. HEADROOM:

MACHINERY

ENGINE:
PROPELLER:
GENERATOR:

SAIL AREA: 261 sq. ft.
FRESH WATER: 0 gals.
FUEL CAPACITY: 0 gals.

COSTS

BASE BOAT: $15,700
DATE: 04/01/85
EST. ON WATER:
DATE:

RATIOS

SAIL AREA/DISP: 19.64
DISP/LENGTH: 172.99
BALLAST RATIO: 30.16
FUEL/DISP: 0.0
FRESH WATER/DISP: 0.0

DECK

STEERING: tiller
WINCHES: 2 Barient winches: 2 primary (#18)
SAFETY: bow and stern pulpits with single lifelines
ANCHOR:
NAV LIGHTS: running lights

RIG

TYPE: fractional rig sloop
RIGGING: wire
MAINSHEET: 4-part with boom-end sheeting

SAILS

SUPPLIED WITH BASE BOAT:

SEIDELMANN 245

DESIGNER:
BUILDER: Seidelmann Yachts

STATISTICS

LOA: 24 ft. 2 ins.
LWL: 20 ft. 6 ins.
BEAM: 8 ft. 0 ins.
DISPLACEMENT
deep keel:
shoal keel:
c/board: 3000 lbs.
BALLAST
deep keel:
shoal keel:
c/board: 1300 lbs.
DRAFT
deep keel:
shoal keel:
c/board up: 1 ft. 11 ins.
c/board down: 4 ft. 5 ins.

INTERIOR

BERTHS: 4 berths: 1 double V forward, 2 settees
TABLE: folding
HEAD(S):
COLD STORAGE: portable
STOVE: 1 burner alcohol
MAX. HEADROOM:

MACHINERY

ENGINE:
PROPELLER:
GENERATOR:

SAIL AREA: 267 sq. ft.
FRESH WATER: 10 gals.
FUEL CAPACITY: 0 gals.

COSTS

BASE BOAT: $20,600
DATE: 09/01/85
EST. ON WATER:
DATE:

RATIOS

SAIL AREA/DISP: 20.5
DISP/LENGTH: 155.5
BALLAST RATIO: 43.3
FUEL/DISP: 0.0
FRESH WATER/DISP: 2.7

DECK

STEERING: tiller
WINCHES: 2 winches
SAFETY: bow pulpit with single lifeline
ANCHOR: anchor well
NAV LIGHTS:

RIG

TYPE: fractional sloop
RIGGING: 1x19 wire
MAINSHEET: 4 part with midboom sheeting

SAILS

SUPPLIED WITH BASE BOAT:

CAL 24

DESIGNER: C. Raymond Hunt Associates
BUILDER: Lear Siegler Marine

STATISTICS

LOA: 24 ft. 4 ins.
LWL: 20 ft. 0 ins.
BEAM: 8 ft. 0 ins.
DISPLACEMENT
deep keel: 3,300 lbs.
shoal keel:
c/board:
BALLAST
deep keel: 1,175 lbs.
shoal keel: 1,400 lbs.
c/board:
DRAFT
deep keel: 4 ft. 3 ins.
shoal keel: 3 ft. 4 ins.
c/board up:
c/board down:

SAIL AREA: 261 sq. ft.
FRESH WATER: 15 gals.
FUEL CAPACITY: 0 gals.

COSTS

BASE BOAT:
DATE:
EST. ON WATER:
DATE:

RATIOS

SAIL AREA/DISP: 18.84
DISP/LENGTH: 184
BALLAST RATIO: 35.60
FUEL/DISP: 0.0
FRESH WATER/DISP: 3.63

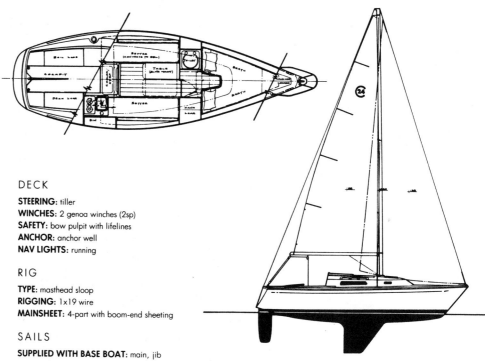

INTERIOR

BERTHS: 5 berths: 1 double V, 1 double convertible settee, 1 single settee
TABLE: bulkhead-mounted dropleaf
HEAD(S): self-contained portable marine toilet
COLD STORAGE: cooler (12 gal.)
STOVE:
MAX. HEADROOM:

MACHINERY

ENGINE:
PROPELLER:
GENERATOR:

DECK

STEERING: tiller
WINCHES: 2 genoa winches (2sp)
SAFETY: bow pulpit with lifelines
ANCHOR: anchor well
NAV LIGHTS: running

RIG

TYPE: masthead sloop
RIGGING: 1x19 wire
MAINSHEET: 4-part with boom-end sheeting

SAILS

SUPPLIED WITH BASE BOAT: main, jib

BUILDER'S COMMENTS A deep water sailboat with trailing sailing capability. A huge cockpit for day sailing and a functional interior that can sleep 5 make this the best 24' Cal we've ever made.

TANZER 7.5

DESIGNER: J. Tanzer
BUILDER: Tanzer Industries, Inc.

STATISTICS

LOA: 24 ft. 7 ins.
LWL: 21 ft. 0 ins.
BEAM: 8 ft. 0 ins.
DISPLACEMENT
deep keel: 3,800 lbs.
shoal keel: 4,150 lbs.
c/board:
BALLAST
deep keel: 1,600 lbs.
shoal keel: 1,950 lbs.
c/board:
DRAFT
deep keel: 4 ft. 0 ins.
shoal keel: 2 ft. 8 ins.
c/board up:
c/board down:

SAIL AREA: 225 sq. ft.
FRESH WATER: 15 gals.
FUEL CAPACITY:

COSTS

BASE BOAT: fin $17,275
shoal $17,500
DATE: 02/01/85
EST. ON WATER: $17,500
shoal $17,750
DATE: 02/01/85

RATIOS

SAIL AREA/DISP: 14.78
DISP/LENGTH: 183.18
BALLAST RATIO: 42.11
FUEL/DISP:
FRESH WATER/DISP: 3.16

DECK

STEERING: tiller
WINCHES: 3 winches: 2 primary, 1 halyard
SAFETY: bow pulpit
ANCHOR:
NAV LIGHTS: running

RIG

TYPE: masthead sloop
RIGGING: wire (5/32")
MAINSHEET: boom-end sheeting

SAILS

SUPPLIED WITH BASE BOAT: main (1 reef), working jib or lapper

INTERIOR

BERTHS: 4 berths: 1 double V, 2 single settees
TABLE: bulkhead-mounted
HEAD(S): 1 head with holding tank
COLD STORAGE: built-in icebox
STOVE: 2-burner alcohol
MAX. HEADROOM: 5 ft. 8 ins.

MACHINERY

ENGINE:
PROPELLER:
GENERATOR:

BUILDER'S COMMENTS A high performance 25 footer that can be trailered. Available with a fin keel for the race-oriented skipper, or a shoal keel for the cruising sailor. Over 700 Tanzer 7.5s have been built to date.

MACGREGOR 25

DESIGNER: Roger MacGregor
BUILDER: MacGregor Yacht Corporation

STATISTICS

LOA: 24 ft. 11 ins.
LWL:
BEAM: 7 ft. 11 ins.
DISPLACEMENT
deep keel:
shoal keel:
c/board: 2,100 lbs.
BALLAST
deep keel:
shoal keel:
c/board: 625 lbs.
DRAFT
deep keel:
shoal keel:
c/board up: 1 ft. 10 ins.
c/board down: 5 ft. 8 ins.

SAIL AREA: 236 sq. ft.
FRESH WATER:
FUEL CAPACITY:

COSTS

BASE BOAT:
DATE:
EST. ON WATER:
DATE:

RATIOS

SAIL AREA/DISP: 23.03
DISP/LENGTH:
BALLAST RATIO: 30.0
FUEL/DISP:
FRESH WATER/DISP:

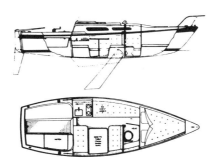

INTERIOR

BERTHS: 5 berths: 1 double V, 1 single settee, 1 double convertible dinette
TABLE: dropleaf
HEAD(S): 1 head
COLD STORAGE: built-in icebox
STOVE: 2-burner
MAX. HEADROOM:

MACHINERY

ENGINE:
PROPELLER:
GENERATOR:

DECK

STEERING: tiller
WINCHES: N/A
SAFETY: bow and stern pulpits with single lifelines
ANCHOR:
NAV LIGHTS: running

RIG

TYPE: fractional rig sloop
RIGGING: N/A
MAINSHEET: boom-end sheeting

SAILS

SUPPLIED WITH BASE BOAT: main, working jib

JEANNEAU EOLIA

DESIGNER: Phillippe Briand
DISTRIBUTOR: Nautique International, Inc. (built in France by Jeanneau, S.A.)

STATISTICS

LOA: 24 ft. 7 ins.
LWL: 21 ft. 8 ins.
BEAM: 9 ft. 2 ins.
DISPLACEMENT
deep keel: 3,750 lbs.
shoal keel:
c/board:
BALLAST
deep keel: 1,550 lbs.
shoal keel:
c/board:
DRAFT
deep keel: 4 ft. 9 ins.
shoal keel:
c/board up: 2 ft. 7 ins.
c/board down: 5 ft. 11 ins.

SAIL AREA: 323 sq. ft.
FRESH WATER: 15 gals.
FUEL CAPACITY: 7 gals.

COSTS

BASE BOAT:
DATE:
EST. ON WATER:
DATE:

RATIOS

SAIL AREA/DISP: 21.41
DISP/LENGTH: 164
BALLAST RATIO: 41.33
FUEL/DISP: 1.400
FRESH WATER/DISP: 3.200

DECK

STEERING: tiller
WINCHES: 2 winches: 1 halyard, 1 reef stopper winch
SAFETY: bow pulpit
ANCHOR: anchor locker
NAV LIGHTS: running

RIG

TYPE: masthead sloop
RIGGING:
MAINSHEET: boom-end sheeting

SAILS

SUPPLIED WITH BASE BOAT: main, genoa

INTERIOR

BERTHS: 4 berths: 1 double V, 1 double quarterberth
TABLE: fold-down
HEAD(S): 1 head
COLD STORAGE: built-in icebox
STOVE: 2-burner
MAX. HEADROOM:

MACHINERY

ENGINE:
PROPELLER:
GENERATOR:

EVELYN 25

DESIGNER: Bob Evelyn
BUILDER: Formula Yachts

STATISTICS

LOA: 24 ft. 9 ins.
LWL: 21 ft. 5 ins.
BEAM: 8 ft. 8 ins.
DISPLACEMENT
deep keel: 2,600 lbs.
shoal keel:
c/board:
BALLAST
deep keel: 1,100 lbs.
shoal keel:
c/board:
DRAFT
deep keel: 4 ft. 4 ins.
shoal keel:
c/board up:
c/board down:

INTERIOR

BERTHS: 4 berths: 1 double V, 2 single settees
TABLE:
HEAD(S):
COLD STORAGE: portable ice chest
STOVE:
MAX. HEADROOM:

MACHINERY

ENGINE:
PROPELLER:
GENERATOR:

SAIL AREA: 293 sq. ft.
FRESH WATER: 0 gals.
FUEL CAPACITY: 0 gals.

COSTS

BASE BOAT: $14,900
DATE: 05/24/85
EST. ON WATER:
DATE:

RATIOS

SAIL AREA/DISP: 24.79
DISP/LENGTH: 118.1
BALLAST RATIO: 42.3
FUEL/DISP: 0.0
FRESH WATER/DISP: 0.0

DECK

STEERING: tiller
WINCHES: 2 Barlow winches (#23A)
SAFETY: bow pulpit with single lifelines
ANCHOR:
NAV LIGHTS:

RIG

TYPE: masthead sloop
RIGGING: 1x19 SS wire
MAINSHEET: boom-end sheeting

SAILS

SUPPLIED WITH BASE BOAT:

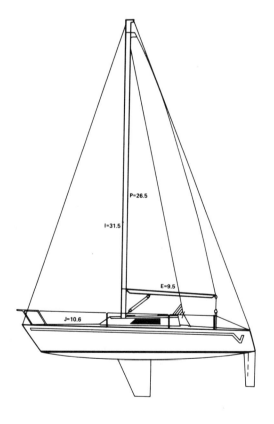

BAVARIA 760

DESIGNER: Axel Mohnhaupt
BUILDER: Bavaria Yachtbau GmbH

STATISTICS

LOA: 25 ft. 0 ins.
LWL: 21 ft. 4 ins.
BEAM: 8 ft. 0 ins.
DISPLACEMENT
deep keel: 3,500 lbs.
shoal keel:
c/board:
BALLAST
deep keel: 1,420 lbs.
shoal keel:
c/board:
DRAFT
deep keel: 4 ft. 3 ins.
shoal keel:
c/board up: 2 ft. 2 ins.
c/board down: 5 ft. 0 ins.

SAIL AREA: 270 sq. ft.
FRESH WATER: 28 gals.
FUEL CAPACITY: 0 gals.

COSTS

BASE BOAT:
DATE:
EST. ON WATER:
DATE:

RATIOS

SAIL AREA/DISP: 18.74
DISP/LENGTH: 160
BALLAST RATIO: 40.57
FUEL/DISP: 0.0
FRESH WATER/DISP: 6.40

INTERIOR

BERTHS: 5 berths: 1 double V, 1 double convertible settee, 1 single settee
TABLE: dropleaf
HEAD(S):
COLD STORAGE: built-in icebox (10 gal.)
STOVE: two-burner alcohol
MAX. HEADROOM: 5 ft. 8 ins.

MACHINERY

ENGINE:
PROPELLER:
GENERATOR:

DECK

STEERING: tiller
WINCHES: 4 Lewmar or Enkes winches: 2 primary, 2 halyard
SAFETY: bow and stern pulpits with double lifelines
ANCHOR: anchor with chain and well
NAV LIGHTS: running and masthead

RIG

TYPE: fractional rig sloop
RIGGING: 1x19 wire
MAINSHEET: 4-part with boom-end sheeting

SAILS

SUPPLIED WITH BASE BOAT: main (2 reefs), working jib

BUILDER'S COMMENTS The Bavaria 760 proves that you get much living space on a compact sailing yacht just without excessive beam. The Bavaria 760 has five berths and a commodious main cabin with a large table and comfortable sofas.

BAYFIELD 25

DESIGNER:
BUILDER: Bayfield Boat Yard, Ltd.

STATISTICS

LOA: 25 ft. 0 ins.
LWL: 19 ft. 8 ins.
BEAM: 8 ft. 0 ins.
DISPLACEMENT
deep keel: 4,300 lbs.
shoal keel:
c/board:
BALLAST
deep keel: 1,500 lbs.
shoal keel:
c/board:
DRAFT
deep keel: 2 ft. 11 ins.
shoal keel:
c/board up:
c/board down:

SAIL AREA: 240 sq. ft.
FRESH WATER: 20 gals.
FUEL CAPACITY: 11 gals.

COSTS

BASE BOAT: $27,950
DATE: 09/84
EST. ON WATER:
DATE:

RATIOS

SAIL AREA/DISP: 14.56
DISP/LENGTH: 252
BALLAST RATIO: 34.9
FUEL/DISP: 1.92
FRESH WATER/DISP: 3.72

INTERIOR

BERTHS: 4 berths: 2 single Vs, 2 single settees
TABLE: bulkhead-mounted
HEAD(S): 1 head with holding tank (20 gal.)
COLD STORAGE: built-in icebox
STOVE: 2-burner alcohol
MAX. HEADROOM: 6 ft. 0 ins.

MACHINERY

ENGINE: 7.5 HP diesel with 3:1 reduction gear
PROPELLER: 3-blade fixed
GENERATOR:

DECK

STEERING: tiller
WINCHES: 2 winches
SAFETY: bow pulpit with single lifelines
ANCHOR: anchor well
NAV LIGHTS: running

RIG

TYPE: masthead sloop
RIGGING: 1x19 wire
MAINSHEET: boom-end sheet

SAILS

SUPPLIED WITH BASE BOAT: main, working jib

CAPE DORY 25D

DESIGNER: Carl Alberg
BUILDER: Cape Dory Yachts

STATISTICS

LOA: 25 ft. 0 ins.
LWL: 19 ft. 0 ins.
BEAM: 8 ft. 0 ins.
DISPLACEMENT
deep keel: 5,120 lbs.
shoal keel:
c/board:
BALLAST
deep keel: 2,050 lbs.
shoal keel:
c/board:
DRAFT
deep keel: 3 ft. 6 ins.
shoal keel:
c/board up:
c/board down:

SAIL AREA: 304 sq. ft.
FRESH WATER: 20 gals.
FUEL CAPACITY: 13 gals.

COSTS

BASE BOAT:
DATE:
EST. ON WATER:
DATE:

RATIOS

SAIL AREA/DISP: 16.21
DISP/LENGTH: 333.0
BALLAST RATIO: 42.0
FUEL/DISP: 2.0
FRESH WATER/DISP: 3.1

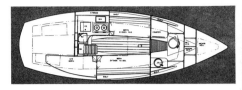

INTERIOR

BERTHS: 4 berths: 2 single settees, 1 double quarterberth
TABLE: pedestal-mounted
HEAD(S): 1 head with holding tank
COLD STORAGE: built-in icebox
STOVE: 2-burner alcohol
MAX. HEADROOM: 5 ft. 11 ins.

MACHINERY

ENGINE: Yanmar diesel with 2.62:1 reduction gear
PROPELLER: 1" shaft
GENERATOR:

DECK

STEERING: tiller
WINCHES: 4 winches: 2 primary, 2 halyard
SAFETY: bow and stern pulpits with single lifelines
ANCHOR: anchor well and roller
NAV LIGHTS: running and masthead

RIG

TYPE: masthead sloop
RIGGING:
MAINSHEET: boom-end sheeting

SAILS

SUPPLIED WITH BASE BOAT: main, working jib

CATALINA 25

DESIGNER:
BUILDER: Catalina Yachts

STATISTICS

LOA: 25 ft. 0 ins.
LWL: 22 ft. 2 ins.
BEAM: 8 ft. 0 ins.
DISPLACEMENT
deep keel: 4,550 lbs.
shoal keel:
c/board: 4,150 lbs.
BALLAST
deep keel: 1,900 lbs.
shoal keel:
c/board: 1,500 lbs.
DRAFT
deep keel: 4 ft. 0 ins.
shoal keel:
c/board up: 2 ft. 8 ins.
c/board down: 5 ft. 0 ins.

SAIL AREA: 270.45 sq. ft.
FRESH WATER: 21 gals.
FUEL CAPACITY: 6 gals.

COSTS

BASE BOAT: $12,995
DATE: 02/01/85
EST. ON WATER:
DATE:

RATIOS

SAIL AREA/DISP: deep 15.76
c/board 16.76
DISP/LENGTH: deep 186.66
c/board 170.25
BALLAST RATIO: deep 41.76
c/board 36.14
FUEL/DISP: deep .99
c/board 1.08
FRESH WATER/DISP: deep 3.69
c/board 4.05

MACHINERY

ENGINE: bracket for outboard engine
PROPELLER:
GENERATOR:

DECK

STEERING: tiller
WINCHES: 2 primary winches
SAFETY: bow and stern pulpits with single lifelines
ANCHOR: anchor well
NAV LIGHTS: running and masthead

RIG

TYPE: masthead sloop
RIGGING: SS wire
MAINSHEET: boom-end sheeting

SAILS

SUPPLIED WITH BASE BOAT: reefable main, 110% jib

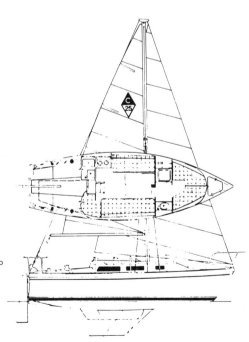

INTERIOR

BERTHS: 5 berths: 1 double V, 1 single settee, 1 double quarterberth
TABLE: dropleaf
HEAD(S): 1 head (WC optional)
COLD STORAGE: built-in icebox
STOVE: 2-burner alcohol
MAX. HEADROOM: 6 ft. 6 ins.

OLSON 25

DESIGNER: George Olson/Peter Smiley
BUILDER: Pacific Boats, Inc.

STATISTICS

LOA: 25 ft. 0 ins.
LWL: 21 ft. 3 ins.
BEAM: 9 ft. 0 ins.
DISPLACEMENT
deep keel: 2,900 lbs.
shoal keel:
c/board:
BALLAST
deep keel: 1,300 lbs.
shoal keel:
c/board:
DRAFT
deep keel: 4 ft. 6 ins.
shoal keel:
c/board up:
c/board down:

INTERIOR

BERTHS: 4 berths: 1 double V, 2 single settees
TABLE:
HEAD(S):
COLD STORAGE:
STOVE:
MAX. HEADROOM:

MACHINERY

ENGINE:
PROPELLER:
GENERATOR:

SAIL AREA: 308 sq. ft.
FRESH WATER:
FUEL CAPACITY:

COSTS

BASE BOAT: $16,995
DATE: 5/22/85
EST. ON WATER:
DATE:

RATIOS

SAIL AREA/DISP: 24.29
DISP/LENGTH: 134.92
BALLAST RATIO: 44.83
FUEL/DISP:
FRESH WATER/DISP:

DECK

STEERING: tiller
WINCHES:
SAFETY: bow and stern pulpits with single lifelines
ANCHOR:
NAV LIGHTS:

RIG

TYPE: masthead sloop
RIGGING:
MAINSHEET: boom-end sheeting

SAILS

SUPPLIED WITH BASE BOAT:

MIRAGE 25

DESIGNER:
BUILDER: Mirage Yachts, Ltd.

STATISTICS

LOA: 25 ft. 2 ins.
LWL: 21 ft. 0 ins.
BEAM: 9 ft. 6 ins.
DISPLACEMENT
deep keel: 4.400 lbs.
shoal keel:
c/board:
BALLAST
deep keel: 1,600 lbs.
shoal keel:
c/board:
DRAFT
deep keel: 4 ft. 4 ins.
shoal keel:
c/board up:
c/board down:

INTERIOR

BERTHS: 4 berths: 1 double V, 2 single settees
TABLE: dropleaf
HEAD(S):
COLD STORAGE: built-in icebox
STOVE:
MAX. HEADROOM: 5 ft. 11 ins.

MACHINERY

ENGINE:
PROPELLER:
GENERATOR:

SAIL AREA: 283 sq. ft.
FRESH WATER: 10 gals.
FUEL CAPACITY:

COSTS

BASE BOAT:
DATE:
EST. ON WATER:
DATE:

RATIOS

SAIL AREA/DISP: 16.86
DISP/LENGTH: 212
BALLAST RATIO: 36.36
FUEL/DISP:
FRESH WATER/DISP: 1.82

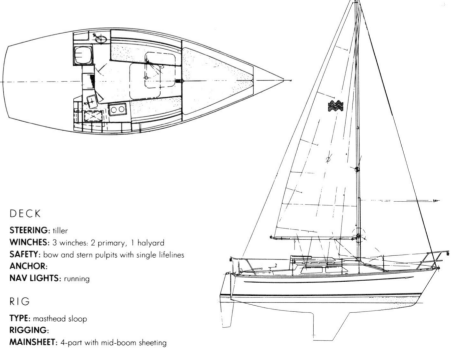

DECK

STEERING: tiller
WINCHES: 3 winches: 2 primary, 1 halyard
SAFETY: bow and stern pulpits with single lifelines
ANCHOR:
NAV LIGHTS: running

RIG

TYPE: masthead sloop
RIGGING:
MAINSHEET: 4-part with mid-boom sheeting

SAILS

SUPPLIED WITH BASE BOAT:

EVELYN 25.5

DESIGNER: Bob Evelyn
BUILDER: Formula Yachts

STATISTICS

LOA: 25 ft. 5 ins.
LWL: 19 ft. 5 ins.
BEAM: 9 ft. 0 ins.
DISPLACEMENT
deep keel: 4,300 lbs.
shoal keel:
c/board:
BALLAST
deep keel: 1,600 lbs.
shoal keel:
c/board:
DRAFT
deep keel: 4 ft. 5 ins.
shoal keel:
c/board up:
c/board down:

INTERIOR

BERTHS: 4 berths: 1 double V, 2 single settees
TABLE:
HEAD(S):
COLD STORAGE: built-in icebox
STOVE:
MAX. HEADROOM:

MACHINERY

ENGINE:
PROPELLER:
GENERATOR:

SAIL AREA:
FRESH WATER:
FUEL CAPACITY:

COSTS

BASE BOAT: $21,800
DATE: 05/24/85
EST. ON WATER:
DATE:

RATIOS

SAIL AREA/DISP:
DISP/LENGTH: 258
BALLAST RATIO: 37.20
FUEL/DISP:
FRESH WATER/DISP:

DECK

STEERING: tiller
WINCHES: 4 Lewmar winches: 2 primary (#30 2sp), 2 halyard (#10)
SAFETY: bow and stern pulpits with lifelines
ANCHOR:
NAV LIGHTS: running

RIG

TYPE: masthead sloop
RIGGING: 1x19 SS wire
MAINSHEET: 4-part with boom-end sheeting

SAILS

SUPPLIED WITH BASE BOAT:

BUILDER'S COMMENTS
1981 MORC International Champion.

ALBIN EXPRESS

DESIGNER: Peter Norlin
BUILDER: Albin Marine, Inc.

STATISTICS

LOA: 25 ft. 6 ins.
LWL: 21 ft. 8 ins.
BEAM: 8 ft. 2 ins.
DISPLACEMENT
deep keel: 3,969 lbs.
shoal keel:
c/board:
BALLAST
deep keel: 1,764 lbs.
shoal keel:
c/board:
DRAFT
deep keel: 4 ft. 9 ins.
shoal keel:
c/board up:
c/board down:

INTERIOR

BERTHS: 4 berths: 1 double V, 2 single settees
TABLE: bulkhead-mounted fold-down
HEAD(S):
COLD STORAGE: portable ice chest
STOVE: 2-burner
MAX. HEADROOM:

MACHINERY

ENGINE: none (outboard mount only)
PROPELLER:
GENERATOR:

SAIL AREA: 344 sq. ft.
FRESH WATER:
FUEL CAPACITY:

COSTS

BASE BOAT: $19,990
DATE: 05/85
EST. ON WATER:
DATE:

RATIOS

SAIL AREA/DISP: 21.96
DISP/LENGTH: 174.36
BALLAST RATIO: 44.44
FUEL/DISP:
FRESH WATER/DISP:

DECK

STEERING: tiller
WINCHES: Lewmar
SAFETY: bow and stern pulpits with lifelines
ANCHOR:
NAV LIGHTS: running

RIG

TYPE: fractional rig sloop with deck-stepped spar
RIGGING: N/A
MAINSHEET: boom-end sheeting

SAILS

SUPPLIED WITH BASE BOAT: working sails

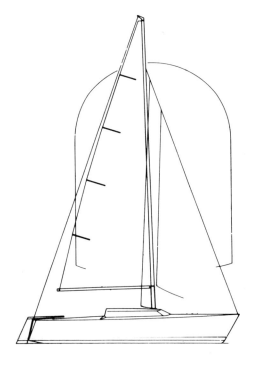

HUNTER 25.5

DESIGNER: Hunter Design Group
BUILDER: Hunter Marine

STATISTICS

LOA: 25 ft. 7 ins.
LWL: 22 ft. 1 ins.
BEAM: 9 ft. 1 ins.
DISPLACEMENT
deep keel: 4,500 lbs.
shoal keel:
c/board:
BALLAST
deep keel: 1,800 lbs.
shoal keel:
c/board:
DRAFT
deep keel: 4 ft. 6 ins.
shoal keel: 3 ft. 3 ins.
c/board up:
c/board down:

SAIL AREA: 282 sq. ft.
FRESH WATER: 12 gals.
FUEL CAPACITY: 0 gals.

COSTS

BASE BOAT:
DATE:
EST. ON WATER: $20,000
DATE: 11/85

RATIOS

SAIL AREA/DISP: 16.55
DISP/LENGTH: 186
BALLAST RATIO: 40.00
FUEL/DISP: 0.0
FRESH WATER/DISP: 2.13

INTERIOR

BERTHS: 5 berths: 1 double V, 1 single settee, 1 double convertible settee
TABLE: dinette
HEAD(S): portable
COLD STORAGE: built-in icebox
STOVE: 2-burner alcohol
MAX. HEADROOM: 6 ft. 6 ins. with pop top up (5'6" with pop top down)

MACHINERY

ENGINE:
PROPELLER:
GENERATOR:

DECK

STEERING: tiller
WINCHES: 3 winches: 2 sheet (ST), 1 halyard
SAFETY: bow and stern pulpits with lifelines
ANCHOR: anchor with anchor well and line
NAV LIGHTS: masthead

RIG

TYPE: masthead sloop
RIGGING:
MAINSHEET: 4-part with boom-end sheeting

SAILS

SUPPLIED WITH BASE BOAT: main, 110% genoa

BUILDER'S COMMENTS The Hunter 25.5' incorporates the innovations from its larger counterparts to offer you a craft with amenities found on larger boats.

She holds six comfortably above and belowdecks. The galley is complete and there's an enclosed head with vanity.

A flush fitting pop top allows additional headroom at sea or moored.

Like all Hunter Boats she comes complete with Cruise Pac (TM), all the gear you need to go sailing.

O'DAY 26

DESIGNER: C. Raymond Hunt Associates
BUILDER: Lear Siegler Marine

STATISTICS

LOA: 25 ft. 8.5 ins.
LWL: 21 ft. 7.0 ins.
BEAM: 8 ft. 0.0 ins.
DISPLACEMENT
deep keel: 4,800 lbs.
shoal keel:
c/board:
BALLAST
deep keel: 1,850 lbs.
shoal keel:
c/board:
DRAFT
deep keel:
shoal keel:
c/board up: 2 ft. 6 ins.
c/board down: 6 ft. 0 ins.

SAIL AREA: 278 sq. ft.
FRESH WATER: 15 gals.
FUEL CAPACITY: 0 gals.

COSTS

BASE BOAT:
DATE:
EST. ON WATER:
DATE:

RATIOS

SAIL AREA/DISP: 15.63
DISP/LENGTH: 213
BALLAST RATIO: 38.54
FUEL/DISP: 0.0
FRESH WATER/DISP: 2.50

INTERIOR

BERTHS: 6 berths: 1 double V, 1 single settee, 1 double convertible settee, 1 single quarterberth
TABLE: bulkhead-mounted
HEAD(S): enclosed Porta Potti
COLD STORAGE: built-in icebox
STOVE:
MAX. HEADROOM: 5 ft. 9 ins.

MACHINERY

ENGINE:
PROPELLER:
GENERATOR:

DECK

STEERING: tiller
WINCHES:
SAFETY: bow and stern pulpits with lifelines
ANCHOR: anchor well
NAV LIGHTS: running and masthead

RIG

TYPE: masthead sloop
RIGGING: 1x19 SS wire
MAINSHEET: mid-boom sheeting

SAILS

SUPPLIED WITH BASE BOAT: main, jib

BUILDER'S COMMENTS Cruising comfort in a trailerable package. The O'Day 26 offers interior room for 5 while still giving the option of over-the-road transport. A crisp sailing keel/centerboard underbody and comfortable deck layout makes this a superb family cruiser.

ERICSON 26

DESIGNER: Bruce King
BUILDER: Ericson Yachts

STATISTICS

LOA: 25 ft. 9 ins.
LWL: 21 ft. 11 ins.
BEAM: 9 ft. 3 ins.
DISPLACEMENT
deep keel: 5,250 lbs.
shoal keel: 5,250 lbs.
c/board:
BALLAST
deep keel: 2,250 lbs.
shoal keel: 2,250 lbs.
c/board:
DRAFT
deep keel: 4 ft. 11 ins.
shoal keel: 3 ft. 11 ins.
c/board up:
c/board down:

SAIL AREA: 325 sq. ft.
FRESH WATER: 18 gals.
FUEL CAPACITY: 15 gals.

COSTS

BASE BOAT:
DATE:
EST. ON WATER:
DATE:

RATIOS

SAIL AREA/DISP: 17.21
DISP/LENGTH: 223
BALLAST RATIO: 42.86
FUEL/DISP: 2.13
FRESH WATER/DISP: 2.74

INTERIOR

BERTHS: 6 berths: 1 double V, 1 double extension settee, 1 single settee, 1 single quarterberth
TABLE: bulkhead-mounted
HEAD(S): 1 head with holding tank
COLD STORAGE: built-in icebox (5 cu. ft.)
STOVE: 2-burner alcohol
MAX. HEADROOM: 6 ft. 1 in.

MACHINERY

ENGINE: 10 HP Westerbeke #2-10 diesel with 2:1 reduction gear
PROPELLER: fixed 12"x10" on 3/4" shaft
GENERATOR:

DECK

STEERING: tiller
WINCHES: 3 Lewmar winches: 2 primary (#16), 1 halyard (#6)
SAFETY: bow and stern pulpits with single lifelines
ANCHOR: anchor well
NAV LIGHTS: running and masthead

RIG

TYPE: fractional rig sloop
RIGGING: wire (3/16")
MAINSHEET: 4-part with mid-boom sheeting

SAILS

SUPPLIED WITH BASE BOAT:

LAGUNA 26

DESIGNER: W. Shad Turner
BUILDER: Laguna Yachts, Inc.

STATISTICS

LOA: 25 ft. 9 ins.
LWL: 21 ft. 6 ins.
BEAM: 8 ft. 4 ins.
DISPLACEMENT
deep keel: 3,900 lbs.
shoal keel:
c/board:
BALLAST
deep keel: 1,500 lbs.
shoal keel:
c/board:
DRAFT
deep keel: 3 ft. 1 ins.
shoal keel:
c/board up:
c/board down:

SAIL AREA: 275 sq. ft.
FRESH WATER: 20 gals.
FUEL CAPACITY: 0 gals.

COSTS

BASE BOAT:
DATE:
EST. ON WATER:
DATE:

RATIOS

SAIL AREA/DISP: 17.75
DISP/LENGTH: 175
BALLAST RATIO: 38.46
FUEL/DISP: 0.0
FRESH WATER/DISP: 4.10

INTERIOR

BERTHS: 6 berths: 1 double V, 1 double convertible dinette, 1 double quarterberth
TABLE: dinette
HEAD(S):
COLD STORAGE: built-in icebox
STOVE: 2-burner alcohol
MAX. HEADROOM: 6 ft. 2 ins.

MACHINERY

ENGINE:
PROPELLER:
GENERATOR:

DECK

STEERING: tiller
WINCHES: 4 winches: 2 sheet, 2 halyard
SAFETY: bow and stern pulpits with lifelines
ANCHOR: anchor
NAV LIGHTS: running masthead

RIG

TYPE: masthead sloop with deck-stepped spar
RIGGING:
MAINSHEET: 4-part with mid-boom sheeting

SAILS

SUPPLIED WITH BASE BOAT: reefable main, working jib

CAPE DORY 26

DESIGNER: Carl Alberg
BUILDER: Cape Dory Yachts

STATISTICS

LOA: 25 ft. 11 ins.
LWL: 19 ft. 3 ins.
BEAM: 8 ft. 0 ins.
DISPLACEMENT
deep keel: 5,300 lbs.
shoal keel:
c/board:
BALLAST
deep keel: 2,400 lbs.
shoal keel:
c/board:
DRAFT
deep keel: 3 ft. 7 ins.
shoal keel:
c/board up:
c/board down:

SAIL AREA: 304 sq. ft.
FRESH WATER: 24 gals.
FUEL CAPACITY: 0 gals.

COSTS

BASE BOAT:
DATE:
EST. ON WATER:
DATE:

RATIOS

SAIL AREA/DISP: 16.00
DISP/LENGTH: 331.69
BALLAST RATIO: 45.28
FUEL/DISP: 0.0
FRESH WATER/DISP: 3.62

INTERIOR

BERTHS: 4 berths: 1 double V, 2 single settees
TABLE:
HEAD(S): 1 head
COLD STORAGE: built-in portable
STOVE:
MAX. HEADROOM: 5 ft. 11 ins.

MACHINERY

ENGINE: 15 HP outboard
PROPELLER:
GENERATOR:

DECK

STEERING: tiller
WINCHES: 4 winches: 2 primary, 2 halyard
SAFETY: bow pulpit
ANCHOR: anchor roller
NAV LIGHTS: running and masthead

RIG

TYPE: masthead sloop
RIGGING:
MAINSHEET: boom-end sheeting

SAILS

SUPPLIED WITH BASE BOAT: main, working jib

S2 7.9/26'

DESIGNER: Graham and Schlageter
BUILDER: S2 Yachts, Inc.

STATISTICS

LOA: 25 ft. 11 ins.
LWL: 21 ft. 8 ins.
BEAM: 9 ft. 0 ins.
DISPLACEMENT
deep keel: 4,250 lbs.
shoal keel:
c/board:
BALLAST
deep keel: 1,750 lbs.
shoal keel:
c/board:
DRAFT
deep keel: 4 ft. 9.0 ins.
shoal keel:
c/board up: 1 ft. 1.5 ins.
c/board down: 5 ft. 0.0 ins.

SAIL AREA: 329 sq. ft.
FRESH WATER: 5 gals.
FUEL CAPACITY: 0 gals.

COSTS

BASE BOAT:
DATE:
EST. ON WATER:
DATE:

RATIOS

SAIL AREA/DISP: 20.06
DISP/LENGTH: 186.71
BALLAST RATIO: 41.17
FUEL/DISP: 0.0
FRESH WATER/DISP: .94

INTERIOR

BERTHS: 4 berths: 1 double V, 2 single settees
TABLE:
HEAD(S): enclosed Porta Potti
COLD STORAGE: built-in icebox
STOVE:
MAX. HEADROOM: 5 ft. 5 ins.

MACHINERY

ENGINE:
PROPELLER:
GENERATOR:

DECK

STEERING: tiller
WINCHES: 4 Lewmar winches: 2 primary (#30 2sp), 2 halyard (#16 2sp)
SAFETY: bow pulpit with lifelines
ANCHOR:
NAV LIGHTS: running and masthead

RIG

TYPE: fractional rig sloop
RIGGING: 1x19 wire on retractable keel model: rod rigging on fixed keel model
MAINSHEET: 4-part with boom-end sheeting

SAILS

SUPPLIED WITH BASE BOAT:

BUILDER'S COMMENTS A serious 26' M.O.R.C. and handicap racer with the advantages of one-design fleets nationwide. The G&S designed 7.9M offers the optimal mix of speed and sailing ease. The vertical retracting keel and kick-up rudder permit easy breaching, launching, and trailering, without a sacrifice in performance. For all her comfort, she never loses the sharp competitive edge that makes her a true racer.

NONSUCH 26 ULTRA

DESIGNER: Mark Ellis Design
BUILDER: Hinterhoeller Yachts, Ltd.

STATISTICS

LOA: 26 ft. 0.0 ins.
LWL: 24 ft. 4.5 ins.
BEAM: 10 ft. 6.0 ins.
DISPLACEMENT
deep keel: 8,500 lbs.
shoal keel:
c/board:
BALLAST
deep keel: 2,750 lbs.
shoal keel:
c/board:
DRAFT
deep keel: 4 ft. 6 ins.
shoal keel:
c/board up:
c/board down:

SAIL AREA / WATER / FUEL

SAIL AREA: 420 sq. ft.
FRESH WATER: 60 gals.
FUEL CAPACITY: 24 gals.

COSTS

BASE BOAT: $50,995
DATE: 08/01/85
EST. ON WATER: $60,000
DATE: 08/01/85

RATIOS

SAIL AREA/DISP: 16.13
DISP/LENGTH: 262
BALLAST RATIO: 32.35
FUEL/DISP: 2.11
FRESH WATER/DISP: 5.64

INTERIOR

BERTHS: 4 berths: 1 double V, 1 convertible dinette
TABLE: dropleaf
HEAD(S): 1 head with shower
COLD STORAGE: built-in icebox
STOVE: 2-burner propane with oven
MAX. HEADROOM: 6 ft. 1 ins.

MACHINERY

ENGINE: 18 HP Westerbeke diesel with 2:1 reduction gear
PROPELLER: 2-blade sailor 15"x10" on 1" SS shaft
GENERATOR:

DECK

STEERING: 28" wheel with emergency tiller
WINCHES:
SAFETY: bow and stern pulpits with lifelines
ANCHOR:
NAV LIGHTS: running and masthead

RIG

TYPE: cat rig
RIGGING:
MAINSHEET: 2-part with boom-end sheeting

SAILS

SUPPLIED WITH BASE BOAT:

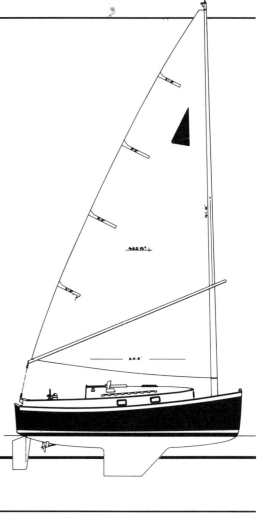

VICTORIA 26

DESIGNER: Chuck Paine
BUILDER: Victoria Marine, Ltd.

STATISTICS

LOA: 26 ft. 0 ins.
LWL: 21 ft. 3 ins.
BEAM: 8 ft. 2 ins.
DISPLACEMENT
deep keel: 6,800 lbs.
shoal keel:
c/board:
BALLAST
deep keel: 3,500 lbs.
shoal keel:
c/board:
DRAFT
deep keel: 3 ft. 10 ins.
shoal keel:
c/board up:
c/board down:

SAIL AREA / WATER / FUEL

SAIL AREA: 340 sq. ft.
FRESH WATER: 25 gals.
FUEL CAPACITY: 12 gals.

COSTS

BASE BOAT:
DATE:
EST. ON WATER:
DATE:

RATIOS

SAIL AREA/DISP: 15.20
DISP/LENGTH: 316.36
BALLAST RATIO: 51.47
FUEL/DISP: 1.32
FRESH WATER/DISP: 2.94

INTERIOR

BERTHS: 4 berths: 1 double V, 1 single settee, 1 single quarterberth
TABLE: bulkhead-mounted
HEAD(S): 1 head
COLD STORAGE: built-in icebox
STOVE:
MAX. HEADROOM: 6 ft. 0 ins.

MACHINERY

ENGINE: 10 HP diesel
PROPELLER: fixed
GENERATOR:

DECK

STEERING: tiller
WINCHES: 4 winches
SAFETY: bow and stern pulpits with double lifelines
ANCHOR: anchor roller
NAV LIGHTS: running and masthead

RIG

TYPE: masthead sloop (cutter also available)
RIGGING:
MAINSHEET: 4-part with mid-boom sheeting

SAILS

SUPPLIED WITH BASE BOAT:

X-79

DESIGNER:
DISTRIBUTOR: Aquarius Performance Yachts, Inc. (built in Denmark by X-Yachts)

STATISTICS

LOA: 26 ft. 1.2 ins.
LWL: 21 ft. 0.0 ins.
BEAM: 9 ft. 6.0 ins.
DISPLACEMENT
deep keel:
shoal keel:
c/board:
BALLAST
deep keel:
shoal keel:
c/board:
DRAFT
deep keel: 4 ft. 4.3 ins.
shoal keel:
c/board up:
c/board down:

SAIL AREA:
FRESH WATER:
FUEL CAPACITY:

COSTS

BASE BOAT:
DATE:
EST. ON WATER:
DATE:

RATIOS

SAIL AREA/DISP:
DISP/LENGTH:
BALLAST RATIO:
FUEL/DISP:
FRESH WATER/DISP:

INTERIOR

BERTHS: 6 berths: 2 single pipe berths, 2 single pilots, 2 single quarterberths
TABLE:
HEAD(S): 1 head
COLD STORAGE:
STOVE:
MAX. HEADROOM:

MACHINERY

ENGINE:
PROPELLER:
GENERATOR:

DECK

STEERING: tiller
WINCHES: 3 Lewmar winches: 2 #7, 1 #6
SAFETY: bow and stern pulpits with single lifelines
ANCHOR:
NAV LIGHTS: masthead

RIG

TYPE: fractional rig sloop
RIGGING: 1x19 wire
MAINSHEET: boom-end sheeting

SAILS

SUPPLIED WITH BASE BOAT:

TANZER 26

DESIGNER: J. Tanzer
BUILDER: Tanzer Industries, Inc.

STATISTICS

LOA: 26 ft. 4 ins.
LWL: 22 ft. 6 ins.
BEAM: 8 ft. 8 ins.
DISPLACEMENT
deep keel: 4,350 lbs.
shoal keel:
c/board:
BALLAST
deep keel: 1,950 lbs.
shoal keel:
c/board:
DRAFT
deep keel: 3 ft. 10 ins.
shoal keel:
c/board up:
c/board down:

SAIL AREA: 260 sq. ft.
FRESH WATER: 15 gals.
FUEL CAPACITY: 12 gals.

COSTS

BASE BOAT: $21,675
DATE: 02/01/85
EST. ON WATER: $22,000
DATE: 02/01/85

RATIOS

SAIL AREA/DISP: 15.61
DISP/LENGTH: 170.49
BALLAST RATIO: 44.82
FUEL/DISP: 2.07
FRESH WATER/DISP: 2.76

INTERIOR

BERTHS: 5 berths: 1 double V, 1 double convertible, 1 single quarterberth
TABLE: bulkhead-mounted
HEAD(S): 1 head with holding tank
COLD STORAGE: built-in icebox
STOVE: 2-burner alcohol
MAX. HEADROOM: 5 ft. 9 ins.

MACHINERY

ENGINE:
PROPELLER:
GENERATOR:

DECK

STEERING: tiller
WINCHES: 3 winches: 2 primary, 1 halyard
SAFETY: bow pulpit and lifelines
ANCHOR: anchor well
NAV LIGHTS:

RIG

TYPE: masthead sloop
RIGGING: wire (5/32")
MAINSHEET: mid-boom sheeting

SAILS

SUPPLIED WITH BASE BOAT: main (1 reef), working jib or lapper

BUILDER'S COMMENTS A family cruiser/racer with performance being a high priority. Sleeps 5 adults in two separate cabins with comfort not always found on a boat this size. Since its introduction, over 800 Tanzer 26s have been built.

C & C 27

DESIGNER: C & C Design Group
BUILDER: C & C Yachts

STATISTICS

LOA: 26 ft. 6 ins.
LWL: 23 ft. 0 ins.
BEAM: 9 ft. 3 ins.
DISPLACEMENT
deep keel: 4,420 lbs.
shoal keel:
c/board:
BALLAST
deep keel: 1,715 lbs.
shoal keel:
c/board:
DRAFT
deep keel: 4 ft. 10 ins.
shoal keel:
c/board up:
c/board down:

SAIL AREA: 342 sq. ft.
FRESH WATER: 20 gals
FUEL CAPACITY: 0 gals.

COSTS

BASE BOAT:
DATE:
EST. ON WATER: $32,200
DATE: 11/85

RATIOS

SAIL AREA/DISP: 20.36
DISP/LENGTH: 162
BALLAST RATIO: 38.80
FUEL/DISP: 0.0
FRESH WATER/DISP: 3.61

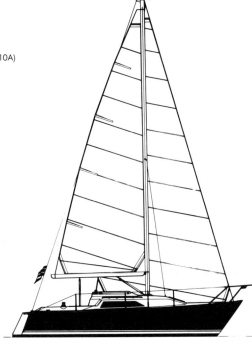

DECK

STEERING: tiller
WINCHES: 4 winches: 2 primary (#18A), 2 halyard (#10A)
SAFETY: bow pulpit with double lifelines
ANCHOR: anchor roller
NAV LIGHTS: running

RIG

TYPE: masthead sloop
RIGGING: 1x19 wire
MAINSHEET: 4-part with mid-boom sheeting

SAILS

SUPPLIED WITH BASE BOAT:

INTERIOR

BERTHS: 5 berths: 1 double V, 1 double convertible settee, 1 single quarterberth
TABLE: bulkhead-mounted
HEAD(S): 1 head with self-contained marine toilet
COLD STORAGE: built-in icebox
STOVE: 2-burner alcohol
MAX. HEADROOM:

MACHINERY

ENGINE:
PROPELLER:
GENERATOR:

BUILDER'S COMMENTS All the performance and live-aboard practicalities that have made the C & C name famous are brought together in this state of the art racer/cruiser.

MERMAID 270

DESIGNER:
DISTRIBUTOR: Anchor Marine, Inc. (built in Denmark by LM Glasfiber, a/s)

STATISTICS

LOA: 26 ft. 7 ins.
LWL: 22 ft. 4 ins.
BEAM: 9 ft. 6 ins.
DISPLACEMENT
deep keel: 7,480 lbs.
shoal keel:
c/board:
BALLAST
deep keel: 2,860 lbs.
shoal keel:
c/board:
DRAFT
deep keel: 4 ft. 1 ins.
shoal keel:
c/board up:
c/board down:

SAIL AREA: 317 sq. ft.
FRESH WATER: 25 gals
FUEL CAPACITY: 15 gals.

COSTS

BASE BOAT: $38,900
DATE: 04/01/85
EST. ON WATER:
DATE:

RATIOS

SAIL AREA/DISP: 13.26
DISP/LENGTH: 300
BALLAST RATIO: 38.2
FUEL/DISP: 1.5
FRESH WATER/DISP: 2.7

DECK

STEERING: tiller
WINCHES:
SAFETY: bow and stern pulpits with double lifelines
ANCHOR: anchor supplied
NAV LIGHTS: running

RIG

TYPE: fractional rig sloop
RIGGING:
MAINSHEET: boom-end sheeting

SAILS

SUPPLIED WITH BASE BOAT: main, working jib

INTERIOR

BERTHS: 6 berths: 1 double V, 2 double convertible settees
TABLE: dropleaf
HEAD(S): 1 head with shower
COLD STORAGE:
STOVE:
MAX. HEADROOM:

MACHINERY

ENGINE: 18 HP Volvo #2002/120 S diesel
PROPELLER: fixed
GENERATOR:

S2 27'

DESIGNER: Graham & Schlageter
BUILDER: S2 Yachts, Inc.

STATISTICS

LOA: 26 ft. 7 ins.
LWL: 23 ft. 4 ins.
BEAM: 9 ft. 3 ins.
DISPLACEMENT
deep keel: 5,000 lbs.
shoal keel:
c/board:
BALLAST
deep keel: 2,000 lbs.
shoal keel:
c/board:
DRAFT
deep keel: 4 ft. 9 ins.
shoal keel:
c/board up:
c/board down:

SAIL AREA: 342 sq. ft.
FRESH WATER: 0 gals.
FUEL CAPACITY: 0 gals.

COSTS

BASE BOAT:
DATE:
EST. ON WATER:
DATE:

RATIOS

SAIL AREA/DISP: 18.71
DISP/LENGTH: 175.78
BALLAST RATIO: 40.00
FUEL/DISP: 0.0
FRESH WATER/DISP: 0.0

INTERIOR

BERTHS: 4 berths: 1 double V, 1 double convertible settee
TABLE: dinette
HEAD(S): Porta Potti
COLD STORAGE: built-in icebox
STOVE: 2-burner
MAX. HEADROOM: 6 ft. 0 ins.

MACHINERY

ENGINE:
PROPELLER:
GENERATOR:

DECK

STEERING: tiller
WINCHES: 4 Lewmar winches: 2 primary (#30), 2 halyard (#8)
SAFETY: bow rail
ANCHOR: anchor well
NAV LIGHTS: running

RIG

TYPE: masthead sloop
RIGGING: 1x19 wire
MAINSHEET: 4-part with mid-boom sheeting led to #8 winch

SAILS

SUPPLIED WITH BASE BOAT:

BUILDER'S COMMENTS Designed around a full, stable hull form, the S2 27' features all the sailing performance that has made the G&S designed 7.9M and 9.1M eminently successful. Engineering excellence and advanced construction techniques that set the standard for the industry assure integrity and enduring value. In her remarkable comfort, incomparable performance, and attention to detail, the S2 27' offers a level of quality that could only be an S2.

TANZER 27

DESIGNER: C. Raymond Hunt & Associates
BUILDER: Tanzer Industries, Inc.

STATISTICS

LOA: 26 ft. 7 ins.
LWL: 22 ft. 6 ins.
BEAM: 9 ft. 6 ins.
DISPLACEMENT
deep keel: 6,200 lbs.
shoal keel: 6,450 lbs.
c/board:
BALLAST
deep keel: 2,250 lbs.
shoal keel: 2,500 lbs.
c/board:
DRAFT
deep keel: 4 ft. 6 ins.
shoal keel: 3 ft. 3 ins.
c/board up:
c/board down:

SAIL AREA: 343 sq. ft.
FRESH WATER: 15 gals.
FUEL CAPACITY:

COSTS

BASE BOAT:
fin keel $27,850
DATE: 02/01/85
shoal keel $28,300
EST. ON WATER:
DATE:

RATIOS

SAIL AREA/DISP: 16.26
DISP/LENGTH: 242.99
BALLAST RATIO: 36.29
FUEL/DISP:
FRESH WATER/DISP: 1.94

INTERIOR

BERTHS: 5 berths: 1 double V, 1 double convertible, 1 single quarterberth
TABLE: bulkhead-mounted
HEAD(S): 1 head with holding tank
COLD STORAGE: built-in icebox
STOVE: 2-burner alcohol
MAX. HEADROOM: 6 ft. 1 ins.

MACHINERY

ENGINE:
PROPELLER:
GENERATOR:

DECK

STEERING: tiller
WINCHES: 3 winches: 2 primary, 1 halyard
SAFETY: bow pulpit and lifelines
ANCHOR: anchor well
NAV LIGHTS: running

RIG

TYPE: masthead sloop
RIGGING: wire (1/4")
MAINSHEET: 4-part with mid-boom sheeting

SAILS

SUPPLIED WITH BASE BOAT: main (1 reef), working jib or lapper

BUILDER'S COMMENTS The Tanzer 27 was designed by John Deknatel of C. Raymond Hunt & Associates as a competitive club racer with cruising comfort as a high priority. Available with either a fin keel or a shoal draft keel that draws only 3'3".

CAL 27 MARK III

DESIGNER: Bill Lapworth
BUILDER: Lear Siegler Marine

STATISTICS

LOA: 26 ft. 8 ins.
LWL: 23 ft. 3 ins.
BEAM: 9 ft. 0 ins.
DISPLACEMENT
deep keel: 5,200 lbs.
shoal keel:
c/board:
BALLAST
deep keel: 2,000 lbs.
shoal keel:
c/board:
DRAFT
deep keel: 5 ft. 0 ins.
shoal keel: 4 ft. 0 ins.
c/board up:
c/board down:

SAIL AREA: 335 sq. ft.
FRESH WATER: 22 gals.
FUEL CAPACITY: 13 gals.

COSTS

BASE BOAT:
DATE:
EST. ON WATER:
DATE:

RATIOS

SAIL AREA/DISP: 17.85
DISP/LENGTH: 184
BALLAST RATIO: 38.46
FUEL/DISP: 1.73
FRESH WATER/DISP: 3.38

INTERIOR

BERTHS: 5 berths: 1 double V, 2 single settees, 1 single quarterberth
TABLE: bulkhead-mounted
HEAD(S): 1 head
COLD STORAGE: built-in icebox (5.4 cu. ft.)
STOVE:
MAX. HEADROOM: 5 ft. 10 ins.

MACHINERY

ENGINE: 7.5 HP diesel
PROPELLER: 2-blade
GENERATOR:

DECK

STEERING: tiller
WINCHES: 4 Barient winches: 2 sheet (#18 2sp), 2 halyard (#10)
SAFETY: bow and stern pulpits with double lifelines
ANCHOR: anchor well
NAV LIGHTS: running and masthead

RIG

TYPE: masthead sloop
RIGGING: 1x19 SS wire
MAINSHEET: 4-part with mid-boom sheeting

SAILS

SUPPLIED WITH BASE BOAT: main, jib

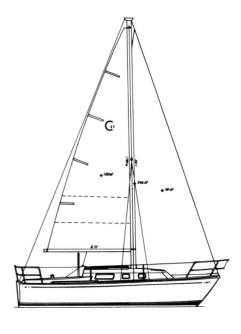

BUILDER'S COMMENTS A comfortable family cruiser in the Cal tradition. Berths for 5, a separate head, and a sea cook's galley are combined with the performance Cals are famous for.

CATALINA 27

DESIGNER:
BUILDER: Catalina Yachts

STATISTICS

LOA: 26 ft. 10 ins.
LWL: 21 ft. 9 ins.
BEAM: 8 ft. 10 ins.
DISPLACEMENT
deep keel: 6,850 lbs.
shoal keel: 7,300 lbs.
c/board:
BALLAST
deep keel: 2,700 lbs.
shoal keel: 3,100 lbs.
c/board:
DRAFT
deep keel: 4 ft. 0 ins.
shoal keel: 3 ft. 5 ins.
c/board up:
c/board down:

SAIL AREA: 340 sq. ft.
FRESH WATER: 20 gals.
FUEL CAPACITY: 15 gals.

COSTS

BASE BOAT: $18,405
DATE: 10/01/84
EST. ON WATER:
DATE:

RATIOS

	deep	shoal
SAIL AREA/DISP:	15.08	14.46
DISP/LENGTH:	297.21	316.74
BALLAST RATIO:	39.42	42.47
FUEL/DISP:	1.64	1.54
FRESH WATER/DISP:	2.34	2.19

INTERIOR

BERTHS: 6 berths: 1 double V, 2 single settees, 1 double quarterberth
TABLE: dropleaf
HEAD(S): 1 head with shower pan
COLD STORAGE: built-in icebox

STOVE: 2-burner alcohol
MAX. HEADROOM: 6 ft. 0 ins.

MACHINERY

ENGINE:
PROPELLER:
GENERATOR:

DECK

STEERING: tiller
WINCHES: 4 winches: 2 primary (2sp), 1 jib halyard, 1 mainsheet (ST)
SAFETY: bow and stern pulpits with double lifelines
ANCHOR: anchor well
NAV LIGHTS: running and masthead

RIG

TYPE: masthead sloop
RIGGING: wire
MAINSHEET: mid-boom sheeting

SAILS

SUPPLIED WITH BASE BOAT:

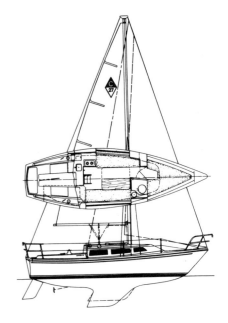

PRIDE 270

DESIGNER: Britton Chance
BUILDER: Tartan Marine Company

STATISTICS

LOA: 26 ft. 10 ins.
LWL: 23 ft. 5 ins.
BEAM: 8 ft. 6 ins.
DISPLACEMENT
deep keel: 3,800 lbs.
shoal keel:
c/board:
BALLAST
deep keel: 1,762 lbs.
shoal keel:
c/board:
DRAFT
deep keel: 4 ft. 11 ins.
shoal keel:
c/board up:
c/board down:

INTERIOR

BERTHS: 4 berths: 1 double V, 2 single settees
TABLE:
HEAD(S):
COLD STORAGE: portable ice chest
STOVE:
MAX. HEADROOM:

MACHINERY

ENGINE:
PROPELLER:
GENERATOR:

SAIL AREA: 404 sq. ft.
FRESH WATER: 15 gals
FUEL CAPACITY:

COSTS

BASE BOAT: $24,600
DATE: 07/01/85
EST. ON WATER: $30,000
DATE: 07/01/85

RATIOS

SAIL AREA/DISP: 26.55
DISP/LENGTH: 132.06
BALLAST RATIO: 46.37
FUEL/DISP:
FRESH WATER/DISP: 3.1

DECK

STEERING: tiller
WINCHES: 4 Lewmar winches
SAFETY: bow and stern pulpits with single lifelines
ANCHOR:
NAV LIGHTS: running

RIG

TYPE: fractional rig sloop with Offshore spar
RIGGING: wire
MAINSHEET: boom-end sheeting

SAILS

SUPPLIED WITH BASE BOAT:

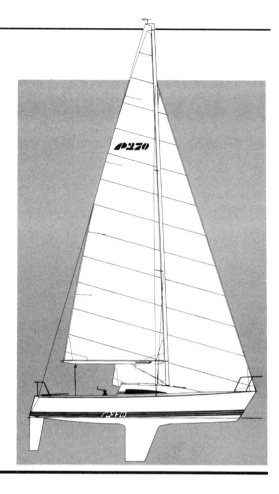

O'DAY 272

DESIGNER: C. Raymond Hunt Associates
BUILDER: Lear Siegler Marine

STATISTICS

LOA: 26 ft. 11 ins.
LWL: 22 ft. 11 ins.
BEAM: 9 ft. 0 ins.
DISPLACEMENT
deep keel:
shoal keel: 4870 lbs.
c/board:
BALLAST
deep keel:
shoal keel: 1870 lbs.
c/board:
DRAFT
deep keel:
shoal keel: 2 ft. 11 ins.
c/board up:
c/board down:

INTERIOR

BERTHS: 6 berths: 1 double V, 1 child settee, 1 settee, 1 double quarterberth
TABLE: folding
HEAD(S): portable chemical head
COLD STORAGE: 3.5 cu. ft. ice box
STOVE:
MAX. HEADROOM: 5 ft. 11 ins.

MACHINERY

ENGINE:
PROPELLER:
GENERATOR:

SAIL AREA: 301.78 sq. ft.
FRESH WATER: 25 gals.
FUEL CAPACITY: 0 gals.

COSTS

BASE BOAT: $19,995
DATE: 11/85
EST. ON WATER:
DATE:

RATIOS

SAIL AREA/DISP: 16.81
DISP/LENGTH: 180.57
BALLAST RATIO: 38.4
FUEL/DISP: 0.0
FRESH WATER/DISP: 4.1

DECK

STEERING: tiller
WINCHES: 3 Barlow winches: 2 primary #16LTC, 1 halyard # 15
SAFETY: bow and stern pulpits with single lifelines
ANCHOR: anchor well
NAV LIGHTS: running lights

RIG

TYPE: masthead sloop
RIGGING: 1x19 wire
MAINSHEET: midboom sheeting

SAILS

SUPPLIED WITH BASE BOAT: mainsail with single reef, 130% genoa

BUILDER'S COMMENTS The O'Day 272 draws just 35" of water with its unique winged keel designed exclusively for cruising. This O'Day was designed to be fast and nimble, moderately light and lively and easily sailed by one or two.

BAVARIA 820

DESIGNER: Axel Mohnhaupt
BUILDER: Bavaria Yachtbau GmbH

STATISTICS

LOA: 27 ft. 0 ins.
LWL: 22 ft. 1 ins.
BEAM: 9 ft. 2 ins.
DISPLACEMENT
deep keel: 4,750 lbs.
shoal keel:
c/board:
BALLAST
deep keel: 2,000 lbs.
shoal keel:
c/board:
DRAFT
deep keel: 4 ft. 3 ins.
shoal keel:
c/board up: 2 ft. 3 ins.
c/board down: 5 ft. 0 ins.

SAIL AREA: 270 sq. ft.
FRESH WATER: 28 gals
FUEL CAPACITY:

COSTS

BASE BOAT:
DATE:
EST. ON WATER:
DATE:

RATIOS

SAIL AREA/DISP: 15.28
DISP/LENGTH: 196
BALLAST RATIO: 42.10
FUEL/DISP:
FRESH WATER/DISP: 4.71

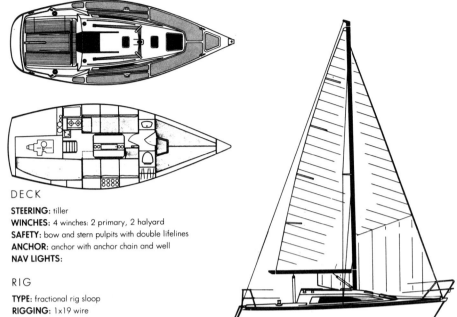

INTERIOR

BERTHS: 6 berths: 1 double V, 1 double convertible settee, 1 single settee, 1 single quarterberth
TABLE: dropleaf
HEAD(S):
COLD STORAGE: built-in icebox (10 gal.)
STOVE: 2-burner alcohol
MAX. HEADROOM: 6 ft. 2 ins.

MACHINERY

ENGINE:
PROPELLER:
GENERATOR:

DECK

STEERING: tiller
WINCHES: 4 winches: 2 primary, 2 halyard
SAFETY: bow and stern pulpits with double lifelines
ANCHOR: anchor with anchor chain and well
NAV LIGHTS:

RIG

TYPE: fractional rig sloop
RIGGING: 1x19 wire
MAINSHEET: mid-boom sheeting

SAILS

SUPPLIED WITH BASE BOAT: main (2 reefs), working jib

BUILDER'S COMMENTS This 27 foot sailboat offers everything that makes life enjoyable onboard even if you are planning longer trips: practical joinery, much room for the crew, essential stowage, and solid construction.

CAPE DORY 270

DESIGNER: Dieter Empacher
BUILDER: Cape Dory Yachts

STATISTICS

LOA: 27 ft. 3 ins.
LWL: 20 ft. 9 ins.
BEAM: 9 ft. 5 ins.
DISPLACEMENT
deep keel:
shoal keel:
c/board: 8,380 lbs.
BALLAST
deep keel:
shoal keel:
c/board: 3,250 lbs.
DRAFT
deep keel:
shoal keel:
c/board up: 3 ft. 0 ins.
c/board down: 7 ft. 0 ins.

SAIL AREA: 398 sq. ft.
FRESH WATER: 46 gals.
FUEL CAPACITY: 15 gals.

COSTS

BASE BOAT:
DATE:
EST. ON WATER:
DATE:

RATIOS

SAIL AREA/DISP: 15.44
DISP/LENGTH: 418.74
BALLAST RATIO: 38.78
FUEL/DISP: 1.34
FRESH WATER/DISP: 4.39

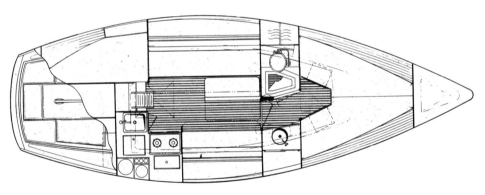

INTERIOR

BERTHS: 6 berths: 1 double V, 2 single settees, 1 double quarterberth
TABLE: fixed double-leaf
HEAD(S): 1 head with holding tank (24 gals.)
COLD STORAGE:
STOVE: 2-burner
MAX. HEADROOM:

MACHINERY

ENGINE: 13 HP Westerbeke diesel with 2:1 reduction gear
PROPELLER: 2-blade on 1" shaft
GENERATOR:

DECK

STEERING: tiller
WINCHES: 4 winches: 2 primary (2sp), 2 halyard
SAFETY: bow and stern pulpits with single lifelines
ANCHOR: anchor well and roller
NAV LIGHTS: running and masthead

RIG

TYPE: masthead sloop
RIGGING:
MAINSHEET: mid-boom sheeting

SAILS

SUPPLIED WITH BASE BOAT: main, working jib

DANA 24

DESIGNER: William Crealock
BUILDER: Pacific Seacraft Corp.

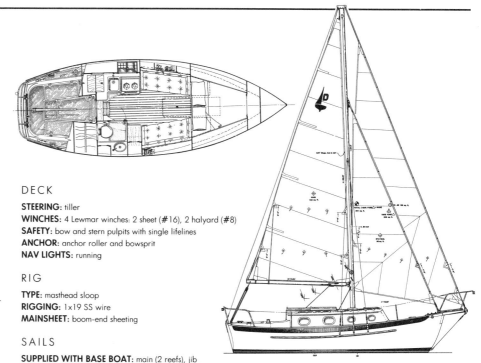

STATISTICS

LOA: 27 ft. 3 ins.
LWL: 21 ft. 5 ins.
BEAM: 8 ft. 7 ins.
DISPLACEMENT
deep keel: 8,000 lbs.
shoal keel:
c/board:
BALLAST
deep keel: 3,100 lbs.
shoal keel:
c/board:
DRAFT
deep keel: 3 ft. 10 ins.
shoal keel:
c/board up:
c/board down:

SAIL AREA: 358 sq. ft.
FRESH WATER: 30 gals.
FUEL CAPACITY: 20 gals.

COSTS

BASE BOAT: $42,900
DATE: 06/85
EST. ON WATER: $46,000
DATE: 06/85

RATIOS

SAIL AREA/DISP: 14.32
DISP/LENGTH: 363
BALLAST RATIO: 38.75
FUEL/DISP: 1.87
FRESH WATER/DISP: 3.00

INTERIOR

BERTHS: 5 berths: 1 double V, 1 single settee, 1 double convertible settee
TABLE: slide-out from under V berth
HEAD(S): 1 head
COLD STORAGE: built-in icebox
STOVE: 2-burner kerosene with oven
MAX. HEADROOM: 6 ft. 2 ins.

MACHINERY

ENGINE: Yanmar #2GM-20 diesel
PROPELLER: 2-blade
GENERATOR:

DECK

STEERING: tiller
WINCHES: 4 Lewmar winches: 2 sheet (#16), 2 halyard (#8)
SAFETY: bow and stern pulpits with single lifelines
ANCHOR: anchor roller and bowsprit
NAV LIGHTS: running

RIG

TYPE: masthead sloop
RIGGING: 1x19 SS wire
MAINSHEET: boom-end sheeting

SAILS

SUPPLIED WITH BASE BOAT: main (2 reefs), jib

BUILDER'S COMMENTS Conceived for cruising and designed for performance, the Dana 24 is the latest design from the board of W.I.B. Crealock. Sophisticated hull design, high ballast ratio, and efficient sail plan provide stability and power for the kind of performance so often lacking in other pocket cruisers. Dana's interior is huge with 6' 2" headroom and more elbow room than most people could imagine in a boat of this length.

HERRESHOFF 27

DESIGNER: Halsey Herreshoff
BUILDER: Cat Ketch Corporation

STATISTICS

LOA: 27 ft. 3 ins.
LWL: 26 ft. 0 ins.
BEAM: 9 ft. 4 ins.
DISPLACEMENT
deep keel: 3,850 lbs.
shoal keel:
c/board:
BALLAST
deep keel: 1,800 lbs.
shoal keel:
c/board:
DRAFT
deep keel: 3 ft. 6 ins.
shoal keel:
c/board up:
c/board down:

SAIL AREA: 312 sq. ft.
FRESH WATER:
FUEL CAPACITY:

COSTS

BASE BOAT: $37,510
DATE: 02/15/85
EST. ON WATER:
DATE:

RATIOS

SAIL AREA/DISP: 20.38
DISP/LENGTH: 98.8
BALLAST RATIO: 46.7
FUEL/DISP:
FRESH WATER/DISP:

INTERIOR

BERTHS: 4 berths: 1 double V, 1 single settee, 1 single quarterberth
TABLE: dropleaf
HEAD(S): 1 head
COLD STORAGE: built-in icebox
STOVE: 2-burner
MAX. HEADROOM:

MACHINERY

ENGINE:
PROPELLER:
GENERATOR:

DECK

STEERING: tiller
WINCHES: none
SAFETY: bow and stern pulpits with double lifelines
ANCHOR: anchor roller
NAV LIGHTS:

RIG

TYPE: cat ketch with unstayed carbon fiber composite masts
RIGGING:
MAINSHEET: 4-part wishbone with boom-end sheeting

SAILS

SUPPLIED WITH BASE BOAT: main, mizzen

BUILDER'S COMMENTS The Herreshoff Cat Ketch features an unstayed, self-tending rig which makes a simple, effortless sailing yacht. The Fiberglass/Airex hull has clean traditional lines and a light displacement, fin keel/skeg configuration. These characteristics result in an agile, quick, easy and fun boat to sail.

JEANNEAU FANTASIA

DESIGNER: Philippe Harle
DISTRIBUTOR: Nautique International, Inc. (built in France by Jeanneau, S.A.)

STATISTICS

LOA: 27 ft. 3 ins.
LWL: 21 ft. 6 ins.
BEAM: 9 ft. 6 ins.
DISPLACEMENT
deep keel: 4,710 lbs.
shoal keel:
c/board:
BALLAST
deep keel: 1,650 lbs.
shoal keel:
c/board:
DRAFT
deep keel: 5 ft. 0 ins.
shoal keel:
c/board up:
c/board down:

SAIL AREA: 341 sq. ft.
FRESH WATER: 13 gals.
FUEL CAPACITY: 7 gals.

COSTS

BASE BOAT:
DATE:
EST. ON WATER:
DATE:

RATIOS

SAIL AREA/DISP: 19.41
DISP/LENGTH: 211
BALLAST RATIO: 35.03
FUEL/DISP: 1.114
FRESH WATER/DISP: 2.208

INTERIOR

BERTHS: 6 berths: 1 double V, 2 single settees, 1 double quarterberth
TABLE: folding dinette
HEAD(S): 1 head
COLD STORAGE: built-in icebox (18 gals.)
STOVE: 2-burner gas
MAX. HEADROOM:

MACHINERY

ENGINE: Yanmar GM diesel
PROPELLER:
GENERATOR:

DECK

STEERING: tiller
WINCHES: 3 winches: 2 primary, 1 halyard
SAFETY: bow and stern pulpits
ANCHOR: anchor well and roller
NAV LIGHTS: running and masthead

RIG

TYPE: masthead sloop
RIGGING:
MAINSHEET: mid-boom sheeting

SAILS

SUPPLIED WITH BASE BOAT: main, intermediate genoa

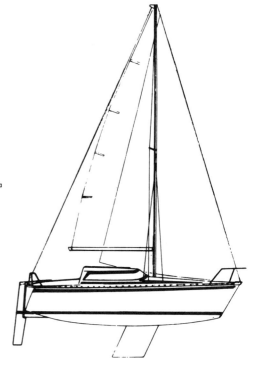

ORION 27 MK II

DESIGNER: Henry Mohrschladt
BUILDER: Pacific Seacraft Corp.

STATISTICS

LOA: 27 ft. 4 ins.
LWL: 22 ft. 2 ins.
BEAM: 9 ft. 3 ins.
DISPLACEMENT
deep keel: 10,000 lbs.
shoal keel:
c/board:
BALLAST
deep keel: 3,500 lbs.
shoal keel:
c/board:
DRAFT
deep keel: 4 ft. 0 ins.
shoal keel:
c/board up:
c/board down:

SAIL AREA: 428 sq. ft.
FRESH WATER: 71 gals.
FUEL CAPACITY: 35 gals.

COSTS

BASE BOAT: $54,500
DATE: 06/85
EST. ON WATER: $58,000
DATE: 06/85

RATIOS

SAIL AREA/DISP: 14.75
DISP/LENGTH: 409
BALLAST RATIO: 35.00
FUEL/DISP: 2.62
FRESH WATER/DISP: 5.86

INTERIOR

BERTHS: 5 berths: 1 double V, 1 double convertible dinette, 1 single quarterberth
TABLE: dinette
HEAD(S): 1 head
COLD STORAGE: built-in icebox
STOVE: 2-burner kerosene with oven
MAX. HEADROOM: 6 ft. 2 ins.

MACHINERY

ENGINE: Yanmar #2GM-20 or #3GM-30 diesel
PROPELLER: 2-blade
GENERATOR:

DECK

STEERING: tiller or wheel
WINCHES: 4 Lewmar winches: 2 primary (#40), 2 halyard (#8)
SAFETY: bow and stern pulpits with single lifelines
ANCHOR: anchor well
NAV LIGHTS: running

RIG

TYPE: masthead sloop
RIGGING: 1x19 SS wire
MAINSHEET: 6-part with mid-boom sheeting

SAILS

SUPPLIED WITH BASE BOAT:

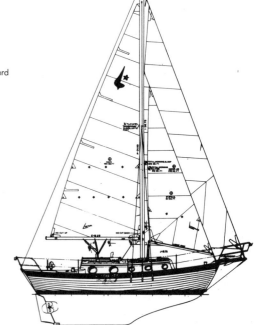

BUILDER'S COMMENTS One of the strongest, most versatile yachts on the market, the Orion 27 Mark II is a rugged world cruiser, an exciting performer, and a comfortable liveaboard for getaway seclusion. Classic bow, wineglass transom, and graceful sheer combine in a yacht that will fill you with pride every time you set eyes on her. Orion's sailing performance is sensational. Her high aspect, well-balanced sail plan and cut-away forefoot make her easy to handle, fast, and responsive, while her full keel provides the directional stability and rudder protection that are so crucial to extended cruising.

LM-27

DESIGNER:
DISTRIBUTOR: Anchor Marine, Inc. (built in Denmark by LM Glasfiber, a/s)

STATISTICS

LOA: 27 ft. 5.0 ins.
LWL: 23 ft. 3.5 ins.
BEAM: 9 ft. 0.5 ins.
DISPLACEMENT
deep keel: 8,800 lbs.
shoal keel:
c/board:
BALLAST
deep keel: 3,960 lbs.
shoal keel:
c/board:
DRAFT
deep keel: 3 ft. 1.5 ins.
shoal keel:
c/board up:
c/board down:

SAIL AREA: 243.0 sq. ft.
FRESH WATER: 26.4 gals.
FUEL CAPACITY: 26.4 gals.

COSTS

BASE BOAT: $45,300
DATE: 04/01/85
EST. ON WATER:
DATE:

RATIOS

SAIL AREA/DISP: 9.12
DISP/LENGTH: 310.98
BALLAST RATIO: 45
FUEL/DISP: 2.25
FRESH WATER/DISP: 2.40

INTERIOR

BERTHS: 6 berths: 1 double V, 2 double convertible settees
TABLE: dropleaf
HEAD(S): 1 head
COLD STORAGE:
STOVE: 2-burner propane
MAX. HEADROOM:

MACHINERY

ENGINE: 36 HP Bukh #DV 36 ME diesel
PROPELLER: fixed
GENERATOR:

DECK

STEERING: tiller
WINCHES:
SAFETY: bow and stern pulpits with double lifelines
ANCHOR: 22 lb. anchor with chain
NAV LIGHTS: running

RIG

TYPE: fractional rig sloop
RIGGING:
MAINSHEET: boom-end sheeting

SAILS

SUPPLIED WITH BASE BOAT: main, working jib

SHOW 27

DESIGNER:
BUILDER: Barberis Cantieri

STATISTICS

LOA: 27 ft. 6 ins.
LWL: 22 ft. 0 ins.
BEAM: 9 ft. 8 ins.
DISPLACEMENT
deep keel: 4,440 lbs.
shoal keel:
c/board:
BALLAST
deep keel: 1,430 lbs.
shoal keel:
c/board:
DRAFT
deep keel: 5 ft. 6 ins.
shoal keel:
c/board up:
c/board down:

SAIL AREA: 298 sq. ft.
FRESH WATER: 15 gals.
FUEL CAPACITY:

COSTS

BASE BOAT:
DATE:
EST. ON WATER:
DATE:

RATIOS

SAIL AREA/DISP: 16.41
DISP/LENGTH: 186.15
BALLAST RATIO: 32.21
FUEL/DISP:
FRESH WATER/DISP: 2.7

INTERIOR

BERTHS: 5 berths: 1 double V, 1 single settee, 1 double convertible dinette
TABLE: hi-lo
HEAD(S): 1 head
COLD STORAGE: built-in icebox
STOVE: 2-burner propane with oven
MAX. HEADROOM:

MACHINERY

ENGINE: Yanmar # GM
PROPELLER: 2-blade fixed
GENERATOR:

DECK

STEERING: wheel
WINCHES: 5 winches: 2 primary, 2 halyard, 1 reefing
SAFETY: bow and stern pulpits with double lifelines
ANCHOR: anchor roller and well
NAV LIGHTS: running and masthead

RIG

TYPE: masthead sloop
RIGGING: 1x19 SS wire
MAINSHEET: 4-part with mid-boom sheeting

SAILS

SUPPLIED WITH BASE BOAT: main (with cover), working jib, medium genoa, storm jib

CALIBER 28

DESIGNER: Michael McCreary
BUILDER: Caliber Yacht Corporation

STATISTICS

LOA: 27 ft. 6 ins.
LWL: 24 ft. 2 ins.
BEAM: 10 ft. 10 ins.
DISPLACEMENT
deep keel: 7,200 lbs.
shoal keel:
c/board:
BALLAST
deep keel: 3,100 lbs.
shoal keel:
c/board:
DRAFT
deep keel: 3 ft. 11 ins.
shoal keel:
c/board up:
c/board down:

SAIL AREA: 428 sq. ft.
FRESH WATER: 25 gals.
FUEL CAPACITY: 21 gals.

COSTS

BASE BOAT:
DATE:
EST. ON WATER:
DATE:

RATIOS

SAIL AREA/DISP: 18.36
DISP/LENGTH: 227
BALLAST RATIO: 43.05
FUEL/DISP: 2.18
FRESH WATER/DISP: 2.77

DECK

STEERING: 30" wheel
WINCHES: 3 Barient winches: 2 primary (#12), 1 halyard (#10)
SAFETY: bow and stern pulpits with double lifelines
ANCHOR: anchor well
NAV LIGHTS: running

RIG

TYPE: masthead sloop
RIGGING: 1x19 wire
MAINSHEET: 6-part with mid-boom sheeting

SAILS

SUPPLIED WITH BASE BOAT: main (1 reef), 110% jib

INTERIOR

BERTHS: 4 berths in 2 cabins: 1 double V, 2 single settees; or 5 berths in 3 cabins: 1 double V, 2 single settees, 1 double quarterberth
TABLE: bulkhead-mounted dropleaf
HEAD(S): 1 head with shower
COLD STORAGE: built-in ice box (6 cu. ft.)
STOVE: 2-burner alcohol
MAX. HEADROOM: 6 ft. 1 ins.

MACHINERY

ENGINE: 18 HP Yanmar diesel
PROPELLER: 14x16
GENERATOR:

J-27

DESIGNER: Rod Johnstone
BUILDER: J Boats, Inc.

STATISTICS

LOA: 27 ft. 6 ins.
LWL: 23 ft. 0 ins.
BEAM: 8 ft. 6 ins.
DISPLACEMENT
deep keel: 3,800 lbs.
shoal keel:
c/board:
BALLAST
deep keel: 1,530 lbs.
shoal keel:
c/board:
DRAFT
deep keel: 4 ft. 10.8 ins.
shoal keel:
c/board up:
c/board down:

SAIL AREA: 362 sq. ft.
FRESH WATER:
FUEL CAPACITY:

COSTS

BASE BOAT: $22,000
DATE: 01/01/85
EST. ON WATER:
DATE:

RATIOS

SAIL AREA/DISP: 23.85
DISP/LENGTH: 139.43
BALLAST RATIO: 40.26
FUEL/DISP:
FRESH WATER/DISP:

DECK

STEERING: tiller
WINCHES: 4 Barient winches: 2 primary (#21), 2 secondary (#18)
SAFETY: bow and stern pulpits with single lifeline
ANCHOR:
NAV LIGHTS: running

RIG

TYPE: fractional rig sloop with Hall spar
RIGGING: wire
MAINSHEET: mid-boom sheeting

SAILS

SUPPLIED WITH BASE BOAT:

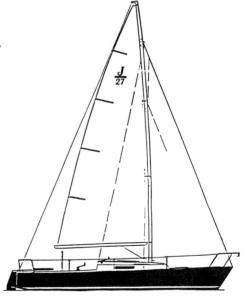

INTERIOR

BERTHS: 5 berths: 1 double V, 1 double convertible settee, 1 single quarterberth
TABLE:
HEAD(S):
COLD STORAGE: cooler (48 qt.)
STOVE:
MAX. HEADROOM:

MACHINERY

ENGINE:
PROPELLER:
GENERATOR:

MIRAGE 27

DESIGNER:
BUILDER: Mirage Yachts, Ltd.

STATISTICS

LOA: 27 ft. 6 ins.
LWL: 21 ft. 8 ins.
BEAM: 9 ft. 3 ins.
DISPLACEMENT
deep keel: 5,200 lbs.
shoal keel:
c/board:
BALLAST
deep keel: 2,200 lbs.
shoal keel:
c/board:
DRAFT
deep keel: 4 ft. 4 ins.
shoal keel:
c/board up:
c/board down:

INTERIOR

BERTHS: 4 berths: 1 double V, 2 single settees
TABLE: dropleaf
HEAD(S):
COLD STORAGE: built-in icebox
STOVE:
MAX. HEADROOM: 6 ft. 1 ins.

MACHINERY

ENGINE:
PROPELLER:
GENERATOR:

SAIL AREA:
FRESH WATER:
FUEL CAPACITY:

COSTS

BASE BOAT:
DATE:
EST. ON WATER:
DATE:

RATIOS

SAIL AREA/DISP:
DISP/LENGTH: 228.44
BALLAST RATIO: 42.30
FUEL/DISP:
FRESH WATER/DISP:

DECK

STEERING: tiller
WINCHES:
SAFETY:
ANCHOR:
NAV LIGHTS:

RIG

TYPE: masthead sloop
RIGGING:
MAINSHEET: mid-boom sheeting

SAILS

SUPPLIED WITH BASE BOAT:

MOODY 28

DESIGNER: Bill Dixon-Angus Primrose, Ltd.
DISTRIBUTOR: A. H. Moody & Son, Ltd. (built in England by Marine Projects, Ltd.)

STATISTICS

LOA: 27 ft. 6 ins.
LWL: 23 ft. 4 ins.
BEAM: 10 ft. 0 ins.
DISPLACEMENT
deep keel: 6,550 lbs.
shoal keel: 6,850 lbs.
c/board:
BALLAST
deep keel: 2,500 lbs.
shoal keel: 2,800 lbs.
c/board:
DRAFT
deep keel: 5 ft. 0 ins.
shoal keel: 3 ft. 6 ins.
c/board up:
c/board down:

RATIOS

	deep	shoal
SAIL AREA/DISP:	16.23	15.75
DISP/LENGTH:	230.28	240.82
BALLAST RATIO:	38.17	40.88
FUEL/DISP:		
FRESH WATER/DISP:		

INTERIOR

BERTHS: 6 berths: 2 single Vs (converting to double), 2 single settees, 1 double quarterberth
TABLE: dropleaf
HEAD(S): 1 head
COLD STORAGE: built-in icebox

SAIL AREA: 355 sq. ft.
FRESH WATER:
FUEL CAPACITY:

COSTS

BASE BOAT:
DATE:
EST. ON WATER:
DATE:

STOVE: 2-burner LPG with oven and grill
MAX. HEADROOM:

MACHINERY

ENGINE: Volvo
PROPELLER: 2-blade fixed
GENERATOR:

DECK

STEERING: tiller
WINCHES: 5 Lewmar winches
SAFETY: bow and stern pulpits with double lifelines
ANCHOR: plough anchor with anchor chain
NAV LIGHTS: running and masthead

RIG

TYPE: masthead sloop with Kemp spar
RIGGING: wire
MAINSHEET: boom-end sheeting

SAILS

SUPPLIED WITH BASE BOAT: main, working jib

MOODY 27

DESIGNER: Bill Dixon-Angus Primrose, Ltd.
DISTRIBUTOR: A. H. Moody & Son, Ltd. (built in England by Marine Projects, Ltd.)

STATISTICS

LOA: 27 ft. 8.0 ins.
LWL: 21 ft. 10.5 ins.
BEAM: 9 ft. 8.0 ins.
DISPLACEMENT
deep keel: 5,750 lbs.
shoal keel:
c/board:
BALLAST
deep keel: 2,530 lbs.
shoal keel:
c/board:
DRAFT
deep keel: 4 ft. 8 ins.
shoal keel:
c/board up:
c/board down:

SAIL AREA: 412 sq. ft.
FRESH WATER: 18 gals.
FUEL CAPACITY: 16 gals.

COSTS

BASE BOAT:
DATE:
EST. ON WATER:
DATE:

RATIOS

SAIL AREA/DISP: 20.53
DISP/LENGTH: 245
BALLAST RATIO: 44.00
FUEL/DISP: 2.08
FRESH WATER/DISP: 2.50

INTERIOR

BERTHS: 6 berths: 1 double V, 2 single settees, 1 double quarterberth
TABLE: dropleaf
HEAD(S): 1 head
COLD STORAGE: built-in icebox
STOVE: 2-burner with oven
MAX. HEADROOM:

MACHINERY

ENGINE: 18 HP Volvo #2002 diesel
PROPELLER: 2-blade
GENERATOR:

DECK

STEERING: tiller
WINCHES: 4 Lewmar winches: 2 primary (#16), 2 halyard
SAFETY: bow and stern pulpit with double lifelines
ANCHOR: anchor well
NAV LIGHTS: running

RIG

TYPE: masthead sloop
RIGGING: 1x19 SS wire
MAINSHEET: mid-boom sheeting

SAILS

SUPPLIED WITH BASE BOAT: main, working jib

ISLANDER 28

DESIGNER: Robert H. Perry
BUILDER: Islander Yachts

STATISTICS

LOA: 27 ft. 11.0 ins.
LWL: 23 ft. 1.0 ins.
BEAM: 9 ft. 10.5 ins.
DISPLACEMENT
deep keel: 7,000 lbs.
shoal keel:
c/board:
BALLAST
deep keel: 3,000 lbs.
shoal keel:
c/board:
DRAFT
deep keel: 5 ft. 0 ins.
shoal keel:
c/board up:
c/board down:

SAIL AREA: 361 sq. ft.
FRESH WATER: 24 gals.
FUEL CAPACITY: 20 gals.

COSTS

BASE BOAT:
DATE:
EST. ON WATER:
DATE:

RATIOS

SAIL AREA/DISP: 15.79
DISP/LENGTH: 253.52
BALLAST RATIO: 42.86
FUEL/DISP: 2.14
FRESH WATER/DISP: 2.74

INTERIOR

BERTHS: 6 berths: 1 double V, 1 double convertible, 1 single settee, 1 single quarterberth
TABLE: bulkhead-mounted
HEAD(S): 1 head
COLD STORAGE: built-in icebox (3.2 cu. ft.)
STOVE: 2-burner alcohol
MAX. HEADROOM:

MACHINERY

ENGINE: 15 HP Yanmar diesel
PROPELLER: 2-blade
GENERATOR:

DECK

STEERING: tiller
WINCHES: 5 Lewmar winches: 2 primary, 1 mainsheet, 2 halyard
SAFETY: bow and stern pulpits with lifelines
ANCHOR: anchor well
NAV LIGHTS: running and masthead

RIG

TYPE: masthead sloop
RIGGING:
MAINSHEET: 4-part with mid-boom sheeting

SAILS

SUPPLIED WITH BASE BOAT: main (1 reef), 110% jib

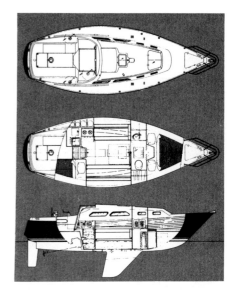

BAHAMA 28

DESIGNER: Robert H. Perry
BUILDER: Islander Yachts

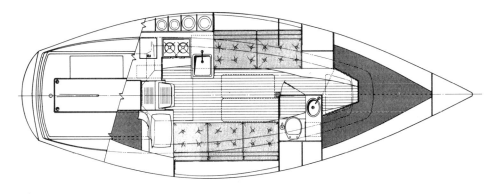

STATISTICS

LOA: 27 ft. 11.0 ins.
LWL: 23 ft. 1.0 ins.
BEAM: 9 ft. 10.5 ins.
DISPLACEMENT
deep keel: 7,000 lbs.
shoal keel:
c/board:
BALLAST
deep keel: 3,000 lbs.
shoal keel:
c/board:
DRAFT
deep keel: 5 ft. 0 ins.
shoal keel:
c/board up:
c/board down:

SAIL AREA: 361 sq. ft.
FRESH WATER: 20 gals.
FUEL CAPACITY: 20 gals.

COSTS

BASE BOAT:
DATE:
EST. ON WATER:
DATE:

RATIOS

SAIL AREA/DISP: 15.79
DISP/LENGTH: 254
BALLAST RATIO: 42.85
FUEL/DISP: 2.142
FRESH WATER/DISP: 2.285

INTERIOR

BERTHS: 5 berths: 1 double V, 2 single settees, 1 single quarterberth
TABLE: bulkhead-mounted
HEAD(S): 1 head
COLD STORAGE: built-in icebox
STOVE: 2-burner alcohol
MAX. HEADROOM:

MACHINERY

ENGINE: 15 Hp Yanmar diesel
PROPELLER: 2-blade
GENERATOR:

DECK

STEERING: tiller
WINCHES: 3 Lewmar winches: 2 primary (#30A), 1 halyard (#8A)
SAFETY: bow and stern pulpits with lifelines
ANCHOR: anchor well
NAV LIGHTS: running and masthead

RIG

TYPE: masthead sloop
RIGGING:
MAINSHEET: mid-boom sheeting

SAILS

SUPPLIED WITH BASE BOAT: main (1 reef), 110% jib

TANZER 8.5

DESIGNER: J. Tanzer
BUILDER: Tanzer Industries, Inc.

STATISTICS

LOA: 27 ft. 11 ins.
LWL: 23 ft. 9 ins.
BEAM: 9 ft. 6 ins.
DISPLACEMENT
deep keel: 7,400 lbs.
shoal keel:
c/board:
BALLAST
deep keel: 3,000 lbs.
shoal keel:
c/board:
DRAFT
deep keel: 4 ft. 4 ins.
shoal keel:
c/board up:
c/board down:

SAIL AREA: 394 sq. ft.
FRESH WATER: 15 gals.
FUEL CAPACITY: 12 gals.

COSTS

BASE BOAT: $28,575
DATE: 02/01/85
EST. ON WATER: $33,000
DATE: 02/01/85

RATIOS

SAIL AREA/DISP: 16.60
DISP/LENGTH: 246.6
BALLAST RATIO: 40.54
FUEL/DISP: 1.22
FRESH WATER/DISP: 1.62

DECK

STEERING: tiller
WINCHES: 3 winches: 2 primary, 1 halyard
SAFETY: bow pulpit with lifelines
ANCHOR: anchor well
NAV LIGHTS: running

RIG

TYPE: masthead sloop
RIGGING: wire (1/4")
MAINSHEET: mid-boom sheeting

SAILS

SUPPLIED WITH BASE BOAT: main (1 reef), working jib or lapper

INTERIOR

BERTHS: 5 berths: 1 double V, 1 double convertible, 1 single quarterberth
TABLE: bulkhead-mounted
HEAD(S): 1 head with holding tank
COLD STORAGE: built-in icebox
STOVE: 2-burner alcohol
MAX. HEADROOM: 6 ft. 4 ins.

MACHINERY

ENGINE: 15 HP Yanmar diesel
PROPELLER:
GENERATOR:

BUILDER'S COMMENTS This 28 footer was designed with the cruising sailor in mind, while not forgetting performance. Close winded, stable, with an interior to satisfy even the most critical cruising family. Its 6'4" headroom, five berths, large galley, and enclosed head all add up to exceptional comfort.

ERICSON 28

DESIGNER: Bruce King
BUILDER: Ericson Yachts

STATISTICS

LOA: 28 ft. 0 ins.
LWL: 23 ft. 4 ins.
BEAM: 10 ft. 0 ins.
DISPLACEMENT
deep keel: 7,500 lbs.
shoal keel:
c/board:
BALLAST
deep keel: 3,200 lbs.
shoal keel:
c/board:
DRAFT
deep keel: 5 ft. 6 ins.
shoal keel: 4 ft. 0 ins.
c/board up:
c/board down:

SAIL AREA: 411 sq. ft.
FRESH WATER: 25 gals.
FUEL CAPACITY: 15 gals.

COSTS

BASE BOAT:
DATE:
EST. ON WATER:
DATE:

RATIOS

SAIL AREA/DISP: 17.16
DISP/LENGTH: 263.68
BALLAST RATIO: 42.67
FUEL/DISP: 1.50
FRESH WATER/DISP: 2.67

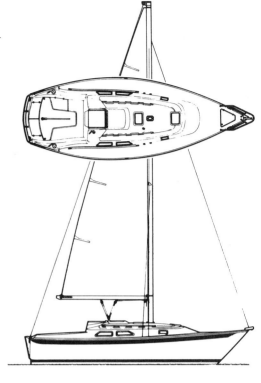

DECK

STEERING: tiller
WINCHES: 4 Barient winches: 2 primary (#21 2sp), 1 halyard (#10), 1 mainsheet (#8)
SAFETY: bow and stern pulpits with single lifelines
ANCHOR: anchor roller and well
NAV LIGHTS: running and masthead

RIG

TYPE: fractional rig sloop with Kenyon spar
RIGGING: wire (1/4")
MAINSHEET: 4-part with mid-boom sheeting

SAILS

SUPPLIED WITH BASE BOAT:

INTERIOR

BERTHS: 6 berths: 1 double V, 1 double extension settee, 1 single settee, 1 aft single
TABLE: bulkhead-mounted
HEAD(S): 1 head with holding tank
COLD STORAGE: built-in icebox (5 cu. ft.)
STOVE: 2-burner alcohol
MAX. HEADROOM: 6 ft. 1 in.

MACHINERY

ENGINE: 10 HP Universal #12 diesel
PROPELLER: fixed 12" × 10" on 3/4" shaft
GENERATOR:

SHANNON 28

DESIGNER: Walter Schulz & Associates
BUILDER: Shannon Boat Company, Inc.

STATISTICS

LOA: 28 ft. 0 ins.
LWL: 22 ft. 11 ins.
BEAM: 9 ft. 6 ins.
DISPLACEMENT
deep keel: 9,300 lbs.
shoal keel:
c/board:
BALLAST
deep keel: 3,600 lbs.
shoal keel:
c/board:
DRAFT
deep keel:
shoal keel:
c/board up:
c/board down:

SAIL AREA: 470 sq. ft.
FRESH WATER: 65 gals.
FUEL CAPACITY: 20 gals.

COSTS

BASE BOAT:
DATE:
EST. ON WATER: $85,000
DATE: 05/31/85

RATIOS

SAIL AREA/DISP: 17.00
DISP/LENGTH: 344
BALLAST RATIO: 38.70
FUEL/DISP: 1.61
FRESH WATER/DISP: 5.59

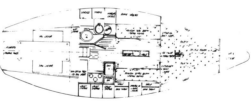

DECK

STEERING: tiller
WINCHES: 6 Lewmar or Barient winches
SAFETY: bow and stern pulpits with lifelines
ANCHOR: anchor roller and bowsprit
NAV LIGHTS: running

RIG

TYPE: cutter
RIGGING: 1x19 SS wire
MAINSHEET: mid-boom sheeting

SAILS

SUPPLIED WITH BASE BOAT: main (2 reef), yankee jib, staysail

INTERIOR

BERTHS: 4 berths: 1 double V, 2 single settees
TABLE: center-mounted dropleaf
HEAD(S):
COLD STORAGE: built-in icebox
STOVE: 2-burner LPG
MAX. HEADROOM: 6 ft. 2 ins.

MACHINERY

ENGINE: 15 HP diesel
PROPELLER: 3-blade
GENERATOR:

BUILDER'S COMMENTS The Shannon 28 is perhaps one of the only boats under 30 feet built in America for serious offshore sailing. Every conceivable item, from hull design to the layout of the galley dish locker, was incorporated to produce the finest yacht possible. It is the contention of Shannon Boat Company that size alone is not a qualifier for structural integrity or ocean sailing.

SIRIUS 28

DESIGNER: Vandestadt & McGruer
BUILDER: Vandestadt & McGruer, Ltd.

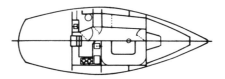
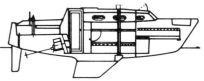
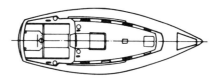
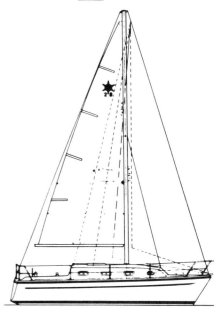

STATISTICS

LOA: 28 ft. 0 ins.
LWL: 24 ft. 0 ins.
BEAM: 9 ft. 8 ins.
DISPLACEMENT
deep keel: 6,700 lbs.
shoal keel:
c/board:
BALLAST
deep keel: 2,600 lbs.
shoal keel:
c/board:
DRAFT
deep keel: 4 ft. 4 ins.
shoal keel:
c/board up:
c/board down:

SAIL AREA: 410 sq. ft.
FRESH WATER: 24 gals.
FUEL CAPACITY: 19 gals.

COSTS

BASE BOAT: $38,950
DATE: 06/24/85
EST. ON WATER: $38,950
DATE: 06/24/85

RATIOS

SAIL AREA/DISP: 18.56
DISP/LENGTH: 216
BALLAST RATIO: 38.80
FUEL/DISP: 2.12
FRESH WATER/DISP: 2.86

INTERIOR

BERTHS: 5 berths: 1 double V, 1 double convertible dinette, 1 single settee
TABLE: dropleaf
HEAD(S): 1 head
COLD STORAGE: built-in icebox (6 cu. ft.)
STOVE: alcohol (pressurized)
MAX. HEADROOM: 6 ft. 3 ins.

MACHINERY

ENGINE: 9 HP Yanmar #1 GM10 diesel
PROPELLER: 2-blade fixed
GENERATOR:

DECK

STEERING: 24" wheel with emergency tiller
WINCHES: 4 Lewmar winches: 2 sheet (#24), 2 halyard (#7)
SAFETY: bow and stern pulpits with double lifelines
ANCHOR: anchor well
NAV LIGHTS: running and masthead

RIG

TYPE: masthead sloop
RIGGING: 1x19 SS wire (7/32")
MAINSHEET: boom-end sheeting

SAILS

SUPPLIED WITH BASE BOAT: Sobstad main (2 reefs), #3 110% genoa

---

MORRIS 28 (LYNDA)

DESIGNER: Chuck Paine
BUILDER: Morris Yachts, Inc.

STATISTICS

LOA: 28 ft. 1 ins.
LWL: 22 ft. 9 ins.
BEAM: 9 ft. 2 ins.
DISPLACEMENT
deep keel: 8,300 lbs.
shoal keel:
c/board:
BALLAST
deep keel: 3,900 lbs.
shoal keel:
c/board:
DRAFT
deep keel: 4 ft. 4 ins.
shoal keel:
c/board up:
c/board down:

SAIL AREA: 410 sq. ft.
FRESH WATER: 37 gals.
FUEL CAPACITY: 16 gals.

COSTS

BASE BOAT: $55,900
DATE: 04/85
EST. ON WATER:
DATE:

RATIOS

SAIL AREA/DISP: 16.00
DISP/LENGTH: 314.69
BALLAST RATIO: 46.99
FUEL/DISP: 1.45
FRESH WATER/DISP: 3.57

INTERIOR

BERTHS: 4 berths: 1 double V, 1 single settee, 1 single quarterberth
TABLE: bulkhead-mounted
HEAD(S): 1 head with holding tank
COLD STORAGE: built-in icebox
STOVE: 2-burner kerosene
MAX. HEADROOM: Over 6 ft.

MACHINERY

ENGINE: 13 HP Westerbeke #W13
PROPELLER: fixed
GENERATOR:

DECK

STEERING: tiller
WINCHES: 4 winches
SAFETY: bow and stern pulpits with double lifelines
ANCHOR: anchor roller
NAV LIGHTS: running

RIG

TYPE: masthead sloop
RIGGING: 1x19 wire (1/4")
MAINSHEET: mid-boom sheeting

SAILS

SUPPLIED WITH BASE BOAT:

CAPE DORY 28

DESIGNER: Carl Alberg
BUILDER: Cape Dory Yachts

STATISTICS

LOA: 28 ft. 1.25 ins.
LWL: 22 ft. 2.50 ins.
BEAM: 8 ft. 10.50 ins.
DISPLACEMENT
deep keel: 9,000 lbs.
shoal keel:
c/board:
BALLAST
deep keel: 3,500 lbs.
shoal keel:
c/board:
DRAFT
deep keel: 4 ft. 0 ins.
shoal keel:
c/board up:
c/board down:

SAIL AREA: 404 sq. ft.
FRESH WATER: 60 gals.
FUEL CAPACITY: 13 gals.

COSTS

BASE BOAT:
DATE:
EST. ON WATER:
DATE:

RATIOS

SAIL AREA/DISP: 14.94
DISP/LENGTH: 364.76
BALLAST RATIO: 38.89
FUEL/DISP: 1.08
FRESH WATER/DISP: 5.33

DECK

STEERING: tiller
WINCHES: 4 winches: 2 primary, 2 halyard
SAFETY: bow and stern pulpits with single lifelines
ANCHOR: anchor roller
NAV LIGHTS: running and masthead

RIG

TYPE: masthead sloop
RIGGING:
MAINSHEET: boom-end sheeting

SAILS

SUPPLIED WITH BASE BOAT: main, working jib

INTERIOR

BERTHS: 5 berths: 1 double V, 1 double convertible settee, 1 single settee
TABLE: bulkhead mounted
HEAD(S): 1 head with holding tank (24 gals.)
COLD STORAGE: built-in icebox
STOVE: 2-burner alcohol
MAX. HEADROOM:

MACHINERY

ENGINE: 13 Hp Volvo #MD7A with 1.91:1 reduction gear
PROPELLER: 1" shaft
GENERATOR:

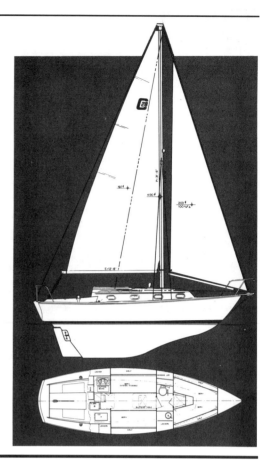

CAL 28

DESIGNER: C. Raymond Hunt Associates
BUILDER: Lear Siegler Marine

STATISTICS

LOA: 28 ft. 3 ins.
LWL: 23 ft. 4 ins.
BEAM: 10 ft. 5 ins.
DISPLACEMENT
deep keel: 7,200 lbs.
shoal keel:
c/board:
BALLAST
deep keel: 2,825 lbs.
shoal keel: 3,150 lbs.
c/board:
DRAFT
deep keel: 5 ft. 3 ins.
shoal keel: 3 ft. 9 ins.
c/board up:
c/board down:

SAIL AREA: 402 sq. ft.
FRESH WATER: 40 gals.
FUEL CAPACITY: 18 gals.

COSTS

BASE BOAT: $44,000
DATE: 11/85
EST. ON WATER:
DATE:

RATIOS

SAIL AREA/DISP: 17.24
DISP/LENGTH: 253
BALLAST RATIO: 39.23
FUEL/DISP: 1.87
FRESH WATER/DISP: 4.44

DECK

STEERING: wheel with emergency tiller
WINCHES: 4 Barient winches: 2 primary, 1 halyard, 1 mainsheet
SAFETY bow and stern pulpits with double lifelines
ANCHOR: anchor roller and well
NAV LIGHTS: running and masthead

RIG

TYPE: masthead sloop
RIGGING: 1x19 ss wire
MAINSHEET: 5-part with mid-boom sheeting

SAILS

SUPPLIED WITH BASE BOAT:

INTERIOR

BERTHS: 6 berths: 1 double V, 2 single settees, 1 double quarterberth
TABLE: dropleaf
HEAD(S): 1 head with shower
COLD STORAGE: built-in icebox (5 cu. ft.)
STOVE: 2-burner propane
MAX. HEADROOM: 6 ft. 3 ins.

MACHINERY

ENGINE: 13 HP Westerbeke diesel
PROPELLER: 2-blade fixed
GENERATOR:

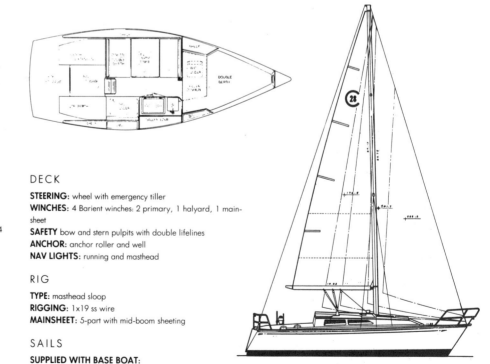

BUILDER'S COMMENTS A very modern cruiser/racer with an aft cabin and aft head. The new Cal 28 also has a full forward cabin. Her modern rig and underbody give the performance Cals are noted for.

O'DAY 28

DESIGNER: C. Raymond Hunt Associates
BUILDER: Lear Siegler Marine

STATISTICS

LOA: 28 ft. 3 ins.
LWL: 22 ft. 11 ins.
BEAM: 10 ft. 3 ins.
DISPLACEMENT
deep keel: 7,300 lbs.
shoal keel: 7,700 lbs.
c/board:
BALLAST
deep keel: 2,550 lbs.
shoal keel: 2,950 lbs.
c/board:
DRAFT
deep keel: 4 ft. 8 ins.
shoal keel: 3 ft. 8 ins.
c/board up:
c/board down:

SAIL AREA: 396.9 sq. ft.
FRESH WATER: 25.0 gals.
FUEL CAPACITY: 18.0 gals.

COSTS

BASE BOAT: $40,700
DATE: 11/85
EST. ON WATER:
DATE:

RATIOS

SAIL AREA/DISP: 16.88
DISP/LENGTH: 270.66
BALLAST RATIO: 34.93
FUEL/DISP: 1.85
FRESH WATER/DISP: 2.74

INTERIOR

BERTHS: 5 berths: 1 double V, 2 single settee, 1 single quarterberth
TABLE: dropleaf
HEAD(S): 1 head with shower and holding tank (15 gals.)
COLD STORAGE: built-in icebox (4 cu. ft.)
STOVE: 2-burner alcohol
MAX. HEADROOM: 6 ft. 0 ins.

MACHINERY

ENGINE: 10 HP Universal #12 diesel
PROPELLER: fixed 12"x11" on 1" shaft
GENERATOR:

DECK

STEERING: tiller
WINCHES: 4 Barlow winches: 2 primary (#23C 2sp), 2 halyard (#16 LT)
SAFETY:
ANCHOR:
NAV LIGHTS: running

RIG

TYPE: masthead sloop
RIGGING: 1x19 wire
MAINSHEET: 4-part with mid-boom sheeting

SAILS

SUPPLIED WITH BASE BOAT: 6.5 oz. main (1 reef), 6.5 oz. working jib

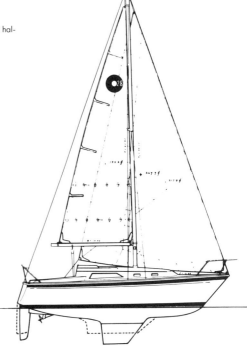

TARTAN 28

DESIGNER: Sparkman & Stephens
BUILDER: Tartan Marine Company

STATISTICS

LOA: 28 ft. 3.0 ins.
LWL: 23 ft. 8.0 ins.
BEAM: 9 ft. 10.5 ins.
DISPLACEMENT
deep keel: 7,450 lbs.
shoal keel: 7,450 lbs.
c/board:
BALLAST
deep keel: 3,200 lbs.
shoal keel: 3,200 lbs.
c/board:
DRAFT
deep keel: 4 ft. 11 ins.
shoal keel: 3 ft. 11 ins.
c/board up:
c/board down:

SAIL AREA: 408 sq. ft.
FRESH WATER: 30 gals.
FUEL CAPACITY: 17 gals.

COSTS

BASE BOAT: $41,250
DATE: 07/01/85
EST. ON WATER: $45,000
DATE: 07/01/85

RATIOS

SAIL AREA/DISP: 17.11
DISP/LENGTH: 251.11
BALLAST RATIO: 42.95
FUEL/DISP: 1.71
FRESH WATER/DISP: 3.22

INTERIOR

BERTHS: 5 berths: 1 double V, 1 double settee, 1 single quarterberth
TABLE: bulkhead-mounted
HEAD(S): 1 head with shower, sump pump, and holding tank
COLD STORAGE: built-in icebox (6 cu. ft.)
STOVE: 2-burner alcohol
MAX. HEADROOM: 6 ft. 0 ins.

MACHINERY

ENGINE: 15 HP Yanmar #26M diesel with 2.6:1 reduction gear
PROPELLER: fixed 12"x14" on 3/4" shaft
GENERATOR:

DECK

STEERING: tiller (wheel optional)
WINCHES: 4 Lewmar winches
SAFETY: bow and stern pulpits with double lifelines
ANCHOR:
NAV LIGHTS: running

RIG

TYPE: masthead sloop with Kenyon spar
RIGGING:
MAINSHEET: boom-end sheeting

SAILS

SUPPLIED WITH BASE BOAT:

HUNTER 28.5

DESIGNER: Hunter Design Group
BUILDER: Hunter Marine

STATISTICS

LOA: 28 ft. 5 ins.
LWL: 23 ft. 9 ins.
BEAM: 10 ft. 6 ins.
DISPLACEMENT
deep keel: 7,000 lbs.
shoal keel: 7,100 lbs.
c/board:
BALLAST
deep keel: 3,000 lbs.
shoal keel: 3,100 lbs.
c/board:
DRAFT
deep keel: 5 ft. 2 ins.
shoal keel: 4 ft. 0 ins.
c/board up:
c/board down:

SAIL AREA: 398 sq. ft.
FRESH WATER: 27 gals.
FUEL CAPACITY: 11 gals.

COSTS

BASE BOAT:
DATE:
EST. ON WATER: $34,000
DATE: 11/85

RATIOS

SAIL AREA/DISP: 17.40
DISP/LENGTH: 233
BALLAST RATIO: 42.85
FUEL/DISP: 1.17
FRESH WATER/DISP: 3.08

INTERIOR

BERTHS: 6 berths: 1 double V, 2 single settees, 1 double quarterberth
TABLE: dropleaf
HEAD(S): 1 head with shower
COLD STORAGE: built-in icebox
STOVE: 2-burner alcohol
MAX. HEADROOM: 6 ft. 2 ins.

MACHINERY

ENGINE: diesel
PROPELLER: 2-blade
GENERATOR:

DECK

STEERING: wheel with emergency tiller
WINCHES: 3 winches: 2 sheet (2sp ST), 1 halyard
SAFETY: bow and stern pulpits with double lifelines
ANCHOR: anchor with anchor well
NAV LIGHTS: running and masthead

RIG

TYPE: masthead sloop
RIGGING:
MAINSHEET: mid-boom sheeting

SAILS

SUPPLIED WITH BASE BOAT: main, 110% genoa

BUILDER'S COMMENTS The Hunter 28.5' is comfort, speed, and economics all engineered into one. Her interior is unique! Horseshoe in design for the maximum use of space below with full galley and enclosed head with hot-water shower. A fresh-water-cooled diesel engine is also standard. Above deck, Cruise Pac (TM) offers all the deck gear and sails required to take you on that long-awaited adventure at sea.

SABRE 28

DESIGNER: Sabre Design Team
BUILDER: Sabre Yachts

STATISTICS

LOA: 28 ft. 5 ins.
LWL: 22 ft. 10 ins.
BEAM: 9 ft. 2 ins.
DISPLACEMENT
deep keel: 7,800 lbs.
shoal keel:
c/board:
BALLAST
deep keel: 3,100 lbs.
shoal keel:
c/board:
DRAFT
deep keel: 4 ft. 8 ins.
shoal keel:
c/board up:
c/board down:

SAIL AREA: 403 sq. ft.
FRESH WATER: 30 gals.
FUEL CAPACITY: 20 gals.

COSTS

BASE BOAT:
DATE:
EST. ON WATER:
DATE:

RATIOS

SAIL AREA/DISP: 15.85
DISP/LENGTH: 296
BALLAST RATIO: 36.70
FUEL/DISP: 1.89
FRESH WATER/DISP: 3.03

INTERIOR

BERTHS: 6 berths: 1 double V, 1 double convertible, 1 single settee, 1 single quarterberth
TABLE: bulkhead-mounted
HEAD(S): 1 head
COLD STORAGE: built-in icebox
STOVE: 2-burner alcohol
MAX. HEADROOM: 6 ft. 0 ins.

MACHINERY

ENGINE: 13 HP Westerbeke diesel with 2:1 reduction gear
PROPELLER: 14"x10"
GENERATOR:

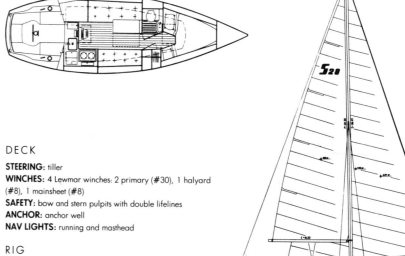

DECK

STEERING: tiller
WINCHES: 4 Lewmar winches: 2 primary (#30), 1 halyard (#8), 1 mainsheet (#8)
SAFETY: bow and stern pulpits with double lifelines
ANCHOR: anchor well
NAV LIGHTS: running and masthead

RIG

TYPE: masthead sloop
RIGGING: 1x19 SS wire
MAINSHEET: 4-part with mid-boom sheeting

SAILS

SUPPLIED WITH BASE BOAT:

PEARSON 28

DESIGNER: Bill Shaw
BUILDER: Pearson Yachts

STATISTICS

LOA: 28 ft. 5.5 ins.
LWL: 24 ft. 4.5 ins.
BEAM: 9 ft. 10.0 ins.
DISPLACEMENT
deep keel: 7,000 lbs.
shoal keel: 7,350 lbs.
c/board:
BALLAST
deep keel: 2,550 lbs.
shoal keel: 2,900 lbs.
c/board:
DRAFT
deep keel: 4 ft. 10 ins.
shoal keel: 3 ft. 6 ins.
c/board up:
c/board down:

SAIL AREA: 384 sq. ft.
FRESH WATER: 25 gals.
FUEL CAPACITY: 18 gals.

COSTS

BASE BOAT:
DATE:
EST. ON WATER:
DATE:

RATIOS

SAIL AREA/DISP: 16.84
DISP/LENGTH: 215.78
BALLAST RATIO: 36.43
FUEL/DISP: 1.93
FRESH WATER/DISP: 2.86

DECK

STEERING: wheel with emergency tiller
WINCHES: 4 Lewmar winches: 2 primary (#30 ST), 2 halyard (#7)
SAFETY: bow and stern pulpits with single lifelines
ANCHOR: anchor well
NAV LIGHTS: running and masthead

RIG

TYPE: masthead sloop
RIGGING: wire
MAINSHEET: mid-boom sheeting

SAILS

SUPPLIED WITH BASE BOAT: main, working jib

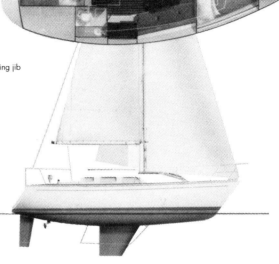

INTERIOR

BERTHS: 6 berths: 1 double V, 2 single settee, 1 double quarterberth
TABLE:
HEAD(S): 1 head with shower, sump pump, and holding tank
COLD STORAGE: built-in icebox (3 cu. ft.)
STOVE: 2-burner alcohol
MAX. HEADROOM:

MACHINERY

ENGINE: diesel
PROPELLER: fixed on 1" shaft
GENERATOR:

C & C 29

DESIGNER: C & C Design Group
BUILDER: C & C Yachts

STATISTICS

LOA: 28 ft. 6 ins.
LWL: 22 ft. 4 ins.
BEAM: 9 ft. 5 ins.
DISPLACEMENT
deep keel: 6,700 lbs.
shoal keel:
c/board:
BALLAST
deep keel: 2,700 lbs.
shoal keel:
c/board:
DRAFT
deep keel: 5 ft. 3 ins.
shoal keel:
c/board up:
c/board down:

SAIL AREA: 305 sq. ft.
FRESH WATER: 32 gals.
FUEL CAPACITY: 20 gals.

COSTS

BASE BOAT:
DATE:
EST. ON WATER: $54,000
DATE: 11/85

RATIOS

SAIL AREA/DISP: 17.78
DISP/LENGTH: 268
BALLAST RATIO: 40.29
FUEL/DISP: 2.23
FRESH WATER/DISP: 3.82

DECK

STEERING: masthead sloop
WINCHES: 4 winches: 2 primary (#18A), 2 halyard (#10A)
SAFETY: bow and stern pulpits with double lifelines
ANCHOR: anchor well
NAV LIGHTS: running and masthead

RIG

TYPE: masthead sloop
RIGGING: 1x19 wire
MAINSHEET: mid-boom sheeting

SAILS

SUPPLIED WITH BASE BOAT:

INTERIOR

BERTHS: 6 berths: 1 double V, 1 double convertible settee, 1 single settee, 1 single quarterberth
TABLE: bulkhead-mounted
HEAD(S): 1 head with shower and holding tank
COLD STORAGE: built-in icebox
STOVE:
MAX. HEADROOM:

MACHINERY

ENGINE: Yanmar #2GM diesel
PROPELLER: 2-blade fixed on 7/8" shaft
GENERATOR:

BUILDER'S COMMENTS In every respect she is one of the most successful yachts we have ever built. Race her to win; cruise her in unparalleled comfort below and above deck. The C & C 29—one of the best values ever.

LM-28

DESIGNER:
DISTRIBUTOR: Anchor Marine, Inc. (built in Denmark by LM Glasfiber, a/s)

STATISTICS

LOA: 28 ft. 8 ins.
LWL: 24 ft. 7 ins.
BEAM: 9 ft. 6 ins.
DISPLACEMENT
deep keel: 8,810 lbs.
shoal keel:
c/board:
BALLAST
deep keel: 3,415 lbs.
shoal keel:
c/board:
DRAFT
deep keel: 4 ft. 5 ins.
shoal keel:
c/board up:
c/board down:

SAIL AREA: 355 sq. ft.
FRESH WATER: 37 gals.
FUEL CAPACITY: 37 gals.

COSTS

BASE BOAT: $49,900
DATE: 04/01/85
EST. ON WATER:
DATE:

RATIOS

SAIL AREA/DISP: 13.32
DISP/LENGTH: 264.84
BALLAST RATIO: 38.76
FUEL/DISP: 3.15
FRESH WATER/DISP: 3.36

INTERIOR

BERTHS: 6 berths: 1 double V, 2 double convertible settees
TABLE: dropleaf
HEAD(S): 1 head with shower
COLD STORAGE:
STOVE: 2-burner propane
MAX. HEADROOM:

MACHINERY

ENGINE: 28 HP Volvo #2003/120 S diesel
PROPELLER: fixed
GENERATOR:

DECK

STEERING: tiller
WINCHES:
SAFETY: bow and stern pulpits with double lifelines
ANCHOR: anchor well
NAV LIGHTS: running

RIG

TYPE: fractional rig sloop
RIGGING:
MAINSHEET: boom-end sheeting

SAILS

SUPPLIED WITH BASE BOAT: main, working jib

BAYFIELD 29

DESIGNER:
BUILDER: Bayfield Boat Yard, Ltd.

STATISTICS

LOA: 29 ft. 0 ins.
LWL: 21 ft. 9 ins.
BEAM: 10 ft. 2 ins.
DISPLACEMENT
deep keel: 7,100 lbs.
shoal keel:
c/board:
BALLAST
deep keel: 3,000 lbs.
shoal keel:
c/board:
DRAFT
deep keel: 3 ft. 6 ins.
shoal keel:
c/board up:
c/board down:

SAIL AREA: 468 sq. ft.
FRESH WATER: 25 gals.
FUEL CAPACITY: 19 gals.

COSTS

BASE BOAT: $46,450
DATE: 09/84
EST. ON WATER:
DATE:

RATIOS

SAIL AREA/DISP: 20.27
DISP/LENGTH: 308.06
BALLAST RATIO: 42.25
FUEL/DISP: 2.01
FRESH WATER/DISP: 2.82

DECK

STEERING: tiller
WINCHES: 4 winches
SAFETY: bow and stern pulpits with single lifelines
ANCHOR: anchor well
NAV LIGHTS: running

RIG

TYPE: masthead cutter
RIGGING: 1x19 wire
MAINSHEET: boom-end sheeting

SAILS

SUPPLIED WITH BASE BOAT: main, staysail, topsail

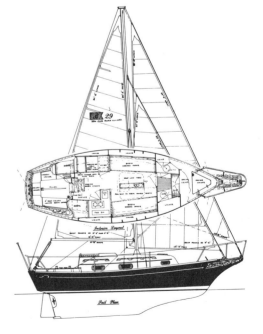

INTERIOR

BERTHS: 5 berths: 1 double settee, 1 single settee, 2 single quarterberths
TABLE: dropleaf
HEAD(S): 1 head with holding tank (20 gals.)
COLD STORAGE: built-in icebox
STOVE: 2-burner alcohol
MAX. HEADROOM:

MACHINERY

ENGINE: 15 HP diesel
PROPELLER: 3-blade fixed
GENERATOR:

VINDO 32

DESIGNER:
DISTRIBUTOR: Vindo North America, Inc. (built in Sweden by Vindo Marin, Ab)

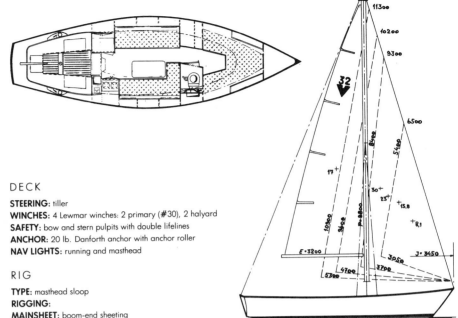

STATISTICS

LOA: 29 ft. 3 ins.
LWL: 22 ft. 0 ins.
BEAM: 9 ft. 1 ins.
DISPLACEMENT
deep keel: 7,040 lbs.
shoal keel:
c/board:
BALLAST
deep keel: 3,300 lbs.
shoal keel:
c/board:
DRAFT
deep keel: 4 ft. 3 ins.
shoal keel:
c/board up:
c/board down:

SAIL AREA: 360.0 sq. ft.
FRESH WATER: 22.5 gals.
FUEL CAPACITY: 12.5 gals.

COSTS

BASE BOAT: $55,000
DATE: 04/85
EST. ON WATER:
DATE:

RATIOS

SAIL AREA/DISP: 15.73
DISP/LENGTH: 295.16
BALLAST RATIO: 46.9
FUEL/DISP: 1.33
FRESH WATER/DISP: 2.56

INTERIOR

BERTHS: 4 berths: 1 double V, 2 single settees
TABLE: dropleaf
HEAD(S): 1 head
COLD STORAGE: built-in icebox
STOVE: 2-burner kerosene
MAX. HEADROOM: 6 ft. 0 ins.

MACHINERY

ENGINE: 13 HP Volvo Penta #MD7 diesel
PROPELLER:
GENERATOR:

DECK

STEERING: tiller
WINCHES: 4 Lewmar winches: 2 primary (#30), 2 halyard
SAFETY: bow and stern pulpits with double lifelines
ANCHOR: 20 lb. Danforth anchor with anchor roller
NAV LIGHTS: running and masthead

RIG

TYPE: masthead sloop
RIGGING:
MAINSHEET: boom-end sheeting

SAILS

SUPPLIED WITH BASE BOAT: main, working jib

ALBIN ALPHA

DESIGNER: Peter Norlin
BUILDER: Albin Marine, Inc.

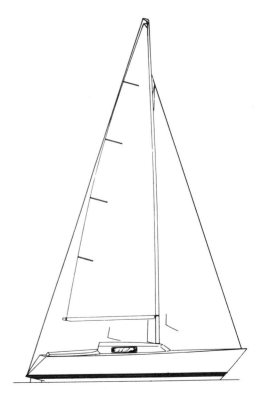

STATISTICS

LOA: 29 ft. 3.5 ins.
LWL: 23 ft. 7.0 ins.
BEAM: 9 ft. 4.0 ins.
DISPLACEMENT
deep keel: 7,055 lbs.
shoal keel:
c/board:
BALLAST
deep keel: 3,042 lbs.
shoal keel:
c/board:
DRAFT
deep keel: 5 ft. 5 ins.
shoal keel:
c/board up:
c/board down:

SAIL AREA: 441.00 sq. ft.
FRESH WATER: 27.75 gals.
FUEL CAPACITY: 14.50 gals.

COSTS

BASE BOAT: $36,900
DATE: 05/85
EST. ON WATER:
DATE:

RATIOS

SAIL AREA/DISP: 19.18
DISP/LENGTH: 240.2
BALLAST RATIO: 43.1
FUEL/DISP: 1.54
FRESH WATER/DISP: 3.15

INTERIOR

BERTHS: 5 berths: 1 double V, 1 single settee, 1 double quarterberth
TABLE: dropleaf
HEAD(S): 1 head
COLD STORAGE: built-in icebox
STOVE: 2-burner with oven
MAX. HEADROOM:

MACHINERY

ENGINE: Yanmar 1GM10 diesel
PROPELLER: 2-blade folding
GENERATOR:

DECK

STEERING: tiller
WINCHES: 4 Lewmar winches
SAFETY: bow and stern pulpits with lifelines
ANCHOR:
NAV LIGHTS: running and masthead

RIG

TYPE: fractional rig sloop with keel-stepped spar
RIGGING:
MAINSHEET: mid-boom sheeting

SAILS

SUPPLIED WITH BASE BOAT: working sails

SEIDELMANN 295

DESIGNER: Seidelmann
BUILDER: Seidelmann Yachts

STATISTICS

LOA: 29 ft. 5 ins.
LWL: 24 ft. 5 ins.
BEAM: 10 ft. 2 ins.
DISPLACEMENT
deep keel: 7,400 lbs.
shoal keel:
c/board:
BALLAST
deep keel: 3,200 lbs.
shoal keel:
c/board:
DRAFT
deep keel:
shoal keel:
c/board up: 3 ft. 3 ins.
c/board down: 6 ft. 2 ins.

SAIL AREA: 408 sq. ft.
FRESH WATER: 30 gals.
FUEL CAPACITY: 12 gals.

COSTS

BASE BOAT:
DATE:
EST. ON WATER:
DATE:

RATIOS

SAIL AREA/DISP: 17.15
DISP/LENGTH: 226
BALLAST RATIO: 43.24
FUEL/DISP: 1.21
FRESH WATER/DISP: 3.24

INTERIOR

BERTHS: 7 berths: 1 double V, 1 double convertible, 1 double quarterberth, 1 berth 5'4"
TABLE: bulkhead-mounted
HEAD(S): 1 self-contained or marine toilet with holding tank
COLD STORAGE: built-in icebox (7 cu. ft.)
STOVE: 2-burner alcohol with oven
MAX. HEADROOM: 6 ft. 3 ins.

MACHINERY

ENGINE:
PROPELLER:
GENERATOR:

DECK

STEERING: tiller or wheel
WINCHES: 2 primary winches
SAFETY: bow and stern pulpits with lifelines
ANCHOR: anchor well
NAV LIGHTS: running and masthead

RIG

TYPE: masthead sloop
RIGGING: stainless steel
MAINSHEET:

SAILS

SUPPLIED WITH BASE BOAT: main, working jib

MORRIS 30 (ANNIE)

DESIGNER: Chuck Paine
BUILDER: Morris Yachts, Inc.

STATISTICS

LOA: 29 ft. 5 ins.
LWL: 24 ft. 6 ins.
BEAM: 9 ft. 5 ins.
DISPLACEMENT
deep keel: 11,027 lbs.
shoal keel:
c/board:
BALLAST
deep keel: 4,400 lbs.
shoal keel:
c/board:
DRAFT
deep keel: 4 ft. 6 ins.
shoal keel:
c/board up:
c/board down:

SAIL AREA: 458 sq. ft.
FRESH WATER: 37 gals.
FUEL CAPACITY: 18 gals.

COSTS

BASE BOAT:
DATE:
EST. ON WATER:
DATE:

RATIOS

SAIL AREA/DISP: 14.78
DISP/LENGTH: 334.74
BALLAST RATIO: 39.90
FUEL/DISP: 1.22
FRESH WATER/DISP: 2.68

DECK

STEERING: tiller
WINCHES: 4 Lewmar winches
SAFETY: bow and stern pulpits with double lifelines
ANCHOR:
NAV LIGHTS: running

RIG

TYPE: masthead sloop
RIGGING: 1x19 wire (1/4")
MAINSHEET: boom-end sheeting

SAILS

SUPPLIED WITH BASE BOAT:

INTERIOR

BERTHS: 4 berths: 1 double V, 1 single settee, 1 single quarterberth
TABLE: dropleaf
HEAD(S): 1 head with sump pump and holding tank
COLD STORAGE: built-in icebox
STOVE: 2-burner kerosene with oven
MAX. HEADROOM: 6 ft. 0 ins.

MACHINERY

ENGINE: Volvo #2002 diesel
PROPELLER:
GENERATOR:

J-29

DESIGNER: Rod Johnstone
BUILDER: J Boats, Inc.

STATISTICS

LOA: 29 ft 6 ins.
LWL: 25 ft. 0 ins.
BEAM: 11 ft. 0 ins.
DISPLACEMENT
deep keel: 6,000 lbs.
shoal keel:
c/board:
BALLAST
deep keel: 2,100 lbs.
shoal keel:
c/board:
DRAFT
deep keel: 5 ft. 6 ins.
shoal keel:
c/board up:
c/board down:

SAIL AREA: 450 sq. ft.
FRESH WATER:
FUEL CAPACITY:

COSTS

BASE BOAT: $29,800
DATE: 04/01/85
EST. ON WATER:
DATE:

RATIOS

SAIL AREA/DISP: 21.81
DISP/LENGTH: 171.43
BALLAST RATIO: 35.00
FUEL/DISP:
FRESH WATER/DISP:

INTERIOR

BERTHS: 4 berths: 1 double V, 2 single settees
TABLE:
HEAD(S):
COLD STORAGE: cooler (48 qt.)
STOVE:
MAX. HEADROOM: 5 ft. 0 ins.

MACHINERY

ENGINE:
PROPELLER:
GENERATOR:

DECK

STEERING: tiller
WINCHES: 4 Barient winches: 2 primary (#25), 2 secondary (#21)
SAFETY: bow and stern pulpits with double lifelines
ANCHOR:
NAV LIGHTS: running

RIG

TYPE: fractional rig sloop
RIGGING: wire
MAINSHEET: 6-part with boom-end sheeting

SAILS

SUPPLIED WITH BASE BOAT:

JEANNEAU ARCADIA

DESIGNER: Tony Castro
DISTRIBUTOR: Nautique International, Inc. (built in France by Jeanneau, S.A.)

STATISTICS

LOA: 29 ft. 6 ins.
LWL: 24 ft. 5 ins.
BEAM: 10 ft. 4 ins.
DISPLACEMENT
deep keel: 6,175 lbs.
shoal keel:
c/board:
BALLAST
deep keel: 2,360 lbs.
shoal keel:
c/board:
DRAFT
deep keel: 5 ft. 4 ins.
shoal keel:
c/board up:
c/board down:

SAIL AREA: 488 sq. ft.
FRESH WATER: 24 gals.
FUEL CAPACITY: 7 gals.

COSTS

BASE BOAT:
outbrd version $34,125
DATE: 02/01/85
EST. ON WATER:
DATE:

RATIOS

SAIL AREA/DISP: 23.19
DISP/LENGTH: 189
BALLAST RATIO: 38.21
FUEL/DISP: 0.85
FRESH WATER/DISP: 3.11

INTERIOR

BERTHS: 6 berths: 1 double V, 2 single settees, 1 double quarterberth
TABLE: folding dinette
HEAD(S): 1 head
COLD STORAGE: built-in icebox (18.5 gals.)
STOVE: 2-burner gas
MAX. HEADROOM:

MACHINERY

ENGINE: (inboard version available)
PROPELLER:
GENERATOR:

DECK

STEERING: tiller
WINCHES: 3 winches: 2 primary, 1 halyard
SAFETY: bow and stern pulpits
ANCHOR: anchor well
NAV LIGHTS: running

RIG

TYPE: masthead sloop
RIGGING:
MAINSHEET: mid-boom sheeting

SAILS

SUPPLIED WITH BASE BOAT: main, medium genoa, storm jib

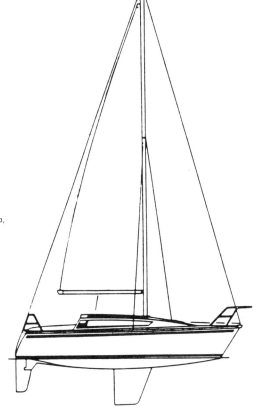

SHOW 30

DESIGNER:
DISTRIBUTOR: Satellite Management, Inc. (built in Italy by Barberis Cantieri)

STATISTICS

LOA: 29 ft. 6 ins.
LWL: 22 ft. 3 ins.
BEAM: 10 ft. 2 ins.
DISPLACEMENT
deep keel: 7,575 lbs.
shoal keel:
c/board:
BALLAST
deep keel: 2,420 lbs.
shoal keel:
c/board:
DRAFT
deep keel: 5 ft. 7 ins.
shoal keel:
c/board up:
c/board down:

SAIL AREA: 350 sq. ft.
FRESH WATER: 25 gals.
FUEL CAPACITY: 10 gals.

COSTS

BASE BOAT:
DATE:
EST. ON WATER:
DATE:

RATIOS

SAIL AREA/DISP: 14.52
DISP/LENGTH: 307
BALLAST RATIO: 31.95
FUEL/DISP: .99
FRESH WATER/DISP: 2.64

INTERIOR

BERTHS: 6 berths: 1 double V, 1 double convertible, 1 single settee, 1 single quarterberth
TABLE: center-mounted
HEAD(S): 1 head
COLD STORAGE: built-in icebox
STOVE: 3-burner propane
MAX. HEADROOM:

MACHINERY

ENGINE: 9.5 HP diesel
PROPELLER:
GENERATOR:

DECK

STEERING: tiller
WINCHES: 4 winches: 2 primary (2sp), 2 halyard
SAFETY: bow and stern pulpits with double lifelines
ANCHOR: anchor with anchor chain, rode, and well
NAV LIGHTS: running and masthead

RIG

TYPE: masthead sloop
RIGGING:
MAINSHEET:

SAILS

SUPPLIED WITH BASE BOAT: main, jib, medium genoa, storm jib

EXPRESS 30-M

DESIGNER: Steve Killing
BUILDER: Express Yachting

STATISTICS

LOA: 29 ft. 7.0 ins.
LWL: 24 ft. 5.5 ins.
BEAM: 10 ft. 0.0 ins.
DISPLACEMENT
deep keel: 6,200 lbs.
shoal keel:
c/board:
BALLAST
deep keel: 3,360 lbs.
shoal keel:
c/board:
DRAFT
deep keel: 5 ft. 4 ins.
shoal keel:
c/board up:
c/board down:

SAIL AREA: 471 sq. ft.
FRESH WATER: 4 gals.
FUEL CAPACITY:

COSTS

BASE BOAT: $37,900
DATE: 07/01/85
EST. ON WATER:
DATE:

RATIOS

SAIL AREA/DISP: 22.32
DISP/LENGTH: 189
BALLAST RATIO: 54.19
FUEL/DISP:
FRESH WATER/DISP: 0.52

DECK

STEERING: tiller
WINCHES: 4 Lewmar winches: 2 primary (#30A), 1 genoa/spinnaker halyard (#24A), 1 main halyard/reefing (#24A)
SAFETY: bow and stern pulpits with lifelines
ANCHOR:
NAV LIGHTS: running and masthead

RIG

TYPE: masthead sloop
RIGGING: Navtec rod
MAINSHEET: 3-part (6:1 ratchet)

SAILS

SUPPLIED WITH BASE BOAT:

INTERIOR

BERTHS: 4 pipe berths
TABLE:
HEAD(S): self-contained marine toilet
COLD STORAGE: portable ice chest
STOVE: 1-burner Kenyon alcohol
MAX. HEADROOM:

MACHINERY

ENGINE: outboard
PROPELLER:
GENERATOR:

VICTORIA 30

DESIGNER: Chuck Painee
BUILDER: Rampart Boatbuilding Co., Ltd.

STATISTICS

LOA: 29 ft. 8 ins.
LWL: 23 ft. 4 ins.
BEAM: 9 ft. 7 ins.
DISPLACEMENT
deep keel: 9,010 lbs.
shoal keel:
c/board:
BALLAST
deep keel: 4,400 lbs.
shoal keel:
c/board:
DRAFT
deep keel: 4 ft. 7 ins.
shoal keel:
c/board up:
c/board down:

SAIL AREA: 420 sq. ft.
FRESH WATER: 30 gals.
FUEL CAPACITY: 12 gals.

COSTS

BASE BOAT:
DATE:
EST. ON WATER:
DATE:

RATIOS

SAIL AREA/DISP: 15.52
DISP/LENGTH: 316.76
BALLAST RATIO: 48.83
FUEL/DISP: 1.00
FRESH WATER/DISP: 2.66

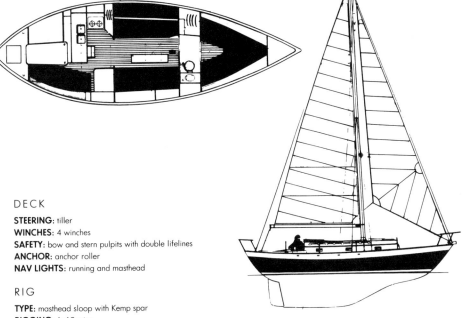

INTERIOR

BERTHS: 6 berths: 1 double V, 2 single settees, 1 single pilots, 1 single quarterberth
TABLE: bulkhead-mounted
HEAD(S): 1 head
COLD STORAGE: built-in icebox
STOVE: 2-burner kerosene
MAX. HEADROOM: 6 ft. 0 ins.

DECK

STEERING: tiller
WINCHES: 4 winches
SAFETY: bow and stern pulpits with double lifelines
ANCHOR: anchor roller
NAV LIGHTS: running and masthead

RIG

TYPE: masthead sloop with Kemp spar
RIGGING: 1x19 wire
MAINSHEET: 4-part with mid-boom sheeting

MACHINERY

ENGINE: 15 HP Yanmar diesel
PROPELLER: fixed
GENERATOR:

SAILS

SUPPLIED WITH BASE BOAT: main, working jib

BABA 30

DESIGNER: Robert H. Perry
BUILDER: Ta-Shing Yacht Building Co., Ltd.

STATISTICS

LOA: 29 ft. 9 ins.
LWL: 24 ft. 6 ins.
BEAM: 10 ft. 3 ins.
DISPLACEMENT
deep keel: 12,500 lbs.
shoal keel:
c/board:
BALLAST
deep keel: 5,000 lbs.
shoal keel:
c/board:
DRAFT
deep keel: 4 ft. 9 ins.
shoal keel:
c/board up:
c/board down:

SAIL AREA: 504 sq. ft.
FRESH WATER:
FUEL CAPACITY:

COSTS

BASE BOAT:
DATE:
EST. ON WATER:
DATE:

RATIOS

SAIL AREA/DISP: 14.97
DISP/LENGTH: 379
BALLAST RATIO: 40.00
FUEL/DISP:
FRESH WATER/DISP:

DECK

STEERING: tiller
WINCHES:
SAFETY:
ANCHOR:
NAV LIGHTS:

RIG

TYPE: masthead sloop
RIGGING:
MAINSHEET: mid-boom sheeting

SAILS

SUPPLIED WITH BASE BOAT:

INTERIOR

BERTHS: 5 berths: 1 double V, 2 single settees, 1 single quarterberth
TABLE: dropleaf
HEAD(S): 1 head with 1 shower
COLD STORAGE: built-in icebox
STOVE: 3-burner LPG
MAX. HEADROOM: 6 ft. 2 ins.

MACHINERY

ENGINE: 22.5 HP Yanmar diesel
PROPELLER:
GENERATOR:

J-30

DESIGNER: Rod Johnstone
BUILDER: J Boats, Inc.

STATISTICS

LOA: 29 ft. 10 ins.
LWL: 25 ft. 0 ins.
BEAM: 11 ft. 2 ins.
DISPLACEMENT
deep keel: 6,500 lbs.
shoal keel:
c/board:
BALLAST
deep keel: 2,100 lbs.
shoal keel:
c/board:
DRAFT
deep keel: 5 ft. 3 ins.
shoal keel:
c/board up:
c/board down:

SAIL AREA: 580 sq. ft.
FRESH WATER: 18 gals.
FUEL CAPACITY: 14 gals.

COSTS

BASE BOAT:
DATE:
EST. ON WATER:
DATE:

RATIOS

SAIL AREA/DISP: 26.64
DISP/LENGTH: 185.71
BALLAST RATIO: 32.30
FUEL/DISP: 1.62
FRESH WATER/DISP: 2.22

DECK

STEERING: tiller
WINCHES: 6 Barient winches: 2 primary (#25), 2 secondary (#21) 2 halyard (#10)
SAFETY: bow and stern pulpits with double lifelines
ANCHOR: anchor well
NAV LIGHTS: running

RIG

TYPE: fractional rig sloop
RIGGING: wire
MAINSHEET: boom-end sheeting

SAILS

SUPPLIED WITH BASE BOAT:

INTERIOR

BERTHS: 6 berths: 1 double V, 2 single settees, 2 single quarterberths
TABLE: center-mount dropleaf
HEAD(S): 1 head
COLD STORAGE: built-in icebox (5 cu. ft.)
STOVE: 2-burner alcohol
MAX. HEADROOM:

MACHINERY

ENGINE: 15 HP diesel
PROPELLER:
GENERATOR:

S2 9.1/30'

DESIGNER: S2 Yachts
BUILDER: S2 Yachts, Inc.

STATISTICS

LOA: 29 ft. 10 ins.
LWL: 25 ft. 0 ins.
BEAM: 10 ft. 6 ins.
DISPLACEMENT
deep keel: 7,850 lbs.
shoal keel:
c/board:
BALLAST
deep keel: 3,200 lbs.
shoal keel:
c/board:
DRAFT
deep keel: 5 ft. 6 ins.
shoal keel:
c/board up:
c/board down:

SAIL AREA: 472 sq. ft.
FRESH WATER: 23 gals.
FUEL CAPACITY: 15 gals.

COSTS

BASE BOAT:
DATE:
EST. ON WATER:
DATE:

RATIOS

SAIL AREA/DISP: 19.12
DISP/LENGTH: 224
BALLAST RATIO: 40.76
FUEL/DISP: 1.43
FRESH WATER/DISP: 2.34

DECK

STEERING: tiller
WINCHES: 4 winches: 2 primary (#40), 2 halyard (#16)
SAFETY: bow and stern pulpits with lifelines
ANCHOR: anchor well
NAV LIGHTS: running and masthead

RIG

TYPE: masthead sloop
RIGGING: Navtec rod
MAINSHEET: 5-part

SAILS

SUPPLIED WITH BASE BOAT:

INTERIOR

BERTHS: 7 berths: 1 double V, 2 single settees, 2 single pilot, 1 single quarterberth
TABLE: centerline removable
HEAD(S): enclosed Porta Potti and shower
COLD STORAGE: built-in ice box
STOVE: 2-burner alcohol
MAX. HEADROOM: 6 ft. 0 ins.

MACHINERY

ENGINE: Yanmar #2 GM diesel
PROPELLER: Martec folding
GENERATOR:

BUILDER'S COMMENTS A fast, competitive 30' M.O.R.C. racer engineered to be extremely stable and easy to sail. Computer designed "mathematically fair" resulting in exceptional stability, excellent pointing ability, and easy handling characteristics. With the S2 9.1M it is not a choice between fast sailing or comfortable cruising. It is a question of how fast and how far.

CATALINA 30

DESIGNER:
BUILDER: Catalina Yachts

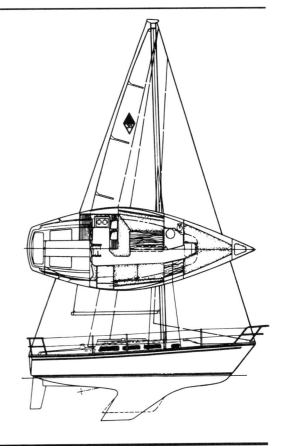

STATISTICS

LOA: 29 ft. 11 ins.
LWL: 25 ft. 0 ins.
BEAM: 10 ft. 10 ins.
DISPLACEMENT
deep keel: 10,200 lbs.
shoal keel: 10,650 lbs.
c/board:
BALLAST
deep keel: 4,200 lbs.
shoal keel: 4,650 lbs.
c/board:
DRAFT
deep keel: 5 ft. 3 ins.
shoal keel: 4 ft. 4 ins.
c/board up:
c/board down:

SAIL AREA: 446 sq. ft.
FRESH WATER: 18 gals.
FUEL CAPACITY: 21 gals.

COSTS

BASE BOAT: $28,495
DATE: 10/01/84
EST. ON WATER:
DATE:

RATIOS

	deep	shoal
SAIL AREA/DISP:	15.17	14.74
DISP/LENGTH:	291.43	304.29
BALLAST RATIO:	41.18	43.66
FUEL/DISP:	1.54	1.48
FRESH WATER/DISP:	1.41	1.35

INTERIOR

BERTHS: 7 berths: 1 double V, 1 single settee, 1 double convertible dinette, 1 double quarterberth
TABLE:
HEAD(S): 1 head
COLD STORAGE: built-in icebox

STOVE: 2-burner alcohol with oven
MAX. HEADROOM: 6 ft. 2 ins.

MACHINERY

ENGINE:
PROPELLER:
GENERATOR:

DECK

STEERING: tiller
WINCHES: 3 winches: 2 primary (2sp), 1 mainsheet
SAFETY: bow and stern pulpits with double lifelines
ANCHOR: anchor roller and locker
NAV LIGHTS: running and masthead

RIG

TYPE: masthead sloop
RIGGING: 1x19 wire
MAINSHEET: 3-part with mid-boom sheeting

SAILS

SUPPLIED WITH BASE BOAT:

ERICSON 30

DESIGNER: Bruce King
BUILDER: Ericson Yachts

STATISTICS

LOA: 29 ft. 11 ins.
LWL: 25 ft. 4 ins.
BEAM: 10 ft. 6 ins.
DISPLACEMENT
deep keel: 9,000 lbs.
shoal keel:
c/board:
BALLAST
deep keel: 4,000 lbs.
shoal keel:
c/board:
DRAFT
deep keel: 5 ft. 10 ins.
shoal keel: 4 ft. 0 ins.
c/board up:
c/board down:

SAIL AREA: 470 sq. ft.
FRESH WATER: 25 gals.
FUEL CAPACITY: 25 gals.

COSTS

BASE BOAT:
DATE:
EST. ON WATER:
DATE:

RATIOS

SAIL AREA/DISP: 17.37
DISP/LENGTH: 247
BALLAST RATIO: 44.44
FUEL/DISP: 2.08
FRESH WATER/DISP: 2.22

DECK

STEERING: 28" wheel with emergency tiller
WINCHES: 5 Barient winches: 2 primary (#21A), 2 halyard (#10), 1 mainsheet (#8)
SAFETY: bow and stern pulpits with double lifelines
ANCHOR: anchor roller and well
NAV LIGHTS: running and masthead

RIG

TYPE: fractional rig sloop with Kenyon spar
RIGGING: wire
MAINSHEET: 4-part with mid-boom sheeting

SAILS

SUPPLIED WITH BASE BOAT:

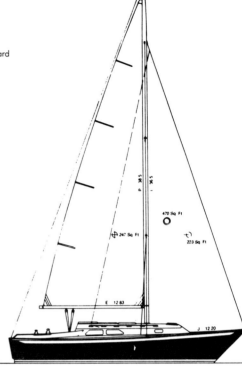

INTERIOR

BERTHS: 6 berths: 1 double V, 1 double convertible dinette, 1 single settee, 1 single quarterberth
TABLE: pedestal-mounted dinette
HEAD(S): 1 head with shower, sump pump, and holding tank
COLD STORAGE: built-in icebox
STOVE: 2-burner alcohol with oven
MAX. HEADROOM: 6 ft. 2 ins.

MACHINERY

ENGINE: 14 HP Universal #18 diesel
PROPELLER: fixed 12"x12" on 1" shaft
GENERATOR:

STELLAR 30

DESIGNER: James H. Kyle
BUILDER: Stellar Technology, Inc.

STATISTICS

LOA: 29 ft. 11 ins.
LWL: 26 ft. 3 ins.
BEAM: 10 ft. 0 ins.
DISPLACEMENT
deep keel: 5,800 lbs.
shoal keel:
c/board:
BALLAST
deep keel: 2,000 lbs.
shoal keel:
c/board:
DRAFT
deep keel: 5 ft. 3 ins.
shoal keel: 4 ft. 0 ins.
c/board up: 2 ft. 3 ins.
c/board down: 5 ft. 6 ins.

SAIL AREA: 400 sq. ft.
FRESH WATER: 24 gals.
FUEL CAPACITY: 12 gals.

COSTS

BASE BOAT:
DATE:
EST. ON WATER:
DATE:

RATIOS

SAIL AREA/DISP: 19.82
DISP/LENGTH: 143
BALLAST RATIO: 34.48
FUEL/DISP: 1.55
FRESH WATER/DISP: 3.31

DECK

STEERING: tiller
WINCHES: 6 Lewmar winches: 2 primary (#30), 2 jib (#7), 2 halyard (#7)
SAFETY: bow and stern pulpits with lifelines
ANCHOR: anchor well
NAV LIGHTS: running

RIG

TYPE: masthead sloop
RIGGING: 1x19 wire (1/4")
MAINSHEET: 4-part with boom-end sheeting

SAILS

SUPPLIED WITH BASE BOAT:

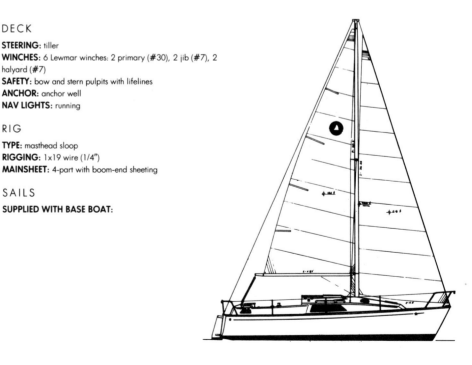

INTERIOR

BERTHS: 6 berths: 1 double V, 1 single settee, 1 child-size settee, 1 double in aft cabin
TABLE: pedestal-mounted
HEAD(S): 1 head
COLD STORAGE: built-in icebox (7.5 cu. ft.)
STOVE: 2-burner alcohol
MAX. HEADROOM: 6 ft. 0 ins.

MACHINERY

ENGINE: 9 HP Yanmar diesel with 2.62:1 reduction gear
PROPELLER: 2-blade on 1" shaft
GENERATOR:

SEIDELMANN 30T

DESIGNER: Seidelmann
BUILDER: Seidelmann Yachts

STATISTICS

LOA: 29 ft. 11 ins.
LWL: 24 ft. 0 ins.
BEAM: 11 ft. 0 ins.
DISPLACEMENT
deep keel: 8,800 lbs.
shoal keel:
c/board:
BALLAST
deep keel: 3,600 lbs.
shoal keel:
c/board:
DRAFT
deep keel: 5 ft. 5 ins.
shoal keel: 4 ft. 2 ins.
c/board up:
c/board down:

SAIL AREA: 420 sq. ft.
FRESH WATER: 30 gals.
FUEL CAPACITY: 12 gals.

COSTS

BASE BOAT:
DATE:
EST. ON WATER:
DATE:

RATIOS

SAIL AREA/DISP: 15.76
DISP/LENGTH: 284
BALLAST RATIO: 40.90
FUEL/DISP: 1.02
FRESH WATER/DISP: 2.73

INTERIOR

BERTHS: 6 berths: 1 double V, 1 double convertible settee, 1 single settee, 1 single quarterberth
TABLE: bulkhead-mounted
HEAD(S): 1 head
COLD STORAGE: built-in icebox (7 cu. ft.)
STOVE: 2-burner alcohol stove
MAX. HEADROOM: 6 ft. 5 ins.

MACHINERY

ENGINE: diesel
PROPELLER: 2 or 3 blade
GENERATOR:

DECK

STEERING: 30" wheel
WINCHES: 4 winches: 2 primary (#30 2sp), 2 halyard
SAFETY:
ANCHOR: anchor well
NAV LIGHTS: running and masthead

RIG

TYPE: masthead sloop
RIGGING: stainless steel
MAINSHEET: mid-boom sheeting

SAILS

SUPPLIED WITH BASE BOAT: main (1 reef), working jib

S2 9.2A/30'

DESIGNER: S2 Yachts
BUILDER: S2 Yachts, Inc.

STATISTICS

LOA: 29 ft. 11 ins.
LWL: 25 ft. 0 ins.
BEAM: 10 ft. 3 ins.
DISPLACEMENT
deep keel: 9,800 lbs.
shoal keel:
c/board:
BALLAST
deep keel: 4,000 lbs.
shoal keel:
c/board:
DRAFT
deep keel: 4 ft. 11 ins.
shoal keel:
c/board up:
c/board down:

SAIL AREA: 468 sq. ft.
FRESH WATER: 37 gals.
FUEL CAPACITY: 31 gals.

COSTS

BASE BOAT:
DATE:
EST. ON WATER:
DATE:

RATIOS

SAIL AREA/DISP: 16.35
DISP/LENGTH: 280
BALLAST RATIO: 40.81
FUEL/DISP: 2.37
FRESH WATER/DISP: 3.02

DECK

STEERING: 28" wheel with emergency tiller
WINCHES: 4 winches: 2 primary (#30 2sp), 2 halyard (#8)
SAFETY: bow and stern pulpits with double lifelines
ANCHOR: anchor well
NAV LIGHTS: running and masthead

RIG

TYPE: masthead sloop
RIGGING: 1x19 wire
MAINSHEET: 6-part with boom-end sheeting

SAILS

SUPPLIED WITH BASE BOAT:

INTERIOR

BERTHS: 6 berths: 1 double V, 1 double convertible, 1 single settee, 1 single quarterberth
TABLE: removable dinette
HEAD(S): 1 head with shower
COLD STORAGE: built-in icebox
STOVE: 2-burner alcohol
MAX. HEADROOM: 6 ft. 3 ins.

MACHINERY

ENGINE: Yanmar #2 GM diesel
PROPELLER:
GENERATOR:

BUILDER'S COMMENTS A classic 30' sailing yacht engineered with the perfect balance of cruising comfort and fast, efficient performance, the 9.2A's open, practical cruising layout has designed-in comfort attuned to eating, sleeping, and socializing under way. Constructed with uncompromising quality throughout. The 9.2A offers a level of quality that could only be an S2.

S2 9.2C/30'

DESIGNER: S2 Yachts
BUILDER: S2 Yachts, Inc.

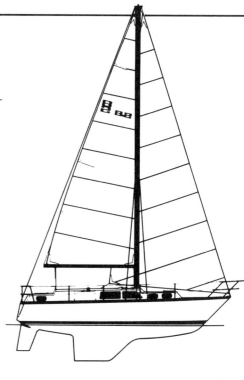

STATISTICS

LOA: 29 ft. 11 ins.
LWL: 25 ft. 0 ins.
BEAM: 10 ft. 3 ins.
DISPLACEMENT
deep keel: 9,800 lbs.
shoal keel:
c/board:
BALLAST
deep keel: 4,000 lbs.
shoal keel:
c/board:
DRAFT
deep keel: 4 ft. 11 ins.
shoal keel:
c/board up:
c/board down:

SAIL AREA: 468 sq. ft.
FRESH WATER: 37 gals.
FUEL CAPACITY: 30 gals.

COSTS

BASE BOAT:
DATE:
EST. ON WATER:
DATE:

RATIOS

SAIL AREA/DISP: 16.35
DISP/LENGTH: 280
BALLAST RATIO: 40.81
FUEL/DISP: 2.29
FRESH WATER/DISP: 3.02

DECK

STEERING: 28" wheel with emergency tiller
WINCHES: 4 Lewmar winches: 2 primary (#30 2sp), 2 halyard (#8)
SAFETY: bow and stern pulpits with double lifelines
ANCHOR: anchor well
NAV LIGHTS: running and masthead

RIG

TYPE: masthead sloop
RIGGING: 1x19 wire
MAINSHEET: 6-part with mid-boom sheeting

SAILS

SUPPLIED WITH BASE BOAT:

INTERIOR

BERTHS: 6 berths: 1 double V, 2 single settees, 1 aft double
TABLE: fixed double-leaf
HEAD(S): 1 head with shower
COLD STORAGE: built-in icebox
STOVE: 2-burner alcohol
MAX. HEADROOM: 6 ft. 2 ins.

MACHINERY

ENGINE: Yanmar #2 GM diesel
PROPELLER:
GENERATOR:

BUILDER'S COMMENTS Performance design co-exists with human dynamics in a swift responsive 30-footer with the privacy of a separate aft cabin. The center cockpit design allows distribution of interior volume, enhancing its function without sacrificing privacy. The assurance of S2 quality is evident in engineering, cruising performance, craftsmanship, and attention to detail throughout.

LAGUNA 30

DESIGNER: W. Shad Turner
BUILDER: Laguna Yachts, Inc.

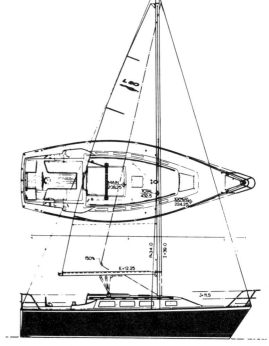

STATISTICS

LOA: 29 ft. 11.5 ins.
LWL: 26 ft. 0.0 ins.
BEAM: 10 ft. 8.0 ins.
DISPLACEMENT
deep keel: 9,040 lbs.
shoal keel:
c/board:
BALLAST
deep keel: 2,800 lbs.
shoal keel:
c/board:
DRAFT
deep keel: 4 ft. 0 ins.
shoal keel:
c/board up:
c/board down:

SAIL AREA: 432 sq. ft.
FRESH WATER: 0 gals.
FUEL CAPACITY: 0 gals.

COSTS

BASE BOAT:
DATE:
EST. ON WATER:
DATE:

RATIOS

SAIL AREA/DISP: 15.94
DISP/LENGTH: 229
BALLAST RATIO: 30.97
FUEL/DISP: 0.0
FRESH WATER/DISP: 0.0

DECK

STEERING: tiller
WINCHES: 4 winches: 2 primary (2sp), 2 halyard
SAFETY: bow and stern pulpits with double lifelines
ANCHOR: anchor well
NAV LIGHTS: running and masthead

RIG

TYPE: masthead sloop
RIGGING:
MAINSHEET: 5-part with mid-boom sheeting

SAILS

SUPPLIED WITH BASE BOAT:
reefable main, working jib

INTERIOR

BERTHS: 7 berths: 1 double V, 1 double convertible dinette, 1 single settee, 1 double quarterberth
TABLE: dropleaf
HEAD(S): 1 head with shower
COLD STORAGE: built-in icebox
STOVE: 2-burner alcohol with oven
MAX. HEADROOM: 6 ft. 3 ins.

MACHINERY

ENGINE: 15 HP Yanmar diesel
PROPELLER: 2-blade
GENERATOR:

TARTAN 3000

DESIGNER: Sparkman & Stephens
BUILDER: Tartan Marine Company

STATISTICS

LOA: 29 ft. 11.5 ins.
LWL: 25 ft. 3.0 ins.
BEAM: 10 ft. 1.0 ins.
DISPLACEMENT
deep keel: 7,950 lbs.
shoal keel:
c/board: 7,950 lbs.
BALLAST
deep keel: 3,830 lbs.
shoal keel:
c/board: 3,830 lbs.
DRAFT
deep keel: 5 ft. 2 ins.
shoal keel:
c/board up: 3 ft. 4 ins.
c/board down: 6 ft. 0 ins.

SAIL AREA: 441 sq. ft.
FRESH WATER: 40 gals.
FUEL CAPACITY: 19 gals.

COSTS

BASE BOAT: $46,000
DATE: 07/01/85
EST. ON WATER: $51,0000
DATE: 07/01/85

RATIOS

SAIL AREA/DISP: 17.71
DISP/LENGTH: 220.46
BALLAST RATIO: 48.18
FUEL/DISP: 1.79
FRESH WATER/DISP: 4.03

DECK

STEERING: tiller (wheel optional)
WINCHES: 4 Lewmar winches
SAFETY: bow and stern pulpits with double lifelines
ANCHOR:
NAV LIGHTS: running and masthead

RIG

TYPE: masthead sloop with Kenyon spar
RIGGING: wire
MAINSHEET:

SAILS

SUPPLIED WITH BASE BOAT:

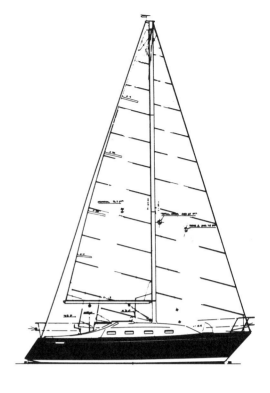

INTERIOR

BERTHS: 5 berths: 1 double V, 1 single settee, 1 double settee
TABLE: bulkhead-mounted
HEAD(S): 1 head with shower, sump pump, and holding tank
COLD STORAGE: built-in icebox (6.5 cu. ft.)
STOVE: 2-burner alcohol
MAX. HEADROOM: 6 ft. 2 ins.

MACHINERY

ENGINE: 18 HP Universal #18 diesel with 2:1 reduction gear
PROPELLER: 3/4" shaft
GENERATOR:

CS 30

DESIGNER: Tony Castro
BUILDER: CS Yachts, Ltd.

STATISTICS

LOA: 30 ft. 0 ins.
LWL: 25 ft. 5 ins.
BEAM: 10 ft. 3 ins.
DISPLACEMENT
deep keel: 8,000 lbs.
shoal keel:
c/board:
BALLAST
deep keel: 3,440 lbs.
shoal keel:
c/board:
DRAFT
deep keel: 5 ft. 6 ins.
shoal keel:
c/board up:
c/board down:

SAIL AREA: 589 sq. ft.
FRESH WATER: 35 gals.
FUEL CAPACITY: 18 gals.

COSTS

BASE BOAT: $49,900
DATE: 06/03/85
EST. ON WATER:
DATE:

RATIOS

SAIL AREA/DISP: 23.56
DISP/LENGTH: 217
BALLAST RATIO: 43.00
FUEL/DISP: 1.68
FRESH WATER/DISP: 3.28

DECK

STEERING: 36" wheel
WINCHES: 4 winches: 2 primary (#40C ST), 2 halyard (#30C ST)
SAFETY: bow and stern pulpits with double lifelines
ANCHOR: anchor roller and well
NAV LIGHTS: running and masthead

RIG

TYPE: masthead sloop
RIGGING: 1x19 wire (1/4")
MAINSHEET: 5-part with mid-boom sheeting

SAILS

SUPPLIED WITH BASE BOAT: North main (2 reefs), #3 genoa (with sail cover)

INTERIOR

BERTHS: 7 berths: 1 double V, 1 double convertible settee, 1 single settee, 1 double quarterberth
TABLE: folding bulkhead-mounted
HEAD(S): 1 head
COLD STORAGE: built-in icebox (6 cu. ft.)
STOVE: 2-burner propane with oven
MAX. HEADROOM: 6 ft. 2 ins.

MACHINERY

ENGINE: Volvo 18 HP diesel
PROPELLER: 15"x15" on 1" shaft
GENERATOR:

EXPRESS 30

DESIGNER: Steve Killing
BUILDER: Express Yachting

STATISTICS

LOA: 30 ft. 0.00 ins.
LWL: 24 ft. 7.25 ins.
BEAM: 10 ft. 0.00 ins.
DISPLACEMENT
deep keel: 8,200 lbs.
shoal keel:
c/board:
BALLAST
deep keel: 3,580 lbs.
shoal keel:
c/board:
DRAFT
deep keel: 5 ft. 6 ins.
shoal keel: 4 ft. 6 ins.
c/board up:
c/board down:

SAIL AREA: 472 sq. ft.
FRESH WATER: 20 gals.
FUEL CAPACITY: 15 gals.

COSTS

BASE BOAT: $52,900
DATE: 07/01/85
EST. ON WATER:
DATE:

RATIOS

SAIL AREA/DISP: 18.57
DISP/LENGTH: 245
BALLAST RATIO: 43.65
FUEL/DISP: 1.37
FRESH WATER/DISP: 1.8

DECK

STEERING: tiller
WINCHES: 4 Lewmar winches: 2 primary (#30A ST), 1 genoa/spinnaker halyard (#24A), 1 main halyard/reefing (#24A)
SAFETY: bow and stern pulpits with lifelines
ANCHOR: anchor well
NAV LIGHTS: running

RIG

TYPE: masthead sloop
RIGGING: Navtec rod
MAINSHEET: 3-part (6:1 ratchet) with boom-end sheeting

SAILS

SUPPLIED WITH BASE BOAT:

INTERIOR

BERTHS: 5 berths: 1 double V, 2 single settees, 1 single pilot
TABLE: dropleaf
HEAD(S): 1 head
COLD STORAGE: icebox
STOVE: 2-burner alcohol
MAX. HEADROOM:

MACHINERY

ENGINE: 15 HP Yanmar diesel
PROPELLER: 2-blade
GENERATOR:

ISLAND PACKET 27

DESIGNER: Robert K. Johnson
BUILDER: Island Packet Yachts

STATISTICS

LOA: 30 ft. 0 ins.
LWL: 24 ft. 3 ins.
BEAM: 10 ft. 6 ins.
DISPLACEMENT
deep keel: 8,000 lbs.
shoal keel:
c/board:
BALLAST
deep keel: 3,000 lbs.
shoal keel:
c/board:
DRAFT
deep keel: 3 ft. 8 ins.
shoal keel:
c/board up: 2 ft. 8 ins.
c/board down: 6 ft. 0 ins.

SAIL AREA: 405 sq. ft.
FRESH WATER: 31 gals.
FUEL CAPACITY: 20 gals.

COSTS

BASE BOAT: $43,950
DATE: 06/85
EST. ON WATER: $47,000
DATE: 06/85

RATIOS

SAIL AREA/DISP: 16.20
DISP/LENGTH: 250
BALLAST RATIO: 37.50
FUEL/DISP: 1.87
FRESH WATER/DISP: 3.10

DECK

STEERING: Edson wheel
WINCHES: 5 Lewmar winches: 2 primary (#16C), 2 halyard (#7C), 1 mainsheet (#7C)
SAFETY: bow and stern pulpits with double lifelines
ANCHOR: anchor roller and bowsprit
NAV LIGHTS: running and masthead

RIG

TYPE: masthead sloop with anodized spar
RIGGING: 1x19 SS wire
MAINSHEET: mid-boom sheeting

SAILS

SUPPLIED WITH BASE BOAT: main (1 reef), 110% jib

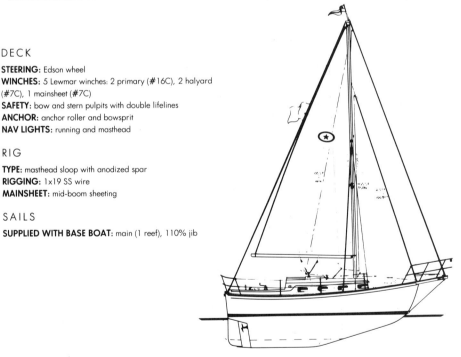

INTERIOR

BERTHS: 6 berths: 1 double V, 1 double convertible settee, 1 single settee, 1 single quarterberth
TABLE: bulkhead-mounted dropleaf
HEAD(S): 1 head with 1 shower
COLD STORAGE: built-in icebox (9 cu. ft.)
STOVE: 2-burner alcohol
MAX. HEADROOM: 6 ft. 2 ins.

MACHINERY

ENGINE: 18 HP Yanmar diesel #2GM20F
PROPELLER: 2-blade fixed 14"x13" on 1" shaft
GENERATOR:

BUILDER'S COMMENTS Modern full keel design with handsome traditional styling, easily managed rig, and an unusually spacious and livable interior. Outstanding performance with moderate or shoal draft. Exceptional quality with extensive standard equipment. Distinctly in a class by itself.

KIRBY 30

DESIGNER:
BUILDER: Mirage Yachts, Ltd.

STATISTICS

LOA: 30 ft. 0 ins.
LWL: 23 ft. 6 ins.
BEAM: 10 ft. 3 ins.
DISPLACEMENT
deep keel: 5,500 lbs.
shoal keel:
c/board:
BALLAST
deep keel: 2,350 lbs.
shoal keel:
c/board:
DRAFT
deep keel: 5 ft. 0 ins.
shoal keel:
c/board up:
c/board down:

INTERIOR

BERTHS: 4 single berths
TABLE:
HEAD(S):
COLD STORAGE: ice chest
STOVE:
MAX. HEADROOM:

MACHINERY

ENGINE: 7.5 HP Yanmar diesel
PROPELLER: 2-blade
GENERATOR:

SAIL AREA: 439 sq. ft.
FRESH WATER:
FUEL CAPACITY:

COSTS

BASE BOAT:
DATE:
EST. ON WATER:
DATE:

RATIOS

SAIL AREA/DISP: 22.54
DISP/LENGTH: 189.2
BALLAST RATIO: 42.72
FUEL/DISP:
FRESH WATER/DISP:

DECK

STEERING: tiller
WINCHES: 4 Lewmar winches: 2 primary (#10), 2 secondary (#8)
SAFETY: bow and stern pulpits with lifelines
ANCHOR:
NAV LIGHTS: running

RIG

TYPE: fractional rig sloop
RIGGING:
MAINSHEET: 4-part with boom-end sheeting

SAILS

SUPPLIED WITH BASE BOAT:

MIRAGE 30

DESIGNER:
BUILDER: Mirage Yachts, Ltd.

STATISTICS

LOA: 30 ft. 0 ins.
LWL: 23 ft. 9 ins.
BEAM: 10 ft. 6 ins.
DISPLACEMENT
deep keel: 7,000 lbs.
shoal keel:
c/board:
BALLAST
deep keel: 2,800 lbs.
shoal keel:
c/board:
DRAFT
deep keel: 4 ft. 10 ins.
shoal keel:
c/board up:
c/board down:

INTERIOR

BERTHS: 6 berths: 1 double V, 2 single settees, 1 double quarterberth
TABLE: centerline dropleaf
HEAD(S):
COLD STORAGE: built-in icebox
STOVE:
MAX. HEADROOM: 6 ft. 3 ins.

MACHINERY

ENGINE: 12 HP diesel
PROPELLER:
GENERATOR:

SAIL AREA: 421 sq. ft.
FRESH WATER: 40 gals.
FUEL CAPACITY: 20 gals.

COSTS

BASE BOAT:
DATE:
EST. ON WATER:
DATE:

RATIOS

SAIL AREA/DISP: 18.41
DISP/LENGTH: 233.27
BALLAST RATIO: 40.00
FUEL/DISP: 2.142
FRESH WATER/DISP: 4.571

DECK

STEERING: wheel
WINCHES: sheet and halyard
SAFETY: bow and stern pulpits with lifelines
ANCHOR: anchor roller and well
NAV LIGHTS: running

RIG

TYPE: masthead sloop
RIGGING:
MAINSHEET:

SAILS

SUPPLIED WITH BASE BOAT: main, 110% jib

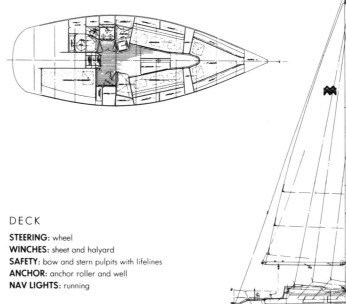

SOVEREIGN 28

DESIGNER: Sovereign Design Group
BUILDER: Sovereign Yacht Co., Inc.

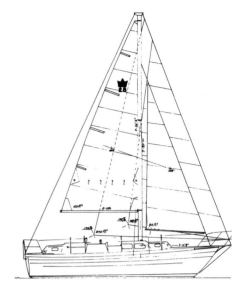

STATISTICS

LOA: 30 ft. 0 ins.
LWL: 23 ft. 0 ins.
BEAM: 8 ft. 4 ins.
DISPLACEMENT
deep keel: 6,800 lbs.
shoal keel:
c/board:
BALLAST
deep keel: 2,400 lbs.
shoal keel:
c/board:
DRAFT
deep keel: 3 ft. 4 ins.
shoal keel:
c/board up:
c/board down:

SAIL AREA: 341 sq. ft.
FRESH WATER: 30 gals.
FUEL CAPACITY: 24 gals.

COSTS

BASE BOAT: $35,500
DATE: 05/01/85
EST. ON WATER: $42,000
DATE: 05/01/85

RATIOS

SAIL AREA/DISP: 15.20
DISP/LENGTH: 249
BALLAST RATIO: 35.29
FUEL/DISP: 2.65
FRESH WATER/DISP: 3.52

DECK

STEERING: 26" Edson wheel
WINCHES: 2 Lewmar genoa sheet winches
SAFETY: bow and stern pulpits with single lifelines
ANCHOR: anchor well
NAV LIGHTS: running

RIG

TYPE: masthead sloop
RIGGING: 1x19 SS wire
MAINSHEET: boom-end sheeting

SAILS

SUPPLIED WITH BASE BOAT: reefable main, lapper

INTERIOR

BERTHS: 5 berths: 1 double V, 1 single settee, 1 aft double
TABLE: folding
HEAD(S): 1 head with self-contained marine toilet and shower
COLD STORAGE: built-in icebox (3 cu. ft.)
STOVE: 2-burner alcohol
MAX. HEADROOM: 6 ft. 2 ins.

MACHINERY

ENGINE: 10 HP Nanni with 2.7:1 reduction gear
PROPELLER: 3-blade
GENERATOR:

CAPE DORY 30

DESIGNER: Carl Alberg
BUILDER: Cape Dory Yachts

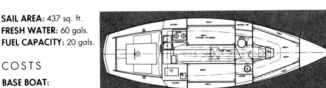

STATISTICS

LOA: 30 ft. 2.5 ins.
LWL: 22 ft. 10.0 ins.
BEAM: 9 ft. 0.0 ins.
DISPLACEMENT
deep keel: 10,000 lbs.
shoal keel:
c/board:
BALLAST
deep keel: 4,000 lbs.
shoal keel:
c/board:
DRAFT
deep keel: 4 ft. 2 ins.
shoal keel:
c/board up:
c/board down:

SAIL AREA: 437 sq. ft.
FRESH WATER: 60 gals.
FUEL CAPACITY: 20 gals.

COSTS

BASE BOAT:
DATE:
EST. ON WATER:
DATE:

RATIOS

SAIL AREA/DISP: 15.06
DISP/LENGTH: 374.68
BALLAST RATIO: 40.00
FUEL/DISP: 1.50
FRESH WATER/DISP: 4.80

DECK

STEERING: wheel with emergency tiller
WINCHES: 7 winches: 2 primary (2sp), 3 halyard, 1 main-sheet, 1 staysail sheet
SAFETY: bow and stern pulpits with lifelines
ANCHOR: anchor roller
NAV LIGHTS: running and masthead

INTERIOR

BERTHS: 5 berths: 1 double V, 1 double convertible settee, 1 single settee (alternate layout available)
TABLE: bulkhead fold-down
HEAD(S): 1 head with holding tank
COLD STORAGE: built-in icebox
STOVE: alcohol with oven
MAX. HEADROOM:

RIG

TYPE: masthead cutter
RIGGING:
MAINSHEET: mid-boom sheeting

SAILS

SUPPLIED WITH BASE BOAT: Ulmer main, yankee jib, staysail

MACHINERY

ENGINE: Universal #18 diesel with 1.91 reduction gear
PROPELLER: 3-blade on 1" shaft
GENERATOR:

PEARSON 303

DESIGNER: Bill Shaw
BUILDER: Pearson Yachts

STATISTICS

LOA: 30 ft. 3.5 ins.
LWL: 25 ft. 4.5 ins.
BEAM: 10 ft. 11.0 ins.
DISPLACEMENT
deep keel: 10,400 lbs.
shoal keel:
c/board:
BALLAST
deep keel: 3,500 lbs.
shoal keel:
c/board:
DRAFT
deep keel: 4 ft. 4 ins.
shoal keel:
c/board up:
c/board down:

SAIL AREA: 457 sq. ft.
FRESH WATER: 38 gals.
FUEL CAPACITY: 22 gals.

COSTS

BASE BOAT:
DATE:
EST. ON WATER:
DATE:

RATIOS

SAIL AREA/DISP: 15.51
DISP/LENGTH: 275
BALLAST RATIO: 34.65
FUEL/DISP: 1.63
FRESH WATER/DISP: 3.16

DECK

STEERING: 28" wheel with emergency tiller
WINCHES: 4 Lewmar winches: 2 sheet (#43 ST), 2 halyard (#16 & #8)
SAFETY: bow and stern pulpits with double lifelines
ANCHOR: anchor well
NAV LIGHTS: running

RIG

TYPE: masthead sloop
RIGGING: 1x19 wire
MAINSHEET: boom-end sheeting

SAILS

SUPPLIED WITH BASE BOAT: main, working jib

INTERIOR

BERTHS: 5 berths: 1 double V, 1 single settee, 1 double convertible settee
TABLE: bulkhead-mounted
HEAD(S): 1 head
COLD STORAGE: built-in icebox (5 cu. ft.)
STOVE: 2-burner propane
MAX. HEADROOM: 6 ft. 3 ins.

MACHINERY

ENGINE: 13 HP Yanmar diesel with 2.6:1 reduction gear
PROPELLER: 2-blade
GENERATOR:

X-95

DESIGNER: Niels Jeppesen
DISTRIBUTOR: Aquarius Performance Yachts, Inc. (built in Denmark by X-Yachts)

STATISTICS

LOA: 30 ft. 3.5 ins.
LWL: 26 ft. 2.5 ins.
BEAM: 10 ft. 7.2 ins.
DISPLACEMENT
deep keel: 6,710 lbs.
shoal keel:
c/board:
BALLAST
deep keel: 3,190 lbs.
shoal keel:
c/board:
DRAFT
deep keel: 5 ft. 8.4 ins.
shoal keel:
c/board up:
c/board down:

SAIL AREA:
FRESH WATER: 28 gals.
FUEL CAPACITY: 13 gals.

COSTS

BASE BOAT:
DATE:
EST. ON WATER:
DATE:

RATIOS

SAIL AREA/DISP:
DISP/LENGTH: 166.37
BALLAST RATIO: 47.54
FUEL/DISP: 1.45
FRESH WATER/DISP: 3.34

INTERIOR

BERTHS: 7 berths: 1 double V, 2 single settees, 2 single pilots, 1 single quarterberth
TABLE:
HEAD(S): 1 head
COLD STORAGE: built-in icebox
STOVE:
MAX. HEADROOM: 6 ft. 0 ins.

MACHINERY

ENGINE: 15 HP Yanmar diesel
PROPELLER: folding
GENERATOR:

DECK

STEERING: tiller
WINCHES: 4 Lewmar winches: 2 #40, 2 #16
SAFETY: bow and stern pulpits with double lifelines
ANCHOR: 27.5 lb. mushroom anchor
NAV LIGHTS: running

RIG

TYPE: fractional rig sloop
RIGGING: 1x19 wire
MAINSHEET: mid-boom sheeting

SAILS

SUPPLIED WITH BASE BOAT:

NONSUCH 30 ULTRA

DESIGNER: Mark Ellis Design, Ltd.
BUILDER: Hinterhoeller Yachts. Ltd.

STATISTICS

LOA: 30 ft. 4 ins.
LWL: 28 ft. 9 ins.
BEAM: 11 ft. 10 ins.
DISPLACEMENT
deep keel: 11,500 lbs.
shoal keel:
c/board:
BALLAST
deep keel: 4,500 lbs.
shoal keel:
c/board:
DRAFT
deep keel: 4 ft. 11.5 ins.
shoal keel:
c/board up:
c/board down:

SAIL AREA: 540 sq. ft.
FRESH WATER: 80 gals.
FUEL CAPACITY: 28 gals.

COSTS

BASE BOAT: $71,900
DATE: 08/01/85
EST. ON WATER: $80,000
DATE: 08/01/85

RATIOS

SAIL AREA/DISP: 16.95
DISP/LENGTH: 216
BALLAST RATIO: 39.13
FUEL/DISP: 1.82
FRESH WATER/DISP: 5.56

DECK

STEERING: 28" wheel with emergency tiller
WINCHES: 4 Barient winches: 1 main halyard (#21), 1 main-sheet (#19 ST), 2 reefing (#10P)
SAFETY: bow and stern pulpits with double lifelines
ANCHOR:
NAV LIGHTS: running and masthead

RIG

TYPE: cat rig
RIGGING:
MAINSHEET: 2-part with boom-end sheeting

SAILS

SUPPLIED WITH BASE BOAT:

INTERIOR

BERTHS: 5 berths: 1 double V, 1 single settee, 1 convertible dinette makes double
TABLE: dropleaf
HEAD(S): 1 head with shower
COLD STORAGE: built-in icebox
STOVE: 2-burner propane with oven
MAX. HEADROOM: 6 ft. 3 ins.

MACHINERY

ENGINE: 27 HP Westerbeke diesel with 2:1 reduction gear
PROPELLER: 2-blade sailer 16" x 14" RH on 1" ss shaft
GENERATOR:

SABRE 30 III

DESIGNER: Sabre Design Team
BUILDER: Sabre Yachts

STATISTICS

LOA: 30 ft. 7 ins.
LWL: 25 ft. 6 ins.
BEAM: 10 ft. 6 ins.
DISPLACEMENT
deep keel: 9,400 lbs.
shoal keel:
c/board:
BALLAST
deep keel: 3,800 lbs.
shoal keel:
c/board:
DRAFT
deep keel: 5 ft. 3 ins.
shoal keel:
c/board up:
c/board down:

SAIL AREA: 462 sq. ft.
FRESH WATER: 47 gals.
FUEL CAPACITY: 20 gals.

COSTS

BASE BOAT:
DATE:
EST. ON WATER:
DATE:

RATIOS

SAIL AREA/DISP: 16.60
DISP/LENGTH: 253.08
BALLAST RATIO: 40.43
FUEL/DISP: 1.63
FRESH WATER/DISP: 4.00

DECK

STEERING: 36" wheel
WINCHES: 5 Lewmar winches: 2 primary (#40), 2 halyard (#8 and #16), 1 mainsheet (#8)
SAFETY: bow and stern pulpits with double lifelines
ANCHOR: anchor well
NAV LIGHTS: running and masthead

RIG

TYPE: masthead sloop
RIGGING: 1x19 SS wire
MAINSHEET: 4-part with mid-boom sheeting

SAILS

SUPPLIED WITH BASE BOAT:

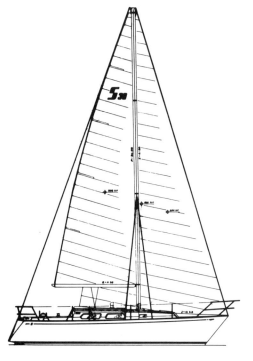

INTERIOR

BERTHS: 6 berths: 1 double V, 1 double convertible, 1 single settee, 1 single quarterberth
TABLE: bulkhead-mounted
HEAD(S): 1 head
COLD STORAGE: built-in icebox
STOVE: 2-burner alcohol
MAX. HEADROOM: 6 ft. 1 ins.

MACHINERY

ENGINE: 18 HP Westerbeke diesel with 2:1 reduction gear
PROPELLER: 14"x12"
GENERATOR:

TANZER 31

DESIGNER: George Cuthbertsson
BUILDER: Tanzer Industries, Inc.

STATISTICS

LOA: 30 ft. 7 ins.
LWL: 25 ft. 0 ins.
BEAM: 10 ft. 6 ins.
DISPLACEMENT
deep keel: 8,300 lbs.
shoal keel:
c/board:
BALLAST
deep keel: 3,300 lbs.
shoal keel: 3,700 lbs.
c/board:
DRAFT
deep keel: 5 ft. 3 ins.
shoal keel: 4 ft. 0 ins.
c/board up:
c/board down:

SAIL AREA: 473 sq. ft.
FRESH WATER: 30 gals.
FUEL CAPACITY: 20 gals.

COSTS

BASE BOAT: $45,380
DATE: 02-01-85
EST. ON WATER:
DATE:

RATIOS

SAIL AREA/DISP: 18.46
DISP/LENGTH: 237.14
BALLAST RATIO:
39.76 (44.58 shoal)
FUEL/DISP: 1.81
FRESH WATER/DISP: 2.89

INTERIOR

BERTHS: 5 berths: 1 double V, 1 double convertible, 1 quarterberth
TABLE: bulkhead-mounted
HEAD(S): 1 head with holding tank
COLD STORAGE: built-in icebox
STOVE: 2-burner alcohol
MAX. HEADROOM: 6 ft. 4 ins.

MACHINERY

ENGINE: 15 HP Yanmar
PROPELLER:
GENERATOR:

DECK

STEERING: wheel
WINCHES: 4 winches: 2 primary (2sp ST), 2 halyard
SAFETY: bow pulpit with double lifelines
ANCHOR: anchor well
NAV LIGHTS: running

RIG

TYPE: masthead sloop
RIGGING: wire (3/16")
MAINSHEET: mid-boom sheeting

SAILS

SUPPLIED WITH BASE BOAT: main (1 reef), working jib or lapper

BUILDER'S COMMENTS The newest addition to the Tanzer line, the Tanzer 31 was designed by George Cuthbertsson to be a fast, but easily handled racer/cruiser. The "Special Edition" 31 is superbly equipped—the only option the owner need consider is whether to have the standing fin keel (draft 5'3") or a shoal keel that draws only 4'0". Even the curtains are standard.

LM-30

DESIGNER:
DISTRIBUTOR: Anchor Marine, Inc. (built in Denmark by LM Glasfiber, a/s)

STATISTICS

LOA: 30 ft. 8 ins.
LWL: 26 ft. 3 ins.
BEAM: 10 ft. 0 ins.
DISPLACEMENT
deep keel: 11,000 lbs.
shoal keel:
c/board:
BALLAST
deep keel: 4,180
shoal keel:
c/board:
DRAFT
deep keel: 4 ft. 11 ins.
shoal keel:
c/board up:
c/board down:

SAIL AREA: 414 sq. ft.
FRESH WATER: 44 gals.
FUEL CAPACITY: 44 gals.

COSTS

BASE BOAT: $63,000
DATE: 04/01/85
EST. ON WATER:
DATE:

RATIOS

SAIL AREA/DISP: 13.39
DISP/LENGTH: 271.49
BALLAST RATIO: 38.00
FUEL/DISP: 3.00
FRESH WATER/DISP: 3.20

INTERIOR

BERTHS: 5 berths: 1 double V, 1 single settee, 1 double convertible settee
TABLE: dropleaf
HEAD(S): 1 head with shower
COLD STORAGE:
STOVE: 2-burner propane
MAX. HEADROOM:

MACHINERY

ENGINE: 36 HP Volvo #MD 17D/120 S diesel
PROPELLER: fixed
GENERATOR:

DECK

STEERING: tiller
WINCHES:
SAFETY: bow and stern pulpits with double lifelines
ANCHOR: 33 lb. anchor with chain
NAV LIGHTS: running

RIG

TYPE: fractional rig sloop
RIGGING:
MAINSHEET: boom-end sheeting

SAILS

SUPPLIED WITH BASE BOAT: main, working jib

MERMAID 315

DESIGNER:
DISTRIBUTOR: Anchor Marine, Inc. (built in Denmark by LM Glasfiber, a/s)

STATISTICS

LOA: 30 ft. 8 ins.
LWL: 26 ft. 3 ins.
BEAM: 10 ft. 0 ins.
DISPLACEMENT
deep keel: 10,340 lbs.
shoal keel:
c/board:
BALLAST
deep keel: 4,180 lbs.
shoal keel:
c/board:
DRAFT
deep keel: 4 ft. 11 ins.
shoal keel:
c/board up:
c/board down:

SAIL AREA: 447.0 sq. ft.
FRESH WATER: 37.0 gals.
FUEL CAPACITY: 18.5 gals.

COSTS

BASE BOAT: $55,800
DATE: 04/01/85
EST. ON WATER:
DATE:

RATIOS

SAIL AREA/DISP: 15.07
DISP/LENGTH: 255.20
BALLAST RATIO: 40.43
FUEL/DISP: 1.34
FRESH WATER/DISP: 2.86

DECK

STEERING: tiller
WINCHES:
SAFETY: bow and stern pulpits with double lifelines
ANCHOR: anchor supplied
NAV LIGHTS: running

RIG

TYPE: fractional rig sloop
RIGGING:
MAINSHEET: boom-end sheeting

SAILS

SUPPLIED WITH BASE BOAT: main, working jib

INTERIOR

BERTHS: 7 berths: 1 double V, 2 double convertible settees, 1 single quarterberth
TABLE: dropleaf
HEAD(S): 1 head with shower
COLD STORAGE:
STOVE:
MAX. HEADROOM:

MACHINERY

ENGINE: 28 HP Volvo #2003/120 S diesel
PROPELLER:
GENERATOR:

OMEGA 30

DESIGNER: Ron Holland
BUILDER: Omega Yachts

STATISTICS

LOA: 30 ft. 8 ins.
LWL: 26 ft. 2 ins.
BEAM: 9 ft. 8 ins.
DISPLACEMENT
deep keel: 6,950 lbs.
shoal keel:
c/board:
BALLAST
deep keel: 2,935 lbs.
shoal keel:
c/board:
DRAFT
deep keel: 5 ft. 1 ins.
shoal keel:
c/board up:
c/board down:

SAIL AREA: 453 sq. ft.
FRESH WATER:
FUEL CAPACITY:

COSTS

BASE BOAT: $43,500
DATE: 05/03/85
EST. ON WATER:
DATE:

RATIOS

SAIL AREA/DISP: 19.90
DISP/LENGTH: 173.3
BALLAST RATIO: 42.23
FUEL/DISP:
FRESH WATER/DISP:

DECK

STEERING: tiller
WINCHES:
SAFETY: bow and stern pulpits with double lifelines
ANCHOR: anchor well
NAV LIGHTS:

RIG

TYPE: fractional rig sloop
RIGGING:
MAINSHEET: mid-boom sheeting

SAILS

SUPPLIED WITH BASE BOAT: main, working jib

INTERIOR

BERTHS: 5 berths: 1 double V, 1 single settee, 2 single quarterberths
TABLE: dropleaf
HEAD(S): 1 head
COLD STORAGE: built-in icebox
STOVE: 2-burner with oven
MAX. HEADROOM:

MACHINERY

ENGINE: Yanmar #16M 10 diesel
PROPELLER: folding
GENERATOR:

ALLMAND 31

DESIGNER: Walter Scott & T. R. Allmand
BUILDER: Allmand Boats, Inc.

STATISTICS

LOA: 30 ft. 9 ins.
LWL: 27 ft. 11 ins.
BEAM: 11 ft. 4 ins.
DISPLACEMENT
deep keel: 12,850 lbs.
shoal keel:
c/board:
BALLAST
deep keel: 4,300 lbs.
shoal keel:
c/board:
DRAFT
deep keel: 4 ft. 0 ins.
shoal keel:
c/board up:
c/board down:

SAIL AREA: 461 sq. ft.
FRESH WATER: 50 gals.
FUEL CAPACITY: 40 gals.

COSTS

BASE BOAT:
DATE:
EST. ON WATER:
DATE:

RATIOS

SAIL AREA/DISP: 13.44
DISP/LENGTH: 263
BALLAST RATIO: 33.46
FUEL/DISP: 2.33
FRESH WATER/DISP: 3.11

INTERIOR

BERTHS: 7 berths: 1 double V, 1 double convertible dinette, 1 single settee, 1 double quarterberth
TABLE: dropleaf
HEAD(S): 1 head with shower and holding tank (25 gals.)
COLD STORAGE: built-in icebox
STOVE: 2-burner alcohol
MAX. HEADROOM: 6 ft. 5 ins.

MACHINERY

ENGINE: 20 HP V-M Group diesel
PROPELLER: on 1" shaft
GENERATOR:

DECK

STEERING: wheel with emergency tiller
WINCHES: 5 Lewmar winches: 2 primary (#30 2sp), 2 halyard (#8), 1 mainsheet (#7)
SAFETY: bow and stern pulpits with double lifelines
ANCHOR: anchor roller and deck pipe
NAV LIGHTS: running and masthead

RIG

TYPE: masthead sloop
RIGGING: 1x19 wire (1/4")
MAINSHEET: mid-boom sheeting

SAILS

SUPPLIED WITH BASE BOAT: main, working jib

MOODY 31

DESIGNER: Bill Dixon-Angus Primrose, Ltd.
DISTRIBUTOR: A. H. Moody & Son, Ltd. (built in England by Marine Projects, Ltd.)

STATISTICS

LOA: 30 ft. 9 ins.
LWL: 25 ft. 5 ins.
BEAM: 10 ft. 6 ins.
DISPLACEMENT
deep keel: 8,750 lbs.
shoal keel:
c/board:
BALLAST
deep keel: 3,675 lbs.
shoal keel:
c/board:
DRAFT
deep keel: 5 ft. 0 ins.
shoal keel:
c/board up:
c/board down:

SAIL AREA: 408 sq. ft.
FRESH WATER: 30 gals.
FUEL CAPACITY: 20 gals.

COSTS

BASE BOAT:
DATE:
EST. ON WATER:
DATE:

RATIOS

SAIL AREA/DISP: 15.37
DISP/LENGTH: 237
BALLAST RATIO: 42.00
FUEL/DISP: 1.71
FRESH WATER/DISP: 2.74

DECK

STEERING: tiller
WINCHES: 4 winches: 2 primary (2sp), 2 halyard
SAFETY: bow and stern pulpits with lifelines
ANCHOR: anchor with anchor roller and well
NAV LIGHTS: running

RIG

TYPE: masthead sloop
RIGGING:
MAINSHEET: mid-boom sheeting

SAILS

SUPPLIED WITH BASE BOAT: main (3 reefs), working jib

INTERIOR

BERTHS: 6 berths: 2 single Vs, 2 single settees, 1 double quarterberth
TABLE: dropleaf
HEAD(S): 1 head
COLD STORAGE: built-in icebox
STOVE: 2-burner gas with oven
MAX. HEADROOM:

MACHINERY

ENGINE: 28 HP Volvo #2003 with 2.34:1 reduction gear
PROPELLER: 2-blade
GENERATOR:

HERRESHOFF 31

DESIGNER: Halsey Herreshoff
BUILDER: Cat Ketch Corporation

STATISTICS

LOA: 30 ft. 10.0 ins.
LWL: 27 ft. 11.5 ins.
BEAM: 10 ft. 4.0 ins.
DISPLACEMENT
deep keel: 8,640 lbs.
shoal keel:
c/board:
BALLAST
deep keel: 3,350 lbs.
shoal keel:
c/board:
DRAFT
deep keel: 4 ft. 0 ins.
shoal keel:
c/board up:
c/board down:

SAIL AREA: 393 sq. ft.
FRESH WATER: 60 gals.
FUEL CAPACITY: 18 gals.

COSTS

BASE BOAT: $60,579
DATE: 09/01/85
EST. ON WATER:
DATE:

RATIOS

SAIL AREA/DISP: 14.93
DISP/LENGTH: 176.5
BALLAST RATIO: 38.77
FUEL/DISP: 1.5
FRESH WATER/DISP: 5.5

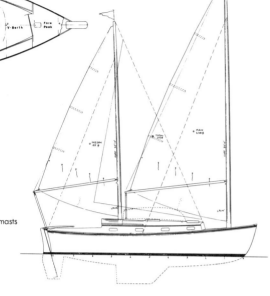

INTERIOR

BERTHS: 5 berths: 1 double V, 1 double convertible settee, 1 single settee
TABLE:
HEAD(S): 1 head with shower and sump pump
COLD STORAGE: built-in icebox
STOVE: 2-burner alcohol
MAX. HEADROOM: 6 ft. 2 ins.

MACHINERY

ENGINE: 15 HP Nannidiesel diesel
PROPELLER: 2-blade fixed 14"x8" on 1" shaft
GENERATOR:

DECK

STEERING: tiller
WINCHES: none
SAFETY: bow and stern pulpits with double lifelines
ANCHOR: teak bow plank anchor storage
NAV LIGHTS: running and masthead

RIG

TYPE: cat ketch with unstayed carbon fiber composite masts
RIGGING:
MAINSHEET: 4-part with boom-end sheeting

SAILS

SUPPLIED WITH BASE BOAT: main, mizzen

BUILDER'S COMMENTS The Herreshoff Cat Ketch features an unstayed, self-tending rig which makes a simple, effortless sailing yacht. The Fiberglass/Airex hull has clean traditional lines and a light displacement, fin keel/skeg configuration. These characteristics result in an agile, quick, easy and fun boat to sail.

SCANMAR 31

DESIGNER: Rolf Magnusson
BUILDER: Scanmar Boats

STATISTICS

LOA: 30 ft. 10 ins.
LWL: 25 ft. 11 ins.
BEAM:
DISPLACEMENT
deep keel: 8,288 lbs.
shoal keel:
c/board:
BALLAST
deep keel:
shoal keel:
c/board:
DRAFT
deep keel: 5 ft. 5 ins.
shoal keel:
c/board up:
c/board down:

SAIL AREA:
FRESH WATER:
FUEL CAPACITY:

COSTS

BASE BOAT:
DATE:
EST. ON WATER:
DATE:

RATIOS

SAIL AREA/DISP:
DISP/LENGTH: 212
BALLAST RATIO:
FUEL/DISP:
FRESH WATER/DISP:

INTERIOR

BERTHS: 4 berths: 1 double V, 2 single settees
TABLE: fixed
HEAD(S): 1 head
COLD STORAGE: built-in icebox
STOVE: 2-burner
MAX. HEADROOM:

MACHINERY

ENGINE:
PROPELLER:
GENERATOR:

DECK

STEERING: tiller
WINCHES:
SAFETY: bow and stern pulpits with double lifelines
ANCHOR:
NAV LIGHTS:

RIG

TYPE: fractional rig sloop
RIGGING:
MAINSHEET:

SAILS

SUPPLIED WITH BASE BOAT:

BRISTOL 31.1

DESIGNER:
BUILDER: Bristol Yacht Co.

STATISTICS

LOA: 31 ft. 1.5 ins.
LWL: 24 ft. 9.0 ins.
BEAM: 10 ft. 2.0 ins.
DISPLACEMENT
deep keel: 11,200 lbs.
shoal keel:
c/board:
BALLAST
deep keel: 4,500 lbs.
shoal keel:
c/board:
DRAFT
deep keel: 5 ft. 3 ins.
shoal keel:
c/board up:
c/board down:

SAIL AREA: 478 sq. ft.
FRESH WATER: 65 gals.
FUEL CAPACITY: 18 gals.

COSTS

BASE BOAT: $60,992
DATE: 09/01/85
EST. ON WATER:
DATE:

RATIOS

SAIL AREA/DISP: 15.33
DISP/LENGTH: 329.8
BALLAST RATIO: 40.0
FUEL/DISP: 1.21
FRESH WATER/DISP: 4.64

DECK

STEERING: wheel
WINCHES: 4 winches: 2 sheet (#30C), 2 halyard (#16C & #8)
SAFETY:
ANCHOR: anchor roller
NAV LIGHTS:

RIG

TYPE: masthead sloop
RIGGING: 1x19 wire
MAINSHEET: boom-end sheeting

SAILS

SUPPLIED WITH BASE BOAT:

INTERIOR

BERTHS: 5 berths: 1 double V, 2 single settees, 1 single pilot
TABLE: bulkhead-mounted
HEAD(S): 1 head
COLD STORAGE: built-in icebox
STOVE: 2-burner alcohol with oven
MAX. HEADROOM:

MACHINERY

ENGINE: Universal #18 diesel
PROPELLER: 2-blade 14"x9" on 1" shaft
GENERATOR:

O'DAY 31

DESIGNER: C. Raymond Hunt Associates
BUILDER: Lear Siegler Marine

STATISTICS

LOA: 30 ft. 1.5 ins.
LWL: 25 ft. 7.0 ins.
BEAM: 10 ft. 9.0 ins.
DISPLACEMENT
deep keel: 10,100 lbs.
shoal keel:
c/board:
BALLAST
deep keel: 3,800 lbs.
shoal keel:
c/board:
DRAFT
deep keel: 5 ft. 3 ins.
shoal keel: 4 ft. 0 ins.
c/board up:
c/board down:

SAIL AREA: 436 sq. ft.
FRESH WATER: 25 gals.
FUEL CAPACITY: 26 gals.

COSTS

BASE BOAT: $48,750
DATE: 11/85
EST. ON WATER:
DATE:

RATIOS

SAIL AREA/DISP: 14.92
DISP/LENGTH: 269
BALLAST RATIO: 37.62
FUEL/DISP: 1.93
FRESH WATER/DISP: 1.98

DECK

STEERING: 28" wheel with emergency tiller
WINCHES: 5 Barlow winches: 2 primary (#24C 2sp ST), 2 halyard ((#16), 1 mainsheet (#19C ST)
SAFETY: bow and stern pulpits with single lifeline
ANCHOR: anchor well and roller
NAV LIGHTS: running and masthead

RIG

TYPE: masthead sloop
RIGGING: 1x19 wire
MAINSHEET: 4-part with mid-boom sheeting

SAILS

SUPPLIED WITH BASE BOAT: main (1 reef), working jib

INTERIOR

BERTHS: 6 berths: 1 double V, 1 double convertible settee, 1 single settee, 1 single quarterberth
TABLE: pedestal-mounted dinette
HEAD(S): 1 head
COLD STORAGE: built-in icebox (4.5 cu. ft.)
STOVE: 2-burner alcohol
MAX. HEADROOM: 6 ft. 3 ins.

MACHINERY

ENGINE: 18 HP Universal diesel
PROPELLER: 2-blade on 1" shaft
GENERATOR:

BUILDER'S COMMENTS An ideal family cruiser for extended horizons, the O'Day offers the convenience of an inboard diesel with the clean deck and smooth underbody of a high performance yacht. The stern boarding platform and comfortable interior makes the 31 a home away from home.

COMFORTINA 32

DESIGNER:
DISTRIBUTOR: Scandvik, Inc. (built in Sweden by Comfort-batar, AB)

STATISTICS

LOA: 31 ft. 2 ins.
LWL: 24 ft. 7 ins.
BEAM: 10 ft. 9 ins.
DISPLACEMENT
deep keel: 9,900 lbs.
shoal keel:
c/board:
BALLAST
deep keel:
shoal keel:
c/board:
DRAFT
deep keel: 5 ft. 7 ins.
shoal keel: 4 ft. 11 ins.
c/board up:
c/board down:

SAIL AREA: 555 sq. ft.
FRESH WATER: 26 gals.
FUEL CAPACITY: 15 gals.

COSTS

BASE BOAT:
DATE:
EST. ON WATER:
DATE:

RATIOS

SAIL AREA/DISP: 19.26
DISP/LENGTH: 297.61
BALLAST RATIO:
FUEL/DISP: 1.14
FRESH WATER/DISP: 2.1

INTERIOR

BERTHS: 6 berths: 1 double V, 2 single settees, 1 double quarterberth
TABLE: dropleaf
HEAD(S): 1 head with holding tank (30 gal.)
COLD STORAGE: built-in icebox
STOVE: 2-burner propane with oven
MAX. HEADROOM:

MACHINERY

ENGINE: 18 HP Volvo Penta #2002 diesel
PROPELLER:
GENERATOR:

DECK

STEERING: tiller
WINCHES: 4 Lewmar winches: 2 #40, 2 #7
SAFETY: bow and stern pulpits with double lifelines
ANCHOR:
NAV LIGHTS: running

RIG

TYPE: fractional rig sloop
RIGGING:
MAINSHEET: mid-boom sheeting

SAILS

SUPPLIED WITH BASE BOAT: main, 110% working jib

IRWIN CITATION 31

DESIGNER: Ted Irwin
BUILDER: Irwin Yacht & Marine Corp.

STATISTICS

LOA: 31 ft. 2.5 ins.
LWL: 28 ft. 3.0 ins.
BEAM: 11 ft. 0.0 ins.
DISPLACEMENT
deep keel:
shoal keel: 9,300 lbs.
c/board:
BALLAST
deep keel:
shoal keel: 3,800 lbs.
c/board:
DRAFT
deep keel: 6 ft. 0 ins.
shoal keel: 4 ft. 0 ins.
c/board up: 4 ft. 0 ins.
c/board down: 8 ft. 1 ins.

SAIL AREA: 495 sq. ft.
FRESH WATER: 35 gals.
FUEL CAPACITY: 31 gals.

COSTS

BASE BOAT: $43,995
DATE: 06/01/85
EST. ON WATER:
DATE:

RATIOS

SAIL AREA/DISP: 17.91
DISP/LENGTH: 184.15
BALLAST RATIO: 40.86
FUEL/DISP: 2.5
FRESH WATER/DISP: 3.0

DECK

STEERING: 36" wheel with emergency tiller
WINCHES: 3 winches: 2 primary, 1 halyard
SAFETY: bow and stern pulpits with double lifelines
ANCHOR: anchor well
NAV LIGHTS: running and masthead

RIG

TYPE: masthead sloop
RIGGING: wire (1/4")
MAINSHEET: 6-part with mid-boom sheeting

SAILS

SUPPLIED WITH BASE BOAT: main, working jib

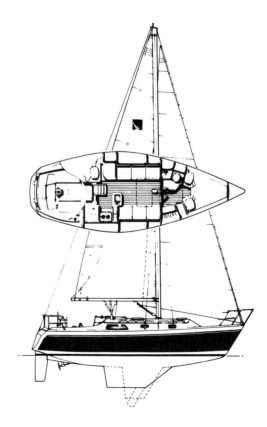

INTERIOR

BERTHS: 6 berths: 1 double V, 1 double settee, 1 single settee, 1 single quarterberth
TABLE: fold-away dinette
HEAD(S): 1 head with shower and holding tank (15 gals.)
COLD STORAGE: built-in icebox (5.5 cu. ft.)
STOVE: 2-burner propane with oven
MAX. HEADROOM:

MACHINERY

ENGINE: 15 HP diesel with 2.62:1 reduction gear
PROPELLER: 2-blade
GENERATOR:

CAPE DORY 31

DESIGNER: Carl Alberg
BUILDER: Cape Dory Yachts

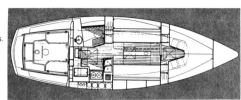

STATISTICS

LOA: 31 ft. 4 ins.
LWL: 23 ft. 3 ins.
BEAM: 9 ft. 9 ins.
DISPLACEMENT
deep keel: 11,500 lbs.
shoal keel:
c/board:
BALLAST
deep keel: 4,350 lbs.
shoal keel:
c/board:
DRAFT
deep keel: 4 ft. 9 ins.
shoal keel:
c/board up:
c/board down:

SAIL AREA: 504 sq. ft.
FRESH WATER: 84 gals.
FUEL CAPACITY: 20 gals.

COSTS

BASE BOAT:
DATE:
EST. ON WATER:
DATE:

RATIOS

SAIL AREA/DISP: 15.83
DISP/LENGTH: 408.49
BALLAST RATIO: 37.83
FUEL/DISP: 1.30
FRESH WATER/DISP: 5.84

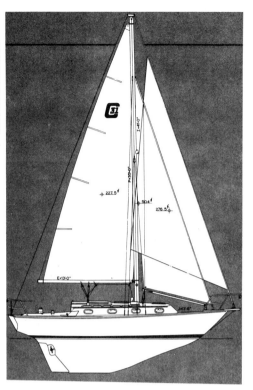

INTERIOR

BERTHS: 6 berths: 1 double V, 1 double convertible settee, 1 single settee, 1 pilot
TABLE: center-mounted dropleaf
HEAD(S): 1 head with shower and holding tank (28 gals.)
COLD STORAGE: built-in icebox
STOVE: 2-burner with oven
MAX. HEADROOM:

DECK

STEERING: wheel with emergency tiller
WINCHES: 8 winches: 2 primary (2sp), 3 halyard, 1 mainsheet, 1 staysail sheet, 1 reefing
SAFETY: bow and stern pulpits with double lifelines
ANCHOR: anchor roller
NAV LIGHTS: running and masthead

RIG

TYPE: masthead cutter
RIGGING:
MAINSHEET: 5-part with mid-boom sheeting

MACHINERY

ENGINE: 25 HP Universal with 2:1 reduction gear
PROPELLER: 1" shaft
GENERATOR:

SAILS

SUPPLIED WITH BASE BOAT:

HUNTER 31

DESIGNER: Hunter Design Group
BUILDER: Hunter Marine

STATISTICS

LOA: 31 ft. 4 ins.
LWL: 26 ft. 3 ins.
BEAM: 10 ft. 11 ins.
DISPLACEMENT
deep keel: 9,700 lbs.
shoal keel: 9,900 lbs.
c/board:
BALLAST
deep keel: 4,000 lbs.
shoal keel: 4,200 lbs.
c/board:
DRAFT
deep keel: 5 ft. 6 ins.
shoal keel: 4 ft. 0 ins.
c/board up:
c/board down:

SAIL AREA: 458 sq. ft.
FRESH WATER: 35 gals.
FUEL CAPACITY: 18 gals.

COSTS

BASE BOAT:
DATE:
EST. ON WATER: $45,000
DATE: 11/85

RATIOS

SAIL AREA/DISP: 16.11
DISP/LENGTH: 239
BALLAST RATIO: 41.23
FUEL/DISP: 1.39
FRESH WATER/DISP: 2.88

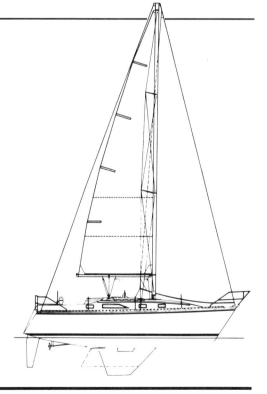

DECK

STEERING: wheel with emergency tiller
WINCHES: 4 winches: 2 sheet (2sp ST), 2 halyard
SAFETY: bow and stern pulpits with lifelines
ANCHOR: anchor well
NAV LIGHTS: running and masthead

RIG

TYPE: masthead sloop
RIGGING:
MAINSHEET: mid-boom sheeting

SAILS

SUPPLIED WITH BASE BOAT: main, 110% genoa

INTERIOR

BERTHS: 7 berths: 1 double V, 1 double convertible settee, 1 single settee, 1 double quarterberth
TABLE: dinette
HEAD(S): 1 head with shower
COLD STORAGE: built-in icebox
STOVE: 2-burner with oven
MAX. HEADROOM: 6 ft. 3 ins.

MACHINERY

ENGINE: diesel
PROPELLER: 2-blade
GENERATOR:

BUILDER'S COMMENTS Like all Hunter sailboats, the 31' offers an unparalleled list of amenities! With innovative designs, the 31 is sleek and built for reliability and enhanced performance. The deck is uncluttered and ready for a crew of seven to utilize her speed. Belowdecks she'll easily handle all seven with a complete galley, enclosed head and shower, and plenty of headroom. From stem to stern the 31' is sheer beauty.

COOPER 316

DESIGNER: S. C. Huntingford
BUILDER: Cooper Yachts

STATISTICS

LOA: 31 ft. 6 ins.
LWL: 25 ft. 6 ins.
BEAM: 10 ft. 11 ins.
DISPLACEMENT
deep keel: 10,500 lbs.
shoal keel:
c/board:
BALLAST
deep keel: 3,600 lbs.
shoal keel:
c/board:
DRAFT
deep keel: 5 ft. 5 ins.
shoal keel:
c/board up:
c/board down:

SAIL AREA: 477 sq. ft.
FRESH WATER: 35 gals.
FUEL CAPACITY: 35 gals.

COSTS

BASE BOAT: $57,500
DATE: 04/85
EST. ON WATER:
DATE:

RATIOS

SAIL AREA/DISP: 15.92
DISP/LENGTH: 282.7
BALLAST RATIO: 34.29
FUEL/DISP: 2.5
FRESH WATER/DISP: 2.67

DECK

STEERING: wheel
WINCHES: 2 Lewmar #30 winches
SAFETY: bow and stern pulpits with double lifelines
ANCHOR:
NAV LIGHTS: running

RIG

TYPE: masthead sloop
RIGGING:
MAINSHEET: mid-boom sheeting

SAILS

SUPPLIED WITH BASE BOAT: main, working jib

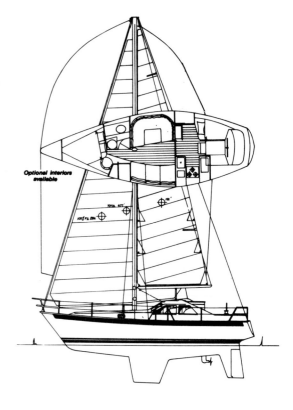

Optional interiors available

INTERIOR

BERTHS: 6 berths: 1 double V, 1 double convertible dinette, 1 single settee, 1 single quarterberth
TABLE:
HEAD(S): 1 head
COLD STORAGE: built-in icebox
STOVE: 3-burner propane or alcohol with oven
MAX. HEADROOM:

MACHINERY

ENGINE: 18 HP Volvo diesel
PROPELLER:
GENERATOR:

BANNER 32

DESIGNER: Stan Huntingford
BUILDER: Cooper Yachts

STATISTICS

LOA: 31 ft. 8 ins.
LWL: 25 ft. 7 ins.
BEAM: 10 ft. 11 ins.
DISPLACEMENT
deep keel: 10,500 lbs.
shoal keel:
c/board:
BALLAST
deep keel: 3,600 lbs.
shoal keel:
c/board:
DRAFT
deep keel: 5 ft. 5 ins.
shoal keel:
c/board up:
c/board down:

SAIL AREA: 477 sq. ft.
FRESH WATER: 30 gals.
FUEL CAPACITY: 30 gals.

COSTS

BASE BOAT: $57,500
DATE: 04/85
EST. ON WATER:
DATE:

RATIOS

SAIL AREA/DISP: 15.92
DISP/LENGTH: 280.05
BALLAST RATIO: 34.29
FUEL/DISP: 2.14
FRESH WATER/DISP: 2.29

DECK

STEERING: wheel
WINCHES: 2 Lewmar #30 winches
SAFETY: bow and stern pulpits with double lifelines
ANCHOR:
NAV LIGHTS: running

RIG

TYPE: masthead sloop
RIGGING:
MAINSHEET: mid-boom sheeting

SAILS

SUPPLIED WITH BASE BOAT: main, working jib

INTERIOR

BERTHS: 6 berths: 1 double V, 1 single settee, 1 double convertible dinette, 1 single quarterberth
TABLE:
HEAD(S): 1 head with shower
COLD STORAGE: built-in icebox (5 cu. ft.)
STOVE: alcohol with oven
MAX. HEADROOM:

MACHINERY

ENGINE: 17 HP Volvo #7C diesel
PROPELLER: fixed
GENERATOR:

UNION 32

DESIGNER: Ted Brewer
BUILDER: Master Mariners Corp.

STATISTICS

LOA: 31 ft. 9 ins.
LWL: 27 ft. 3 ins.
BEAM: 10 ft. 10 ins.
DISPLACEMENT
deep keel: 11,500 lbs.
shoal keel:
c/board:
BALLAST
deep keel: 4,600 lbs.
shoal keel:
c/board:
DRAFT
deep keel: 4 ft. 10 ins.
shoal keel:
c/board up:
c/board down:

SAIL AREA:
FRESH WATER: 60 gals.
FUEL CAPACITY: 25 gals.

COSTS

BASE BOAT:
   West coast $67,000
DATE: 04/85
   East coast $69,000
DATE: 04/85

RATIOS

SAIL AREA/DISP:
DISP/LENGTH: 253.72
BALLAST RATIO: 40.00
FUEL/DISP: 1.63
FRESH WATER/DISP: 4.17

DECK

STEERING: tiller
WINCHES:
SAFETY:
ANCHOR:
NAV LIGHTS:

RIG

TYPE: masthead sloop
RIGGING:
MAINSHEET: mid-boom sheeting

SAILS

SUPPLIED WITH BASE BOAT:

INTERIOR

BERTHS: 4 berths: 1 double V, 2 single settees
TABLE: dropleaf
HEAD(S): 1 head with shower
COLD STORAGE: fixed
STOVE: 3-burner
MAX. HEADROOM:

MACHINERY

ENGINE: 25 HP Volvo diesel
PROPELLER:
GENERATOR:

JEANNEAU ATTALIA

DESIGNER: Joubert/Nivelt
DISTRIBUTOR: Nautique International, Inc. (built in France by Jeanneau, S. A.)

STATISTICS

LOA: 31 ft. 10 ins.
LWL: 25 ft. 11 ins.
BEAM: 10 ft. 5 ins.
DISPLACEMENT
deep keel: 7,493 lbs.
shoal keel:
c/board: 7,493 lbs.
BALLAST
deep keel: 2,644 lbs.
shoal keel:
c/board: 2,909 lbs.
DRAFT
deep keel: 5 ft. 8 ins.
shoal keel:
c/board up: 3 ft. 7 ins.
c/board down: 6 ft. 6 ins.

SAIL AREA: 556 sq. ft.
FRESH WATER: 26 gals.
FUEL CAPACITY: 10 gals.

COSTS

BASE BOAT:
DATE:
EST. ON WATER:
DATE:

RATIOS

SAIL AREA/DISP: 23.23
DISP/LENGTH: 192.09
BALLAST RATIO:
35.28 38.82 (c/brd)
FUEL/DISP: 1.00
FRESH WATER/DISP: 2.78

DECK

STEERING: tiller
WINCHES: 1 halyard winch
SAFETY: bow pulpit with double lifelines
ANCHOR: double anchor rollers
NAV LIGHTS: bow light

RIG

TYPE: masthead sloop
RIGGING:
MAINSHEET: mid-boom sheeting

SAILS

SUPPLIED WITH BASE BOAT: main, light/medium genoa, storm jib

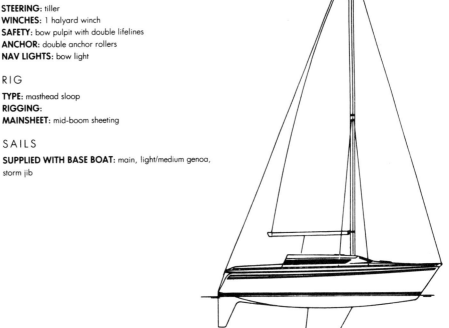

INTERIOR

BERTHS: 6 berths: 1 double V, 2 single settees, 1 double quarterberth
TABLE: dropleaf
HEAD(S): 1 head with shower
COLD STORAGE: built-in icebox (18 gals.)
STOVE: 2-burner gas with oven
MAX. HEADROOM:

MACHINERY

ENGINE: Yanmar #2GM diesel
PROPELLER:
GENERATOR:

BAYFIELD 32

DESIGNER:
BUILDER: Bayfield Boat Yard, Ltd.

STATISTICS

LOA: 32 ft. 0 ins.
LWL: 23 ft. 3 ins.
BEAM: 10 ft. 6 ins.
DISPLACEMENT
deep keel: 9,600 lbs.
shoal keel:
c/board:
BALLAST
deep keel: 4,000 lbs.
shoal keel:
c/board:
DRAFT
deep keel: 3 ft. 9 ins.
shoal keel:
c/board up:
c/board down:

SAIL AREA: 525 sq. ft.
FRESH WATER: 20 gals.
FUEL CAPACITY: 20 gals.

COSTS

BASE BOAT: $58,750
DATE: 09/84
EST. ON WATER:
DATE:

RATIOS

SAIL AREA/DISP: 18.60
DISP/LENGTH: 341
BALLAST RATIO: 41.67
FUEL/DISP: 1.56
FRESH WATER/DISP: 1.69

DECK

STEERING: wheel with emergency tiller
WINCHES: 4 winches
SAFETY: bow and stern pulpits with double lifelines
ANCHOR: anchor roller and well
NAV LIGHTS: running and masthead

RIG

TYPE: cutter
RIGGING: 1x19 wire
MAINSHEET: boom-end sheeting

SAILS

SUPPLIED WITH BASE BOAT: main, topsail, staysail

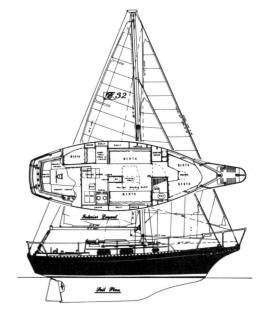

INTERIOR

BERTHS: 6 berths: 1 double V, 1 double settee, 1 single settee, 1 single quarterberth
TABLE: dropleaf
HEAD(S): 1 head with holding tank (20 gal.)
COLD STORAGE: built-in icebox (4 cu. ft.)
STOVE: 2-burner alcohol with oven
MAX. HEADROOM:

MACHINERY

ENGINE: 21 HP Yanmar with 2:1 reduction gear
PROPELLER: 3-blade fixed
GENERATOR:

LM-32

DESIGNER:
DISTRIBUTOR: Anchor Marine, Inc. (built in Denmark by LM Glasfiber, a/s)

STATISTICS

LOA: 32 ft. 0 ins.
LWL: 27 ft. 10 ins.
BEAM: 10 ft. 8 ins.
DISPLACEMENT
deep keel: 13,200 lbs.
shoal keel:
c/board:
BALLAST
deep keel: 4,840 lbs.
shoal keel:
c/board:
DRAFT
deep keel: 4 ft. 11 ins.
shoal keel:
c/board up:
c/board down:

SAIL AREA: 494 sq. ft.
FRESH WATER: 55 gals.
FUEL CAPACITY: 55 gals.

COSTS

BASE BOAT: $71,300
DATE: 04/01/85
EST. ON WATER:
DATE:

RATIOS

SAIL AREA/DISP: 14.15
DISP/LENGTH: 273.1
BALLAST RATIO: 36.67
FUEL/DISP: 3.13
FRESH WATER/DISP: 3.33

INTERIOR

BERTHS: 6 berths: 1 double V, 2 double convertible settees
TABLE: dropleaf
HEAD(S): 1 head with shower and holding tank (15 gals.)
COLD STORAGE: refrigerator (19.8 gals.)
STOVE: 2-burner propane
MAX. HEADROOM:

MACHINERY

ENGINE: 36 HP Volvo #MD 17D/120 S diesel
PROPELLER: fixed
GENERATOR:

DECK

STEERING: tiller
WINCHES:
SAFETY: bow and stern pulpits with double lifelines
ANCHOR: 33 lb. anchor with chain
NAV LIGHTS: running

RIG

TYPE: fractional rig sloop
RIGGING:
MAINSHEET: boom-end sheeting

SAILS

SUPPLIED WITH BASE BOAT: main, working jib

EVELYN 32

DESIGNER: Bob Evelyn
DISTRIBUTOR: Formula Yachts

STATISTICS

LOA: 32 ft. 1 ins.
LWL: 28 ft. 2 ins.
BEAM: 9 ft. 8 ins.
DISPLACEMENT
deep keel: 4,500 lbs.
shoal keel:
c/board:
BALLAST
deep keel: 2,000 lbs.
shoal keel:
c/board:
DRAFT
deep keel: 6 ft. 0 ins.
shoal keel:
c/board up:
c/board down:

SAIL AREA: 441 sq. ft.
FRESH WATER:
FUEL CAPACITY:

COSTS

BASE BOAT: $32,900
DATE: 05/24/85
EST. ON WATER:
DATE:

RATIOS

SAIL AREA/DISP: 25.88
DISP/LENGTH: 89
BALLAST RATIO: 44.44
FUEL/DISP:
FRESH WATER/DISP:

INTERIOR

BERTHS: 6 berths: 1 double V, 2 single settees, 2 single quarterberths
TABLE: fold-down
HEAD(S): enclosed portable
COLD STORAGE: built-in icebox
STOVE:
MAX. HEADROOM:

MACHINERY

ENGINE:
PROPELLER:
GENERATOR:

DECK

STEERING: tiller
WINCHES: 4 Lewmar winches: 2 primary (#40), 2 secondary/halyard
SAFETY: bow and stern pulpits with double lifelines
ANCHOR:
NAV LIGHTS: running

RIG

TYPE: masthead sloop
RIGGING: 1x19 wire
MAINSHEET: 5-part with boom-end sheeting

SAILS

SUPPLIED WITH BASE BOAT:

BUILDER'S COMMENTS Overall winner Block Island Week 1984.

VALIANT 32

DESIGNER: Robert H. Perry
BUILDER: Valiant Yachts

STATISTICS

LOA: 32 ft. 1.25 ins.
LWL: 26 ft. 0.00 ins.
BEAM: 10 ft. 5.00 ins.
DISPLACEMENT
deep keel: 11,800 lbs.
shoal keel:
c/board:
BALLAST
deep keel: 4,700 lbs.
shoal keel:
c/board:
DRAFT
deep keel: 5 ft. 2 ins.
shoal keel:
c/board up:
c/board down:

SAIL AREA: 531 sq. ft.
FRESH WATER: 80 gals.
FUEL CAPACITY: 30 gals.

COSTS

BASE BOAT:
DATE:
EST. ON WATER:
DATE:

RATIOS

SAIL AREA/DISP: 16.39
DISP/LENGTH: 283
BALLAST RATIO: 40
FUEL/DISP: 1.9
FRESH WATER/DISP: 5.4

INTERIOR

BERTHS: 5 berths: 1 double V, 1 single settee, 1 double quarterberth
TABLE: dropleaf
HEAD(S): 1 head with shower
COLD STORAGE: refrigerator/freezer and built-in icebox
STOVE: 3-burner with oven
MAX. HEADROOM: 6 ft. 4 ins.

MACHINERY

ENGINE: diesel with 2:1 reduction gear
PROPELLER:
GENERATOR:

DECK

STEERING: wheel with emergency tiller
WINCHES: complete package
SAFETY: bow and stern pulpits with double lifelines
ANCHOR:
NAV LIGHTS: running

RIG

TYPE: masthead sloop
RIGGING: wire
MAINSHEET: mid-boom sheeting

SAILS

SUPPLIED WITH BASE BOAT:

BUILDER'S COMMENTS An ocean proven yacht in the Valiant tradition. Features all the attributes of the famous Valiant 40 at an affordable price.

SABRE 32

DESIGNER: Sabre Design Team
BUILDER: Sabre Yachts

STATISTICS

LOA: 32 ft. 2 ins.
LWL: 26 ft. 2 ins.
BEAM: 10 ft. 4 ins.
DISPLACEMENT
deep keel: 10,500 lbs.
shoal keel:
c/board:
BALLAST
deep keel: 4,100 lbs.
shoal keel:
c/board:
DRAFT
deep keel: 5 ft. 7 ins.
shoal keel:
c/board up: 3 ft. 8 ins.
c/board down: 7 ft. 0 ins.

SAIL AREA: 481 sq. ft.
FRESH WATER: 63 gals.
FUEL CAPACITY: 20 gals.

COSTS

BASE BOAT:
DATE:
EST. ON WATER:
DATE:

RATIOS

SAIL AREA/DISP: 16.05
DISP/LENGTH: 261
BALLAST RATIO: 39.04
FUEL/DISP: 1.42
FRESH WATER/DISP: 4.80

INTERIOR

BERTHS: 8 berths: 1 double V, 1 double convertible, 1 single settee, 1 double quarterberth, 1 single quarterberth
TABLE: centerline dropleaf
HEAD(S): 1 head
COLD STORAGE: built-in icebox
STOVE: 2-burner alcohol with oven
MAX. HEADROOM: 6 ft. 2 ins.

MACHINERY

ENGINE: 21 HP Westerbeke diesel with 2:1 reduction gear
PROPELLER: 14"x12"
GENERATOR:

DECK

STEERING: wheel
WINCHES: 4 Lewmar winches: 2 primary (#42), 2 halyard (#8 and #16)
SAFETY: bow and stern pulpits with lifelines
ANCHOR: anchor well
NAV LIGHTS: running and masthead

RIG

TYPE: masthead sloop
RIGGING: 1x19 SS wire
MAINSHEET: 4-part with mid-boom sheeting

SAILS

SUPPLIED WITH BASE BOAT:

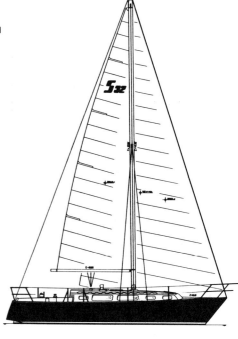

ALBIN 10 METER

DESIGNER: Peter Norlin
BUILDER: Albin Marine, Inc.

STATISTICS

LOA: 32 ft. 5 ins.
LWL: 26 ft. 3 ins.
BEAM: 10 ft. 4 ins.
DISPLACEMENT
deep keel: 8,177 lbs.
shoal keel:
c/board:
BALLAST
deep keel: 3,868 lbs.
shoal keel:
c/board:
DRAFT
deep keel: 5 ft. 6 ins.
shoal keel:
c/board up:
c/board down:

SAIL AREA: 505 sq. ft.
FRESH WATER: 26 gals.
FUEL CAPACITY: 13 gals.

COSTS

BASE BOAT: $49,900
DATE: 05/85
EST. ON WATER:
DATE:

RATIOS

SAIL AREA/DISP: 19.91
DISP/LENGTH: 201.82
BALLAST RATIO: 48.5
FUEL/DISP: 1.19
FRESH WATER/DISP: 2.54

INTERIOR

BERTHS: 6 berths: 1 double V, 2 single settees, 1 double quarterberth
TABLE: centerline dropleaf
HEAD(S): 1 head with 1 shower
COLD STORAGE: built-in icebox
STOVE: 2-burner LPG with oven
MAX. HEADROOM:

MACHINERY

ENGINE: 15 HP Yanmar diesel
PROPELLER: 2-blade folding
GENERATOR:

DECK

STEERING: wheel
WINCHES: 4 Lewmar winches: 2 primary (#40), 2 halyard (#30)
SAFETY: bow and stern pulpits with double lifelines
ANCHOR: anchor locker
NAV LIGHTS: running and masthead

RIG

TYPE: fractional rig sloop with keel-stepped spar
RIGGING:
MAINSHEET: mid-boom sheeting

SAILS

SUPPLIED WITH BASE BOAT: working sails

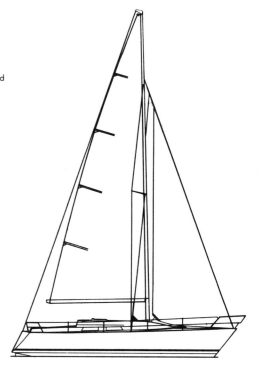

BUILDER'S COMMENTS Introducing a Norlin designed racer/cruiser already very popular in Scandinavia and Northern Europe. High aspect 7/8 rig gives it excellent light wind performance, yet it is a stiff, weatherly yacht in a blow.

CALIBER 33

DESIGNER: Michael McCreary
BUILDER: Caliber Yacht Corporation

STATISTICS

LOA: 32 ft. 6 ins.
LWL: 29 ft. 6 ins.
BEAM: 11 ft. 4 ins.
DISPLACEMENT
deep keel: 11,400 lbs.
shoal keel:
c/board:
BALLAST
deep keel: 5,200 lbs.
shoal keel:
c/board:
DRAFT
deep keel: 4 ft. 6 ins.
shoal keel:
c/board up:
c/board down:

SAIL AREA: 525 sq. ft.
FRESH WATER: 68 gals.
FUEL CAPACITY: 30 gals.

COSTS

BASE BOAT: $62,950
DATE: 04/85
EST. ON WATER:
DATE:

RATIOS

SAIL AREA/DISP: 16.58
DISP/LENGTH: 198
BALLAST RATIO: 45.61
FUEL/DISP: 1.97
FRESH WATER/DISP: 4.77

DECK

STEERING: 32" wheel
WINCHES: 4 Barient winches: 2 primary (#24 2 sp), 2 halyard (#10)
SAFETY: bow and stern pulpits with double lifelines
ANCHOR: bowsprit and anchor well
NAV LIGHTS: running and masthead

RIG

TYPE: masthead sloop
RIGGING: 1x19 SS wire
MAINSHEET: 6-part with mid-boom sheeting

SAILS

SUPPLIED WITH BASE BOAT:
main (1 reef), 110% jib

INTERIOR

BERTHS: 7 berths: 1 double V, 1 double convertible dinette, 1 single settee, 1 double quarterberth
TABLE: bulkhead-mounted
HEAD(S): 1 head with shower
COLD STORAGE: built-in icebox (10 cu. ft.)
STOVE: 2-burner alcohol with oven
MAX. HEADROOM: 6 ft. 2 ins.

MACHINERY

ENGINE: 28 HP diesel
PROPELLER:
GENERATOR:

ERICSON 32

DESIGNER: Bruce King
BUILDER: Ericson Yachts

STATISTICS

LOA: 32 ft. 6 ins.
LWL: 25 ft. 10 ins.
BEAM: 10 ft. 10 ins.
DISPLACEMENT
deep keel: 9,800 lbs.
shoal keel:
c/board:
BALLAST
deep keel: 4,200 lbs.
shoal keel:
c/board:
DRAFT
deep keel: 6 ft. 2 ins.
shoal keel: 4 ft. 4 ins.
c/board up:
c/board down:

SAIL AREA: 496 sq. ft.
FRESH WATER: 32 gals.
FUEL CAPACITY: 22 gals.

COSTS

BASE BOAT:
DATE:
EST. ON WATER:
DATE:

RATIOS

SAIL AREA/DISP: 17.33
DISP/LENGTH: 253.57
BALLAST RATIO: 42.86
FUEL/DISP: 1.88
FRESH WATER/DISP: 2.61

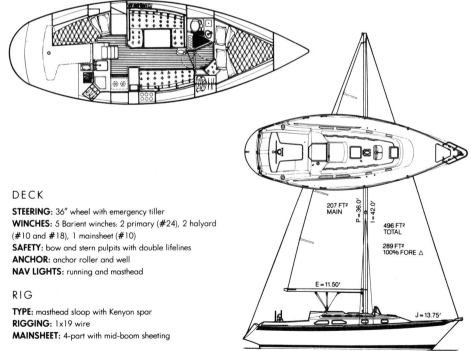

DECK

STEERING: 36" wheel with emergency tiller
WINCHES: 5 Barient winches: 2 primary (#24), 2 halyard (#10 and #18), 1 mainsheet (#10)
SAFETY: bow and stern pulpits with double lifelines
ANCHOR: anchor roller and well
NAV LIGHTS: running and masthead

RIG

TYPE: masthead sloop with Kenyon spar
RIGGING: 1x19 wire
MAINSHEET: 4-part with mid-boom sheeting

SAILS

SUPPLIED WITH BASE BOAT:

INTERIOR

BERTHS: 6 berths: 1 double V, 1 double convertible dinette, 1 single settee, 1 single quarterberth
TABLE: pedestal-mounted dinette
HEAD(S): 1 head with shower, sump pump, and holding tank
COLD STORAGE: built-in icebox (6 cu. ft.)
STOVE: 2-burner alcohol with oven
MAX. HEADROOM: 6 ft. 2 ins.

MACHINERY

ENGINE: 21 HP Universal #25 diesel
PROPELLER: 2-blade 15"x11" on 1" shaft
GENERATOR:

C & C 33

DESIGNER: C & C Design Group
BUILDER: C & C Yachts

STATISTICS

LOA: 32 ft. 7.0 ins.
LWL: 26 ft. 2.0 ins.
BEAM: 10 ft. 6.5 ins.
DISPLACEMENT
deep keel: 9,450 lbs.
shoal keel:
c/board:
BALLAST
deep keel: 3,975 lbs.
shoal keel:
c/board:
DRAFT
deep keel: 6 ft. 4 ins.
shoal keel:
c/board up: 4 ft. 4 ins.
c/board down: 6 ft. 6 ins.

INTERIOR

BERTHS: 7 berths: 1 double V, 1 single settee, 1 double convertible settee, 1 double quarterberth
TABLE: centerline
HEAD(S): 1 head with shower, sump pump, and holding tank
COLD STORAGE: built-in icebox
STOVE: 2-burner alcohol
MAX. HEADROOM:

MACHINERY

ENGINE: Yanmar #2GM diesel
PROPELLER: 2-blade fixed
GENERATOR:

SAIL AREA:
FRESH WATER: 30 gals.
FUEL CAPACITY: 20 gals.

COSTS

BASE BOAT:
DATE:
EST. ON WATER: $75,000
DATE: 11/85

RATIOS

SAIL AREA/DISP:
DISP/LENGTH: 235
BALLAST RATIO: 42.06
FUEL/DISP: 1.59
FRESH WATER/DISP: 2.54

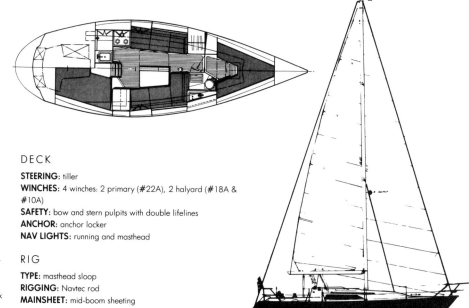

DECK

STEERING: tiller
WINCHES: 4 winches: 2 primary (#22A), 2 halyard (#18A & #10A)
SAFETY: bow and stern pulpits with double lifelines
ANCHOR: anchor locker
NAV LIGHTS: running and masthead

RIG

TYPE: masthead sloop
RIGGING: Navtec rod
MAINSHEET: mid-boom sheeting

SAILS

SUPPLIED WITH BASE BOAT:

BUILDER'S COMMENTS A hard-driving racing yacht that knows how to relax. Design, engineering, and craftsmanship skillfully combine the science of performance and the art of living well.

ENDEAVOUR 33

DESIGNER: Bruce Kelley
BUILDER: Endeavour Yacht Corporation

STATISTICS

LOA: 32 ft. 7 ins.
LWL: 27 ft. 6 ins.
BEAM: 11 ft. 6 ins.
DISPLACEMENT
deep keel: 11,350 lbs.
shoal keel:
c/board:
BALLAST
deep keel: 4,600 lbs.
shoal keel:
c/board:
DRAFT
deep keel: 4 ft. 6 ins.
shoal keel:
c/board up:
c/board down:

INTERIOR

BERTHS: 6 berths: 1 double V, 1 double convertible, 1 double quarterberth
TABLE: centerline dropleaf
HEAD(S): 1 head with shower
COLD STORAGE: built-in icebox
STOVE: 2-burner with oven
MAX. HEADROOM: 6 ft. 2 ins.

MACHINERY

ENGINE: 22 HP Yanmar diesel with 2.6:1 reduction gear
PROPELLER: 2-blade on 1" shaft
GENERATOR:

SAIL AREA: 539 sq. ft.
FRESH WATER: 70 gals.
FUEL CAPACITY: 36 gals.

COSTS

BASE BOAT:
DATE:
EST. ON WATER:
DATE:

RATIOS

SAIL AREA/DISP: 17.07
DISP/LENGTH: 243.
BALLAST RATIO: 40.52
FUEL/DISP: 2.37
FRESH WATER/DISP: 4.9

DECK

STEERING: 38" wheel
WINCHES: 4 winches: 2 sheet, 2 halyard
SAFETY: bow and stern pulpits with double lifelines
ANCHOR: anchor well
NAV LIGHTS: running and masthead

RIG

TYPE: masthead sloop
RIGGING:
MAINSHEET: mid-boom sheeting

SAILS

SUPPLIED WITH BASE BOAT:

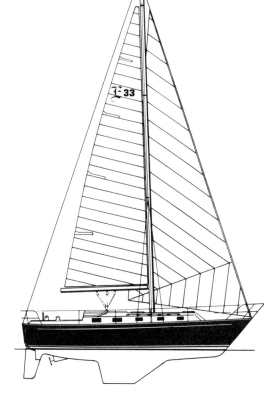

CS 33

DESIGNER: Raymond Wall
BUILDER: CS Yachts, Ltd.

STATISTICS

LOA: 32 ft. 8 ins.
LWL: 26 ft. 5 ins.
BEAM: 10 ft. 8 ins.
DISPLACEMENT
deep keel: 10,000 lbs.
shoal keel:
c/board:
BALLAST
deep keel: 4,200 lbs.
shoal keel:
c/board:
DRAFT
deep keel: 5 ft. 9 ins.
shoal keel:
c/board up:
c/board down:

SAIL AREA: 505 sq. ft.
FRESH WATER: 50 gals.
FUEL CAPACITY: 21 gals.

COSTS

BASE BOAT: $59,900
DATE: 06/03/85
EST. ON WATER:
DATE:

RATIOS

SAIL AREA/DISP: 17.40
DISP/LENGTH: 242
BALLAST RATIO: 42.00
FUEL/DISP: 1.57
FRESH WATER/DISP: 4.00

INTERIOR

BERTHS: 5 berths: 1 double V, 1 double convertible settee, 1 single settee
TABLE: fixed dropleaf or folding bulkhead-mounted
HEAD(S): 1 head with shower and sump pump
COLD STORAGE: built-in icebox (6 cu. ft.)
STOVE: 2-burner propane with oven
MAX. HEADROOM: 6 ft. 2 ins.

MACHINERY

ENGINE: 20 HP Bukh diesel with 2.25:1 reduction gear
PROPELLER: 2-blade
GENERATOR:

DECK

STEERING: 32" wheel
WINCHES: 5 winches: 2 primary (Lewmar #40C 2sp), 1 main halyard (Lewmar #16C 2sp), 1 jib halyard (Lewmar #30C 2 sp), 1 mainsheet (Gibb #7)
SAFETY: bow and stern pulpits with double lifelines
ANCHOR: anchor roller and well
NAV LIGHTS: running and masthead

RIG

TYPE: masthead sloop
RIGGING: 1x19 wire (¼")
MAINSHEET: 5-part with mid-boom sheeting

SAILS

SUPPLIED WITH BASE BOAT:

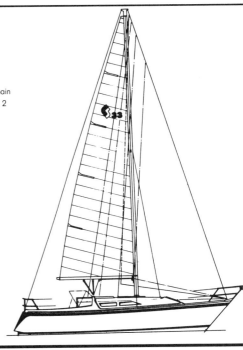

BUILDER'S COMMENTS The CS 33 is a beautiful cruising yacht that incorporates comfort and amenities and can more than hold her own in local and club racing competition. Designed with an eye to light air performance, she nevertheless carries a better than 42% ballast/weight ratio for real stiffness when the wind pipes up. Her fine entry and state-of-the-art fin keel tell you that she is extremely close winded and highly maneuverable. The fullness of her after sections lets her track beautifully downwind, and gives her plenty of room in the cockpit and below.

FREEDOM 32

DESIGNER: Gary Hoyt
BUILDER: Freedom Yachts International, Inc.

STATISTICS

LOA: 32 ft. 8 ins.
LWL: 25 ft. 9 ins.
BEAM: 12 ft. 3 ins.
DISPLACEMENT
deep keel: 9,000 lbs.
shoal keel:
c/board:
BALLAST
deep keel: 3,500 lbs.
shoal keel:
c/board:
DRAFT
deep keel: 6 ft. 0 ins.
shoal keel: 4 ft. 11 ins.
c/board up:
c/board down:

SAIL AREA: 500 sq. ft.
FRESH WATER:
FUEL CAPACITY:

COSTS

BASE BOAT: $66,900
DATE: 11/85
EST. ON WATER:
DATE:

RATIOS

SAIL AREA/DISP: 18.49
DISP/LENGTH: 235.32
BALLAST RATIO: 38.89
FUEL/DISP:
FRESH WATER/DISP:

INTERIOR

BERTHS: 5 berths: 1 double V, 1 single settee, 2 single quarterberths
TABLE: dropleaf
HEAD(S): 1 head with 1 shower
COLD STORAGE: built-in icebox
STOVE:
MAX. HEADROOM:

MACHINERY

ENGINE: 22.5 HP diesel
PROPELLER:
GENERATOR:

DECK

STEERING: wheel
WINCHES:
SAFETY: bow and stern pulpits with double lifelines
ANCHOR:
NAV LIGHTS:

RIG

TYPE: cat rig sloop
RIGGING: unstayed
MAINSHEET: mid-boom sheeting

SAILS

SUPPLIED WITH BASE BOAT:

GLADIATOR

DESIGNER: Holman & Pye
BUILDER: Chantiers Henri Wauquiez

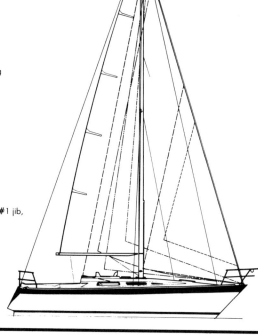

STATISTICS

LOA: 32 ft. 10 ins.
LWL: 27 ft. 3 ins.
BEAM: 11 ft. 0 ins.
DISPLACEMENT
deep keel: 11,000 lbs.
shoal keel:
c/board:
BALLAST
deep keel: 4,800 lbs.
shoal keel:
c/board:
DRAFT
deep keel: 6 ft. 0 ins.
shoal keel:
c/board up:
c/board down:

SAIL AREA: 511 sq. ft.
FRESH WATER: 66 gals.
FUEL CAPACITY: 20 gals.

COSTS

BASE BOAT: 446,000 francs
DATE: 02/25/85
EST. ON WATER:
DATE:

RATIOS

SAIL AREA/DISP: 16.52
DISP/LENGTH: 242
BALLAST RATIO: 43.63
FUEL/DISP: 1.36
FRESH WATER/DISP: 4.8

DECK

STEERING: tiller
WINCHES: 5 winches: 2 primary, 2 halyard, 1 reefing
SAFETY: double lifelines
ANCHOR: CQR anchor with anchor locker
NAV LIGHTS: running and masthead

RIG

TYPE: masthead sloop
RIGGING:
MAINSHEET: mid-boom sheeting

SAILS

SUPPLIED WITH BASE BOAT: main, 150% genoa, #1 jib, storm jib

INTERIOR

BERTHS: 7 berths: 1 double V, 1 single settee, 1 double convertible dinette, 1 double quarterberth
TABLE: centerline dropleaf
HEAD(S): 1 head with shower
COLD STORAGE: built-in icebox
STOVE: 2-burner with oven
MAX. HEADROOM: 6 ft. 2 ins.

MACHINERY

ENGINE: 88 HP Volvo sail drive
PROPELLER: 2-blade fixed
GENERATOR:

BUILDER'S COMMENTS After the success of the 380 Centurions, we thought that we ought to offer a faster and roomier cruising yacht to satisfy the needs of enthusiastic yachtsmen. This boat should, in our mind, have the same qualities as the Centurion, but even more: strong construction, lovely lines, and excellent finish. Brilliantly designed by the same team, Holman & Pye, the Gladiator is already a great success. Going through the water like a dream, she points remarkably well and can maintain a high speed in all conditions.

X-102

DESIGNER: Niels Jeppesen
DISTRIBUTOR: Aquarius Performance Yachts, Inc. (built in Denmark by X-Yachts)

STATISTICS

LOA: 32 ft. 10.8 ins.
LWL: 25 ft. 7.2 ins.
BEAM: 11 ft. 1.2 ins.
DISPLACEMENT
deep keel: 7,700 lbs.
shoal keel:
c/board:
BALLAST
deep keel: 3,520 lbs.
shoal keel:
c/board:
DRAFT
deep keel: 6 ft. 2.4 ins.
shoal keel:
c/board up:
c/board down:

SAIL AREA: 602 sq. ft.
FRESH WATER: 28 gals.
FUEL CAPACITY: 13 gals.

COSTS

BASE BOAT:
DATE:
EST. ON WATER:
DATE:

RATIOS

SAIL AREA/DISP: 24.70
DISP/LENGTH: 204.99
BALLAST RATIO: 45.21
FUEL/DISP: 1.27
FRESH WATER/DISP: 2.91

INTERIOR

BERTHS: 9 berths: 1 double V, 2 single settees, 2 single pilots, 1 double quarterberth, 1 single quarterberth
TABLE: dropleaf
HEAD(S): 1 head
COLD STORAGE: built-in icebox
STOVE:
MAX. HEADROOM: 6 ft. 2 ins.

MACHINERY

ENGINE: 15 HP Yanmar diesel
PROPELLER: folding
GENERATOR:

DECK

STEERING: tiller
WINCHES: 6 Lewmar winches: 2 #40, 2 #24, 2 #16 ST
SAFETY: bow and stern pulpits with double lifelines
ANCHOR: 27.5 lb. mushroom anchor with anchor roller
NAV LIGHTS: running and masthead

RIG

TYPE: fractional rig sloop with Nordic spar
RIGGING: 1x19 wire
MAINSHEET: mid-boom sheeting

SAILS

SUPPLIED WITH BASE BOAT:

BAVARIA 960

DESIGNER: Axel Mohnhaupt
BUILDER: Bavaria Yachtbau GmbH

STATISTICS

LOA: 33 ft. 0 ins.
LWL: 26 ft. 2 ins.
BEAM: 10 ft. 0 ins.
DISPLACEMENT
deep keel: 8,500 lbs.
shoal keel:
c/board:
BALLAST
deep keel: 3,400 lbs.
shoal keel:
c/board:
DRAFT
deep keel: 5 ft. 6 ins.
shoal keel:
c/board up:
c/board down:

SAIL AREA:
FRESH WATER: 55.0 gals.
FUEL CAPACITY: 27.5 gals.

COSTS

BASE BOAT:
DATE:
EST. ON WATER:
DATE:

RATIOS

SAIL AREA/DISP:
DISP/LENGTH: 211
BALLAST RATIO: 40.00
FUEL/DISP: 5.2
FRESH WATER/DISP: 2.4

INTERIOR

BERTHS: 6 berths: 1 double V, 2 single settees, 1 double quarterberth
TABLE: dropleaf
HEAD(S): 1 head
COLD STORAGE: built-in icebox
STOVE: 2-burner gas
MAX. HEADROOM:

MACHINERY

ENGINE: 18 HP Volvo diesel
PROPELLER:
GENERATOR:

DECK

STEERING:
WINCHES: 4 Enkes winches: 2 primary, 2 halyard
SAFETY: bow and stern pulpits with double lifelines
ANCHOR: anchor with anchor chain, roller, and well
NAV LIGHTS: running and masthead

RIG

TYPE: fractional rig sloop
RIGGING: 1x19 wire
MAINSHEET: mid-boom sheeting

SAILS

SUPPLIED WITH BASE BOAT: main (2 reefs), working jib

BUILDER'S COMMENTS Bavaria 960, the consequent continuation in design of Bavaria 1060, has a high quality interior accommodation. The best possible choice of fittings and arrangement of fittings are of course part of the Bavaria standard.

CAL 33

DESIGNER: C. Raymond Hunt Associates
BUILDER: Lear Siegler Marine

STATISTICS

LOA: 33 ft. 0 ins.
LWL: 27 ft. 6 ins.
BEAM: 11 ft. 4 ins.
DISPLACEMENT
deep keel: 10,800 lbs.
shoal keel:
c/board:
BALLAST
deep keel: 4,475 lbs.
shoal keel: 4,750 lbs.
c/board:
DRAFT
deep keel: 6 ft. 2 ins.
shoal keel: 4 ft. 8 ins.
c/board up:
c/board down:

SAIL AREA: 552 sq. ft.
FRESH WATER: 50 gals.
FUEL CAPACITY: 24 gals.

COSTS

BASE BOAT: $66,500
DATE: 11/85
EST. ON WATER:
DATE:

RATIOS

SAIL AREA/DISP: 18.07
DISP/LENGTH: 231
BALLAST RATIO: 43.98
FUEL/DISP: 1.66
FRESH WATER/DISP: 3.70

INTERIOR

BERTHS: 7 berths: 1 double V, 1 single settee, 1 double convertible settee, 1 double quarterberth
TABLE: centerline dropleaf
HEAD(S): 1 head with shower
COLD STORAGE: built-in icebox (6 cu. ft.)
STOVE: 2-burner alcohol with oven
MAX. HEADROOM: 6 ft. 2 ins.

MACHINERY

ENGINE: 22 HP Yanmar diesel
PROPELLER: 2-blade on 1¼" shaft
GENERATOR:

DECK

STEERING: 38" wheel
WINCHES: 6 Barient winches: 2 primary (#23C ST), 2 halyard #21 & #18), 1 mainsheet (#19 ST), 1 reefing (#10 P)
SAFETY: bow and stern pulpits with double lifelines
ANCHOR: anchor roller and well
NAV LIGHTS: running

RIG

TYPE: masthead sloop
RIGGING: 1x19 wire
MAINSHEET: mid-boom sheeting

SAILS

SUPPLIED WITH BASE BOAT:

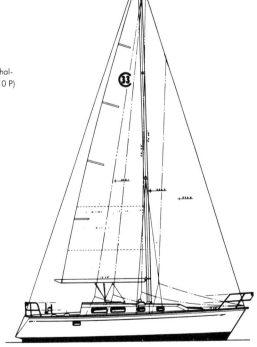

BUILDER'S COMMENTS A unique blend of performance and civilized creature comfort. A wide open feeling below due to its twin double berth interior. The hull form was designed for performance, and the deck also reflects this with aft-led halyards and a double-spreader tapered rig.

HOBIE 33

DESIGNER: Hobie Design Department
BUILDER: Hobie Cat

STATISTICS

LOA: 33 ft. 0 ins.
LWL: 30 ft. 6 ins.
BEAM: 8 ft. 0 ins.
DISPLACEMENT
deep keel: 4,000 lbs.
shoal keel:
c/board:
BALLAST
deep keel: 1,800 lbs.
shoal keel:
c/board:
DRAFT
deep keel: 5 ft. 6 ins.
shoal keel:
c/board up:
c/board down:

SAIL AREA: 428 sq. ft.
FRESH WATER: 5 gals.
FUEL CAPACITY: 0 gals.

COSTS

BASE BOAT: $34,000
DATE: 01/01/85
EST. ON WATER: $38,000
DATE: 01/01/85

RATIOS

SAIL AREA/DISP: 27.17
DISP/LENGTH: 62.94
BALLAST RATIO: 45.0
FUEL/DISP: 0.0
FRESH WATER/DISP: 1.00

INTERIOR

BERTHS: 6 berths: 1 double V, 1 double, 2 quarterberths
TABLE: dinette/chart table combination
HEAD(S): 1 portable head
COLD STORAGE: cooler (48 qt.)
STOVE: 2-burner alcohol
MAX. HEADROOM:

MACHINERY

ENGINE:
PROPELLER:
GENERATOR:

DECK

STEERING: tiller
WINCHES: 5 Lewmar winches: 2 primary (2sp), 3 halyard
SAFETY: bow and stern pulpits with lifelines
ANCHOR: anchor well
NAV LIGHTS: running

RIG

TYPE: fractional rig sloop
RIGGING: SS
MAINSHEET: 4-part with boom-end sheeting

SAILS

SUPPLIED WITH BASE BOAT:

BUILDER'S COMMENTS The Hobie 33's unique bulb keel enables the boat to sail upwind with the 40 footers. Its ultralight weight maintains that advantage downwind with speeds in excess of 20 knots.

FREEDOM 33

DESIGNER: J. Paris & Gary Hoyt
BUILDER: Freedom Yachts International, Inc.

STATISTICS

LOA: 33 ft. 0 ins.
LWL: 30 ft. 0 ins.
BEAM: 11 ft. 0 ins.
DISPLACEMENT
deep keel:
shoal keel:
c/board: 12,000 lbs.
BALLAST
deep keel:
shoal keel:
c/board: 3,800 lbs.
DRAFT
deep keel:
shoal keel:
c/board up: 3 ft. 6 ins.
c/board down: 6 ft. 0 ins.

SAIL AREA: 516 sq. ft.
FRESH WATER: 83 gals.
FUEL CAPACITY: 25 gals.

COSTS

BASE BOAT:
DATE:
EST. ON WATER:
DATE:

RATIOS

SAIL AREA/DISP: 15.75
DISP/LENGTH: 198.41
BALLAST RATIO: 31.67
FUEL/DISP: 1.56
FRESH WATER/DISP: 5.53

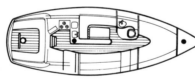

INTERIOR

BERTHS: 6 berths: 1 double V, 1 double convertible dinette, 1 single settee, 1 single quarterberth
TABLE:
HEAD(S): 1 head with shower and holding tank
COLD STORAGE: built-in icebox (7 cu. ft.)
STOVE: 3-burner LPG with oven
MAX. HEADROOM: 6 ft. 1 ins.

MACHINERY

ENGINE: Yanmar #3GM diesel
PROPELLER: 2-blade
GENERATOR:

DECK

STEERING: 32" wheel with emergency tiller
WINCHES: 2 Barient winches: 2 primary (#23 ST)
SAFETY: bow and stern pulpits with double lifelines
ANCHOR:
NAV LIGHTS:

RIG

TYPE: cat ketch
RIGGING: unstayed
MAINSHEET:

SAILS

SUPPLIED WITH BASE BOAT: main, mizzen

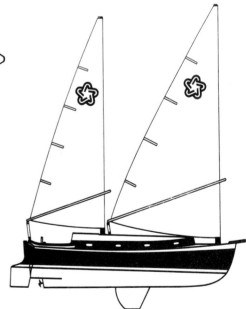

SOVEREL 33

DESIGNER: Mark Soverel
BUILDER: Soverel Marine, Inc.

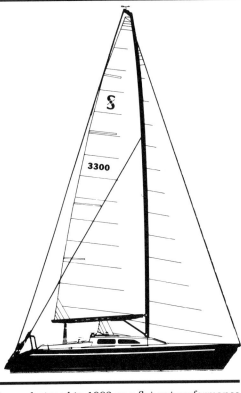

STATISTICS

LOA: 33 ft. 0 ins.
LWL: 30 ft. 6 ins.
BEAM: 11 ft. 0 ins.
DISPLACEMENT
deep keel: 5,800 lbs.
shoal keel:
c/board:
BALLAST
deep keel: 2,800 lbs.
shoal keel:
c/board:
DRAFT
deep keel: 5 ft. 10.75 ins.
shoal keel:
c/board up:
c/board down:

SAIL AREA: 537 sq. ft.
FRESH WATER: 0 gals.
FUEL CAPACITY: 9 gals.

COSTS

BASE BOAT: $44,990
DATE: 05/23/85
EST. ON WATER: $60,000
DATE: 05/23/85

RATIOS

SAIL AREA/DISP: 28.62
DISP/LENGTH: 81
BALLAST RATIO: 53.84
FUEL/DISP: 0.0
FRESH WATER/DISP: 1.16

DECK

STEERING: tiller
WINCHES: 4 Lewmar winches: 2 primary (#43), 2 halyard/spinnaker (#40A)
SAFETY: bow and stern pulpits with lifelines
ANCHOR:
NAV LIGHTS: running

RIG

TYPE: fractional rig sloop with Kenyon spar
RIGGING: rod
MAINSHEET: 4-part with boom-end sheeting

SAILS

SUPPLIED WITH BASE BOAT:

INTERIOR

BERTHS: 4 berths: 2 single settees, 2 single quarterberths
TABLE:
HEAD(S):
COLD STORAGE:
STOVE:
MAX. HEADROOM: 5 ft. 10 ins.

MACHINERY

ENGINE: 9.5 HP Yanmar diesel
PROPELLER: Martec folding
GENERATOR:

BUILDER'S COMMENTS The Soverel 33 was designed in 1983 as a flat-out performance racer/cruiser to excel under all conditions in the PHRF and one-design racing classes. No compromises were made to any particular handicap rule, and consequently the Soverel 33 is an extremely attractive yacht and possibly the fastest 33 footer afloat.

X-³/₄ Ton

DESIGNER: Niels Jeppesen
DISTRIBUTOR: Aquarius Performance Yachts, Inc. (built in Denmark by X-Yachts)

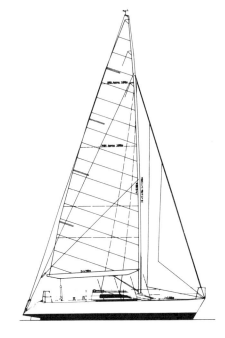

STATISTICS

LOA: 33 ft. 0.0 ins.
LWL: 25 ft. 7.2 ins.
BEAM: 11 ft. 1.2 ins.
DISPLACEMENT
deep keel: 7,275 lbs.
shoal keel:
c/board:
BALLAST
deep keel: 4,850 lbs.
shoal keel:
c/board:
DRAFT
deep keel: 6 ft. 2.4 ins.
shoal keel:
c/board up:
c/board down:

SAIL AREA: 626 sq. ft.
FRESH WATER:
FUEL CAPACITY:

COSTS

BASE BOAT:
DATE:
EST. ON WATER:
DATE:

RATIOS

SAIL AREA/DISP: 26.68
DISP/LENGTH: 193.58
BALLAST RATIO: 66.67
FUEL/DISP:
FRESH WATER/DISP:

DECK

STEERING: tiller
WINCHES:
SAFETY:
ANCHOR:
NAV LIGHTS:

RIG

TYPE: fractional rig sloop
RIGGING:
MAINSHEET: mid-boom sheeting

SAILS

SUPPLIED WITH BASE BOAT:

INTERIOR

BERTHS: 8 berths: 2 single settees, 4 pipe berths, 2 pilots
TABLE:
HEAD(S): 1 head
COLD STORAGE:
STOVE:
MAX. HEADROOM: 6 ft. 0 ins.

MACHINERY

ENGINE: 20 HP Bukh diesel
PROPELLER:
GENERATOR:

CAPE DORY 33

DESIGNER: Carl Alberg
BUILDER: Cape Dory Yachts

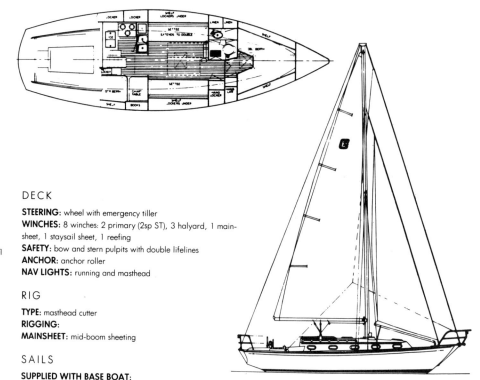

STATISTICS

LOA: 33 ft. 0.5 ins.
LWL: 24 ft. 6.0 ins.
BEAM: 10 ft. 3.0 ins.
DISPLACEMENT
deep keel: 13,300 lbs.
shoal keel:
c/board:
BALLAST
deep keel: 5,500 lbs.
shoal keel:
c/board:
DRAFT
deep keel: 4 ft. 10 ins.
shoal keel:
c/board up:
c/board down:

SAIL AREA: 546 sq. ft.
FRESH WATER: 74 gals.
FUEL CAPACITY: 21 gals.

COSTS

BASE BOAT:
DATE:
EST. ON WATER:
DATE:

RATIOS

SAIL AREA/DISP: 15.56
DISP/LENGTH: 403.74
BALLAST RATIO: 41.35
FUEL/DISP: 1.18
FRESH WATER/DISP: 4.45

INTERIOR

BERTHS: 6 berths: 1 double V, 1 double convertible settee, 1 single settee, 1 single quarterberth
TABLE: bulkhead-mounted
HEAD(S): 1 head with shower and holding tank (35 gals.)
COLD STORAGE: built-in icebox
STOVE: 3-burner
MAX. HEADROOM:

MACHINERY

ENGINE: Universal #30 diesel with 2:1 reduction gear
PROPELLER: 3-blade on 1" shaft
GENERATOR:

DECK

STEERING: wheel with emergency tiller
WINCHES: 8 winches: 2 primary (2sp ST), 3 halyard, 1 mainsheet, 1 staysail sheet, 1 reefing
SAFETY: bow and stern pulpits with double lifelines
ANCHOR: anchor roller
NAV LIGHTS: running and masthead

RIG

TYPE: masthead cutter
RIGGING:
MAINSHEET: mid-boom sheeting

SAILS

SUPPLIED WITH BASE BOAT:

OFFSHORE 33

DESIGNER: Walter H. Scott
BUILDER: Offshore Yachts

STATISTICS

LOA: 33 ft. 1 ins.
LWL: 26 ft. 9 ins.
BEAM: 11 ft. 0 ins.
DISPLACEMENT
deep keel: 13,000 lbs.
shoal keel:
c/board:
BALLAST
deep keel: 5,000 lbs.
shoal keel:
c/board:
DRAFT
deep keel: 5 ft. 0 ins.
shoal keel: 4 ft. 0 ins.
c/board up:
c/board down:

SAIL AREA: 500 sq. ft.
FRESH WATER: 80 gals.
FUEL CAPACITY: 30 gals.

COSTS

BASE BOAT:
DATE:
EST. ON WATER:
DATE:

RATIOS

SAIL AREA/DISP: 14.52
DISP/LENGTH: 303.2
BALLAST RATIO: 38.46
FUEL/DISP: 1.73
FRESH WATER/DISP: 4.92

DECK

STEERING: wheel
WINCHES: Lewmar winches
SAFETY: bow and stern pulpits with double lifelines
ANCHOR:
NAV LIGHTS: running and masthead

RIG

TYPE: cat ketch
RIGGING:
MAINSHEET:

SAILS

SUPPLIED WITH BASE BOAT:

INTERIOR

BERTHS: 4 berths: 1 double V, 1 single settee, 1 single pilot
TABLE: dropleaf
HEAD(S): 1 head with shower, sump pump, and holding tank
COLD STORAGE: built-in icebox (6.5 cu. ft.)
STOVE: 2-burner alcohol with oven
MAX. HEADROOM: 6 ft. 2 ins.

MACHINERY

ENGINE: 21 HP Universal diesel
PROPELLER: 16" on 1" shaft
GENERATOR:

DEHLER 34

DESIGNER: Van de Stadt
DISTRIBUTOR: Southwest Marine Sales, Inc. (built in Germany by Dehler Yachts)

STATISTICS

LOA: 33 ft. 1.5 ins.
LWL: 27 ft. 3.0 ins.
BEAM: 11 ft. 2.0 ins.
DISPLACEMENT
deep keel: 8,378 lbs.
shoal keel:
c/board:
BALLAST
deep keel: 3,968 lbs.
shoal keel:
c/board:
DRAFT
deep keel: 5 ft. 7 ins.
shoal keel:
c/board up:
c/board down:

INTERIOR

BERTHS: 8 berths: 1 double V, 2 double convertibles, 1 aft double
TABLE: centerline dropleaf
HEAD(S): 1 head
COLD STORAGE: built-in icebox
STOVE: 2-burner propane with oven
MAX. HEADROOM:

MACHINERY

ENGINE: 18 HP Yanmar diesel
PROPELLER:
GENERATOR:

SAIL AREA: 485 sq. ft.
FRESH WATER: 20 gals.
FUEL CAPACITY:

COSTS

BASE BOAT:
DATE:
EST. ON WATER:
DATE:

RATIOS

SAIL AREA/DISP: 18.81
DISP/LENGTH: 184
BALLAST RATIO: 47.36
FUEL/DISP:
FRESH WATER/DISP: 1.91

DECK

STEERING: wheel
WINCHES:
SAFETY:
ANCHOR:
NAV LIGHTS:

RIG

TYPE: fractional rig sloop
RIGGING:
MAINSHEET: boom-end sheeting

SAILS

SUPPLIED WITH BASE BOAT:

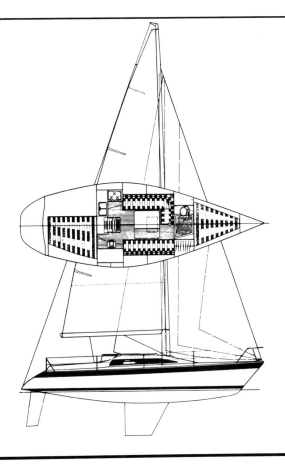

TARTAN TEN

DESIGNER: Sparkman & Stephens
BUILDER: Tartan Marine Company

STATISTICS

LOA: 33 ft. 1.75 ins.
LWL: 27 ft. 0.00 ins.
BEAM: 9 ft. 3.00 ins.
DISPLACEMENT
deep keel: 6,700 lbs.
shoal keel:
c/board:
BALLAST
deep keel: 3,300 lbs.
shoal keel:
c/board:
DRAFT
deep keel: 5 ft. 10.5 ins.
shoal keel:
c/board up:
c/board down:

INTERIOR

BERTHS: 6 berths: 1 double V, 4 single settees
TABLE: dropleaf
HEAD(S): portable marine toilet
COLD STORAGE: portable ice chest
STOVE:
MAX. HEADROOM: sitting room

MACHINERY

ENGINE: 15 HP Yanmar #26M diesel with 2.6:1 reduction gear
PROPELLER: folding 12"x12" on ¾" shaft
GENERATOR:

SAIL AREA: 481 sq. ft.
FRESH WATER: 19 gals.
FUEL CAPACITY: 12 gals.

COSTS

BASE BOAT: $36,900
DATE: 07/26/85
EST. ON WATER: $43,000
DATE: 07/26/85

RATIOS

SAIL AREA/DISP: 21.65
DISP/LENGTH: 131.96
BALLAST RATIO: 49.25
FUEL/DISP: 1.34
FRESH WATER/DISP: 2.27

DECK

STEERING: tiller
WINCHES:
SAFETY: bow and stern pulpits with double lifelines
ANCHOR:
NAV LIGHTS: running

RIG

TYPE: fractional rig sloop with Annapolis spar
RIGGING: wire
MAINSHEET: 8-part with boom-end sheeting

SAILS

SUPPLIED WITH BASE BOAT:

GIB'SEA 96 MASTER

DESIGNER: Joubert & Nivelt
BUILDER: Gilbert Marine, S.A.

STATISTICS

LOA: 33 ft. 2 ins.
LWL: 27 ft. 3 ins.
BEAM: 10 ft. 10 ins.
DISPLACEMENT
deep keel: 8,600 lbs.
shoal keel:
c/board:
BALLAST
deep keel: 2,800 lbs.
shoal keel:
c/board:
DRAFT
deep keel: 5 ft. 7 ins.
shoal keel:
c/board up: 4 ft. 1 ins.
c/board down: 7 ft. 10 ins.

SAIL AREA:
FRESH WATER: 65 gals.
FUEL CAPACITY: 25 gals.

COSTS

BASE BOAT:
DATE:
EST. ON WATER:
DATE:

RATIOS

SAIL AREA/DISP:
DISP/LENGTH: 189.7
BALLAST RATIO: 30.0
FUEL/DISP: 2.2
FRESH WATER/DISP: 6.0

DECK

STEERING: wheel
WINCHES: 4 self-tailing winches
SAFETY: bow and stern pulpits with double lifelines
ANCHOR: anchor well
NAV LIGHTS: running and masthead

RIG

TYPE: masthead sloop
RIGGING:
MAINSHEET: 4-part with boom-end sheeting

SAILS

SUPPLIED WITH BASE BOAT: main, 150% genoa, storm jib

INTERIOR

BERTHS: 6 berths: 1 double V, 2 single settees, 1 double quarterberth
TABLE:
HEAD(S): 1 head with shower, sump pump, and holding tank (25 cu. ft.)
COLD STORAGE: built-in icebox and refrigerator/freezer (2.1 cu. ft. + 1.4 cu. ft. = 3.5 cu. ft. total)
STOVE: 2-burner propane with oven
MAX. HEADROOM: 6 ft. 0 ins.

MACHINERY

ENGINE: diesel
PROPELLER: 2-blade
GENERATOR:

SCANMAR 33

DESIGNER: Rolf Magnusson
BUILDER:

STATISTICS

LOA: 33 ft. 2 ins.
LWL: 27 ft. 3 ins.
BEAM: 10 ft. 10 ins.
DISPLACEMENT
deep keel: 10,138 lbs.
shoal keel:
c/board:
BALLAST
deep keel:
shoal keel:
c/board:
DRAFT
deep keel: 5 ft. 9 ins.
shoal keel:
c/board up:
c/board down:

SAIL AREA:
FRESH WATER:
FUEL CAPACITY:

COSTS

BASE BOAT:
DATE:
EST. ON WATER:
DATE:

RATIOS

SAIL AREA/DISP:
DISP/LENGTH: 223.67
BALLAST RATIO:
FUEL/DISP:
FRESH WATER/DISP:

INTERIOR

BERTHS: 5 berths: 1 double V, 1 single settee, 1 double convertible dinette
TABLE: fixed
HEAD(S): 1 head
COLD STORAGE:
STOVE: 3-burner with oven
MAX. HEADROOM: ft. ins.

MACHINERY

ENGINE: 28 HP Volvo Penta #2003/120B diesel
PROPELLER:
GENERATOR:

DECK

STEERING: wheel
WINCHES:
SAFETY: bow and stern pulpits with double lifelines
ANCHOR:
NAV LIGHTS:

RIG

TYPE: fractional rig sloop
RIGGING:
MAINSHEET: boom-end sheeting

SAILS

SUPPLIED WITH BASE BOAT:

MOODY 34

DESIGNER: Bill Dixon-Angus Primrose, Ltd.
DISTRIBUTOR: A. H. Moody & Son, Ltd. (built in England by Marine Projects, Ltd.)

STATISTICS

LOA: 33 ft. 5 ins.
LWL: 27 ft. 9 ins.
BEAM: 11 ft. 8 ins.
DISPLACEMENT
deep keel: 11,200 lbs.
shoal keel:
c/board:
BALLAST
deep keel: 4,500 lbs.
shoal keel:
c/board:
DRAFT
deep keel: 5 ft. 0 ins.
shoal keel:
c/board up:
c/board down:

SAIL AREA: 514 sq. ft.
FRESH WATER: 40 gals.
FUEL CAPACITY: 35 gals.

COSTS

BASE BOAT:
DATE:
EST. ON WATER:
DATE:

RATIOS

SAIL AREA/DISP: 16.42
DISP/LENGTH: 233
BALLAST RATIO: 40.17
FUEL/DISP: 2.34
FRESH WATER/DISP: 2.85

INTERIOR

BERTHS: 6 berths: 2 single Vs, 2 single settees, 1 double quarterberth
TABLE: dropleaf
HEAD(S): 1 head with shower
COLD STORAGE: built-in icebox
STOVE: 2-burner gas with oven
MAX. HEADROOM:

MACHINERY

ENGINE: 35 HP Thornycroft #T-90 diesel
PROPELLER: 2-blade
GENERATOR:

DECK

STEERING: wheel with emergency tiller
WINCHES: 5 winches: 2 primary (2sp), 2 halyard, 1 reefing
SAFETY: bow and stern pulpits with double lifelines
ANCHOR: plough anchor with anchor roller and well
NAV LIGHTS: running and masthead

RIG

TYPE: masthead sloop
RIGGING: 1x19 SS wire
MAINSHEET: 4-part with boom-end sheeting

SAILS

SUPPLIED WITH BASE BOAT: main (3 reefs), working jib

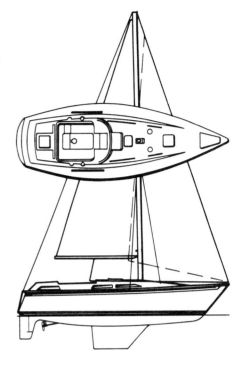

MIRAGE 33

DESIGNER:
BUILDER: Mirage Yachts, Ltd.

STATISTICS

LOA: 33 ft. 6 ins.
LWL: 26 ft. 9 ins.
BEAM: 11 ft. 8 ins.
DISPLACEMENT
deep keel: 9,300 lbs.
shoal keel:
c/board:
BALLAST
deep keel: 3,500 lbs.
shoal keel:
c/board:
DRAFT
deep keel: 5 ft. 0 ins.
shoal keel:
c/board up:
c/board down:

SAIL AREA: 460 sq. ft.
FRESH WATER: 40 gals.
FUEL CAPACITY: 20 gals.

COSTS

BASE BOAT:
DATE:
EST. ON WATER:
DATE:

RATIOS

SAIL AREA/DISP: 16.64
DISP/LENGTH: 216.9
BALLAST RATIO: 37.63
FUEL/DISP: 1.612
FRESH WATER/DISP: 3.440

INTERIOR

BERTHS: 6 berths: 1 double V, 1 single settee, 1 double convertible, 1 single quarterberth
TABLE: dinette
HEAD(S): 1 head with shower
COLD STORAGE: built-in icebox
STOVE:
MAX. HEADROOM: 6 ft. 5 ins.

MACHINERY

ENGINE: 20 HP Volvo diesel
PROPELLER:
GENERATOR:

DECK

STEERING: wheel
WINCHES: 2 primary winches: #40 2sp
SAFETY: bow and stern pulpits with lifelines
ANCHOR: anchor with anchor roller and well
NAV LIGHTS: running

RIG

TYPE: masthead sloop
RIGGING: 1x19 wire
MAINSHEET: mid-boom sheeting

SAILS

SUPPLIED WITH BASE BOAT: main, 105% genoa

SWEDEN YACHTS C34

DESIGNER:
DISTRIBUTOR: Westover Yachts (built in Sweden by Sweden Yachts)

STATISTICS

LOA: 33 ft. 6 ins.
LWL: 28 ft. 8 ins.
BEAM: 11 ft. 5 ins.
DISPLACEMENT
deep keel: 13,300 lbs.
shoal keel:
c/board:
BALLAST
deep keel: 4,650 lbs.
shoal keel:
c/board:
DRAFT
deep keel: 6 ft. 0 ins.
shoal keel:
c/board up:
c/board down:

SAIL AREA:
FRESH WATER: 42 gals.
FUEL CAPACITY: 26 gals.

COSTS

BASE BOAT:
DATE:
EST. ON WATER:
DATE:

RATIOS

SAIL AREA/DISP:
DISP/LENGTH: 256.48
BALLAST RATIO: 34.96
FUEL/DISP: 1.46
FRESH WATER/DISP: 2.53

DECK

STEERING: 36" wheel with emergency tiller
WINCHES: 4 Lewmar winches
SAFETY: bow and stern pulpits with double lifelines
ANCHOR: anchor well
NAV LIGHTS: running

RIG

TYPE: masthead sloop
RIGGING: wire
MAINSHEET: mid-boom sheeting

SAILS

SUPPLIED WITH BASE BOAT:

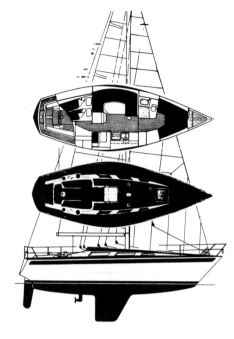

INTERIOR

BERTHS: 6 berths: 1 double V, 1 double convertible dinette, 1 double quarterberth
TABLE: fixed
HEAD(S): 1 head with shower, sump pump, and holding tank
COLD STORAGE: built-in icebox
STOVE: 2-burner LPG with oven
MAX. HEADROOM:

MACHINERY

ENGINE: 25 HP Volvo diesel
PROPELLER: folding
GENERATOR:

C & C 35

DESIGNER: C & C Design Group
BUILDER: C & C Yachts

STATISTICS

LOA: 34 ft. 7.5 ins.
LWL: 28 ft. 0.0 ins.
BEAM: 11 ft. 2.0 ins.
DISPLACEMENT
deep keel: 10,825 lbs.
shoal keel:
c/board:
BALLAST
deep keel: 4,354 lbs.
shoal keel:
c/board:
DRAFT
deep keel: 6 ft. 5 ins.
shoal keel:
c/board up: 4 ft. 2 ins.
c/board down:

SAIL AREA: 571 sq. ft.
FRESH WATER: 30 gals.
FUEL CAPACITY: 20 gals.

COSTS

BASE BOAT:
DATE:
EST. ON WATER: $95,000
DATE: 11/85

RATIOS

SAIL AREA/DISP: 18.67
DISP/LENGTH: 220
BALLAST RATIO: 40.22
FUEL/DISP: 1.38
FRESH WATER/DISP: 2.22

DECK

STEERING: wheel
WINCHES: 5 winches: 2 primary (#25A), 2 halyard (#18A), 1 mainsheet (#18A)
SAFETY: bow and stern pulpits with double lifelines
ANCHOR: anchor locker
NAV LIGHTS: running and masthead

RIG

TYPE: masthead sloop
RIGGING: rod
MAINSHEET: mid-boom sheeting

SAILS

SUPPLIED WITH BASE BOAT:

INTERIOR

BERTHS: 7 berths: 1 double V, 1 single settee, 1 double convertible dinette, 1 double quarterberth
TABLE: dinette
HEAD(S): 1 head with shower, sump pump, and holding tank
COLD STORAGE: built-in icebox
STOVE: 3-burner alcohol with oven
MAX. HEADROOM:

MACHINERY

ENGINE: Yanmar #3 GM with 2.8:1 reduction gear
PROPELLER: 2-blade on 1" shaft
GENERATOR:

BUILDER'S COMMENTS A pedigree of design that works to win—the C & C 35. Swift off the mark and as comfortable as she is fast. The 35 sets standards for others to aspire to, yet with striking style and comfort that conspire to make winning look easy.

MIRAGE 34

DESIGNER: Bruce Kelley
BUILDER: Mirage Manufacturing Co.

STATISTICS

LOA: 33 ft. 8 ins.
LWL: 28 ft. 10 ins.
BEAM: 10 ft. 8 ins.
DISPLACEMENT
deep keel: 4,480 lbs.
shoal keel:
c/board:
BALLAST
deep keel: 2,400 lbs.
shoal keel:
c/board:
DRAFT
deep keel: 6 ft. 0 ins.
shoal keel:
c/board up:
c/board down:

INTERIOR

BERTHS:
TABLE:
HEAD(S):
COLD STORAGE:
STOVE:
MAX. HEADROOM:

MACHINERY

ENGINE:
PROPELLER:
GENERATOR:

SAIL AREA: 510 sq. ft.
FRESH WATER:
FUEL CAPACITY:

COSTS

BASE BOAT: $31,950
DATE: 04/85
EST. ON WATER:
DATE:

RATIOS

SAIL AREA/DISP: 30.04
DISP/LENGTH: 83.38
BALLAST RATIO: 53.57
FUEL/DISP:
FRESH WATER/DISP:

DECK

STEERING: tiller
WINCHES: 8 winches: 6 2sp, 2 1sp
SAFETY: bow and stern pulpits with double lifelines
ANCHOR:
NAV LIGHTS: running

RIG

TYPE: fractional rig sloop
RIGGING: rod
MAINSHEET: boom-end sheeting

SAILS

SUPPLIED WITH BASE BOAT:

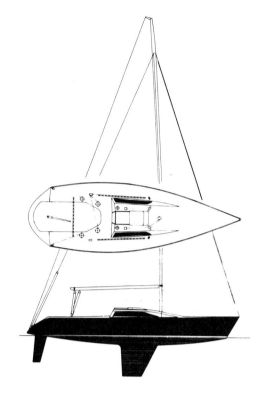

SABRE 34

DESIGNER: Sabre Design Team
BUILDER: Sabre Yachts

STATISTICS

LOA: 33 ft. 8 ins.
LWL: 26 ft. 3 ins.
BEAM: 10 ft. 6 ins.
DISPLACEMENT
deep keel: 11,300 lbs.
shoal keel:
c/board:
BALLAST
deep keel: 4,500 lbs.
shoal keel:
c/board:
DRAFT
deep keel: 5 ft. 10 ins.
shoal keel:
c/board up: 3 ft. 11 ins.
c/board down: 7 ft. 9 ins.

INTERIOR

BERTHS: 6 berths: 1 double V, 1 double convertible, 1 single settee, 1 single quarterberth
TABLE: bulkhead-mounted double-leaf
HEAD(S): 1 head
COLD STORAGE: built-in icebox
STOVE: 2-burner alcohol with oven
MAX. HEADROOM: 6 ft. 3 ins.

MACHINERY

ENGINE: 27 HP Westerbeke diesel with 2:1 reduction gear
PROPELLER: 16"x10"
GENERATOR:

SAIL AREA: 507 sq. ft.
FRESH WATER: 76 gals.
FUEL CAPACITY: 20 gals.

COSTS

BASE BOAT:
DATE:
EST. ON WATER:
DATE:

RATIOS

SAIL AREA/DISP: 16.10
DISP/LENGTH: 278
BALLAST RATIO: 39.82
FUEL/DISP: 1.32
FRESH WATER/DISP: 5.38

DECK

STEERING: 28" wheel
WINCHES: 5 Lewmar winches: 2 primary (#42), 2 halyard (#16), 1 mainsheet (#16)
SAFETY: bow and stern pulpits with double lifelines
ANCHOR: anchor well
NAV LIGHTS: running and masthead

RIG

TYPE: masthead sloop
RIGGING: 1x19 SS wire
MAINSHEET: 4-part with mid-boom sheeting

SAILS

SUPPLIED WITH BASE BOAT:

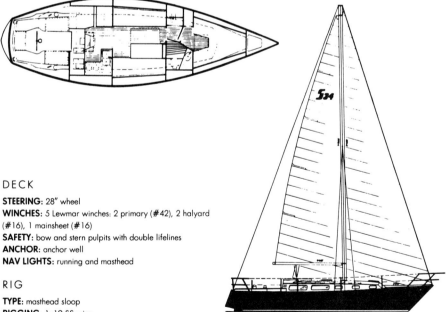

SHOW 34

DESIGNER: Barberis/Franco
DISTRIBUTOR: Satellite Management, Inc. (built in Italy by Barberis Cantieri)

STATISTICS

LOA: 33 ft. 8 ins.
LWL: 27 ft. 2 ins.
BEAM: 11 ft. 2 ins.
DISPLACEMENT
deep keel: 10,780 lbs.
shoal keel:
c/board:
BALLAST
deep keel: 4,400 lbs.
shoal keel:
c/board:
DRAFT
deep keel: 6 ft. 0 ins.
shoal keel:
c/board up:
c/board down:

SAIL AREA: 487 sq. ft.
FRESH WATER: 70 gals.
FUEL CAPACITY: 30 gals.

COSTS

BASE BOAT:
DATE:
EST. ON WATER:
DATE:

RATIOS

SAIL AREA/DISP: 15.96
DISP/LENGTH: 240
BALLAST RATIO: 40.81
FUEL/DISP: 2.09
FRESH WATER/DISP: 5.19

DECK

STEERING: wheel
WINCHES: 4 winches: 2 primary, 2 halyard
SAFETY: bow and stern pulpits with double lifelines
ANCHOR: anchor with anchor chain, rode, and well
NAV LIGHTS: running and masthead

RIG

TYPE: masthead sloop
RIGGING:
MAINSHEET: mid-boom sheeting

SAILS

SUPPLIED WITH BASE BOAT: main, medium genoa, jib, storm jib

INTERIOR

BERTHS: 6 berths: 1 double V, 1 double convertible, 1 single settee, 1 single quarterberth
TABLE: dinette
HEAD(S): 1 head with shower
COLD STORAGE: built-in icebox
STOVE: 2-burner propane with oven
MAX. HEADROOM: 6 ft. 3 ins.

MACHINERY

ENGINE: Yanmar #3 GM
PROPELLER:
GENERATOR:

VINDO 45

DESIGNER:
DISTRIBUTOR: Vindo North America, Inc. (built in Sweden by Vindo Marin, Ab)

STATISTICS

LOA: 33 ft. 8 ins.
LWL: 26 ft. 9 ins.
BEAM: 10 ft. 10 ins.
DISPLACEMENT
deep keel: 13,000 lbs.
shoal keel:
c/board:
BALLAST
deep keel: 5,510 lbs.
shoal keel:
c/board:
DRAFT
deep keel: 5 ft. 2 ins.
shoal keel:
c/board up:
c/board down:

SAIL AREA: 489 sq. ft.
FRESH WATER: 70 gals.
FUEL CAPACITY: 25 gals.

COSTS

BASE BOAT: $84,900
DATE: 04/85
EST. ON WATER:
DATE:

RATIOS

SAIL AREA/DISP: 14.15
DISP/LENGTH: 303.2
BALLAST RATIO: 42.38
FUEL/DISP: 1.44
FRESH WATER/DISP: 4.31

DECK

STEERING: wheel
WINCHES: 4 Lewmar winches: 2 primary (#42 ST), 2 halyard (#2sp)
SAFETY: bow and stern pulpits with double lifelines
ANCHOR: 25 lb. Danforth anchor with anchor well and roller
NAV LIGHTS: running and masthead

RIG

TYPE: masthead sloop
RIGGING:
MAINSHEET: boom-end sheeting

SAILS

SUPPLIED WITH BASE BOAT: main, working jib

INTERIOR

BERTHS: 6 berths: 1 double V, 1 double convertible dinette, 1 double quarterberth (alternate layout available)
TABLE: dropleaf
HEAD(S): 1 head
COLD STORAGE: built-in icebox
STOVE: 2-burner propane with oven
MAX. HEADROOM: 6 ft. 3 ins.

MACHINERY

ENGINE: 28 HP Volvo Penta #2003 diesel
PROPELLER:
GENERATOR:

MASON 33

DESIGNER: Al Mason
BUILDER: Pacific Asian Enterprises, Inc.

STATISTICS

LOA: 33 ft. 9 ins.
LWL: 25 ft. 5 ins.
BEAM: 10 ft. 10 ins.
DISPLACEMENT
deep keel: 14,269 lbs.
shoal keel:
c/board:
BALLAST
deep keel: 5,040 lbs.
shoal keel:
c/board:
DRAFT
deep keel: 5 ft. 0 ins.
shoal keel:
c/board up:
c/board down:

SAIL AREA: 608 sq. ft.
FRESH WATER: 65 gals.
FUEL CAPACITY: 35 gals.

COSTS

BASE BOAT:
DATE:
EST. ON WATER:
DATE:

RATIOS

SAIL AREA/DISP: 16.53
DISP/LENGTH: 387
BALLAST RATIO: 35.32
FUEL/DISP: 1.83
FRESH WATER/DISP: 3.64

INTERIOR

BERTHS: 4 berths: 1 forward double, 2 single settees
TABLE: dropleaf
HEAD(S): 1 head with shower
COLD STORAGE: built-in icebox
STOVE: 2-burner
MAX. HEADROOM:

MACHINERY

ENGINE: Westerbeke #21 diesel
PROPELLER: 3-blade
GENERATOR:

DECK

STEERING: tiller (wheel available)
WINCHES: 5 Lewmar winches: 2 primary (#40 2sp), 2 halyard (#24 2sp), 1 mainsheet (#16 2sp)
SAFETY: bow and stern pulpits with double lifelines
ANCHOR: anchor roller
NAV LIGHTS: running

RIG

TYPE: masthead sloop
RIGGING:
MAINSHEET: mid-boom sheeting

SAILS

SUPPLIED WITH BASE BOAT: main (2 reefs), jib

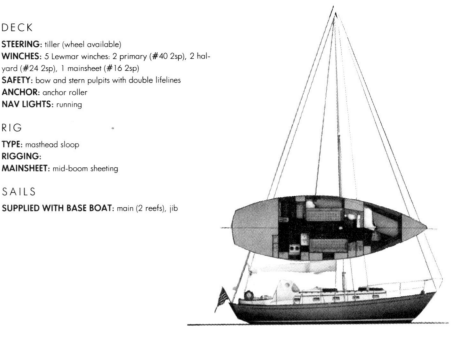

S2 10.3/34'

DESIGNER: Graham & Schlageter
BUILDER: S2 Yachts, Inc.

STATISTICS

LOA: 33 ft. 9 ins.
LWL: 28 ft. 0 ins.
BEAM: 11 ft. 4 ins.
DISPLACEMENT
deep keel: 10,500 lbs.
shoal keel:
c/board:
BALLAST
deep keel: 4,350 lbs.
shoal keel:
c/board:
DRAFT
deep keel: 6 ft. 1 ins.
shoal keel:
c/board up:
c/board down:

SAIL AREA: 553 sq. ft.
FRESH WATER: 40 gals.
FUEL CAPACITY: 22 gals.

COSTS

BASE BOAT:
DATE:
EST. ON WATER:
DATE:

RATIOS

SAIL AREA/DISP: 18.45
DISP/LENGTH: 213
BALLAST RATIO: 41.42
FUEL/DISP: 1.57
FRESH WATER/DISP: 3.04

INTERIOR

BERTHS: 7 berths: 1 double V, 2 single settees, 2 single pilots, 1 single quarterberth
TABLE: fixed centerline dinette
HEAD(S): 1 head with shower
COLD STORAGE: built-in icebox
STOVE: 2-burner alcohol
MAX. HEADROOM: 6 ft. 2 ins.

MACHINERY

ENGINE: Yanmar #2 GM diesel
PROPELLER: Martec folding
GENERATOR:

DECK

STEERING: tiller
WINCHES: 4 Lewmar winches: 2 primary (#43 2sp), 2 halyard (#30)
SAFETY: bow and stern pulpits with double lifelines
ANCHOR: anchor well
NAV LIGHTS: running and masthead

RIG

TYPE: masthead sloop
RIGGING: rod
MAINSHEET: 6-part with mid-boom sheeting

SAILS

SUPPLIED WITH BASE BOAT:

BUILDER'S COMMENTS The S2 10.3M is a swift, powerful 10R racer created with the potential of a serious offshore cruiser. The G&S designed 10.3M is a quality made dual-purpose boat for those who enjoy the pleasures of cruising in the fast lane.

PEARSON 34

DESIGNER: Bill Shaw
BUILDER: Pearson Yachts

STATISTICS

LOA: 33 ft. 9.5 ins.
LWL: 28 ft. 1.5 ins.
BEAM: 11 ft. 2.0 ins.
DISPLACEMENT
deep keel: 11,240 lbs.
shoal keel:
c/board:
BALLAST
deep keel: 4,250 lbs.
shoal keel:
c/board:
DRAFT
deep keel:
shoal keel:
c/board up: 3 ft. 10 ins.
c/board down: 7 ft. 6 ins.

SAIL AREA: 550 sq. ft.
FRESH WATER: 50 gals.
FUEL CAPACITY: 22 gals.

COSTS

BASE BOAT:
DATE:
EST. ON WATER:
DATE:

RATIOS

SAIL AREA/DISP: 17.53
DISP/LENGTH: 225
BALLAST RATIO: 37.81
FUEL/DISP: 1.46
FRESH WATER/DISP: 3.56

DECK

STEERING: wheel
WINCHES: 5 winches: 2 primary (#43 ST), 2 halyard (#16 & #8), 1 mainsheet (#30 ST)
SAFETY: bow and stern pulpits with double lifelines
ANCHOR: anchor well
NAV LIGHTS: running

RIG

TYPE: masthead sloop
RIGGING:
MAINSHEET: mid-boom sheeting

SAILS

SUPPLIED WITH BASE BOAT:

INTERIOR

BERTHS: 6 berths: 1 double V, 2 single settees, 1 double quarterberth
TABLE: bulkhead-mounted
HEAD(S): 1 head
COLD STORAGE: built-in icebox
STOVE: 2-burner propane with oven
MAX. HEADROOM: 6 ft. 4 ins.

MACHINERY

ENGINE: 22 HP Yanmar diesel
PROPELLER: 2-blade
GENERATOR:

SCHOCK 34 (Performance Cruiser)

DESIGNER: Nelson/Marek
BUILDER: W. D. Schock Corp.

STATISTICS

LOA: 33 ft. 10.0 ins.
LWL: 28 ft. 8.4 ins.
BEAM: 11 ft. 7.2 ins.
DISPLACEMENT
deep keel: 9,800 lbs.
shoal keel: 10,100 lbs.
c/board:
BALLAST
deep keel: 3,220 lbs.
shoal keel: 5,550 lbs.
c/board:
DRAFT
deep keel: 6 ft. 6 ins.
shoal keel: 4 ft. 6 ins.
c/board up:
c/board down:

SAIL AREA: 554 sq. ft.
FRESH WATER: 30 gals.
FUEL CAPACITY: 20 gals.

COSTS

BASE BOAT: $59,995
DATE: 07/25/85
EST. ON WATER:
DATE:

RATIOS

SAIL AREA/DISP: 19.36
DISP/LENGTH: 185.26
BALLAST RATIO: 32.8
FUEL/DISP: 1.53
FRESH WATER/DISP: 2.45

DECK

STEERING: 32" wheel with emergency tiller
WINCHES: 4 Lewmar winches: 2 primary (#40 2sp ST), 1 halyard (#16 2sp), 1 mainsheet (#16 2sp ST)
SAFETY: bow and stern pulpits with double lifelines
ANCHOR: anchor roller and well
NAV LIGHTS: running and masthead

RIG

TYPE: masthead sloop
RIGGING: 1x19 SS wire
MAINSHEET: mid-boom sheeting

SAILS

SUPPLIED WITH BASE BOAT:

INTERIOR

BERTHS: 5 berths: 1 double V, 2 single settees, 1 double quarterberth ("Grand Prix" racing version also available)
TABLE: fixed dinette
HEAD(S): 1 head with holding tank
COLD STORAGE: built-in icebox
STOVE: 2-burner
MAX. HEADROOM:

MACHINERY

ENGINE: 18 HP Yanmar #2GM20 diesel
PROPELLER: on 1" shaft
GENERATOR:

NASSAU 34

DESIGNER: George Stadell III
DISTRIBUTOR: Nassau Yacht Corp. (built in Taiwan by President Marine, Ltd.) also distributed by Southern Offshore Yachts, Inc.

STATISTICS

LOA: 33 ft. 11 ins.
LWL: 28 ft. 6 ins.
BEAM: 10 ft. 9 ins.
DISPLACEMENT
deep keel: 14,250 lbs.
shoal keel:
c/board:
BALLAST
deep keel: 5,300 lbs.
shoal keel:
c/board:
DRAFT
deep keel: 5 ft. 0 ins.
shoal keel:
c/board up:
c/board down:

SAIL AREA: 600 sq. ft.
FRESH WATER: 45 gals.
FUEL CAPACITY: 35 gals.

COSTS

BASE BOAT: $61,500
DATE: 06/28/85
EST. ON WATER: $64,700
DATE: 06/28/85

RATIOS

SAIL AREA/DISP: 16.33
DISP/LENGTH: 274.81
BALLAST RATIO: 37.19
FUEL/DISP: 1.84
FRESH WATER/DISP: 2.53

INTERIOR

BERTHS: 5 berths: 1 double V, 2 single settees, 1 single quarterberth
TABLE: bulkhead-mounted
HEAD(S): 1 head with shower and holding tank
COLD STORAGE: built-in icebox
STOVE:
MAX. HEADROOM: 6 ft. 1.25 ins.

MACHINERY

ENGINE: 33 HP Yanmar #3QM30F diesel
PROPELLER: fixed on 1" shaft
GENERATOR:

DECK

STEERING: wheel with emergency tiller
WINCHES: 6 Barlow winches: 2 jib sheet (#20), 3 halyard (#15), 1 mainsheet (#15)
SAFETY: bow and stern pulpits with double lifelines
ANCHOR: anchor well
NAV LIGHTS: running and masthead

RIG

TYPE: masthead sloop with TM of Japan spar
RIGGING: wire
MAINSHEET: 5-part with mid-boom sheeting

SAILS

SUPPLIED WITH BASE BOAT: main, working jib, staysail, topsail

BUILDER'S COMMENTS The fine lines in the forward sections make this perfectly balanced hull unusually fast for a full keel cruising boat. Good hardware and outstanding craftsmanship are obvious in the Nassau 34, resulting in a very attractive value.

J-34

DESIGNER: Rod Johnstone
BUILDER: J Boats, Inc.

STATISTICS

LOA: 34 ft. 0 ins.
LWL: 26 ft. 0 ins.
BEAM: 11 ft. 2 ins.
DISPLACEMENT
deep keel: 8,100 lbs.
shoal keel:
c/board:
BALLAST
deep keel: 3,400 lbs.
shoal keel:
c/board:
DRAFT
deep keel: 6 ft. 2 ins.
shoal keel:
c/board up:
c/board down:

SAIL AREA: 615 sq. ft.
FRESH WATER:
FUEL CAPACITY:

COSTS

BASE BOAT: $56,500
DATE: 04/01/85
EST. ON WATER:
DATE:

RATIOS

SAIL AREA/DISP: 24.40
DISP/LENGTH: 205.40
BALLAST RATIO: 41.97
FUEL/DISP:
FRESH WATER/DISP:

INTERIOR

BERTHS: 2 berths: 2 single settees
TABLE:
HEAD(S):
COLD STORAGE: built-in icebox
STOVE:
MAX. HEADROOM:

MACHINERY

ENGINE: 18 HP Volvo diesel
PROPELLER: Martec folding
GENERATOR:

DECK

STEERING: tiller
WINCHES: 6 Lewmar winches: 2 primary (#46)
SAFETY: bow and stern pulpits
ANCHOR:
NAV LIGHTS: running

RIG

TYPE: masthead sloop
RIGGING: Navtec rod
MAINSHEET: boom-end sheeting

SAILS

SUPPLIED WITH BASE BOAT:

RIVAL 34

DESIGNER: Peter Brett
DISTRIBUTOR: Rival Yachts, Inc. (built in England by Rival Yachts, Ltd.)

STATISTICS

LOA: 34 ft. 0 ins.
LWL: 24 ft. 10 ins.
BEAM: 9 ft. 8 ins.
DISPLACEMENT
deep keel: 10,900 lbs.
shoal keel:
c/board:
BALLAST
deep keel: 4,370 lbs.
shoal keel:
c/board:
DRAFT
deep keel: 5 ft. 10 ins.
shoal keel: 4 ft. 8 ins.
c/board up:
c/board down:

SAIL AREA: 482 sq. ft.
FRESH WATER: 48 gals.
FUEL CAPACITY: 36 gals.

COSTS

BASE BOAT:
DATE:
EST. ON WATER: $75,000
DATE: 07/08/85

RATIOS

SAIL AREA/DISP: 15.69
DISP/LENGTH: 317.49
BALLAST RATIO: 40.09
FUEL/DISP: 2.06
FRESH WATER/DISP:
2.64/small 3.52/large

INTERIOR

BERTHS: 8 berths: 2 single Vs, 1 double convertible dinette, 1 single settee, 3 pipe berths
TABLE: hi-lo
HEAD(S): 1 head
COLD STORAGE: built-in icebox
STOVE: 2-burner LPG with oven
MAX. HEADROOM: 6 ft. 1.25 ins.

MACHINERY

ENGINE: 20 HP Bukh with 3:1 reduction gear
PROPELLER: 2-blade 17"x12"
GENERATOR:

DECK

STEERING: tiller
WINCHES: 4 Lewmar winches: 2 primary (#40C), 2 halyard (#16C 2sp & #8C)
SAFETY: bow and stern pulpits with double lifelines
ANCHOR: 33 lb. Bruce & 25 lb. CQR anchors with 30 fthm. chain, windlass, and anchor well
NAV LIGHTS:

RIG

TYPE: masthead sloop with Kemp spar
RIGGING: 1x19 wire
MAINSHEET: boom-end sheeting

SAILS

SUPPLIED WITH BASE BOAT: Hood main (3 reefs), working jib

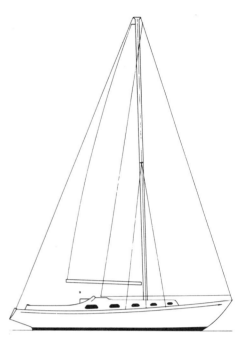

BUILDER'S COMMENTS All complete Rivals are built as standard to Lloyd's Register + 100 A-1 classification and are sold fully equipped to sail. The Lloyd's requirements apply to all elements of construction including design, materials, construction conditions, and equipment. A Lloyd's surveyor oversees each yacht's construction to ensure these standards are maintained.

SEIDELMANN 34

DESIGNER: Seidelmann
BUILDER: Seidelmann Yachts

STATISTICS

LOA: 34 ft. 0 ins.
LWL: 26 ft. 6 ins.
BEAM: 11 ft. 10 ins.
DISPLACEMENT
deep keel: 11,000 lbs.
shoal keel:
c/board:
BALLAST
deep keel: 5,000 lbs.
shoal keel:
c/board:
DRAFT
deep keel: 5 ft. 5 ins.
shoal keel: 3 ft. 11 ins.
c/board up:
c/board down:

SAIL AREA: 516 sq. ft.
FRESH WATER: 100 gals.
FUEL CAPACITY: 18 gals.

COSTS

BASE BOAT:
DATE:
EST. ON WATER:
DATE:

RATIOS

SAIL AREA/DISP: 16.69
DISP/LENGTH: 263
BALLAST RATIO: 45.45
FUEL/DISP: 1.22
FRESH WATER/DISP: 7.27

INTERIOR

BERTHS: 5 berths: 1 double V, 1 double convertible settee, 1 single quarterberth
TABLE: bulkhead-mounted
HEAD(S): 1 head with shower
COLD STORAGE: built-in icebox (9 cu. ft.)
STOVE: 2-burner alcohol with oven
MAX. HEADROOM: 6 ft. 5 ins.

MACHINERY

ENGINE: diesel
PROPELLER: 2 or 3 blade
GENERATOR:

DECK

STEERING: 30" wheel
WINCHES: 4 winches: 2 sheet (#40 2sp), 2 halyard
SAFETY: bow and stern pulpits with double lifelines
ANCHOR: anchor well
NAV LIGHTS:

RIG

TYPE: masthead sloop
RIGGING: stainless steel
MAINSHEET: mid-boom sheeting

SAILS

SUPPLIED WITH BASE BOAT: main (1 reef), working jib

CREALOCK 34

DESIGNER: William Crealock
BUILDER: Pacific Seacraft Corp.

STATISTICS

LOA: 34 ft. 1.0 ins.
LWL: 26 ft. 2.5 ins.
BEAM: 10 ft. 0.0 ins.
DISPLACEMENT
deep keel: 12,000 lbs.
shoal keel:
c/board:
BALLAST
deep keel: 4,700 lbs.
shoal keel:
c/board:
DRAFT
deep keel: 4 ft. 11 ins.
shoal keel: 4 ft. 1 ins.
c/board up:
c/board down:

SAIL AREA: 534 sq. ft.
FRESH WATER: 80 gals.
FUEL CAPACITY: 35 gals.

COSTS

BASE BOAT: $75,900
DATE: 06/85
EST. ON WATER: $85,000
DATE: 06/85

RATIOS

SAIL AREA/DISP: 16.30
DISP/LENGTH: 297
BALLAST RATIO: 39.16
FUEL/DISP: 2.18
FRESH WATER/DISP: 5.33

INTERIOR

BERTHS: 6 berths: 1 double V, 1 single settee, 1 double convertible dinette, 1 single quarterberth
TABLE: dropleaf, bulkhead-mounted, or dinette
HEAD(S): 1 head
COLD STORAGE: built-in icebox
STOVE: 2-burner kerosene with oven
MAX. HEADROOM: 6 ft. 3 ins.

MACHINERY

ENGINE: 29 HP Westerbeke diesel
PROPELLER: 2-blade
GENERATOR:

DECK

STEERING: tiller
WINCHES: 5 Lewmar winches: 2 primary (#43), 2 halyard (#8), 1 mainsheet (#8)
SAFETY: bow and stern pulpits with double lifelines
ANCHOR: anchor rollers and double locker
NAV LIGHTS: running

RIG

TYPE: masthead sloop
RIGGING: 1x19 SS wire
MAINSHEET: mid-boom sheeting

SAILS

SUPPLIED WITH BASE BOAT:

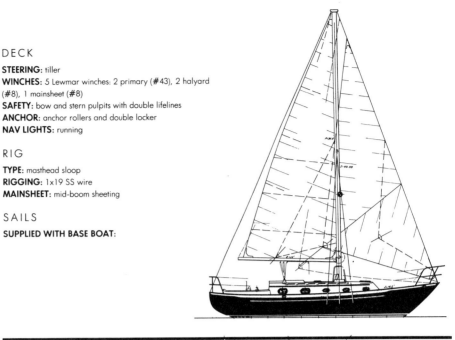

BUILDER'S COMMENTS From the graceful overhang of her bow to her sophisticated canoe stern, the clean, perfectly proportioned lines of the Crealock 34 reveal a boat that will take you anywhere you want to go. The 34 is seakindly, easily handled by a small crew or cruising couple, and fast. Her highly efficient cruising fin keel and skeg rudder are combined with a slippery underbody that is at the leading edge of current technology. Construction is of the very highest caliber with bronze hardware and fine teak joinery used throughout.

ISLAND PACKET 31

DESIGNER: Robert K. Johnson
BUILDER: Island Packet Yachts

STATISTICS

LOA: 34 ft. 4 ins.
LWL: 27 ft. 9 ins.
BEAM: 11 ft. 6 ins.
DISPLACEMENT
deep keel: 11,000 lbs.
shoal keel:
c/board:
BALLAST
deep keel: 4,500 lbs.
shoal keel:
c/board:
DRAFT
deep keel: 4 ft. 0 ins.
shoal keel:
c/board up: 3 ft. 0 ins.
c/board down: 7 ft. 0 ins.

SAIL AREA: 531 sq. ft.
FRESH WATER: 60 gals.
FUEL CAPACITY: 25 gals.

COSTS

BASE BOAT: $61,950
DATE: 06/85
EST. ON WATER: $65,000
DATE: 06/85

RATIOS

SAIL AREA/DISP: 17.17
DISP/LENGTH: 229
BALLAST RATIO: 40.90
FUEL/DISP: 1.70
FRESH WATER/DISP: 4.36

INTERIOR

BERTHS: 7 berths: 1 double V, 1 double convertible settee, 1 single settee, 1 double quarterberth
TABLE: bulkhead-mounted dropleaf
HEAD(S): 1 head with shower
COLD STORAGE: built-in icebox (11 cu. ft.)
STOVE: 2-burner alcohol with oven
MAX. HEADROOM: 6 ft. 3 ins.

MACHINERY

ENGINE: 27 HP Yanmar #3GM30F diesel
PROPELLER: 2-blade fixed 15"x13" on 1" shaft
GENERATOR:

DECK

STEERING: Edson wheel
WINCHES: 5 Lewmar winches: 2 primary (#40C 2sp), 2 halyard (#7C), 1 mainsheet (#7C)
SAFETY: bow and stern pulpits with double lifelines
ANCHOR: anchor roller and bowsprit
NAV LIGHTS: running and masthead

RIG

TYPE: masthead sloop with anodized spar (cutter option)
RIGGING: 1x19 SS wire
MAINSHEET: mid-boom sheeting

SAILS

SUPPLIED WITH BASE BOAT: main (1 reef), 110% jib

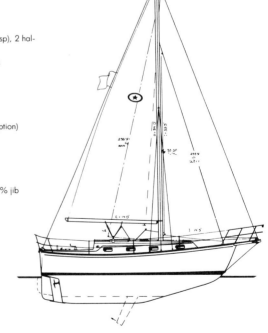

BUILDER'S COMMENTS Modern full keel design with handsome traditional styling, easily managed rig, and an unusually spacious and livable interior. Outstanding performance with moderate or shoal draft. Exceptional quality with extensive standard equipment. Distinctly in a class by itself.

HUNTER 34

DESIGNER: Hunter Design Group
BUILDER: Hunter Marine

STATISTICS

LOA: 34 ft. 5 ins.
LWL: 28 ft. 3 ins.
BEAM: 11 ft. 7 ins.
DISPLACEMENT
deep keel: 11,820 lbs.
shoal keel: 11,920 lbs.
c/board:
BALLAST
deep keel: 5,000 lbs.
shoal keel: 5,200 lbs.
c/board:
DRAFT
deep keel: 5 ft. 6 ins.
shoal keel: 4 ft. 3 ins.
c/board up:
c/board down:

SAIL AREA: 557 sq. ft.
FRESH WATER: 65 gals.
FUEL CAPACITY: 25 gals.

COSTS

BASE BOAT:
DATE:
EST. ON WATER: $55,000
DATE: 11/85

RATIOS

SAIL AREA/DISP: 18.12
DISP/LENGTH: 215
BALLAST RATIO: 41.65
FUEL/DISP: 1.72
FRESH WATER/DISP: 4.77

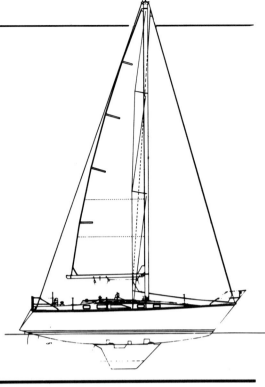

DECK

STEERING: wheel
WINCHES: 4 winches: 2 primary (2sp ST), 2 halyard
SAFETY: bow and stern pulpits with double lifelines
ANCHOR: anchor with anchor roller, well, and line
NAV LIGHTS: running and masthead

RIG

TYPE: masthead sloop
RIGGING:
MAINSHEET: mid-boom sheeting

SAILS

SUPPLIED WITH BASE BOAT: main, 110% genoa

INTERIOR

BERTHS: 7 berths: 1 double V, 1 double convertible dinette, 1 single settee, 1 double quarterberth
TABLE: dinette
HEAD(S): 1 head with shower
COLD STORAGE: built-in icebox
STOVE: 2-burner with oven
MAX. HEADROOM: 6 ft. 3 ins.

MACHINERY

ENGINE: diesel
PROPELLER: 2-blade
GENERATOR:

BUILDER'S COMMENTS Hunter's "Commitment to Better Engineering" offers the 34' with a unidirectional fiberglass frame to carry all major rig and keel loads. The cockpit area features contoured seats, pedestal steering, and a helmsman's seat. Below, the cabin area comes complete with full galley, chart table, and the port quarter sports an enclosed private stateroom, complete with double berth. The Hunter 34 comes complete with Cruise Pac (TM), everything you need to sail.

TANZER 10.5

DESIGNER: Dick Carter
BUILDER: Tanzer Industries, Inc.

STATISTICS

LOA: 34 ft. 5 ins.
LWL: 27 ft. 6 ins.
BEAM: 11 ft. 6 ins.
DISPLACEMENT
deep keel: 13,000 lbs.
shoal keel:
c/board:
BALLAST
deep keel: 5,500 lbs.
shoal keel:
c/board:
DRAFT
deep keel: 5 ft. 11 ins.
shoal keel: 4 ft. 6 ins.
lifting keel up: 2 ft. 1 ins.
lifting keel dn: 6 ft. 6 ins.

SAIL AREA: 592 sq. ft.
FRESH WATER: 70 gals.
FUEL CAPACITY: 35 gals.

COSTS

BASE BOAT: fin $74,620
DATE: 02/01/85
shoal $74,620
DATE: 02/01/85
lifting $79,000
DATE: 02/01/85

RATIOS

SAIL AREA/DISP: 17.13
DISP/LENGTH: 279
BALLAST RATIO: 42.30
FUEL/DISP: 2.01
FRESH WATER/DISP: 4.31

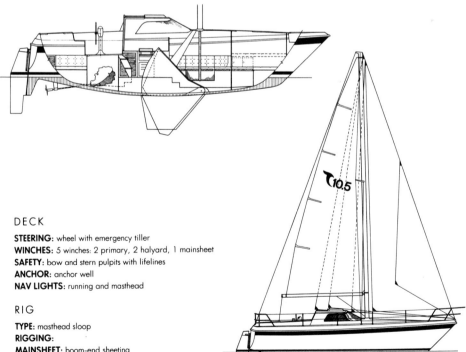

INTERIOR

BERTHS: 8 berths: 4 single forward upper and lowers, 2 single settees, 1 double quarterberth
TABLE: dinette
HEAD(S): 1 head with shower
COLD STORAGE: built-in icebox (9 cu. ft.)
STOVE: 3-burner propane with oven
MAX. HEADROOM:

MACHINERY

ENGINE: 30 HP diesel
PROPELLER:
GENERATOR:

DECK

STEERING: wheel with emergency tiller
WINCHES: 5 winches: 2 primary, 2 halyard, 1 mainsheet
SAFETY: bow and stern pulpits with lifelines
ANCHOR: anchor well
NAV LIGHTS: running and masthead

RIG

TYPE: masthead sloop
RIGGING:
MAINSHEET: boom-end sheeting

SAILS

SUPPLIED WITH BASE BOAT: main, 110% working jib

TARTAN 34

DESIGNER: Sparkman & Stephens
BUILDER: Tartan Marine Company

STATISTICS

LOA: 34 ft. 5.0 ins.
LWL: 28 ft. 10.0 ins.
BEAM: 10 ft. 11.5 ins.
DISPLACEMENT
deep keel: 11,000 lbs.
Scheel keel: 11,000 lbs.
c/board:
BALLAST
deep keel: 4,400 lbs.
scheel keel: 4,400 lbs.
c/board:
DRAFT
deep keel: 6 ft. 3.0 ins.
shoal keel: 4 ft. 5.5 ins.
c/board up:
c/board down:

SAIL AREA: 536 sq. ft.
FRESH WATER: 57 gals.
FUEL CAPACITY: 23 gals.

COSTS

BASE BOAT: $68,000
DATE: 07/01/85
EST. ON WATER: $75,000
DATE: 07/01/85

RATIOS

SAIL AREA/DISP: 17.34
DISP/LENGTH: 204.72
BALLAST RATIO: 40.0
FUEL/DISP: 1.57
FRESH WATER/DISP: 4.15

INTERIOR

BERTHS: 7 berths: 1 double V, 1 single settee, 1 double settee, 1 double quarterberth
TABLE: bulkhead-mounted
HEAD(S): 1 head with shower, sump pump, and holding tank
COLD STORAGE: built-in icebox
STOVE: 3-burner alcohol with oven
MAX. HEADROOM: 6 ft. 4 ins.

MACHINERY

ENGINE: 27 HP Yanmar #3 GM diesel with 2.6:1 reduction gear
PROPELLER: fixed 16" diameter on 1" shaft
GENERATOR:

DECK

STEERING: wheel with emergency tiller
WINCHES: 4 Lewmar winches
SAFETY: bow and stern pulpits with double lifelines
ANCHOR:
NAV LIGHTS: running and masthead

RIG

TYPE: masthead sloop with Kenyon spar
RIGGING: wire
MAINSHEET: boom-end sheeting

SAILS

SUPPLIED WITH BASE BOAT:

CATALINA 34

DESIGNER:
BUILDER: Catalina Yachts

STATISTICS

LOA: 34 ft. 6 ins.
LWL: 29 ft. 10 ins.
BEAM: 11 ft. 9 ins.
DISPLACEMENT
deep keel: 11,950 lbs.
shoal keel: 12,600 lbs.
c/board:
BALLAST
deep keel: 5,000 lbs.
shoal keel: 5,650 lbs.
c/board:
DRAFT
deep keel: 5 ft. 7 ins.
shoal keel: 4 ft. 8 ins.
c/board up:
c/board down:

SAIL AREA: 523 sq. ft.
FRESH WATER: 70 gals.
FUEL CAPACITY: 30 gals.

COSTS

BASE BOAT: $46,985
DATE: 10/01/84
EST. ON WATER:
DATE:

RATIOS

	deep	shoal
SAIL AREA/DISP:	16.07	15.45
DISP/LENGTH:	200.78	211.70
BALLAST RATIO:	41.84	44.84
FUEL/DISP:	1.88	1.79
FRESH WATER/DISP:	4.69	4.44

INTERIOR

BERTHS: 6 berths
TABLE:
HEAD(S): 1 head with shower and holding tank
COLD STORAGE: built-in icebox
STOVE: 2-burner with oven
MAX. HEADROOM: 6 ft. 6 ins.

MACHINERY

ENGINE: 21 HP Universal #25 diesel with 2:1 reduction gear
PROPELLER:
GENERATOR:

DECK

STEERING: 32" wheel
WINCHES: 4 winches
SAFETY: bow and stern pulpits with double lifelines
ANCHOR: anchor well
NAV LIGHTS: running

RIG

TYPE: masthead sloop
RIGGING:
MAINSHEET: mid-boom sheeting

SAILS

SUPPLIED WITH BASE BOAT: main, 130% jib

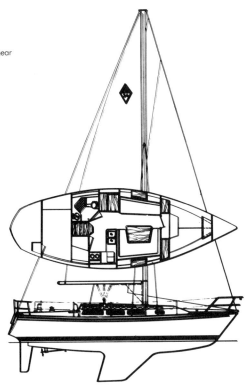

JEANNEAU SUNRISE 34

DESIGNER: Jacques Fauroux
DISTRIBUTOR: Nautique International, Inc. (built in France by Jeanneau, S. A.)

STATISTICS

LOA: 34 ft. 7 ins.
LWL: 28 ft. 0 ins.
BEAM: 11 ft. 6 ins.
DISPLACEMENT
deep keel: 10,362 lbs.
shoal keel:
c/board:
BALLAST
deep keel: 3,395 lbs.
shoal keel:
c/board:
DRAFT
deep keel: 5 ft. 11 ins.
shoal keel:
c/board up: 5 ft. 3 ins.
c/board down: 7 ft. 0 ins.

SAIL AREA: 700 sq. ft.
FRESH WATER: 53 gals.
FUEL CAPACITY: 0 gals.

COSTS

BASE BOAT:
DATE:
EST. ON WATER:
DATE:

RATIOS

SAIL AREA/DISP: 23.56
DISP/LENGTH: 210
BALLAST RATIO: 32.76
FUEL/DISP: 0.0
FRESH WATER/DISP: 4.091

INTERIOR

BERTHS: 6 berths: 1 double V, 1 single settee, 1 double quarterberth
TABLE: dropleaf
HEAD(S): 1 head with shower
COLD STORAGE: built-in icebox (26 gals.)
STOVE: 2-burner gas with oven
MAX. HEADROOM:

MACHINERY

ENGINE:
PROPELLER:
GENERATOR:

DECK

STEERING: tiller
WINCHES: 4 winches: 2 primary, 1 halyard, 1 reefing
SAFETY: bow and stern pulpits with double lifelines
ANCHOR: anchor roller
NAV LIGHTS: running

RIG

TYPE: masthead sloop
RIGGING:
MAINSHEET: 5-part with mid-boom sheeting

SAILS

SUPPLIED WITH BASE BOAT: main, intermediate genoa, storm jib

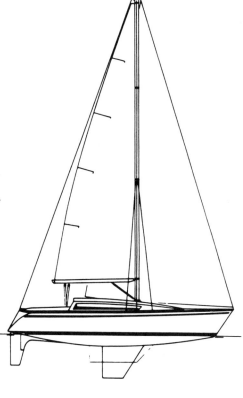

IRWIN CITATION 34

DESIGNER: Ted Irwin
BUILDER: Irwin Yacht & Marine Corp.

STATISTICS

LOA: 34 ft. 7.5 ins.
LWL: 27 ft. 4.0 ins.
BEAM: 11 ft. 3.0 ins.
DISPLACEMENT
deep keel:
shoal keel: 11,500 lbs.
c/board:
BALLAST
deep keel:
shoal keel: 4,500 lbs.
c/board:
DRAFT
deep keel: 5 ft. 4 ins.
shoal keel: 4 ft. 0 ins.
c/board up: 4 ft. 0 ins.
c/board down: 8 ft. 1 ins.

SAIL AREA: 573 sq. ft.
FRESH WATER: 80 gals.
FUEL CAPACITY: 31 gals.

COSTS

BASE BOAT: $50,795
DATE: 06/01/85
EST. ON WATER:
DATE:

RATIOS

SAIL AREA/DISP: 17.99
DISP/LENGTH: 251.5
BALLAST RATIO: 39.13
FUEL/DISP: 2.02
FRESH WATER/DISP: 5.56

INTERIOR

BERTHS: 6 berths: 1 double V, 1 single settee, 1 double convertible dinette, 1 single quarterberth
TABLE: hi-lo
HEAD(S): 1 head with shower and holding tank (15 gals.)
COLD STORAGE: built-in icebox (4.2 cu. ft.)
STOVE: 3-burner propane with oven
MAX. HEADROOM:

MACHINERY

ENGINE: 15 HP diesel with 2.62:1 reduction gear
PROPELLER: 2-blade
GENERATOR:

DECK

STEERING: 28" wheel with emergency tiller
WINCHES: 3 winches: 2 primary, 1 halyard
SAFETY: bow and stern pulpits with double lifelines
ANCHOR: anchor well
NAV LIGHTS: running and masthead

RIG

TYPE: masthead sloop
RIGGING: wire (3/16" double lowers, 1/4" uppers)
MAINSHEET: 6-part with mid-boom sheeting

SAILS

SUPPLIED WITH BASE BOAT: main, working jib

ALLMAND 35

DESIGNER: Walter Scott & J. R. Allmand
BUILDER: Allmand Boats, Inc.

STATISTICS

LOA: 34 ft. 9 ins.
LWL: 29 ft. 7 ins.
BEAM: 11 ft. 8 ins.
DISPLACEMENT
deep keel: 15,100 lbs.
shoal keel:
c/board:
BALLAST
deep keel: 4,300 lbs.
shoal keel:
c/board:
DRAFT
deep keel: 5 ft. 2 ins.
shoal keel:
c/board up:
c/board down:

INTERIOR

BERTHS: 6 berths: 1 double V, 2 single settees, 1 double quarterberth
TABLE: dropleaf
HEAD(S): 1 head with shower and holding tank
COLD STORAGE: built-in icebox (8 cu. ft.)
STOVE: 3-burner alcohol with oven
MAX. HEADROOM:

MACHINERY

ENGINE: Universal #30 diesel
PROPELLER: fixed on 1" shaft
GENERATOR:

SAIL AREA: 550 sq. ft.
FRESH WATER: 95 gals.
FUEL CAPACITY: 40 gals.

COSTS

BASE BOAT:
DATE:
EST. ON WATER:
DATE:

RATIOS

SAIL AREA/DISP: 14.4
DISP/LENGTH: 260.5
BALLAST RATIO: 38.5
FUEL/DISP: 2.0
FRESH WATER/DISP: 5.0

DECK

STEERING: wheel
WINCHES: 5 Lewmar winches 2 #40 2sp, 3 #8
SAFETY: bow and stern pulpits with double lifelines
ANCHOR: anchor roller
NAV LIGHTS: running and masthead

RIG

TYPE: masthead sloop
RIGGING: 1x19 wire
MAINSHEET:

SAILS

SUPPLIED WITH BASE BOAT: main, 100% working jib

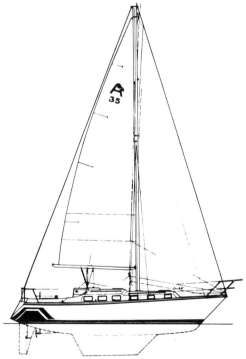

BABA 35

DESIGNER: Robert H. Perry
BUILDER: Ta-Shing Yacht Building Co., Ltd.

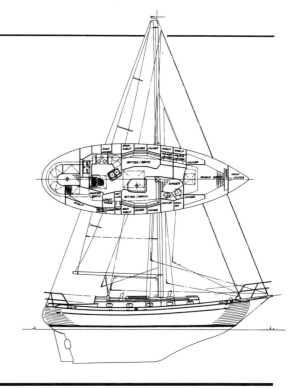

STATISTICS

LOA: 34 ft. 10.5 ins.
LWL: 29 ft. 7.5 ins.
BEAM: 11 ft. 2.0 ins.
DISPLACEMENT
deep keel: 21,200 lbs.
shoal keel:
c/board:
BALLAST
deep keel: 9,400 lbs.
shoal keel:
c/board:
DRAFT
deep keel: 5 ft. 6 ins.
shoal keel:
c/board up:
c/board down:

SAIL AREA: 674 sq. ft.
FRESH WATER:
FUEL CAPACITY:

COSTS

BASE BOAT:
DATE:
EST. ON WATER:
DATE:

RATIOS

SAIL AREA/DISP: 14.13
DISP/LENGTH: 364
BALLAST RATIO: 44.34
FUEL/DISP:
FRESH WATER/DISP:

DECK

STEERING: wheel
WINCHES:
SAFETY:
ANCHOR:
NAV LIGHTS:

RIG

TYPE:
RIGGING:
MAINSHEET: mid-boom sheeting

SAILS

SUPPLIED WITH BASE BOAT:

INTERIOR

BERTHS: 5 berths: 1 double V, 2 single settees, 1 single quarterberth
TABLE: fixed
HEAD(S): 1 head with shower
COLD STORAGE: built-in icebox
STOVE: 2-burner with oven
MAX. HEADROOM:

MACHINERY

ENGINE:
PROPELLER:
GENERATOR:

BUILDER'S COMMENTS The BABA 35 has just enough charm and beauty of the old ways, blended with the practicality and efficiency of new technology. Topside she is a classic passage maker, while her computer-updated canoe body is easily driven with optimal distribution of volume for excellent performance. The cruising interior of the BABA 35 displays a thoughtfulness of design and a degree of Ta-Shing craftsmanship uncommon in most contemporary yachts.

O'DAY 35

DESIGNER: C. Raymond Hunt Associates
BUILDER: Lear Siegler Marine

STATISTICS

LOA: 34 ft. 11.5 ins.
LWL: 28 ft. 9.0 ins.
BEAM: 11 ft. 3.0 ins.
DISPLACEMENT
deep keel: 11,500 lbs.
shoal keel:
c/board:
BALLAST
deep keel: 4,600 lbs.
shoal keel:
c/board:
DRAFT
deep keel: 5 ft. 7 ins.
shoal keel: 4 ft. 5 ins.
c/board up:
c/board down:

SAIL AREA: 524 sq. ft.
FRESH WATER: 50 gals.
FUEL CAPACITY: 30 gals.

COSTS

BASE BOAT: $84,900
DATE: 11/85
EST. ON WATER:
DATE:

RATIOS

SAIL AREA/DISP: 16.45
DISP/LENGTH: 216
BALLAST RATIO: 40.00
FUEL/DISP: 1.95
FRESH WATER/DISP: 3.47

DECK

STEERING: wheel with emergency tiller
WINCHES: 5 Barlow winches: 2 primary (#25 ST), 2 halyard (#16C LT & #19), 1 mainsheet (#24C ST)
SAFETY: bow and stern pulpits with lifelines
ANCHOR: anchor well and roller
NAV LIGHTS: running and masthead

RIG

TYPE: masthead sloop
RIGGING: 1x19 wire
MAINSHEET: mid-boom sheeting

SAILS

SUPPLIED WITH BASE BOAT: main (2 reefs), working jib

INTERIOR

BERTHS: 6 berths: 1 double V, 1 single settee, 1 double convertible settee, 1 single quarterberth
TABLE: centerline dropleaf
HEAD(S): 1 head
COLD STORAGE: 2 built-in iceboxes (8 cu. ft. total)
STOVE: 2-burner propane with oven
MAX. HEADROOM: 6 ft. 2 ins.

MACHINERY

ENGINE: 21 HP Universal diesel with 2:1 reduction gear
PROPELLER: 2-blade 16"x9" on 1" shaft
GENERATOR:

BUILDER'S COMMENTS An extremely well formed and proportioned vessel in the popular mid 30' range, the O'Day 35 offers a transom boarding platform to make boarding easier. Her easily driven hull and large but easy to handle sloop rig will give spritely performance.

CAL 35

DESIGNER: Bill Lapworth
BUILDER: Lear Siegler Marine

STATISTICS

LOA: 35 ft. 0 ins.
LWL: 28 ft. 9 ins.
BEAM: 10 ft. 11 ins.
DISPLACEMENT
deep keel: 13,000 lbs.
shoal keel:
c/board:
BALLAST
deep keel: 5,200 lbs.
shoal keel:
c/board:
DRAFT
deep keel: 6 ft. 0 ins.
shoal keel: 5 ft. 0 ins.
c/board up:
c/board down:

SAIL AREA: 595 sq. ft.
FRESH WATER: 90 gals.
FUEL CAPACITY: 33 gals.

COSTS

BASE BOAT:
DATE:
EST. ON WATER:
DATE:

RATIOS

SAIL AREA/DISP: 17.21
DISP/LENGTH: 244
BALLAST RATIO: 40.00
FUEL/DISP: 1.90
FRESH WATER/DISP: 5.53

DECK

STEERING: 28" wheel with emergency tiller
WINCHES: 6 Barient winches: 2 primary (#24), 2 halyard (#18 & #10P), 1 mainsheet (#18), 1 reefing (#10P)
SAFETY: bow and stern pulpits with double lifelines
ANCHOR: anchor well and double anchor rollers
NAV LIGHTS: running

RIG

TYPE: masthead sloop
RIGGING: 1x19 wire
MAINSHEET: 5-part with mid-boom sheeting

SAILS

SUPPLIED WITH BASE BOAT:

INTERIOR

BERTHS: 6 berths: 1 double V, 1 double convertible settee, 1 single settee, 1 single quarterberth
TABLE: centerline dropleaf
HEAD(S): 1 head with shower and sump pump
COLD STORAGE: built-in icebox (5 cu. ft.)
STOVE: 3-burner propane with oven
MAX. HEADROOM: 6 ft. 3 ins.

MACHINERY

ENGINE: 32 HP Universal diesel
PROPELLER: 2-blade on 1" shaft
GENERATOR:

BUILDER'S COMMENTS A comfortable cruising sloop in the Cal tradition. This Lapworth design gives tremendous living room with good performance. The abundant stowage and separate stall shower make extended cruising a joy.

EXPRESS 35

DESIGNER: Steve Killing
BUILDER: Express Yachting

STATISTICS

LOA: 35 ft. 0 ins.
LWL: 29 ft. 0 ins.
BEAM: 11 ft. 6 ins.
DISPLACEMENT
deep keel: 10,600 lbs.
shoal keel:
c/board:
BALLAST
deep keel: 5,300 lbs.
shoal keel:
c/board:
DRAFT
deep keel: 6 ft. 6 ins.
shoal keel: 5 ft. 0 ins.
c/board up:
c/board down:

SAIL AREA: 643 sq. ft.
FRESH WATER: 33 gals.
FUEL CAPACITY: 30 gals.

COSTS

BASE BOAT: $85,400
DATE: 07/01/85
EST. ON WATER:
DATE:

RATIOS

SAIL AREA/DISP: 21.32
DISP/LENGTH: 194
BALLAST RATIO: 50.00
FUEL/DISP: 2.12
FRESH WATER/DISP: 2.49

DECK

STEERING: tiller
WINCHES: 4 Lewmar winches: 2 primary (#52A ST), 1 genoa/spinnaker halyard ((#45A ST), 1 main halyard/reefing (#43A ST)
SAFETY: bow and stern pulpits with double lifelines
ANCHOR:
NAV LIGHTS: running and masthead

RIG

TYPE: masthead sloop
RIGGING: rod
MAINSHEET: 3-part (6:1 ratchet) with boom-end sheeting

SAILS

SUPPLIED WITH BASE BOAT:

INTERIOR

BERTHS: 7 berths: 1 double V, 2 single settees, 1 single pilot, 1 double quarterberth
TABLE: center-mounted dropleaf
HEAD(S): 1 head
COLD STORAGE: built-in icebox
STOVE: 2-burner alcohol
MAX. HEADROOM:

MACHINERY

ENGINE: 23 HP Yanmar diesel
PROPELLER: 2-blade
GENERATOR:

SCHOCK 35

DESIGNER:
BUILDER: W. D. Schock Corp.

STATISTICS

LOA: 35 ft. 0.0 ins.
LWL: 29 ft. 6.0 ins.
BEAM: 11 ft. 10.8 ins.
DISPLACEMENT
deep keel: 10,000 lbs.
shoal keel:
c/board:
BALLAST
deep keel: 4,500 lbs.
shoal keel:
c/board:
DRAFT
deep keel: 4 ft. 10.8 ins.
shoal keel:
c/board up:
c/board down:

SAIL AREA: 639 sq. ft.
FRESH WATER: 20 gals.
FUEL CAPACITY: 20 gals.

COSTS

BASE BOAT: $49,500
DATE: 06/01/85
EST. ON WATER:
DATE:

RATIOS

SAIL AREA/DISP: 22.03
DISP/LENGTH: 173.89
BALLAST RATIO: 45.00
FUEL/DISP: 1.5
FRESH WATER/DISP: 1.6

DECK

STEERING: tiller
WINCHES: 6 Lewmar winches: 2 primary (#46), 2 halyard (#30), 2 spinnaker sheet/running backstay (#40)
SAFETY: bow and stern pulpits with double lifelines
ANCHOR:
NAV LIGHTS: running

RIG

TYPE: masthead sloop
RIGGING: rod
MAINSHEET: boom-end sheeting

SAILS

SUPPLIED WITH BASE BOAT:

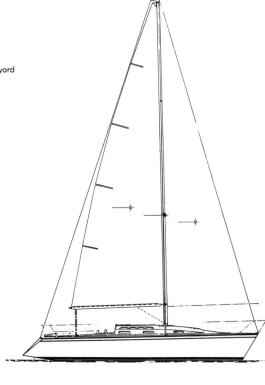

INTERIOR

BERTHS: 6 berths: 2 single settees, 2 single pilots, 2 single quarterberths
TABLE:
HEAD(S):
COLD STORAGE: built-in icebox
STOVE:
MAX. HEADROOM: 6 ft. 2 ins.

MACHINERY

ENGINE: 18 HP Yanmar 26M
PROPELLER: folding on 1" shaft
GENERATOR:

NIAGARA 35 ENCORE

DESIGNER: Mark Ellis Design, Ltd.
BUILDER: Hinterhoeller Yachts, Ltd.

STATISTICS

LOA: 35 ft. 1 ins.
LWL: 26 ft. 8 ins.
BEAM: 11 ft. 5 ins.
DISPLACEMENT
deep keel: 15,000 lbs.
shoal keel:
c/board:
BALLAST
deep keel:
shoal keel:
c/board:
DRAFT
deep keel: 5 ft. 2 ins.
shoal keel:
c/board up:
c/board down:

SAIL AREA: 598 sq. ft.
FRESH WATER: 80 gals.
FUEL CAPACITY: 28 gals.

COSTS

BASE BOAT: $79,600
DATE: 08/01/85
EST. ON WATER: $90,000
DATE: 08/01/85

RATIOS

SAIL AREA/DISP: 15.73
DISP/LENGTH: 353.4
BALLAST RATIO:
FUEL/DISP: 1.4
FRESH WATER/DISP: 4.27

DECK

STEERING: 28" wheel with emergency tiller
WINCHES: 5 Barient winches: 2 sheet (#25), 2 halyard (#21 & #18), 1 reefing (#10P)
SAFETY: bow and stern pulpits with double lifelines
ANCHOR: bowsprit with anchor rollers
NAV LIGHTS: running and masthead

RIG

TYPE: sloop
RIGGING: Navtec rod
MAINSHEET: 4-part

SAILS

SUPPLIED WITH BASE BOAT:

INTERIOR

BERTHS: 5 berths: 1 forward double, 2 single settees, 1 single quarterberth,
TABLE: dropleaf
HEAD(S): 1 head with shower
COLD STORAGE: built-in icebox (7.5 cu. ft.)
STOVE: 3-burner propane with oven
MAX. HEADROOM: 6 ft. 3 ins.

MACHINERY

ENGINE: 27 HP Westerbeke with 2:1 reduction gear
PROPELLER: 2-blade sailer 16"x14" on 1" SS shaft
GENERATOR:

PRETORIEN

DESIGNER: Holman & Pye
BUILDER: Chantiers Henri Wauquiez

STATISTICS

LOA: 35 ft. 1 ins.
LWL: 30 ft. 4 ins.
BEAM: 11 ft. 7 ins.
DISPLACEMENT
deep keel: 14,326 lbs.
shoal keel:
c/board:
BALLAST
deep keel: 6,612 lbs.
shoal keel:
c/board:
DRAFT
deep keel: 6 ft. 0 ins.
shoal keel:
c/board up:
c/board down:

SAIL AREA: 527 sq. ft.
FRESH WATER: 66 gals.
FUEL CAPACITY: 25 gals.

COSTS

BASE BOAT: 629,500 francs
DATE: 02/25/85
EST. ON WATER:
DATE:

RATIOS

SAIL AREA/DISP: 14.29
DISP/LENGTH: 229
BALLAST RATIO: 46.15
FUEL/DISP: 1.09
FRESH WATER/DISP: 3.07

INTERIOR

BERTHS: 7 berths: 1 double V, 1 double convertible dinette, 1 single settee, 1 double quarterberth
TABLE: centerline dropleaf
HEAD(S): 1 head with shower
COLD STORAGE: built-in icebox
STOVE: 2-burner stove with oven
MAX. HEADROOM: 6 ft. 2 ins.

MACHINERY

ENGINE: 28 HP Volvo diesel
PROPELLER: 2-blade fixed
GENERATOR:

DECK

STEERING: wheel
WINCHES: 5 winches: 2 primary (Lewmar #46), 2 halyard, 1 reefing
SAFETY: bow and stern pulpits with double lifelines
ANCHOR: 35 lbs. anchor with anchor chain and locker
NAV LIGHTS: running and masthead

RIG

TYPE: masthead sloop
RIGGING:
MAINSHEET: Mid-boom sheeting

SAILS

SUPPLIED WITH BASE BOAT: main, medium genoa, #1 jib, storm jib

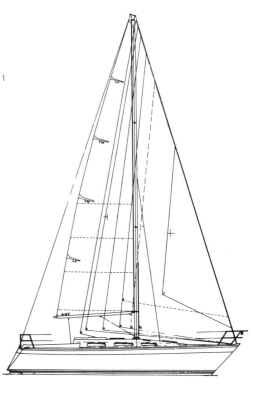

SCANMAR 35

DESIGNER: Rolf Magnusson
BUILDER: Scanmar Boats

STATISTICS

LOA: 35 ft. 1.75 ins.
LWL: 27 ft. 7.00 ins.
BEAM: 10 ft. 10.00 ins.
DISPLACEMENT
deep keel: 10,579 lbs.
shoal keel:
c/board:
BALLAST
deep keel:
shoal keel:
c/board:
DRAFT
deep keel: 5 ft. 9.75 ins.
shoal keel:
c/board up:
c/board down:

SAIL AREA:
FRESH WATER:
FUEL CAPACITY:

COSTS

BASE BOAT:
DATE:
EST. ON WATER:
DATE:

RATIOS

SAIL AREA/DISP:
DISP/LENGTH: 225.12
BALLAST RATIO:
FUEL/DISP:
FRESH WATER/DISP:

INTERIOR

BERTHS: 7 berths: 1 double V, 1 single settee, 1 double convertible dinette, 2 single quarterberths
TABLE:
HEAD(S): 1 head
COLD STORAGE: built-in icebox
STOVE: 2-burner with oven
MAX. HEADROOM:

MACHINERY

ENGINE: 28 HP Volvo Penta #2003/120B diesel
PROPELLER:
GENERATOR:

DECK

STEERING: wheel
WINCHES:
SAFETY: bow and stern pulpits with double lifelines
ANCHOR:
NAV LIGHTS:

RIG

TYPE: fractional rig sloop
RIGGING:
MAINSHEET:

SAILS

SUPPLIED WITH BASE BOAT:

ENDEAVOUR 35

DESIGNER: Bruce Kelley
BUILDER: Endeavour Yacht Corporation

STATISTICS

LOA: 35 ft. 5 ins.
LWL: 29 ft. 6 ins.
BEAM: 12 ft. 2 ins.
DISPLACEMENT
deep keel: 13,250 lbs.
shoal keel:
c/board:
BALLAST
deep keel: 5,630 lbs.
shoal keel:
c/board:
DRAFT
deep keel: 4 ft. 11 ins.
shoal keel:
c/board up:
c/board down:

SAIL AREA: 671 sq. ft.
FRESH WATER: 76 gals.
FUEL CAPACITY: 33 gals.

COSTS

BASE BOAT:
DATE:
EST. ON WATER:
DATE:

RATIOS

SAIL AREA/DISP: 19.17
DISP/LENGTH: 230
BALLAST RATIO: 42.49
FUEL/DISP: 1.86
FRESH WATER/DISP: 4.58

INTERIOR

BERTHS: 7 berths: 1 double V, 1 double convertible, 1 single settee, 1 double quarterberth
TABLE: centerline dropleaf
HEAD(S): 1 head with shower
COLD STORAGE: built-in icebox (8 cu. ft.) with refrigeration system
STOVE: 2-burner with oven
MAX. HEADROOM:

MACHINERY

ENGINE: 30 HP Yanmar diesel with 2:1 reduction gear
PROPELLER: 2-blade on 1 1/4" shaft
GENERATOR:

DECK

STEERING: 38" wheel with emergency tiller
WINCHES: 4 winches: 2 sheet (ST), 2 halyard
SAFETY: bow and stern pulpits with double lifelines
ANCHOR: anchor well
NAV LIGHTS: running and masthead

RIG

TYPE: masthead sloop
RIGGING:
MAINSHEET: mid-boom sheeting

SAILS

SUPPLIED WITH BASE BOAT:

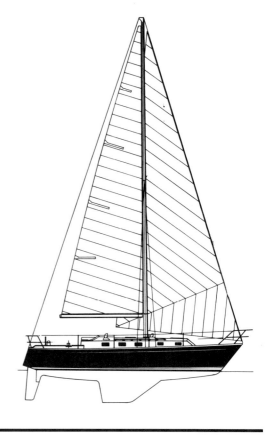

SHOW 36

DESIGNER: Fontana/Maletto/Navone
BUILDER: Barberis Cantieri

STATISTICS

LOA: 35 ft. 5.0 ins.
LWL: 28 ft. 9.6 ins.
BEAM: 11 ft. 9.6 ins.
DISPLACEMENT
deep keel: 10,800 lbs.
shoal keel:
c/board:
BALLAST
deep keel: 3,800 lbs.
shoal keel:
c/board:
DRAFT
deep keel: 6 ft. 0 ins.
shoal keel:
c/board up:
c/board down:

SAIL AREA: 542 sq. ft.
FRESH WATER: 50 gals.
FUEL CAPACITY:

COSTS

BASE BOAT: $85,000
DATE: 05/85
EST. ON WATER:
DATE:

RATIOS

SAIL AREA/DISP: 17.75
DISP/LENGTH: 201.84
BALLAST RATIO: 35.19
FUEL/DISP:
FRESH WATER/DISP: 3.70

INTERIOR

BERTHS: 6 berths: 1 double V, 2 double quarterberths
TABLE: dropleaf
HEAD(S): 1 head
COLD STORAGE: built-in icebox
STOVE: 3-burner propane with oven
MAX. HEADROOM:

MACHINERY

ENGINE: Volvo #2002 diesel
PROPELLER: 2-blade fixed
GENERATOR:

DECK

STEERING: tiller
WINCHES: 5 winches
SAFETY: bow and stern pulpits with double lifelines
ANCHOR: anchor roller and well
NAV LIGHTS: running and masthead

RIG

TYPE: masthead sloop
RIGGING: 1x19 wire
MAINSHEET:

SAILS

SUPPLIED WITH BASE BOAT:

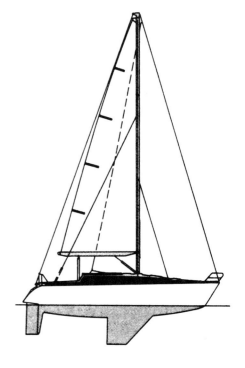

J-35

DESIGNER: Rod Johnstone
BUILDER: J Boats, Inc.

STATISTICS

LOA: 35 ft. 5.25 ins.
LWL: 30 ft. 0.00 ins.
BEAM: 11 ft. 9.00 ins.
DISPLACEMENT
deep keel: 10,000 lbs.
shoal keel:
c/board:
BALLAST
deep keel: 4,400 lbs.
shoal keel:
c/board:
DRAFT
deep keel: 6 ft. 10.75 ins.
shoal keel:
c/board up:
c/board down:

INTERIOR

BERTHS: 2 berths: 2 single settees
TABLE: dropleaf
HEAD(S):
COLD STORAGE: cooler (48 qt.)
STOVE:
MAX. HEADROOM:

MACHINERY

ENGINE: 22.5 Yanmar diesel
PROPELLER: Martec folding 16"x12"
GENERATOR:

SAIL AREA: 632 sq. ft.
FRESH WATER:
FUEL CAPACITY:

COSTS

BASE BOAT: $55,400
DATE: 04/01/85
EST. ON WATER:
DATE:

RATIOS

SAIL AREA/DISP: 21.78
DISP/LENGTH: 165
BALLAST RATIO: 44.00
FUEL/DISP:
FRESH WATER/DISP:

DECK

STEERING: tiller
WINCHES: 6 Barient winches: 2 primary (#28)
SAFETY:
ANCHOR:
NAV LIGHTS: running

RIG

TYPE: masthead sloop
RIGGING: Navtec rod
MAINSHEET: 6-part boom-end

SAILS

SUPPLIED WITH BASE BOAT:

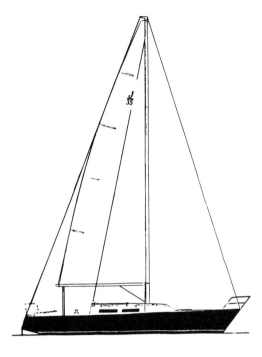

BRISTOL 35.5

DESIGNER: Ted Hood
BUILDER: Bristol Yacht Co.

STATISTICS

LOA: 35 ft. 6 ins.
LWL: 27 ft. 6 ins.
BEAM: 10 ft. 10 ins.
DISPLACEMENT
deep keel: 15,000 lbs.
shoal keel:
c/board:
BALLAST
deep keel: 6,500 lbs.
shoal keel:
c/board:
DRAFT
deep keel: 5 ft. 9 ins.
shoal keel:
c/board up:
c/board down:

SAIL AREA: 589 sq. ft.
FRESH WATER: 56 gals.
FUEL CAPACITY: 31 gals

COSTS

BASE BOAT: $85,020
DATE: 09/01/85
EST. ON WATER:
DATE:

RATIOS

SAIL AREA/DISP: 15.49
DISP/LENGTH: 321.99
BALLAST RATIO: 43.33
FUEL/DISP: 1.55
FRESH WATER/DISP: 1.99

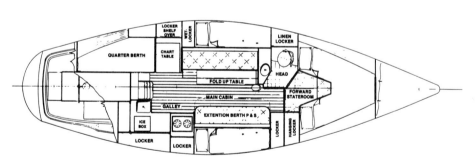

INTERIOR

BERTHS: 7 berths: 1 double V, 2 single extension settees, 2 single pilots, 1 single quarterberth
TABLE: bulkhead-mounted
HEAD(S): 1 head
COLD STORAGE: built-in icebox
STOVE: 2-burner
MAX. HEADROOM:

MACHINERY

ENGINE: 22 HP Yanmar diesel
PROPELLER:
GENERATOR:

DECK

STEERING: wheel
WINCHES: 4 Lewmar winches: 2 #40, 1 #16, 1 #8
SAFETY: bow and stern pulpits with lifelines
ANCHOR: anchor roller
NAV LIGHTS: running and masthead

RIG

TYPE: masthead sloop
RIGGING:
MAINSHEET: boom-end sheeting

SAILS

SUPPLIED WITH BASE BOAT:

ERICSON 35

DESIGNER: Bruce King
BUILDER: Ericson Yachts

STATISTICS

LOA: 35 ft. 6.0 ins.
LWL: 28 ft. 10.5 ins.
BEAM: 11 ft. 4.0 ins.
DISPLACEMENT
deep keel: 13,000 lbs.
shoal keel:
c/board:
BALLAST
deep keel: 5,800 lbs.
shoal keel:
c/board:
DRAFT
deep keel: 6 ft. 2.0 ins.
shoal keel: 4 ft. 11.5 ins.
c/board up:
c/board down:

SAIL AREA: 598 sq. ft.
FRESH WATER: 50 gals.
FUEL CAPACITY: 40 gals.

COSTS

BASE BOAT:
DATE:
EST. ON WATER:
DATE:

RATIOS

SAIL AREA/DISP: 17.31
DISP/LENGTH: 240.94
BALLAST RATIO: 44.6
FUEL/DISP: 2.31
FRESH WATER/DISP: 3.08

INTERIOR

BERTHS: 7 berths: 1 double V, 1 double convertible dinette, 1 single settee, 1 double quarterberth
TABLE: pedestal-mounted dinette
HEAD(S): 1 head with shower, sump pump and holding tank
COLD STORAGE: built-in icebox (6.5 cu. ft.)
STOVE: 3-burner alcohol with oven
MAX. HEADROOM: 6 ft. 3 ins.

MACHINERY

ENGINE: 21 HP Universal #25 diesel
PROPELLER: 2-blade 15"x11" on 1" shaft
GENERATOR:

DECK

STEERING: 36" wheel with emergency tiller
WINCHES: 5 Barient winches: 2 primary (#27 ST), 2 halyard (#18), 1 mainsheet (#19 ST)
SAFETY: bow and stern pulpits with double lifelines
ANCHOR: anchor roller and well
NAV LIGHTS: running and masthead

RIG

TYPE: masthead sloop with Kenyon spar
RIGGING: 1x19 wire
MAINSHEET: 5-part with mid-boom sheeting

SAILS

SUPPLIED WITH BASE BOAT:

MIRAGE 35

DESIGNER:
BUILDER: Mirage Yachts, Ltd.

STATISTICS

LOA: 35 ft. 6 ins.
LWL: 26 ft. 9 ins.
BEAM: 11 ft. 8 ins.
DISPLACEMENT
deep keel: 9,300 lbs.
shoal keel:
c/board:
BALLAST
deep keel: 3,500 lbs.
shoal keel:
c/board:
DRAFT
deep keel: 5 ft. 0 ins.
shoal keel:
c/board up:
c/board down:

SAIL AREA: 460 sq. ft.
FRESH WATER: 40 gals.
FUEL CAPACITY: 20 gals.

COSTS

BASE BOAT:
DATE:
EST. ON WATER:
DATE:

RATIOS

SAIL AREA/DISP: 16.65
DISP/LENGTH: 216.9
BALLAST RATIO: 37.63
FUEL/DISP: 1.61
FRESH WATER/DISP: 3.44

INTERIOR

BERTHS: 6 berths: 1 double V, 1 single settee, 1 double convertible, 1 single quarterberth
TABLE: dinette
HEAD(S): 1 head
COLD STORAGE: built-in icebox
STOVE:
MAX. HEADROOM: 6 ft. 5 ins.

MACHINERY

ENGINE: diesel
PROPELLER:
GENERATOR:

DECK

STEERING: wheel
WINCHES: 4 winches: 2 primary (#40), 2 halyard
SAFETY: bow and stern pulpits with lifelines
ANCHOR: anchor roller and well
NAV LIGHTS: running

RIG

TYPE: masthead sloop
RIGGING:
MAINSHEET: mid-boom sheeting

SAILS

SUPPLIED WITH BASE BOAT:

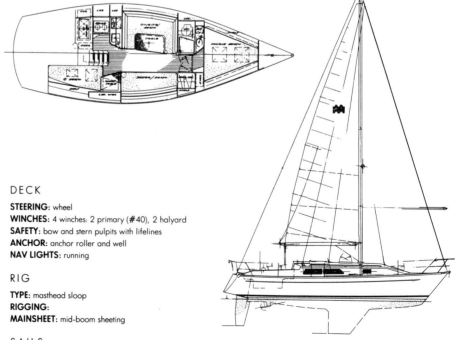

NEW YORK 36

DESIGNER: William E. Cook
BUILDER: W. D. Schock Corp

STATISTICS

LOA: 35 ft. 8 ins.
LWL: 29 ft. 6 ins.
BEAM: 11 ft. 8 ins.
DISPLACEMENT
deep keel: 10,500 lbs.
shoal keel:
c/board:
BALLAST
deep keel: 4,200 lbs.
shoal keel:
c/board:
DRAFT
deep keel: 6 ft. 4 ins.
shoal keel:
c/board up:
c/board down:

SAIL AREA: 650 sq. ft.
FRESH WATER: 20 gals.
FUEL CAPACITY: 20 gals.

COSTS

BASE BOAT: $84,950
DATE: 09/01/84
EST. ON WATER:
DATE:

RATIOS

SAIL AREA/DISP: 21.69
DISP/LENGTH: 182.59
BALLAST RATIO: 40.00
FUEL/DISP: 1.43
FRESH WATER/DISP: 1.52

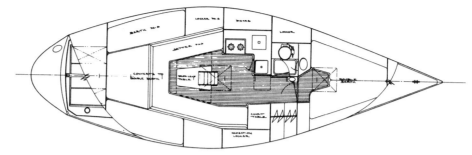

INTERIOR

BERTHS: 8 berths: 1 double V, 2 single settees, 1 double convertible, 2 single quarterberths
TABLE: dropleaf
HEAD(S): 1 head with shower and holding tank
COLD STORAGE: built-in icebox
STOVE: 2-burner CNG with alcohol oven
MAX. HEADROOM:

MACHINERY

ENGINE: 15 HP MD7B diesel
PROPELLER: on 1" SS shaft
GENERATOR:

DECK

STEERING: tiller
WINCHES: 8 Lewmar winches
SAFETY: bow and stern pulpits with double lifelines
ANCHOR:
NAV LIGHTS: running

RIG

TYPE: fractional rig sloop
RIGGING: Navtec rod
MAINSHEET: mid-boom sheeting

SAILS

SUPPLIED WITH BASE BOAT:

FREEPORT 36 CENTER COCKPIT

DESIGNER: Robert H. Perry
BUILDER: Islander Yachts

STATISTICS

LOA: 35 ft. 9 ins.
LWL: 27 ft. 6 ins.
BEAM: 12 ft. 0 ins.
DISPLACEMENT
deep keel: 17,000 lbs.
shoal keel:
c/board:
BALLAST
deep keel: 6,300 lbs.
shoal keel:
c/board:
DRAFT
deep keel: 5 ft. 3 ins.
shoal keel:
c/board up:
c/board down:

SAIL AREA: 653 sq. ft.
FRESH WATER: 120 gals.
FUEL CAPACITY: 50 gals.

COSTS

BASE BOAT:
DATE:
EST. ON WATER:
DATE:

RATIOS

SAIL AREA/DISP: 15.80
DISP/LENGTH: 364.92
BALLAST RATIO: 37.06
FUEL/DISP: 2.21
FRESH WATER/DISP: 5.65

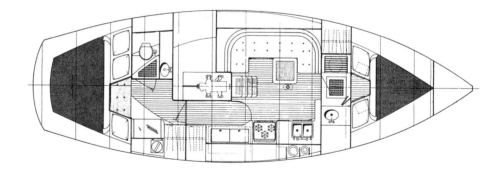

INTERIOR

BERTHS: 7 berths: 1 double V, 1 double settee, 1 double pilot, 1 single pilot
TABLE: dinette
HEAD(S): 2 heads with 2 showers
COLD STORAGE: built-in icebox (7.8 cu. ft.)
STOVE: 3-burner propane with oven
MAX. HEADROOM:

MACHINERY

ENGINE: 42 HP Pathfinder diesel
PROPELLER: 2-blade
GENERATOR:

DECK

STEERING: 28" wheel with emergency tiller
WINCHES: 5 winches: 2 jib sheet (#27A ST), 1 mainsheet (#10A), 2 halyard (#21C and #22C)
SAFETY: bow and stern pulpits with double lifelines
ANCHOR: anchor roller and well
NAV LIGHTS: running and masthead

RIG

TYPE: masthead sloop
RIGGING:
MAINSHEET: mid-boom sheeting

SAILS

SUPPLIED WITH BASE BOAT:

RIVAL 36

DESIGNER: Peter Brett
DISTRIBUTOR: Rival Yachts, Inc. (built in England by Rival Yachts, Ltd.)

STATISTICS

LOA: 35 ft. 10 ins.
LWL: 27 ft. 2 ins.
BEAM: 11 ft. 0 ins.
DISPLACEMENT
deep keel: 14,250 lbs.
shoal keel:
c/board:
BALLAST
deep keel: 5,400 lbs.
shoal keel: 5,700 lbs.
c/board:
DRAFT
deep keel: 6 ft. 0 ins.
shoal keel: 4 ft. 11 ins.
c/board up: 3 ft. 11 ins.
c/board down: 6 ft. 11 ins.

SAIL AREA: 505 sq. ft.
FRESH WATER: 85 gals.
FUEL CAPACITY: 48 gals.

COSTS

BASE BOAT:
DATE:
EST. ON WATER: $99,000
DATE: 07/10/85

RATIOS

SAIL AREA/DISP: 13.75
DISP/LENGTH: 317.52
BALLAST RATIO: 37.89
FUEL/DISP: 2.53
FRESH WATER/DISP: 4.77

INTERIOR

BERTHS: 7 berths: 2 single Vs, 2 single settees, 2 single pipe berths, 1 single quarterberth
TABLE: centerline dropleaf
HEAD(S): 1 head with shower
COLD STORAGE: built-in icebox
STOVE: 2-burner LPG with oven
MAX. HEADROOM: 6 ft. 1.25 ins.

MACHINERY

ENGINE: 20 HP Bukh diesel with 3:1 reduction gear
PROPELLER: 2-blade 17"x12"
GENERATOR:

DECK

STEERING: wheel with emergency tiller fitted
WINCHES: 3 Lewmar winches: 2 sheet (#43C), 1 halyard (#16C)
SAFETY: bow and stern pulpits with double lifelines
ANCHOR: 35 lb. & 45 lb. CQR anchors with 30 fthm. chain, 2sp windlass, and anchor well
NAV LIGHTS: running and masthead

RIG

TYPE: masthead sloop with Kemp spar
RIGGING: 1x19 wire
MAINSHEET: mid-boom sheeting

SAILS

SUPPLIED WITH BASE BOAT: Hood main (3 reefs), working jib

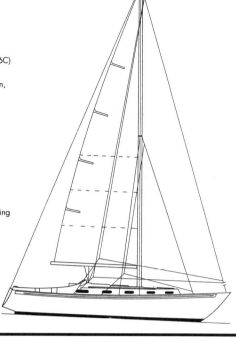

BUILDER'S COMMENTS All complete Rivals are built as standard to Lloyd's Register +100 A-1 classification and are sold fully equipped to sail. The Lloyd's requirements apply to all elements of construction including design, materials, construction conditions, and equipment. A Lloyd's surveyor oversees each yacht's construction to ensure these standards are maintained.

TAYANA-MARINER 36

DESIGNER: William Garden
DISTRIBUTOR: Southern Offshore Yachts, Inc. (built in Taiwan by TaYang Yacht Building Co.)

STATISTICS

LOA: 35 ft. 10 ins.
LWL: 27 ft. 11 ins.
BEAM: 11 ft. 0 ins.
DISPLACEMENT
deep keel: 21,000 lbs.
shoal keel:
c/board:
BALLAST
deep keel: 7,500 lbs.
shoal keel:
c/board:
DRAFT
deep keel:
shoal keel:
c/board up:
c/board down:

SAIL AREA: 685 sq. ft. (cutter)
696 sq. ft. (ketch)
FRESH WATER: 80 gals.
FUEL CAPACITY: 70 gals.

COSTS

BASE BOAT: $67,000
DATE: 07/85
EST. ON WATER:
DATE:

RATIOS

SAIL AREA/DISP: 14.40 (cutter)
14.63 (ketch)
DISP/LENGTH: 430.75
BALLAST RATIO: 35.71
FUEL/DISP: 2.50
FRESH WATER/DISP: 3.05

INTERIOR

BERTHS: 6 berths: 1 double V, 2 double quarterberths
TABLE: dropleaf
HEAD(S): 1 head with 1 shower, 1 sump pump, and 2 holding tanks
COLD STORAGE: built-in icebox
STOVE:
MAX. HEADROOM: 6 ft. 3 ins.

MACHINERY

ENGINE: 36 HP Yanmar #3QM diesel
PROPELLER: 3-blade fixed 18"x13" on 1 1/4" shaft
GENERATOR:

DECK

STEERING: wheel with emergency tiller
WINCHES: 6 Barlow winches: 2 #24, 2 #20, 2 #15
SAFETY: bow and stern pulpits with double lifelines
ANCHOR:
NAV LIGHTS: running and masthead

RIG

TYPE: masthead cutter or ketch
RIGGING: wire (3/8")
MAINSHEET:

SAILS

SUPPLIED WITH BASE BOAT: main, yankee, staysail

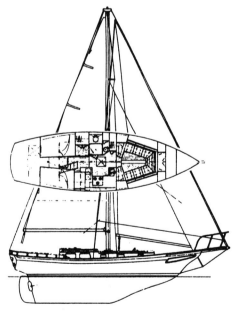

J-36

DESIGNER: Rod Johnstone
BUILDER: J Boats, Inc.

STATISTICS

LOA: 35 ft. 11.75 ins.
LWL: 30 ft. 6.00 ins.
BEAM: 11 ft. 10.00 ins.
DISPLACEMENT
deep keel: 10,570 lbs. IOR
11,500 lbs. sailing
shoal keel:
c/board:
BALLAST
deep keel: 4,600 lbs.
shoal keel:
c/board:
DRAFT
deep keel: 6 ft. 7.25 ins.
shoal keel:
c/board up:
c/board down:

INTERIOR

BERTHS: 8 berths: 2 forward singles, 2 single settees, 2 single
extension berths, 2 single pipe berths
TABLE: centerline dropleaf
HEAD(S): 1 head with shower and holding tank
COLD STORAGE: built-in icebox (5 cu. ft.)
STOVE: 2-burner propane with oven
MAX. HEADROOM:

MACHINERY

ENGINE: 22.5 HP Yanmar diesel
PROPELLER: Martec folding 6"x12"
GENERATOR:

SAIL AREA: 675 sq. ft.
FRESH WATER: 30 gals.
FUEL CAPACITY: 20 gals.

COSTS

BASE BOAT: 84,500
DATE: 04/01/85
EST. ON WATER:
DATE:

RATIOS

SAIL AREA/DISP: 23.20
DISP/LENGTH: 158.07
BALLAST RATIO: 45.78
FUEL/DISP: 1.493
FRESH WATER/DISP: 2.389

DECK

STEERING: 40" wheel with emergency tiller
WINCHES: 8 Barient winches: 2 primary (#26), 2 secondary
(#25), 2 halyard/vang (#21), 2 mainsheet (#27 ST)
SAFETY: bow and stern pulpits with double lifelines
ANCHOR: anchor well
NAV LIGHTS: running and masthead

RIG

TYPE: fractional rig sloop
RIGGING: Navtec rod
MAINSHEET: 2-part with boom-end sheeting

SAILS

SUPPLIED WITH BASE BOAT:

COMFORTINA 36

DESIGNER:
DISTRIBUTOR: Scandvik, Inc. (built in Sweden by Comfort-
batar, AB)

STATISTICS

LOA: 36 ft. 0 ins.
LWL: 31 ft. 2 ins.
BEAM: 10 ft. 0 ins.
DISPLACEMENT
deep keel: 10,000 lbs.
shoal keel:
c/board:
BALLAST
deep keel: 4,400 lbs.
shoal keel:
c/board:
DRAFT
deep keel: 5 ft. 7 ins.
shoal keel: 4 ft. 11 ins.
c/board up:
c/board down:

INTERIOR

BERTHS: 6 berths: 1 double V, 2 single settees, 1 double
quarterberth
TABLE: dropleaf
HEAD(S): 1 head
COLD STORAGE: built-in icebox
STOVE:
MAX. HEADROOM:

MACHINERY

ENGINE: 27 HP Yanmar diesel
PROPELLER:
GENERATOR:

SAIL AREA:
FRESH WATER: 33 gals.
FUEL CAPACITY: 21 gals.

COSTS

BASE BOAT: $55,500
DATE: 05/85
EST. ON WATER:
DATE:

RATIOS

SAIL AREA/DISP:
DISP/LENGTH: 147.56
BALLAST RATIO: 44.00
FUEL/DISP: 1.58
FRESH WATER/DISP: 2.64

DECK

STEERING: tiller
WINCHES:
SAFETY:
ANCHOR:
NAV LIGHTS:

RIG

TYPE: fractional rig sloop
RIGGING:
MAINSHEET: mid-boom sheeting

SAILS

SUPPLIED WITH BASE BOAT:

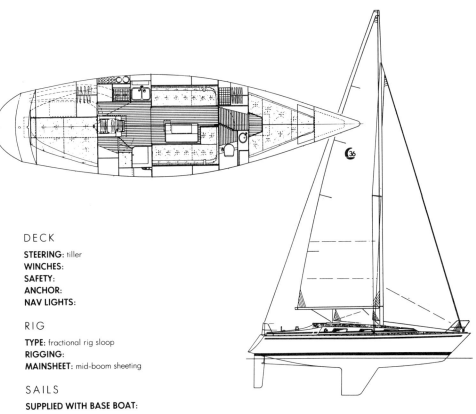

MARINER POLARIS 36

DESIGNER: Robert H. Perry
BUILDER: Master Mariners Corp.

STATISTICS

LOA: 36 ft. 0 ins.
LWL: 32 ft. 0 ins.
BEAM: 11 ft. 4 ins.
DISPLACEMENT
deep keel: 19,000 lbs.
shoal keel:
c/board:
BALLAST
deep keel: 8,200 lbs.
shoal keel:
c/board:
DRAFT
deep keel: 5 ft. 6 ins.
shoal keel:
c/board up:
c/board down:

SAIL AREA: 786 sq. ft.
FRESH WATER: 140 gals.
FUEL CAPACITY: 100 gals.

COSTS

BASE BOAT:
West coast $84,500
DATE: 04/85
East coast $87,000
DATE: 04/85

RATIOS

SAIL AREA/DISP: 17.67
DISP/LENGTH: 258.85
BALLAST RATIO: 43.16
FUEL/DISP: 3.95
FRESH WATER/DISP: 5.9

INTERIOR

BERTHS: 8 berths: 1 double V, 1 double convertible dinette, 2 single pilots, 1 double quarterberth
TABLE: fixed
HEAD(S): 1 head with shower
COLD STORAGE: refrigerator/freezer
STOVE:
MAX. HEADROOM:

MACHINERY

ENGINE: 50 HP diesel with 2.5:1 reduction gear
PROPELLER: on 1 1/4" shaft
GENERATOR: 2.5 kW

DECK

STEERING: wheel
WINCHES: 5 winches
SAFETY: bow and stern pulpits with double lifelines
ANCHOR: anchor roller
NAV LIGHTS: running and masthead

RIG

TYPE: masthead cutter with Isomet spar
RIGGING:
MAINSHEET: boom-end sheeting

SAILS

SUPPLIED WITH BASE BOAT:
main, 100% working jib

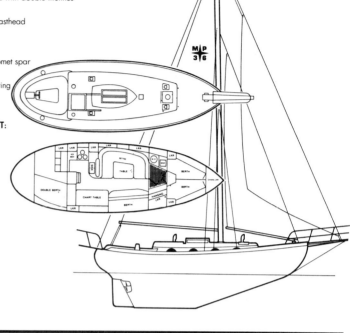

NONSUCH 36

DESIGNER:
BUILDER: Hinterhoeller Yachts, Ltd.

STATISTICS

LOA: 36 ft. 0 ins.
LWL: 33 ft. 9 ins.
BEAM: 12 ft. 8 ins.
DISPLACEMENT
deep keel: 17,000 lbs.
shoal keel:
c/board:
BALLAST
deep keel: 6,600 lbs.
shoal keel:
c/board:
DRAFT
deep keel: 5 ft. 6 ins.
shoal keel:
c/board up:
c/board down:

SAIL AREA: 742 sq. ft.
FRESH WATER: 112 gals.
FUEL CAPACITY: 49 gals.

COSTS

BASE BOAT: $107,500
DATE: 08/01/85
EST. ON WATER: $125,000
DATE: 08/01/85

RATIOS

SAIL AREA/DISP: 17.95
DISP/LENGTH: 197
BALLAST RATIO: 38.82
FUEL/DISP: 2.16
FRESH WATER/DISP: 5.27

INTERIOR

BERTHS: 6 berths: 1 forward double, 2 single settees, 1 double quarterberth
TABLE: centerline dropleaf
HEAD(S): 1 head with shower and sump pump
COLD STORAGE: built-in icebox (8.5 cu. ft.)
STOVE: 3-burner propane with oven
MAX. HEADROOM: 6 ft. 6 ins.

MACHINERY

ENGINE: 46 HP Westerbeke diesel with 2:1 reduction gear
PROPELLER: 2-blade sailor 18"x14" RH on 1 1/8" SS shaft
GENERATOR:

DECK

STEERING: 32" wheel with emergency tiller
WINCHES: 4 winches: 1 main halyard (#23), 1 mainsheet (#27 ST), 2 choker/reefing (#19)
SAFETY: bow and stern pulpits with double lifelines
ANCHOR:
NAV LIGHTS: running and masthead

RIG

TYPE: cat rig
RIGGING:
MAINSHEET: 2-part with boom-end sheeting

SAILS

SUPPLIED WITH BASE BOAT:

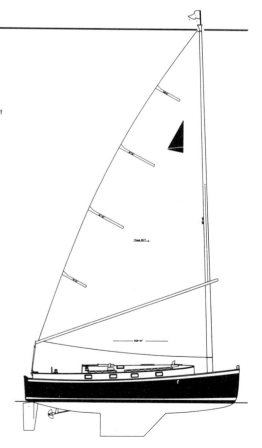

SABRE 36

DESIGNER: Sabre Design Team
BUILDER: Sabre Yachts

STATISTICS

LOA: 36 ft. 0 ins.
LWL: 29 ft. 4 ins.
BEAM: 11 ft. 3 ins.
DISPLACEMENT
deep keel: 13,200 lbs.
shoal keel:
c/board:
BALLAST
deep keel: 5,400 lbs.
shoal keel:
c/board:
DRAFT
deep keel: 6 ft. 4 ins.
shoal keel:
c/board up: 4 ft. 2 ins.
c/board down: 7 ft. 8 ins.

SAIL AREA: 612 sq. ft.
FRESH WATER: 77 gals.
FUEL CAPACITY: 20 gals.

COSTS

BASE BOAT:
DATE:
EST. ON WATER:
DATE:

RATIOS

SAIL AREA/DISP: 17.53
DISP/LENGTH: 233
BALLAST RATIO: 40.90
FUEL/DISP: 1.13
FRESH WATER/DISP: 4.66

DECK

STEERING: wheel
WINCHES: 5 Lewmar winches: 2 primary (#46), 2 halyard (#16 and #24), 1 mainsheet (#24)
SAFETY: bow and stern pulpits with double lifelines
ANCHOR: anchor well
NAV LIGHTS: running and masthead

RIG

TYPE: masthead sloop
RIGGING: Navtec rod
MAINSHEET: 4-part with mid-boom sheeting

SAILS

SUPPLIED WITH BASE BOAT:

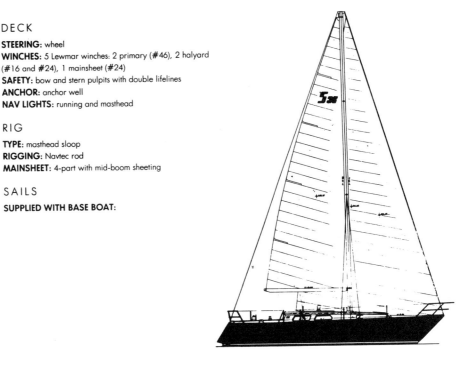

INTERIOR

BERTHS: 7 berths: 1 double V, 1 double convertible, 1 single settee, 1 double quarterberth
TABLE: dinette
HEAD(S): 1 head
COLD STORAGE: built-in icebox
STOVE: 2-burner alcohol with oven
MAX. HEADROOM: 6 ft. 3 ins.

MACHINERY

ENGINE: 27 HP Westerbeke diesel with 2:1 reduction gear
PROPELLER: 16"x10"
GENERATOR:

S2 11.0A/36'

DESIGNER: S2 Yachts
BUILDER: S2 Yachts, Inc.

STATISTICS

LOA: 36 ft. 0 ins.
LWL: 28 ft. 3 ins.
BEAM: 11 ft. 11 ins.
DISPLACEMENT
deep keel: 15,000 lbs.
shoal keel:
c/board:
BALLAST
deep keel: 6,000 lbs.
shoal keel:
c/board:
DRAFT
deep keel: 5 ft. 6 ins.
shoal keel:
c/board up:
c/board down:

SAIL AREA: 632 sq. ft.
FRESH WATER: 80 gals.
FUEL CAPACITY: 50 gals.

COSTS

BASE BOAT:
DATE:
EST. ON WATER:
DATE:

RATIOS

SAIL AREA/DISP: 16.62
DISP/LENGTH: 297
BALLAST RATIO: 40.00
FUEL/DISP: 2.50
FRESH WATER/DISP: 4.26

DECK

STEERING: 36" wheel with emergency tiller
WINCHES: 4 Lewmar winches: 2 primary (#40 2sp), 1 jib halyard (#16 2sp), 1 main halyard (#8)
SAFETY: bow and stern pulpits with double lifelines
ANCHOR: anchor roller and locker
NAV LIGHTS:

RIG

TYPE: masthead sloop
RIGGING: 1x19 wire
MAINSHEET: 6-part with mid-boom sheeting

SAILS

SUPPLIED WITH BASE BOAT:

INTERIOR

BERTHS: 7 berths: 1 double V, 1 double convertible, 1 single settee, 1 double quarterberth
TABLE: pedestal-mounted double-leaf
HEAD(S): 1 head with shower
COLD STORAGE: built-in icebox (9 cu. ft.)
STOVE: 2-burner with oven
MAX. HEADROOM: 6 ft. 3 ins.

MACHINERY

ENGINE: 30 HP Yanmar
PROPELLER: 2-blade
GENERATOR:

BUILDER'S COMMENTS A proven, formidable 36' cruising yacht bred with spirited performance, responsiveness, and easy sailing characteristics. The large interior volume made possible by a wide beam is planned for living ease and cruising comfort.

ISLANDER 36

DESIGNER: Alan Gurney
BUILDER: Islander Yachts

STATISTICS

LOA: 36 ft. 1 ins.
LWL: 28 ft. 3 ins.
BEAM: 11 ft. 2 ins.
DISPLACEMENT
deep keel: 13,450 lbs.
shoal keel:
c/board:
BALLAST
deep keel: 5,450 lbs.
shoal keel:
c/board:
DRAFT
deep keel: 6 ft. 0 ins.
shoal keel:
c/board up:
c/board down:

SAIL AREA: 612 sq. ft.
FRESH WATER: 56 gals.
FUEL CAPACITY: 30 gals.

COSTS

BASE BOAT:
DATE:
EST. ON WATER:
DATE:

RATIOS

SAIL AREA/DISP: 17.31
DISP/LENGTH: 266
BALLAST RATIO: 40.52
FUEL/DISP: 1.672
FRESH WATER/DISP: 3.330

DECK

STEERING: 28" wheel with emergency tiller
WINCHES: 5 Barient winches: 2 primary (#28A), 1 main halyard (#21C), 1 jib halyard (#22C), 1 mainsheet (#18A)
SAFETY: bow and stern pulpits with double lifelines
ANCHOR: anchor roller and well
NAV LIGHTS: running and masthead

RIG

TYPE: masthead sloop
RIGGING:
MAINSHEET: mid-boom sheeting

SAILS

SUPPLIED WITH BASE BOAT:

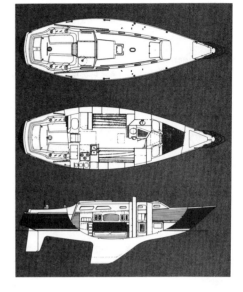

INTERIOR

BERTHS: 6 berths: 1 double V, 1 double convertible, 1 single settee, 1 single quarterberth
TABLE: bulkhead-mounted
HEAD(S): 1 head with shower and sump pump
COLD STORAGE: built-in icebox (5 cu. ft.)
STOVE: 3-burner LPG with oven
MAX. HEADROOM:

MACHINERY

ENGINE: 30 HP Yanmar diesel with 2.1:4 reduction gear
PROPELLER: 2-blade 16" diameter
GENERATOR:

SWEDEN YACHTS 36

DESIGNER: Norlin/Ostmann
DISTRIBUTOR: Westover Yachts (built in Sweden by Sweden Yachts)

STATISTICS

LOA: 36 ft. 1.2 ins.
LWL: 29 ft. 6.0 ins.
BEAM: 12 ft. 0.0 ins.
DISPLACEMENT
deep keel: 14,000 lbs.
shoal keel:
c/board:
BALLAST
deep keel: 5,900 lbs.
shoal keel:
c/board:
DRAFT
deep keel: 6 ft. 8.4 ins.
shoal keel:
c/board up:
c/board down:

SAIL AREA:
FRESH WATER: 50 gals.
FUEL CAPACITY: 26 gals.

COSTS

BASE BOAT:
DATE:
EST. ON WATER:
DATE:

RATIOS

SAIL AREA/DISP:
DISP/LENGTH: 245.44
BALLAST RATIO: 42.14
FUEL/DISP: 1.39
FRESH WATER/DISP: 2.86

DECK

STEERING: 36" wheel with emergency tiller
WINCHES: 7 Lewmar winches: 2 #46C ST, 2 #43C, 2 #30C, 1 #16C
SAFETY: bow and stern pulpits with double lifelines
ANCHOR: anchor roller
NAV LIGHTS: running

RIG

TYPE: masthead sloop
RIGGING: wire
MAINSHEET: boom-end sheeting

SAILS

SUPPLIED WITH BASE BOAT:

INTERIOR

BERTHS: 5 berths: 1 double V, 1 single quarterberth, 1 double quarterberth
TABLE: dropleaf
HEAD(S): 1 head with shower, sump pump, and holding tank
COLD STORAGE: built-in icebox
STOVE: 2-burner LPG with oven
MAX. HEADROOM:

MACHINERY

ENGINE: 28 HP Volvo Penta #2003 diesel
PROPELLER: folding
GENERATOR:

CAPE DORY 36

DESIGNER: Carl Alberg
BUILDER: Cape Dory Yachts

STATISTICS

LOA: 36 ft. 1.5 ins.
LWL: 27 ft. 0.0 ins.
BEAM: 10 ft. 8.0 ins.
DISPLACEMENT
deep keel: 16,100 lbs.
shoal keel:
c/board:
BALLAST
deep keel: 6,050 lbs.
shoal keel:
c/board:
DRAFT
deep keel: 5 ft. 0 ins.
shoal keel:
c/board up:
c/board down:

SAIL AREA: 622 sq. ft.
FRESH WATER: 90 gals.
FUEL CAPACITY: 43 gals.

COSTS

BASE BOAT:
DATE:
EST. ON WATER:
DATE:

RATIOS

SAIL AREA/DISP: 15.61
DISP/LENGTH: 365.16
BALLAST RATIO: 37.58
FUEL/DISP: 2.00
FRESH WATER/DISP: 4.47

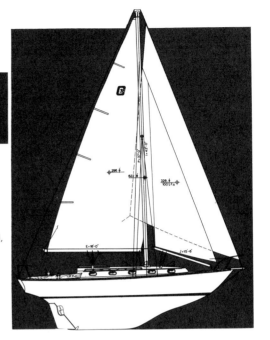

INTERIOR

BERTHS: 6 berths: 1 double V, 1 double cconvertible settee, 1 single settee, 1 single quarterberth
TABLE: bulkhead-mounted
HEAD(S): 1 head with shower, sump pump, and holding tank (35 gals.)
COLD STORAGE: built-in icebox
STOVE: 3-burner alcohol with oven
MAX. HEADROOM:

DECK

STEERING: wheel with emergency tiller
WINCHES: 8 winches: 2 primary (2sp ST), 3 halyard, 1 mainsheet (2sp), 1 staysail sheet, 1 reefing
SAFETY: bow and stern pulpits with double lifelines
ANCHOR: double anchor rollers
NAV LIGHTS: running and masthead

RIG

TYPE: masthead cutter
RIGGING:
MAINSHEET:

MACHINERY

ENGINE: Perkins #4-108 diesel with 2.1:1 reduction gear
PROPELLER: 1" shaft
GENERATOR:

SAILS

SUPPLIED WITH BASE BOAT:

F-36

DESIGNER: German Frers
BUILDER: Carroll Marine

STATISTICS

LOA: 36 ft. 3 ins.
LWL: 29 ft. 6 ins.
BEAM: 11 ft. 11 ins.
DISPLACEMENT
deep keel: 10,900 lbs.
shoal keel:
c/board:
BALLAST
deep keel: 5,400 lbs.
shoal keel:
c/board:
DRAFT
deep keel: 6 ft. 11 ins.
shoal keel:
c/board up:
c/board down:

SAIL AREA: 662 sq. ft.
FRESH WATER: 35 gals.
FUEL CAPACITY: 20 gals.

COSTS

BASE BOAT: $75,000
DATE: 11/85
EST. ON WATER: $93,500
DATE: 11/85

RATIOS

SAIL AREA/DISP: 21.55
DISP/LENGTH: 189.55
BALLAST RATIO: 49.54
FUEL/DISP: 1.38
FRESH WATER/DISP: 2.57

DECK

STEERING: tiller
WINCHES: 6 Barient winches: 2 primaries (#28A), 2 halyard (#22A), 2 utility and reefing (#18A)
SAFETY: bow and stern pulpits with double lifelines
ANCHOR:
NAV LIGHTS: running and masthead

RIG

TYPE: masthead sloop
RIGGING: Navtec rod
MAINSHEET: mid-boom sheeting

SAILS

SUPPLIED WITH BASE BOAT:

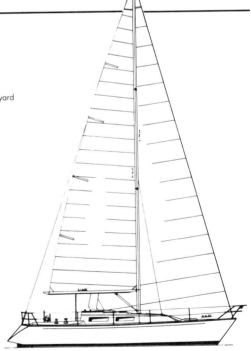

INTERIOR

BERTHS: 6 berths: 1 double V, 2 single settees, 1 double quuarterberth
TABLE:
HEAD(S): 1 head with 1 holding tank
COLD STORAGE: built-in icebox
STOVE: 2-burner LPG with oven
MAX. HEADROOM:

MACHINERY

ENGINE: 22 HP Westerbeke diesel with 2:1 reduction gear
PROPELLER: 2-blade fixed on 1" shaft
GENERATOR:

BUILDER'S COMMENTS Very seldom does a yacht receive the research that has been incorporated into this Frers-36. Over the two and a half years that we have been sailing the semi-custom F-3, we have been in the process of developing a family cruiser/racer recognizing the benefits of a hull that weighs under 11,000 pounds. In terms of easy handling, extremely manageable control and a good deal of luxurious interior volume, the Frers-36 represents the most developed family racer/cruiser in many years.

MORRIS 36 (JUSTINE)

DESIGNER: Chuck Paine
BUILDER: Morris Yachts, Inc.

STATISTICS

LOA: 36 ft. 3 ins.
LWL: 29 ft. 6 ins.
BEAM: 11 ft. 7 ins.
DISPLACEMENT
deep keel: 15,602 lbs.
shoal keel:
c/board:
BALLAST
deep keel: 6,500 lbs.
shoal keel:
c/board:
DRAFT
deep keel: 5 ft. 4 ins.
shoal keel: opt. 4 ft. 4 ins.
c/board up:
c/board down:

SAIL AREA: 627 sq. ft.
FRESH WATER: 106 gals.
FUEL CAPACITY: 37 gals.

COSTS

BASE BOAT: $112,500
DATE: 04/85
EST. ON WATER:
DATE:

RATIOS

SAIL AREA/DISP: 16.06
DISP/LENGTH: 271
BALLAST RATIO: 41.66
FUEL/DISP: 1.77
FRESH WATER/DISP: 5.43

DECK

STEERING: wheel
WINCHES: primary and halyard
SAFETY: bow and stern pulpits with double lifelines
ANCHOR:
NAV LIGHTS: running

RIG

TYPE: masthead sloop
RIGGING: 1x19 SS wire
MAINSHEET: mid-boom sheeting

SAILS

SUPPLIED WITH BASE BOAT:

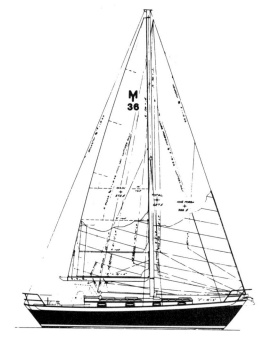

INTERIOR

BERTHS: 5 berths: 1 double V, 2 single extension berths, 1 single quarterberth
TABLE: dropleaf
HEAD(S): 1 head with holding tank
COLD STORAGE: built-in icebox
STOVE: 2-burner kerosene with oven
MAX. HEADROOM: 6 ft. 3 ins.

MACHINERY

ENGINE: Volvo #2003 diesel with 2:1 reduction gear
PROPELLER:
GENERATOR:

CATALINA 36

DESIGNER:
BUILDER: Catalina Yachts

STATISTICS

LOA: 36 ft. 4 ins.
LWL: 30 ft. 3 ins.
BEAM: 11 ft. 11 ins.
DISPLACEMENT
deep keel: 13,500 lbs.
shoal keel: 14,300 lbs.
c/board:
BALLAST
deep keel: 6,000 lbs.
shoal keel: 6,800 lbs.
c/board:
DRAFT
deep keel: 5 ft. 5 ins.
shoal keel: 4 ft. 7 ins.
c/board up:
c/board down:

SAIL AREA: 554.6 sq. ft.
FRESH WATER: 48.0 gals.
FUEL CAPACITY: 33.0 gals.

COSTS

BASE BOAT: $54,995
DATE: 10/01/84
EST. ON WATER:
DATE:

STOVE: 2-burner alcohol with oven
MAX. HEADROOM: 6 ft. 7 ins.

MACHINERY

ENGINE: 21 HP Universal #25 diesel with 2:1 reduction gear
PROPELLER:
GENERATOR:

DECK

STEERING: 32" wheel
WINCHES: 4 winches: 2 primary (3sp), 1 halyard, 1 mainsheet
SAFETY: bow and stern pulpits with double lifelines
ANCHOR: anchor locker
NAV LIGHTS: running and masthead

RIG

TYPE: masthead sloop
RIGGING:
MAINSHEET: mid-boom sheeting

SAILS

SUPPLIED WITH BASE BOAT:

RATIOS

	deep	shoal
SAIL AREA/DISP:	15.65	15.06
DISP/LENGTH:	217.73	230.63
BALLAST RATIO:	44.44	47.55
FUEL/DISP:	1.83	1.73
FRESH WATER/DISP:	2.84	2.69

INTERIOR

BERTHS: 7 berths: 1 double V, 1 double convertible, 1 single quarterberth, 1 center aft double
TABLE: center aft
HEAD(S): 1 head with shower
COLD STORAGE: built-in icebox

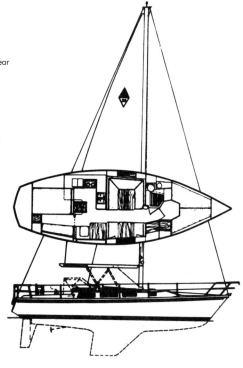

JEANNEAU SUN-SHINE

DESIGNER: Tony Castro
DISTRIBUTOR: Nautique International, Inc. (built in France by Jeanneau, S. A.)

STATISTICS

LOA: 36 ft. 5 ins.
LWL: 30 ft. 8 ins.
BEAM: 12 ft. 7 ins.
DISPLACEMENT
deep keel: 11,681 lbs.
shoal keel:
c/board: 11,681 lbs.
BALLAST
deep keel: 4,848 lbs.
shoal keel:
c/board: 5,510 lbs.
DRAFT
deep keel: 6 ft. 3 ins.
shoal keel:
c/board up: 4 ft. 1 ins.
c/board down: 6 ft. 11 ins.

SAIL AREA: 678 sq. ft.
FRESH WATER: 44 gals.
FUEL CAPACITY: 19 gals.

COSTS

BASE BOAT:
DATE:
EST. ON WATER:
DATE:

RATIOS

SAIL AREA/DISP: 21.07
DISP/LENGTH: 190.08
BALLAST RATIO:
41.50 47.17 (c/brd)
FUEL/DISP: 1.22
FRESH WATER/DISP: 3.01

DECK

STEERING: tiller
WINCHES: 4 winches
SAFETY: bow and stern pulpits with double lifelines
ANCHOR: anchor roller and locker
NAV LIGHTS: running lights

RIG

TYPE: masthead sloop
RIGGING:
MAINSHEET: mid-boom sheeting

SAILS

SUPPLIED WITH BASE BOAT: main, intermediate genoa, storm jib

INTERIOR

BERTHS: 8 berths: 1 double V, 2 single settees, 2 double quarterberths, 2 single pilots
TABLE: dropleaf
HEAD(S): 1 head with shower
COLD STORAGE: built-in icebox
STOVE: 2-burner gas with oven
MAX. HEADROOM: 6 ft. 2 ins.

MACHINERY

ENGINE: Yanmar #3GM diesel
PROPELLER:
GENERATOR:

CS 36

DESIGNER: Raymond Wall
BUILDER: CS Yachts, Ltd.

STATISTICS

LOA: 36 ft. 6 ins.
LWL: 29 ft. 3 ins.
BEAM: 11 ft. 6 ins.
DISPLACEMENT
deep keel: 15,500 lbs.
shoal keel:
c/board:
BALLAST
deep keel: 6,500 lbs.
shoal keel:
c/board:
DRAFT
deep keel: 6 ft. 3 ins.
shoal keel: 4 ft. 11 ins.
c/board up:
c/board down:

SAIL AREA: 822 sq. ft.
FRESH WATER: 83 gals.
FUEL CAPACITY: 35 gals.

COSTS

BASE BOAT: $79,900
DATE: 06/03/85
EST. ON WATER:
DATE:

RATIOS

SAIL AREA/DISP: 21.15
DISP/LENGTH: 276
BALLAST RATIO: 41.93
FUEL/DISP: 1.69
FRESH WATER/DISP: 4.28

DECK

STEERING: 36" wheel with emergency tiller
WINCHES: 6 Lewmar winches: 2 primary (#42), 1 main halyard (#30) 1 genoa halyard (#40), 1 mainsheet (#16), 1 reefing (#16)
SAFETY: bow and stern pulpits with double lifelines
ANCHOR: anchor well
NAV LIGHTS: running and masthead

RIG

TYPE: masthead sloop
RIGGING: 1x19 wire
MAINSHEET: boom-end or mid-boom sheeting

SAILS

SUPPLIED WITH BASE BOAT:

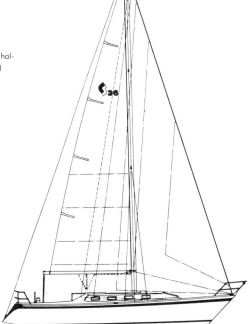

INTERIOR

BERTHS: 6 berths: 1 double V, 1 double convertible settee, 1 single settee, 1 single quarterberth
TABLE: centerline dropleaf or folding bulkhead-mounted
HEAD(S): 1 head with shower and sump pump
COLD STORAGE: built-in icebox (9 cu. ft.)
STOVE: 3-burner propane with oven
MAX. HEADROOM: 6 ft. 4 ins.

MACHINERY

ENGINE: 25 HP Westerbeke #30 diesel with 2:1 reduction gear
PROPELLER: 2-blade on 1" shaft
GENERATOR:

BUILDER'S COMMENTS The CS 36 anticipates in every specification, in quality of construction, and in handling characteristics the requirements of the sailor who is well seasoned in coastal and offshore cruising as well as club and local racing. But, at the same time, she's designed to be easily handled by a husband and wife crew. Below decks the CS 36 is warm, rich and comfortable—a luxurious blending of form and function.

PEARSON 36

DESIGNER: Bill Shaw
BUILDER: Pearson Yachts

STATISTICS

LOA: 36 ft. 6 ins.
LWL: 29 ft. 7 ins.
BEAM: 12 ft. 4 ins.
DISPLACEMENT
deep keel: 15,000 lbs.
shoal keel:
c/board: 15,850 lbs.
BALLAST
deep keel: 5,800 lbs.
shoal keel:
c/board: 6,550 lbs.
DRAFT
deep keel: 6 ft. 6 ins.
shoal keel:
c/board up: 4 ft. 2 ins.
c/board down: 8 ft. 3 ins.

SAIL AREA: 665 sq. ft.
FRESH WATER: 100 gals.
FUEL CAPACITY: 22 gals.

COSTS

BASE BOAT:
DATE:
EST. ON WATER:
DATE:

RATIOS

SAIL AREA/DISP: 17.49
DISP/LENGTH: 258.73
BALLAST RATIO: 38.67
FUEL/DISP: 1.1
FRESH WATER/DISP: 5.33

DECK

STEERING: wheel with emergency tiller
WINCHES: 6 Lewmar winches:
2 primary (#48 ST), 2 halyard (#16), 1 mainsheet
(#30 ST), 1 reefing (#8)
SAFETY: bow and stern pulpits
with double lifelines
ANCHOR: anchor well
NAV LIGHTS: running and masthead

RIG

TYPE: masthead sloop
RIGGING: wire
MAINSHEET: mid-boom sheeting

SAILS

SUPPLIED WITH BASE BOAT:

INTERIOR

BERTHS: 7 berths: 1 double V, 1 single settee, 1 double settee, 1 double quarterberth
TABLE: fixed
HEAD(S): 1 head with shower, sump pump, and holding tank
COLD STORAGE: built-in icebox (8 cu. ft.)
STOVE: 2-burner propane with oven
MAX. HEADROOM:

MACHINERY

ENGINE: 30 HP diesel
PROPELLER: fixed on 1 1/4" shaft
GENERATOR:

BANNER 37

DESIGNER: Stan Huntingford
BUILDER: Cooper Yachts

STATISTICS

LOA: 36 ft. 7 ins.
LWL: 28 ft. 10 ins.
BEAM: 12 ft. 0 ins.
DISPLACEMENT
deep keel: 13,500 lbs.
shoal keel:
c/board:
BALLAST
deep keel: 5,500 lbs.
shoal keel:
c/board:
DRAFT
deep keel: 5 ft. 0 ins.
shoal keel:
c/board up:
c/board down:

SAIL AREA: 655 sq. ft.
FRESH WATER: 40 gals.
FUEL CAPACITY: 40 gals.

COSTS

BASE BOAT: $77,500
DATE: 04/85
EST. ON WATER:
DATE:

RATIOS

SAIL AREA/DISP: 18.48
DISP/LENGTH: 251.25
BALLAST RATIO: 40.74
FUEL/DISP: 2.22
FRESH WATER/DISP: 2.37

DECK

STEERING: wheel
WINCHES: 5 Lewmar winches: 2 #42 ST, 2 #30, 1 #16
SAFETY: bow and stern pulpits with double lifelines
ANCHOR:
NAV LIGHTS: running

RIG

TYPE: masthead sloop
RIGGING:
MAINSHEET: mid-boom sheeting

SAILS

SUPPLIED WITH BASE BOAT: main, working jib

INTERIOR

BERTHS: 6 berths: 1 double V, 1 double convertible dinette, 1 single settee, 1 single quarterberth
TABLE:
HEAD(S): 1 head with shower and holding tank
COLD STORAGE: built-in icebox (5 cu. ft.)
STOVE: 3 burner propane with oven
MAX. HEADROOM:

MACHINERY

ENGINE: 23 HP Volvo diesel
PROPELLER: fixed
GENERATOR:

COOPER 367

DESIGNER: Stan Huntingford
BUILDER: Cooper Yachts

STATISTICS

LOA: 36 ft. 7 ins.
LWL: 28 ft. 6 ins.
BEAM: 12 ft. 0 ins.
DISPLACEMENT
deep keel: 13,250 lbs.
shoal keel:
c/board:
BALLAST
deep keel: 5,250 lbs.
shoal keel:
c/board:
DRAFT
deep keel: 5 ft. 10 ins.
shoal keel:
c/board up:
c/board down:

SAIL AREA: 561 sq. ft.
FRESH WATER: 80 gals.
FUEL CAPACITY: 40 gals.

COSTS

BASE BOAT: $82,500
DATE: 04/85
EST. ON WATER:
DATE:

RATIOS

SAIL AREA/DISP: 16.03
DISP/LENGTH: 255.52
BALLAST RATIO: 39.62
FUEL/DISP: 2.26
FRESH WATER/DISP: 4.83

DECK

STEERING: wheel
WINCHES: 5 Lewmar winches: 2 #40, 3 #10
SAFETY: bow and stern pulpits with double lifelines
ANCHOR:
NAV LIGHTS: running

RIG

TYPE: masthead sloop
RIGGING:
MAINSHEET: mid-boom sheeting

SAILS

SUPPLIED WITH BASE BOAT: main, working jib

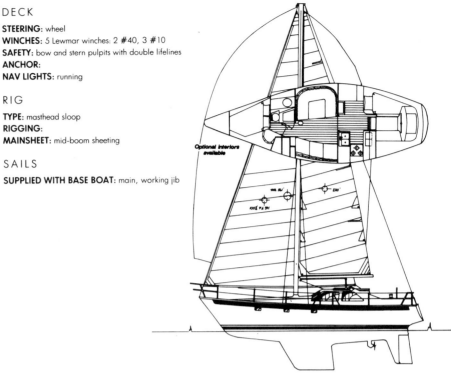

INTERIOR

BERTHS: 6 berths: 1 double V, 1 single settee, 1 double convertible dinette, 1 single quarterberth
TABLE:
HEAD(S): 1 head with shower
COLD STORAGE: built-in icebox (6 cu. ft.)
STOVE: 3-burner propane with oven
MAX. HEADROOM:

MACHINERY

ENGINE: 25 HP diesel
PROPELLER:
GENERATOR:

TAYANA 37

DESIGNER: Robert H. Perry
DISTRIBUTOR: Southern Offshore Yachts, Inc. (built in Taiwan by TaYang Yacht Building Co.)

STATISTICS

LOA: 36 ft. 8 ins.
LWL: 31 ft. 0 ins.
BEAM: 11 ft. 6 ins.
DISPLACEMENT
deep keel: 22,500 lbs.
shoal keel:
c/board:
BALLAST
deep keel: 7,340 lbs.
shoal keel:
c/board:
DRAFT
deep keel: 5 ft. 8 ins.
shoal keel:
c/board up:
c/board down:

SAIL AREA: 861 sq. ft. (cutter)
768 sq. ft. (ketch)
FRESH WATER: 100 gals.
FUEL CAPACITY: 90 gals.

COSTS

BASE BOAT: $67,500
DATE: 07/85
EST. ON WATER: $80,000
DATE: 07/85

RATIOS

SAIL AREA/DISP: 17.28 (cutter)
15.42 (ketch)
DISP/LENGTH: 337.17
BALLAST RATIO: 32.62
FUEL/DISP: 3.00
FRESH WATER/DISP: 3.56

DECK

STEERING: wheel with emergency tiller
WINCHES: 8 Barlow winches: 2 #22, 1 #18, 1 #16, 4 #15
SAFETY: bow and stern pulpits with double lifelines
ANCHOR: anchor roller and well
NAV LIGHTS: running and masthead

RIG

TYPE: masthead cutter or ketch
RIGGING: wire (3/8")
MAINSHEET: 6-part with mid-boom sheeting

SAILS

SUPPLIED WITH BASE BOAT: main (2 reefs), yankee, staysail, mizzen

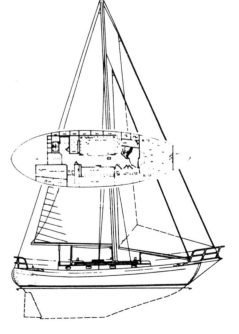

INTERIOR

BERTHS: 7 berths
TABLE:
HEAD(S): 1 head with 1 shower, 1 sump pump, and 2 holding tanks
COLD STORAGE: built-in icebox (10–12 cu. ft.)
STOVE:
MAX. HEADROOM: 6 ft. 4 ins.

MACHINERY

ENGINE: 36 HP Yanmar #3QM diesel
PROPELLER: 3-blade fixed 18"x13" on 1 1/4" shaft
GENERATOR:

H. T. GOZZARD 36

DESIGNER: H. Ted Gozzard
BUILDER: North Castle Marine, Ltd.

STATISTICS

LOD: 36 ft. 9 ins.
LWL: 29 ft. 6 ins.
BEAM: 12 ft. 0 ins.
DISPLACEMENT
deep keel: 17,200 lbs.
shoal keel:
c/board:
BALLAST
deep keel: 6,700 lbs.
shoal keel:
c/board:
DRAFT
deep keel: 4 ft. 9 ins.
shoal keel:
c/board up:
c/board down:

SAIL AREA: 810 sq. ft.
FRESH WATER:
FUEL CAPACITY:

COSTS

BASE BOAT: $103,000
DATE: 04/01/85
EST. ON WATER:
DATE:

RATIOS

SAIL AREA/DISP: 19.45
DISP/LENGTH: 299.1
BALLAST RATIO: 38.96
FUEL/DISP:
FRESH WATER/DISP:

DECK

STEERING: wheel with emergency tiller
WINCHES: 4 Lewmar winches: 1 #40A ST 2sp, 1 #30A ST 2sp, 2 #16 2sp
SAFETY: bow and stern pulpits with double lifelines
ANCHOR: anchor roller
NAV LIGHTS: running and masthead

RIG

TYPE: masthead cutter
RIGGING: 1x19 wire
MAINSHEET: boom-end sheeting

SAILS

SUPPLIED WITH BASE BOAT:

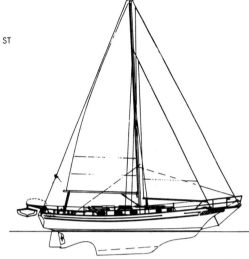

INTERIOR

BERTHS: 6 berths: 1 double V, 1 double convertible settee, 1 double convertible dinette
TABLE: bulkhead-mounted
HEAD(S): 1 head with shower and sump pump
COLD STORAGE: built-in icebox
STOVE: 3-burner propane with oven
MAX. HEADROOM:

MACHINERY

ENGINE: 52 HP Westerbeke diesel
PROPELLER: fixed
GENERATOR:

SEA BIRD 37 C.C.

DESIGNER:
BUILDER: Cooper Yachts

STATISTICS

LOA: 36 ft. 10 ins.
LWL: 32 ft. 6 ins.
BEAM: 11 ft. 8 ins.
DISPLACEMENT
deep keel: 18,000 lbs.
shoal keel:
c/board:
BALLAST
deep keel: 6,000 lbs.
shoal keel:
c/board:
DRAFT
deep keel: 4 ft. 0 ins.
shoal keel:
c/board up:
c/board down:

SAIL AREA: cutter 639 sq. ft.
ketch 650 sq. ft.
FRESH WATER: 100 gals.
FUEL CAPACITY: 90 gals.

COSTS

BASE BOAT: $92,500
DATE: 04/85
EST. ON WATER:
DATE:

RATIOS

SAIL AREA/DISP: 15.14
DISP/LENGTH: 234.09
BALLAST RATIO: 33.33
FUEL/DISP: 3.75
FRESH WATER/DISP: 4.44

DECK

STEERING: wheel
WINCHES: 4 Lewmar winches: 2 #30, 2 #10
SAFETY: bow and stern pulpits with double lifelines
ANCHOR: 40 lb. anchor
NAV LIGHTS:

RIG

TYPE: cutter or ketch
RIGGING:
MAINSHEET:

SAILS

SUPPLIED WITH BASE BOAT: main, working jib, staysail, 135% genoa

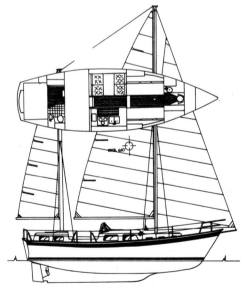

INTERIOR

BERTHS: 4 berths: 2 single settees, 1 center aft double
TABLE:
HEAD(S): 2 heads with 1 shower and 2 holding tanks
COLD STORAGE: built-in icebox (6 cu. ft.)
STOVE: 3-burner propane with oven
MAX. HEADROOM:

MACHINERY

ENGINE: 40 HP diesel
PROPELLER:
GENERATOR:

SEA BIRD 37 MOTOR SAILER

DESIGNER:
BUILDER: Cooper Yachts

STATISTICS

LOA: 36 ft. 10 ins.
LWL: 32 ft. 6 ins.
BEAM: 11 ft. 8 ins.
DISPLACEMENT
deep keel: 18,000 lbs.
shoal keel:
c/board:
BALLAST
deep keel: 6,000 lbs.
shoal keel:
c/board:
DRAFT
deep keel: 4 ft. 0 ins.
shoal keel:
c/board up:
c/board down:

SAIL AREA: 560 sq. ft.
FRESH WATER: 100 gals.
FUEL CAPACITY: 100 gals.

COSTS

BASE BOAT: $92,500
DATE: 04/85
EST. ON WATER:
DATE:

RATIOS

SAIL AREA/DISP: 13.05
DISP/LENGTH: 234.09
BALLAST RATIO: 33.33
FUEL/DISP: 4.17
FRESH WATER/DISP: 4.44

DECK

STEERING: wheel
WINCHES: 5 Lewmar winches: 2 #30 ST, 3 #10
SAFETY: bow and stern pulpits with double lifelines
ANCHOR:
NAV LIGHTS: running

RIG

TYPE: masthead sloop
RIGGING:
MAINSHEET:

SAILS

SUPPLIED WITH BASE BOAT: main

INTERIOR

BERTHS: 4 berths: 2 single Vs, 1 single settee, 1 single pilot
TABLE:
HEAD(S): 1 head with shower and holding tank
COLD STORAGE: built-in icebox (6 cu. ft.)
STOVE: 3-burner propane with oven
MAX. HEADROOM:

MACHINERY

ENGINE: 50 HP diesel
PROPELLER:
GENERATOR:

SEIDELMANN 37

DESIGNER: Seidelmann
BUILDER: Seidelmann Yachts

STATISTICS

LOA: 36 ft. 10 ins.
LWL: 29 ft. 6 ins.
BEAM: 12 ft. 0 ins.
DISPLACEMENT
deep keel: 13,500 lbs.
shoal keel:
c/board:
BALLAST
deep keel: 6,000 lbs.
shoal keel:
c/board:
DRAFT
deep keel: 5 ft. 11 ins.
shoal keel: 4 ft. 6 ins.
c/board up:
c/board down:

SAIL AREA: 6,000 sq. ft.
FRESH WATER: 100 gals.
FUEL CAPACITY: 18 gals.

COSTS

BASE BOAT:
DATE:
EST. ON WATER:
DATE:

RATIOS

SAIL AREA/DISP: 18.14
DISP/LENGTH: 234
BALLAST RATIO: 44.44
FUEL/DISP: 1.00
FRESH WATER/DISP: 4.14

INTERIOR

BERTHS: 6 berths: 1 double V, 1 double convertible settee, 1 single settee, 1 single quarterberth
TABLE: bulkhead-mounted
HEAD(S): 1 head with shower
COLD STORAGE: built-in icebox
STOVE: 2-burner alcohol with oven
MAX. HEADROOM: 6 ft. 7 ins.

MACHINERY

ENGINE: diesel
PROPELLER: 2 or 3 blade
GENERATOR:

DECK

STEERING: 30" wheel;
WINCHES: 4 winches: 2 sheet (#24), 2 halyard
SAFETY: bow and stern pulpits with double lifelines
ANCHOR: anchor well
NAV LIGHTS: running and masthead

RIG

TYPE: masthead sloop
RIGGING: stainless steel
MAINSHEET: mid-boom sheeting

SAILS

SUPPLIED WITH BASE BOAT: main (1 reef), working jib

BAVARIA 1060

DESIGNER: Axel Mohnhaupt
BUILDER: Bavaria Yachtbau GmbH

STATISTICS

LOA: 36 ft. 10.88 ins.
LWL: 28 ft. 2.63 ins.
BEAM: 11 ft. 1.88 ins.
DISPLACEMENT
deep keel: 10,580 lbs.
shoal keel:
c/board:
BALLAST
deep keel: 4,408 lbs.
shoal keel:
c/board:
DRAFT
deep keel: 5 ft. 9.25 ins.
shoal keel: 4 ft. 7.00 ins.
c/board up:
c/board down:

SAIL AREA: 614.14 sq. ft.
FRESH WATER: 55.00 gals.
FUEL CAPACITY: 27.60 gals.

COSTS

BASE BOAT:
DATE:
EST. ON WATER:
DATE:

RATIOS

SAIL AREA/DISP: 20.39
DISP/LENGTH: 210.16
BALLAST RATIO: 41.7
FUEL/DISP: 4.17
FRESH WATER/DISP: 1.95

INTERIOR

BERTHS: 7 berths: 1 double V, 1 double convertible settee, 1 single settee, 2 single quarterberths
TABLE: dropleaf
HEAD(S):
COLD STORAGE: built-in icebox
STOVE: 2-burner gas
MAX. HEADROOM: 6 ft. 1 ins.

MACHINERY

ENGINE: 18 HP Volvo with 2.2:1 reduction gear
PROPELLER:
GENERATOR:

DECK

STEERING: tiller
WINCHES: 4 Lewmar or Enkes winches: 2 primary, 2 halyard
SAFETY: bow and stern pulpits with double lifelines
ANCHOR: anchor with anchor chain, roller, and well
NAV LIGHTS: running and masthead

RIG

TYPE: fractional rig sloop
RIGGING: 1x19 wire
MAINSHEET: mid-boom sheeting

SAILS

SUPPLIED WITH BASE BOAT:
main (2 reefs), working jib

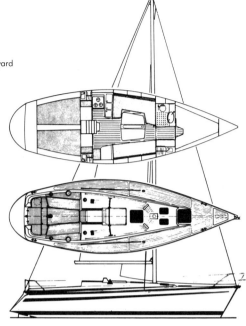

BUILDER'S COMMENTS The Bavaria 1060 has everything that makes sailing faster, safer, and more pleasant. Just looking at the hull form you can see that this is a very fast boat. The teak deck is both beautiful and very safe because of its non-slip covering. The main-sheet traveler has been positioned on the coachroof, where it does not hinder activities in the cockpit.

CREALOCK 37

DESIGNER: William Crealock
BUILDER: Pacific Seacraft Corp.

STATISTICS

LOA: 36 ft. 11 ins.
LWL: 27 ft. 9 ins.
BEAM: 10 ft. 10 ins.
DISPLACEMENT
deep keel: 16,000 lbs.
shoal keel:
c/board:
BALLAST
deep keel: 6,200 lbs.
shoal keel:
c/board:
DRAFT
deep keel: 5 ft. 6 ins.
shoal keel: 4 ft. 5 ins.
c/board up:
c/board down:

SAIL AREA: 619 sq. ft.
FRESH WATER: 90 gals.
FUEL CAPACITY: 40 gals.

COSTS

BASE BOAT: $102,800
DATE: 06/85
EST. ON WATER: $120,000
DATE: 06/85

RATIOS

SAIL AREA/DISP: 15.6
DISP/LENGTH: 334
BALLAST RATIO: 38.75
FUEL/DISP: 1.87
FRESH WATER/DISP: 4.50

INTERIOR

BERTHS: 6 berths: 1 forward double, 1 double convertible settee, 1 single settee, 1 single quarterberth
TABLE: folding
HEAD(S): 1 head
COLD STORAGE: built-in icebox
STOVE: 2-burner kerosene with oven
MAX. HEADROOM: 6 ft. 4 ins.

MACHINERY

ENGINE: 32 HP Universal #40 diesel
PROPELLER: 2-blade
GENERATOR:

DECK

STEERING: tiller
WINCHES: 5 Lewmar winches: 2 primaries (#46), 2 halyard (#16), 1 mainsheet (#16)
SAFETY: bow and stern pulpits with double lifelines
ANCHOR: double anchor rollers and wells
NAV LIGHTS: running

RIG

TYPE: masthead sloop, cutter, or yawl
RIGGING: 1x19 SS wire
MAINSHEET: mid-boom sheeting

SAILS

SUPPLIED WITH BASE BOAT:

BUILDER'S COMMENTS The Crealock 37 is a superb high performance cruising yacht which incorporates all the qualities an experienced sailor looks for in "a proper yacht"—seaworthiness, premium quality, exceptional performance, comfort, and beauty. Her designer, W.I.B. Crealock, has utilized a modern split keel and skeg rudder underbody. She's sleek, beautiful, and a brilliant performer in all conditions, as was proven by her remarkable performance in the recent Single-Handed Trans-Pacific Yacht Race. She'll accommodate six and has features specifically designed for extended cruising.

BAVARIA 1130

DESIGNER: Axel Mohnhaupt
BUILDER: Bavaria Yachtbau GmbH

STATISTICS

LOA: 37 ft. 0 ins.
LWL: 29 ft. 10 ins.
BEAM: 11 ft. 4 ins.
DISPLACEMENT
deep keel: 15,000 lbs.
shoal keel:
c/board:
BALLAST
deep keel: 6,700 lbs.
shoal keel:
c/board:
DRAFT
deep keel: 6 ft. 2 ins.
shoal keel:
c/board up:
c/board down:

SAIL AREA: 580 sq. ft.
FRESH WATER: 80 gals.
FUEL CAPACITY: 28 gals.

COSTS

BASE BOAT:
DATE:
EST. ON WATER:
DATE:

RATIOS

SAIL AREA/DISP: 15.25
DISP/LENGTH: 252
BALLAST RATIO: 44.66
FUEL/DISP: 1.40
FRESH WATER/DISP: 4.26

INTERIOR

BERTHS: 7 berths: 1 double V, 2 single settees, 1 single pilot berth, 1 double aft
TABLE: dropleaf
HEAD(S): 2 heads
COLD STORAGE: built-in icebox (21 gal.)
STOVE: 2-burner gas
MAX. HEADROOM:

MACHINERY

ENGINE: 28 HP Volvo diesel with 2.2:1 reduction gear
PROPELLER:
GENERATOR:

DECK

STEERING: wheel
WINCHES: 3 Lewmar or Enkes winches: 2 primary (2sp ST), 1 mainsheet (#16 ST)
SAFETY: bow and stern pulpits with double lifelines
ANCHOR: anchor with anchor chain and well
NAV LIGHTS: running and masthead

RIG

TYPE: masthead sloop
RIGGING: 1x19 wire
MAINSHEET:

SAILS

SUPPLIED WITH BASE BOAT: main (2 reefs), working jib

BUILDER'S COMMENTS The Bavaria 1130, "Made in Germany," is a secure investment in a quality yacht. Its construction is based on extensive modern yacht building knowledge

DICKERSON 37 AFT COCKPIT

DESIGNER: George Hazen
BUILDER: Dickerson Boatbuilders, Inc.

STATISTICS

LOA: 37 ft. 0 ins.
LWL: 28 ft. 10 ins.
BEAM: 11 ft. 6 ins.
DISPLACEMENT
deep keel: 15,950 lbs.
shoal keel:
c/board:
BALLAST
deep keel: 6,000 lbs.
shoal keel:
c/board:
DRAFT
deep keel: 4 ft. 6 ins.
shoal keel:
c/board up:
c/board down:

SAIL AREA: 675 sq. ft.
FRESH WATER: 90 gals.
FUEL CAPACITY: 40 gals.

COSTS

BASE BOAT:
DATE:
EST. ON WATER:
DATE:

RATIOS

SAIL AREA/DISP: 17.04
DISP/LENGTH: 296.84
BALLAST RATIO: 37.61
FUEL/DISP: 1.88
FRESH WATER/DISP: 4.51

DECK

STEERING: wheel
WINCHES: 4 winches: 2 primary, 2 halyard
SAFETY: bow and stern pulpits with lifelines
ANCHOR: anchor well, roller, and bowsprit
NAV LIGHTS: running

RIG

TYPE: masthead sloop, cutter, or ketch
RIGGING: 1x19 wire
MAINSHEET:

SAILS

SUPPLIED WITH BASE BOAT:

INTERIOR

BERTHS: 6 berths: 1 double V, 2 single settees, 1 double quarterberth
TABLE: bulkhead-mounted
HEAD(S): 1 head with shower
COLD STORAGE: built-in icebox
STOVE: 3-burner alcohol with oven
MAX. HEADROOM:

MACHINERY

ENGINE: Perkins #4-108 diesel
PROPELLER: 3-blade
GENERATOR:

DICKERSON 37 CENTER COCKPIT KETCH

DESIGNER: George Hazen
BUILDER: Dickerson Boatbuilders, Inc.

STATISTICS

LOA: 37 ft. 0 ins.
LWL: 28 ft. 10 ins.
BEAM: 11 ft. 6 ins.
DISPLACEMENT
deep keel: 15,950 lbs.
shoal keel:
c/board:
BALLAST
deep keel: 6,000 lbs.
shoal keel:
c/board:
DRAFT
deep keel: 4 ft. 6 ins.
shoal keel:
c/board up:
c/board down:

SAIL AREA: 675 sq. ft.
FRESH WATER: 90 gals.
FUEL CAPACITY: 40 gals.

COSTS

BASE BOAT:
DATE:
EST. ON WATER:
DATE:

RATIOS

SAIL AREA/DISP: 17.04
DISP/LENGTH: 296.04
BALLAST RATIO: 37.61
FUEL/DISP: 1.88
FRESH WATER/DISP: 4.51

DECK

STEERING: wheel
WINCHES: 4 winches: 2 primary, 2 halyard
SAFETY: bow and stern pulpits with lifelines
ANCHOR: anchor well, roller, and bowsprit
NAV LIGHTS: running

RIG

TYPE: masthead ketch
RIGGING: 1x19 wire
MAINSHEET:

SAILS

SUPPLIED WITH BASE BOAT:

INTERIOR

BERTHS: 6 berths: 1 double V, 1 double convertible, 1 aft double
TABLE: bulkhead-mounted
HEAD(S): 1 head with shower
COLD STORAGE: built-in icebox
STOVE: 3-burner alcohol with oven
MAX. HEADROOM:

MACHINERY

ENGINE: Perkins #4-108 diesel
PROPELLER: 3-bladed
GENERATOR:

MOODY 37

DESIGNER: Bill Dixon-Angus Primrose, Ltd.
DISTRIBUTOR: A. H. Moody & Son, Ltd. (built in England by Marine Projects, Ltd.)

STATISTICS

LOA: 37 ft. 0 ins.
LWL:
BEAM: 12 ft. 5 ins.
DISPLACEMENT
deep keel: 16,250 lbs.
shoal keel:
c/board:
BALLAST
deep keel: 6,500 lbs.
shoal keel:
c/board:
DRAFT
deep keel: 5 ft. 5 ins.
shoal keel:
c/board up:
c/board down:

SAIL AREA:
FRESH WATER: 55 gals.
FUEL CAPACITY: 45 gals.

COSTS

BASE BOAT:
DATE:
EST. ON WATER:
DATE:

RATIOS

SAIL AREA/DISP: 20.95
DISP/LENGTH:
BALLAST RATIO: 40.00
FUEL/DISP: 2.08
FRESH WATER/DISP: 2.71

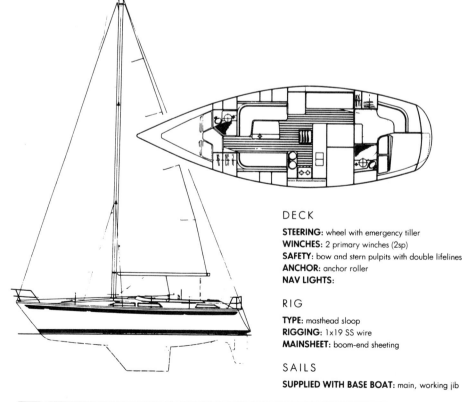

INTERIOR

BERTHS: 7 berths: 2 single Vs (converting to double), 3 single settees, 1 center aft double
TABLE: dropleaf
HEAD(S): 2 heads with 2 showers
COLD STORAGE: refrigerator/freezer
STOVE: 2-burner LPG with oven
MAX. HEADROOM: 6 + ft.

MACHINERY

ENGINE: 38 HP Thornycroft #T-90 diesel
PROPELLER: fixed
GENERATOR:

DECK

STEERING: wheel with emergency tiller
WINCHES: 2 primary winches (2sp)
SAFETY: bow and stern pulpits with double lifelines
ANCHOR: anchor roller
NAV LIGHTS:

RIG

TYPE: masthead sloop
RIGGING: 1x19 SS wire
MAINSHEET: boom-end sheeting

SAILS

SUPPLIED WITH BASE BOAT: main, working jib

VALIANT 37

DESIGNER: Robert H. Perry
BUILDER: Valiant Yachts

STATISTICS

LOA: 37 ft. 0 ins.
LWL: 31 ft. 7 ins.
BEAM: 11 ft. 5 ins.
DISPLACEMENT
deep keel: 17,000 lbs.
shoal keel:
c/board:
BALLAST
deep keel: 6,600 lbs.
shoal keel:
c/board:
DRAFT
deep keel: 5 ft. 9 ins.
shoal keel:
c/board up:
c/board down:

SAIL AREA: 667 sq. ft.
FRESH WATER:
FUEL CAPACITY:

COSTS

BASE BOAT:
DATE:
EST. ON WATER:
DATE:

RATIOS

SAIL AREA/DISP: 16.14
DISP/LENGTH: 239
BALLAST RATIO: 38.82
FUEL/DISP:
FRESH WATER/DISP:

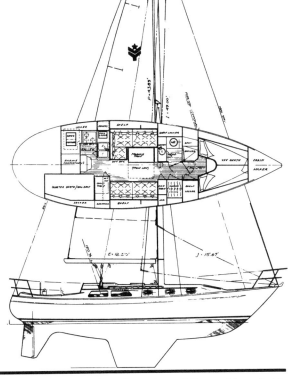

DECK

STEERING: wheel with emergency tiller
WINCHES: complete package
SAFETY: bow and stern pulpits with lifelines
ANCHOR:
NAV LIGHTS: running

RIG

TYPE: masthead sloop
RIGGING: rod
MAINSHEET: mid-boom sheeting

SAILS

SUPPLIED WITH BASE BOAT:

INTERIOR

BERTHS: 6 berths: 1 double V, 2 single settees, 1 double quarterberth
TABLE: center double-leaf
HEAD(S): 2 heads with 2 showers
COLD STORAGE: refrigerator/freezer and built-in icebox
STOVE: 3-burner with oven
MAX. HEADROOM: 6 ft. 4 ins.

MACHINERY

ENGINE: diesel with 2:1 reduction gear
PROPELLER:
GENERATOR:

BUILDER'S COMMENTS This beautiful yacht is the culmination of the vast knowledge that can only be gained by experience. The new Valiant 37 embodies all that has made Valiant the "ultimate" in sailing yachts. It is a contemporary statement of the Valiant tradition.

EXPRESS 37

DESIGNER: Carl Schumacher
BUILDER: Alsberg Brothers Boatworks

STATISTICS

LOA: 37 ft. 1 ins.
LWL: 30 ft. 10 ins.
BEAM: 11 ft. 6 ins.
DISPLACEMENT
deep keel: 9,500 lbs.
shoal keel:
c/board:
BALLAST
deep keel: 4,500 lbs.
shoal keel:
c/board:
DRAFT
deep keel: 7 ft. 3 ins.
shoal keel:
c/board up:
c/board down:

SAIL AREA: 638 sq. ft.
FRESH WATER:
FUEL CAPACITY:

COSTS

BASE BOAT:
DATE:
EST. ON WATER:
DATE:

RATIOS

SAIL AREA/DISP: 22.77
DISP/LENGTH: 144.6
BALLAST RATIO: 47.4
FUEL/DISP:
FRESH WATER/DISP:

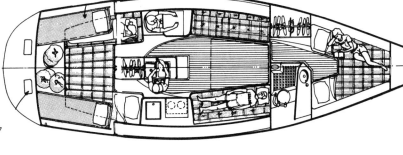

INTERIOR

BERTHS: 6 berths: 1 double V, 2 single settees, 1 center aft double
TABLE:
HEAD(S): 1 head with shower
COLD STORAGE: built-in icebox
STOVE: 2-burner
MAX. HEADROOM: 6 ft. 2 ins.

MACHINERY

ENGINE: 15 HP Yanmar diesel
PROPELLER:
GENERATOR:

DECK

STEERING: tiller
WINCHES:
SAFETY: bow and stern pulpits with double lifelines
ANCHOR:
NAV LIGHTS:

RIG

TYPE: masthead sloop
RIGGING:
MAINSHEET: mid-boom sheeting

SAILS

SUPPLIED WITH BASE BOAT:

GIB'SEA 106 MASTER

DESIGNER: Joubert & Nivelt
BUILDER: Gilbert Marine, S. A.

STATISTICS

LOA: 37 ft. 1 ins.
LWL: 29 ft. 11 ins.
BEAM: 11 ft. 10 ins.
DISPLACEMENT
deep keel: 10,600 lbs.
shoal keel:
c/board:
BALLAST
deep keel: 3,750 lbs.
shoal keel:
c/board:
DRAFT
deep keel: 5 ft. 11 ins.
shoal keel:
c/board up: 4 ft. 0 ins.
c/board down: 6 ft. 11 ins.

SAIL AREA: 600 sq. ft.
FRESH WATER: 80 gals.
FUEL CAPACITY: 40 gals.

COSTS

BASE BOAT:
DATE:
EST. ON WATER:
DATE:

RATIOS

SAIL AREA/DISP: 19.89
DISP/LENGTH: 176
BALLAST RATIO: 35.37
FUEL/DISP: 2.83
FRESH WATER/DISP: 6.03

DECK

STEERING: wheel with emergency tiller
WINCHES: 4 winches: 2 primary (2sp ST), 2 halyard (2sp ST)
SAFETY: bow and stern pulpits with double lifelines
ANCHOR: double bow roller and anchor well
NAV LIGHTS: running and masthead

RIG

TYPE: masthead sloop
RIGGING:
MAINSHEET: mid-boom sheeting

SAILS

SUPPLIED WITH BASE BOAT:

INTERIOR

BERTHS: 6 berths: 1 double V, 2 single settees, 1 double quarterberth
TABLE: dropleaf
HEAD(S): 1 head with shower and sump pump
COLD STORAGE: built-in icebox (4.6 cu. ft.); refrigerator (2.5 cu. ft.)
STOVE: 2-burner LPG with oven
MAX. HEADROOM: 6 ft. 1 ins.

MACHINERY

ENGINE: 28 HP diesel
PROPELLER: 2-blade
GENERATOR:

ALBERG 37

DESIGNER: Carl A. Alberg
BUILDER: Whitby Boat Works, Ltd.

STATISTICS

LOA: 37 ft. 2 ins.
LWL: 26 ft. 6 ins.
BEAM: 10 ft. 2 ins.
DISPLACEMENT
deep keel: 16,800 lbs.
shoal keel:
c/board:
BALLAST
deep keel: 6,500 lbs.
shoal keel:
c/board:
DRAFT
deep keel: 5 ft. 6 ins.
shoal keel:
c/board up:
c/board down:

SAIL AREA: 646 sq. ft.
FRESH WATER: 51 gals.
FUEL CAPACITY: 35 gals.

COSTS

BASE BOAT:
DATE:
EST. ON WATER:
DATE:

RATIOS

SAIL AREA/DISP: 15.76
DISP/LENGTH: 403
BALLAST RATIO: 38.69
FUEL/DISP: 1.56
FRESH WATER/DISP: 2.43

DECK

STEERING: 24" wheel with emergency tiller
WINCHES: 6 Lewmar winches
SAFETY: bow and stern pulpits with double lifelines
ANCHOR: Danforth 22-S
NAV LIGHTS: running and masthead

RIG

TYPE: masthead sloop (yawl also available)
RIGGING: 1x19 wire
MAINSHEET: boom-end sheeting

SAILS

SUPPLIED WITH BASE BOAT:

INTERIOR

BERTHS: 7 berths: 1 double V, 1 single settee, 1 double convertible dinette, 1 single pilot, 1 single quarterberth
TABLE: bulkhead-mounted dropleaf
HEAD(S): 1 head with shower and holding tank (33 gals.)
COLD STORAGE: built-in icebox
STOVE: 2-burner propane with oven
MAX. HEADROOM:

MACHINERY

ENGINE: 28 HP Volvo #2003 diesel with 2.38:1 reduction gear
PROPELLER: 3-blade fixed 13"x14" on 1" shaft
GENERATOR:

JEANNEAU SELECTION

DESIGNER: Joubert/Nivelt
DISTRIBUTOR: Nautique International, Inc. (built in France by Jeanneau, S. A.)

STATISTICS

LOA: 37 ft. 3 ins.
LWL: 29 ft. 4 ins.
BEAM: 10 ft. 8 ins.
DISPLACEMENT
deep keel: 6,800 lbs.
shoal keel:
c/board:
BALLAST
deep keel: 2,425 lbs.
shoal keel:
c/board:
DRAFT
deep keel: 6 ft. 3 ins.
shoal keel:
c/board up:
c/board down:

SAIL AREA: 578.0 sq. ft.
FRESH WATER: 13.2 gals.
FUEL CAPACITY: 10.0 gals.

COSTS

BASE BOAT: $65,500
DATE: 08/01/84
EST. ON WATER:
DATE:

RATIOS

SAIL AREA/DISP: 23.89
DISP/LENGTH: 134.75
BALLAST RATIO: 31.84
FUEL/DISP: .98
FRESH WATER/DISP: 1.39

DECK

STEERING: tiller
WINCHES:
SAFETY:
ANCHOR:
NAV LIGHTS: running and masthead

RIG

TYPE: fractional rig sloop
RIGGING:
MAINSHEET: boom-end sheeting

SAILS

SUPPLIED WITH BASE BOAT:

INTERIOR

BERTHS: 8 berths: 1 double V, 2 single settees, 2 single quarter-berths, 2 pilot berths
TABLE: dropleaf
HEAD(S): 1 head with shower and holding tank
COLD STORAGE: built-in icebox
STOVE: 2-burner
MAX. HEADROOM:

MACHINERY

ENGINE: Yanmar #2GM diesel
PROPELLER: fixed
GENERATOR:

TARTAN 37

DESIGNER: Sparkman & Stephens
BUILDER: Tartan Marine Company

STATISTICS

LOA: 37 ft. 3.5 ins.
LWL: 31 ft. 7.0 ins.
BEAM: 12 ft. 8.4 ins.
DISPLACEMENT
deep keel: 15,500 lbs.
shoal keel:
c/board: 15,500 lbs.
BALLAST
deep keel: 7.500 lbs.
shoal keel:
c/board: 7,500 lbs.
DRAFT
deep keel: 6 ft. 4 ins.
shoal keel:
c/board up: 4 ft. 2 ins.
c/board down: 7 ft. 9 ins.

SAIL AREA: 625 sq. ft.
FRESH WATER: 90 gals.
FUEL CAPACITY: 50 gals.

COSTS

BASE BOAT: $94,000
DATE: 07/01/85
EST. ON WATER: $105,000
DATE: 07/01/85

RATIOS

SAIL AREA/DISP: 16.09
DISP/LENGTH: 219.71
BALLAST RATIO: 48.39
FUEL/DISP: 2.42
FRESH WATER/DISP: 4.65

DECK

STEERING: wheel with emergency tiller
WINCHES: 4 Lewmar winches
SAFETY: bow and stern pulpits with double lifelines
ANCHOR:
NAV LIGHTS: running and masthead

RIG

TYPE: masthead sloop with Annapolis spar
RIGGING: wire
MAINSHEET: mid-boom sheeting

SAILS

SUPPLIED WITH BASE BOAT:

INTERIOR

BERTHS: 6 berths: 1 double V, 2 single settees, 1 double quarterberth
TABLE: bulkhead-mounted
HEAD(S): 1 head with shower, sump pump, and holding tank
COLD STORAGE: 1 built-in icebox (7 cu. ft.)
STOVE: 3-burner alcohol with oven
MAX. HEADROOM: 6 ft. 5 ins.

MACHINERY

ENGINE: 33 HP Universal #40 diesel with 2:1 reduction gear
PROPELLER: fixed 16" diameter on 1" shaft
GENERATOR:

RIVAL 38 & 38A

DESIGNER: Peter Brett
BUILDER: Rival Yachts, Inc. (built in England by Rival Yachts, Ltd.)

STATISTICS

LOA: 37 ft. 7 ins.
LWL: 29 ft. 6 ins.
BEAM: 11 ft. 3 ins.
DISPLACEMENT
deep keel: 17,196 lbs.
shoal keel:
c/board:
BALLAST
deep keel: 6,850 lbs.
shoal keel:
c/board:
DRAFT
deep keel: 5 ft. 4 ins.
shoal keel:
c/board up:
c/board down:

SAIL AREA: 595 sq. ft.
FRESH WATER: 90 gals.
FUEL CAPACITY: 48 gals.

COSTS

BASE BOAT:
DATE:
EST. ON WATER: $125,000
DATE: 07/08/85

RATIOS

SAIL AREA/DISP: 14.29
DISP/LENGTH: 299.00
BALLAST RATIO: 39.83
FUEL/DISP: 2.09
FRESH WATER/DISP: 4.19

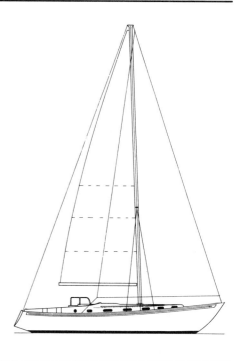

DECK

STEERING: wheel with emergency tiller
WINCHES: 4 Lewmar winches: 2 #43C, 1 #16C, 1 #30C 2 sp
SAFETY: bow and stern pulpits with double lifelines
ANCHOR: 45 lb. & 35 lb. CQR anchors with 30 fthm. chain and 2sp windlass
NAV LIGHTS: running and masthead

RIG

TYPE: masthead sloop or cutter with Kemp spar
RIGGING: 1x19 wire
MAINSHEET: mid-boom sheeting

SAILS

SUPPLIED WITH BASE BOAT: Hood main (3 reefs), working jib (or yankee & staysail)

INTERIOR

BERTHS: 6 berths: 1 double V, 2 single settees, 2 aft singles
TABLE: dropleaf
HEAD(S): 1 head with shower
COLD STORAGE: built-in icebox
STOVE: 2-burner with oven
MAX. HEADROOM: 6 ft. 2 ins.

MACHINERY

ENGINE: 36 HP Bukh diesel with 3:1 reduction gear
PROPELLER: 2-blade 20"x12"
GENERATOR:

BUILDER'S COMMENTS All complete Rivals are built as standard to Lloyd's Register +100 A-1 classification and are sold fully equipped to sail. The Lloyd's requirements apply to all elements of construction including design, materials, construction conditions, and equipment. A Lloyd's surveyor oversees each yacht's construction to ensure these standards are maintained.

ERICSON 38

DESIGNER: Bruce King
BUILDER: Ericson Yachts

STATISTICS

LOA: 37 ft. 8 ins.
LWL: 30 ft. 6 ins.
BEAM: 12 ft. 0 ins.
DISPLACEMENT
deep keel: 14,900 lbs.
shoal keel:
c/board:
BALLAST
deep keel: 6,300 lbs.
shoal keel:
c/board:
DRAFT
deep keel: 6 ft. 6 ins.
shoal keel: 4 ft. 11 ins.
c/board up:
c/board down:

SAIL AREA: 709 sq. ft.
FRESH WATER: 80 gals.
FUEL CAPACITY: 55 gals.

COSTS

BASE BOAT:
DATE:
EST. ON WATER:
DATE:

RATIOS

SAIL AREA/DISP: 18.73
DISP/LENGTH: 234.44
BALLAST RATIO: 42.28
FUEL/DISP: 2.77
FRESH WATER/DISP: 4.29

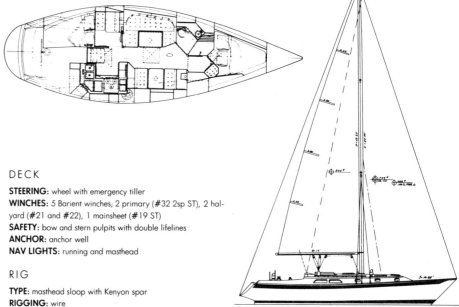

INTERIOR

BERTHS: 7 berths: 1 double V, 1 double convertible dinette, 1 single convertible dinette, 1 double quarterberth
TABLE: pedestal-mounted dinette
HEAD(S): 1 head with shower, sump pump, and holding tank
COLD STORAGE: built-in icebox (12 cu. ft.)
STOVE: 3-burner alcohol with oven
MAX. HEADROOM: 6 ft. 3 ins.

DECK

STEERING: wheel with emergency tiller
WINCHES: 5 Barient winches; 2 primary (#32 2sp ST), 2 halyard (#21 and #22), 1 mainsheet (#19 ST)
SAFETY: bow and stern pulpits with double lifelines
ANCHOR: anchor well
NAV LIGHTS: running and masthead

RIG

TYPE: masthead sloop with Kenyon spar
RIGGING: wire
MAINSHEET: 5-part with mid-boom sheeting

MACHINERY

ENGINE: 32 HP Universal #40 diesel with 2:1 reduction gear
PROPELLER: fixed 16"x13" on 1" shaft
GENERATOR:

SAILS

SUPPLIED WITH BASE BOAT:

ERICSON 28-200 SERIES

DESIGNER: Bruce King
BUILDER: Ericson Yachts

STATISTICS

LOA: 37 ft. 8 ins.
LWL: 30 ft. 6 ins.
BEAM: 12 ft. 0 ins.
DISPLACEMENT
deep keel: 14,900 lbs.
shoal keel:
c/board:
BALLAST
deep keel: 6,300 lbs.
shoal keel:
c/board:
DRAFT
deep keel: 6 ft. 6 ins.
shoal keel: 4 ft. 11 ins.
c/board up:
c/board down:

SAIL AREA: 709 sq. ft.
FRESH WATER: 60 gals.
FUEL CAPACITY: 59 gals.

COSTS

BASE BOAT:
DATE:
EST. ON WATER:
DATE:

RATIOS

SAIL AREA/DISP: 18.73
DISP/LENGTH: 234
BALLAST RATIO: 42.28
FUEL/DISP: 2.96
FRESH WATER/DISP: 3.22

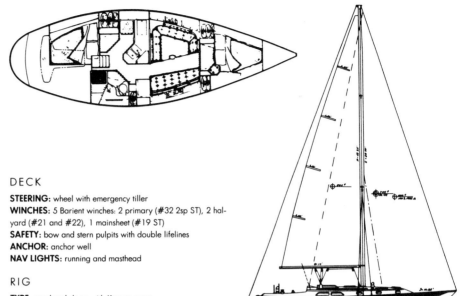

INTERIOR

BERTHS: 7 berths: 1 double V, 1 double convertible dinette, 1 single settee, 1 double quarterberth
TABLE: mast-mounted dinette
HEAD(S): 1 head with shower, sump pump, and holding tank
COLD STORAGE: built-in icebox (6 cu. ft.)
STOVE: 3-burner alcohol with oven
MAX. HEADROOM: 6 ft. 3 ins.

MACHINERY

ENGINE: 32 HP Universal #40 diesel with 2:1 reduction gear
PROPELLER: fixed 16"x13" on 1" shaft
GENERATOR:

DECK

STEERING: wheel with emergency tiller
WINCHES: 5 Barient winches: 2 primary (#32 2sp ST), 2 halyard (#21 and #22), 1 mainsheet (#19 ST)
SAFETY: bow and stern pulpits with double lifelines
ANCHOR: anchor well
NAV LIGHTS: running and masthead

RIG

TYPE: masthead sloop with Kenyon spar
RIGGING: wire
MAINSHEET: 5-part with mid-boom sheeting

SAILS

SUPPLIED WITH BASE BOAT:

ERICSON 381

DESIGNER: Bruce King
BUILDER: Ericson Yachts

STATISTICS

LOA: 37 ft. 8 ins.
LWL: 30 ft. 6 ins.
BEAM: 12 ft. 0 ins.
DISPLACEMENT
deep keel: 14,400 lbs.
shoal keel:
c/board:
BALLAST
deep keel: 6,300 lbs.
shoal keel:
c/board:
DRAFT
deep keel: 6 ft. 6 ins.
shoal keel: 4 ft. 11 ins.
c/board up:
c/board down:

SAIL AREA: 663 sq. ft.
FRESH WATER: 50 gals.
FUEL CAPACITY: 60 gals.

COSTS

BASE BOAT:
DATE:
EST. ON WATER:
DATE:

RATIOS

SAIL AREA/DISP: 17.92
DISP/LENGTH: 226
BALLAST RATIO: 43.75
FUEL/DISP: 3.12
FRESH WATER/DISP: 2.77

DECK

STEERING: 36" wheel with emergency tiller
WINCHES: 5 Barient winches: 2 primary (#28 ST), 2 halyard (#21 and #18), 1 mainsheet (#19 ST)
SAFETY: bow and stern pulpits with double lifelines
ANCHOR: anchor roller and well
NAV LIGHTS: running and masthead

RIG

TYPE: masthead sloop with Kenyon spar
RIGGING: 1x19 wire
MAINSHEET: 5-part with mid-boom sheeting

SAILS

SUPPLIED WITH BASE BOAT:

INTERIOR

BERTHS: 6 berths: 1 double V, 2 single settees, 1 double quarterberth
TABLE: centerline dropleaf
HEAD(S): 1 head with shower, sump pump, and holding tank
COLD STORAGE: built-in icebox (7.5 cu. ft.)
STOVE: 3-burner alcohol with oven
MAX. HEADROOM: 6 ft. 3 ins.

MACHINERY

ENGINE: 32 HP Universal #40 diesel
PROPELLER: 2-blade 16"x13" on 1" shaft
GENERATOR:

SHOW 38

DESIGNER: Fontana/Maletto/Navone
BUILDER: Satellite Management, Inc. (built in Italy by Barberis Cantieri)

STATISTICS

LOA: 37 ft. 8 ins.
LWL: 30 ft. 11 ins.
BEAM: 12 ft. 7 ins.
DISPLACEMENT
deep keel: 11,220 lbs.
shoal keel:
c/board:
BALLAST
deep keel: 5,280 lbs.
shoal keel:
c/board:
DRAFT
deep keel: 6 ft. 3 ins.
shoal keel:
c/board up:
c/board down:

SAIL AREA: 662 sq. ft.
FRESH WATER: 79 gals.
FUEL CAPACITY: 26 gals.

COSTS

BASE BOAT:
DATE:
EST. ON WATER:
DATE:

RATIOS

SAIL AREA/DISP: 21.13
DISP/LENGTH: 169
BALLAST RATIO: 47.05
FUEL/DISP: 1.73
FRESH WATER/DISP: 5.63

INTERIOR

BERTHS: 9 berths: 1 double V or 2 single pipe berths, 2 doubles, 1 double convertible settee, 1 single settee
TABLE: dropleaf
HEAD(S): 2 heads with shower
COLD STORAGE: built-in icebox
STOVE: propane with oven
MAX. HEADROOM:

MACHINERY

ENGINE: Yanmar #3GMF diesel
PROPELLER: 2-blade
GENERATOR:

DECK

STEERING: wheel
WINCHES: 4 winches: 2 primary (2sp), 2 halyard (2sp)
SAFETY: bow and stern pulpits with lifelines
ANCHOR: anchor and anchor windlass
NAV LIGHTS: running and masthead

RIG

TYPE: masthead sloop
RIGGING:
MAINSHEET: 4-part with boom-end sheeting

SAILS

SUPPLIED WITH BASE BOAT:

C & C 38

DESIGNER: C & C Design Group
BUILDER: C & C Yachts

STATISTICS

LOA: 37 ft. 9 ins.
LWL: 31 ft. 0 ins.
BEAM: 12 ft. 9 ins.
DISPLACEMENT
deep keel: 14,250 lbs.
shoal keel:
c/board:
BALLAST
deep keel: 6,250 lbs.
shoal keel:
c/board:
DRAFT
deep keel: 7 ft. 6 ins.
shoal keel:
c/board up: 5 ft. 0 ins.
c/board down: 7 ft. 9 ins.

SAIL AREA: 729 sq. ft.
FRESH WATER: 60 gals.
FUEL CAPACITY: 20 gals.

COSTS

BASE BOAT:
DATE:
EST. ON WATER: $112,000
DATE: 11/85

RATIOS

SAIL AREA/DISP: 19.84
DISP/LENGTH: 213.5
BALLAST RATIO: 43.86
FUEL/DISP: 1.05
FRESH WATER/DISP: 3.37

INTERIOR

BERTHS: 8 berths: 1 double V, 2 single settees, 2 single pilots, 1 double quarterberth
TABLE:
HEAD(S): 1 head with 1 shower, 1 sump pump, and 1 holding tank (24 gals.)
COLD STORAGE: fixed icebox
STOVE: 3-burner alcohol with oven
MAX. HEADROOM:

MACHINERY

ENGINE: Yanmar #3HM diesel with 2.83 reduction gear
PROPELLER: 2-blade fixed 18"x13" on 1 ⅛" shaft
GENERATOR:

DECK

STEERING: wheel
WINCHES: 5 winches: 2 primary (#28A), 1 main halyard/outhaul (#18A), 1 center halyard/reefing (#22A), 1 mainsheet (#18A)
SAFETY: bow and stern pulpits with double lifelines
ANCHOR:
NAV LIGHTS: running

RIG

TYPE:
RIGGING: Navtec rod
MAINSHEET:

SAILS

SUPPLIED WITH BASE BOAT:

BUILDER'S COMMENTS The new 38 is a sleek, swift, "no compromise" machine that delivers more competitive excitement and cruising convenience for its size than any other yacht.

CT 38 SLOOP

DESIGNER: Alan Warwick
DISTRIBUTOR: Ta Chiao USA, Inc. (built in Taiwan by Ta Chiao Bros. Yacht Building Co.)

STATISTICS

LOA: 37 ft. 9 ins.
LWL: 30 ft. 10 ins.
BEAM: 11 ft. 6 ins.
DISPLACEMENT
deep keel: 16,755 lbs.
shoal keel:
c/board:
BALLAST
deep keel: 8,527 lbs.
shoal keel:
c/board:
DRAFT
deep keel: 6 ft. 7 ins.
shoal keel:
c/board up:
c/board down:

SAIL AREA: 647 sq. ft.
FRESH WATER: 60 gals.
FUEL CAPACITY: 50 gals.

COSTS

BASE BOAT: $72,900
DATE: 07/15/85
EST. ON WATER: $80,200
DATE: 07/15/85

RATIOS

SAIL AREA/DISP: 15.81
DISP/LENGTH: 255.00
BALLAST RATIO: 50.89
FUEL/DISP: 2.24
FRESH WATER/DISP: 2.86

INTERIOR

BERTHS: 6 berths: 1 double V, 1 double quarterberth, 2 single pilots
TABLE: dropleaf
HEAD(S): 1 head with shower, sump pump, and holding tank (20 gals.)
COLD STORAGE: built-in icebox
STOVE: 2-burner gas with oven
MAX. HEADROOM: 6 ft. 4 ins.

MACHINERY

ENGINE: 30 HP Yanmar #30M30F diesel
PROPELLER: fixed
GENERATOR:

DECK

STEERING: wheel
WINCHES: 6 Barlow winches
SAFETY: bow and stern pulpits with double lifelines
ANCHOR: anchor with anchor well
NAV LIGHTS: running and masthead

RIG

TYPE: masthead sloop
RIGGING: wire
MAINSHEET:

SAILS

SUPPLIED WITH BASE BOAT: main, working jib, 135% genoa

BUILDER'S COMMENTS The CT-38 is a very modern, fast cruising boat. Thirty-seven have been built to date and the boat is popular for offshore passages. There is a choice of one or two staterooms.

SHANNON 38

DESIGNER: Stadel, Schulz & Associates
BUILDER: Shannon Boat Company, Inc.

STATISTICS

LOA: 37 ft. 9 ins.
LWL: 30 ft. 10 ins.
BEAM: 11 ft. 6 ins.
DISPLACEMENT
deep keel: 18,500 lbs.
shoal keel:
c/board:
BALLAST
deep keel: 6,500 lbs.
shoal keel:
c/board:
DRAFT
deep keel: 5 ft. 0 ins.
shoal keel:
c/board up:
c/board down:

SAIL AREA: 703 sq. ft.
FRESH WATER: 120 gals
FUEL CAPACITY: 70 gals.

COSTS

EST. ON WATER:
cutter: $180,000
DATE: 05/31/85
ketch: $195,000
DATE: 05/31/85

RATIOS

SAIL AREA/DISP: 16.07
DISP/LENGTH: 281
BALLAST RATIO: 35.00
FUEL/DISP: 2.83
FRESH WATER/DISP: 5.19

INTERIOR

BERTHS: 7 berths: 1 forward double, 2 single settees, 1 single pilot, 1 double quarterberth
TABLE: dropleaf
HEAD(S): 1 head with 1 shower
COLD STORAGE: ice/refrigeration compartment (9 cu. ft.)
STOVE: 3-burner LPG with oven
MAX. HEADROOM: 6 ft. 5 ins.

MACHINERY

ENGINE: 40 HP diesel with 2:1 reduction gear
PROPELLER: 3-blade in aperture
GENERATOR:

DECK

STEERING: wheel
WINCHES: 7 (cutter) or 9 (ketch) Lewmar or Barient winches
SAFETY: bow and stern pulpits with double lifelines
ANCHOR: double anchor rollers
NAV LIGHTS: running and masthead

RIG

TYPE: masthead cutter or double headsail ketch
RIGGING: Navtec rod
MAINSHEET: mid-boom sheeting

SAILS

SUPPLIED WITH BASE BOAT: main (2 reefs), 150% genoa, yankee jib, staysail, mizzen (for ketch)

BUILDER'S COMMENTS Since its introduction ten years ago, the Shannon 38 has created the standard for quality offshore cruising yachts. Designed and laid out for a couple to traverse the globe in comfort and safety, Shannon 38s have proven their merits on the two major oceans of the world in all wind and sea conditions. A truly personal yacht built to a specific owner's requirements, the Shannon 38 is the perfect blend of elegance and rugged construction.

HERRESHOFF 38

DESIGNER: Halsey Herreshoff
BUILDER: Cat Ketch Corporation

STATISTICS

LOA: 37 ft. 9.5 ins.
LWL: 34 ft. 0.0 ins.
BEAM: 11 ft. 6.0 ins.
DISPLACEMENT
deep keel: 13,080 lbs.
shoal keel:
c/board:
BALLAST
deep keel: 5,500 lbs.
shoal keel:
c/board:
DRAFT
deep keel: 4 ft. 6 ins.
shoal keel:
c/board up:
c/board down:

SAIL AREA: 593 sq. ft.
FRESH WATER: 100 gals.
FUEL CAPACITY: 40 gals.

COSTS

BASE BOAT: $108,928
DATE: 09/15/85
EST. ON WATER: $115,000
DATE: 06/01/85

RATIOS

SAIL AREA/DISP: 17.09
DISP/LENGTH: 148
BALLAST RATIO: 42.04
FUEL/DISP: 2.29
FRESH WATER/DISP: 6.16

DECK

STEERING: 30" wheel with emergency tiller
WINCHES: none
SAFETY: bow and stern pulpits with double lifelines
ANCHOR: teak bow plank anchor storage
NAV LIGHTS: running and masthead

RIG

TYPE: cat ketch with unstayed carbon fiber composite masts
RIGGING:
MAINSHEET: 4-part with boom-end sheeting

SAILS

SUPPLIED WITH BASE BOAT: main (with reefs), mizzen

INTERIOR

BERTHS: 7 berths: 1 double V, 1 single settee, 1 double convertible dinette, 1 double quarterberth
TABLE: dinette with 3 drawers under
HEAD(S): 1 head with stall shower, sump pump, and tank
COLD STORAGE: built-in icebox
STOVE: 2-burner alcohol with oven
MAX. HEADROOM: 6 ft. 6 ins.

MACHINERY

ENGINE: 32 HP Nannidiesel #4.110HE diesel
PROPELLER: 2-blade fixed 16"x9" on 1" shaft
GENERATOR:

BUILDER'S COMMENTS The Herreshoff Cat Ketch features an unstayed, self-tending rig which makes a simple, effortless sailing yacht. The Fiberglass/Airex hull has clean traditional lines and a light displacement, fin keel/skeg configuration. These characteristics result in an agile, quick, easy and fun boat to sail.

SABRE 38

DESIGNER: Sabre Design Team
BUILDER: Sabre Yachts

STATISTICS

LOA: 37 ft. 10 ins.
LWL: 31 ft. 2 ins.
BEAM: 11 ft. 6 ins.
DISPLACEMENT
deep keel: 15,200 lbs.
shoal keel:
c/board:
BALLAST
deep keel: 6,400 lbs.
shoal keel:
c/board:
DRAFT
deep keel: 6 ft. 6 ins.
shoal keel:
c/board up: 4 ft. 3 ins.
c/board down: 8 ft. 0 ins.

SAIL AREA: 688 sq. ft.
FRESH WATER: 94 gals.
FUEL CAPACITY: 30 gals.

COSTS

BASE BOAT:
DATE:
EST. ON WATER:
DATE:

RATIOS

SAIL AREA/DISP: 17.94
DISP/LENGTH: 224
BALLAST RATIO: 42.10
FUEL/DISP: 1.48
FRESH WATER/DISP: 4.95

DECK

STEERING: wheel
WINCHES: 6 Lewmar winches: 2 primary (#48C ST), 2 halyard (#24 and #30) 1 mainsheet (#24), 1 reefing (#24)
SAFETY: bow and stern pulpits with double lifelines
ANCHOR: anchor well
NAV LIGHTS: running and masthead

RIG

TYPE: masthead sloop
RIGGING: 1x19 SS wire
MAINSHEET: 5-part with mid-boom sheeting

SAILS

SUPPLIED WITH BASE BOAT:

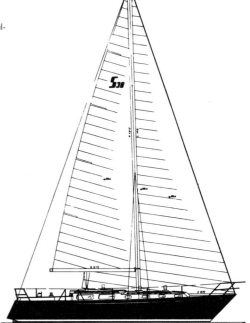

INTERIOR

BERTHS: 6 berths: 1 double V, 1 double convertible settee, 1 single settee, 1 single quarterberth (aft cabin layout available)
TABLE: bulkhead-mounted
HEAD(S): 1 head
COLD STORAGE: built-in icebox
STOVE: 3-burner stove with oven
MAX. HEADROOM: 6 ft. 3 ins.

MACHINERY

ENGINE: 33 HP Westerbeke diesel with 2:1 reduction gear
PROPELLER: 16"x12"
GENERATOR:

HOOD 38

DESIGNER: Ted Hood
BUILDER: Chantier Henri Wauquiez

STATISTICS

LOA: 38 ft. 0 ins.
LWL: 31 ft. 0 ins.
BEAM: 11 ft. 9 ins.
DISPLACEMENT
deep keel: 22,046 lbs.
shoal keel:
c/board:
BALLAST
deep keel: 11,023 lbs.
shoal keel:
c/board:
DRAFT
deep keel:
shoal keel:
c/board up: 4 ft. 6 ins.
c/board down: 10 ft. 8 ins.

SAIL AREA: 691 sq. ft.
FRESH WATER: 105 gals.
FUEL CAPACITY: 37 gals.

COSTS

BASE BOAT: 781,500 francs
DATE: 02/25/85
EST. ON WATER:
DATE:

RATIOS

SAIL AREA/DISP: 14.06
DISP/LENGTH: 330
BALLAST RATIO: 50.00
FUEL/DISP: 1.12
FRESH WATER/DISP: 3.19

DECK

STEERING: wheel
WINCHES: 5 Lewmar winches; 1 Merriman centerboard winch
SAFETY:
ANCHOR: 44 lbs. anchor with anchor chain and well
NAV LIGHTS: running and masthead

RIG

TYPE: masthead sloop
RIGGING:
MAINSHEET: mid-boom sheeting

SAILS

SUPPLIED WITH BASE BOAT: main, genoa, storm jib

INTERIOR

BERTHS: 8 berths: 1 double V, 1 double convertible dinette, 1 single settee, 1 single pilot, 1 double quarterberth
TABLE: centerline dropleaf
HEAD(S): 2 heads with 1 shower
COLD STORAGE: refrigerator
STOVE: 2-burner with oven
MAX. HEADROOM: 6 ft. 6 ins.

MACHINERY

ENGINE: 47 HP Perkins diesel
PROPELLER: fixed
GENERATOR:

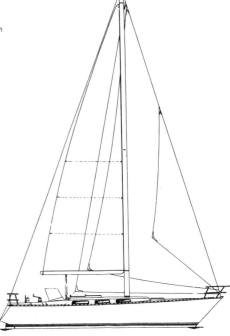

ISLANDER 38C

DESIGNER: Robert H. Perry
BUILDER: Islander Yachts

STATISTICS

LOA: 38 ft. 0 ins.
LWL: 27 ft. 6 ins.
BEAM: 12 ft. 0 ins.
DISPLACEMENT
deep keel: 17,000 lbs.
shoal keel:
c/board:
BALLAST
deep keel: 7,700 lbs.
shoal keel:
c/board:
DRAFT
deep keel: 5 ft. 3 ins.
shoal keel:
c/board up:
c/board down:

SAIL AREA: 673 sq. ft.
FRESH WATER: 100 gals.
FUEL CAPACITY: 55 gals.

COSTS

BASE BOAT:
DATE:
EST. ON WATER:
DATE:

RATIOS

SAIL AREA/DISP: 16.29
DISP/LENGTH: 364
BALLAST RATIO: 45.29
FUEL/DISP: 2.426
FRESH WATER/DISP: 4.705

DECK

STEERING: 36" wheel with emergency tiller
WINCHES: 5 winches: 2 primary, 1 main halyard, 1 jib halyard, 1 mainsheet
SAFETY: bow and stern pulpits with double lifelines
ANCHOR: anchor roller and well
NAV LIGHTS: running and masthead

RIG

TYPE: masthead sloop
RIGGING:
MAINSHEET: 5-part with mid-boom sheeting

SAILS

SUPPLIED WITH BASE BOAT:

INTERIOR

BERTHS: 5 berths: 1 forward double, 1 double convertible dinette, 1 single quarterberth
TABLE: bulkhead-mounted
HEAD(S): 1 head with shower and sump pump
COLD STORAGE: built-in icebox (cu. ft.)
STOVE: 3-burner LPG with oven
MAX. HEADROOM:

MACHINERY

ENGINE: 42 HP Pathfinder diesel with 1.8:1 reduction gear
PROPELLER: 2-blade
GENERATOR:

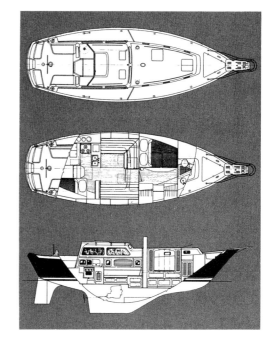

CATALINA 38

DESIGNER: Frank Butler
BUILDER: Catalina Yachts

STATISTICS

LOA: 38 ft. 2 ins.
LWL: 30 ft. 3 ins.
BEAM: 11 ft. 10 ins.
DISPLACEMENT
deep keel: 15,900 lbs.
shoal keel: 16,700 lbs.
c/board:
BALLAST
deep keel: 6,850 lbs.
shoal keel: 7,650 lbs.
c/board:
DRAFT
deep keel: 6 ft. 9 ins.
shoal keel: 4 ft. 11 ins.
c/board up:
c/board down:

SAIL AREA: 639 sq. ft.
FRESH WATER: 35 gals.
FUEL CAPACITY: 36 gals.

COSTS

BASE BOAT: $54,495
DATE: 10/01/84
EST. ON WATER:
DATE:

RATIOS

	deep	shoal
SAIL AREA/DISP:	16.17	15.65
DISP/LENGTH:	256.43	269.33
BALLAST RATIO:	43.08	45.81
FUEL/DISP:	1.70	1.62
FRESH WATER/DISP:	1.76	1.68

INTERIOR

BERTHS: 6 berths: 1 double V, 1 single settee, 1 single quarterberth, 1 double quarterberth
TABLE: fixed
HEAD(S): 1 head with shower and holding tank (21 gals.)
COLD STORAGE: built-in icebox
STOVE: 2-burner alcohol with oven
MAX. HEADROOM: 6 ft. 3 ins.

MACHINERY

ENGINE: Universal #30 diesel with 2:1 reduction gear
PROPELLER: fixed 15"x13" on 1" shaft
GENERATOR:

DECK

STEERING: 32" wheel
WINCHES: 4 winches
SAFETY: bow and stern pulpits with double lifelines
ANCHOR: anchor well
NAV LIGHTS: running

RIG

TYPE: masthead sloop
RIGGING:
MAINSHEET: mid-boom sheeting

SAILS

SUPPLIED WITH BASE BOAT:

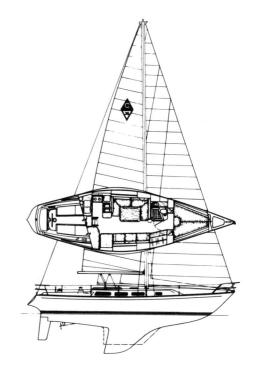

KROGEN 38 CUTTER

DESIGNER:
BUILDER: Kadey-Krogen Yachts, Inc.

STATISTICS

LOA: 38 ft. 2 ins.
LWL: 32 ft. 1 ins.
BEAM: 12 ft. 8 ins.
DISPLACEMENT
deep keel: 24,000 lbs.
shoal keel:
c/board:
BALLAST
deep keel: 7,000 lbs.
shoal keel:
c/board:
DRAFT
deep keel: 5 ft. 0 ins.
shoal keel:
c/board up: 3 ft. 2 ins.
c/board down: 6 ft. 8 ins.

SAIL AREA: 858 sq. ft.
FRESH WATER: 140 gals.
FUEL CAPACITY: 80 gals.

COSTS

BASE BOAT: $95,750
DATE: 06/01/85
EST. ON WATER: $105,000
DATE: 06/01/85

RATIOS

SAIL AREA/DISP: 16.51
DISP/LENGTH: 324.5
BALLAST RATIO: 29.2
FUEL/DISP: 2.5
FRESH WATER/DISP: 4.67

INTERIOR

BERTHS: 7 berths: 1 double V, 1 single settee, 1 double convertible dinette, 1 double quarterberth
TABLE: hi-lo
HEAD(S): 1 head with separate shower
COLD STORAGE: 11 cu. ft.
STOVE: 3-burner propane
MAX. HEADROOM: 6 ft. 4 ins.

MACHINERY

ENGINE: Perkins #4-108 diesel
PROPELLER: 18"x13"
GENERATOR:

DECK

STEERING: Edson wheel
WINCHES: 5 winches: 2 primary (ST), 2 halyard, 1 mainsheet
SAFETY: bow and stern pulpits with lifelines
ANCHOR: anchor with anchor rode and bowsprit
NAV LIGHTS: running and masthead

RIG

TYPE: cutter
RIGGING:
MAINSHEET:

SAILS

SUPPLIED WITH BASE BOAT: main, genoa, staysail

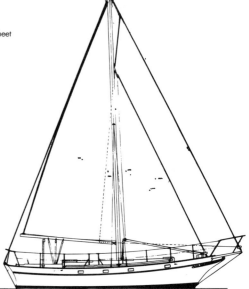

ENDEAVOUR 38 C

DESIGNER: Johan Valentijn
BUILDER: Endeavour Yacht Corporation

STATISTICS

LOA: 38 ft. 3 ins.
LWL: 32 ft. 0 ins.
BEAM: 12 ft. 6 ins.
DISPLACEMENT
deep keel: 17,600 lbs.
shoal keel:
c/board:
BALLAST
deep keel: 8,800 lbs.
shoal keel:
c/board:
DRAFT
deep keel: 4 ft. 11 ins.
shoal keel:
c/board up:
c/board down:

SAIL AREA: 704 sq. ft.
FRESH WATER: 70 gals.
FUEL CAPACITY: 30 gals.

COSTS

BASE BOAT:
DATE:
EST. ON WATER:
DATE:

RATIOS

SAIL AREA/DISP: 16.64
DISP/LENGTH: 239
BALLAST RATIO: 50.00
FUEL/DISP: 1.27
FRESH WATER/DISP: 3.45

INTERIOR

BERTHS: 7 berths: 1 double V, 1 single settee, 1 double convertible, 1 aft double
TABLE: pedestal-mounted dropleaf
HEAD(S): 2 heads with shower
COLD STORAGE: built-in icebox with refrigeration system (10 cu. ft.)
STOVE: 3-burner alcohol with oven
MAX. HEADROOM: 6 ft. 4 ins.

MACHINERY

ENGINE: 40 HP Yanmar diesel
PROPELLER: 3-blade
GENERATOR:

DECK

STEERING: 34" wheel with emergency tiller
WINCHES: 5 winches: 2 primary (ST), 2 halyard, 1 mainsheet
SAFETY: bow and stern pulpits with double lifelines
ANCHOR: anchor well for 2 anchors
NAV LIGHTS: running and masthead

RIG

TYPE: masthead sloop
RIGGING:
MAINSHEET: mid-boom sheeting

SAILS

SUPPLIED WITH BASE BOAT:

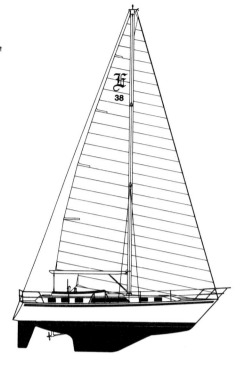

PEARSON 385

DESIGNER: Bill Shaw
BUILDER: Pearson Yachts

STATISTICS

LOA: 38 ft. 3.5 ins.
LWL: 30 ft. 0.0 ins.
BEAM: 11 ft. 7.0 ins.
DISPLACEMENT
deep keel: 19,000 lbs.
shoal keel:
c/board: 20,575 lbs.
BALLAST
deep keel: 8,200 lbs.
shoal keel:
c/board: 9,675 lbs.
DRAFT
deep keel: 5 ft. 6 ins.
shoal keel:
c/board up: 4 ft. 4 ins.
c/board down:

SAIL AREA: 612 sq. ft.
FRESH WATER: 170 gals.
FUEL CAPACITY: 45 gals.

COSTS

BASE BOAT:
DATE:
EST. ON WATER:
DATE:

RATIOS

SAIL AREA/DISP: 13.70
DISP/LENGTH: 315.8
BALLAST RATIO: 42.93
FUEL/DISP: 1.77
FRESH WATER/DISP: 7.72

INTERIOR

BERTHS: 6 berths: 1 double V, 2 single settee, 1 aft double (transverse)
TABLE: dropleaf
HEAD(S): 2 heads with 2 showers, 1 sump pump, and 2 holding tanks
COLD STORAGE: built-in icebox (8 cu. ft.)
STOVE: 3-burner propane with oven
MAX. HEADROOM: 6 ft. 4 ins.

MACHINERY

ENGINE: 42 HP diesel with 2:1 reduction gear
PROPELLER: fixed
GENERATOR:

DECK

STEERING: wheel with emergency tiller
WINCHES: 6 Lewmar winches:
2 primary (#48 ST), 2 halyard (#16 and #8), 1 mainsheet (#30 ST), 1 reefing (#6)
SAFETY: bow and stern pulpits with double lifelines
ANCHOR: anchor well
NAV LIGHTS: running and masthead

RIG

TYPE: masthead sloop
RIGGING:
MAINSHEET: boom-end sheeting

SAILS

SUPPLIED WITH BASE BOAT:

PEARSON 386

DESIGNER: Bill Shaw
BUILDER: Pearson Yachts

STATISTICS

LOA: 38 ft. 3.5 ins.
LWL: 30 ft. 0.0 ins.
BEAM: 11 ft. 7.0 ins.
DISPLACEMENT
deep keel: 16,915 lbs.
shoal keel:
c/board:
BALLAST
deep keel: 7,000 lbs.
shoal keel:
c/board:
DRAFT
deep keel: 5 ft. 6 ins.
shoal keel:
c/board up: 4 ft. 4 ins.
c/board down:

SAIL AREA: 684 sq. ft.
FRESH WATER: 150 gals.
FUEL CAPACITY: 45 gals.

COSTS

BASE BOAT:
DATE:
EST. ON WATER:
DATE:

RATIOS

SAIL AREA/DISP: 16.61
DISP/LENGTH: 279.68
BALLAST RATIO: 41.38
FUEL/DISP: 1.99
FRESH WATER/DISP: 7.09

DECK

STEERING: wheel with emergency tiller
WINCHES: 6 Lewmar winches: 2 primary
(#46 ST), 2 halyard (#16 & #8),
1 mainsheet (#30), 1 reefing (#6)
SAFETY: bow and stern pulpits
with single lifelines
ANCHOR: anchor well
NAV LIGHTS: running

RIG

TYPE: masthead sloop
RIGGING: wire
MAINSHEET: mid-boom sheeting

SAILS

SUPPLIED WITH BASE BOAT:

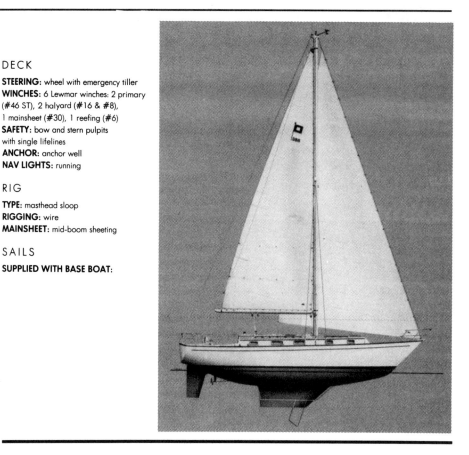

INTERIOR

BERTHS: 6 berths: 1 double V, 2 single extension settees, 1
double quarterberth
TABLE: dropleaf
HEAD(S): 1 head with shower, sump pump, and holding tank
COLD STORAGE: built-in icebox (8.5 cu. ft.)
STOVE: 3-burner alcohol with oven
MAX. HEADROOM: 6 ft. 3 ins.

MACHINERY

ENGINE: diesel with 2:1 reduction gear
PROPELLER:
GENERATOR:

SOVEREL 39

DESIGNER: Mark Soverel
BUILDER: Soverel Marine, Inc.

STATISTICS

LOA: 38 ft. 5 ins.
LWL: 34 ft. 9 ins.
BEAM: 12 ft. 6 ins.
DISPLACEMENT
deep keel: 11,640 lbs.
shoal keel:
c/board:
BALLAST
deep keel: 6,820 lbs.
shoal keel:
c/board:
DRAFT
deep keel: 7 ft. 8 ins.
shoal keel:
c/board up:
c/board down:

SAIL AREA: 760 sq. ft.
FRESH WATER: 25 gals.
FUEL CAPACITY: 25 gals.

COSTS

BASE BOAT: $99,990
DATE: 05/85
EST. ON WATER:
DATE:

RATIOS

SAIL AREA/DISP: 23.67
DISP/LENGTH: 123
BALLAST RATIO: 58.59
FUEL/DISP: 1.61
FRESH WATER/DISP: 1.71

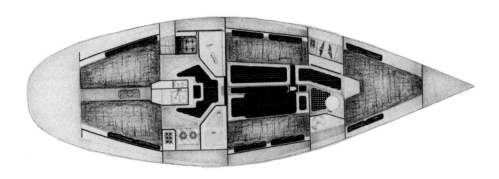

INTERIOR

BERTHS: 8 berths: 1 double V, 2 single settees, 2 double
quarterberths
TABLE: dinette
HEAD(S): 1 head
COLD STORAGE: built-in icebox
STOVE: 2-burner CNG with oven
MAX. HEADROOM:

MACHINERY

ENGINE: 22 HP Yanmar diesel
PROPELLER: Martex 17" folding
GENERATOR:

DECK

STEERING: tiller
WINCHES: 8 Lewmar winches: 2 primary (#48), 2 secondary
(#43), 2 halyard (#40), 2 running back (#30)
SAFETY: bow and stern pulpits with double lifelines
ANCHOR:
NAV LIGHTS: running

RIG

TYPE: fractional rig sloop with Proctor spar
RIGGING: rod
MAINSHEET: 4-part with boom-end sheeting

SAILS

SUPPLIED WITH BASE BOAT:

BUILDER'S COMMENTS The Soverel 39 racer/cruiser, while designed to rate 30.5 under
the IOR handicap rule, contains a complete and functional cruising interior. The boat is
ideal for those who wish to cruise in style to their favorite haunts as well as for the serious
racing yachtsman.

VINDO 65

DESIGNER:
DISTRIBUTOR: Vindo North America, Inc. (built in Sweden by Vindo Martin, Ab)

STATISTICS

LOA: 38 ft. 6 ins.
LWL: 31 ft. 3 ins.
BEAM: 12 ft. 2 ins.
DISPLACEMENT
deep keel: 21,000 lbs.
shoal keel:
c/board:
BALLAST
deep keel: 8,440 lbs.
shoal keel:
c/board:
DRAFT
deep keel: 6 ft. 3 ins.
shoal keel:
c/board up:
c/board down:

SAIL AREA: 632 sq. ft.
FRESH WATER: 100 gals.
FUEL CAPACITY: 70 gals.

COSTS

BASE BOAT:
DATE:
EST. ON WATER:
DATE:

RATIOS

SAIL AREA/DISP: 13.28
DISP/LENGTH: 307.20
BALLAST RATIO: 40.19
FUEL/DISP: 2.50
FRESH WATER/DISP: 3.81

DECK

STEERING: wheel
WINCHES: 5 Lewmar winches: 2 primary (#48), 2 halyard (2sp), 1 reefing
SAFETY: bow and stern pulpits with double lifelines
ANCHOR: 25 lb. Danforth anchor with anchor well and roller
NAV LIGHTS: running and masthead

RIG

TYPE: masthead ketch (sloop also available)
RIGGING:
MAINSHEET: boom-end sheeting

SAILS

SUPPLIED WITH BASE BOAT: main, working jib

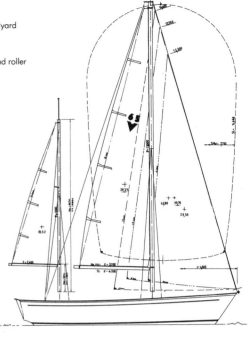

INTERIOR

BERTHS: 8 berths: 1 double V, 1 double convertible dinette, 2 double quarterberths
TABLE: dropleaf
HEAD(S): 1 head with shower
COLD STORAGE: refrigerator/freezer
STOVE: 3-burner propane with oven
MAX. HEADROOM: 6 ft. 5 ins.

MACHINERY

ENGINE: 51 HP Volvo Penta #MD 21 diesel
PROPELLER:
GENERATOR:

X-1 TON

DESIGNER: Niels Jeppesen
DISTRIBUTOR: Aquarius Performance Yachts, Inc. (built in Denmark by X-Yachts)

STATISTICS

LOA: 39 ft. 6.4 ins.
LWL: 33 ft. 1.7 ins.
BEAM: 12 ft. 11.5 ins.
DISPLACEMENT
deep keel: 12,676 lbs.
shoal keel:
c/board:
BALLAST
deep keel: 7,716 lbs.
shoal keel:
c/board:
DRAFT
deep keel: 7 ft. 0.6 ins.
shoal keel:
c/board up:
c/board down:

SAIL AREA: 905 sq. ft.
FRESH WATER:
FUEL CAPACITY:

COSTS

BASE BOAT:
DATE:
EST. ON WATER:
DATE:

RATIOS

SAIL AREA/DISP: 26.63
DISP/LENGTH: 155.48
BALLAST RATIO: 60.87
FUEL/DISP:
FRESH WATER/DISP:

DECK

STEERING: tiller
WINCHES:
SAFETY:
ANCHOR:
NAV LIGHTS:

RIG

TYPE: fractional rig sloop
RIGGING:
MAINSHEET: mid-boom sheeting

SAILS

SUPPLIED WITH BASE BOAT:

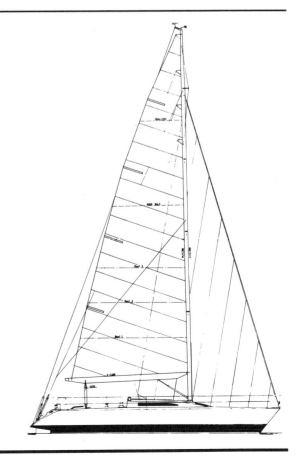

INTERIOR

BERTHS: 8 berths: 2 single settees, 2 single pilots, 4 pipe berths
TABLE:
HEAD(S): 1 head
COLD STORAGE:
STOVE:
MAX. HEADROOM: 6 ft. 1 ins.

MACHINERY

ENGINE: 36 HP diesel
PROPELLER:
GENERATOR:

X-402

DESIGNER: Niels Jeppesen
DISTRIBUTOR: Aquarius Performance Yachts, Inc. (built in Denmark by X-Yachts)

STATISTICS

LOA: 39 ft. 8.4 ins.
LWL: 33 ft. 1.7 ins.
BEAM: 12 ft. 11.4 ins.
DISPLACEMENT
deep keel: 13,200 lbs.
shoal keel:
c/board:
BALLAST
deep keel: 6,820 lbs.
shoal keel:
c/board:
DRAFT
deep keel: 6 ft. 10.7 ins.
shoal keel:
c/board up:
c/board down:

SAIL AREA: 669 sq. ft.
FRESH WATER: 54 gals.
FUEL CAPACITY: 26 gals.

COSTS

BASE BOAT:
DATE:
EST. ON WATER:
DATE:

RATIOS

SAIL AREA/DISP: 19.16
DISP/LENGTH: 161.91
BALLAST RATIO: 51.67
FUEL/DISP: 1.48
FRESH WATER/DISP: 3.27

INTERIOR

BERTHS: 8 berths: 2 single pipe berths, 2 single pilots, 2 double quarterberths
TABLE: dropleaf
HEAD(S): 1 head with shower
COLD STORAGE: built-in icebox
STOVE: 3-burner gas with oven
MAX. HEADROOM: 6 ft. 2.4 ins.

MACHINERY

ENGINE: 28 HP Volvo diesel
PROPELLER: folding
GENERATOR:

DECK

STEERING: tiller
WINCHES: 7 Lewmar winches: 2 #55 ST, 2 #43 St, 2 #43, 1 #30 ST
SAFETY: bow and stern pulpits with double lifelines
ANCHOR: 33 lb. mushroom anchor with anchor roller
NAV LIGHTS: masthead

RIG

TYPE: masthead sloop
RIGGING: rod
MAINSHEET: mid-boom sheeting

SAILS

SUPPLIED WITH BASE BOAT:

SWEDEN YACHTS 38

DESIGNER: Norlin/Ostmann
DISTRIBUTOR: Westover Yachts (built in Sweden by Sweden Yachts)

STATISTICS

LOA: 38 ft. 8 ins.
LWL: 31 ft. 2 ins.
BEAM: 12 ft. 8 ins.
DISPLACEMENT
deep keel: 16,320 lbs.
shoal keel:
c/board:
BALLAST
deep keel: 6,945 lbs.
shoal keel:
c/board:
DRAFT
deep keel: 7 ft. 4 ins.
shoal keel: 6 ft. 7 ins.
c/board up:
c/board down:

SAIL AREA:
FRESH WATER: 85 gals.
FUEL CAPACITY: 26 gals.

COSTS

BASE BOAT:
DATE:
EST. ON WATER:
DATE:

RATIOS

SAIL AREA/DISP:
DISP/LENGTH: 240.81
BALLAST RATIO: 42.56
FUEL/DISP: 1.19
FRESH WATER/DISP: 4.17

INTERIOR

BERTHS: 5 berths: 1 double V, 1 single quarterberth, 1 double quarterberth
TABLE: dropleaf
HEAD(S): 1 head with shower, sump pump, and holding tank
COLD STORAGE: built-in icebox
STOVE: 2-burner LPG with oven
MAX. HEADROOM:

MACHINERY

ENGINE: 28 HP Volvo #2003 diesel
PROPELLER: folding
GENERATOR:

DECK

STEERING: 40" wheel with emergency tiller
WINCHES: 9 Lewmar winches: 2 #48C ST, 2 #44C, 4 #40C ST, 1 #30C
SAFETY: bow and stern pulpits with double lifelines
ANCHOR: anchor roller
NAV LIGHTS: running

RIG

TYPE: masthead sloop
RIGGING:
MAINSHEET: boom-end sheeting

SAILS

SUPPLIED WITH BASE BOAT:

LANDFALL 39

DESIGNER: C & C Design Group
BUILDER: C & C Yachts

STATISTICS

LOA: 38 ft. 9.0 ins.
LWL: 33 ft. 6.0 ins.
BEAM: 12 ft. 2.5 ins.
DISPLACEMENT
deep keel: 19,483 lbs.
shoal keel: 20,257 lbs.
c/board:
BALLAST
deep keel: 6,250 lbs.
shoal keel: 7,002 lbs.
c/board:
DRAFT
deep keel: 5 ft. 6 ins.
shoal keel: 4 ft. 3 ins.
c/board up:
c/board down:

SAIL AREA: 666.7 sq. ft.
FRESH WATER: 103.0 gals.
FUEL CAPACITY: 40.0 gals.

COSTS

BASE BOAT:
DATE:
EST. ON WATER: $139,000
DATE: 11/85

RATIOS

SAIL AREA/DISP: 14.7
DISP/LENGTH: 231
BALLAST RATIO: 32
FUEL/DISP: 1.54
FRESH WATER/DISP: 4.2

INTERIOR

BERTHS: 6 berths: 1 double V, 2 single settees, 1 center aft double (transverse)
TABLE: dropleaf
HEAD(S): 2 heads with 2 showers, and 2 holding tanks (24 gals.)
COLD STORAGE: built-in icebox
STOVE: 3-burner propane with oven
MAX. HEADROOM:

MACHINERY

ENGINE: 44 HP Yanmar #4JHE diesel with 2.17:1 reduction gear
PROPELLER: 2-blade fixed
GENERATOR:

DECK

STEERING: 36" wheel with emergency tiller
WINCHES: 6 winches: 2 primary (#28A), 1 genoa halyard (#22A), 1 main halyard (#18A), 1 mainsheet (#19A), 1 outhaul/reefing (#10HA)
SAFETY: bow and stern pulpits with double lifelines
ANCHOR: anchor locker
NAV LIGHTS: running

RIG

TYPE: masthead sloop
RIGGING: Navtec rod
MAINSHEET: boom-end sheeting

SAILS

SUPPLIED WITH BASE BOAT:

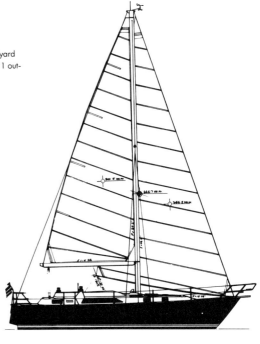

BUILDER'S COMMENTS By any criterion, this new C & C Landfall is a thoroughbred cruiser. A center cockpit cruising yacht that moves through blue water or in her harbor with an easy grace and an impeccable sense of style.

CAL 39

DESIGNER: Bill Lapworth
BUILDER: Lear Siegler Marine

STATISTICS

LOA: 39 ft. 0 ins.
LWL: 32 ft. 1 ins.
BEAM: 12 ft. 0 ins.
DISPLACEMENT
deep keel: 19,000 lbs.
shoal keel:
c/board:
BALLAST
deep keel: 7,000 lbs.
shoal keel:
c/board:
DRAFT
deep keel: 6 ft. 8 ins.
shoal keel: 5 ft. 6 ins.
c/board up:
c/board down:

SAIL AREA: 720 sq. ft.
FRESH WATER: 152 gals.
FUEL CAPACITY: 45 gals.

COSTS

BASE BOAT:
DATE:
EST. ON WATER:
DATE:

RATIOS

SAIL AREA/DISP: 16.17
DISP/LENGTH: 256
BALLAST RATIO: 36.84
FUEL/DISP: 1.77
FRESH WATER/DISP: 6.40

INTERIOR

BERTHS: 7 berths: 1 double V, 1 double settee, 1 single settee, 1 double quarterberth
TABLE: dropleaf
HEAD(S): 2 heads with shower
COLD STORAGE: built-in icebox (8 cu. ft.)
STOVE: 3-burner propane with oven
MAX. HEADROOM: 6 ft. 3 ins.

MACHINERY

ENGINE: 44 HP Universal diesel
PROPELLER:
GENERATOR:

DECK

STEERING: 32" wheel
WINCHES: 5 Barient winches: 2 primary (#28), 2 halyard (#22 & #18), 1 mainsheet (#18)
SAFETY: bow and stern pulpits with lifelines
ANCHOR: anchor well
NAV LIGHTS: running

RIG

TYPE: masthead sloop
RIGGING: 1x19 wire
MAINSHEET: 5-part with mid-boom sheeting

SAILS

SUPPLIED WITH BASE BOAT:

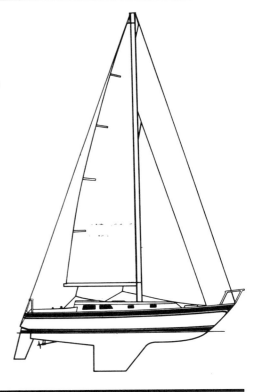

BUILDER'S COMMENTS The Cal 39 gives traditional Cal performance with a two-cabin cruising interior. A high performance Lapworth design gives superb handling and a spacious interior with a huge galley. Comfort at sea or at rest.

COMFORTINA 39

DESIGNER:
DISTRIBUTOR: Scandvik, Inc. (built in Sweden by Comfort-batar, AB)

STATISTICS

LOA: 39 ft. 0 ins.
LWL: 33 ft. 0 ins.
BEAM: 12 ft. 9 ins.
DISPLACEMENT
deep keel: 15,600 lbs.
shoal keel:
c/board:
BALLAST
deep keel: 6,850 lbs.
shoal keel:
c/board:
DRAFT
deep keel: 6 ft. 8 ins.
shoal keel: 5 ft. 10 ins.
c/board up:
c/board down:

SAIL AREA:
FRESH WATER: 38 gals.
FUEL CAPACITY: 22 gals.

COSTS

BASE BOAT: $98,500
DATE: 05/85
EST. ON WATER:
DATE:

RATIOS

SAIL AREA/DISP:
DISP/LENGTH: 193.79
BALLAST RATIO: 43.91
FUEL/DISP: 1.06
FRESH WATER/DISP: 1.95

DECK

STEERING: tiller
WINCHES:
SAFETY:
ANCHOR:
NAV LIGHTS:

RIG

TYPE:
RIGGING:
MAINSHEET:

SAILS

SUPPLIED WITH BASE BOAT:

INTERIOR

BERTHS:
TABLE:
HEAD(S):
COLD STORAGE:
STOVE:
MAX. HEADROOM:

MACHINERY

ENGINE: 28 HP Volvo #2002 diesel
PROPELLER:
GENERATOR:

FREEDOM 39 EXPRESS

DESIGNER: Gary Hoyt/Ron Holland
BUILDER: Freedom Yachts International, Inc.

STATISTICS

LOA: 39 ft. 0 ins.
LWL: 31 ft. 1 ins.
BEAM: 12 ft. 10 ins.
DISPLACEMENT
deep keel: 18,500 lbs.
shoal keel:
c/board:
BALLAST
deep keel: 6,000 lbs.
shoal keel:
c/board:
DRAFT
deep keel: 5 ft. 6 ins.
shoal keel: 4 ft. 6 ins.
c/board up:
c/board down:

SAIL AREA: 857 sq. ft.
FRESH WATER: 130 gals.
FUEL CAPACITY: 80 gals.

COSTS

BASE BOAT: $129,900
DATE: 11/85
EST. ON WATER:
DATE:

RATIOS

SAIL AREA/DISP: 19.60
DISP/LENGTH: 274.56
BALLAST RATIO: 32.43
FUEL/DISP: 3.24
FRESH WATER/DISP: 5.62

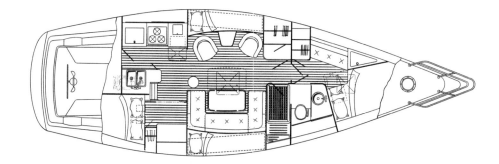

INTERIOR

BERTHS: 6 berths: 1 double V, 1 double quarterberth, 2 single pilots
TABLE: dropleaf
HEAD(S): 1 head with shower and holding tank (25 gals.)
COLD STORAGE: built-in icebox
STOVE: 3-burner with oven
MAX. HEADROOM: 6 ft. 4 ins.

MACHINERY

ENGINE: 50 HP Perkins #4-108 diesel
PROPELLER:
GENERATOR:

DECK

STEERING: wheel
WINCHES:
SAFETY: bow and stern pulpits with single lifelines
ANCHOR:
NAV LIGHTS:

RIG

TYPE: cat ketch
RIGGING: unstayed
MAINSHEET: boom-end sheeting

SAILS

SUPPLIED WITH BASE BOAT:

FREEDOM 39 PILOTHOUSE SCHOONER

DESIGNER: Gary Hoyt/Ron Holland
BUILDER: Freedom Yachts International, Inc.

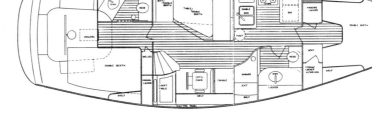

STATISTICS

LOA: 39 ft. 0 ins.
LWL: 31 ft. 0 ins.
BEAM: 12 ft. 10 ins.
DISPLACEMENT
deep keel: 18,500 lbs.
shoal keel:
c/board:
BALLAST
deep keel: 5,300 lbs.
shoal keel:
c/board:
DRAFT
deep keel: 5 ft. 6 ins.
shoal keel: 4 ft. 11 ins.
c/board up:
c/board down:

SAIL AREA: 818 sq. ft.
FRESH WATER: 160 gals.
FUEL CAPACITY: 100 gals.

COSTS

BASE BOAT: $141,900.00
DATE: 11/85
EST. ON WATER:
DATE:

RATIOS

SAIL AREA/DISP: 18.71
DISP/LENGTH: 277.23
BALLAST RATIO: 28.65
FUEL/DISP: 4.05
FRESH WATER/DISP: 6.92

INTERIOR

BERTHS: 6 berths: 2 double V, 1 double convertible dinette, 1 double quarterberth
TABLE: dropleaf
HEAD(S): 2 heads with 1 shower and holding tank (30 gals.)
COLD STORAGE: built-in icebox
STOVE: 3-burner with oven
MAX. HEADROOM: 6 ft. 6 ins.

MACHINERY

ENGINE: 50 HP Perkins #4-108 diesel
PROPELLER:
GENERATOR:

DECK

STEERING: wheel
WINCHES: Barient
SAFETY: bow and stern pulpits with double lifelines
ANCHOR:
NAV LIGHTS: running and masthead

RIG

TYPE: cat schooner
RIGGING: unstayed
MAINSHEET: mid-boom sheeting

SAILS

SUPPLIED WITH BASE BOAT:

GRENADIER 119

DESIGNER: Laurent Giles and Partners, Ltd.
BUILDER: A. H. Moody & Son, Ltd.

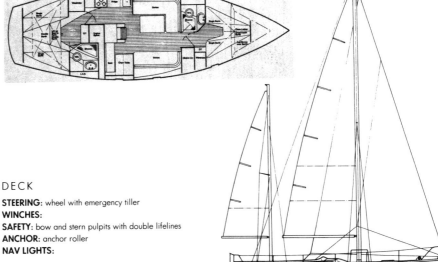

STATISTICS

LOA: 39 ft. 2.0 ins.
LWL: 29 ft. 0.0 ins.
BEAM: 12 ft. 5.5 ins.
DISPLACEMENT
deep keel: 21,728 lbs.
shoal keel:
c/board:
BALLAST
deep keel: 10,080 lbs.
shoal keel:
c/board:
DRAFT
deep keel: 6 ft. 0 ins.
shoal keel:
c/board up:
c/board down:

SAIL AREA: 736 sq. ft.
FRESH WATER: 119 gals.
FUEL CAPACITY: 112 gals.

COSTS

BASE BOAT:
DATE:
EST. ON WATER:
DATE:

RATIOS

SAIL AREA/DISP: 15.12
DISP/LENGTH: 397.72
BALLAST RATIO: 46.39
FUEL/DISP: 3.87
FRESH WATER/DISP: 4.38

INTERIOR

BERTHS: 6 berths: 2 single Vs, 2 single settees, 2 single quarterberths
TABLE: dropleaf
HEAD(S): 2 heads with 2 showers
COLD STORAGE: refrigerator/freezer
STOVE: 3-burner LPG with oven
MAX. HEADROOM:

MACHINERY

ENGINE: 47 shaft HP Perkins #4.108 diesel with 1.8:1 reduction gear
PROPELLER:
GENERATOR:

DECK

STEERING: wheel with emergency tiller
WINCHES:
SAFETY: bow and stern pulpits with double lifelines
ANCHOR: anchor roller
NAV LIGHTS:

RIG

TYPE: masthead ketch (sloop also available)
RIGGING: wire
MAINSHEET: boom-end sheeting

SAILS

SUPPLIED WITH BASE BOAT:

JEANNEAU REGATTA 39

DESIGNER: Tony Castro
DISTRIBUTOR: Nautique International, Inc. (built in France by Jeanneau, S.A.)

STATISTICS

LOA: 39 ft. 2 ins.
LWL: 30 ft. 5 ins.
BEAM: 12 ft. 7 ins.
DISPLACEMENT
deep keel: 11,872 lbs.
shoal keel:
c/board:
BALLAST
deep keel: 5,824 lbs.
shoal keel:
c/board:
DRAFT
deep keel: 6 ft. 3 ins.
shoal keel:
c/board up:
c/board down:

SAIL AREA: 570 sq. ft.
FRESH WATER: 44 gals.
FUEL CAPACITY: 19 gals.

COSTS

BASE BOAT: $79,250
DATE: 02/01/85
EST. ON WATER:
DATE:

RATIOS

SAIL AREA/DISP: 17.52
DISP/LENGTH: 188.28
BALLAST RATIO: 49.06
FUEL/DISP: 1.20
FRESH WATER/DISP: 1.96

DECK

STEERING: tiller
WINCHES: 5 winches
SAFETY: bow and stern pulpits with double lifelines
ANCHOR: anchor roller
NAV LIGHTS: running and masthead

RIG

TYPE: masthead sloop (fractional rig also available)
RIGGING:
MAINSHEET: mid-boom sheeting

SAILS

SUPPLIED WITH BASE BOAT:

INTERIOR

BERTHS: 10 berths: 1 double V, 4 single settees, 2 double quarterberths
TABLE: dropleaf
HEAD(S): 1 head with shower
COLD STORAGE: built-in icebox (26 gals.)
STOVE: 2-burner with oven
MAX. HEADROOM: 6 ft. 1 ins.

MACHINERY

ENGINE: Yanmar #3GM diesel
PROPELLER: folding
GENERATOR:

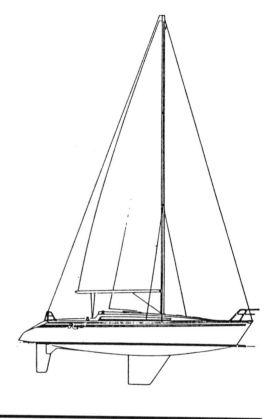

OFFSHORE 39

DESIGNER: Yves-Marie Tanton
BUILDER: Offshore Yachts

STATISTICS

LOA: 39 ft. 3 ins.
LWL: 35 ft. 2 ins.
BEAM: 12 ft. 9 ins.
DISPLACEMENT
deep keel: 18,200 lbs.
shoal keel:
c/board:
BALLAST
deep keel: 8,000 lbs.
shoal keel:
c/board:
DRAFT
deep keel: 4 ft. 10 ins.
shoal keel:
c/board up:
c/board down:

SAIL AREA: 720 sq. ft.
FRESH WATER:
FUEL CAPACITY:

COSTS

BASE BOAT:
DATE:
EST. ON WATER:
DATE:

RATIOS

SAIL AREA/DISP: 16.65
DISP/LENGTH: 186.93
BALLAST RATIO: 43.96
FUEL/DISP:
FRESH WATER/DISP:

DECK

STEERING:
WINCHES:
SAFETY:
ANCHOR:
NAV LIGHTS:

RIG

TYPE: cat ketch
RIGGING:
MAINSHEET:

SAILS

SUPPLIED WITH BASE BOAT:

INTERIOR

BERTHS: 5 berths: 1 double V, 1 single pilot, 1 double quarterberth
TABLE: fixed
HEAD(S): 2 heads with 2 showers
COLD STORAGE:
STOVE:
MAX. HEADROOM: 6 ft. 5 ins.

MACHINERY

ENGINE:
PROPELLER:
GENERATOR:

Designer: Yves-Marie Tanton, N.A.

ISLANDER 40

DESIGNER: Doug Peterson
BUILDER: Islander Yachts

STATISTICS

LOA: 39 ft. 6.5 ins.
LWL: 30 ft. 10.0 ins.
BEAM: 11 ft. 10.0 ins.
DISPLACEMENT
deep keel: 17,000 lbs.
shoal keel:
c/board:
BALLAST
deep keel: 7,700 lbs.
shoal keel:
c/board:
DRAFT
deep keel: 7 ft. 2 ins.
shoal keel:
c/board up:
c/board down:

INTERIOR

BERTHS: 6 berths: 1 double V, 2 single settees, 1 pilot berth, 1 single quarterberth
TABLE: dropleaf
HEAD(S): 1 head with shower
COLD STORAGE: built-in icebox (10 cu. ft.)
STOVE: 3-burner propane with oven
MAX. HEADROOM:

MACHINERY

ENGINE: 42 HP Pathfinder diesel
PROPELLER: 2-blade
GENERATOR:

SAIL AREA: 734 sq. ft.
FRESH WATER: 60 gals.
FUEL CAPACITY: 35 gals.

COSTS

BASE BOAT:
DATE:
EST. ON WATER:
DATE:

RATIOS

SAIL AREA/DISP: 17.76
DISP/LENGTH: 258
BALLAST RATIO: 45.29
FUEL/DISP: 1.54
FRESH WATER/DISP: 2.82

DECK

STEERING: 40" wheel with emergency tiller
WINCHES: 5 Barient or Lewmar winches: 2 jib sheet, 2 halyard, 1 mainsheet
SAFETY: bow and stern pulpits with double lifelines
ANCHOR: anchor well
NAV LIGHTS: running and masthead

RIG

TYPE: masthead sloop
RIGGING:
MAINSHEET: mid-boom sheeting

SAILS

SUPPLIED WITH BASE BOAT:

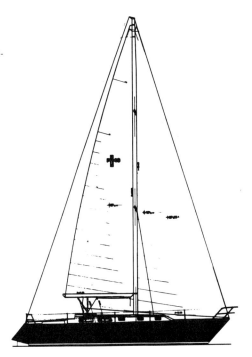

O'DAY 40

DESIGNER: Philippe Briand & Hunt Assoc.
BUILDER: Lear Siegler Marine

STATISTICS

LOA: 39 ft. 7.0 ins.
LWL: 33 ft. 6.0 ins.
BEAM: 12 ft. 7.5 ins.
DISPLACEMENT
deep keel: 18,000 lbs.
shoal keel:
c/board:
BALLAST
deep keel: 6,600 lbs.
shoal keel:
c/board:
DRAFT
deep keel: 6 ft. 4 ins.
shoal keel:
c/board up:
c/board down:

INTERIOR

BERTHS: 7 berths: 1 double V, 1 single settee, 1 double convertible settee, 1 double quarterberth
TABLE: centerline dropleaf
HEAD(S): 1 head with shower
COLD STORAGE: built-in icebox (6.5 cu. ft.)
STOVE: 2-burner propane with oven
MAX. HEADROOM: 6 ft. 5 ins.

MACHINERY

ENGINE: 46 HP Westerbeke diesel
PROPELLER: 2-blade 18"x13" on 1¼" shaft
GENERATOR:

SAIL AREA: 698 sq. ft.
FRESH WATER: 107 gals.
FUEL CAPACITY: 40 gals.

COSTS

BASE BOAT: $90,500
DATE: 11/85
EST. ON WATER:
DATE:

RATIOS

SAIL AREA/DISP: 16.26
DISP/LENGTH: 213
BALLAST RATIO: 36.66
FUEL/DISP: 1.66
FRESH WATER/DISP: 4.75

DECK

STEERING: 30" wheel with emergency tiller
WINCHES: 5 Barlow winches: 2 primary (#27 ST), 1 halyard #23C ST), 1 mainsheet (#23 ST), 1 reefing/outhaul (#16C ST)
SAFETY: bow and stern pulpits with double lifelines
ANCHOR: double anchor rollers
NAV LIGHTS: running and masthead

RIG

TYPE: masthead sloop
RIGGING: 1x19 wire
MAINSHEET: mid-boom sheeting

SAILS

SUPPLIED WITH BASE BOAT: main (2 reefs), working jib

BUILDER'S COMMENTS A brand new design for Lear Siegler Marine, the O'Day 40 gives great sailing performance with fantastic comfort for two couples. Her tall sloop rig and fin keel give great performance under sail. The huge saloon and galley give cruising and living comforts not found in other yachts of her size.

HUNTER 40

DESIGNER: Hunter Design Group
BUILDER: Hunter Marine

STATISTICS

LOA: 39 ft. 7.5 ins.
LWL: 32 ft. 6.0 ins.
BEAM: 13 ft. 5.0 ins.
DISPLACEMENT
deep keel: 17,400 lbs.
shoal keel: 17,900 lbs.
c/board:
BALLAST
deep keel: 7,900 lbs.
shoal keel: 8,400 lbs.
c/board:
DRAFT
deep keel: 6 ft. 6 ins.
shoal keel: 5 ft. 0 ins.
c/board up:
c/board down:

INTERIOR

BERTHS: 6 berths: 1 double V, 2 single settees, 1 center aft double
TABLE: dropleaf
HEAD(S): 2 heads with shower
COLD STORAGE: refrigerator and built-in icebox
STOVE: 3-burner CNG with oven
MAX. HEADROOM: 6 ft. 6 ins.

MACHINERY

ENGINE: diesel
PROPELLER: 2-blade
GENERATOR:

SAIL AREA: 787 sq. ft.
FRESH WATER: 105 gals.
FUEL CAPACITY: 38 gals.

COSTS

BASE BOAT:
DATE:
EST. ON WATER: $92,000
DATE: 11/85

RATIOS

SAIL AREA/DISP: 18.75
DISP/LENGTH: 226
BALLAST RATIO: 45.40
FUEL/DISP: 1.63
FRESH WATER/DISP: 4.82

DECK

STEERING: wheel with emergency tiller
WINCHES: 6 winches: 2 primary (2sp ST), 2 halyard (2sp ST), 1 mainsheet (2sp ST), 1 reefing/outhaul (ST)
SAFETY: bow and stern pulpits with double lifelines
ANCHOR: anchor with anchor well
NAV LIGHTS: running and masthead

RIG

TYPE: masthead sloop
RIGGING:
MAINSHEET: mid-boom sheeting

SAILS

SUPPLIED WITH BASE BOAT: main, 110% genoa (furling)

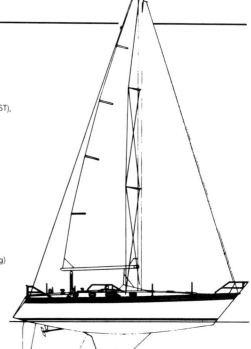

BUILDER'S COMMENTS The Hunter 40' excels in innovations, technology, and amenities, above and below decks.

Above deck is all the gear you could ever ask for, including: roller furling and the patented B&R rigging (No. 3862613).

Belowdecks there's a large double bed aft with private head and shower, AM/FM cassette stereo, and a complete galley.

The Hunter 40 will stand out in any port of call.

NORDIC 40

DESIGNER: Robert H. Perry
BUILDER: Nordic Yachts, Inc.

STATISTICS

LOA: 39 ft. 8 ins.
LWL: 32 ft. 6 ins.
BEAM: 12 ft. 5 ins.
DISPLACEMENT
deep keel: 18,000 lbs.
shoal keel:
c/board:
BALLAST
deep keel: 7,091 lbs.
shoal keel:
c/board:
DRAFT
deep keel: 6 ft. 4 ins.
shoal keel:
c/board up:
c/board down:

INTERIOR

BERTHS: 6 berths: 1 double V, 2 single settees, 1 double quarterberth
TABLE: bulkhead-mounted with leaf
HEAD(S): 1 head with shower
COLD STORAGE: built-in icebox (9 cu. ft.)
STOVE: 3-burner propane with oven
MAX. HEADROOM: 6 ft. 3 ins.

MACHINERY

ENGINE: Universal #40 diesel
PROPELLER: 2-blade
GENERATOR:

SAIL AREA: 756 sq. ft.
FRESH WATER: 130 gals.
FUEL CAPACITY: 56 gals.

COSTS

BASE BOAT:
DATE:
EST. ON WATER:
DATE:

RATIOS

SAIL AREA/DISP: 17.61
DISP/LENGTH: 234
BALLAST RATIO: 39.39
FUEL/DISP: 2.1
FRESH WATER/DISP: 5.8

DECK

STEERING: 40" wheel
WINCHES: 7 Lewmar winches: 2 primary (#55), 2 halyard (#43), 1 mainsheet (#43), 1 reefing (#30), 1 outhaul (#8)
SAFETY: bow and stern pulpits with double lifelines
ANCHOR:
NAV LIGHTS: running and masthead

RIG

TYPE: masthead sloop
RIGGING: rod
MAINSHEET: mid-boom sheeting

SAILS

SUPPLIED WITH BASE BOAT:

BUILDER'S COMMENTS The Nordic 40 is a Robert H. Perry design which combines outstanding cruising performance with luxurious interior accommodations. Each yacht is built with craftsmanship, precision, and quality that are unsurpassed by other production yachts. Whether racing or cruising, the Nordic 40 offers a combination of world class quality and value that is unequaled.

PANDA 40

DESIGNER: Robert H. Perry
BUILDER: Ta-Shing Yacht Building Co., Ltd.

STATISTICS

LOA: 39 ft. 10 ins.
LWL: 36 ft. 2 ins.
BEAM: 12 ft. 10 ins.
DISPLACEMENT
deep keel: 29,000 lbs.
shoal keel:
c/board:
BALLAST
deep keel: 12,000 lbs.
shoal keel:
c/board:
DRAFT
deep keel: 6 ft. 0 ins.
shoal keel:
c/board up:
c/board down:

INTERIOR

BERTHS: 7 berths: 1 double V, 1 single settee, 1 convertible dinette, 1 double quarterberth
TABLE: fixed pedestal-mounted
HEAD(S): 1 head with shower and sump pump
COLD STORAGE: built-in double icebox
STOVE: optional
MAX. HEADROOM:

MACHINERY

ENGINE: 52 HP Volvo diesel
PROPELLER:
GENERATOR:

SAIL AREA: 910 sq. ft.
FRESH WATER: 160 gals.
FUEL CAPACITY: 85 gals.

COSTS

BASE BOAT:
DATE:
EST. ON WATER:
DATE:

RATIOS

SAIL AREA/DISP: 15.42
DISP/LENGTH: 273
BALLAST RATIO: 41.37
FUEL/DISP: 2.2
FRESH WATER/DISP: 4.4

DECK

STEERING: wheel with emergency tiller
WINCHES: 9 Lewmar winches
SAFETY: bow and stern pulpits with double lifelines
ANCHOR: anchor rollers
NAV LIGHTS: running

RIG

TYPE: cutter or ketch
RIGGING: 1x19 wire
MAINSHEET: mid-boom sheeting

SAILS

SUPPLIED WITH BASE BOAT: main (2 reefs), staysail, yankee, mizzen (for ketch)

JONMERI 40

DESIGNER: Jorma Nyman
DISTRIBUTOR: Dodson Boat Yard (built in Finland by Jonmeri Oy)

STATISTICS

LOA: 39 ft. 10.5 ins.
LWL: 32 ft. 9.5 ins.
BEAM: 12 ft. 7.5 ins.
DISPLACEMENT
deep keel: 18,900 lbs.
shoal keel:
c/board:
BALLAST
deep keel: 8,900 lbs.
shoal keel:
c/board:
DRAFT
deep keel:
shoal keel:
c/board up:
c/board down:

SAIL AREA: 727 sq. ft.
FRESH WATER: 100 gals.
FUEL CAPACITY: 56 gals.

COSTS

BASE BOAT:
DATE:
EST. ON WATER:
DATE:

RATIOS

SAIL AREA/DISP: 16.39
DISP/LENGTH: 239
BALLAST RATIO: 47.0
FUEL/DISP: 2.2
FRESH WATER/DISP: 4.2

DECK

STEERING: wheel
WINCHES: 10 Barient or Equal winches: 2 #32, 2 #28, 6 #18
SAFETY: bow and stern pulpits with lifelines
ANCHOR:
NAV LIGHTS: running and masthead

RIG

TYPE: masthead sloop
RIGGING: rod
MAINSHEET: mid-boom sheeting

SAILS

SUPPLIED WITH BASE BOAT:

INTERIOR

BERTHS: 7 berths: 1 double V, 2 single settees, 1 double quarterberth, 1 single quarterberth
TABLE: dropleaf
HEAD(S): 1 head
COLD STORAGE: built-in icebox
STOVE: 3-burner gas with oven
MAX. HEADROOM: 6 ft. 10.6 ins.

MACHINERY

ENGINE: 45 HP BMW diesel
PROPELLER: folding
GENERATOR:

VALIANT 40

DESIGNER: Robert H. Perry
BUILDER: Valiant Yachts

STATISTICS

LOA: 39 ft. 10.75 ins.
LWL: 34 ft. 0.00 ins.
BEAM: 12 ft. 4.00 ins.
DISPLACEMENT
deep keel: 22,500 lbs.
shoal keel:
c/board:
BALLAST
deep keel: 7,700 lbs.
shoal keel:
c/board:
DRAFT
deep keel: 6 ft. 0 ins.
shoal keel:
c/board up:
c/board down:

SAIL AREA: 772 sq. ft.
FRESH WATER: 150 gals.
FUEL CAPACITY: 89 gals.

COSTS

BASE BOAT:
DATE:
EST. ON WATER:
DATE:

RATIOS

SAIL AREA/DISP: 15.2
DISP/LENGTH: 255
BALLAST RATIO: 34.22
FUEL/DISP: 3.00
FRESH WATER/DISP: 5.33

DECK

STEERING: wheel with emergency tiller
WINCHES: complete package
SAFETY: bow and stern pulpits with double lifelines
ANCHOR:
NAV LIGHTS: running

RIG

TYPE:
RIGGING: rod
MAINSHEET: mid-boom sheeting

SAILS

SUPPLIED WITH BASE BOAT:

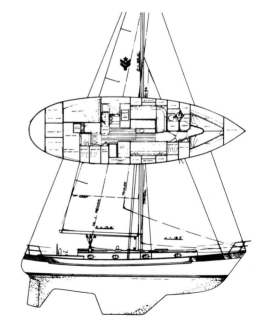

INTERIOR

BERTHS: 6 berths: 1 double V, 2 single settees, 1 double quarterberth (in aft stateroom)
TABLE: center dropleaf
HEAD(S): 1 head with shower
COLD STORAGE: refrigerator/freezer
STOVE: 3-burner with oven
MAX. HEADROOM: 6 ft. 4 ins.

MACHINERY

ENGINE: diesel with 2:1 reduction gear
PROPELLER:
GENERATOR:

BUILDER'S COMMENTS Voted the "Offshore Cruiser of the Decade" by the readers of *Sail* magazine. Winner of many world records and survivor of numerous storms. Truly the proven "ultimate" ocean sailing yacht.

VALIANT PH 40

DESIGNER: Robert H. Perry
BUILDER: Valiant Yachts

STATISTICS

LOA: 39 ft. 10.75 ins.
LWL: 34 ft. 0.00 ins.
BEAM: 12 ft. 4.00 ins.
DISPLACEMENT
deep keel: 22,500 lbs.
shoal keel:
c/board:
BALLAST
deep keel: 7,700 lbs.
shoal keel:
c/board:
DRAFT
deep keel: 6 ft. 0 ins.
shoal keel:
c/board up:
c/board down:

INTERIOR

BERTHS: 5 berths: 1 double V, 1 single settee, 1 double quarterberth (in aft stateroom)
TABLE: center dropleaf
HEAD(S): 1 head with tub and shower
COLD STORAGE: refrigerator/freezer and built-in icebox
STOVE: 3-burner with oven
MAX. HEADROOM: 6 ft. 6 ins.

MACHINERY

ENGINE: diesel with 2:1 reduction gear
PROPELLER:
GENERATOR:

SAIL AREA: 753 sq. ft.
FRESH WATER:
FUEL CAPACITY:

COSTS

BASE BOAT:
DATE:
EST. ON WATER:
DATE:

RATIOS

SAIL AREA/DISP: 15.12
DISP/LENGTH: 255
BALLAST RATIO: 34.22
FUEL/DISP:
FRESH WATER/DISP:

DECK

STEERING: 2 wheels (1 inside) with emergency tiller
WINCHES: complete package
SAFETY: bow and stern pulpits with double lifelines
ANCHOR:
NAV LIGHTS: running

RIG

TYPE: masthead sloop
RIGGING: rod
MAINSHEET: mid-boom sheeting

SAILS

SUPPLIED WITH BASE BOAT:

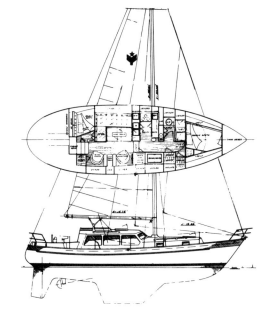

BUILDER'S COMMENTS The hull and performance of the "Cruiser of the Decade" *plus* an inside helm. One of the few ocean-going pilot houses.

SWAN 391

DESIGNER: Ron Holland
BUILDER: Navtor

STATISTICS

LOA: 39 ft. 11.9 ins.
LWL: 33 ft. 1.2 ins.
BEAM: 12 ft. 5.6 ins.
DISPLACEMENT
deep keel: 18,900 lbs.
shoal keel:
c/board:
BALLAST
deep keel: 6,800 lbs.
shoal keel:
c/board:
DRAFT
deep keel: 7 ft. 2 ins.
shoal keel:
c/board up:
c/board down:

INTERIOR

BERTHS: 9 berths: 2 single settees, 2 single pilots, 1 single quarterberth, 1 double quarterberth, 2 single pipe berths
TABLE: dropleaf
HEAD(S): 1 head with shower and sump pump
COLD STORAGE: built-in icebox
STOVE:
MAX. HEADROOM:

MACHINERY

ENGINE: 40 HP Perkins diesel with 2.6:1 reduction gear
PROPELLER: folding
GENERATOR:

SAIL AREA:
FRESH WATER: 93 gals.
FUEL CAPACITY: 47 gals.

COSTS

BASE BOAT:
DATE:
EST. ON WATER:
DATE:

RATIOS

SAIL AREA/DISP:
DISP/LENGTH: 232.24
BALLAST RATIO: 35.98
FUEL/DISP: 1.87
FRESH WATER/DISP: 3.88

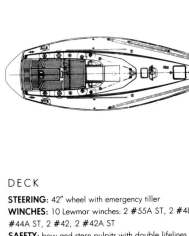

DECK

STEERING: 42" wheel with emergency tiller
WINCHES: 10 Lewmar winches: 2 #55A ST, 2 #48, 2 #44A ST, 2 #42, 2 #42A ST
SAFETY: bow and stern pulpits with double lifelines
ANCHOR: Danforth 20H anchor with anchor well
NAV LIGHTS: running and masthead

RIG

TYPE: masthead sloop
RIGGING: rod
MAINSHEET: mid-boom sheeting

SAILS

SUPPLIED WITH BASE BOAT:

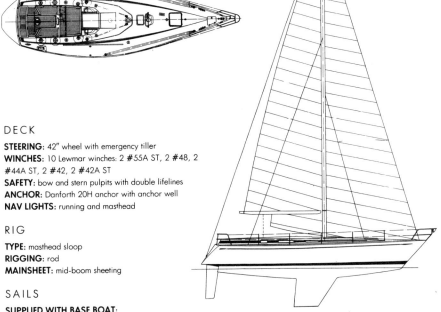

ADVANCE 40

DESIGNER: Sparkman & Stephens
DISTRIBUTOR: Concordia Yacht Sales (built in Finland by Oy Avance Yachts, Ab)

STATISTICS

LOA: 40 ft. 0.0 ins.
LWL: 32 ft. 0.0 ins.
BEAM: 12 ft. 7.1 ins.
DISPLACEMENT
deep keel: 19,600 lbs.
shoal keel:
c/board:
BALLAST
deep keel: 8,400 lbs.
shoal keel:
c/board:
DRAFT
deep keel: 7 ft. .02 ins.
shoal keel:
c/board up: 4 ft. .91 ins.
c/board down: 8 ft. .83 ins.

SAIL AREA:
FRESH WATER: 79 gals.
FUEL CAPACITY: 34 gals.

COSTS

BASE BOAT: $105,650
DATE: 04/01/85
EST. ON WATER:
DATE:

RATIOS

SAIL AREA/DISP:
DISP/LENGTH: 267
BALLAST RATIO: 4.3
FUEL/DISP: 1.30
FRESH WATER/DISP: 3.22

DECK

STEERING: wheel
WINCHES: 9 Lewmar winches: 2 #46C, 2 #43C, 5 #40C
SAFETY: bow and stern pulpits with double lifelines
ANCHOR: anchor roller
NAV LIGHTS: running and masthead

RIG

TYPE: fractional rig sloop
RIGGING: 1x19 wire
MAINSHEET:

SAILS

SUPPLIED WITH BASE BOAT:

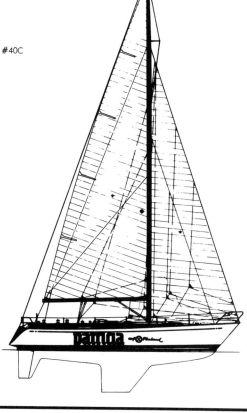

INTERIOR

BERTHS: 6 berths: 1 double V, 1 single pilot, 1 quarterberth, 1 double quarterberth
TABLE: dropleaf
HEAD(S): 1 head with shower and sump pump
COLD STORAGE: built-in icebox
STOVE: 3-burner gas with oven
MAX. HEADROOM:

MACHINERY

ENGINE: 36 HP Volvo #MD 17D 36 diesel with 2.4:1 reduction gear
PROPELLER: folding
GENERATOR:

INTREPID 40

DESIGNER: C. W. Paine
BUILDER: Intrepid Yachts

STATISTICS

LOA: 40 ft. 0 ins.
LWL: 32 ft. 9 ins.
BEAM: 12 ft. 7 ins.
DISPLACEMENT
deep keel: 20,065 lbs.
shoal keel:
c/board:
BALLAST
deep keel: 7,422 lbs.
shoal keel:
c/board:
DRAFT
deep keel: 5 ft. 8 ins.
shoal keel:
c/board up:
c/board down:

SAIL AREA: 775 sq. ft.
FRESH WATER: 200 gals.
FUEL CAPACITY: 90 gals.

COSTS

BASE BOAT:
DATE:
EST. ON WATER:
DATE:

RATIOS

SAIL AREA/DISP: 16.79
DISP/LENGTH: 255
BALLAST RATIO: 36.98
FUEL/DISP: 3.36
FRESH WATER/DISP: 7.97

DECK

STEERING: wheel
WINCHES: 6 Lewmar winches: 2 primary (#55), 2 halyard (#30 & #16), 1 mainsheet (#42), 1 reefing (#8)
SAFETY: bow and stern pulpits with double lifelines
ANCHOR: double anchor rollers, windlass, and anchor well
NAV LIGHTS: running and masthead

RIG

TYPE: masthead sloop
RIGGING: 1x19 wire
MAINSHEET: 4-part with mid-boom sheeting

SAILS

SUPPLIED WITH BASE BOAT:

INTERIOR

BERTHS: 6 berths: 1 double V, 2 single settees, 1 aft double
TABLE: centerline dropleaf
HEAD(S): 2 heads with 2 showers and 2 sump pumps
COLD STORAGE: refrigerator/freezer
STOVE: 3-burner propane with oven
MAX. HEADROOM:

MACHINERY

ENGINE: 50 HP Perkins #4109 with 2.1:1 reduction gear
PROPELLER:
GENERATOR:

J-41

DESIGNER: Rod Johnstone
BUILDER: J Boats, Inc.

STATISTICS

LOA: 40 ft. 1.0 ins.
LWL: 34 ft. 2.5 ins.
BEAM: 13 ft. 2.5 ins.
DISPLACEMENT
deep keel: 15,400 lbs.
shoal keel:
c/board:
BALLAST
deep keel: 6,500 lbs.
shoal keel:
c/board:
DRAFT
deep keel: 7 ft. 4 ins.
shoal keel:
c/board up:
c/board down:

SAIL AREA: 905 sq. ft.
FRESH WATER: 30 gals.
FUEL CAPACITY: 20 gals.

COSTS

BASE BOAT: $134,000
DATE: 01/01/85
EST. ON WATER:
DATE:

RATIOS

SAIL AREA/DISP: 23.39
DISP/LENGTH: 171
BALLAST RATIO: 42.20
FUEL/DISP: 0.974
FRESH WATER/DISP: 1.558

DECK

STEERING: tiller
WINCHES: 8 Barient winches: 2 primary (#632A 3sp), 2 secondary/runner (#28A ST), 4 halyard/pole/reefing (#23A ST)
SAFETY: bow and stern pulpits with double lifelines
ANCHOR:
NAV LIGHTS: running

RIG

TYPE: masthead sloop
RIGGING: Navtec rod
MAINSHEET:

SAILS

SUPPLIED WITH BASE BOAT:

INTERIOR

BERTHS: 10 berths: 2 single settees, 8 single pipe berths
TABLE:
HEAD(S):
COLD STORAGE: built-in icebox
STOVE: 2-burner alcohol
MAX. HEADROOM:

MACHINERY

ENGINE: 28 HP Volvo #2003 with 2.38:1 reduction gear
PROPELLER: 20" feathering on 1¼" shaft
GENERATOR:

IRWIN CRUISING 38

DESIGNER: Ted Irwin
BUILDER: Irwin Yacht & Marine Corp.

STATISTICS

LOA: 40 ft. 1.25 ins.
LWL: 32 ft. 6.00 ins.
BEAM: 12 ft. 3.00 ins.
DISPLACEMENT
deep keel:
shoal keel: 20,000 lbs.
c/board:
BALLAST
deep keel:
shoal keel: 7,000 lbs.
c/board:
DRAFT
deep keel: 6 ft. 3 ins.
shoal keel: 4 ft. 6 ins.
c/board up: 4 ft. 6 ins.
c/board down: 9 ft. 8 ins.

SAIL AREA: 771 sq. ft.
FRESH WATER: 145 gals.
FUEL CAPACITY: 60 gals.

COSTS

BASE BOAT: $86,995
DATE: 06/01/85
EST. ON WATER:
DATE:

RATIOS

SAIL AREA/DISP: 16.74
DISP/LENGTH: 260.09
BALLAST RATIO: 35
FUEL/DISP: 2.25
FRESH WATER/DISP: 5.8

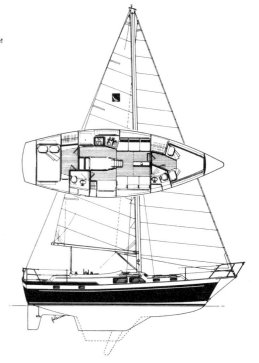

DECK

STEERING: 28" wheel with emergency tiller
WINCHES: 5 winches: 2 primary, 2 halyard, 1 mainsheet
SAFETY: bow and stern pulpits with double lifelines
ANCHOR: anchor locker
NAV LIGHTS: running and masthead

RIG

TYPE: masthead sloop
RIGGING: wire (¼" double lowers, ⁵⁄₁₆" uppers)
MAINSHEET: 4-part with mid-boom sheeting

SAILS

SUPPLIED WITH BASE BOAT: main, working jib

INTERIOR

BERTHS: 1 double V, 2 single settees, 1 center aft double (transverse)
TABLE: dropleaf
HEAD(S): 2 heads with 2 showers and 2 holding tanks (15 gals. each)
COLD STORAGE: built-in icebox (9.5 cu. ft.)
STOVE: 3-burner propane with oven
MAX. HEADROOM:

MACHINERY

ENGINE: 50 HP diesel with 2:1 reduction gear
PROPELLER: 2-blade
GENERATOR:

BRISTOL 40

DESIGNER: Ted Hood
BUILDER: Bristol Yacht Co.

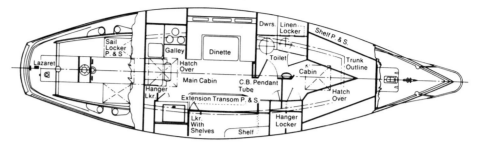

STATISTICS

LOA: 40 ft. 2.0 ins.
LWL: 27 ft. 6.5 ins.
BEAM: 10 ft. 9.0 ins.
DISPLACEMENT
deep keel: 17,580 lbs.
shoal keel:
c/board:
BALLAST
deep keel: 6,500 lbs.
shoal keel:
c/board:
DRAFT
deep keel: 5 ft. 4.5 ins.
shoal keel:
c/board up:
c/board down:

SAIL AREA: 694 sq. ft.
FRESH WATER: 130 gals.
FUEL CAPACITY: 31 gals.

COSTS

BASE BOAT: $89,872
DATE: 09/01/85
EST. ON WATER:
DATE:

RATIOS

SAIL AREA/DISP: 16.42
DISP/LENGTH: 375.73
BALLAST RATIO: 36.97
FUEL/DISP: 1.32
FRESH WATER/DISP: 5.92

INTERIOR

BERTHS: 8 berths: 1 double V, 1 double convertible dinette, 2 single extension berths, 1 single pilot, 1 single pipe berth (other layouts available)
TABLE: bulkhead-mounted
HEAD(S): 1 head with shower
COLD STORAGE: built-in icebox
STOVE: 3-burner alcohol with oven
MAX. HEADROOM:

MACHINERY

ENGINE: Westerbeke #4-108
PROPELLER:
GENERATOR:

DECK

STEERING: wheel
WINCHES: 5 Lewmar winches: 2 #40, 2 #8, 1 #16
SAFETY: bow and stern pulpits with lifelines
ANCHOR: anchor roller
NAV LIGHTS: running and masthead

RIG

TYPE: masthead sloop or yawl
RIGGING:
MAINSHEET: boom-end sheeting

SAILS

SUPPLIED WITH BASE BOAT:

CAPE DORY 40

DESIGNER: Carl Alberg
BUILDER: Cape Dory Yachts

STATISTICS

LOA: 40 ft. 2 ins.
LWL: 30 ft. 0 ins.
BEAM: 11 ft. 8 ins.
DISPLACEMENT
deep keel: 19,500 lbs.
shoal keel:
c/board:
BALLAST
deep keel: 7,600 lbs.
shoal keel:
c/board:
DRAFT
deep keel: 5 ft. 8 ins.
shoal keel:
c/board up:
c/board down:

SAIL AREA: 776 sq. ft.
FRESH WATER: 106 gals.
FUEL CAPACITY: 53 gals.

COSTS

BASE BOAT:
DATE:
EST. ON WATER:
DATE:

RATIOS

SAIL AREA/DISP: 17.14
DISP/LENGTH: 322.42
BALLAST RATIO: 38.97
FUEL/DISP: 2.04
FRESH WATER/DISP: 4.35

INTERIOR

BERTHS: 7 berths: 1 double V, 1 double convertible dinette, 1 single settee, 1 double quarterberth
TABLE:
HEAD(S): 1 head with shower, sump pump, and holding tank (50 gals.)
COLD STORAGE: built-in icebox (10 cu. ft.)
STOVE: 3-burner propane with oven
MAX. HEADROOM:

MACHINERY

ENGINE: Perkins #4-108 diesel with 2.1:1 reduction gear
PROPELLER: 3-blade on 1" shaft
GENERATOR:

DECK

STEERING: wheel with emergency tiller
WINCHES: 7 winches: 2 primary (2sp ST), 3 halyard, 1 mainsheet (2sp), 1 staysail sheet
SAFETY: bow and stern pulpits with double lifelines
ANCHOR: double anchor rollers
NAV LIGHTS: running and masthead

RIG

TYPE: masthead cutter
RIGGING:
MAINSHEET: 5-part with mid-boom sheeting

SAILS

SUPPLIED WITH BASE BOAT:

TARTAN 40

DESIGNER: Sparkman & Stephens
BUILDER: Tartan Marine Company

STATISTICS

LOA: 40 ft. 3.0 ins.
LWL: 31 ft. 7.0 ins.
BEAM: 12 ft. 8.4 ins.
DISPLACEMENT
deep keel: 17,250 lbs.
shoal keel:
c/board: 17,800 lbs.
BALLAST
deep keel: 7,600 lbs.
shoal keel:
c/board: 7,600 lbs.
DRAFT
deep keel: 7 ft. 6 ins.
shoal keel:
c/board up: 4 ft. 9 ins.
c/board down: 8 ft. 5 ins.

SAIL AREA: 727 sq. ft.
FRESH WATER: 110 gals.
FUEL CAPACITY: 47 gals.

COSTS

BASE BOAT: $131,250
DATE: 07/01/85
EST. ON WATER: $155,000
DATE: 07/01/85

RATIOS

SAIL AREA/DISP: 17.42
DISP/LENGTH: 244.51
BALLAST RATIO: 44.06
FUEL/DISP: 2.04
FRESH WATER/DISP: 5.1

DECK

STEERING: wheel with emergency tiller
WINCHES: 5 Lewmar winches
SAFETY: bow and stern pulpits with double lifelines
ANCHOR:
NAV LIGHTS: running and masthead

RIG

TYPE: masthead sloop with Annapolis spar
RIGGING: wire
MAINSHEET: mid-boom sheeting

SAILS

SUPPLIED WITH BASE BOAT:

INTERIOR

BERTHS: 7 berths: 1 double V, 1 single settee, 1 double convertible dinette, 1 double quarterberth
TABLE: dropleaf
HEAD(S): 1 head with shower, sump pump, and holding tank
COLD STORAGE: built-in icebox (10 cu. ft.)
STOVE: 3-burner CNG with oven
MAX. HEADROOM: 6 ft. 5 ins.

MACHINERY

ENGINE: 33 HP Universal #40 diesel with 2:1 reduction gear (other models available)
PROPELLER: 17" diameter on 1" shaft
GENERATOR:

GIB'SEA 116 MASTER

DESIGNER: Joubert & Nivelt
BUILDER: Gilbert Marine, S.A.

STATISTICS

LOA: 40 ft. 4 ins.
LWL: 31 ft. 8 ins.
BEAM: 12 ft. 6 ins.
DISPLACEMENT
deep keel: 16,500 lbs.
shoal keel:
c/board:
BALLAST
deep keel: 6,200 lbs.
shoal keel:
c/board:
DRAFT
deep keel: 6 ft. 5 ins.
shoal keel:
c/board up:
c/board down:

SAIL AREA: 590 sq. ft.
FRESH WATER: 100 gals.
FUEL CAPACITY: 40 gals.

COSTS

BASE BOAT:
DATE:
EST. ON WATER:
DATE:

RATIOS

SAIL AREA/DISP: 14.56
DISP/LENGTH: 231
BALLAST RATIO: 37.57
FUEL/DISP: 1.81
FRESH WATER/DISP: 4.84

INTERIOR

BERTHS: 6 berths: 1 double V, 2 single settees, 1 double quarterberth
TABLE: centerline dropleaf
HEAD(S): 2 heads with 2 showers
COLD STORAGE: built-in icebox (5.6 cu. ft.) and refrigerator (2.5 cu. ft.)
STOVE: 2-burner LPG with oven
MAX. HEADROOM: 6 ft. 3 ins.

MACHINERY

ENGINE: 50 HP diesel
PROPELLER: 2-blade
GENERATOR:

DECK

STEERING: wheel with emergency tiller
WINCHES: 6 self-tailing winches: 2 primary, 2 halyard, 1 mainsheet, 1 kicking strap
SAFETY: bow and stern pulpits with double lifelines
ANCHOR: anchor well
NAV LIGHTS: running and masthead

RIG

TYPE: masthead sloop
RIGGING:
MAINSHEET: mid-boom sheeting

SAILS

SUPPLIED WITH BASE BOAT:

CT-41 KETCH

DESIGNER: Garden
DISTRIBUTOR: Ta Chiao USA, Inc. (built in Taiwan by Ta Chaio Bros. Yacht Building Co.)

STATISTICS

LOA: 40 ft. 8 ins.
LWL: 31 ft. 8 ins.
BEAM: 12 ft. 2 ins.
DISPLACEMENT
deep keel: 28,000 lbs.
shoal keel:
c/board:
BALLAST
deep keel: 9,000 lbs.
shoal keel:
c/board:
DRAFT
deep keel: 6 ft. 0 ins.
shoal keel:
c/board up:
c/board down:

SAIL AREA: 800 sq. ft.
FRESH WATER: 100 gals.
FUEL CAPACITY: 120 gals.

COSTS

BASE BOAT: $80,900
DATE: 07/01/85
EST. ON WATER: $90,000
DATE: 07/01/85

RATIOS

SAIL AREA/DISP: 13.94
DISP/LENGTH: 393.89
BALLAST RATIO: 32.14
FUEL/DISP: 3.21
FRESH WATER/DISP: 2.86

INTERIOR

BERTHS: 9 berths: 2 single Vs, 1 forward double, 1 single settee, 1 double settee, 1 double convertible dinette (other layouts available)
TABLE: dropleaf
HEAD(S): 1 or 2 heads with 1 or 2 showers and sump pumps and 1 holding tank
COLD STORAGE: built-in icebox or refrigerator/freezer
STOVE: 3-burner with oven
MAX. HEADROOM: 6 ft. 5 ins.

MACHINERY

ENGINE: 50 HP Perkins #4-108 diesel

PROPELLER: fixed
GENERATOR:

DECK

STEERING: wheel with emergency tiller
WINCHES: 6 Barlow winches: 2 #25 ST, 1 #20, 2 #19, 1 #15
SAFETY: bow and stern pulpits with double lifelines
ANCHOR: anchor roller
NAV LIGHTS: running and masthead

RIG

TYPE: masthead ketch
RIGGING: wire
MAINSHEET:

SAILS

SUPPLIED WITH BASE BOAT: main, working jib, mizzen

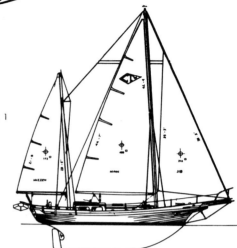

BUILDER'S COMMENTS The CT-41 is part of our ocean clipper line of cruising boats. Over 250 have been built. Current construction is all fiberglass one-piece molded hull and one-piece molded, cored deck and housetop. This boat has sailed on every ocean of the world and many have made circumnavigation. Interior customizing is possible.

BERMUDA 40

DESIGNER: William Tripp
BUILDER: Henry R. Hinckley & Co.

STATISTICS

LOA: 40 ft. 9 ins.
LWL: 28 ft. 10 ins.
BEAM: 11 ft. 9 ins.
DISPLACEMENT
deep keel: 20,000 lbs.
shoal keel:
c/board:
BALLAST
deep keel: 6,500 lbs.
shoal keel:
c/board:
DRAFT
deep keel:
shoal keel:
c/board up: 4 ft. 3 ins.
c/board down: 8 ft. 9 ins.

SAIL AREA: 727 sq. ft.
FRESH WATER: 110 gals.
FUEL CAPACITY: 48 gals.

COSTS

BASE BOAT: $189,000
DATE: 06/85
EST. ON WATER: $225,000
DATE: 06/85

RATIOS

SAIL AREA/DISP: 15.78
DISP/LENGTH: 372
BALLAST RATIO: 32.50
FUEL/DISP: 1.80
FRESH WATER/DISP: 4.40

INTERIOR

BERTHS: 6 berths: 1 double V, 2 single pilots, 2 single extensions (or 1 double convertible dinette instead of pilot and extension)
TABLE: centerline dropleaf
HEAD(S): 1 head with shower
COLD STORAGE: refrigerator (8 cu. ft.)
STOVE: 3-burner LPG with oven
MAX. HEADROOM:

MACHINERY

ENGINE: 40 HP Westerbeke diesel with 2:1 reduction gear
PROPELLER: 2-blade on 1" bronze shaft
GENERATOR:

DECK

STEERING: 28" wheel with emergency tiller
WINCHES: 7 Barient winches: 2 primary (#28), 2 secondary (#22), 2 halyard (#18 & #22), 1 mainsheet (#22)
SAFETY: bow and stern pulpits with double lifelines
ANCHOR:
NAV LIGHTS: running

RIG

TYPE: masthead sloop
RIGGING: 1x19 wire
MAINSHEET: mid-boom sheeting

SAILS

SUPPLIED WITH BASE BOAT:

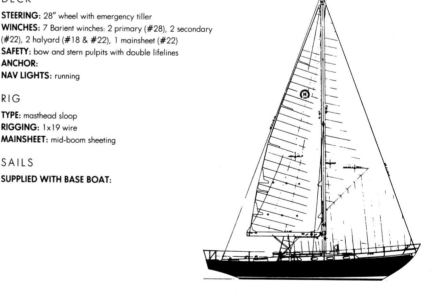

BUILDER'S COMMENTS The B-40 has been in continuous production longer than any other sailing auxilliary. Comfortable, easily handled by a couple, she is thought by many to be the finest shoal draft cruising boat available in her size range.

C & C 41

DESIGNER: C & C Design Group
BUILDER: C & C Yachts

STATISTICS

LOA: 40 ft. 9 ins.
LWL: 33 ft. 4 ins.
BEAM: 12 ft. 11 ins.
DISPLACEMENT
deep keel: 17,500
shoal keel:
c/board:
BALLAST
deep keel: 8,000
shoal keel:
c/board:
DRAFT
deep keel: 7 ft. 10 ins.
shoal keel:
c/board up: 4 ft. 11 ins.
c/board down: 7 ft. 10 ins.

SAIL AREA: 812 sq. ft.
FRESH WATER: 60 gals.
FUEL CAPACITY: 20 gals.

COSTS

BASE BOAT:
DATE:
EST. ON WATER: $145,000
DATE: 11/85

RATIOS

SAIL AREA/DISP: 19.27
DISP/LENGTH: 210
BALLAST RATIO: 45.71
FUEL/DISP: 0.8
FRESH WATER/DISP: 2.74

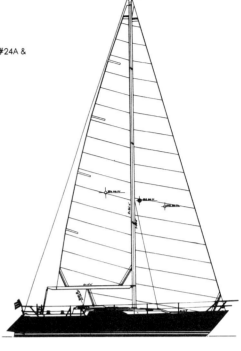

DECK

STEERING: 40" wheel
WINCHES: 5 winches: 2 primary (#32A), 2 halyard (#24A & #21A), 1 mainsheet (#21A)
SAFETY: bow and stern pulpits with double lifelines
ANCHOR: anchor locker
NAV LIGHTS: running

RIG

TYPE: masthead sloop
RIGGING: rod
MAINSHEET: mid-boom sheeting

SAILS

SUPPLIED WITH BASE BOAT:

INTERIOR

BERTHS: 7 berths: 1 double V, 2 single settees, 1 single pilot, 1 double quarterberth
TABLE: dinette
HEAD(S): 1 head with shower, sump pump, and holding tank
COLD STORAGE: built-in icebox
STOVE: 3-burner propane with oven
MAX. HEADROOM:

MACHINERY

ENGINE: Yanmar #3HM diesel
PROPELLER: 2-blade fixed on 1⅛" shaft
GENERATOR:

BUILDER'S COMMENTS Bred in the traditional winning experience of the C & C custom 39s, 40s and 41s, the C & C 41 is a performance racer/cruiser that heralds her breeding with outstanding achievement.

JEANNEAU SUN LEGEND 41

DESIGNER: Doug Peterson
DISTRIBUTOR: Nautique International, Inc. (built in France by Jeanneau, S.A.)

STATISTICS

LOA: 40 ft. 10 ins.
LWL: 32 ft. 9 ins.
BEAM: 12 ft. 11 ins.
DISPLACEMENT
deep keel: 18,144 lbs.
shoal keel:
c/board:
BALLAST
deep keel: 7,616 lbs.
shoal keel:
c/board: 7,840 lbs.
DRAFT
deep keel: 6 ft. 5 ins.
shoal keel:
c/board up: 4 ft. 2 ins.
c/board down: 7 ft. 2 ins.

SAIL AREA:
FRESH WATER: 95 gals.
FUEL CAPACITY: 40 gals.

COSTS

BASE BOAT:
DATE:
EST. ON WATER:
DATE:

RATIOS

SAIL AREA/DISP:
DISP/LENGTH: 230.60
BALLAST RATIO: 41.98
FUEL/DISP: 1.65
FRESH WATER/DISP: 4.19

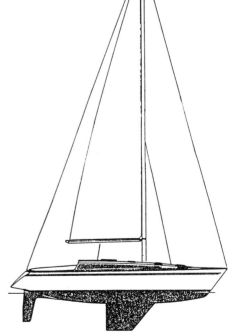

DECK

STEERING: tiller
WINCHES: 7 winches
SAFETY: bow and stern pulpits
ANCHOR: anchor well and roller
NAV LIGHTS: running and masthead

RIG

TYPE: masthead sloop
RIGGING:
MAINSHEET: mid-boom sheeting

SAILS

SUPPLIED WITH BASE BOAT:

INTERIOR

BERTHS: 5 berths: 1 double V, 1 single settee, 1 double quarterberth
TABLE: dropleaf
HEAD(S): 2 heads with 2 showers, 1 sump pump, and 2 holding tanks
COLD STORAGE: built-in icebox and refrigerator
STOVE: 2-burner gas with oven
MAX. HEADROOM:

MACHINERY

ENGINE:
PROPELLER:
GENERATOR:

HANS CHRISTIAN 41 T (TRADITIONAL)

DESIGNER: Scott Sprague
BUILDER: Hans Christian Yachts, Inc.

STATISTICS

LOA: 40 ft. 11 ins.
LWL: 35 ft. 10 ins.
BEAM: 13 ft. 3 ins.
DISPLACEMENT
deep keel: 35,500 lbs.
shoal keel:
c/board:
BALLAST
deep keel: 12,300 lbs.
shoal keel:
c/board:
DRAFT
deep keel: 6 ft. 5 ins.
shoal keel:
c/board up:
c/board down:

SAIL AREA: 1,148 sq. ft.
FRESH WATER:
FUEL CAPACITY:

COSTS

BASE BOAT:
DATE:
EST. ON WATER:
DATE:

RATIOS

SAIL AREA/DISP: 17.00
DISP/LENGTH: 344.25
BALLAST RATIO: 34.65
FUEL/DISP:
FRESH WATER/DISP:

INTERIOR

BERTHS: 5 berths: 1 double V, 1 double quarterberth, 1 single quarterberth
TABLE: dropleaf table
HEAD(S): 1 head with shower
COLD STORAGE: built-in icebox (7 cu. ft.)
STOVE: propane stove with oven
MAX. HEADROOM:

MACHINERY

ENGINE: 72 HP Mercedes-Benz diesel with 2.7:1 reduction gear
PROPELLER: fixed
GENERATOR:

DECK

STEERING: wheel with emergency tiller
WINCHES: Maxwell and Lewmar
SAFETY: bow pulpit
ANCHOR:
NAV LIGHTS: running and masthead

RIG

TYPE: masthead sloop with Kenyon spar
RIGGING: 1x19 wire (⅜")
MAINSHEET: 4-part with mid-boom sheeting

SAILS

SUPPLIED WITH BASE BOAT: main and working jibs

MARINER NEPTUNE 41 (CUTTER)

DESIGNER: Jay R. Benford
BUILDER: Master Mariners Corp.

STATISTICS

LOA: 41 ft. 0 ins.
LWL: 36 ft. 0 ins.
BEAM: 14 ft. 0 ins.
DISPLACEMENT
deep keel: 22,000 lbs.
shoal keel:
c/board:
BALLAST
deep keel: 9,000 lbs.
shoal keel:
c/board:
DRAFT
deep keel: 6 ft. 0 ins.
shoal keel:
c/board up:
c/board down:

SAIL AREA: 949 sq. ft.
FRESH WATER: 255 gals.
FUEL CAPACITY: 275 gals.

COSTS

BASE BOAT:
West coast $127,000
DATE: 04/85
East Coast $129,500
DATE: 04/85

RATIOS

SAIL AREA/DISP: 19.34
DISP/LENGTH: 210.51
BALLAST RATIO: 40.91
FUEL/DISP: 9.38
FRESH WATER/DISP: 9.27

INTERIOR

BERTHS: 6 berths: 1 double V, 2 single settees, 1 double quarterberth
TABLE:
HEAD(S): 1 head
COLD STORAGE: refrigerator/freezer
STOVE:
MAX. HEADROOM:

MACHINERY

ENGINE: 60 HP diesel with 2.75:1 reduction gear
PROPELLER:
GENERATOR: 3.5 kW

DECK

STEERING: wheel
WINCHES: 5 winches
SAFETY: bow and stern pulpits with double lifelines
ANCHOR: roller
NAV LIGHTS:

RIG

TYPE: cutter with Isomat spar
RIGGING:
MAINSHEET:

SAILS

SUPPLIED WITH BASE BOAT: main, working jib, staysail, yankee

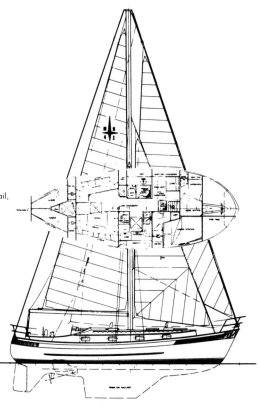

RIVAL 41 & 41A

DESIGNER: Peter Brett
DISTRIBUTOR: Rival Yachts, Inc. (built in England by Rival Yachts, Ltd.)

STATISTICS

LOA: 41 ft. 0 ins.
LWL: 32 ft. 8 ins.
BEAM: 12 ft. 3 ins.
DISPLACEMENT
deep keel: 22,046 lbs.
shoal keel:
c/board:
BALLAST
deep keel: 9,250 lbs.
shoal keel:
c/board:
DRAFT
deep keel: 5 ft. 11 ins.
shoal keel: 4 ft. 11 ins.
c/board up:
c/board down:

SAIL AREA: 728 sq. ft.
FRESH WATER: 144 gals.
FUEL CAPACITY: 90 gals.

COSTS

BASE BOAT:
DATE:
EST. ON WATER: $159,000
DATE: 07/08/85

RATIOS

SAIL AREA/DISP: 15.6
DISP/LENGTH: 282
BALLAST RATIO: 41.96
FUEL/DISP: 3.06
FRESH WATER/DISP: 5.23

INTERIOR

BERTHS: 7 berths: 1 double V, 2 single settees, 1 single pilot, 2 singles or 1 double in aft cabin
TABLE: dropleaf
HEAD(S): 2 heads with 2 showers
COLD STORAGE: engine-driven refrigeration
STOVE: 3-burner with oven
MAX. HEADROOM: 6 ft. 4 ins.

MACHINERY

ENGINE: 50 HP Perkins diesel with 2:1 reduction gear
PROPELLER: 2-blade 18"x12"
GENERATOR:

DECK

STEERING: wheel with emergency tiller
WINCHES: 4 Lewmar winches: 2 #46C, 1 #16C, 1 #30C 2sp
SAFETY: bow and stern pulpits with double lifelines
ANCHOR: 60 lb. and 45 lb. CQR anchors with 30 fthm. chain and electric windlass
NAV LIGHTS: running and masthead

RIG

TYPE: masthead sloop, cutter, or ketch with Kemp spars
RIGGING: 1x19 wire
MAINSHEET: mid-boom sheeting

SAILS

SUPPLIED WITH BASE BOAT: Hood main (3 reefs), working jib

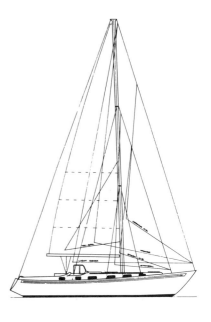

BUILDER'S COMMENTS All complete Rivals are built as standard to Lloyd's Register +100 A-1 classification and are sold fully equipped to sail. The Lloyd's requirements apply to all elements of construction including design, materials, construction conditions, and equipment. A Lloyd's surveyor oversees each yacht's construction to ensure these standards are maintained.

SWEDEN YACHTS 41

DESIGNER: Norlin/Ostmann
DISTRIBUTOR: Westover Yachts (built in Sweden by Sweden Yachts)

STATISTICS

LOA: 41 ft. 0 ins.
LWL: 32 ft. 10 ins.
BEAM: 13 ft. 0 ins.
DISPLACEMENT
deep keel: 18,740 lbs.
shoal keel:
c/board:
BALLAST
deep keel: 8,160 lbs.
shoal keel:
c/board:
DRAFT
deep keel: 7 ft. 4 ins.
shoal keel:
c/board up:
c/board down:

SAIL AREA:
FRESH WATER: 85 gals.
FUEL CAPACITY: 40 gals.

COSTS

BASE BOAT:
DATE:
EST. ON WATER:
DATE:

RATIOS

SAIL AREA/DISP:
DISP/LENGTH: 236.22
BALLAST RATIO: 43.54
FUEL/DISP: 1.60
FRESH WATER/DISP: 3.63

INTERIOR

BERTHS: 4 berths: 1 double V, 1 center aft double
TABLE: dropleaf
HEAD(S): 1 head with shower, sump pump, and holding tank
COLD STORAGE: refrigerator
STOVE: 2-burner LPG with oven
MAX. HEADROOM:

MACHINERY

ENGINE: 36 HP Volvo #3000 diesel
PROPELLER: folding
GENERATOR:

DECK

STEERING: wheel with emergency tiller
WINCHES: 12 Lewmar winches: 2 #55C, 2 #46C, 7 #40C, 1 #30C
SAFETY: bow and stern pulpits with double lifelines
ANCHOR: anchor well and roller
NAV LIGHTS: running

RIG

TYPE: masthead sloop
RIGGING:
MAINSHEET: mid-boom sheeting

SAILS

SUPPLIED WITH BASE BOAT:

BRISTOL 41.1

DESIGNER: Ted Hood
BUILDER: Bristol Yacht Co.

STATISTICS

LOA: 41 ft. 1.75 ins.
LWL: 33 ft. 4.00 ins.
BEAM: 12 ft. 11.00 ins.
DISPLACEMENT
deep keel: 26,530 lbs.
shoal keel:
c/board:
BALLAST
deep keel: 10,500 lbs.
shoal keel:
c/board:
DRAFT
deep keel:
shoal keel:
c/board up: 4 ft. 6 ins.
c/board down: 10 ft. 0 ins.

SAIL AREA: 830 sq. ft.
FRESH WATER:
FUEL CAPACITY: 100 gals.

COSTS

BASE BOAT:
DATE:
EST. ON WATER:
DATE:

RATIOS

SAIL AREA/DISP: 14.93
DISP/LENGTH: 319.88
BALLAST RATIO: 39.58
FUEL/DISP: 2.83
FRESH WATER/DISP:

INTERIOR

BERTHS: 7 berths: 1 double V, 1 single settee, 1 single extension berth, 1 single quarterberth, 1 double quarterberth
TABLE: dropleaf
HEAD(S): 2 heads with shower and sump pump
COLD STORAGE: refrigerator
STOVE: 3-burner alcohol with oven
MAX. HEADROOM:

MACHINERY

ENGINE: Westerbeke #50 with 2:1 reduction gear
PROPELLER: 3-blade on 1¼" shaft
GENERATOR:

DECK

STEERING: wheel
WINCHES: 5 winches: 2 jib sheet (#44C), 2 halyard (#42C & 40C), 1 mainsheet (#40C)
SAFETY: bow and stern pulpits with double lifelines
ANCHOR:
NAV LIGHTS: running

RIG

TYPE: masthead sloop
RIGGING:
MAINSHEET: boom-end sheeting

SAILS

SUPPLIED WITH BASE BOAT:

BUILDER'S COMMENTS Aft or center cockpit versions available.

BAYFIELD 36

DESIGNER:
BUILDER: Bayfield Boat Yard, Ltd.

STATISTICS

LOA: 41 ft. 3 ins.
LWL: 30 ft. 6 ins.
BEAM: 12 ft. 0 ins.
DISPLACEMENT
deep keel: 18,500 lbs.
shoal keel:
c/board:
BALLAST
deep keel: 6,500 lbs.
shoal keel:
c/board:
DRAFT
deep keel: 5 ft. 0 ins.
shoal keel:
c/board up:
c/board down:

SAIL AREA:
FRESH WATER: 100 gals.
FUEL CAPACITY:

COSTS

BASE BOAT:
DATE:
EST. ON WATER:
DATE:

RATIOS

SAIL AREA/DISP:
DISP/LENGTH: 291.1
BALLAST RATIO: 35.14
FUEL/DISP:
FRESH WATER/DISP: 4.32

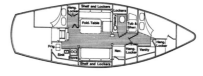

INTERIOR

BERTHS: 5 berths: 1 double V, 1 single settee, 1 double quarterberth
TABLE: dropleaf
HEAD(S): 1 head with shower and tub, 1 sump pump, and 1 holding tank
COLD STORAGE: refrigerator/freezer
STOVE: 2-burner alcohol with oven
MAX. HEADROOM: 6 ft. 3 ins.

MACHINERY

ENGINE: 44 HP Yanmar diesel with 2.17:1 reduction gear
PROPELLER: 3-blade
GENERATOR:

DECK

STEERING: wheel with emergency tiller
WINCHES: 10 Lewmar winches: 4 #40, 5 #16, 1 #8
SAFETY: bow and stern pulpits with double lifelines
ANCHOR: anchor roller and well
NAV LIGHTS: running and masthead

RIG

TYPE: cutter with Isomat spar
RIGGING: wire (⁹⁄₁₆")
MAINSHEET: mid-boom sheeting

SAILS

SUPPLIED WITH BASE BOAT: main, yankee, and staysail

MERMAID 42

DESIGNER: Ta Chiao Design Department
DISTRIBUTOR: Ta Chiao USA, Inc. (built in Taiwan by Ta Chiao Bros. Yacht Building Co.)

STATISTICS

LOA: 41 ft. 5 ins.
LWL: 32 ft. 2 ins.
BEAM: 12 ft. 2 ins.
DISPLACEMENT
deep keel: 29,300 lbs.
shoal keel:
c/board:
BALLAST
deep keel: 9,400 lbs.
shoal keel:
c/board:
DRAFT
deep keel: 6 ft. 3 ins.
shoal keel:
c/board up:
c/board down:

SAIL AREA: 800 sq. ft.
FRESH WATER: 120 gals.
FUEL CAPACITY: 120 gals.

COSTS

BASE BOAT: $89,000
DATE: 04/01/85
EST. ON WATER:
DATE:

RATIOS

SAIL AREA/DISP: 13.47
DISP/LENGTH: 393.25
BALLAST RATIO: 32.08
FUEL/DISP: 3.07
FRESH WATER/DISP: 3.27

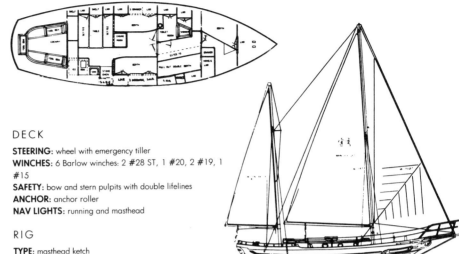

INTERIOR

BERTHS: 10 berths in aft cockpit version: 2 single Vs, 2 single settees, 1 double convertible dinette, 1 double quarterberth, 1 double pilot (center cockpit version also available)
TABLE: fixed
HEAD(S): 1 head with shower and sump pump
COLD STORAGE: built-in icebox
STOVE: 3-burner with oven
MAX. HEADROOM:

MACHINERY

ENGINE: 50 HP Perkins #4-108 diesel
PROPELLER: fixed
GENERATOR:

DECK

STEERING: wheel with emergency tiller
WINCHES: 6 Barlow winches: 2 #28 ST, 1 #20, 2 #19, 1 #15
SAFETY: bow and stern pulpits with double lifelines
ANCHOR: anchor roller
NAV LIGHTS: running and masthead

RIG

TYPE: masthead ketch
RIGGING: wire
MAINSHEET: mid-boom sheeting

SAILS

SUPPLIED WITH BASE BOAT: main, working jib, mizzen

BUILDER'S COMMENTS This boat was designed after the CT-41 and has a slightly greater volume, which allows her interior to be constructed with either one or two staterooms. She is an exceptional sailing vessel and is a favorite among passage-makers. Custom interiors can be accommodated.

SHOW 42

DESIGNER: Andrea Valicelli
DISTRIBUTOR: Satellite Management, Inc. (built in Italy by Barberis Cantieri)

STATISTICS

LOA: 41 ft. 5 ins.
LWL: 34 ft. 4 ins.
BEAM: 13 ft. 0 ins.
DISPLACEMENT
deep keel: 18,480 lbs.
shoal keel:
c/board:
BALLAST
deep keel: 9,240 lbs.
shoal keel:
c/board:
DRAFT
deep keel: 6 ft. 10 ins.
shoal keel:
c/board up:
c/board down:

SAIL AREA: 792 sq. ft.
FRESH WATER: 119 gals.
FUEL CAPACITY: 66 gals.

COSTS

BASE BOAT:
DATE:
EST. ON WATER:
DATE:

RATIOS

SAIL AREA/DISP: 18.12
DISP/LENGTH: 203
BALLAST RATIO: 50.00
FUEL/DISP: 2.67
FRESH WATER/DISP: 5.15

INTERIOR

BERTHS: 7 berths: 1 double V, 2 single settees, 1 single pilot, 1 aft double
TABLE: dinette
HEAD(S): 2 heads with shower
COLD STORAGE: built-in icebox with refrigeration system
STOVE: 4-burner propane with oven
MAX. HEADROOM:

MACHINERY

ENGINE: 48 HP diesel
PROPELLER: 2-blade
GENERATOR:

DECK

STEERING: wheel
WINCHES: 6 winches: 2 primary (2sp), 2 halyard (2sp), 1 mainsheet (2sp), 1 reefing (2sp)
SAFETY: bow and stern pulpits with lifelines
ANCHOR: anchor with anchor chain, well, and electric windlass
NAV LIGHTS: running and masthead

RIG

TYPE: masthead sloop
RIGGING:
MAINSHEET: mid-boom sheeting

SAILS

SUPPLIED WITH BASE BOAT:

ALBIN NIMBUS 42

DESIGNER: Kaufman & Ladd
BUILDER: Albin Marine, Inc.

STATISTICS

LOA: 41 ft. 6 ins.
LWL: 34 ft. 2 ins.
BEAM: 12 ft. 6 ins.
DISPLACEMENT
deep keel: 21,500 lbs.
shoal keel:
c/board:
BALLAST
deep keel: 10,000 lbs.
shoal keel:
c/board:
DRAFT
deep keel: 5 ft. 10 ins.
shoal keel:
c/board up:
c/board down:

SAIL AREA: 872 sq. ft.
FRESH WATER: 120 gals.
FUEL CAPACITY: 60 gals.

COSTS

BASE BOAT: $138,500
DATE: 05/28/85
EST. ON WATER:
DATE:

RATIOS

SAIL AREA/DISP: 18.04
DISP/LENGTH: 240
BALLAST RATIO: 46.51
FUEL/DISP: 2.09
FRESH WATER/DISP: 4.46

DECK

STEERING: wheel
WINCHES: 8 Barient winches: 2 primary (ST), 2 secondary (ST), 4 halyard
SAFETY: bow and stern pulpits with double lifelines
ANCHOR: anchor well
NAV LIGHTS:

RIG

TYPE: masthead sloop
RIGGING:
MAINSHEET: mid-boom sheeting

SAILS

SUPPLIED WITH BASE BOAT: working sails

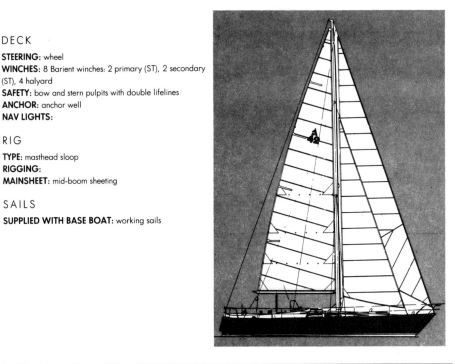

INTERIOR

BERTHS: 8 berths: 1 double V, 1 double convertible dinette, 1 single settee, 1 double quarterberth, 1 single quarterberth
TABLE: dropleaf
HEAD(S): 2 heads with 2 showers
COLD STORAGE: built-in ice box
STOVE: 3-burner LPG with oven
MAX. HEADROOM:

MACHINERY

ENGINE: 50 HP Pathfinder diesel
PROPELLER: 2-blade folding
GENERATOR:

BUILDER'S COMMENTS A yacht whose performance capability has been proven from Block Island Race Week to the Lauderdale-Key West events, but not by sacrificing cruising accommodations and comfort. Flexible rig, instantly converting powerful masthead sloop to cutter.

COOPER 416

DESIGNER: Stan Huntingford
BUILDER: Cooper Yachts

STATISTICS

LOA: 41 ft. 6 ins.
LWL: 32 ft. 6 ins.
BEAM: 14 ft. 0 ins.
DISPLACEMENT
deep keel: 24,000 lbs.
shoal keel:
c/board:
BALLAST
deep keel: 10,500 lbs.
shoal keel:
c/board:
DRAFT
deep keel: 6 ft. 7 ins.
shoal keel:
c/board up:
c/board down:

SAIL AREA: 723 sq. ft.
FRESH WATER: 150 gals.
FUEL CAPACITY: 150 gals.

COSTS

BASE BOAT: $117,500
DATE: 04/85
EST. ON WATER:
DATE:

RATIOS

SAIL AREA/DISP: 13.90
DISP/LENGTH: 312.11
BALLAST RATIO: 43.75
FUEL/DISP: 4.69
FRESH WATER/DISP: 5.00

DECK

STEERING: wheel
WINCHES: 5 Lewmar winches: 2 #42, 2 #30, 1 #1
SAFETY: bow and stern pulpits with double lifelines
ANCHOR:
NAV LIGHTS: running

RIG

TYPE: masthead sloop
RIGGING:
MAINSHEET: mid-boom sheeting

SAILS

SUPPLIED WITH BASE BOAT: main, working jib

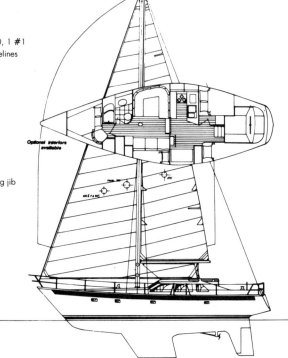

INTERIOR

BERTHS: 6 berths: 1 double V, 1 single settee, 1 single quarterberth, 1 double quarterberth
TABLE:
HEAD(S): 1 head with shower
COLD STORAGE: built-in icebox (8 cu. ft.)
STOVE: 3-burner propane with oven
MAX. HEADROOM:

MACHINERY

ENGINE: 50 HP Lehman diesel
PROPELLER: fixed
GENERATOR:

FREEPORT 41

DESIGNER:
BUILDER: Islander Yachts

STATISTICS

LOA: 41 ft. 6 ins.
LWL: 32 ft. 6 ins.
BEAM: 13 ft. 2 ins.
DISPLACEMENT
deep keel: 22,000 lbs.
shoal keel:
c/board:
BALLAST
deep keel: 7,000 lbs.
shoal keel:
c/board:
DRAFT
deep keel: 5 ft. 0 ins.
shoal keel:
c/board up:
c/board down:

SAIL AREA: 817 sq. ft.
FRESH WATER: 188 gals.
FUEL CAPACITY: 188 gals.

COSTS

BASE BOAT:
DATE:
EST. ON WATER:
DATE:

RATIOS

SAIL AREA/DISP: 16.66
DISP/LENGTH: 286
BALLAST RATIO: 31.81
FUEL/DISP: 6.409
FRESH WATER/DISP: 6.836

DECK

STEERING: wheel
WINCHES: 7 winches
SAFETY: bow and stern pulpits with double lifelines
ANCHOR: anchor roller
NAV LIGHTS: running and masthead

RIG

TYPE: ketch
RIGGING:
MAINSHEET: boom-end sheeting

SAILS

SUPPLIED WITH BASE BOAT:

INTERIOR

BERTHS: 7 berths: 1 double V, 1 single V, 1 double convertible dinette, 1 center aft double (transverse)
TABLE: dinette
HEAD(S): 1 head
COLD STORAGE: built-in icebox (13 cu. ft.)
STOVE: 3-burner propane with oven
MAX. HEADROOM:

MACHINERY

ENGINE: 85 HP Pathfinder diesel
PROPELLER: 3-blade on 1¼" shaft
GENERATOR:

ISLAND PACKET 38

DESIGNER: Robert K. Johnson
BUILDER: Island Packet Yachts

STATISTICS

LOA: 41 ft. 6 ins.
LWL: 33 ft. 0 ins.
BEAM: 12 ft. 8 ins.
DISPLACEMENT
deep keel: 19,000 lbs.
shoal keel:
c/board:
BALLAST
deep keel: 7,600 lbs.
shoal keel:
c/board:
DRAFT
deep keel: 5 ft. 0 ins.
shoal keel:
c/board up: 4 ft. 0 ins.
c/board down: 7 ft. 7 ins.

SAIL AREA: 735 sq. ft.
FRESH WATER: 150 gals.
FUEL CAPACITY: 50 gals.

COSTS

BASE BOAT: $109,950
DATE: 06/85
EST. ON WATER: $115,000
DATE: 06/85

RATIOS

SAIL AREA/DISP: 16.51
DISP/LENGTH: 236
BALLAST RATIO: 40.00
FUEL/DISP: 1.97
FRESH WATER/DISP: 6.3

DECK

STEERING: Edson wheel
WINCHES: 5 Lewmar winches: 2 primary (#43C), 2 halyard (#16C), 1 mainsheet (#16C)
SAFETY: bow and stern pulpits with double lifelines
ANCHOR: anchor roller and bowsprit
NAV LIGHTS: running and masthead

RIG

TYPE: masthead sloop with anodized spar (cutter option)
RIGGING: 1x19 SS wire
MAINSHEET: mid-boom sheeting

SAILS

SUPPLIED WITH BASE BOAT: main (1 reef), 110% jib

INTERIOR

BERTHS: 7 berths: 1 forward double, 1 double convertible settee, 1 single settee, 1 aft double
TABLE: bulkhead-mounted dropleaf
HEAD(S): 1 head with shower
COLD STORAGE: built-in icebox (14 cu. ft.)
STOVE: 3-burner LPG with oven
MAX. HEADROOM: 6 ft. 4 ins.

MACHINERY

ENGINE: 44 HP Yanmar #4JHE diesel
PROPELLER: 2-blade fixed on 1¼" shaft
GENERATOR:

BUILDER'S COMMENTS Modern full keel design with handsome traditional styling, easily managed rig, and an unusually spacious and livable interior. Outstanding performance with moderate or shoal draft. Exceptional quality with extensive standard equipment. Distinctly in a class by itself.

MOODY 419

DESIGNER: Bill Dixon-Angus Primrose, Ltd.
DISTRIBUTOR: A. H. Moody & Son, Ltd. (built in England by Marine Projects, Ltd.)

STATISTICS

LOA: 41 ft. 9.0 ins.
LWL: 33 ft. 11.5 ins.
BEAM: 13 ft. 2.0 ins.
DISPLACEMENT
deep keel: 20,600 lbs.
shoal keel:
c/board:
BALLAST
deep keel: 8,700 lbs.
shoal keel:
c/board:
DRAFT
deep keel: 6 ft. 0 ins.
shoal keel:
c/board up:
c/board down:

SAIL AREA: 724 sq. ft.
FRESH WATER: 100 gals.
FUEL CAPACITY: 50 gals.

COSTS

BASE BOAT:
DATE:
EST. ON WATER:
DATE:

RATIOS

SAIL AREA/DISP: 15.41
DISP/LENGTH: 234
BALLAST RATIO: 42.23
FUEL/DISP: 1.82
FRESH WATER/DISP: 3.88

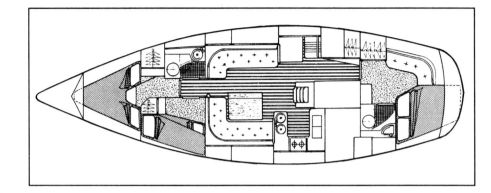

INTERIOR

BERTHS: 8 berths: 2 single Vs, 2 single upper and lowers, 2 single settees, 1 aft double
TABLE: dropleaf
HEAD(S): 2 heads with 1 shower and sump pump
COLD STORAGE: refrigerator
STOVE: 2-burner gas with oven
MAX. HEADROOM:

MACHINERY

ENGINE: 50 HP Thornycroft #T-108 diesel with 1.8:1 reduction gear
PROPELLER: 2-blade
GENERATOR:

DECK

STEERING: wheel with emergency tiller
WINCHES: 6 winches: 2 primary (2sp), 2 halyard, 1 mainsheet, 1 slab reefing
SAFETY: bow and stern pulpits with lifelines
ANCHOR: anchor well, roller, and manual windlass
NAV LIGHTS: running

RIG

TYPE: masthead sloop
RIGGING: 1x19 SS wire
MAINSHEET: boom-end sheeting

SAILS

SUPPLIED WITH BASE BOAT: main, (3 reefs), working jib

SIGMA 41 MH

DESIGNER: David Thomas
BUILDER: Cruise Away Yacht Sales

STATISTICS

LOA: 41 ft. 9 ins.
LWL: 33 ft. 4 ins.
BEAM: 12 ft. 10 ins.
DISPLACEMENT
deep keel: 19,000 lbs.
shoal keel:
c/board:
BALLAST
deep keel:
shoal keel:
c/board:
DRAFT
deep keel: 5 ft. 11 ins.
shoal keel:
c/board up:
c/board down:

SAIL AREA:
FRESH WATER: 87 gals.
FUEL CAPACITY: 36 gals.

COSTS

BASE BOAT:
DATE:
EST. ON WATER:
DATE:

RATIOS

SAIL AREA/DISP:
DISP/LENGTH: 229
BALLAST RATIO:
FUEL/DISP: 1.4
FRESH WATER/DISP: 3.7

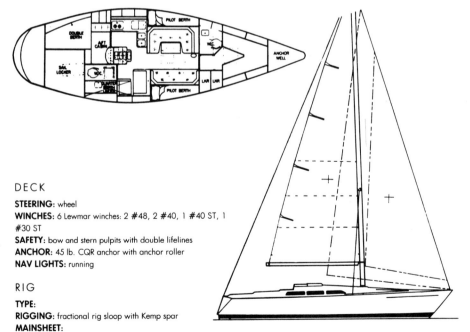

INTERIOR

BERTHS: 9 berths: 2 single Vs, 2 single settees, 2 single pilots, 1 double quarterberth, 1 single quarterberth
TABLE: dropleaf
HEAD(S): 2 heads with 1 shower and 2 holding tanks
COLD STORAGE: built-in icebox
STOVE: 2-burner propane with oven
MAX. HEADROOM:

MACHINERY

ENGINE: Perkins #4-108 diesel
PROPELLER:
GENERATOR:

DECK

STEERING: wheel
WINCHES: 6 Lewmar winches: 2 #48, 2 #40, 1 #40 ST, 1 #30 ST
SAFETY: bow and stern pulpits with double lifelines
ANCHOR: 45 lb. CQR anchor with anchor roller
NAV LIGHTS: running

RIG

TYPE:
RIGGING: fractional rig sloop with Kemp spar
MAINSHEET:

SAILS

SUPPLIED WITH BASE BOAT: main, working jib, #2 genoa

TAYANA-V-42

DESIGNER: Robert H. Harris
DISTRIBUTOR: Southern Offshore Yachts, Inc. (built in Taiwan by TaYang Yacht Building Co.)

STATISTICS

LOA: 41 ft. 9 ins.
LWL: 33 ft. 0 ins.
BEAM: 12 ft. 6 ins.
DISPLACEMENT
deep keel: 29,157 lbs.
shoal keel:
c/board:
BALLAST
deep keel: 11,800 lbs.
shoal keel:
c/board:
DRAFT
deep keel: 5 ft. 10 ins.
shoal keel:
c/board up:
c/board down:

INTERIOR

BERTHS: 7 berths: 1 double V, 1 double settee, 1 single settee, 1 center aft double
TABLE:
HEAD(S): 2 heads with 2 showers, 2 sump pumps, and 2 holding tanks
COLD STORAGE: built-in icebox
STOVE:
MAX. HEADROOM: 6 ft. 5 ins.

MACHINERY

ENGINE: 36 HP Yanmar #3QM diesel
PROPELLER: 3-blade fixed 18"x13" on 1 1/4" shaft
GENERATOR:

SAIL AREA: 942 sq. ft.
FRESH WATER: 140 gals.
FUEL CAPACITY: 120 gals.

COSTS

BASE BOAT: $92,700
DATE: 07/85
EST. ON WATER:
DATE:

RATIOS

SAIL AREA/DISP: 15.91
DISP/LENGTH: 362.20
BALLAST RATIO: 40.47
FUEL/DISP: 3.09
FRESH WATER/DISP: 3.84

DECK

STEERING: wheel with emergency tiller
WINCHES: 9 Lewmar winches: 2 #42 ST, 2 #34 ST, 1 #16, 1 #10, 3 #8
SAFETY: bow and stern pulpits with double lifelines
ANCHOR: anchor roller and well
NAV LIGHTS:

RIG

TYPE: masthead sloop
RIGGING:
MAINSHEET: mid-boom sheeting

SAILS

SUPPLIED WITH BASE BOAT: main (2 reefs), yankee, staysail

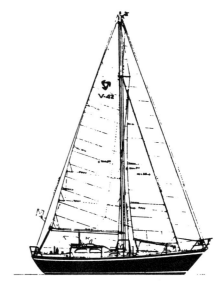

NASSAU 42

DESIGNER: Robert H. Perry
DISTRIBUTOR: Nassau Yacht Corp. (built in Taiwan by Angel Marine) also distributed by Southern Offshore Yachts, Inc.

STATISTICS

LOA: 41 ft. 10 ins.
LWL: 34 ft. 7 ins.
BEAM: 12 ft. 9 ins.
DISPLACEMENT
deep keel: 21,250 lbs.
shoal keel:
c/board:
BALLAST
deep keel: 8,870 lbs.
shoal keel:
c/board:
DRAFT
deep keel: 5 ft. 10 ins.
shoal keel:
c/board up:
c/board down:

INTERIOR

BERTHS: 5 berths: 1 double V, 1 single quarterberth, 1 double quarterberth
TABLE: dropleaf
HEAD(S): 2 heads with 1 shower, 1 sump pump, and 2 holding tanks
COLD STORAGE: built-in icebox
STOVE: stove with oven
MAX. HEADROOM: 6 ft. 4.75 ins.

MACHINERY

ENGINE: 49 HP Perkins #4-108 diesel with 2:1:1 reduction gear

SAIL AREA: 800 sq. ft.
FRESH WATER: 160 gals.
FUEL CAPACITY: 70 gals.

COSTS

BASE BOAT: $111,200
DATE: 06/28/85
EST. ON WATER: $115,300
DATE: 06/28/85

RATIOS

SAIL AREA/DISP: 16.69
DISP/LENGTH: 229.4
BALLAST RATIO: 41.7
FUEL/DISP: 2.5
FRESH WATER/DISP: 6.0

PROPELLER: fixed
GENERATOR:

DECK

STEERING: wheel with emergency tiller
WINCHES: 5 Lewmar winches: 2 #55A 2sp ST, 1 #42A 2sp ST, 1 #30A ST, 1 #44A 2sp ST
SAFETY: bow and stern pulpits with double lifelines
ANCHOR:
NAV LIGHTS: running and masthead

RIG

TYPE: masthead
RIGGING: 1x19 wire
MAINSHEET: 5-part with mid-boom sheeting

SAILS

SUPPLIED WITH BASE BOAT: main, 110% working jib

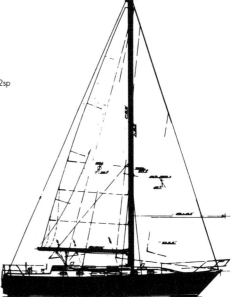

BUILDER'S COMMENTS The exquisitely finished "two bedroom, two bath" accommodations of the Nassau 42 make it difficult to believe the outstanding performance of this cruising boat. Believe it! She races competitively at a 114 PHRF handicap and cruises two couples in luxury.

SOUTHERN OFFSHORE 42

DESIGNER: Robert H. Perry
BUILDER: Southern Offshore Yachts, Inc.

STATISTICS

LOA: 41 ft. 10 ins.
LWL: 36 ft. 5 ins.
BEAM: 12 ft. 9 ins.
DISPLACEMENT
deep keel: 21,258 lbs.
shoal keel:
c/board:
BALLAST
deep keel: 8,700 lbs.
shoal keel:
c/board:
DRAFT
deep keel: 5 ft. 10 ins.
shoal keel:
c/board up:
c/board down:

INTERIOR

BERTHS: 5 berths: 1 double V, 1 single quarterberth, 1 double quarterberth
TABLE: dropleaf
HEAD(S): 2 heads with 1 shower
COLD STORAGE: built-in icebox
STOVE: 3-burner
MAX. HEADROOM:

MACHINERY

ENGINE: 42 HP Pathfinder
PROPELLER:
GENERATOR:

SAIL AREA: 800 sq. ft.
FRESH WATER:
FUEL CAPACITY:

COSTS

BASE BOAT:
DATE:
EST. ON WATER:
DATE:

RATIOS

SAIL AREA/DISP: 16.69
DISP/LENGTH: 196.45
BALLAST RATIO: 40.93
FUEL/DISP:
FRESH WATER/DISP:

DECK

STEERING: wheel
WINCHES:
SAFETY: bow and stern pulpits with double lifelines
ANCHOR:
NAV LIGHTS:

RIG

TYPE: masthead sloop
RIGGING:
MAINSHEET: mid-boom sheeting

SAILS

SUPPLIED WITH BASE BOAT:

BREWER 12.8 METER

DESIGNER: Ted Brewer
BUILDER: Ft. Myers Yacht & Shipbuilding

STATISTICS

LOA: 42 ft. 0 ins.
LWL: 33 ft. 9 ins.
BEAM: 13 ft. 6 ins.
DISPLACEMENT
deep keel: 23,850 lbs.
shoal keel:
c/board:
BALLAST
deep keel: 9,000 lbs.
shoal keel:
c/board:
DRAFT
deep keel:
shoal keel:
c/board up: 4 ft. 6 ins.
c/board down: 9 ft. 0 ins.

INTERIOR

BERTHS: 6 berths: 1 double V, 2 single settees, 2 aft singles
TABLE: dropleaf
HEAD(S): 2 heads with 2 showers
COLD STORAGE: refrigerator/freezer (15 cu. ft.)
STOVE: 3-burner propane with oven
MAX. HEADROOM: 6 ft. 3 ins.

MACHINERY

ENGINE: 72 HP Mercedes-Benz (Nanni)
PROPELLER: 3-blade on 1 1/4" shaft
GENERATOR:

SAIL AREA: 867 sq. ft.
FRESH WATER: 200 gals.
FUEL CAPACITY: 125 gals.

COSTS

BASE BOAT: $109,600
DATE: 05/01/85
EST. ON WATER: $130,000
DATE: 05/01/85

RATIOS

SAIL AREA/DISP: 16.74
DISP/LENGTH: 276
BALLAST RATIO: 37.73
FUEL/DISP: 3.93
FRESH WATER/DISP: 6.70

DECK

STEERING: wheel with emergency tiller
WINCHES: 6 Lewmar winches: 2 primaries (#52 ST), 2 halyard (#30) 1 mainsheet (#30A ST), 1 outhaul/reefing (#8)
SAFETY: bow and stern pulpits with lifelines
ANCHOR: anchor and anchor line
NAV LIGHTS: running and masthead

RIG

TYPE: cutter or ketch
RIGGING: 1x19 wire
MAINSHEET: 4-part with boom-end sheeting

SAILS

SUPPLIED WITH BASE BOAT:

BUILDER'S COMMENTS Truly a blue water cruiser with performance plus. We specialize in modifications for the experienced yachtsman.

CENTURION 42

DESIGNER: Edward Dubois
BUILDER: Chantier Henri Wasquiez

STATISTICS

LOA: 42 ft. 0 ins.
LWL: 33 ft. 2 ins.
BEAM: 13 ft. 3 ins.
DISPLACEMENT
deep keel: 24,300 lbs.
shoal keel:
c/board:
BALLAST
deep keel: 9,600 lbs.
shoal keel:
c/board:
DRAFT
deep keel: 7 ft. 5 ins.
shoal keel: 5 ft. 5 ins.
c/board up:
c/board down:

SAIL AREA:
FRESH WATER: 68 gals.
FUEL CAPACITY: 105 gals.

COSTS

BASE BOAT:
DATE:
EST. ON WATER:
DATE:

RATIOS

SAIL AREA/DISP:
DISP/LENGTH: 297.5
BALLAST RATIO: 39.5
FUEL/DISP: 2.1
FRESH WATER/DISP: 3.5

DECK

STEERING: wheel
WINCHES: 7 Lewmar winches: 2 primary (#55 ST), 1 genoa halyard (#46 ST), 1 main halyard (#43 ST), 1 mainsheet (#43 ST), 1 reefing (#43 ST), 1 spinnaker boom (#40 ST)
SAFETY: bow and stern pulpits with double lifelines
ANCHOR: 35 lb. CQR anchor with anchor well and locker
NAV LIGHTS: running and masthead

RIG

TYPE: masthead sloop with Kemp spar
RIGGING:
MAINSHEET: mid-boom sheeting

SAILS

SUPPLIED WITH BASE BOAT:

INTERIOR

BERTHS: 6 berths: 1 double V, 2 single pilots, 1 double quarterberth
TABLE: fixed
HEAD(S): 2 heads with 2 showers
COLD STORAGE: refrigerator/freezer
STOVE: 2-burner propane or butane with oven
MAX. HEADROOM:

MACHINERY

ENGINE: 47 HP Perkins #4 108 diesel
PROPELLER:
GENERATOR:

BUILDER'S COMMENTS The Centurion 42 is the same breed of prestigious racer/cruiser that the Henri Wauquiez shipyard is known for. It has three separate cabins in addition to a sumptuous saloon, with also an enormous sail locker too often forgotten. The Centurion 42 will thrill you with speed in the greatest of comfort.

WHITBY 42

DESIGNER: Edward S. Brewer & Associates, Inc.
BUILDER: Whitby Boat Works, Ltd.

STATISTICS

LOA: 42 ft. 0 ins.
LWL: 32 ft. 8 ins.
BEAM: 13 ft. 0 ins.
DISPLACEMENT
deep keel: 23,500 lbs.
shoal keel:
c/board:
BALLAST
deep keel:
shoal keel:
c/board:
DRAFT
deep keel: 5 ft. 0 ins.
shoal keel:
c/board up:
c/board down:

SAIL AREA: 875 sq. ft.
FRESH WATER: 290 gals.
FUEL CAPACITY: 210 gals.

COSTS

BASE BOAT:
DATE:
EST. ON WATER:
DATE:

RATIOS

SAIL AREA/DISP: 17.06
DISP/LENGTH: 301.14
BALLAST RATIO:
FUEL/DISP: 6.7
FRESH WATER/DISP: 9.87

DECK

STEERING: wheel with emergency tiller
WINCHES: 7 Lewmar winches
SAFETY: bow and stern pulpits with double lifelines
ANCHOR: Danforth 20-H anchor with anchor roller
NAV LIGHTS: running and masthead

RIG

TYPE: masthead ketch
RIGGING: 1x19 wire
MAINSHEET: boom-end sheeting

SAILS

SUPPLIED WITH BASE BOAT:

INTERIOR

BERTHS: 7 berths: 1 double V, 1 single settee, 1 double convertible dinette, 2 singles or 1 double in aft cabin
TABLE: bulkhead-mounted dropleaf
HEAD(S): 2 heads with 2 showers and 1 holding tank
COLD STORAGE: refrigerator/freezer (12.5 cu. ft.)
STOVE: 3-burner propane with oven
MAX. HEADROOM:

MACHINERY

ENGINE: Volvo MD 30 diesel with 2.37:1 reduction gear
PROPELLER: fixed 18"x12" on 1 1/4" shaft
GENERATOR:

LANDFALL 43

DESIGNER: C & C Design Group
BUILDER: C & C Yachts

STATISTICS

LOA: 42 ft. 1 ins.
LWL: 34 ft. 5 ins.
BEAM: 12 ft. 7 ins.
DISPLACEMENT
deep keel: 24,600 lbs.
shoal keel:
c/board:
BALLAST
deep keel: 9,075 lbs.
shoal keel:
c/board:
DRAFT
deep keel: 5 ft. 6 ins.
shoal keel:
c/board up:
c/board down:

SAIL AREA: 796 sq. ft.
FRESH WATER: 175 gals.
FUEL CAPACITY: 70 gals.

COSTS

BASE BOAT:
DATE:
EST. ON WATER:
DATE:

RATIOS

SAIL AREA/DISP: 15.05
DISP/LENGTH: 269
BALLAST RATIO: 36.89
FUEL/DISP: 2.13
FRESH WATER/DISP: 5.69

INTERIOR

BERTHS: 7 berths: 1 double V, 1 double convertible dinette, 1 single-settee, 1 center aft double
TABLE: dropleaf
HEAD(S): 2 heads with 1 shower, 1 sump pump, and 2 holding tanks (20 gal)
COLD STORAGE: refrigerator
STOVE: 3-burner propane with oven
MAX. HEADROOM:

MACHINERY

ENGINE: 40 HP Westerbeke diesel
PROPELLER: 2-blade fixed
GENERATOR:

DECK

STEERING: 36" Edson wheel
WINCHES: 6 Barient winches: 2 primaries (#28A), 2 halyard (#24C), 2 halyard (#23A ST), 1 outhaul/reefing (#18A)
SAFETY: bow and stern pulpits with double lifelines
ANCHOR: anchor well
NAV LIGHTS: running and masthead

RIG

TYPE: masthead sloop
RIGGING: Navtec rod
MAINSHEET: mid-boom sheeting

SAILS

SUPPLIED WITH BASE BOAT:

BUILDER'S COMMENTS The C & C Landfall 43 is a sleek and swift cruising vessel from the boards of the C & C design group. Her heritage is the powerful Landfall 48 and the custom 67 foot Archangel. The C & C Landfall 43—no other center cockpit looks and moves like her.

NIAGARA 42

DESIGNER: Mark Ellis Design, Ltd.
BUILDER: Henterhoeller Yachts, Ltd.

STATISTICS

LOA: 42 ft. 2 ins.
LWL: 32 ft. 6 ins.
BEAM: 12 ft. 9 ins.
DISPLACEMENT
deep keel: 20,000 lbs.
shoal keel:
c/board:
BALLAST
deep keel:
shoal keel:
c/board:
DRAFT
deep keel: 5 ft. 8 ins.
shoal keel:
c/board up:
c/board down:

SAIL AREA: 850 sq. ft.
FRESH WATER: 150 gals.
FUEL CAPACITY: 65 gals.

COSTS

BASE BOAT: $130,750
DATE: 08/01/85
EST. ON WATER: $150,000
DATE: 08/01/85

RATIOS

SAIL AREA/DISP: 18.46
DISP/LENGTH: 260.09
BALLAST RATIO:
FUEL/DISP: 2.44
FRESH WATER/DISP: 6.00

INTERIOR

BERTHS: 6 berths: 1 forward double berth, 2 settees, 1 double quarterberth
TABLE: dropleaf
HEAD(S): 2 heads with 1 shower
COLD STORAGE: built-in icebox (10 cu. ft.)
STOVE: 3-burner propane with oven
MAX. HEADROOM: 6 ft. 6 ins.

MACHINERY

ENGINE: 46 HP Westerbeke diesel with 2:1 V drive
PROPELLER: 2-blade 18"x16" RH on 1 1/8" SS shaft
GENERATOR:

DECK

STEERING: 32" wheel with emergency tiller
WINCHES: 7 Barient winches: 2 primary (#32 ST), 2 mainsheet (#17 ST), 2 halyard (#24 & #21), 1 reefing (#18)
SAFETY: bow and stern pulpits with double lifelines
ANCHOR: bowsprit with anchor rollers
NAV LIGHTS: running and masthead

RIG

TYPE: sloop (optional cutter)
RIGGING: Navtec rod
MAINSHEET: 4-part

SAILS

SUPPLIED WITH BASE BOAT:

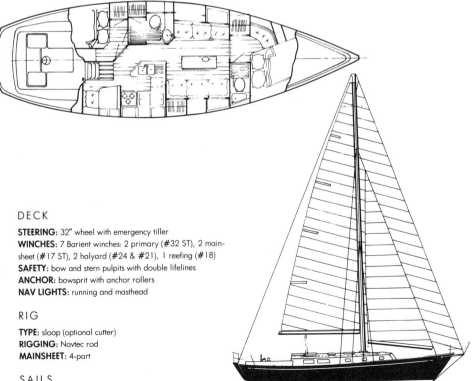

PEARSON 422

DESIGNER: Bill Shaw
BUILDER: Pearson Yachts

STATISTICS

LOA: 42 ft. 2 ins.
LWL: 33 ft. 8 ins.
BEAM: 13 ft. 0 ins.
DISPLACEMENT
deep keel: 22,000 lbs.
shoal keel:
c/board:
BALLAST
deep keel: 7,630 lbs.
shoal keel:
c/board:
DRAFT
deep keel: 5 ft. 3 ins.
shoal keel:
c/board up:
c/board down:

SAIL AREA: 719 sq. ft.
FRESH WATER: 160 gals.
FUEL CAPACITY: 80 gals.

COSTS

BASE BOAT:
DATE:
EST. ON WATER:
DATE:

RATIOS

SAIL AREA/DISP: 14.65
DISP/LENGTH: 257.53
BALLAST RATIO: 34.68
FUEL/DISP: 2.73
FRESH WATER/DISP: 5.82

DECK

STEERING: wheel with emergency tiller
WINCHES: 6 Lewmar winches: 2 primary (#48 ST), 2 halyard (#16), 1 mainsheet, 1 reefing (#6)
SAFETY: bow and stern pulpits with double lifelines
ANCHOR: anchor locker
NAV LIGHTS: running and masthead

RIG

TYPE: masthead sloop
RIGGING: wire
MAINSHEET: boom-end sheeting

SAILS

SUPPLIED WITH BASE BOAT:

INTERIOR

BERTHS: 6 berths: 1 double V, 2 single settee, 1 center aft double
TABLE: dropleaf
HEAD(S): 2 heads with 2 showers and 2 holding tanks
COLD STORAGE: built-in icebox
STOVE: 3-burner propane with oven
MAX. HEADROOM:

MACHINERY

ENGINE: diesel
PROPELLER:
GENERATOR:

ENDEAVOUR 42

DESIGNER:
BUILDER: Endeavour Yacht Corporation

STATISTICS

LOA: 42 ft. 3 ins.
LWL: 33 ft. 4 ins.
BEAM: 13 ft. 0 ins.
DISPLACEMENT
deep keel: 25,500 lbs.
shoal keel:
c/board:
BALLAST
deep keel: 9,000 lbs.
shoal keel:
c/board:
DRAFT
deep keel: 5 ft. 0 ins.
shoal keel:
c/board up:
c/board down:

SAIL AREA: 788 sq. ft.
FRESH WATER:
FUEL CAPACITY: 75 gals.

COSTS

BASE BOAT:
DATE:
EST. ON WATER:
DATE:

RATIOS

SAIL AREA/DISP: 14.55
DISP/LENGTH: 307
BALLAST RATIO: 35.29
FUEL/DISP: 2.20
FRESH WATER/DISP:

DECK

STEERING: 38" wheel
WINCHES: 4 winches: 2 sheet, 2 halyard
SAFETY: bow and stern pulpits with lifelines
ANCHOR: anchor well
NAV LIGHTS: running and masthead

RIG

TYPE: masthead sloop
RIGGING:
MAINSHEET: boom-end sheeting

SAILS

SUPPLIED WITH BASE BOAT:

INTERIOR

BERTHS: 7 berths: 1 double V, 1 single settee, 1 double convertible settee, 1 aft double
TABLE: centerline dropleaf
HEAD(S): 2 heads with 2 showers
COLD STORAGE: built-in icebox with refrigeration system
STOVE: 3-burner propane with oven
MAX. HEADROOM: 6 ft. 4 ins.

MACHINERY

ENGINE: 62 HP Perkins #4-154 diesel
PROPELLER: 3-blade
GENERATOR:

RH-43 SLOOP

DESIGNER: Ron Holland
DISTRIBUTOR: Ta Chiao USA, Inc. (built in Taiwan by Ta Chiao Bros. Yacht Building Co.)

STATISTICS

LOA: 42 ft. 8.0 ins.
LWL: 33 ft. 10.5 ins.
BEAM: 13 ft. 0.0 ins.
DISPLACEMENT
deep keel: 23,780 lbs.
shoal keel:
c/board:
BALLAST
deep keel: 9,390 lbs.
shoal keel:
c/board:
DRAFT
deep keel: 6 ft. 8 ins.
shoal keel: 5 ft. 7 ins.
c/board up:
c/board down:

INTERIOR

BERTHS: 6 berths in interior A: 1 double V, 2 single settees, 1 double quarterberth (3 additional single berths available with interior B)
TABLE: dropleaf
HEAD(S): 2 heads with 1 shower, 1 bathtub, 1 sump pump, 1 holding tank
COLD STORAGE: built-in icebox
STOVE: 3-burner gas with oven
MAX. HEADROOM: 6 ft. 4 ins.

MACHINERY

ENGINE: 50 HP Perkins #4-108 diesel

SAIL AREA: 800-950 sq. ft.
FRESH WATER: 80 gals.
FUEL CAPACITY: 90 gals.

COSTS

BASE BOAT: $122,000
DATE: 07/01/85
EST. ON WATER:
DATE:

RATIOS

SAIL AREA/DISP: 15.48
DISP/LENGTH: 273.46
BALLAST RATIO: 39.49
FUEL/DISP: 2.84
FRESH WATER/DISP: 2.69

PROPELLER: folding or fixed
GENERATOR:

DECK

STEERING: wheel with emergency tiller
WINCHES: 10 Lewmar winches: 2 #55A ST, 5 #46A ST, 3 #40A ST
SAFETY: bow and stern pulpits with double lifelines
ANCHOR: anchor roller
NAV LIGHTS: running and masthead

RIG

TYPE: masthead sloop with Kemp spar
RIGGING: rod
MAINSHEET: mid-boom sheeting

SAILS

SUPPLIED WITH BASE BOAT: main, working jib, 135% genoa

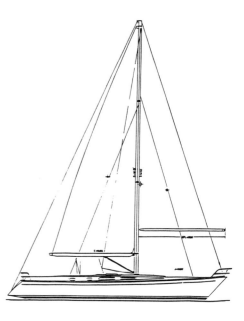

BUILDER'S COMMENTS The RH-43 sloop is an exceptionally fast cruising boat which could be classed as a club racer. She is competitive under PHRF or IOR. In addition, she has a full cruising layout, including two excellent staterooms.

HANS CHRISTIAN 44 PILOT HOUSE

DESIGNER: Harwood S. Ives
BUILDER: Hans Christian Yachts, Inc.

STATISTICS

LOA: 42 ft. 9 ins.
LWL: 37 ft. 6 ins.
BEAM: 14 ft. 7 ins.
DISPLACEMENT
deep keel: 44,000 lbs.
shoal keel:
c/board:
BALLAST
deep keel: 15,000 lbs.
shoal keel:
c/board:
DRAFT
deep keel: 5 ft. 6 ins.
shoal keel:
c/board up:
c/board down:

INTERIOR

BERTHS: 6 berths: 1 double V, 1 double pilot, 1 double quarterberth
TABLE: fixed
HEAD(S): 2 heads with 2 showers and 1 holding tank
COLD STORAGE: built-in icebox
STOVE: 3-burner with oven
MAX. HEADROOM:

MACHINERY

ENGINE: 110-120 HP diesel with 3.1:1 reduction gear
PROPELLER: fixed 27"x14°
GENERATOR:

SAIL AREA: 1,150 sq. ft.
FRESH WATER: 400 gals.
FUEL CAPACITY: 450 gals.

COSTS

BASE BOAT:
DATE:
EST. ON WATER:
DATE:

RATIOS

SAIL AREA/DISP: 14.76
DISP/LENGTH: 372.49
BALLAST RATIO: 34.09
FUEL/DISP: 7.67
FRESH WATER/DISP: 7.27

DECK

STEERING: wheel
WINCHES:
SAFETY: bow and stern pulpits with double lifelines
ANCHOR: anchor roller
NAV LIGHTS:

RIG

TYPE: masthead ketch
RIGGING: 1x19 wire (⅜")
MAINSHEET: boom-end sheeting

SAILS

SUPPLIED WITH BASE BOAT:

SOU'WESTER 42

DESIGNER: McCurdy & Rhodes, Inc.
BUILDER: Henry R. Hinckley & Co.

STATISTICS

LOA: 42 ft. 9 ins.
LWL: 31 ft. 3 ins.
BEAM: 12 ft. 6 ins.
DISPLACEMENT
deep keel: 21,000 lbs.
shoal keel:
c/board:
BALLAST
deep keel: 8,500 lbs.
shoal keel:
c/board:
DRAFT
deep keel:
shoal keel:
c/board up: 5 ft. 0 ins.
c/board down: 9 ft. 0 ins.

SAIL AREA: 818 sq. ft.
FRESH WATER: 155 gals.
FUEL CAPACITY: 60 gals.

COSTS

BASE BOAT: $245,000
DATE: 06/85
EST. ON WATER: $300,000
DATE: 06/85

RATIOS

SAIL AREA/DISP: 17.19
DISP/LENGTH: 307
BALLAST RATIO: 28.57
FUEL/DISP: 2.14
FRESH WATER/DISP: 5.90

DECK

STEERING: 32" wheel
WINCHES: 7 Barient winches: 4 primary/secondary (#28), 2 halyard (#22), 1 mainsheet (#22)
SAFETY: bow and stern pulpits with double lifelines
ANCHOR:
NAV LIGHTS: running

RIG

TYPE: masthead sloop
RIGGING: 1x19 wire
MAINSHEET: mid-boom sheeting

SAILS

SUPPLIED WITH BASE BOAT:

INTERIOR

BERTHS: 6 berths: 1 double V, 2 single pilots, 2 single extensions (or 1 double convertible instead of pilot and extension)
TABLE: dining
HEAD(S): 1 head with shower
COLD STORAGE: built-in icebox
STOVE: 3-burner LPG with oven
MAX. HEADROOM:

MACHINERY

ENGINE: 40 HP Westerbeke diesel
PROPELLER: 2-blade
GENERATOR:

BUILDER'S COMMENTS The SW-42 is a comfortable modern cruising yacht. Traditional lines above the water are wed to a high performance fin keel underbody which make her fast on all points of sail.

SWAN 43

DESIGNER: Ron Holland
BUILDER: Nautor

STATISTICS

LOA: 42 ft. 11.3 ins.
LWL: 34 ft. 1.6 ins.
BEAM: 13 ft. 1.4 ins.
DISPLACEMENT
deep keel: 23,400 lbs.
shoal keel:
c/board:
BALLAST
deep keel: 9,000 lbs.
shoal keel:
c/board:
DRAFT
deep keel: 7 ft. 6 ins.
shoal keel:
c/board up:
c/board down:

SAIL AREA:
FRESH WATER: 92 gals.
FUEL CAPACITY: 71 gals.

COSTS

BASE BOAT:
DATE:
EST. ON WATER:
DATE:

RATIOS

SAIL AREA/DISP:
DISP/LENGTH: 262.76
BALLAST RATIO: 38.46
FUEL/DISP: 2.28
FRESH WATER/DISP: 3.15

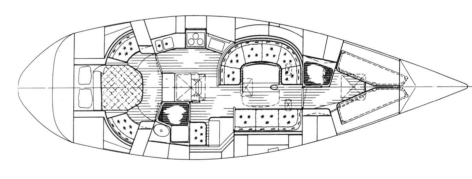

INTERIOR

BERTHS: 5 berths: 1 single settee, 1 center aft double, 2 pipe berths
TABLE: dropleaf
HEAD(S): 1 head with shower, 1 separate shower stall only, 2 sump pumps
COLD STORAGE: built-in icebox (5.3 cu. ft.) and refrigerator (4.6 cu. ft.)
STOVE: 3-burner gas with oven
MAX. HEADROOM:

MACHINERY

ENGINE: 45 HP Volvo Penta #2003 diesel with 3.0:1 reduction gear

PROPELLER: 21" folding
GENERATOR:

DECK

STEERING: 42" wheel with emergency tiller
WINCHES: 12 Lewmar winches: 4 #48A ST, 2 #65AP, 4 #40A ST, 2 #44A ST
SAFETY: bow and stern pulpits with double lifelines
ANCHOR: Danforth 40S anchor with anchor well

NAV LIGHTS: running and masthead

RIG

TYPE: masthead sloop
RIGGING: rod
MAINSHEET:

SAILS

SUPPLIED WITH BASE BOAT:

AMPHITRITE

DESIGNER: Holman & Pye
BUILDER: Chantier Henri Wauquiez

STATISTICS

LOA: 43 ft. 0 ins.
LWL: 34 ft. 0 ins.
BEAM: 13 ft. 8 ins.
DISPLACEMENT
deep keel: 28,600 lbs.
shoal keel:
c/board:
BALLAST
deep keel: 9,900 lbs.
shoal keel:
c/board:
DRAFT
deep keel: 5 ft. 10 ins.
shoal keel:
c/board up:
c/board down:

SAIL AREA:
FRESH WATER: 210 gals.
FUEL CAPACITY: 120 gals.

COSTS

BASE BOAT: 1,165,000 francs
DATE: 02/25/85
EST. ON WATER:
DATE:

RATIOS

SAIL AREA/DISP:
DISP/LENGTH: 324.8
BALLAST RATIO: 34.6
FUEL/DISP: 5.81
FRESH WATER/DISP: 3.15

DECK

STEERING: wheel
WINCHES: 8 winches
SAFETY: bow and stern pulpits with double lifelines
ANCHOR: 44 lbs. anchor with anchor chain and locker
NAV LIGHTS: running and masthead

RIG

TYPE: masthead ketch
RIGGING:
MAINSHEET: boom-end sheeting

SAILS

SUPPLIED WITH BASE BOAT: main, genoa, mizzen, storm jib

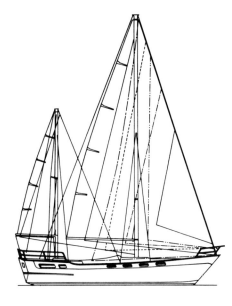

INTERIOR

BERTHS: 10 berths: 1 double V, 1 single settee, 1 double convertible dinette, 3 single pilots, 1 double quarterberth
TABLE: dropleaf
HEAD(S): 2 heads with 2 showers
COLD STORAGE: icebox
STOVE: 2-burner propane or butane with oven
MAX. HEADROOM: 6 ft. 4 ins.

MACHINERY

ENGINE: 62 HP Perkins diesel
PROPELLER:
GENERATOR:

BUILDER'S COMMENTS The Amphitrite is one of the most exceptional offshore cruising ketches. It can sail at 35 degrees from the apparent wind without losing speed. The sail area is divided for ease of handling, even with a family crew of only two. There are but few boats of the same size offering such comfort: three big separate cabins with two berths each and two toilets—plus a saloon. Every detail has been thought of for this very special boat.

CT-44 CUTTER

DESIGNER: Yves-Marie Tanton
DISTRIBUTOR: Ta Chiao USA, Inc. (built in Taiwan by Ta Chiao Bros. Yacht Building Co.)

STATISTICS

LOA: 43 ft. 2.0 ins.
LWL: 37 ft. 7.0 ins.
BEAM: 13 ft. 1.5 ins.
DISPLACEMENT
deep keel: 20,216 lbs.
shoal keel:
c/board:
BALLAST
deep keel: 9,267 lbs.
shoal keel:
c/board:
DRAFT
deep keel: 6 ft. 0 ins.
shoal keel: 5 ft. 0 ins.
c/board up:
c/board down:

SAIL AREA: 865 sq. ft.
FRESH WATER: 120 gals.
FUEL CAPACITY: 100 gals.

COSTS

BASE BOAT: $116,000
DATE: 07/01/85
EST. ON WATER:
DATE:

RATIOS

SAIL AREA/DISP: 18.65
DISP/LENGTH: 170.05
BALLAST RATIO: 45.84
FUEL/DISP: 3.70
FRESH WATER/DISP: 4.75

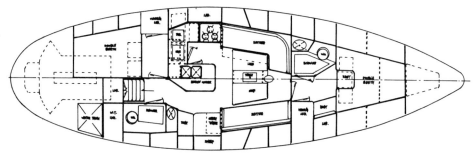

INTERIOR

BERTHS: 6 berths: 1 double V, 1 single settee, 1 single convertible dinette, 1 double quarterberth
TABLE: dropleaf
HEAD(S): 2 heads with 2 showers, 1 sump pump, and 1 holding tank
COLD STORAGE: built-in icebox
STOVE: 3-burner with oven
MAX. HEADROOM: 6 ft. 4 ins.

MACHINERY

ENGINE: 50 HP Perkins #4-108 diesel
PROPELLER: fixed
GENERATOR:

DECK

STEERING: wheel with emergency tiller
WINCHES: 7 Barlow winches: 3 #27 ST, 4 #24 ST
SAFETY: bow and stern pulpits with double lifelines
ANCHOR: anchor roller and well
NAV LIGHTS: running and masthead

RIG

TYPE: masthead cutter
RIGGING: wire
MAINSHEET: mid-boom sheeting

SAILS

SUPPLIED WITH BASE BOAT: main, working jib, staysail

BUILDER'S COMMENTS The CT-44 is a medium displacement cutter designed by Tanton for fast cruising passages. She is exceptionally well laid out with one of the best cruising cockpits in the industry. The layout below has a U-shaped galley, two heads, two staterooms, and an easy entry from deck level.

OFFSHORE 43

DESIGNER: Yves-Marie Tanton
BUILDER: Offshore Yachts

STATISTICS

LOA: 43 ft. 2 ins.
LWL: 37 ft. 7 ins.
BEAM: 13 ft. 1 ins.
DISPLACEMENT
deep keel: 20,216 lbs.
shoal keel:
c/board:
BALLAST
deep keel: 9,000 lbs.
shoal keel:
c/board:
DRAFT
deep keel: 4 ft. 10 ins.
shoal keel:
c/board up:
c/board down:

SAIL AREA: 794 sq. ft.
FRESH WATER: 120 gals.
FUEL CAPACITY: 80 gals.

COSTS

BASE BOAT:
DATE:
EST. ON WATER:
DATE:

RATIOS

SAIL AREA/DISP: 17.12
DISP/LENGTH: 170.05
BALLAST RATIO: 44.52
FUEL/DISP: 2.97
FRESH WATER/DISP: 4.75

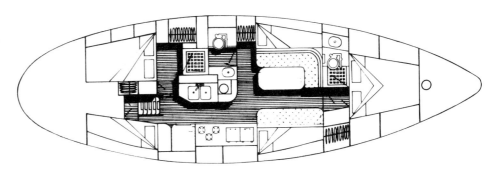

INTERIOR

BERTHS: 7 berths: 1 double V, 2 single pilots, 1 single quarterberth, 1 double quarterberth
TABLE:
HEAD(S): 2 heads with showers and 1 sump pump
COLD STORAGE: built-in icebox
STOVE: 3-burner propane with oven
MAX. HEADROOM: 6 ft. 5 ins.

MACHINERY

ENGINE: 50 HP Perkins #4-108M diesel
PROPELLER: folding or fixed
GENERATOR:

DECK

STEERING: wheel with emergency tiller
WINCHES:
SAFETY: bow and stern pulpits with double lifelines
ANCHOR: anchor roller
NAV LIGHTS: running and masthead

RIG

TYPE: cat ketch
RIGGING:
MAINSHEET:

SAILS

SUPPLIED WITH BASE BOAT: main, mizzen

CAL 44

DESIGNER: C. Raymond Hunt Associates
BUILDER: Lear Siegler Marine

STATISTICS

LOA: 43 ft. 6 ins.
LWL: 36 ft. 3 ins.
BEAM: 13 ft. 6 ins.
DISPLACEMENT
deep keel: 25,000 lbs.
shoal keel:
c/board:
BALLAST
deep keel: 10,000 lbs.
shoal keel:
c/board:
DRAFT
deep keel: 6 ft. 6 ins.
shoal keel: 5 ft. 6 ins.
c/board up:
c/board down:

SAIL AREA: 860 sq. ft.
FRESH WATER: 200 gals.
FUEL CAPACITY: 80 gals.

COSTS

BASE BOAT:
DATE:
EST. ON WATER:
DATE:

RATIOS

SAIL AREA/DISP: 16.09
DISP/LENGTH: 234
BALLAST RATIO: 40.00
FUEL/DISP: 2.40
FRESH WATER/DISP: 6.40

DECK

STEERING: 40" wheel
WINCHES: 6 Barient winches: 2 primary (#32 ST), 2 halyard (#21 & #18) 1 mainsheet (#23), 1 reefing (#18)
SAFETY: bow and stern pulpits with lifelines
ANCHOR: bowsprit with dual rollers and anchor well
NAV LIGHTS: running and masthead

RIG

TYPE: masthead sloop
RIGGING: 1x19 wire
MAINSHEET: mid-boom sheeting

SAILS

SUPPLIED WITH BASE BOAT:

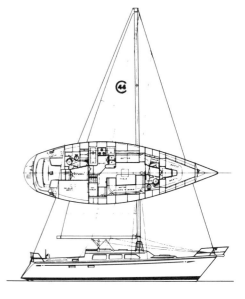

INTERIOR

BERTHS: 7 berths: 1 double V, 1 double convertible settee, 1 single settee, 1 double quarterberth
TABLE: pedestal-mounted dinette
HEAD(S): 2 heads with 2 showers and 2 sump pumps
COLD STORAGE: built-in icebox (11 cu. ft.)
STOVE: 3-burner propane with oven
MAX. HEADROOM: 6 ft. 5.5 ins.

MACHINERY

ENGINE: 58 HP Westerbeke diesel with 2.7:1 reduction gear
PROPELLER: 3-blade on 1 1/4" shaft
GENERATOR:

BUILDER'S COMMENTS The Cal 44 is a unique statement about the modern cruising sailboat. Two spacious cabins and a raised deckhouse give comfort never before found in an aft cockpit sailboat. Her modern rig and fin keel give sprightly performance that will surprise even the sailing sophisticate.

NORDIC 44

DESIGNER: Robert H. Perry
BUILDER: Nordic Yachts, Inc.

STATISTICS

LOA: 43 ft. 10 ins.
LWL: 35 ft. 5 ins.
BEAM: 12 ft. 11 ins.
DISPLACEMENT
deep keel: 24,000 lbs.
shoal keel:
c/board:
BALLAST
deep keel: 9,340 lbs.
shoal keel:
c/board:
DRAFT
deep keel: 7 ft. 0 ins.
shoal keel:
c/board up:
c/board down:

SAIL AREA: 907 sq. ft.
FRESH WATER: 140 gals.
FUEL CAPACITY: 76 gals.

COSTS

BASE BOAT.
DATE:
EST. ON WATER:
DATE:

RATIOS

SAIL AREA/DISP: 17.44
DISP/LENGTH: 241
BALLAST RATIO: 38.91
FUEL/DISP: 2.37
FRESH WATER/DISP: 4.66

INTERIOR

BERTHS: 6 berths: 1 double V, 2 single settees, 1 double quarterberth
TABLE: fixed with leaf
HEAD(S): 2 heads with 2 showers
COLD STORAGE: built-in icebox (9 cu. ft.)
STOVE: 3-burner propane with oven
MAX. HEADROOM: 6 ft. 6 ins.

MACHINERY

ENGINE: Universal #50 diesel
PROPELLER: 2-blade
GENERATOR:

DECK

STEERING: 40" wheel
WINCHES: 8 Lewmar winches: 2 primary (#65), 3 halyard (#43), 1 mainsheet (#43), 1 reefing (#30), 1 outhaul (#8)
SAFETY: bow and stern pulpits with double lifelines
ANCHOR.
NAV LIGHTS: running and masthead

RIG

TYPE: masthead sloop
RIGGING: rod
MAINSHEET: mid-boom sheeting

SAILS

SUPPLIED WITH BASE BOAT:

BUILDER'S COMMENTS The Nordic 44, designed by Robert H. Perry to be a combination of beauty, functional interior arrangement, and superior sailing performance, has proven its sailing ability both on the race course and in thousands of miles of successful ocean sailing. For 1986 an exciting new interior arrangement has been introduced.

SHANNON 43

DESIGNER: Walter Schulz & Associates
BUILDER: Shannon Boat Company, Inc.

STATISTICS

LOA: 43 ft. 10 ins.
LWL: 36 ft. 7 ins.
BEAM: 13 ft. 0 ins.
DISPLACEMENT
deep keel: 27,000 lbs.
shoal keel:
c/board:
BALLAST
deep keel:
shoal keel:
c/board:
DRAFT
deep keel:
shoal keel:
c/board up: 4 ft. 9 ins.
c/board down: 6 ft. 6 ins.

SAIL AREA: 950 sq. ft.
FRESH WATER: 200 gals.
FUEL CAPACITY: 100 gals.

COSTS

BASE BOAT:
DATE:
EST. ON WATER:
DATE:

RATIOS

SAIL AREA/DISP: 16.96
DISP/LENGTH: 246.25
BALLAST RATIO:
FUEL/DISP: 2.78
FRESH WATER/DISP: 5.93

INTERIOR

BERTHS: 8 berths: 1 double V, 1 double settee, 1 single settee, 1 single pilot berth, 1 double quarterberth
TABLE: dropleaf
HEAD(S): 2 heads with 2 showers and 2 sump pumps
COLD STORAGE: refrigerator/freezer (12 cu. ft.)
STOVE: 3-burner propane with oven
MAX. HEADROOM:

MACHINERY

ENGINE: 55 HP Perkins #4.154 diesel
PROPELLER: 3-blade
GENERATOR:

DECK

STEERING: wheel
WINCHES: 8 Barient or Lewmar winches
SAFETY: bow and stern pulpits with double lifelines
ANCHOR: 45 lb. CQR and 20 HT Danforth anchors with anchor roller
NAV LIGHTS:

RIG

TYPE: ketch or cutter
RIGGING: rod
MAINSHEET: mid-boom sheeting

SAILS

SUPPLIED WITH BASE BOAT: main, 150% genoa, staysail, yankee, mizzen

MASON 43

DESIGNER: Al Mason
BUILDER: Pacific Asian Enterprises, Inc.

STATISTICS

LOA: 43 ft. 10.5 ins.
LWL: 31 ft. 3.0 ins.
BEAM: 12 ft. 3.5 ins.
DISPLACEMENT
deep keel: 25,000 lbs.
shoal keel:
c/board:
BALLAST
deep keel: 8,400 lbs.
shoal keel:
c/board:
DRAFT
deep keel: 6 ft. 3 ins.
shoal keel:
c/board up:
c/board down:

SAIL AREA: 899 sq. ft. (cutter)
916 sq. ft. (ketch)
FRESH WATER: 206 gals.
FUEL CAPACITY: 104 gals.

COSTS

BASE BOAT:
DATE:
EST. ON WATER:
DATE:

RATIOS

SAIL AREA/DISP: 16.83
DISP/LENGTH: 365.71
BALLAST RATIO: 33.6
FUEL/DISP: 3.12
FRESH WATER/DISP: 6.59

GENERATOR:

DECK

STEERING: 28" wheel with emergency tiller
WINCHES: 9 winches: 2 primary (Lewmar #48C ST), 2 secondary (#30C), 3 halyard (2 #30C & 1 #24C), 1 mainsheet (#30C), 1 reefing
SAFETY: bow and stern pulpits with double lifelines
ANCHOR:
NAV LIGHTS: running and masthead

RIG

TYPE: masthead cutter (ketch available)
RIGGING: wire
MAINSHEET: boom-end sheeting

SAILS

SUPPLIED WITH BASE BOAT: main, working jib, staysail

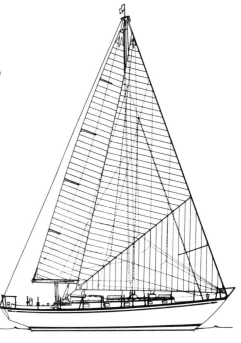

INTERIOR

BERTHS: 9 berths: 1 forward double, 1 single settee, 1 double convertible dinette, 1 pilot berth, 1 single quarterberth, 1 double quarterberth
TABLE: fixed
HEAD(S): 1 head with shower, sump pump, and holding tank (30 gal.)
COLD STORAGE: built-in icebox and refrigerator/freezer
STOVE: 3-burner
MAX. HEADROOM:

MACHINERY

ENGINE: Perkins #4-108 diesel with 2:1 reduction gear
PROPELLER: 1 1/4" shaft

MASON 44

DESIGNER: Al Mason
BUILDER: Pacific Asian Enterprises, Inc.

STATISTICS

LOA: 43 ft. 10.50 ins.
LWL: 31 ft. 9.00 ins.
BEAM: 12 ft. 3.25 ins.
DISPLACEMENT
deep keel: 27,400 lbs.
shoal keel:
c/board:
BALLAST
deep keel: 9,400 lbs.
shoal keel:
c/board:
DRAFT
deep keel: 6 ft. 5 ins.
shoal keel:
c/board up:
c/board down:

SAIL AREA: 899 sq. ft.
FRESH WATER: 205 gals.
FUEL CAPACITY: 130 gals.

COSTS

BASE BOAT:
DATE:
EST. ON WATER:
DATE:

RATIOS

SAIL AREA/DISP: 15.82
DISP/LENGTH: 382.2
BALLAST RATIO: 34.3
FUEL/DISP: 3.56
FRESH WATER/DISP: 6.0

DECK

STEERING: 34" wheel with emergency tiller
WINCHES: 9 winches: 2 primary (#48C), 2 secondary (#30C), 3 halyard (#30C ST), 1 mainsheet (#30C), 1 reefing (#30C ST)
SAFETY: bow and stern pulpits with double lifelines
ANCHOR:
NAV LIGHTS: running and masthead

RIG

TYPE: cutter with Forespar spar (ketch available)
RIGGING: wire
MAINSHEET:

SAILS

SUPPLIED WITH BASE BOAT: main, working jib, staysail

INTERIOR

BERTHS: 7 berths: 1 double V, 1 single settee, 1 double convertible dinette, and 1 aft double
TABLE:
HEAD(S): 1 head with shower, sump pump, and holding tank
COLD STORAGE: built-in icebox
STOVE:
MAX. HEADROOM:

MACHINERY

ENGINE: Westerbeke #58 with 2:1 reduction gear
PROPELLER: 1 1/4" shaft
GENERATOR:

FREEDOM 44

DESIGNER: Gary Hoyt
BUILDER: Freedom Yachts International, Inc.

STATISTICS

LOA: 44 ft. 0 ins.
LWL: 39 ft. 6 ins.
BEAM: 12 ft. 0 ins.
DISPLACEMENT
deep keel: 24,000 lbs
shoal keel:
c/board:
BALLAST
deep keel: 6,000 lbs.
shoal keel:
c/board:
DRAFT
deep keel: 7 ft. 8 ins.
shoal keel: 6 ft. 0 ins.
c/board up:
c/board down:

SAIL AREA: 1,002 sq. ft.
FRESH WATER: 200 gals.
FUEL CAPACITY: 107 gals.

COSTS

BASE BOAT:
DATE:
EST. ON WATER:
DATE:

RATIOS

SAIL AREA/DISP: 19.27
DISP/LENGTH: 173.85
BALLAST RATIO: 25.00
FUEL/DISP: 3.34
FRESH WATER/DISP: 6.67

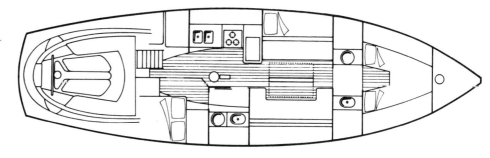

INTERIOR

BERTHS: 5 berths: 1 double V, 1 double quarterberth, 1 single pilot
TABLE: dropleaf
HEAD(S): 2 heads with 1 shower
COLD STORAGE: built-in icebox
STOVE: 3-burner with oven
MAX. HEADROOM:

MACHINERY

ENGINE: 50 HP diesel
PROPELLER:
GENERATOR:

DECK

STEERING: wheel
WINCHES:
SAFETY: bow and stern pulpits with single lifelines
ANCHOR:
NAV LIGHTS:

RIG

TYPE: cat ketch
RIGGING: unstayed
MAINSHEET:

SAILS

SUPPLIED WITH BASE BOAT:

GRENADIER 134

DESIGNER: Laurent Giles & Partners, Ltd.
BUILDER: A. H. Moody & Son, Ltd.

STATISTICS

LOA: 44 ft. 0 ins.
LWL: 34 ft. 6 ins.
BEAM: 13 ft. 7 ins.
DISPLACEMENT
deep keel: 32,480 lbs.
shoal keel:
c/board:
BALLAST
deep keel: 12,992 lbs.
shoal keel:
c/board:
DRAFT
deep keel: 7 ft. 0 ins.
shoal keel:
c/board up:
c/board down:

SAIL AREA: 1,037 sq. ft.
FRESH WATER: 200 gals.
FUEL CAPACITY: 188 gals.

COSTS

BASE BOAT:
DATE:
EST. ON WATER:
DATE:

RATIOS

SAIL AREA/DISP: 16.3
DISP/LENGTH: 353.1
BALLAST RATIO: 40
FUEL/DISP: 4.3
FRESH WATER/DISP: 4.9

DECK

STEERING: wheel
WINCHES:
SAFETY: bow and stern pulpits with double lifelines
ANCHOR:
NAV LIGHTS:

RIG

TYPE: ketch (sloop also available)
RIGGING: wire
MAINSHEET: boom-end sheeting

SAILS

SUPPLIED WITH BASE BOAT:

INTERIOR

BERTHS: 6 berths: 1 double V, 2 single settees, 1 double quarterberth
TABLE: 2 dropleaf
HEAD(S): 2 heads with 2 showers
COLD STORAGE: refrigerator/freezer
STOVE: 3-burner LPG with oven
MAX. HEADROOM:

MACHINERY

ENGINE: 73 shaft HP Perkins #4.23G diesel
PROPELLER: fixed
GENERATOR:

HORIZON 44

DESIGNER: German Frers
BUILDER: Windward Maritime Affiliates Corp.

STATISTICS

LOA: 44 ft. 1.9 ins.
LWL: 34 ft. 10.0 ins.
BEAM: 13 ft. 5.5 ins.
DISPLACEMENT
deep keel: 22,320 lbs.
shoal keel:
c/board:
BALLAST
deep keel: 11,020 lbs.
shoal keel:
c/board:
DRAFT
deep keel: 6 ft. 0 ins.
shoal keel:
c/board up:
c/board down:

SAIL AREA: 864 sq. ft.
FRESH WATER: 200 gals.
FUEL CAPACITY: 110 gals.

COSTS

BASE BOAT:
DATE:
EST. ON WATER:
DATE:

RATIOS

SAIL AREA/DISP: 17.45
DISP/LENGTH: 235.62
BALLAST RATIO: 49.37
FUEL/DISP: 3.7
FRESH WATER/DISP: 7.17

DECK

STEERING: wheel
WINCHES: 7 Barient winches: 2 #55 ST, 1 #43 ST, 1 #30 ST, 1 #43C, 1 #43C, 1 #40C
SAFETY: bow and stern pulpits with double lifelines
ANCHOR: anchor roller and well
NAV LIGHTS: running and masthead

RIG

TYPE: masthead sloop
RIGGING:
MAINSHEET: boom-end sheeting

SAILS

SUPPLIED WITH BASE BOAT:

INTERIOR

BERTHS: 6 berths: 1 double V, 2 single settees, 1 double quarterberth
TABLE: dropleaf
HEAD(S): 2 heads with 2 showers, 1 sump pump, and 2 holding tanks
COLD STORAGE: refrigerator/freezer (14 cu. ft.)
STOVE: 3-burner propane with oven
MAX. HEADROOM:

MACHINERY

ENGINE: 70 HP Westerbeke diesel
PROPELLER: fixed on 1 1/2" shaft
GENERATOR:

C & C 44

DESIGNER: C & C Design Group
BUILDER: C & C Yachts

STATISTICS

LOA: 44 ft. 2 ins.
LWL: 35 ft. 3 ins.
BEAM: 13 ft. 3 ins.
DISPLACEMENT
deep keel: 20,800 lbs.
shoal keel:
c/board:
BALLAST
deep keel: 9,850 lbs.
shoal keel:
c/board:
DRAFT
deep keel: 8 ft. 3 ins.
shoal keel:
c/board up: 5 ft. 6 ins.
c/board down: 8 ft. 6 ins.

SAIL AREA: 909 sq. ft.
FRESH WATER: 100 gals.
FUEL CAPACITY: 50 gals.

COSTS

BASE BOAT:
DATE:
EST. ON WATER: $170,000
DATE: 11/85

RATIOS

SAIL AREA/DISP: 19.23
DISP/LENGTH: 21.2
BALLAST RATIO: 47.4
FUEL/DISP: 3.85
FRESH WATER/DISP: 1.8

GENERATOR:

DECK

STEERING: 48" wheel with emergency tiller
WINCHES: 5 winches: 2 primary (#36A), 2 halyard (#24), 1 mainsheet (#24)
SAFETY: bow and stern pulpits with double lifelines
ANCHOR: anchor locker
NAV LIGHTS: running

RIG

TYPE: masthead
RIGGING: rod
MAINSHEET: mid-boom sheeting

SAILS

SUPPLIED WITH BASE BOAT:

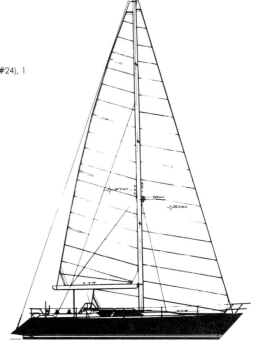

INTERIOR

BERTHS: 8 berths: 1 double V, 2 single settees, 2 single pilots, 1 center aft double (double aft cabin layout available)
TABLE: folding
HEAD(S): 2 heads with 2 showers, 2 sump pumps, 2 holding tanks (20 gals.)
COLD STORAGE: fixed icebox
STOVE: 3-burner propane with oven
MAX. HEADROOM:

MACHINERY

ENGINE: 44 HP Yanmar #4JHE diesel with 2.17:1 reduction gear
PROPELLER: 2-blade on 1 1/4" shaft

BUILDER'S COMMENTS Bred from C & C's vast custom expertise, the new 44 racer/cruiser is an exhilarating blend of pure performance and live-aboard luxury.

LA FITTE 44

DESIGNER: Robert H. Perry
BUILDER: La Fitte Yachts, Inc.

STATISTICS

LOA: 44 ft. 4 ins.
LWL: 35 ft. 5 ins.
BEAM: 12 ft. 8 ins.
DISPLACEMENT
deep keel: 28,000 lbs.
shoal keel:
c/board:
BALLAST
deep keel: 11,000 lbs.
shoal keel:
c/board:
DRAFT
deep keel: 6 ft. 4 ins.
shoal keel:
c/board up:
c/board down:

SAIL AREA: 927 sq. ft.
FRESH WATER: 160 gals.
FUEL CAPACITY: 130 gals.

COSTS

BASE BOAT: $198,750
DATE: 06/01/85
EST. ON WATER:
DATE:

RATIOS

SAIL AREA/DISP: 16.08
DISP/LENGTH: 281
BALLAST RATIO: 39.28
FUEL/DISP: 3.48
FRESH WATER/DISP: 4.57

DECK

STEERING: wheel with emergency tiller
WINCHES: 8 winches: 2 primary (#55 ST), 2 staysail sheet (#40 ST), 1 mainsheet (#44 ST), 3 halyard (#40 ST)
SAFETY: bow and stern pulpits with lifelines
ANCHOR: anchor rollers and electric windlass
NAV LIGHTS: running

RIG

TYPE: masthead sloop
RIGGING: 1x19 Nitronic 50 wire
MAINSHEET: mid-boom sheeting

SAILS

SUPPLIED WITH BASE BOAT:

INTERIOR

BERTHS: 7 berths: 1 double V, 2 single settees, 1 double quarterberth, 1 single quarterberth
TABLE: dropleaf
HEAD(S): 2 heads with 2 showers
COLD STORAGE: built-in refrigerator/freezer
STOVE: 4-burner propane with oven
MAX. HEADROOM: 6 ft. 6 ins.

MACHINERY

ENGINE: 60 HP Perkins diesel with 2:1 reduction gear
PROPELLER: 2-blade fixed
GENERATOR: 3.5 kW Entec

CS 44

DESIGNER: Tony Castro
BUILDER: CS Yachts, Ltd.

STATISTICS

LOA: 44 ft. 5.0 ins.
LWL: 34 ft. 8.0 ins.
BEAM: 13 ft. 8.0 ins.
DISPLACEMENT
deep keel: 22,000 lbs.
shoal keel:
c/board:
BALLAST
deep keel: 9,000 lbs.
shoal keel:
c/board:
DRAFT
deep keel: 7 ft. 6 ins.
shoal keel: 5 ft. 6 ins.
c/board up:
c/board down:

SAIL AREA: 1,224 sq. ft.
FRESH WATER: 100 gals.
FUEL CAPACITY: 60 gals.

COSTS

BASE BOAT:
DATE:
EST. ON WATER:
DATE:

RATIOS

SAIL AREA/DISP: 24.94
DISP/LENGTH: 235
BALLAST RATIO: 40.98
FUEL/DISP: 2.04
FRESH WATER/DISP: 3.63

DECK

STEERING: 54" wheel with emergency tiller
WINCHES: 11 Lewmar winches: 2 primary (#65), 2 secondary (#65), 4 halyard (#46), 1 mainsheet (#46), 2 utility (#40)
SAFETY: bow and stern pulpits with double lifelines
ANCHOR: anchor rollers, windlass, and well
NAV LIGHTS: bow and stern and masthead

RIG

TYPE: masthead sloop
RIGGING: 1x19 SS wire
MAINSHEET: mid-boom sheeting

SAILS

SUPPLIED WITH BASE BOAT:

INTERIOR

BERTHS: 7 berths: 1 double V, 1 double convertible settee, 1 single settee, 1 center aft double
TABLE: fixed
HEAD(S): 2 heads with 2 showers, 2 sump pumps, and 1 bathtub
COLD STORAGE: 2 refrigerator/freezer
STOVE: 3-burner propane with oven and microwave
MAX. HEADROOM: 6 ft. 5 ins.

MACHINERY

ENGINE: Westerbeke #46 diesel, 2.68:1 reduction gear
PROPELLER: 2-blade on 1 1/4" shaft
GENERATOR: 4 kW Mariner #4000

BUILDER'S COMMENTS Our latest model, designed by Tony Castro, is a true tri-cabin offshore sloop with a cutter rig as an option. The hull design and deck layout represent the latest thinking in efficient hull shape and ease of handling. The deck hardware and interior appointments show a high level of sophistication, appreciated by serious sailors interested in good craftsmanship and design detailing.

KANTER ATLANTIC 45

DESIGNER: Ted Brewer Designs, Ltd.
BUILDER: Kanter Yachts Corp.

STATISTICS

LOA: 44 ft. 6.0 ins.
LWL: 36 ft. 8.0 ins.
BEAM: 13 ft. 10.5 ins.
DISPLACEMENT
deep keel: 36,000 lbs.
shoal keel:
c/board:
BALLAST
deep keel:
shoal keel:
c/board:
DRAFT
deep keel: 6 ft. 10 ins.
shoal keel: 6 ft. 0 ins.
c/board up:
c/board down:

INTERIOR

BERTHS:
TABLE: dropleaf
HEAD(S): 1 head with shower and sump pump
COLD STORAGE: refrigerator/freezer
STOVE: 3-burner propane with oven
MAX. HEADROOM:

MACHINERY

ENGINE: 90 HP Volvo diesel
PROPELLER:
GENERATOR:

SAIL AREA: 1,021 sq. ft. (cutter)
1,077 sq. ft. (ketch)
FRESH WATER: 300 gals.
FUEL CAPACITY: 300 gals.

COSTS

BASE BOAT: $138,000 (cutter)
DATE: 04/85
EST. ON WATER:
DATE:

RATIOS

SAIL AREA/DISP: 15.05
DISP/LENGTH: 326.2
BALLAST RATIO:
FUEL/DISP: 6.25
FRESH WATER/DISP: 6.67

DECK

STEERING: wheel
WINCHES: 8 Lewmar winches: 2 #48, 3 #30, 3 #10
SAFETY: bow and stern pulpits with double lifelines
ANCHOR: anchor roller
NAV LIGHTS: running and masthead

RIG

TYPE: masthead cutter or ketch
RIGGING: 3/8"
MAINSHEET: boom-end sheeting

SAILS

SUPPLIED WITH BASE BOAT:

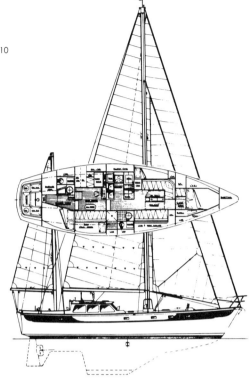

NORSEMAN 447

DESIGNER: Robert H. Perry
BUILDER: Norseman Yachts, Inc.

STATISTICS

LOA: 44 ft. 7 ins.
LWL: 37 ft. 6 ins.
BEAM: 13 ft. 0 ins.
DISPLACEMENT
deep keel: 28,000 lbs.
shoal keel:
c/board:
BALLAST
deep keel: 12,000 lbs.
shoal keel:
c/board:
DRAFT
deep keel: 6 ft. 4 ins.
shoal keel:
c/board up:
c/board down:

INTERIOR

BERTHS: 7 berths: 1 double V, 1 double convertible dinette, 1 single settee, 1 double quarterberth
TABLE: dinette
HEAD(S): 1 head with shower and sump pump
COLD STORAGE: built-in icebox
STOVE:
MAX. HEADROOM: 6 ft. 4 ins.

MACHINERY

ENGINE: 61 HP Lehman diesel with 2:1 reduction gear
PROPELLER: 2-blade
GENERATOR:

SAIL AREA: 937 sq. ft.
FRESH WATER: 120 gals.
FUEL CAPACITY: 100 gals.

COSTS

BASE BOAT:
DATE:
EST. ON WATER:
DATE:

RATIOS

SAIL AREA/DISP: 16.26
DISP/LENGTH: 237
BALLAST RATIO: 42.82
FUEL/DISP: 2.62
FRESH WATER/DISP: 3.35

DECK

STEERING: 32" wheel
WINCHES: 6 Lewmar winches: 2 primary (#55 ST), 2 halyard (#43), 1 mainsheet (#46), 1 reefing (#30)
SAFETY: bow and stern pulpits with double lifelines
ANCHOR: double anchor roller
NAV LIGHTS: running

RIG

TYPE: masthead cutter
RIGGING:
MAINSHEET: mid-boom sheeting

SAILS

SUPPLIED WITH BASE BOAT: main (2 reefs), 110% genoa

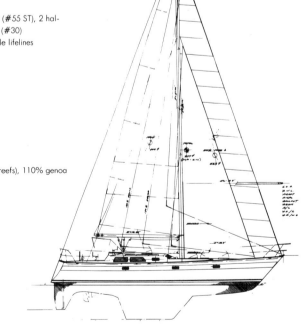

BUILDER'S COMMENTS Two versions of the Norseman 447 are available—a center cockpit and an aft cockpit.

GIB'SEA 126 MASTER

DESIGNER: Joubert & Nivelt
BUILDER: Gibert Marine, S. A.

STATISTICS

LOA: 44 ft. 8 ins.
LWL: 33 ft. 10 ins.
BEAM: 13 ft. 4 ins.
DISPLACEMENT
deep keel: 19,900 lbs.
shoal keel:
c/board:
BALLAST
deep keel: 6,850 lbs.
shoal keel:
c/board:
DRAFT
deep keel: 5 ft. 11 ins.
shoal keel:
c/board up:
c/board down:

SAIL AREA: 715 sq. ft.
FRESH WATER: 160 gals.
FUEL CAPACITY: 53 gals.

COSTS

BASE BOAT:
DATE:
EST. ON WATER:
DATE:

RATIOS

SAIL AREA/DISP: 15.57
DISP/LENGTH: 229
BALLAST RATIO: 34.42
FUEL/DISP: 1.99
FRESH WATER/DISP: 6.43

INTERIOR

BERTHS: 7 berths: 1 forward double, 1 single settee, 2 double quarterberths
TABLE: fixed
HEAD(S): 2 heads with 2 showers
COLD STORAGE: built-in icebox (5.6 cu. ft.) and refrigerator (3 cu. ft.)
STOVE: 2-burner LPG with oven
MAX. HEADROOM: 6 ft. 5 ins.

MACHINERY

ENGINE: 50 HP diesel
PROPELLER: 3-blade
GENERATOR:

DECK

STEERING: wheel with emergency tiller
WINCHES: 8 winches: 2 primary, 3 halyard, 1 mainsheet, 1 reefing, 1 kicking strap
SAFETY: bow and stern pulpits with double lifelines
ANCHOR: anchor well and double roller
NAV LIGHTS: running and masthead

RIG

TYPE: masthead sloop
RIGGING:
MAINSHEET: mid-boom sheeting

SAILS

SUPPLIED WITH BASE BOAT:

NASSAU 45

DESIGNER: Robert H. Perry
DISTRIBUTOR: Nassau Yacht Corp. (built in Taiwan by Angel Marine)

STATISTICS

LOA: 44 ft. 11 ins.
LWL: 34 ft. 7 ins.
BEAM: 12 ft. 9 ins.
DISPLACEMENT
deep keel: 21,250 lbs.
shoal keel:
c/board:
BALLAST
deep keel: 8,870 lbs.
shoal keel:
c/board:
DRAFT
deep keel: 5 ft. 10 ins.
shoal keel:
c/board up:
c/board down:

SAIL AREA: 800 sq. ft.
FRESH WATER: 160 gals.
FUEL CAPACITY: 70 gals.

COSTS

BASE BOAT: $116,100
DATE: 06/28/85
EST. ON WATER: $120,200
DATE: 06/28/85

RATIOS

SAIL AREA/DISP: 16.69
DISP/LENGTH: 229.4
BALLAST RATIO: 41.7
FUEL/DISP: 2.5
FRESH WATER/DISP: 6.0

INTERIOR

BERTHS: 5 berths: 1 double V, 1 single quarterberth, 1 double quarterberth
TABLE: dropleaf
HEAD(S): 2 heads with 1 shower, 1 sump pump, and 2 holding tanks
COLD STORAGE: built-in icebox
STOVE: stove with oven
MAX. HEADROOM: 6 ft. 4 3/4 ins.

MACHINERY

ENGINE: 49 HP Perkins #4-108 diesel with 2.1:1 reduction gear

PROPELLER: fixed
GENERATOR:

DECK

STEERING: wheel with emergency tiller
WINCHES: 5 Lewmar winches: 2 #55A ST 2sp, 1 #42A ST, 1 #30A ST, 1 #44A ST 2sp
SAFETY: bow and stern pulpits with double lifelines
ANCHOR:
NAV LIGHTS: running and masthead

RIG

TYPE: masthead sloop with Isomat spar
RIGGING: 1x19 wire
MAINSHEET: 5-part with mid-boom sheeting

SAILS

SUPPLIED WITH BASE BOAT: main, 110% jib

BUILDER'S COMMENTS At least 25 parts of the interior of the Nassau 45 are molded from 1/8" teak battens. No finer joiner work can be found anywhere in the world. It is a truly performance oriented cruising boat.

HERRESHOFF 45

DESIGNER: Halsey Herreshoff
BUILDER: Cat Ketch Corporation

STATISTICS

LOA: 45 ft. 0 ins.
LWL: 40 ft. 0 ins.
BEAM: 13 ft. 5 ins.
DISPLACEMENT
deep keel: 18,500 lbs.
shoal keel:
c/board:
BALLAST
deep keel: 7,500 ft. ins.
shoal keel:
c/board:
DRAFT
deep keel: 5 ft. 0 ins.
shoal keel:
c/board up:
c/board down:

INTERIOR

BERTHS: 6 berths: 1 double forward, 1 double convertible dinette, 1 double quarterberth
TABLE: dinette with 3 drawers under
HEAD(S): 2 heads with 2 showers, sump pump, and tank
COLD STORAGE: built-in icebox with separate freezer compartment
STOVE: 3-burner LPG
MAX. HEADROOM: 6 ft. 6 ins.

MACHINERY

ENGINE: 42 HP Nannidiesel #4.60HE diesel
PROPELLER: 2-blade fixed 18"x10" on 1" shaft
GENERATOR:

SAIL AREA: 830 sq. ft.
FRESH WATER: 200 gals.
FUEL CAPACITY: 100 gals.

COSTS

BASE BOAT: $148,750
DATE: 02/15/85
EST. ON WATER: $158,000
DATE: 06/01/85

RATIOS

SAIL AREA/DISP: 18.99
DISP/LENGTH: 129
BALLAST RATIO: 40.5
FUEL/DISP: 4.05
FRESH WATER/DISP: 8.64

DECK

STEERING: wheel with emergency tiller
WINCHES: none
SAFETY: bow and stern pulpits with double lifelines
ANCHOR: double anchor roller and teak bow plank anchor storage
NAV LIGHTS: running and masthead

RIG

TYPE: cat ketch with unstayed carbon fiber composite masts
RIGGING:
MAINSHEET: 6-part with boom-end sheeting

SAILS

SUPPLIED WITH BASE BOAT: main, mizzen

BUILDER'S COMMENTS The Herreshoff Cat Ketch features an unstayed, self-tending rig which makes a simple, effortless sailing yacht. The Fiberglass/Airex hull has clean traditional lines and a light displacement, fin keel/skeg rudder configuration. These characteristics result in an agile, quick, easy and fun boat to sail.

MAPLE LEAF 45

DESIGNER: S. C. Huntingford
BUILDER: Cooper Yachts

STATISTICS

LOA: 45 ft. 0 ins.
LWL: 37 ft. 9 ins.
BEAM: 14 ft. 0 ins.
DISPLACEMENT
deep keel:
shoal keel:
c/board:
BALLAST
deep keel: 9,200 lbs.
shoal keel:
c/board:
DRAFT
deep keel: 6 ft. 3 ins.
shoal keel: 5 ft. 0 ins.
c/board up:
c/board down:

SAIL AREA: 862 sq. ft.
FRESH WATER: 175 gals.
FUEL CAPACITY: 125 gals.

COSTS

BASE BOAT: $137,500
DATE: 04/85
EST. ON WATER: $147,500
DATE: 11/85

RATIOS

SAIL AREA/DISP: 16.18
DISP/LENGTH: 207.5
BALLAST RATIO: 36.8
FUEL/DISP: 3.75
FRESH WATER/DISP: 5.6

INTERIOR

BERTHS: 6 berths: 1 double V, 1 single convertible dinette, 1 single settee, 1 center aft double
TABLE: fixed
HEAD(S): 2 heads with 2 showers, 1 tub, and 1 holding tank
COLD STORAGE: built-in icebox (10–12 cu. ft.)
STOVE: 3-burner propane with oven
MAX. HEADROOM:

MACHINERY

ENGINE: 50 HP diesel
PROPELLER: fixed 16"x15" on 1 1/4" shaft
GENERATOR:

DECK

STEERING: 36" wheel with emergency tiller
WINCHES: 5 Lewmar winches: 2 #43 ST, 1 #40 ST, 2 #30
SAFETY: bow and stern pulpits with double lifelines
ANCHOR:
NAV LIGHTS: running and masthead

RIG

TYPE: masthead sloop
RIGGING: wire (5/16"–3/8")
MAINSHEET: 5-part with boom-end sheeting

SAILS

SUPPLIED WITH BASE BOAT: main, 110% working jib

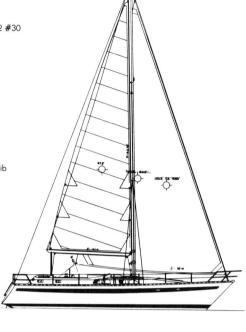

JEANNEAU SUN-KISS

DESIGNER: Phillippe Briand
DISTRIBUTOR: Nautique International, Inc. (built in France by Jeanneau, S. A.)

STATISTICS

LOA: 45 ft. 1 ins.
LWL: 37 ft. 3 ins.
BEAM: 14 ft. 5 ins.
DISPLACEMENT
deep keel: 24,905 lbs.
shoal keel:
c/board: 24,905 lbs.
BALLAST
deep keel: 9,036 lbs.
shoal keel:
c/board: 10,138 lbs.
DRAFT
deep keel: 6 ft. 6 ins.
shoal keel:
c/board up: 5 ft. 0 ins.
c/board down: 8 ft. 10 ins.

SAIL AREA: 1,097 sq. ft.
FRESH WATER: 165 gals.
FUEL CAPACITY: 47 gals.

COSTS

BASE BOAT:
DATE:
EST. ON WATER:
DATE:

RATIOS

SAIL AREA/DISP: 20.58
DISP/LENGTH: 215.11
BALLAST RATIO:
36.28 40.71 (c/brd)
FUEL/DISP: 1.42
FRESH WATER/DISP: 5.30

INTERIOR

BERTHS: 6 berths: 1 double forward berth, 2 double quarter-berths
TABLE: fixed
HEAD(S): 2 heads with 2 showers
COLD STORAGE: built-in icebox (26 gals.) and refrigerator (58 gals.)
STOVE: 2-burner gas with oven
MAX. HEADROOM:

MACHINERY

ENGINE:

PROPELLER:
GENERATOR:

DECK

STEERING: wheel with emergency tiller
WINCHES: 7 winches: 2 primary, 2 secondary, 1 halyard, 1 mainsheet, 1 reefing
SAFETY: bow and stern pulpits with double lifelines
ANCHOR: anchor locker, roller, and electric windlass
NAV LIGHTS:

RIG

TYPE: masthead sloop
RIGGING:
MAINSHEET: mid-boom sheeting

SAILS

SUPPLIED WITH BASE BOAT:

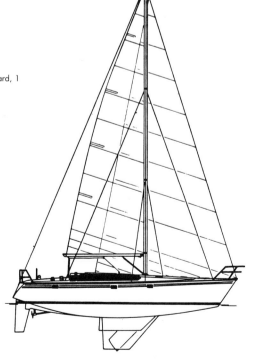

CAPE DORY 45

DESIGNER: Carl Alberg
BUILDER: Cape Dory Yachts

STATISTICS

LOA: 45 ft. 2 ins.
LWL: 33 ft. 6 ins.
BEAM: 13 ft. 0 ins.
DISPLACEMENT
deep keel: 24,000 lbs.
shoal keel:
c/board:
BALLAST
deep keel: 9,400 lbs.
shoal keel:
c/board:
DRAFT
deep keel: 6 ft. 3 ins.
shoal keel:
c/board up:
c/board down:

SAIL AREA: ketch 936 sq. ft.
cutter 882 sq. ft.
FRESH WATER: 200 gals.
FUEL CAPACITY: 125 gals.

COSTS

BASE BOAT:
DATE:
EST. ON WATER:
DATE:

RATIOS

SAIL AREA/DISP: 18.00
DISP/LENGTH: 284.99
BALLAST RATIO: 39.17
FUEL/DISP: 3.91
FRESH WATER/DISP: 6.67

INTERIOR

BERTHS: 8 berths: 1 double V, 1 double convertible dinette, 1 single settee, 1 pilot, 1 double quarterberth
TABLE: center-mount dropleaf
HEAD(S): 2 heads with 2 showers, sump pump, and holding tank (60 gals.)
COLD STORAGE: built-in icebox (10 cu. ft.) and refrigeration system
STOVE: 3-burner propane with oven
MAX. HEADROOM:

MACHINERY

ENGINE: 62 HP Perkins #4.54 diesel with 2:1 reduction gear

PROPELLER: 1 1/4" shaft
GENERATOR:

DECK

STEERING: wheel with emergency tiller
WINCHES: 9 Lewmar winches: 2 primary (#48 ST), 4 halyard (2–#16, 1–#30, 1–#8), 1 mainsheet (#42 ST), 1 staysail sheet (#16 ST), 1 reefing (#8)
SAFETY: bow and stern pulpits with double lifelines
ANCHOR: anchor locker and double rollers
NAV LIGHTS: running and masthead

RIG

TYPE: ketch or cutter
RIGGING: 1x19 wire (3/8"; 9/32" on staysail stay)
MAINSHEET:

SAILS

SUPPLIED WITH BASE BOAT:

BRISTOL 45.5

DESIGNER: Ted Hood
BUILDER: Bristol Yacht Co.

STATISTICS

LOA: 45 ft. 3.0 ins.
LWL: 37 ft. 3.0 ins.
BEAM: 13 ft. 2.5 ins.
DISPLACEMENT
deep keel: 34,660 lbs.
shoal keel:
c/board:
BALLAST
deep keel: 15,000 lbs.
shoal keel:
c/board:
DRAFT
deep keel:
shoal keel:
c/board up: 4 ft. 11 ins.
c/board down: 11 ft. 0 ins.

SAIL AREA: 1,125 sq. ft.
FRESH WATER: 180 gals.
FUEL CAPACITY: 100 gals.

COSTS

BASE BOAT:
AFT cockpit $200,022,
center cockpit $214,500
DATE: 09/01/85
EST. ON WATER:
DATE:

RATIOS

SAIL AREA/DISP: 16.93
DISP/LENGTH: 299.37
BALLAST RATIO: 43.27
FUEL/DISP: 2.16
FRESH WATER/DISP: 4.15

INTERIOR

BERTHS: 5 berths: 1 double V, 1 single extension berth, 1 aft double
TABLE: pedestal-mounted dropleaf
HEAD(S): 2 heads with 2 showers and 2 sump pumps
COLD STORAGE: built-in icebox and refrigerator
STOVE: 3-burner propane with oven
MAX. HEADROOM:

MACHINERY

ENGINE: Westerbeke #58 with 2:1 reduction gear
PROPELLER: 3-blade on 1 1/4" shaft
GENERATOR:

DECK

STEERING: wheel
WINCHES: 5 Lewmar winches: 2 jib sheet (#55), 2 halyard (#44 & #40), 1 mainsheet (#40)
SAFETY: bow and stern pulpits with double lifelines
ANCHOR:
NAV LIGHTS:

RIG

TYPE: masthead sloop
RIGGING:
MAINSHEET: boom-end sheeting

SAILS

SUPPLIED WITH BASE BOAT:

BUILDER'S COMMENTS Center or aft cockpit versions available.

HUNTER 45

DESIGNER: Hunter Design Group
BUILDER: Hunter Marine

STATISTICS

LOA: 45 ft. 5 ins.
LWL: 38 ft. 4 ins.
BEAM: 13 ft. 10 ins.
DISPLACEMENT
deep keel: 21,950 lbs.
shoal keel: 22,450 lbs.
c/board:
BALLAST
deep keel: 10,380 lbs.
shoal keel: 10,900 lbs.
c/board:
DRAFT
deep keel: 6 ft. 6 ins.
shoal keel: 5 ft. 0 ins.
c/board up:
c/board down:

SAIL AREA: 950 sq. ft.
FRESH WATER: 105 gals.
FUEL CAPACITY: 50 gals.

COSTS

BASE BOAT:
DATE:
EST. ON WATER: $120,000
DATE: 11/85

RATIOS

SAIL AREA/DISP: 19.38
DISP/LENGTH: 174
BALLAST RATIO: 47.3
FUEL/DISP: 1.7
FRESH WATER/DISP: 3.8

INTERIOR

BERTHS: 6 berths: 1 forward double, 2 single settees, 1 double quarterberth
TABLE:
HEAD(S): 2 heads with 2 showers
COLD STORAGE: built-in icebox and refrigerator/freezer
STOVE: 3-burner CNG with oven
MAX. HEADROOM: 6 ft. 6 ins.

MACHINERY

ENGINE: diesel
PROPELLER:
GENERATOR:

DECK

STEERING: wheel with emergency tiller
WINCHES: 4 winches: 2 sheet (ST), 2 halyard (ST)
SAFETY: bow and stern pulpits with double lifelines
ANCHOR: anchor and anchor well
NAV LIGHTS: running and masthead

RIG

TYPE: masthead
RIGGING:
MAINSHEET: boom-end sheeting

SAILS

SUPPLIED WITH BASE BOAT: main, working jib

BUILDER'S COMMENTS The new Hunter 45' has the most complete sailing package ever offered to the sailing public! A complete instrumentation package is included, VHF radio, Loran, Digital Knotmeter, Depthfinder, and a Digital Windspeed Indicator. There's an auxiliary generator and microwave as well as complete AM/FM stereo cassette. She's spacious, elegant, and built to travel long distances in full and complete comfort. Hunter's proof of its "Commitment to Better Engineering."

BAYFIELD 40

DESIGNER:
BUILDER: Bayfield Boat Yard, Ltd.

STATISTICS

LOA: 45 ft. 6 ins.
LWL: 30 ft. 6 ins.
BEAM:
DISPLACEMENT
deep keel: 21,000 lbs.
shoal keel:
c/board:
BALLAST
deep keel: 8,200 lbs.
shoal keel:
c/board:
DRAFT
deep keel: 4 ft. 11 ins.
shoal keel:
c/board up:
c/board down:

SAIL AREA: 1,009 sq. ft.
FRESH WATER:
FUEL CAPACITY:

COSTS

BASE BOAT:
DATE:
EST. ON WATER:
DATE:

RATIOS

SAIL AREA/DISP: 21.21
DISP/LENGTH: 330.42
BALLAST RATIO: 39.05
FUEL/DISP:
FRESH WATER/DISP:

INTERIOR

BERTHS: 6 berths: 2 double Vs, 1 double convertible dinette
TABLE: dropleaf
HEAD(S): 1 head with shower
COLD STORAGE: refrigerator/freezer
STOVE: 2-burner propane
MAX. HEADROOM:

MACHINERY

ENGINE: 52 HP Westerbeke
PROPELLER:
GENERATOR:

DECK

STEERING: wheel
WINCHES: 11 winches
SAFETY:
ANCHOR:
NAV LIGHTS:

RIG

TYPE: masthead ketch
RIGGING:
MAINSHEET:

SAILS

SUPPLIED WITH BASE BOAT: main, mizzen, topsail, staysail

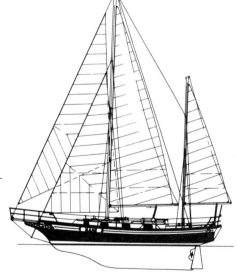

IRWIN CRUISING 43

DESIGNER: Ted Irwin
BUILDER: Irwin Yacht & Marine Corp.

STATISTICS

LOA: 45 ft. 6 ins.
LWL: 35 ft. 6 ins.
BEAM: 13 ft. 7 ins.
DISPLACEMENT
deep keel:
shoal keel: 26,000 lbs.
c/board:
BALLAST
deep keel:
shoal keel: 8,000 lbs.
c/board:
DRAFT
deep keel:
shoal keel: 4 ft. 11 ins.
c/board up: 4 ft. 10 ins.
c/board down: 9 ft. 8 ins.

SAIL AREA:
FRESH WATER: 183 gals.
FUEL CAPACITY: 107 gals.

COSTS

BASE BOAT: $114,950
DATE: 06/01/85
EST. ON WATER:
DATE:

RATIOS

SAIL AREA/DISP:
DISP/LENGTH: 259.94
BALLAST RATIO: 30.77
FUEL/DISP: 3.08
FRESH WATER/DISP: 5.63

DECK

STEERING: 28" wheel with emergency tiller
WINCHES: 5 winches: 2 primary, 2 halyard, 1 mainsheet
SAFETY: bow and stern pulpits with double lifelines
ANCHOR: anchor locker
NAV LIGHTS: running and masthead

RIG

TYPE: masthead sloop
RIGGING: wire (5/16")
MAINSHEET: 5-part with boom-end sheeting

SAILS

SUPPLIED WITH BASE BOAT: main, working jib

INTERIOR

BERTHS: 6 berths: 1 double V, 1 single settee, 1 single pilot, 1 center aft double (transverse)
TABLE: fixed
HEAD(S): 2 heads with 2 showers and 2 holding tanks
COLD STORAGE: built-in icebox (6.6 cu. ft.)
STOVE: 3-burner propane
MAX. HEADROOM:

MACHINERY

ENGINE: 62 HP diesel with 2:1 reduction gear
PROPELLER: 3-blade
GENERATOR:

LITTLE HARBOR 46

DESIGNER: Ted Hood
BUILDER: Little Harbor Custom Yachts

STATISTICS

LOA: 45 ft. 8 ins.
LWL: 36 ft. 6 ins.
BEAM: 13 ft. 8 ins.
DISPLACEMENT
deep keel: 32,500 lbs.
shoal keel:
c/board:
BALLAST
deep keel: 13,800 lbs.
shoal keel:
c/board:
DRAFT
deep keel:
shoal keel:
c/board up: 5 ft. 0 ins.
c/board down: 10 ft. 2 ins.

SAIL AREA: 1,036 sq. ft.
FRESH WATER: 170 gals.
FUEL CAPACITY: 100 gals.

COSTS

BASE BOAT:
aft cockpit $227,450
DATE: 04/85
center cockpit $241,150
DATE: 04/85

RATIOS

SAIL AREA/DISP: 16.28
DISP/LENGTH: 298.37
BALLAST RATIO: 42.46
FUEL/DISP: 2.31
FRESH WATER/DISP: 4.18

DECK

STEERING: wheel
WINCHES:
SAFETY:
ANCHOR: electric windlass
NAV LIGHTS:

RIG

TYPE: ketch (sloop or cutter also available)
RIGGING: rod
MAINSHEET: mid-boom sheeting

SAILS

SUPPLIED WITH BASE BOAT:

INTERIOR

BERTHS:
TABLE: dropleaf
HEAD(S): 2 heads with 2 showers and 1 holding tank
COLD STORAGE: refrigerator/freezer
STOVE:
MAX. HEADROOM:

MACHINERY

ENGINE:
PROPELLER: folding
GENERATOR:

CAMBRIA 44

DESIGNER: David Walters
BUILDER: David Walters Yachts, Ltd.

STATISTICS

LOA: 45 ft. 10.5 ins.
LWL: 36 ft. 0.0 ins.
BEAM: 13 ft. 5.5 ins.
DISPLACEMENT
deep keel: 28,600 lbs.
shoal keel:
c/board:
BALLAST
deep keel: 11,500 lbs.
shoal keel:
c/board:
DRAFT
deep keel: 7 ft. 6 ins.
shoal keel: 5 ft. 11 ins.
c/board up: 5 ft. 3 ins.
c/board down: 10 ft. 6 ins.

SAIL AREA: 943 sq. ft.
FRESH WATER: 175 gals.
FUEL CAPACITY: 85 gals.

COSTS

BASE BOAT: $262,150
DATE: 05/01/85
EST. ON WATER:
DATE:

RATIOS

SAIL AREA/DISP: 16.13
DISP/LENGTH: 273
BALLAST RATIO: 40.20
FUEL/DISP: 2.22
FRESH WATER/DISP: 4.89

DECK

STEERING: wheel
WINCHES: 12 Lewmar or Barient winches
SAFETY: bow and stern pulpits with double lifelines
ANCHOR: 2 anchors
NAV LIGHTS: running

RIG

TYPE: masthead cutter
RIGGING: rod
MAINSHEET: mid-boom sheeting

SAILS

SUPPLIED WITH BASE BOAT: main (2 reefs), fore staysail and jib topsail (both roller furling)

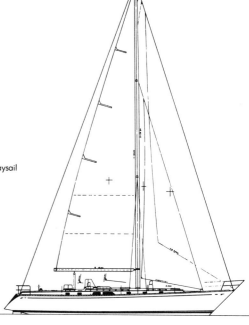

INTERIOR

BERTHS: 9 berths: 1 double V, 2 single settees, 2 single pilots, 1 single quarterberth, 1 aft double
TABLE: centerline dropleaf
HEAD(S): 2 heads with 2 showers
COLD STORAGE: refrigerator/freezer
STOVE: 4-burner Dickinson propane with oven
MAX. HEADROOM: 6 ft. 3 ins.

MACHINERY

ENGINE: 62 HP Perkins diesel
PROPELLER: 2-blade Michigan 11"x17" on 1 1/4" shaft
GENERATOR:

TAYANA-SURPRISE 45

DESIGNER: Pieter Beeldsnijder
DISTRIBUTOR: Southern Offshore Yachts, Inc. (built in Taiwan by TaYang Yacht Building Co.)

STATISTICS

LOA: 45 ft. 11 ins.
LWL: 35 ft. 7 ins.
BEAM: 13 ft. 5 ins.
DISPLACEMENT
deep keel: 26,400 lbs.
shoal keel:
c/board:
BALLAST
deep keel: 11,000 lbs.
shoal keel:
c/board:
DRAFT
deep keel: 6 ft. 5 ins.
shoal keel:
c/board up:
c/board down:

SAIL AREA: 919 sq. ft.
FRESH WATER: 150 gals.
FUEL CAPACITY: 85 gals.

COSTS

BASE BOAT: $135,000
DATE: 07/85
EST. ON WATER: $150,000
DATE: 07/85

RATIOS

SAIL AREA/DISP: 16.58
DISP/LENGTH: 261.66
BALLAST RATIO: 41.67
FUEL/DISP: 2.41
FRESH WATER/DISP: 4.55

DECK

STEERING: wheel with emergency tiller
WINCHES: 10 winches
SAFETY: bow and stern pulpits with double lifelines
ANCHOR: 40 lb. CQR anchor with anchor roller and well
NAV LIGHTS: running and masthead

RIG

TYPE: sloop or schooner
RIGGING: 1x19 wire
MAINSHEET: mid-boom sheeting

SAILS

SUPPLIED WITH BASE BOAT: main, working jib, mizzen

INTERIOR

BERTHS: 6 berths: 1 forward double, 2 double quarterberths
TABLE: fixed
HEAD(S): 2 heads with 2 showers, 2 sump pumps, and 1 holding tank
COLD STORAGE: refrigerator/freezer
STOVE: 3-burner gas with oven
MAX. HEADROOM: 6 ft. 5 ins.

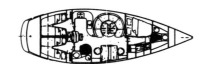

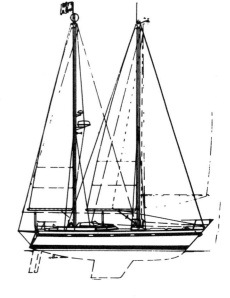

MACHINERY

ENGINE: 65 HP Perkins diesel with 2.1:1 reduction gear
PROPELLER: 3-blade fixed 12"x12"
GENERATOR:

HANS CHRISTIAN 39 PILOT HOUSE

DESIGNER: Harwood S. Ives
BUILDER: Hans Christian Yachts, Inc.

STATISTICS

LOA: 46 ft. 0 ins.
LWL: 33 ft. 0 ins.
BEAM: 12 ft. 6.6 ins.
DISPLACEMENT
deep keel: 27,585 lbs.
shoal keel:
c/board:
BALLAST
deep keel: 10,287 lbs.
shoal keel:
c/board:
DRAFT
deep keel: 6 ft. 0 ins.
shoal keel:
c/board up:
c/board down:

INTERIOR

BERTHS: 5 berths: 1 double V, 1 single pilot, 1 double quarterberth
TABLE: dropleaf
HEAD(S): 1 head with shower
COLD STORAGE: built-in icebox
STOVE: 3-burner with oven
MAX. HEADROOM:

MACHINERY

ENGINE: 120–155 HP diesel with 3:1 reduction gear
PROPELLER: fixed
GENERATOR:

SAIL AREA: 634 sq. ft.
FRESH WATER: 200 gals.
FUEL CAPACITY: 250 gals.

COSTS

BASE BOAT:
DATE:
EST. ON WATER:
DATE:

RATIOS

SAIL AREA/DISP: 11.1
DISP/LENGTH: 343
BALLAST RATIO: 37.3
FUEL/DISP: 6.8
FRESH WATER/DISP: 5.8

DECK

STEERING: wheel
WINCHES:
SAFETY: bow and stern pulpits with double lifelines
ANCHOR: anchor roller
NAV LIGHTS:

RIG

TYPE: masthead cutter
RIGGING:
MAINSHEET: mid-boom sheeting

SAILS

SUPPLIED WITH BASE BOAT:

MOODY 47

DESIGNER: Bill Dixon
BUILDER: A. H. Moody & Son, Ltd.

STATISTICS

LOA: 46 ft. 6 ins.
LWL: 38 ft. 9 ins.
BEAM: 14 ft. 8 ins.
DISPLACEMENT
deep keel:
shoal keel:
c/board:
BALLAST
deep keel: 11,000 lbs.
shoal keel:
c/board:
DRAFT
deep keel: 6 ft. 9 ins.
shoal keel:
c/board up:
c/board down:

INTERIOR

BERTHS: 6 berths: 4 single pilots, 1 center aft double
TABLE: dropleaf
HEAD(S): 2 heads with 2 showers
COLD STORAGE: refrigerator/freezer (4.5 cu. ft.)
STOVE: 2-burner gas with oven
MAX. HEADROOM:

MACHINERY

ENGINE: 60 HP Thornycroft #T-140 diesel with 2:1 reduction gear
PROPELLER: fixed
GENERATOR:

SAIL AREA: 911 sq. ft.
FRESH WATER: 120 gals.
FUEL CAPACITY: 70 gals.

COSTS

BASE BOAT:
DATE:
EST. ON WATER:
DATE:

RATIOS

SAIL AREA/DISP:
DISP/LENGTH:
BALLAST RATIO:
FUEL/DISP:
FRESH WATER/DISP:

DECK

STEERING: wheel with emergency tiller
WINCHES: 3 Lewmar winches
SAFETY: bow and stern pulpits with double lifelines
ANCHOR: anchor roller
NAV LIGHTS: running and masthead

RIG

TYPE: masthead sloop (cutter or ketch also available)
RIGGING: 1x19 wire
MAINSHEET: boom-end sheeting

SAILS

SUPPLIED WITH BASE BOAT: main, working jib

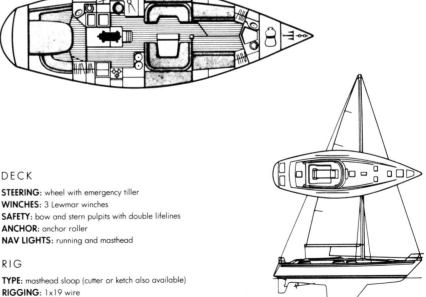

CT-47

DESIGNER: Kaufman & Ladd
DISTRIBUTOR; Ta Chiao USA, Inc. (built in Taiwan by Ta Chiao Bros. Yacht Building Co.)

STATISTICS

LOA: 46 ft. 11.75 ins.
LWL: 37 ft. 6.00 ins.
BEAM: 13 ft. 2.00 ins.
DISPLACEMENT
deep keel: 29,395 lbs.
shoal keel:
c/board:
BALLAST
deep keel: 12,000 lbs.
shoal keel:
c/board:
DRAFT
deep keel: 6 ft. 0 ins.
shoal keel:
c/board up:
c/board down:

SAIL AREA: 1,099 sq. ft.
FRESH WATER: 160 gals.
FUEL CAPACITY: 150 gals.

COSTS

BASE BOAT:
cutter $133,800
DATE: 04/01/85
ketch $136,000
DATE: 04/01/85
EST. ON WATER:

RATIOS

SAIL AREA/DISP: 18.46
DISP/LENGTH: 248.85
BALLAST RATIO: 40.82
FUEL/DISP: 3.83
FRESH WATER/DISP: 4.36

INTERIOR

BERTHS: 6 berths in center cockpit version: 1 double V, 1 double quarterberth, 2 pilots (aft cockpit version available)
TABLE: fixed
HEAD(S): 2 heads with 2 showers, 2 sump pumps, and 1 holding tank
COLD STORAGE: built-in icebox
STOVE: 3-burner with oven
MAX. HEADROOM: 6 ft. 4 ins.

MACHINERY

ENGINE: 62 HP Perkins #4-154 diesel
PROPELLER: fixed
GENERATOR:

DECK

STEERING: wheel with emergency tiller
WINCHES: 8 Barlow winches: 2 #32, 2 #27, 4 #23
SAFETY: bow and stern pulpits with double lifelines
ANCHOR: anchor roller
NAV LIGHTS: running and masthead

RIG

TYPE: cutter or ketch
RIGGING: wire
MAINSHEET:

SAILS

SUPPLIED WITH BASE BOAT: main, working jib, 120% genoa, spinnaker, staysail

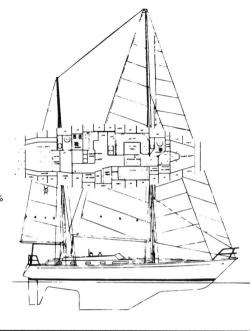

BUILDER'S COMMENTS In excess of eighty of these boats have been constructed. The boat can be either 47 feet or 49 feet, with either a conventional transom or a reversed contemporary transom. In addition, the cockpit can be either center or aft and the rig can be either cutter or ketch. In all versions, the accommodations contain two staterooms, two heads and showers, a large main cabin, generator area, U-shaped galley, and large chart table area. Sailing characteristics are excellent. The boat is fast and comfortable.

VALIANT 47

DESIGNER: Robert H. Perry
BUILDER: Valiant Yachts

STATISTICS

LOA: 47 ft. 0 ins.
LWL: 40 ft. 0 ins.
BEAM: 13 ft. 10 ins.
DISPLACEMENT
deep keel: 30,000 lbs.
shoal keel:
c/board:
BALLAST
deep keel: 11,000 lbs.
shoal keel:
c/board:
DRAFT
deep keel: 6 ft. 3 ins.
shoal keel:
c/board up:
c/board down:

SAIL AREA: 1,100 sq. ft.
FRESH WATER: 200 gals.
FUEL CAPACITY: 160 gals.

COSTS

BASE BOAT:
DATE:
EST. ON WATER:
DATE:

RATIOS

SAIL AREA/DISP: 18.23
DISP/LENGTH: 209
BALLAST RATIO: 36.66
FUEL/DISP: 4.00
FRESH WATER/DISP: 5.33

INTERIOR

BERTHS: 7 berths: 1 forward double; 1 double convertible settee, 1 single settee, 1 double quarterberth
TABLE: center-mounted
HEAD(S): 2 heads with 2 showers
COLD STORAGE: built-in icebox
STOVE: 3-burner with oven
MAX. HEADROOM: 6 ft. 6 ins.

MACHINERY

ENGINE: diesel
PROPELLER:
GENERATOR:

DECK

STEERING: wheel with emergency tiller
WINCHES: complete package
SAFETY: bow and stern pulpits with lifelines
ANCHOR:
NAV LIGHTS: running

RIG

TYPE: masthead sloop
RIGGING: rod
MAINSHEET: mid-boom sheeting

SAILS

SUPPLIED WITH BASE BOAT:

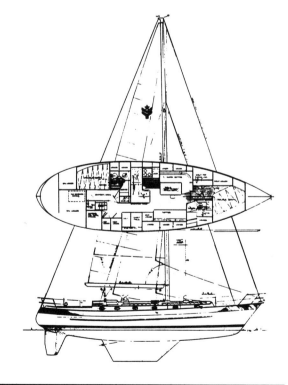

BUILDER'S COMMENTS All the famous attributes of the "Cruiser of the Decade" (our Valiant 40) plus sheer luxury. Available as a semi-custom yacht with endless interior possibilities.

SWAN 46 (Cruising Version)

DESIGNER: German Frers
BUILDER: Nautor

STATISTICS

LOA: 47 ft. 1.4 ins.
LWL: 37 ft. 10.7 ins.
BEAM: 14 ft. 5.6 ins.
DISPLACEMENT
deep keel: 31,300 lbs.
shoal keel:
c/board:
BALLAST
deep keel: 11,400 lbs.
shoal keel:
c/board:
DRAFT
deep keel: 8 ft. 2.4 ins.
shoal keel:
c/board up:
c/board down:

SAIL AREA:
FRESH WATER: 127 gals.
FUEL CAPACITY: 98 gals.

COSTS

BASE BOAT:
DATE:
EST. ON WATER:
DATE:

RATIOS

SAIL AREA/DISP:
DISP/LENGTH: 256.88
BALLAST RATIO: 36.42
FUEL/DISP: 2.35
FRESH WATER/DISP: 3.25

DECK

STEERING: 60" wheel with emergency tiller
WINCHES: 14 Lewmar winches: 2 #65AP, 2 #55A ST, 6 #44A ST, 4 #48AP
SAFETY: bow and stern pulpits with double lifelines
ANCHOR: Danforth 35H anchor with anchor well
NAV LIGHTS: running and masthead

RIG

TYPE: masthead sloop
RIGGING: rod
MAINSHEET: mid-boom sheet

SAILS

SUPPLIED WITH BASE BOAT:

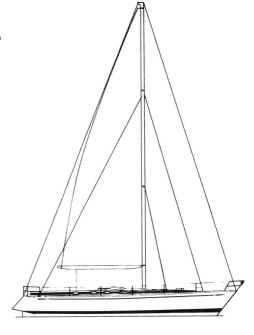

INTERIOR

BERTHS: 6 berths: 1 double V, 1 single pilot, 1 single quarterberth, 1 double quarterberth
TABLE: dropleaf
HEAD(S): 2 heads with 2 showers and 2 sump pumps
COLD STORAGE: refrigerator/freezer (10.8 cu. ft.)
STOVE: 3-burner gas with oven
MAX. HEADROOM:

MACHINERY

ENGINE: 58 HP Perkins #4.154 diesel
PROPELLER: 23" folding
GENERATOR:

ISLANDER 48

DESIGNER: Ted Brewer
BUILDER: Islander Yachts

STATISTICS

LOA: 47 ft. 6 ins.
LWL: 37 ft. 0 ins.
BEAM: 13 ft. 10 ins.
DISPLACEMENT
deep keel: 29,125 lbs.
shoal keel:
c/board:
BALLAST
deep keel: 11,000 lbs.
shoal keel:
c/board:
DRAFT
deep keel: 5 ft. 10.5 ins.
shoal keel:
c/board up:
c/board down:

SAIL AREA: 997 sq. ft.
FRESH WATER:
FUEL CAPACITY: 100 gals.

COSTS

BASE BOAT:
DATE:
EST. ON WATER:
DATE:

RATIOS

SAIL AREA/DISP: 16.85
DISP/LENGTH: 256.69
BALLAST RATIO: 37.77
FUEL/DISP: 2.58
FRESH WATER/DISP:

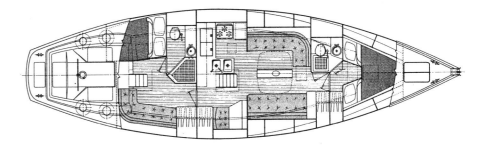

INTERIOR

BERTHS: 7 berths: 1 double V, 3 single settees, 1 center aft double
TABLE: fixed
HEAD(S): 2 heads with 2 showers and sump pump
COLD STORAGE: built-in icebox (11 cu. ft.)
STOVE: 3-burner propane with oven
MAX. HEADROOM:

MACHINERY

ENGINE: 82 HP Pathfinder diesel
PROPELLER: 2-blade on 1 1/2" shaft
GENERATOR:

DECK

STEERING: 40" wheel with emergency tiller
WINCHES: 5 Barient winches: 2 primary (#32 2sp ST), 2 halyard (#24 2sp) 1 mainsheet (#23 2sp ST)
SAFETY: bow and stern pulpits with double lifelines
ANCHOR: anchor well
NAV LIGHTS: running and masthead

RIG

TYPE: masthead sloop
RIGGING:
MAINSHEET: mid-boom sheeting

SAILS

SUPPLIED WITH BASE BOAT:

CENTURION 47

DESIGNER: Edward Dubois
BUILDER: Chantier Henri Wauquiez

STATISTICS

LOA: 47 ft. 7 ins.
LWL: 38 ft. 0 ins.
BEAM: 14 ft. 8 ins.
DISPLACEMENT
deep keel: 30,000 lbs.
shoal keel:
c/board:
BALLAST
deep keel: 12,800 lbs.
shoal keel:
c/board:
DRAFT
deep keel: 8 ft. 6 ins.
shoal keel: 5 ft. 10 ins.
c/board up:
c/board down:

SAIL AREA:
FRESH WATER: 142 gals.
FUEL CAPACITY: 90 gals.

COSTS

BASE BOAT: 1,813,350 francs
DATE: 01/01/85
EST. ON WATER:
DATE:

RATIOS

SAIL AREA/DISP:
DISP/LENGTH: 244
BALLAST RATIO: 42.7
FUEL/DISP: 2.25
FRESH WATER/DISP: 3.8

INTERIOR

BERTHS: 6 berths: 1 forward double, 2 single pilot, 1 double quarterberth
TABLE: fixed
HEAD(S): 2 heads with 2 showers
COLD STORAGE: refrigerator/freezer
STOVE: 4-burner propane or butane with oven
MAX. HEADROOM:

MACHINERY

ENGINE: 60 HP Perkins #4 154 diesel
PROPELLER:
GENERATOR:

DECK

STEERING: wheel
WINCHES: 7 Lewmar self-tailing winches: 2 primary (#65), 1 genoa halyard (#48), 1 main halyard (#46), 1 mainsheet (#46), 1 reefing (#46), 1 spinnaker boom (#43)
SAFETY: bow and stern pulpits with double lifelines
ANCHOR: 45 lbs. CQR anchor with electric anchor winch and locker
NAV LIGHTS: running and masthead

RIG

TYPE: masthead sloop with Kemp spar
RIGGING:
MAINSHEET: mid-boom sheeting

SAILS

SUPPLIED WITH BASE BOAT:

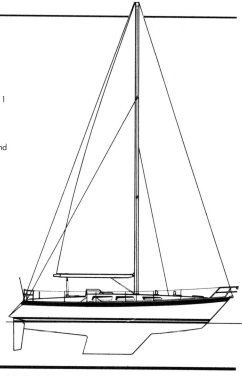

BUILDER'S COMMENTS The Centurion 47 is an exceptional boat. The hull shape, the deck plan, and the rig are designed for performance. With a following wind, you will flirt with speeds of 12 or 15 knots, without any fear, as the balance is so perfect. The Centurion 47 is very comfortable, with two, three, or four independent cabins according to your choice. It is also very comfortable at sea, a stiff, powerful boat with kind motion. The construction techniques demonstrate the mastery of quality for which the yard is famous.

JEANNEAU TRINIDAD

DESIGNER: Guy Ribadeau-Dumas
DISTRIBUTOR: Nautique International, Inc. (built by Jeanneau S.A.)

STATISTICS

LOA: 47 ft. 7 ins.
LWL: 41 ft. 4 ins.
BEAM: 15 ft. 1 ins.
DISPLACEMENT
deep keel: 25,000 lbs.
shoal keel:
c/board:
BALLAST
deep keel: 9,400 lbs.
shoal keel:
c/board:
DRAFT
deep keel: 7 ft. 4.50 ins.
shoal keel:
c/board up: 4 ft. 6.75 ins.
c/board down: 8 ft. 8.25 ins.
SAIL AREA: 1,334 sq. ft.
FRESH WATER: 209 gals.
(250 U.S. gal.)

FUEL CAPACITY: 110 gals.

COSTS

BASE BOAT:
sloop $169,900
DATE: 02/01/85
ketch $175,200
DATE: 02/01/85
EST. ON WATER:
DATE:

RATIOS

SAIL AREA/DISP: 24.96
DISP/LENGTH: 158.09
BALLAST RATIO: 37.60
FUEL/DISP: 3.300
FRESH WATER/DISP: 6.688

INTERIOR

BERTHS: 10 berths in 5 cabins: 1 convertible double forward, 2 single upper and lowers to starboard, 1 double to port, 2 double quarterberths aft (alternate layout available)
TABLE: fold-away
HEAD(S): 3 heads with 3 showers
COLD STORAGE: built-in icebox and refrigerator (58 gals.)
STOVE: 3-burner gas with oven
MAX. HEADROOM: 6 ft. 5 ins.

MACHINERY

ENGINE: 82 HP Perkins diesel
PROPELLER:
GENERATOR:

DECK

STEERING: wheel and emergency tiller
WINCHES: 6 winches: 2 primary (ST), 2 halyard, 1 mainsheet, 1 reefing
SAFETY: bow and stern pulpits with double lifelines
ANCHOR: anchor locker and windlass
NAV LIGHTS: running

RIG

TYPE: sloop or ketch
RIGGING:
MAINSHEET: boom-end sheeting

SAILS

SUPPLIED WITH BASE BOAT:

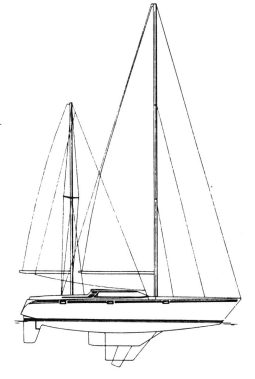

MAPLE LEAF 48

DESIGNER:
BUILDER: Cooper Yachts

STATISTICS

LOA: 47 ft. 8 ins.
LWL: 40 ft. 6 ins.
BEAM: 14 ft. 6 ins.
DISPLACEMENT
deep keel: 34,000 lbs.
shoal keel:
c/board:
BALLAST
deep keel: 9,500 lbs.
shoal keel:
c/board:
DRAFT
deep keel: 6 ft. 6 ins.
shoal keel:
c/board up:
c/board down:

SAIL AREA: 933 sq. ft.
FRESH WATER: 350 gals.
FUEL CAPACITY: 350 gals.

COSTS

BASE BOAT:
DATE:
EST. ON WATER:
DATE:

RATIOS

SAIL AREA/DISP: 14.22
DISP/LENGTH: 228.49
BALLAST RATIO: 27.94
FUEL/DISP: 7.72
FRESH WATER/DISP: 8.24

INTERIOR

BERTHS: 7 berths: 1 double V, 1 single settee, 1 single convertible dinette, 1 single pilot, 1 center aft double
TABLE: fixed
HEAD(S): 2 heads with 2 showers, 2 sump pumps, and 1 holding tank
COLD STORAGE: refrigerator/freezer
STOVE: 4-burner LPG with oven
MAX. HEADROOM: 6 ft. 4 ins.

MACHINERY

ENGINE: 85 HP Ford or Perkins diesel
PROPELLER: fixed 18"x18" on 1 1/2" shaft
GENERATOR:

DECK

STEERING: wheel
WINCHES:
SAFETY: bow and stern pulpits with double lifelines
ANCHOR:
NAV LIGHTS: running and masthead

RIG

TYPE: masthead sloop
RIGGING: wire (7/16"–5/6")
MAINSHEET: 5-part with boom-end sheeting

SAILS

SUPPLIED WITH BASE BOAT: main and working jib

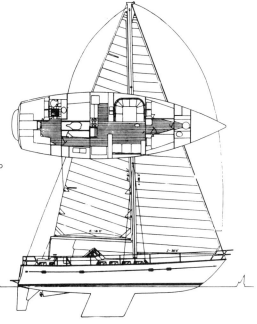

HANS CHRISTIAN 48 (Cruising Version)

DESIGNER: Scott Sprague
BUILDER: Hans Christian Yachts, Inc.

STATISTICS

LOA: 47 ft. 10 ins.
LWL: 41 ft. 3 ins.
BEAM: 14 ft. 3 ins.
DISPLACEMENT
deep keel: 44,000 lbs.
shoal keel:
c/board:
BALLAST
deep keel: 14,700 lbs.
shoal keel:
c/board:
DRAFT
deep keel: 7 ft. 0 ins.
shoal keel: 4 ft. 6 ins.
c/board up:
c/board down:

SAIL AREA: 1,387 sq. ft.
FRESH WATER: 300 gals.
FUEL CAPACITY: 140 gals.

COSTS

BASE BOAT:
DATE:
EST. ON WATER:
DATE:

RATIOS

SAIL AREA/DISP: 17.81
DISP/LENGTH: 279.85
BALLAST RATIO: 33.41
FUEL/DISP: 2.39
FRESH WATER/DISP: 5.49

INTERIOR

BERTHS: 5 berths: 1 double V, 1 single pilot, 2 double quarterberths
TABLE: fixed
HEAD(S): 1 head with shower, sump pump, and holding tank
COLD STORAGE: built-in icebox (10 cu. ft.)
STOVE:
MAX. HEADROOM:

MACHINERY

ENGINE: Mercedes-Benz or BMW diesel
PROPELLER: fixed on 2" shaft
GENERATOR:

DECK

STEERING: wheel with emergency tiller
WINCHES:
SAFETY: bow and stern pulpits with double lifelines
ANCHOR: anchor roller
NAV LIGHTS: running and masthead

RIG

TYPE: cutter or ketch
RIGGING:
MAINSHEET: boom-end sheeting

SAILS

SUPPLIED WITH BASE BOAT:

ORION 50

DESIGNER: Gary Mull
BUILDER: Ta-Shing Yacht Building Co., Ltd.

STATISTICS

LOA: 49 ft. 5 ins.
LWL: 42 ft. 5 ins.
BEAM: 14 ft. 5 ins.
DISPLACEMENT
deep keel: 36,600 lbs.
shoal keel:
c/board:
BALLAST
deep keel: 14,000 lbs.
shoal keel:
c/board:
DRAFT
deep keel: 6 ft. 5 ins.
shoal keel:
c/board up:
c/board down:

INTERIOR

BERTHS: 7 berths: 1 double V, 1 single pilot, 1 double pilot,
1 double quarterberth
TABLE:
HEAD(S): 2 heads with 2 showers
COLD STORAGE: built-in icebox
STOVE: 3-burner with oven
MAX. HEADROOM:

MACHINERY

ENGINE:
PROPELLER:
GENERATOR:

SAIL AREA: 1,118 sq. ft.
FRESH WATER:
FUEL CAPACITY:

COSTS

BASE BOAT:
DATE:
EST. ON WATER:
DATE:

RATIOS

SAIL AREA/DISP: 16.23
DISP/LENGTH: 212.85
BALLAST RATIO: 38.25
FUEL/DISP:
FRESH WATER/DISP:

DECK

STEERING: wheel
WINCHES:
SAFETY: bow and stern pulpits with double lifelines
ANCHOR:
NAV LIGHTS:

RIG

TYPE: ketch
RIGGING:
MAINSHEET: mid-boom sheeting

SAILS

SUPPLIED WITH BASE BOAT:

BUILDER'S COMMENTS The "Orion 50," carefully developed as a moderate displacement yacht with relatively shoal draft, provides a combination of very impressive performance under sail, particularly with the wind free and steady, and easily driven cruising under power. The resulting long waterline and generous beam reap the additional benefit of a very spacious and stable hull form affording excellent accommodations in a surprisingly roomy and open interior.

DICKERSON 50

DESIGNER: Kaufman & Associates
BUILDER: Dickerson Boatbuilders, Inc.

STATISTICS

LOA: 50 ft. 0 ins.
LWL: 38 ft. 9 ins.
BEAM: 13 ft. 9 ins.
DISPLACEMENT
deep keel: 33,900 lbs.
shoal keel:
c/board:
BALLAST
deep keel: 14,000 lbs.
shoal keel:
c/board:
DRAFT
deep keel: 6 ft. 6 ins.
shoal keel:
c/board up: 5 ft. 2 ins.
c/board down: 11 ft. 0 ins.

SAIL AREA: 1,142 sq. ft.
FRESH WATER: 200 gals.
FUEL CAPACITY: 135 gals.

COSTS

BASE BOAT:
DATE:
EST. ON WATER:
DATE:

RATIOS

SAIL AREA/DISP: 17.45
DISP/LENGTH: 260
BALLAST RATIO: 41.3
FUEL/DISP: 3.0
FRESH WATER/DISP: 4.7

DECK

STEERING: wheel with emergency tiller
WINCHES: 11 Barient winches: 2 primary (#32 ST), 2 secondary (#28 ST), 1 mainsheet (#28 ST), 3 halyard (#25), 1 staysail sheet (#27), 2 mizzen halyard (#21)
SAFETY: bow and stern pulpits with double lifelines
ANCHOR: anchor roller
NAV LIGHTS: running and masthead

RIG

TYPE: masthead staysail ketch
RIGGING: 1x19 wire
MAINSHEET: mid-boom sheeting

SAILS

SUPPLIED WITH BASE BOAT:

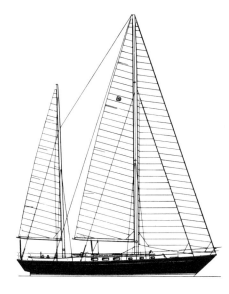

INTERIOR

BERTHS: all custom designed
TABLE:
HEAD(S): 2 heads with 2 showers and 1 sump pump
COLD STORAGE: refrigerator/freezer (14.5 cu. ft.)
STOVE: 3-burner propane with oven
MAX. HEADROOM:

MACHINERY

ENGINE: 85 HP Perkins #4-236 diesel with 2:1 reduction gear
PROPELLER: fixed 24"x16" on 1½" shaft
GENERATOR: 3.5 kW Onan

STEVENS CUSTOM 50

DESIGNER: Sparkman & Stephens
BUILDER: Stevens Yachts of Annapolis

STATISTICS

LOA: 50 ft. 1.75 ins.
LWL: 37 ft. 9.00 ins.
BEAM: 14 ft. 4.00 ins.
DISPLACEMENT
deep keel: 31,220 lbs.
shoal keel:
c/board:
BALLAST
deep keel: 12,000 lbs.
shoal keel:
c/board:
DRAFT
deep keel: 6 ft. 0 ins.
shoal keel:
c/board up:
c/board down:

SAIL AREA: 1,055 sq. ft.
FRESH WATER: 300 gals.
FUEL CAPACITY: 150 gals.

COSTS

BASE BOAT: $250,000
DATE: 05/29/85
EST. ON WATER: $275,000
DATE: 05/29/85

RATIOS

SAIL AREA/DISP: 17.03
DISP/LENGTH: 259.08
BALLAST RATIO: 38.44
FUEL/DISP: 3.60
FRESH WATER/DISP: 7.69

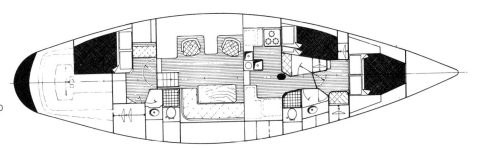

INTERIOR

BERTHS: 8 berths: 1 double V, 2 forward single upper and lowers, 2 single settees, 1 aft double
TABLE: hi-lo dinette
HEAD(S): 2 heads with 2 showers
COLD STORAGE: refrigerator/freezer
STOVE: Shipmate
MAX. HEADROOM: 6 ft. 7 ins.

MACHINERY

ENGINE: 70 HP Westerbeke diesel
PROPELLER: 2-blade
GENERATOR:

DECK

STEERING: wheel
WINCHES: 12 Lewmar ST winches
SAFETY: bow and stern pulpits with double lifelines
ANCHOR: 50 lb. Bruce and 35 lb. Danforth anchors
NAV LIGHTS:

RIG

TYPE: cutter
RIGGING:
MAINSHEET: boom-end sheeting

SAILS

SUPPLIED WITH BASE BOAT:

BUILDER'S COMMENTS Optional below-deck steering station. Unlimited other options.

MAPLE LEAF 50

DESIGNER: S. C. Huntingford
BUILDER: Cooper Yachts

STATISTICS

LOA: 50 ft. 4 ins.
LWL: 42 ft. 0 ins.
BEAM: 14 ft. 6 ins.
DISPLACEMENT
deep keel: 35,000 lbs.
shoal keel:
c/board:
BALLAST
deep keel: 10,000 lbs.
shoal keel:
c/board:
DRAFT
deep keel: 6 ft. 6 ins.
shoal keel:
c/board up:
c/board down:

SAIL AREA: 970 sq. ft.
FRESH WATER: 400 gals.
FUEL CAPACITY: 400 gals.

COSTS

BASE BOAT: $205,000
DATE: 01/85
EST. ON WATER: $240,000
DATE: 08/85

RATIOS

SAIL AREA/DISP: 14.50
DISP/LENGTH: 210.9
BALLAST RATIO: 28.57
FUEL/DISP: 8.57
FRESH WATER/DISP: 9.14

INTERIOR

BERTHS: 7 berths: 1 double V, 1 single settee, 1 single convertible dinette, 1 single pilot, 1 center aft double
TABLE: fixed
HEAD(S): 2 heads with 2 showers, 2 sump pumps, and 1 holding tank
COLD STORAGE: refrigerator/freezer
STOVE: 4-burner LPG with oven
MAX. HEADROOM: 6 ft. 4 ins.

MACHINERY

ENGINE: 85 HP Ford or Perkins diesel with 2.1:1 reduction gear
PROPELLER: fixed 18"x18" on 1½" shaft
GENERATOR:

DECK

STEERING: wheel with emergency tiller
WINCHES: 6 Lewmar winches: 2 #55, 1 #43, 3 #40
SAFETY: bow and stern pulpits with double lifelines
ANCHOR:
NAV LIGHTS: running and masthead

RIG

TYPE: masthead sloop
RIGGING: wire (⁷/₁₆"–⅝")
MAINSHEET: boom-end sheeting

SAILS

SUPPLIED WITH BASE BOAT: main, working jib

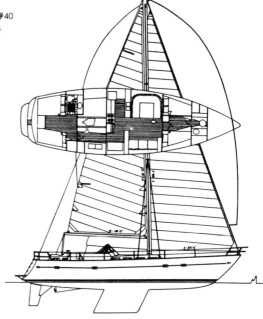

BANNER 51

DESIGNER: Stan Huntingford
BUILDER: Cooper Yachts

STATISTICS

LOA: 50 ft. 8 ins.
LWL: 44 ft. 0 ins.
BEAM: 15 ft. 0 ins.
DISPLACEMENT
deep keel: 37,000 lbs.
shoal keel:
c/board:
BALLAST
deep keel: 16,500 lbs.
shoal keel:
c/board:
DRAFT
deep keel: 8 ft. 0 ins.
shoal keel:
c/board up:
c/board down:

SAIL AREA:
FRESH WATER: 150 gals.
FUEL CAPACITY: 150 gals.

COSTS

BASE BOAT: $200,000
DATE: 04/85
EST. ON WATER:
DATE:

RATIOS

SAIL AREA/DISP:
DISP/LENGTH: 193.91
BALLAST RATIO: 44.59
FUEL/DISP: 3.04
FRESH WATER/DISP: 3.24

INTERIOR

BERTHS:
TABLE:
HEAD(S): 2 heads with 2 showers
COLD STORAGE: built-in icebox
STOVE: 3-burner propane with oven
MAX. HEADROOM:

MACHINERY

ENGINE: 85 HP diesel
PROPELLER:
GENERATOR:

DECK

STEERING: wheel
WINCHES: 5 Lewmar winches: 2 #55 ST, 2 #34, 1 #34 ST
SAFETY: bow and stern pulpits with double lifelines
ANCHOR:
NAV LIGHTS: running

RIG

TYPE: masthead sloop
RIGGING:
MAINSHEET: mid-boom sheeting

SAILS

SUPPLIED WITH BASE BOAT: main, working jib, 150% genoa

COOPER 508

DESIGNER: Stan Huntingford
BUILDER: Cooper Yachts

STATISTICS

LOA: 50 ft. 8 ins.
LWL: 44 ft. 0 ins.
BEAM: 15 ft. 0 ins.
DISPLACEMENT
deep keel: 38,350 lbs.
shoal keel:
c/board:
BALLAST
deep keel: 16,500 lbs.
shoal keel:
c/board:
DRAFT
deep keel: 8 ft. 0 ins.
shoal keel:
c/board up:
c/board down:

SAIL AREA:
FRESH WATER: 150 gals.
FUEL CAPACITY: 150 gals.

COSTS

BASE BOAT: $217,500
DATE: 04/85
EST. ON WATER:
DATE:

RATIOS

SAIL AREA/DISP:
DISP/LENGTH: 200.98
BALLAST RATIO: 43.02
FUEL/DISP: 2.93
FRESH WATER/DISP: 3.13

DECK

STEERING: wheel
WINCHES: 5 Lewmar winches: 2 #55 ST, 2 #34, 1 #34 ST
SAFETY: bow and stern pulpits with double lifelines
ANCHOR:
NAV LIGHTS: running

RIG

TYPE: masthead sloop
RIGGING:
MAINSHEET: boom-end sheeting

SAILS

SUPPLIED WITH BASE BOAT: main, working jib, 150%
genoa

INTERIOR

BERTHS: 6 berths: 1 forward double, 1 mid-ship double, 1
double quarterberth
TABLE:
HEAD(S): 2 heads with 2 showers
COLD STORAGE: built-in icebox (8 cu. ft.)
STOVE: 3-burner propane with oven
MAX. HEADROOM:

MACHINERY

ENGINE: diesel
PROPELLER:
GENERATOR:

SHANNON 50

DESIGNER: Walter Schulz & Associates
BUILDER: Shannon Boat Company, Inc.

STATISTICS

LOA: 50 ft. 11 ins.
LWL: 42 ft. 9 ins.
BEAM: 14 ft. 3 ins.
DISPLACEMENT
deep keel: 39,000 lbs.
shoal keel:
c/board:
BALLAST
deep keel: 15,500 lbs.
shoal keel:
c/board:
DRAFT
deep keel:
shoal keel:
c/board up:
c/board down:

SAIL AREA: 1,227 sq. ft.
FRESH WATER: 300 gals.
FUEL CAPACITY: 150 gals.

COSTS

BASE BOAT:
DATE:
EST. ON WATER: $415,000
DATE: 05/30/85

RATIOS

SAIL AREA/DISP: 17.07
DISP/LENGTH: 222
BALLAST RATIO: 39.75
FUEL/DISP: 2.88
FRESH WATER/DISP: 6.15

DECK

STEERING: wheel
WINCHES: 12 Lewmar or Barient winches
SAFETY: bow and stern pulpits with double lifelines
ANCHOR: double anchor rollers with hydraulic windlass
NAV LIGHTS: running and masthead

RIG

TYPE: double headsail ketch
RIGGING: Navtec rod
MAINSHEET: mid-boom sheeting

SAILS

SUPPLIED WITH BASE BOAT: main (2 reefs), 150% genoa,
yankee jib, staysail, mizzen

INTERIOR

BERTHS: 9 berths: 1 double V, 1 double convertible dinette, 1
single settee, 2 single pilots, 1 double quarterberth
TABLE: dropleaf
HEAD(S): 2 heads with 2 showers and 1 bathtub
COLD STORAGE: refrigerator (10 cu. ft.) freezer (4.5 cu. ft.)
STOVE: 3-burner with oven and microwave
MAX. HEADROOM: 6 ft. 7 ins.

MACHINERY

ENGINE: 85 HP Perkins or 86 HP Mercedes diesel
PROPELLER: 3-blade in aperture
GENERATOR:

BUILDER'S COMMENTS The Shannon 50 offers two private staterooms for guests plus
a completely private aft owner's stateroom. The two heads have separate shower stalls,
and the galley is designed for gourmet cooking. A navigator's station is designed to handle
the most sophisticated equipment, and the Shannon 50 cockpit design is considered the
most well thought out in the industry.

SHANNON 51 CC

DESIGNER: Walter Schulz & Assoc.
BUILDER: Shannon Boat Company, Inc.

STATISTICS

LOA: 50 ft. 11 ins.
LWL: 42 ft. 9 ins.
BEAM: 14 ft. 3 ins.
DISPLACEMENT
deep keel: 39,000 lbs.
shoal keel:
c/board:
BALLAST
deep keel: 15,500 lbs.
shoal keel:
c/board:
DRAFT
deep keel:
shoal keel:
c/board up: 5 ft. 8 ins.
c/board down: 9 ft. 9 ins.

SAIL AREA: 1,227 sq. ft.
FRESH WATER: 300 gals.
FUEL CAPACITY: 150 gals.

COSTS

BASE BOAT:
DATE:
EST. ON WATER: $425,000
DATE: 05/30/85

RATIOS

SAIL AREA/DISP: 17.07
DISP/LENGTH: 222
BALLAST RATIO: 39.74
FUEL/DISP: 2.88
FRESH WATER/DISP: 6.15

INTERIOR

BERTHS: 9 berths: 1 double V, 1 double convertible settee, 1 single settee, 2 single pilots, 1 center aft double
TABLE: dropleaf
HEAD(S): 2 heads with 2 showers
COLD STORAGE: refrigerator (11 cu. ft.) and freezer (4 cu. ft.)
STOVE: 3-burner LPG with oven
MAX. HEADROOM: 6 ft. 7 ins.

MACHINERY

ENGINE: 85 HP diesel with 2:1 reduction gear
PROPELLER: 3-blade
GENERATOR:

DECK

STEERING: wheel
WINCHES: 13 Lewmar or Barient winches
SAFETY: bow and stern pulpits with double lifelines
ANCHOR: 2 anchors with anchor roller, bowsprit, and hydraulic windlass
NAV LIGHTS: running

RIG

TYPE: double headsail ketch
RIGGING: Navtec rod
MAINSHEET: boom-end sheeting

SAILS

SUPPLIED WITH BASE BOAT: main (2 reefs) 150% genoa, yankee jib, club staysail, mizzen (1 reef)

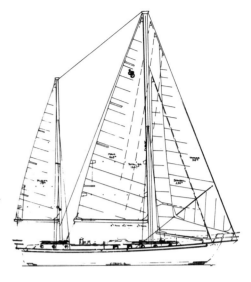

BUILDER'S COMMENTS The Shannon center cockpit 51 is designed for those who prefer a midcockpit configuration. Utilizing the ocean-proven hull and rig of the aft cockpit Shannon 50, the 51 cc is a fast, seakindly yacht.

ENDEAVOUR 51

DESIGNER: Johan Valentijin
BUILDER: Endeavour Yacht Corporation

STATISTICS

LOA: 51 ft. 0 ins.
LWL: 42 ft. 3 ins.
BEAM: 15 ft. 0 ins.
DISPLACEMENT
deep keel: 37,500 lbs.
shoal keel:
c/board:
BALLAST
deep keel: 17,300 lbs.
shoal keel:
c/board:
DRAFT
deep keel: 7 ft. 6 ins.
shoal keel: 5 ft. 0 ins.
c/board up:
c/board down:

SAIL AREA: 1,238 sq. ft.
FRESH WATER: 300 gals.
FUEL CAPACITY: 125 gals.

COSTS

BASE BOAT:
DATE:
EST. ON WATER:
DATE:

RATIOS

SAIL AREA/DISP: 17.68
DISP/LENGTH: 221.98
BALLAST RATIO: 46.13
FUEL/DISP: 2.5
FRESH WATER/DISP: 6.4

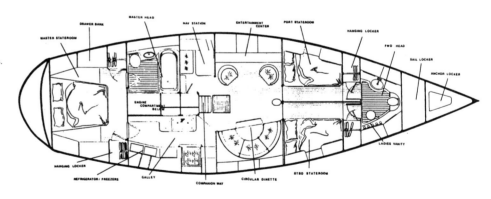

INTERIOR

BERTHS: 6 berths: 1 forward double, 1 port double, 1 aft double
TABLE:
HEAD(S): 2 heads with 2 showers
COLD STORAGE: refrigerator/freezer
STOVE: 3-burner propane with oven
MAX. HEADROOM:

MACHINERY

ENGINE: 85 HP Perkins #4-236 diesel
PROPELLER: 3-blade
GENERATOR:

DECK

STEERING: wheel
WINCHES: 4 winches: 2 sheet (ST), 2 halyard
SAFETY: double bow pulpit and stern rail
ANCHOR: anchor well
NAV LIGHTS: running and masthead

RIG

TYPE: masthead sloop
RIGGING:
MAINSHEET:

SAILS

SUPPLIED WITH BASE BOAT:

GRENADIER 158

DESIGNER: Laurent Giles & Partners, Ltd.
BUILDER: A. H. Moody & Son, Ltd.

STATISTICS

LOA: 51 ft. 3 ins.
LWL: 39 ft. 0 ins.
BEAM: 14 ft. 2 ins.
DISPLACEMENT
deep keel: 42,829 lbs.
shoal keel:
c/board:
BALLAST
deep keel: 16,800 lbs.
shoal keel:
c/board:
DRAFT
deep keel: 7 ft. 5 ins.
shoal keel:
c/board up:
c/board down:

SAIL AREA: 1,562 sq. ft.
FRESH WATER: 375 gals.
FUEL CAPACITY: 375 gals.

COSTS

BASE BOAT:
DATE:
EST. ON WATER:
DATE:

RATIOS

SAIL AREA/DISP: 20.42
DISP/LENGTH: 322.33
BALLAST RATIO: 39.23
FUEL/DISP: 6.57
FRESH WATER/DISP: 7.00

DECK

STEERING: wheel
WINCHES:
SAFETY: bow and stern pulpits with double lifelines
ANCHOR:
NAV LIGHTS:

RIG

TYPE: ketch
RIGGING:
MAINSHEET: boom-end sheeting

SAILS

SUPPLIED WITH BASE BOAT:

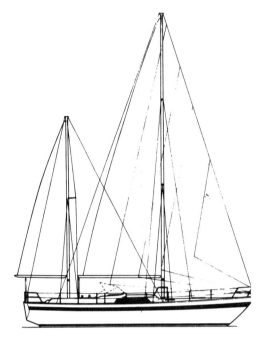

INTERIOR

BERTHS: 8 berths: 1 double V, 2 single settees, 4 single pilots, 1 double quarterberth
TABLE: dropleaf
HEAD(S): 2 heads with 2 showers
COLD STORAGE: refrigerator/freezer
STOVE: 3-burner LPG with oven
MAX. HEADROOM:

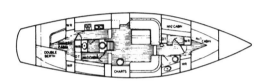

MACHINERY

ENGINE: 109 shaft HP Perkins #G3544 diesel
PROPELLER:
GENERATOR:

SOU'WESTER 51

DESIGNER: McCurdy & Rhodes, Inc.
BUILDER: Henry R. Hinckley & Co.

STATISTICS

LOA: 51 ft. 3 ins.
LWL: 37 ft. 6 ins.
BEAM: 14 ft. 0 ins.
DISPLACEMENT
deep keel: 38,000 lbs.
shoal keel:
c/board:
BALLAST
deep keel: 14,600 lbs.
shoal keel:
c/board:
DRAFT
deep keel: 8 ft. 0.0 ins.
shoal keel:
c/board up: 5 ft. 10.5 ins.
c/board down: 11 ft. 0.0 ins.

SAIL AREA: 1,135 sq. ft.
FRESH WATER: 250 gals.
FUEL CAPACITY: 120 gals.

COSTS

BASE BOAT: $415,000
DATE: 06/85
EST. ON WATER: $475,000
DATE: 06/85

RATIOS

SAIL AREA/DISP: 16.07
DISP/LENGTH: 321.69
BALLAST RATIO: 38.42
FUEL/DISP: 2.37
FRESH WATER/DISP: 5.26

DECK

STEERING: wheel with emergency tiller
WINCHES: 11 Barient winches
SAFETY: bow and stern pulpits with double lifelines
ANCHOR: anchor well
NAV LIGHTS: running

RIG

TYPE: masthead cutter
RIGGING: 1x19 SS wire
MAINSHEET: mid-boom sheeting

SAILS

SUPPLIED WITH BASE BOAT:

INTERIOR

BERTHS: 2 berths in 3 cabins: 1 double V in forward cabin, 2 single settees in main cabin, 1 double quarterberth in aft cabin
TABLE: dropleaf
HEAD(S): 1 head with shower
COLD STORAGE: built-in icebox (11 cu. ft.)
STOVE: 3-burner with oven
MAX. HEADROOM:

MACHINERY

ENGINE: 85 HP Perkins diesel with 2:1 reduction gear
PROPELLER: 2-blade
GENERATOR:

BUILDER'S COMMENTS A high performance cruising yacht designed for long distance passage-making.

SWAN 51

DESIGNER: German Frers
BUILDER: Nautor

STATISTICS

LOA: 51 ft. 3.0 ins.
LWL: 42 ft. 4.7 ins.
BEAM: 14 ft. 8.8 ins.
DISPLACEMENT
deep keel: 39,600 lbs.
shoal keel:
c/board:
BALLAST
deep keel: 16,500 lbs.
shoal keel:
c/board:
DRAFT
deep keel: 8 ft. 10.8 ins.
shoal keel:
c/board up:
c/board down:

SAIL AREA:
FRESH WATER: 170 gals.
FUEL CAPACITY: 74 gals.

COSTS

BASE BOAT:
DATE:
EST. ON WATER:
DATE:

RATIOS

SAIL AREA/DISP:
DISP/LENGTH: 232.09
BALLAST RATIO: 41.67
FUEL/DISP: 1.4
FRESH WATER/DISP: 3.43

DECK

STEERING: 48" wheel with emergency tiller
WINCHES: 14 Lewmar winches: 2 #55A ST, 2 #65AP, 6 #44A ST, 4 #48AP
SAFETY: bow and stern pulpits with double lifelines
ANCHOR: Danforth 60H anchor
NAV LIGHTS: running and masthead

RIG

TYPE: masthead sloop
RIGGING: rod
MAINSHEET: boom-end sheeting

SAILS

SUPPLIED WITH BASE BOAT:

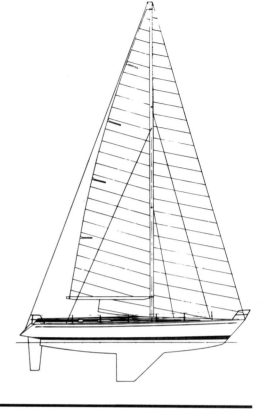

INTERIOR

BERTHS: 9 berths: 3 single pilots, 1 single quarterberth, 1 double quarterberth, 3 single pipe berths
TABLE: dropleaf
HEAD(S): 2 heads with 2 showers and 2 sump pumps
COLD STORAGE: refrigerator/freezer
STOVE: 3-burner gas with oven
MAX. HEADROOM:

MACHINERY

ENGINE: 73 HP Perkins #4.236M diesel with 2.0:1 reduction gear
PROPELLER: 25" folding
GENERATOR:

RON HOLLAND 52

DESIGNER: Ron Holland
BUILDER: Ta Chiao Bros. Yacht Building Co.

STATISTICS

LOA: 51 ft. 6 ins.
LWL: 42 ft. 6 ins.
BEAM: 14 ft. 7 ins.
DISPLACEMENT
deep keel: 38,000 lbs.
shoal keel:
c/board:
BALLAST
deep keel: 13,700 lbs.
shoal keel:
c/board:
DRAFT
deep keel: 8 ft. 2 ins.
shoal keel:
c/board up: 5 ft. 11 ins.
c/board down:

SAIL AREA:
FRESH WATER:
FUEL CAPACITY: 150 gals.

COSTS

BASE BOAT: $185,000
DATE:
EST. ON WATER: $225,000
DATE:

RATIOS

SAIL AREA/DISP:
DISP/LENGTH: 220
BALLAST RATIO: 36.05
FUEL/DISP: 2.96
FRESH WATER/DISP:

DECK

STEERING: 44" wheel with emergency tiller
WINCHES: 7 winches: 4 Barient primary & secondary (#36 3sp ST), 2 halyard (#28), 1 mainsheet (#27 ST)
SAFETY: bow and stern pulpits with double lifelines
ANCHOR: 45 lb. anchor with anchor rollers and windlass
NAV LIGHTS: running and masthead

RIG

TYPE: masthead ketch or cutter
RIGGING: 1x19 wire
MAINSHEET:

SAILS

SUPPLIED WITH BASE BOAT:

INTERIOR

BERTHS: 9 berths: 1 double V, 2 forward singles, 2 single settees, 1 single quarterberth, 1 double quarterberth
TABLE: center-mounted
HEAD(S): 2 heads with 2 showers and 2 sump pumps
COLD STORAGE: refrigerator/freezer
STOVE: 3-burner propane with oven
MAX. HEADROOM: 6 ft. 8 ins.

MACHINERY

ENGINE: 130 HP Perkins diesel
PROPELLER: 3-blade folding
GENERATOR:

MOODY CARBINEER 52

DESIGNER: Laurent Giles & Partners, Ltd.
BUILDER: A. H. Moody & Son, Ltd.

STATISTICS

LOA: 51 ft. 9 ins.
LWL: 39 ft. 0 ins.
BEAM: 14 ft. 2 ins.
DISPLACEMENT
deep keel: 42,851 lbs.
shoal keel:
c/board:
BALLAST
deep keel: 16,800 lbs.
shoal keel:
c/board:
DRAFT
deep keel: 7 ft. 5 ins.
shoal keel:
c/board up:
c/board down:

SAIL AREA: 1,123 sq. ft.
FRESH WATER: 375 gals.
FUEL CAPACITY: 375 gals.

COSTS

BASE BOAT:
DATE:
EST. ON WATER:
DATE:

RATIOS

SAIL AREA/DISP: 14.67
DISP/LENGTH: 322.49
BALLAST RATIO: 39.21
FUEL/DISP: 6.56
FRESH WATER/DISP: 7.00

DECK

STEERING: wheel
WINCHES:
SAFETY: bow and stern pulpits with double lifelines
ANCHOR: anchor roller
NAV LIGHTS:

RIG

TYPE: ketch
RIGGING:
MAINSHEET: boom-end sheeting

SAILS

SUPPLIED WITH BASE BOAT:

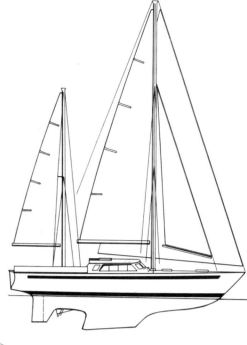

Deck Saloon

INTERIOR

BERTHS: 8 berths: 1 double V, 4 single pilots, 2 single quarterberths
TABLE: dropleaf
HEAD(S): 2 heads with 2 showers
COLD STORAGE: refrigerator/freezer
STOVE: 3-burner with oven
MAX. HEADROOM:

MACHINERY

ENGINE: 109 shaft HP Perkins #63544 diesel
PROPELLER:
GENERATOR:

TAYANA 52

DESIGNER: Robert H. Perry
DISTRIBUTOR: Southern Offshore Yachts, Inc. (built in Taiwan by TaYang Yacht Building Co.)

STATISTICS

LOA: 52 ft. 5.5 ins.
LWL: 42 ft. 1.0 ins.
BEAM: 15 ft. 1.0 ins.
DISPLACEMENT
deep keel: 38,570 lbs.
shoal keel:
c/board:
BALLAST
deep keel: 14,800 lbs.
shoal keel:
c/board:
DRAFT
deep keel: 6 ft. 6 ins.
shoal keel: 5 ft. 4 ins.
c/board up:
c/board down:

SAIL AREA: 1,156 sq. ft.
FRESH WATER: 180 gals.
FUEL CAPACITY: 160 gals.

COSTS

BASE BOAT: $181,200
DATE: 04/85
EST. ON WATER:
DATE:

RATIOS

SAIL AREA/DISP: 16.20
DISP/LENGTH: 230.76
BALLAST RATIO: 38.37
FUEL/DISP: 3.11
FRESH WATER/DISP: 3.73

MACHINERY

ENGINE: 72 HP Perkins #4-236M diesel with 2.1:1 reduction gear
PROPELLER: fixed on 1½" shaft
GENERATOR:

DECK

STEERING: 44" wheel with emergency tiller
WINCHES: 7 Lewmar winches: 2 #55 ST, 4 #40 ST, 1 #30 ST
SAFETY: bow and stern pulpits with double lifelines
ANCHOR: anchor roller
NAV LIGHTS: running and masthead

RIG

TYPE: double headsail masthead sloop with Kemp spar
RIGGING: 1x19 wire
MAINSHEET: mid-boom sheeting

SAILS

SUPPLIED WITH BASE BOAT: main, staysail, yankee

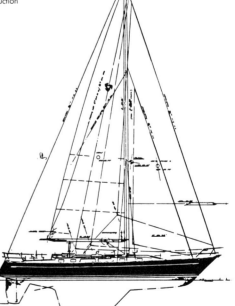

INTERIOR

BERTHS: 10 berths: 1 double V, 1 single convertible dinette, 1 double convertible dinette, 2 double quarterberths, 1 single quarterberth
TABLE: fixed
HEAD(S): 2 heads with 2 showers, 1 sump pump, and 1 holding tank (30 gal.)
COLD STORAGE: built-in icebox
STOVE:
MAX. HEADROOM:

LITTLE HARBOR 53

DESIGNER: Ted Hood
BUILDER: Little Harbor Custom Yachts

STATISTICS

LOA: 52 ft. 8 ins.
LWL: 42 ft. 2 ins.
BEAM: 15 ft. 1 ins.
DISPLACEMENT
deep keel:
shoal keel:
c/board: 43,200 lbs.
BALLAST
deep keel:
shoal keel:
c/board: 18,000 lbs.
DRAFT
deep keel:
shoal keel:
c/board up: 5 ft. 6 ins.
c/board down: 11 ft. 4 ins.

RATIOS

SAIL AREA/DISP: 16.61   17.82 (ketch)
DISP/LENGTH: 257.36
BALLAST RATIO: 41.7
FUEL/DISP: 3.04
FRESH WATER/DISP: 5.74

INTERIOR

BERTHS: 9 berths: 1 double V, 4 single pilots, 1 single quarterberth, 1 double quarterberth
TABLE:
HEAD(S): 3 heads with 1 holding tank
COLD STORAGE: refrigerator/freezer
STOVE:

SAIL AREA:
sloop: 1,278 sq. ft.
ketch: 1,371 sq. ft.
FRESH WATER: 310 gals.
FUEL CAPACITY: 175 gals.

COSTS

BASE BOAT:
sloop: $386,500
DATE: 12/84
ketch: $391,450
DATE: 12/84

MAX. HEADROOM:

MACHINERY

ENGINE:
PROPELLER: folding
GENERATOR:

DECK

STEERING: wheel
WINCHES:
SAFETY:
ANCHOR: electric windlass
NAV LIGHTS:

RIG

TYPE: masthead
RIGGING:
MAINSHEET:

SAILS

SUPPLIED WITH BASE BOAT:

MASON 53

DESIGNER: Al Mason
BUILDER: Pacific Asian Enterprises, Inc.

STATISTICS

LOA: 53 ft. 6.0 ins.
LWL: 39 ft. 8.5 ins.
BEAM: 14 ft. 10.0 ins.
DISPLACEMENT
deep keel: 38,600 lbs.
shoal keel:
c/board:
BALLAST
deep keel:
shoal keel:
c/board:
DRAFT
deep keel: 6 ft. 8 ins.
shoal keel: 5 ft. 9 ins.
c/board up:
c/board down:

INTERIOR

BERTHS: 3 interior options
TABLE:
HEAD(S): 2 heads
COLD STORAGE:
STOVE:
MAX. HEADROOM:

MACHINERY

ENGINE: Perkins #236
PROPELLER:
GENERATOR: 4.4 kW Westerbeke

SAIL AREA:
FRESH WATER: 333 gals.
FUEL CAPACITY: 204 gals.

COSTS

BASE BOAT:
DATE:
EST. ON WATER:
DATE:

RATIOS

SAIL AREA/DISP:
DISP/LENGTH: 275.2
BALLAST RATIO:
FUEL/DISP: 4.0
FRESH WATER/DISP: 6.9

DECK

STEERING: wheel
WINCHES:
SAFETY: bow and stern pulpits with double lifelines
ANCHOR:
NAV LIGHTS: running and masthead

RIG

TYPE: masthead ketch
RIGGING:
MAINSHEET: mid-boom sheeting

SAILS

SUPPLIED WITH BASE BOAT: working sails

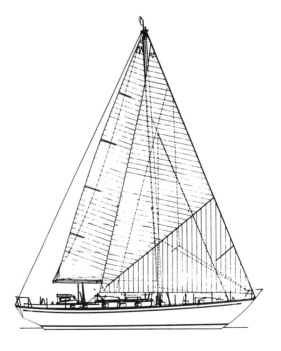

CT-54

DESIGNER: Robert H. Perry
DISTRIBUTOR: Ta Chiao USA, Inc. (built in Taiwan by Ta Chiao Bros. Yacht Building Co.)

STATISTICS

LOA: 53 ft. 7 ins.
LWL: 42 ft. 6 ins.
BEAM: 15 ft. 1 ins.
DISPLACEMENT
deep keel: 54,000 lbs.
shoal keel:
c/board:
BALLAST
deep keel: 16,500 lbs.
shoal keel:
c/board:
DRAFT
deep keel: 6 ft. 6 ins.
shoal keel:
c/board up:
c/board down:

SAIL AREA: 1,455 sq. ft.
FRESH WATER: 200 gals.
FUEL CAPACITY: 200 gals.

COSTS

BASE BOAT: $191,000
DATE: 04/01/85
EST. ON WATER: $210,100
DATE:

RATIOS

SAIL AREA/DISP: 16.29
DISP/LENGTH: 314.04
BALLAST RATIO: 30.56
FUEL/DISP: 2.78
FRESH WATER/DISP: 2.96

INTERIOR

BERTHS: 10 berths in model II: 1 double V, 1 single quarter-berth, 1 double quarterberth, 3 single pilots, 1 double pilot
TABLE: fixed
HEAD(S): 2 heads with 2 showers, 2 sump pumps, and 2 holding tanks
COLD STORAGE: refrigerator/freezer
STOVE: 3-burner gas with oven
MAX. HEADROOM: 6 ft. 6 ins.

MACHINERY

ENGINE: 120 HP Lehman Ford diesel
PROPELLER: fixed
GENERATOR:

DECK

STEERING: wheel with emergency tiller
WINCHES: 6 Barlow winches: 2 #32 ST, 1 #28 ST, 2 #5 ST, 1 #4 ST
SAFETY: bow and stern pulpits with double lifelines
ANCHOR: anchor rollers and teak storage platform
NAV LIGHTS: running and masthead

RIG

TYPE: fractional rig ketch
RIGGING: wire
MAINSHEET: mid-boom sheeting

SAILS

SUPPLIED WITH BASE BOAT: main, working jib, staysail, mizzen

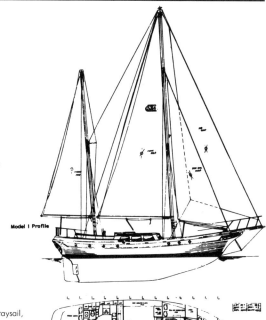

Model I Profile

Model I Layout

BUILDER'S COMMENTS The CT-54 is a classic and one of the most beautiful cruising boats ever developed. Nearly one hundred have been built and this vessel has been used successfully in charter, for circumnavigation, and has literally sailed every ocean of the world. She is strong, comfortable and fast, easily handled by two people.

MAPLE LEAF 54

DESIGNER:
BUILDER: Cooper Yachts

STATISTICS

LOA: 54 ft. 5 ins.
LWL: 47 ft. 4 ins.
BEAM: 14 ft. 9 ins.
DISPLACEMENT
deep keel: 42,000 lbs.
shoal keel:
c/board:
BALLAST
deep keel: 11,500 lbs.
shoal keel:
c/board:
DRAFT
deep keel: 7 ft. 2 ins.
shoal keel:
c/board up:
c/board down:

SAIL AREA: 1,030 sq. ft.
FRESH WATER: 550 gals.
FUEL CAPACITY: 550 gals.

COSTS

BASE BOAT: $235,000
DATE: 06/85
EST. ON WATER: $270,000
DATE: 11/85

RATIOS

SAIL AREA/DISP: 13.64
DISP/LENGTH: 176.84
BALLAST RATIO: 27.38
FUEL/DISP: 9.82
FRESH WATER/DISP: 10.48

INTERIOR

BERTHS: 6 berths: 1 double V, 1 single settee, 1 single pilot, 1 center aft double
TABLE: fixed
HEAD(S): 2 heads with 2 showers, 2 sump pumps, and 1 holding tank
COLD STORAGE: refrigerator/freezer (12 cu. ft)
STOVE: 4-burner LPG with oven
MAX. HEADROOM: 6 ft. 4 ins.

MACHINERY

ENGINE: 120 HP Ford or Perkins diesel
PROPELLER: fixed 24"x16" on 1 3/4" shaft
GENERATOR:

DECK

STEERING: wheel with emergency tiller
WINCHES: 6 Lewmar winches: 2 #55, 1 #48, 3 #36
SAFETY: bow and stern pulpits with double lifelines
ANCHOR: 45 lb. CQR anchor with anchor chain and winch
NAV LIGHTS:

RIG

TYPE: masthead ketch or sloop
RIGGING: wire (5/16"–1/2")
MAINSHEET: 4-part with boom-end sheeting

SAILS

SUPPLIED WITH BASE BOAT: main, working jib, 150% genoa

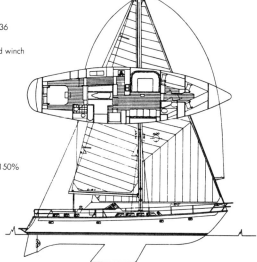

TAYANA 55

DESIGNER: Pieter Beeldsnijder
DISTRIBUTOR: Southern Offshore Yachts, Inc. (built in Taiwan by TaYang Yacht Building Co.)

STATISTICS

LOA: 55 ft. 0.00 ins.
LWL: 45 ft. 11.00 ins.
BEAM: 16 ft. 0.75 ins.
DISPLACEMENT
deep keel: 48,400 lbs.
shoal keel:
c/board:
BALLAST
deep keel: 17,600 lbs.
shoal keel:
c/board: 16,940 lbs.
DRAFT
deep keel: 6 ft. 7 ins.
shoal keel:
c/board up: 5 ft. 3 ins.
c/board down: 9 ft. 10 ins.
SAIL AREA: 1,022 sq. ft.
(schooner)
1,635 sq. ft. (cutter)
FRESH WATER: 250 gals.

FUEL CAPACITY: 150 gals.

COSTS

BASE BOAT:
schooner-keel $215,000
DATE: 07/01/85
schooner-c/brd $232,700
cutter-keel $205,000
cutter-c/brd $224,300
EST. ON WATER: + $25,000
DATE: 07/01/85

RATIOS

SAIL AREA/DISP:
12.32 (schooner)
19.7 (cutter)
DISP/LENGTH: 223.15
BALLAST RATIO: 36.36
FUEL/DISP: 2.32
FRESH WATER/DISP: 4.13

INTERIOR

BERTHS: 8 berths: 1 forward double, 1 double convertible settee, 1 double, 2 single pilots (custom layouts available)
TABLE: dinette
HEAD(S): 3 heads with 3 showers, 2 sump pumps, and 1 holding tank (30 gals.)
COLD STORAGE: built-in icebox
STOVE:
MAX. HEADROOM: 6 ft. 6 ins.

MACHINERY

ENGINE: 120 HP Perkins or Ford diesel
PROPELLER: 2- or 3-blade 23"x12" on a 2" shaft
GENERATOR:

DECK

STEERING: wheel with emergency tiller
WINCHES: 10 or 8 Lewmar winches:
schooner: 2 #65A ST, 4 #48A ST, 4 #30A
cutter: 2 #65A ST, 2 #42A ST, 1 #30A ST, 3 #30A
SAFETY: bow and stern pulpits with double lifelines
ANCHOR:
NAV LIGHTS:

RIG

TYPE: staysail schooner or cutter
RIGGING:
MAINSHEET:

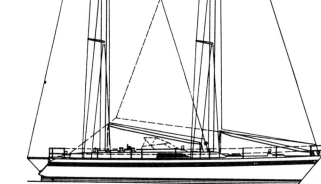

SAILS

SUPPLIED WITH BASE BOAT: schooner: 2 dacron staysails
cutter: main, staysail, yankee

WHITBY 55

DESIGNER:
BUILDER: Whitby Boat Works, Ltd.

STATISTICS

LOA: 55 ft. 0 ins.
LWL: 45 ft. 0 ins.
BEAM: 15 ft. 5 ins.
DISPLACEMENT
deep keel: 42,000 lbs.
shoal keel:
c/board:
BALLAST
deep keel: 16,800 lbs.
shoal keel:
c/board:
DRAFT
deep keel: 6 ft. 7.5 ins.
shoal keel:
c/board up:
c/board down:

SAIL AREA: 1,359 sq. ft.
FRESH WATER: 350 gals.
FUEL CAPACITY: 400 gals.

COSTS

BASE BOAT:
DATE:
EST. ON WATER:
DATE:

RATIOS

SAIL AREA/DISP: 17.99
DISP/LENGTH: 205
BALLAST RATIO: 40.00
FUEL/DISP: 7.14
FRESH WATER/DISP: 6.66

INTERIOR

BERTHS: 7 berths in 4 cabins: 1 single V pipe berth, 1 forward double, 2 single upper and lowers, 1 center aft double
TABLE: dinette
HEAD(S): 3 heads with 3 showers and 3 sump pumps
COLD STORAGE: refrigerator/freezer
STOVE: 3-burner LPG with oven
MAX. HEADROOM:

MACHINERY

ENGINE: 105 HP Volvo #MD30 diesel
PROPELLER: folding Weesco
GENERATOR:

DECK

STEERING: Edson wheel
WINCHES: 14 Barient winches: 2 primary (#36A ST), 2 secondary (#32A ST), 6 halyard (3 #27C & 3 #18), 1 mainsheet (#27A ST), 1 mizzen sheet (#19A ST), 2 outhaul/reefing (#12 & #10)
SAFETY: bow and stern pulpits with double lifelines
ANCHOR: 44 lb. Bruce anchor & 60 lb. Danforth anchor with anchor rollers and electric windlass
NAV LIGHTS: running and masthead

RIG

TYPE: masthead ketch
RIGGING: 1x19 SS wire
MAINSHEET: mid-boom sheeting

SAILS

SUPPLIED WITH BASE BOAT:

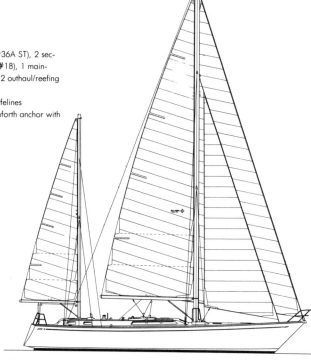

IRWIN CRUISING KETCH 52

DESIGNER: Ted Irwin
BUILDER: Irwin Yacht & Marine Corp.

STATISTICS

LOA: 56 ft. 0 ins.
LWL: 44 ft. 0 ins.
BEAM: 15 ft. 4 ins.
DISPLACEMENT
deep keel:
shoal keel: 46,500 lbs.
c/board:
BALLAST
deep keel:
shoal keel: 16,100 lbs.
c/board:
DRAFT
deep keel:
shoal keel: 5 ft. 6 ins.
c/board up: 5 ft. 6 ins.
c/board down: 12 ft. 6 ins.

SAIL AREA: 1,246 sq. ft.
FRESH WATER: 375 gals.
FUEL CAPACITY: 260 gals.

COSTS

BASE BOAT: $205,450
DATE: 06/01/85
EST. ON WATER:
DATE:

RATIOS

SAIL AREA/DISP: 15.42
DISP/LENGTH: 243.7
BALLAST RATIO: 34.62
FUEL/DISP: 4.19
FRESH WATER/DISP: 6.45

INTERIOR

BERTHS: 7 berths: 1 double V, 1 single settee, 1 double settee, 1 center aft double
TABLE: hi-lo
HEAD(S): 3 heads with 3 showers and 3 holding tanks (15 gals. each)
COLD STORAGE: built-in icebox (7.5 cu. ft.)
STOVE: 3-burner propane with oven
MAX. HEADROOM:

MACHINERY

ENGINE: 85 HP diesel with 2.5:1 reduction gear
PROPELLER: 3-blade
GENERATOR: 7.7 kW

DECK

STEERING: 28" wheel with emergency tiller
WINCHES: 8 winches: 2 primary, 3 halyard, 1 mainsheet, 1 mizzen sheet, 1 reefing
SAFETY: bow and stern pulpits with double lifelines
ANCHOR: anchor locker
NAV LIGHTS: running and masthead

RIG

TYPE: masthead ketch
RIGGING: wire (5/16")
MAINSHEET: 8-part with mid-boom sheeting

SAILS

SUPPLIED WITH BASE BOAT: main, working jib, mizzen

MAPLE LEAF 56

DESIGNER:
BUILDER: Cooper Yachts

STATISTICS

LOA: 56 ft. 4 ins.
LWL: 48 ft. 0 ins.
BEAM: 14 ft. 9 ins.
DISPLACEMENT
deep keel: 44,000 lbs.
shoal keel:
c/board:
BALLAST
deep keel: 12,500 lbs.
shoal keel:
c/board:
DRAFT
deep keel: 7 ft. 2 ins.
shoal keel:
c/board up:
c/board down:

SAIL AREA: 1,030 sq. ft.
FRESH WATER: 550 gals.
FUEL CAPACITY: 550 gals.

COSTS

BASE BOAT: $245,000
DATE:
EST. ON WATER: $275,000
DATE:

RATIOS

SAIL AREA/DISP: 13.22
DISP/LENGTH: 177.62
BALLAST RATIO: 28.41
FUEL/DISP: 9.38
FRESH WATER/DISP: 10.00

INTERIOR

BERTHS: 7 berths: 1 double V, 1 double convertible dinette, 1 single quarterberth, 1 center aft double
TABLE: fixed
HEAD(S): 2 heads with 2 showers, 2 sump pumps, and 1 holding tank
COLD STORAGE: refrigerator/freezer (12 cu. ft.)
STOVE: 4-burner LPG with oven
MAX. HEADROOM: 6 ft. 4 ins.

MACHINERY

ENGINE: 120 HP Ford or Perkins diesel
PROPELLER: fixed 24"x16" on 1 3/4" shaft
GENERATOR:

DECK

STEERING: wheel with emergency tiller
WINCHES: 6 Lewmar winches: 2 #55, 1 #43, 3 #36
SAFETY: bow and stern pulpits with double lifelines
ANCHOR: 45 lb. CQR anchor with anchor chain and winch
NAV LIGHTS: running and masthead

RIG

TYPE: masthead ketch
RIGGING: wire (5/16"–3/8")
MAINSHEET: 4-part with boom-end sheeting

SAILS

SUPPLIED WITH BASE BOAT: main, working jib, 150% genoa

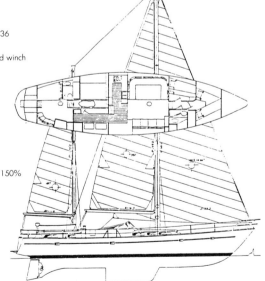

MOODY 58

DESIGNER: Bill Dixon-Angus Primrose, Ltd.
BUILDER: A. H. Moody & Son, Ltd.

STATISTICS

LOA: 57 ft. 6 ins.
LWL: 48 ft. 0 ins.
BEAM: 16 ft. 3 ins.
DISPLACEMENT
deep keel: 50,000 lbs.
shoal keel:
c/board:
BALLAST
deep keel: 20,000 lbs.
shoal keel:
c/board:
DRAFT
deep keel: 7 ft. 4 ins.
shoal keel:
c/board up:
c/board down:

SAIL AREA: 1,721 sq. ft.
FRESH WATER: 200 gals.
FUEL CAPACITY: 120 gals.

COSTS

BASE BOAT:
DATE:
EST. ON WATER:
DATE:

RATIOS

SAIL AREA/DISP: 20.29
DISP/LENGTH: 201.84
BALLAST RATIO: 40.00
FUEL/DISP: 1.80
FRESH WATER/DISP: 3.20

INTERIOR

BERTHS: 7 berths: 1 double settee, 3 single pilots, 1 double quarterberth, (other layouts available)
TABLE: dropleaf
HEAD(S): 2 heads with 2 showers and 2 sump pumps
COLD STORAGE: refrigerator/freezer (10 cu. ft.)
STOVE: 4-burner with oven
MAX. HEADROOM:

MACHINERY

ENGINE: 120 HP Perkins #G/3544 diesel with 2:1 reduction gear
PROPELLER: fixed on 2" shaft
GENERATOR:

DECK

STEERING: wheel with emergency tiller
WINCHES: 10 Lewmar winches: 2 #65, 3 #43 ST, 2 #43, 1 #48, 1 #16 ST, 1 #40
SAFETY: bow and stern pulpits with double lifelines
ANCHOR: anchor roller
NAV LIGHTS: running and masthead

RIG

TYPE: masthead sloop
RIGGING: wire
MAINSHEET:

SAILS

SUPPLIED WITH BASE BOAT:

SWAN 59

DESIGNER: German Frers
BUILDER: Nautor

STATISTICS

LOA: 58 ft. 10.6 ins.
LWL: 48 ft. 1.8 ins.
BEAM: 16 ft. 4.8 ins.
DISPLACEMENT
deep keel: 60,000 lbs.
shoal keel:
c/board:
BALLAST
deep keel: 20,300 lbs.
shoal keel:
c/board:
DRAFT
deep keel: 9 ft. 9.6 ins.
shoal keel:
c/board up:
c/board down:

SAIL AREA:
FRESH WATER: 277 gals.
FUEL CAPACITY: 185 gals.

COSTS

BASE BOAT:
DATE:
EST. ON WATER:
DATE:

RATIOS

SAIL AREA/DISP:
DISP/LENGTH: 239.95
BALLAST RATIO: 33.95
FUEL/DISP: 1.31
FRESH WATER/DISP: 3.69

INTERIOR

BERTHS: 8 berths: 4 single pilots, 1 center aft double or 2 single quarterberths, 2 pipe berths
TABLE: dropleaf
HEAD(S): 2 heads with 2 showers and 2 sump pumps
COLD STORAGE: built-in icebox and refrigerator/freezer (17.1 cu. ft. total)
STOVE: 3-burner gas with oven
MAX. HEADROOM:

MACHINERY

ENGINE: 86 HP Volvo #TMD 30 diesel with 2.73:1 reduction gear

PROPELLER: 23" folding
GENERATOR:

DECK

STEERING: 44" wheel with emergency tiller
WINCHES: 10 Lewmar winches: 3 #55A ST, 2 #65A ST, 4 #48A ST, 1 #46A ST
SAFETY: bow and stern pulpits with double lifelines
ANCHOR: Danforth 60H and CQR anchors with anchor roller and well
NAV LIGHTS: running and masthead

RIG

TYPE: masthead sloop
RIGGING: rod
MAINSHEET: mid-boom sheeting

SAILS

SUPPLIED WITH BASE BOAT:

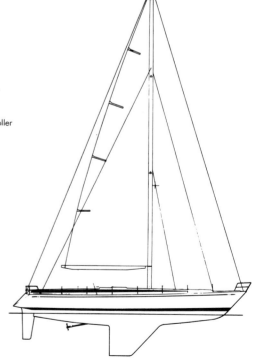

SOU'WESTER 59

DESIGNER: Hinckley
BUILDER: Henry R. Hinckley & Co.

STATISTICS

LOA: 59 ft. 3 ins.
LWL: 44 ft. 2 ins.
BEAM: 15 ft. 6 ins.
DISPLACEMENT
deep keel: 57,350 lbs.
shoal keel:
c/board:
BALLAST
deep keel: 23,250 lbs.
shoal keel:
c/board:
DRAFT
deep keel: 8 ft. 0 ins.
shoal keel:
c/board up: 6 ft. 6 ins.
c/board down: 12 ft. 6 ins.

SAIL AREA: 1,556 sq. ft.
FRESH WATER: 450 gals.
FUEL CAPACITY: 300 gals.

COSTS

BASE BOAT: $605,000
DATE: 06/85
EST. ON WATER: $685,000
DATE: 06/85

RATIOS

SAIL AREA/DISP: 16.74
DISP/LENGTH: 297
BALLAST RATIO: 40.54
FUEL/DISP: 3.92
FRESH WATER/DISP: 6.28

INTERIOR

BERTHS: 9 berths in 4 cabins: 2 sets of upper and lower singles in 2 forward cabins, 1 double extension in main cabin, 1 double and 1 single quarterberth in aft cabin
TABLE: hi-lo
HEAD(S): 3 heads with showers
COLD STORAGE: built-in icebox
STOVE: 3-burner LPG with oven
MAX. HEADROOM:

MACHINERY

ENGINE: Perkins #6.354 diesel with 2:1 reduction gear
PROPELLER: 3-blade 22" on 1 1/2" shaft
GENERATOR:

DECK

STEERING: 44" wheel with emergency tiller
WINCHES: 14 Barient winches
SAFETY: bow and stern pulpits with double lifelines
ANCHOR: anchor roller and well
NAV LIGHTS: running

RIG

TYPE: masthead ketch
RIGGING:
MAINSHEET: boom-end sheeting

SAILS

SUPPLIED WITH BASE BOAT:

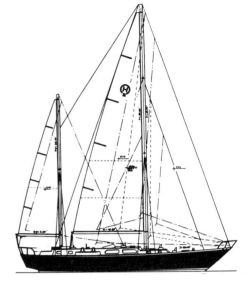

BUILDER'S COMMENTS An extremely comfortable mid-cockpit shoal draft cruising boat with a powerful rig. This large yacht can still be handled by an experienced couple. For the yachtsman who insists upon a minimum of compromise.

GRENADIER 183

DESIGNER: Laurent Giles & Partners, Ltd.
BUILDER: A. H. Moody & Son, Ltd.

STATISTICS

LOA: 60 ft. 0 ins.
LWL: 48 ft. 0 ins.
BEAM: 16 ft. 3 ins.
DISPLACEMENT
deep keel: 79,520 lbs.
shoal keel:
c/board:
BALLAST
deep keel: 28,000 lbs.
shoal keel:
c/board:
DRAFT
deep keel: 8 ft. 0 ins.
shoal keel:
c/board up:
c/board down:

SAIL AREA: 1,492 sq. ft.
FRESH WATER:
FUEL CAPACITY:

COSTS

BASE BOAT:
DATE:
EST. ON WATER:
DATE:

RATIOS

SAIL AREA/DISP: 12.91
DISP/LENGTH: 321.00
BALLAST RATIO: 35.21
FUEL/DISP:
FRESH WATER/DISP:

INTERIOR

BERTHS: 9 berths in 5 cabins: 2 single Vs, 1 forward single, 1 forward double, 2 single aft upper and lowers, 1 double quarterberth
TABLE: dropleaf
HEAD(S): 3 heads with 3 showers
COLD STORAGE: refrigerator/freezer (3.8 cu. ft.)
STOVE: 3-burner with oven
MAX. HEADROOM:

MACHINERY

ENGINE: owner's choice
PROPELLER:
GENERATOR:

DECK

STEERING: wheel
WINCHES:
SAFETY: bow and stern pulpits with double lifelines
ANCHOR: anchor roller
NAV LIGHTS:

RIG

TYPE: ketch
RIGGING:
MAINSHEET: boom-end sheeting

SAILS

SUPPLIED WITH BASE BOAT:

GULFSTAR 60 MARK II

DESIGNER: Richard C. Lazzara
BUILDER: Gulfstar Yacht Sales

STATISTICS

LOA: 60 ft. 6 ins.
LWL: 48 ft. 4 ins.
BEAM: 16 ft. 0 ins.
DISPLACEMENT
deep keel: 60,200 lbs.
shoal keel:
c/board:
BALLAST
deep keel: 16,800 lbs.
shoal keel:
c/board:
DRAFT
deep keel: 6 ft. 2 ins.
shoal keel:
c/board up:
c/board down:

SAIL AREA: 1,576 sq. ft.
FRESH WATER: 250 gals.
FUEL CAPACITY: 330 gals.

COSTS

BASE BOAT: $289,500
DATE: 04/85
EST. ON WATER:
DATE:

RATIOS

SAIL AREA/DISP: 16.4
DISP/LENGTH: 239.3
BALLAST RATIO: 28.
FUEL/DISP: 4.1
FRESH WATER/DISP: 3.3

DECK

STEERING: 48" wheel with emergency tiller
WINCHES: 6 Barient winches: 2 primary (#35 2sp ST), 2 halyard (#27 2sp and #25 2sp), 1 mainsheet (#27 2sp ST), 1 reefing (#25 2sp)
SAFETY: bow and stern pulpits with double lifelines
ANCHOR: anchor roller
NAV LIGHTS: running and masthead

RIG

TYPE: masthead sloop
RIGGING:
MAINSHEET: mid-boom sheeting

SAILS

SUPPLIED WITH BASE BOAT:

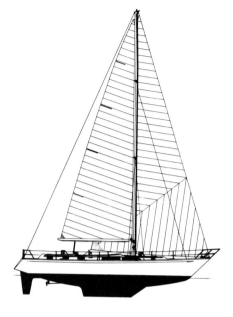

INTERIOR

BERTHS: 11 berths in 4 cabins: 3 single uppers and 3 double convertible lowers, 1 center aft double
TABLE: dropleaf
HEAD(S): 3 heads with 3 showers
COLD STORAGE: built-in icebox and refrigerator/freezer
STOVE: 3-burner propane with oven, broiler, and microwave
MAX. HEADROOM:

MACHINERY

ENGINE: 135 HP Perkins #6-354.4 diesel with 2.5:1 reduction gear
PROPELLER: 3-blade on 1½" shaft
GENERATOR: 8 kW Onan

SWAN 61

DESIGNER: German Frers
BUILDER: Nautor

STATISTICS

LOA: 60 ft. 6.00 ins.
LWL: 48 ft. 1.75 ins.
BEAM: 16 ft. 1.75 ins.
DISPLACEMENT
deep keel: 61,000 lbs.
shoal keel:
c/board:
BALLAST
deep keel: 20,300 lbs.
shoal keel:
c/board:
DRAFT
deep keel: 9 ft. 9 ins.
shoal keel:
c/board up:
c/board down:

SAIL AREA:
FRESH WATER: 277 gals.
FUEL CAPACITY: 185 gals.

COSTS

BASE BOAT:
DATE:
EST. ON WATER:
DATE:

RATIOS

SAIL AREA/DISP:
DISP/LENGTH: 244.1
BALLAST RATIO: 33.28
FUEL/DISP: 2.27
FRESH WATER/DISP: 3.63

DECK

STEERING: 44" wheel with emergency tiller
WINCHES: 9 Lewmar winches: 3 #55A ST, 4 #48A ST, 2 #46A ST
SAFETY: bow and stern pulpits with double lifelines
ANCHOR: 60 lb. Danforth and 75 lb. CQR anchors with anchor roller and well
NAV LIGHTS: running and masthead

RIG

TYPE: masthead sloop
RIGGING: rod
MAINSHEET:

SAILS

SUPPLIED WITH BASE BOAT:

INTERIOR

BERTHS: 10 berths
TABLE: folding
HEAD(S): 2 heads with 2 showers and 2 sump pumps
COLD STORAGE: refrigerator/freezer (5.3 cu. ft.)
STOVE: 3-burner gas with oven
MAX. HEADROOM:

MACHINERY

ENGINE: Volvo diesel with 2.73:1 reduction gear
PROPELLER: feathering
GENERATOR:

MASON 63

DESIGNER: Al Mason
BUILDER: Pacific Asian Enterprises, Inc.

STATISTICS

LOA: 63 ft. 7 ins.
LWL: 46 ft. 8 ins.
BEAM: 16 ft. 6 ins.
DISPLACEMENT
deep keel: 64,400 lbs.
shoal keel:
c/board:
BALLAST
deep keel: 15,000 lbs.
shoal keel:
c/board:
DRAFT
deep keel: 7 ft. 0 ins.
shoal keel:
c/board up:
c/board down:

SAIL AREA: 1,632 sq. ft.
FRESH WATER: 400 gals.
FUEL CAPACITY: 700 gals.

COSTS

BASE BOAT:
DATE:
EST. ON WATER:
DATE:

RATIOS

SAIL AREA/DISP: 16.25
DISP/LENGTH: 283.0
BALLAST RATIO: 23.3
FUEL/DISP: 4.7
FRESH WATER/DISP: 8.7

DECK

STEERING: wheel
WINCHES: Lewmar self-tailing with electric sheeting
SAFETY: bow and stern pulpits with double lifelines
ANCHOR:
NAV LIGHTS: running and masthead

RIG

TYPE: masthead ketch with Forespar spars
RIGGING:
MAINSHEET: boom-end sheeting

SAILS

SUPPLIED WITH BASE BOAT: main, mizzen, staysail, topsail

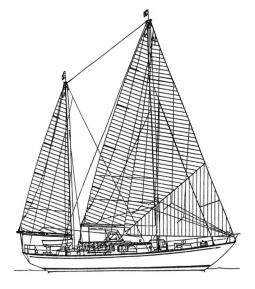

INTERIOR

BERTHS: 3 interior options
TABLE:
HEAD(S): 2 heads with 2 showers
COLD STORAGE:
STOVE:
MAX. HEADROOM:

MACHINERY

ENGINE: 140 HP GMC #4 53 diesel
PROPELLER:
GENERATOR: 7.7 kW Westerbeke

CT-65

DESIGNER: Robert H. Perry
DISTRIBUTOR: Ta Chiao USA, Inc. (built in Taiwan by Ta Chiao Bros. Yacht Building Co.)

STATISTICS

LOA: 64 ft. 10 ins.
LWL: 50 ft. 10 ins.
BEAM: 17 ft. 6 ins.
DISPLACEMENT
deep keel: 77,383 lbs.
shoal keel:
c/board:
BALLAST
deep keel: 26,000 lbs.
shoal keel:
c/board:
DRAFT
deep keel: 7 ft. 0 ins.
shoal keel:
c/board up:
c/board down:

SAIL AREA: 1,800 sq. ft.
FRESH WATER: 500 gals.
FUEL CAPACITY: 600 gals.

COSTS

BASE BOAT: $415,000
DATE: 07/15/85
EST. ON WATER: $456,500
DATE: 07/15/85

RATIOS

SAIL AREA/DISP: 15.86
DISP/LENGTH: 262.89
BALLAST RATIO: 33.6
FUEL/DISP: 5.82
FRESH WATER/DISP: 5.17

DECK

STEERING: wheel with emergency tiller
WINCHES: 19 Barlow 2sp ST winches
SAFETY: bow and stern pulpits with double lifelines
ANCHOR: anchor roller and well
NAV LIGHTS: running and masthead

RIG

TYPE: masthead ketch
RIGGING: wire
MAINSHEET: mid-boom sheeting

SAILS

SUPPLIED WITH BASE BOAT: main, staysail, yankee, mizzen

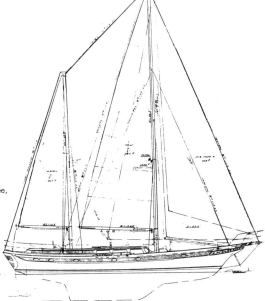

INTERIOR

BERTHS: 8–10 berths: 1 double V, 4–6 single pilots, 1 center aft double
TABLE: fixed
HEAD(S): 4 heads with 3 showers, 3 sump pumps, and 2 holding tanks
COLD STORAGE: refrigerator/freezer (15–18 cu. ft.)
STOVE: 3-burner propane with oven
MAX. HEADROOM: 6 ft. 10 ins.

MACHINERY

ENGINE: 200 HP Perkins diesel with 2.9:1 reduction gear
PROPELLER: fixed on 2" shaft
GENERATOR: 12.5 kW Onan

BUILDER'S COMMENTS The CT-65 is one of Bob Perry's finest designs. An extension of the CT-54, she is part of the ocean clipper line of cruising boats. Traditional in appearance, she is nevertheless a very modern boat with a long fin keel and skeg rudder capable of speeds of eleven knots. She is an exceptional sailer. Seven boats have been sold in the first two years. She is being built with a Lloyd's, ABS, or Bureau Veritas 100A1 Certificate. Beautiful on deck and below.

MACGREGOR 65

DESIGNER:
BUILDER: MacGregor Yacht Corporation

STATISTICS

LOA: 65 ft. 0 ins.
LWL: 63 ft. 0 ins.
BEAM: 11 ft. 8 ins.
DISPLACEMENT
deep keel: 21,000 lbs.
shoal keel:
c/board:
BALLAST
deep keel: 9,000 lbs.
shoal keel:
c/board:
DRAFT
deep keel:
shoal keel:
c/board up:
c/board down:

SAIL AREA: 1,632 sq. ft.
FRESH WATER:
FUEL CAPACITY:

COSTS

BASE BOAT:
DATE:
EST. ON WATER:
DATE:

RATIOS

SAIL AREA/DISP: 34.31
DISP/LENGTH: 37.49
BALLAST RATIO: 42.86
FUEL/DISP:
FRESH WATER/DISP:

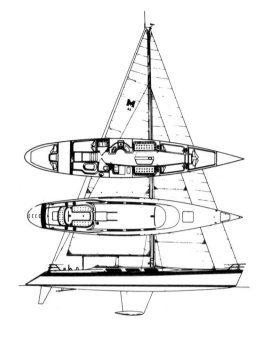

DECK

STEERING: wheel
WINCHES:
SAFETY: bow and stern pulpits with double lifelines
ANCHOR:
NAV LIGHTS:

RIG

TYPE: masthead cutter
RIGGING:
MAINSHEET: mid-boom sheeting

SAILS

SUPPLIED WITH BASE BOAT: main, working jib

INTERIOR

BERTHS: 10 berths: 1 double V, 2 single settees, 1 double quarterberth, 2 single pilots, 1 center aft double
TABLE: dropleaf
HEAD(S): 1 head with bathtub
COLD STORAGE:
STOVE: 3-burner
MAX. HEADROOM: 6 ft. 7 ins.

MACHINERY

ENGINE: 80 HP Pathfinder diesel
PROPELLER:
GENERATOR:

GRENADIER 206

DESIGNER: hull and sail plan—Nicholson 70, deck and interior—Laurent Giles
BUILDER: A. H. Moody & Son, Ltd.

STATISTICS

LOA: 67 ft. 6 ins.
LWL: 54 ft. 6 ins.
BEAM: 17 ft. 1 ins.
DISPLACEMENT
deep keel:
shoal keel:
c/board:
BALLAST
deep keel:
shoal keel:
c/board:
DRAFT
deep keel: 8 ft. 6 ins.
shoal keel:
c/board up:
c/board down:

SAIL AREA: 2,148 sq. ft.
FRESH WATER:
FUEL CAPACITY:

COSTS

BASE BOAT:
DATE:
EST. ON WATER:
DATE:

RATIOS

SAIL AREA/DISP:
DISP/LENGTH:
BALLAST RATIO:
FUEL/DISP:
FRESH WATER/DISP:

MACHINERY

ENGINE:
PROPELLER:
GENERATOR:

DECK

STEERING: wheel
WINCHES:
SAFETY:
ANCHOR:
NAV LIGHTS:

RIG

TYPE: ketch
RIGGING:
MAINSHEET:

SAILS

SUPPLIED WITH BASE BOAT:

INTERIOR

BERTHS: 13 berths in 8 cabins: 2 single Vs, 1 forward single, 2 forward single upper and lowers, 1 forward double, 1 single pilot, 1 aft single, 2 single aft upper and lowers, 1 double quarterberth
TABLE: 2 dropleaf
HEAD(S): 3 heads with 3 showers
COLD STORAGE: refrigerator/freezer
STOVE: 4-burner with oven
MAX. HEADROOM:

SWAN 651

DESIGNER: German Frers
BUILDER: Nautor

STATISTICS

LOA: 65 ft. 6.6 ins.
LWL: 55 ft. 1.4 ins.
BEAM: 17 ft. 4.7 ins.
DISPLACEMENT
deep keel: 75,000 lbs.
shoal keel:
c/board
BALLAST
deep keel: 31,700 lbs.
shoal keel:
c/board:
DRAFT
deep keel: 11 ft. 6 ins.
shoal keel:
c/board up:
c/board down:

SAIL AREA:
FRESH WATER: 370 gals.
FUEL CAPACITY: 264 gals.

COSTS

BASE BOAT:
DATE:
EST. ON WATER:
DATE:

RATIOS

SAIL AREA/DISP:
DISP/LENGTH: 199.93
BALLAST RATIO: 42.27
FUEL/DISP: 2.64
FRESH WATER/DISP: 3.95

DECK

STEERING: 70" wheel with emergency tiller
WINCHES: 18 Lewmar winches: 2 grinders (#98), 3 #55 AP, 2 #65 AP, 2 #70A ST, 2 #65A ST, 2 #44A ST, 5 #48A ST
SAFETY: bow and stern pulpits with double lifelines
ANCHOR: Danforth 60H and 75 lb. CQR anchors with anchor well
NAV LIGHTS: running and masthead

RIG

TYPE: masthead sloop (ketch also available)
RIGGING: rod
MAINSHEET: boom-end sheeting

SAILS

SUPPLIED WITH BASE BOAT:

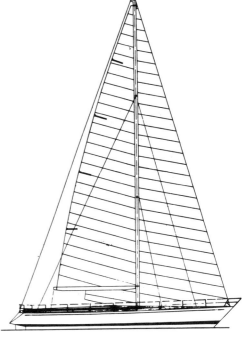

INTERIOR

BERTHS: 10 berths: 5 single pilots, 1 single quarterberth, 1 double quarterberth, 2 single pipe berths
TABLE: dropleaf
HEAD(S): 3 heads with 3 showers and 3 sump pumps
COLD STORAGE: refrigerator/freezer
STOVE: 4-burner gas with oven
MAX. HEADROOM:

MACHINERY

ENGINE: 115 HP Perkins #6.3544 diesel with 3:1 reduction gear
PROPELLER: 30" folding
GENERATOR: 8 kW G&M

LA FITTE 66

DESIGNER: Robert H. Perry
BUILDER: La Fitte Yachts, Inc.

STATISTICS

LOA: 66 ft. 0.00 ins.
LWL: 52 ft. 3.25 ins.
BEAM: 16 ft. 8.00 ins.
DISPLACEMENT
deep keel: 66,794 lbs.
shoal keel:
c/board:
BALLAST
deep keel: 23,000 lbs.
shoal keel:
c/board:
DRAFT
deep keel: 6 ft. 9 ins.
shoal keel:
c/board up:
c/board down:

SAIL AREA: 1,623 sq. ft.
FRESH WATER: 700 gals.
FUEL CAPACITY: 700 gals.

COSTS

BASE BOAT: $650,000
DATE: 07/01/85
EST. ON WATER:
DATE:

RATIOS

SAIL AREA/DISP: 15.77
DISP/LENGTH: 208.79
BALLAST RATIO: 34.43
FUEL/DISP: 7.86
FRESH WATER/DISP: 8.38

DECK

STEERING: 44" wheel
WINCHES: 13 Lewmar winches: 6 sheet, 5 halyard, 2 outhaul and reefing
SAFETY: bow and stern pulpits with double lifelines
ANCHOR: anchor with anchor chain, double rollers, and electric windlass
NAV LIGHTS: running and masthead

RIG

TYPE: masthead ketch
RIGGING: 1x19 Nitronic 50 wire
MAINSHEET: boom-end sheeting

SAILS

SUPPLIED WITH BASE BOAT:

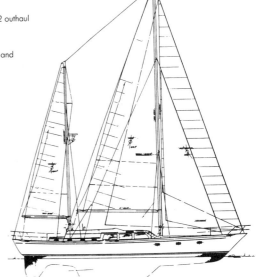

INTERIOR

BERTHS: 8 berths in 4 staterooms: 2 single Vs, 1 forward double, 2 single pilots, 1 center aft double
TABLE: dinette
HEAD(S): 5 heads with 5 showers and 1 bathtub
COLD STORAGE: refrigerator/freezer (12 cu. ft.)
STOVE: LPG with oven
MAX. HEADROOM: 6 ft. 6 ins.

MACHINERY

ENGINE: 130 HP Perkins #6.354 diesel with 2:1 reduction gear
PROPELLER: three-blade on 1½" shaft
GENERATOR: Koehler and Power Genny

MAPLE LEAF 68

DESIGNER:
BUILDER: Cooper Yachts

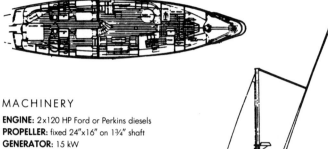

STATISTICS

LOA: 67 ft. 8 ins.
LWL: 56 ft. 0 ins.
BEAM: 17 ft. 10 ins.
DISPLACEMENT
deep keel: 72,000 lbs.
shoal keel:
c/board:
BALLAST
deep keel: 21,000 lbs.
shoal keel:
c/board:
DRAFT
deep keel: 6 ft. 6 ins.
shoal keel:
c/board up:
c/board down:

SAIL AREA: 1,855 sq. ft.
FRESH WATER: 1,000 gals.
FUEL CAPACITY: 1,000 gals.

COSTS

BASE BOAT:
DATE:
EST. ON WATER:
DATE:

RATIOS

SAIL AREA/DISP: 17.15
DISP/LENGTH: 183.03
BALLAST RATIO: 29.17
FUEL/DISP: 10.42
FRESH WATER/DISP: 11.11

INTERIOR

BERTHS: 10 berths in 5 cabins: 2 sets of single upper and lowers in 2 forward cabins, 2 pairs of singles in port and starboard cabins, 1 center double in aft cabin
TABLE: fixed
HEAD(S): 3 heads with 3 showers, 3 sump pumps, and 2 holding tanks
COLD STORAGE: refrigerator/freezer (20 cu. ft.)
STOVE: 4-burner LPG with oven
MAX. HEADROOM: 6 ft. 6 ins.

MACHINERY

ENGINE: 2x120 HP Ford or Perkins diesels
PROPELLER: fixed 24"x16" on 1¾" shaft
GENERATOR: 15 kW

DECK

STEERING: wheel with emergency tiller
WINCHES: 8 Lewmar winches: 2 #65, 2 #48, 2 #40, 2 #36
SAFETY: bow and stern pulpits with double lifelines
ANCHOR: 65 lb. CQR anchor with anchor chain and winch
NAV LIGHTS: running and masthead

RIG

TYPE: masthead ketch
RIGGING: wire (⅜"–⁹⁄₁₆")
MAINSHEET: 4-part with boom-end sheeting

SAILS

SUPPLIED WITH BASE BOAT: main, working jib, 150% genoa, mizzen

---

IRWIN CRUISING KETCH 65

DESIGNER: Ted Irwin
BUILDER: Irwin Yacht & Marine Corp.

STATISTICS

LOA: 72 ft. 2 ins.
LWL: 54 ft. 0 ins.
BEAM: 17 ft. 4 ins.
DISPLACEMENT
deep keel:
shoal keel: 78,500 lbs.
c/board:
BALLAST
deep keel:
shoal keel: 23,000 lbs.
c/board:
DRAFT
deep keel:
shoal keel: 5 ft. 9 ins.
c/board up: 5 ft. 9 ins.
c/board down: 14 ft. 6 ins.

SAIL AREA:
FRESH WATER: 900 gals.
FUEL CAPACITY: 620 gals.

COSTS

BASE BOAT: $395,450
DATE: 06/01/85
EST. ON WATER:
DATE:

RATIOS

SAIL AREA/DISP:
DISP/LENGTH: 222.56
BALLAST RATIO: 29.29
FUEL/DISP: 5.92
FRESH WATER/DISP: 9.17

INTERIOR

BERTHS: 9 berths: 1 double V, 1 forward double, 1 single settee, 2 single pilots, 1 center aft double (other interiors available)
TABLE: hi-lo
HEAD(S): 3 heads with 3 showers and 3 holding tanks (15 gals. each)
COLD STORAGE: refrigerator/freezer (14 cu. ft.)
STOVE: 3-burner propane with oven
MAX. HEADROOM:

MACHINERY

ENGINE: 130 HP diesel with 2.5:1 reduction gear
PROPELLER: 3-blade
GENERATOR: 12.5 kW

DECK

STEERING: 36" wheel with emergency tiller
WINCHES: 9 winches: 2 primary, 3 halyard, 1 mainsheet, 1 mizzen sheet, 2 reefing
SAFETY: bow and stern pulpits with double lifelines
ANCHOR: anchor locker
NAV LIGHTS: running and masthead

RIG

TYPE: masthead ketch
RIGGING: wire (½")
MAINSHEET: 8-part with mid-boom sheeting

SAILS

SUPPLIED WITH BASE BOAT: main, working jib, mizzen

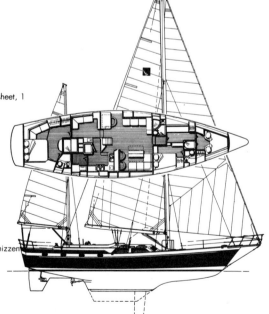

HARTMANN—PALMER 75 MOTORSAILER ──────────

DESIGNER: Ted Hood, Seaton and Neville
BUILDER: Hartmann—Palmer Yachts, Inc.

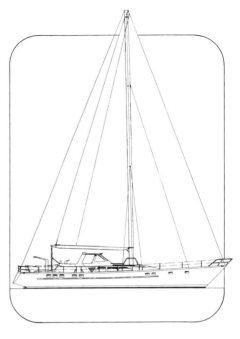

STATISTICS

LOA: 75 ft. 0 ins.
LWL: 62 ft. 6 ins.
BEAM: 18 ft. 5 ins.
DISPLACEMENT
deep keel: 118,000 lbs.
shoal keel:
c/board:
BALLAST
deep keel:
shoal keel:
c/board:
DRAFT
deep keel:
shoal keel:
c/board up: 6 ft. 1 ins.
c/board down: 13 ft. 9 ins.

SAIL AREA: 2,428 sq. ft.
FRESH WATER: 900 gals.
FUEL CAPACITY: 1,000 gals.

COSTS

BASE BOAT:
DATE:
EST. ON WATER:
DATE:

RATIOS

SAIL AREA/DISP: 16.15
DISP/LENGTH: 221.0
BALLAST RATIO:
FUEL/DISP: 6.3
FRESH WATER/DISP: 5.7

DECK

STEERING:
WINCHES:
SAFETY: bow and stern pulpits with double lifelines
ANCHOR:
NAV LIGHTS:

RIG

TYPE: masthead sloop
RIGGING:
MAINSHEET: boom-end sheeting

SAILS

SUPPLIED WITH BASE BOAT:

INTERIOR

BERTHS: 8 berths: 1 double, 6 singles
TABLE: dropleaf
HEAD(S): 4 heads with 2 showers
COLD STORAGE:
STOVE: 4-burner with oven
MAX. HEADROOM:

MACHINERY

ENGINE:
PROPELLER:
GENERATOR:

Appendixes

BLANK DATA SHEETS ───

BOAT NAME:
DESIGNER:
BUILDER:

STATISTICS

LOA:
LWL:
BEAM:
DISPLACEMENT
deep keel:
shoal keel:
c/board:
BALLAST
deep keel:
shoal keel:
c/board:
DRAFT
deep keel:
shoal keel:
c/board up:
c/board down:
SAIL AREA:
FRESH WATER:
FUEL CAPACITY:

COSTS

BASE BOAT:
DATE:
EST. ON WATER:
DATE:

RATIOS

SAIL AREA/DISP:
DISP/LENGTH:
BALLAST RATIO:
FUEL/DISP:
FRESH WATER/DISP:

INTERIOR

BERTHS:
TABLE:
HEAD (S):
COLD STORAGE:
STOVE:
MAX. HEADROOM:

MACHINERY

ENGINE:
PROPELLER:
GENERATOR:

DECK

STEERING:
WINCHES:
SAFETY:
ANCHOR:
NAV LIGHTS:

RIG

TYPE:
RIGGING:
MAINSHEET:

SAILS

SUPPLIED WITH BASE BOAT:

BLANK DATA SHEETS ───

BOAT NAME:
DESIGNER:
BUILDER:

STATISTICS

LOA:
LWL:
BEAM:
DISPLACEMENT
deep keel:
shoal keel:
c/board:
BALLAST
deep keel:
shoal keel:
c/board:
DRAFT
deep keel:
shoal keel:
c/board up:
c/board down:
SAIL AREA:
FRESH WATER:
FUEL CAPACITY:

COSTS

BASE BOAT:
DATE:
EST. ON WATER:
DATE:

RATIOS

SAIL AREA/DISP:
DISP/LENGTH:
BALLAST RATIO:
FUEL/DISP:
FRESH WATER/DISP:

INTERIOR

BERTHS:
TABLE:
HEAD (S):
COLD STORAGE:
STOVE:
MAX. HEADROOM:

MACHINERY

ENGINE:
PROPELLER:
GENERATOR:

DECK

STEERING:
WINCHES:
SAFETY:
ANCHOR:
NAV LIGHTS:

RIG

TYPE:
RIGGING:
MAINSHEET:

SAILS

SUPPLIED WITH BASE BOAT:

APPENDIX A

BLANK DATA SHEETS

BOAT NAME:
DESIGNER:
BUILDER:

STATISTICS

LOA:
LWL:
BEAM:
DISPLACEMENT
deep keel:
shoal keel:
c/board:
BALLAST
deep keel:
shoal keel:
c/board:
DRAFT
deep keel:
shoal keel:
c/board up:
c/board down:
SAIL AREA:
FRESH WATER:
FUEL CAPACITY:

COSTS

BASE BOAT:
DATE:
EST. ON WATER:
DATE:

RATIOS

SAIL AREA/DISP:
DISP/LENGTH:
BALLAST RATIO:
FUEL/DISP:
FRESH WATER/DISP:

INTERIOR

BERTHS:
TABLE:
HEAD (S):
COLD STORAGE:
STOVE:
MAX. HEADROOM:

MACHINERY

ENGINE:
PROPELLER:
GENERATOR:

DECK

STEERING:
WINCHES:
SAFETY:
ANCHOR:
NAV LIGHTS:

RIG

TYPE:
RIGGING:
MAINSHEET:

SAILS

SUPPLIED WITH BASE BOAT:

BLANK DATA SHEETS

BOAT NAME:
DESIGNER:
BUILDER:

STATISTICS

LOA:
LWL:
BEAM:
DISPLACEMENT
deep keel:
shoal keel:
c/board:
BALLAST
deep keel:
shoal keel:
c/board:
DRAFT
deep keel:
shoal keel:
c/board up:
c/board down:
SAIL AREA:
FRESH WATER:
FUEL CAPACITY:

COSTS

BASE BOAT:
DATE:
EST. ON WATER:
DATE:

RATIOS

SAIL AREA/DISP:
DISP/LENGTH:
BALLAST RATIO:
FUEL/DISP:
FRESH WATER/DISP:

INTERIOR

BERTHS:
TABLE:
HEAD (S):
COLD STORAGE:
STOVE:
MAX. HEADROOM:

MACHINERY

ENGINE:
PROPELLER:
GENERATOR:

DECK

STEERING:
WINCHES:
SAFETY:
ANCHOR:
NAV LIGHTS:

RIG

TYPE:
RIGGING:
MAINSHEET:

SAILS

SUPPLIED WITH BASE BOAT:

BLANK DATA SHEETS

BOAT NAME:
DESIGNER:
BUILDER:

STATISTICS

LOA:
LWL:
BEAM:
DISPLACEMENT
deep keel:
shoal keel:
c/board:
BALLAST
deep keel:
shoal keel:
c/board:
DRAFT
deep keel:
shoal keel:
c/board up:
c/board down:
SAIL AREA:
FRESH WATER:
FUEL CAPACITY:

COSTS

BASE BOAT:
DATE:
EST. ON WATER:
DATE:

RATIOS

SAIL AREA/DISP:
DISP/LENGTH:
BALLAST RATIO:
FUEL/DISP:
FRESH WATER/DISP:

INTERIOR

BERTHS:
TABLE:
HEAD (S):
COLD STORAGE:
STOVE:
MAX. HEADROOM:

MACHINERY

ENGINE:
PROPELLER:
GENERATOR:

DECK

STEERING:
WINCHES:
SAFETY:
ANCHOR:
NAV LIGHTS:

RIG

TYPE:
RIGGING:
MAINSHEET:

SAILS

SUPPLIED WITH BASE BOAT:

BLANK DATA SHEETS

BOAT NAME:
DESIGNER:
BUILDER:

STATISTICS

LOA:
LWL:
BEAM:
DISPLACEMENT
deep keel:
shoal keel:
c/board:
BALLAST
deep keel:
shoal keel:
c/board:
DRAFT
deep keel:
shoal keel:
c/board up:
c/board down:
SAIL AREA:
FRESH WATER:
FUEL CAPACITY:

COSTS

BASE BOAT:
DATE:
EST. ON WATER:
DATE:

RATIOS

SAIL AREA/DISP:
DISP/LENGTH:
BALLAST RATIO:
FUEL/DISP:
FRESH WATER/DISP:

INTERIOR

BERTHS:
TABLE:
HEAD (S):
COLD STORAGE:
STOVE:
MAX. HEADROOM:

MACHINERY

ENGINE:
PROPELLER:
GENERATOR:

DECK

STEERING:
WINCHES:
SAFETY:
ANCHOR:
NAV LIGHTS:

RIG

TYPE:
RIGGING:
MAINSHEET:

SAILS

SUPPLIED WITH BASE BOAT:

BLANK DATA SHEETS —————————————————

BOAT NAME:
DESIGNER:
BUILDER:

STATISTICS

LOA:
LWL:
BEAM:
DISPLACEMENT
deep keel:
shoal keel:
c/board:
BALLAST
deep keel:
shoal keel:
c/board:
DRAFT
deep keel:
shoal keel:
c/board up:
c/board down:
SAIL AREA:
FRESH WATER:
FUEL CAPACITY:

COSTS

BASE BOAT:
DATE:
EST. ON WATER:
DATE:

RATIOS

SAIL AREA/DISP:
DISP/LENGTH:
BALLAST RATIO:
FUEL/DISP:
FRESH WATER/DISP:

INTERIOR

BERTHS:
TABLE:
HEAD (S):
COLD STORAGE:
STOVE:
MAX. HEADROOM:

MACHINERY

ENGINE:
PROPELLER:
GENERATOR:

DECK

STEERING:
WINCHES:
SAFETY:
ANCHOR:
NAV LIGHTS:

RIG

TYPE:
RIGGING:
MAINSHEET:

SAILS

SUPPLIED WITH BASE BOAT:

BLANK DATA SHEETS —————————————————

BOAT NAME:
DESIGNER:
BUILDER:

STATISTICS

LOA:
LWL:
BEAM:
DISPLACEMENT
deep keel:
shoal keel:
c/board:
BALLAST
deep keel:
shoal keel:
c/board:
DRAFT
deep keel:
shoal keel:
c/board up:
c/board down:
SAIL AREA:
FRESH WATER:
FUEL CAPACITY:

COSTS

BASE BOAT:
DATE:
EST. ON WATER:
DATE:

RATIOS

SAIL AREA/DISP:
DISP/LENGTH:
BALLAST RATIO:
FUEL/DISP:
FRESH WATER/DISP:

INTERIOR

BERTHS:
TABLE:
HEAD (S):
COLD STORAGE:
STOVE:
MAX. HEADROOM:

MACHINERY

ENGINE:
PROPELLER:
GENERATOR:

DECK

STEERING:
WINCHES:
SAFETY:
ANCHOR:
NAV LIGHTS:

RIG

TYPE:
RIGGING:
MAINSHEET:

SAILS

SUPPLIED WITH BASE BOAT:

BLANK DATA SHEETS ———

BOAT NAME:
DESIGNER:
BUILDER:

STATISTICS

LOA:
LWL:
BEAM:
DISPLACEMENT
deep keel:
shoal keel:
c/board:
BALLAST
deep keel:
shoal keel:
c/board:
DRAFT
deep keel:
shoal keel:
c/board up:
c/board down:
SAIL AREA:
FRESH WATER:
FUEL CAPACITY:

COSTS

BASE BOAT:
DATE:
EST. ON WATER:
DATE:

RATIOS

SAIL AREA/DISP:
DISP/LENGTH:
BALLAST RATIO:
FUEL/DISP:
FRESH WATER/DISP:

INTERIOR

BERTHS:
TABLE:
HEAD (S):
COLD STORAGE:
STOVE:
MAX. HEADROOM:

MACHINERY

ENGINE:
PROPELLER:
GENERATOR:

DECK

STEERING:
WINCHES:
SAFETY:
ANCHOR:
NAV LIGHTS:

RIG

TYPE:
RIGGING:
MAINSHEET:

SAILS

SUPPLIED WITH BASE BOAT:

BLANK DATA SHEETS ———

BOAT NAME:
DESIGNER:
BUILDER:

STATISTICS

LOA:
LWL:
BEAM:
DISPLACEMENT
deep keel:
shoal keel:
c/board:
BALLAST
deep keel:
shoal keel:
c/board:
DRAFT
deep keel:
shoal keel:
c/board up:
c/board down:
SAIL AREA:
FRESH WATER:
FUEL CAPACITY:

COSTS

BASE BOAT:
DATE:
EST. ON WATER:
DATE:

RATIOS

SAIL AREA/DISP:
DISP/LENGTH:
BALLAST RATIO:
FUEL/DISP:
FRESH WATER/DISP:

INTERIOR

BERTHS:
TABLE:
HEAD (S):
COLD STORAGE:
STOVE:
MAX. HEADROOM:

MACHINERY

ENGINE:
PROPELLER:
GENERATOR:

DECK

STEERING:
WINCHES:
SAFETY:
ANCHOR:
NAV LIGHTS:

RIG

TYPE:
RIGGING:
MAINSHEET:

SAILS

SUPPLIED WITH BASE BOAT:

BLANK DATA SHEETS

BOAT NAME:
DESIGNER:
BUILDER:

STATISTICS

LOA:
LWL:
BEAM:
DISPLACEMENT
deep keel:
shoal keel:
c/board:
BALLAST
deep keel:
shoal keel:
c/board:
DRAFT
deep keel:
shoal keel:
c/board up:
c/board down:
SAIL AREA:
FRESH WATER:
FUEL CAPACITY:

COSTS

BASE BOAT:
DATE:
EST. ON WATER:
DATE:

RATIOS

SAIL AREA/DISP:
DISP/LENGTH:
BALLAST RATIO:
FUEL/DISP:
FRESH WATER/DISP:

INTERIOR

BERTHS:
TABLE:
HEAD (S):
COLD STORAGE:
STOVE:
MAX. HEADROOM:

MACHINERY

ENGINE:
PROPELLER:
GENERATOR:

DECK

STEERING:
WINCHES:
SAFETY:
ANCHOR:
NAV LIGHTS:

RIG

TYPE:
RIGGING:
MAINSHEET:

SAILS

SUPPLIED WITH BASE BOAT:

BLANK DATA SHEETS

BOAT NAME:
DESIGNER:
BUILDER:

STATISTICS

LOA:
LWL:
BEAM:
DISPLACEMENT
deep keel:
shoal keel:
c/board:
BALLAST
deep keel:
shoal keel:
c/board:
DRAFT
deep keel:
shoal keel:
c/board up:
c/board down:
SAIL AREA:
FRESH WATER:
FUEL CAPACITY:

COSTS

BASE BOAT:
DATE:
EST. ON WATER:
DATE:

RATIOS

SAIL AREA/DISP:
DISP/LENGTH:
BALLAST RATIO:
FUEL/DISP:
FRESH WATER/DISP:

INTERIOR

BERTHS:
TABLE:
HEAD (S):
COLD STORAGE:
STOVE:
MAX. HEADROOM:

MACHINERY

ENGINE:
PROPELLER:
GENERATOR:

DECK

STEERING:
WINCHES:
SAFETY:
ANCHOR:
NAV LIGHTS:

RIG

TYPE:
RIGGING:
MAINSHEET:

SAILS

SUPPLIED WITH BASE BOAT:

ADDRESSES OF BUILDERS AND DISTRIBUTORS

A. H. Moody & Son, Ltd.
Swanwick Shore Rd., Swanwick
Southampton, Hampshire
S03 7ZL England

Albin Marine, Inc.
143 River Road
Cos Cob, CT 06807
(203) 661-4341

Allmand Boats, Inc.
6969 West 20th Ave.
Hialeah, FL 33014
(305) 821-4070

Alsberg Brothers Boatworks
953-A Tower Place
Santa Cruz, CA 95062
(408) 476-0529

Anchor Marine, Inc.
10967 N. Bayshore Dr.
Sister Bay, WI 54234
(414) 854-2124

Aquarius Performance Yachts, Inc.
P.O. Box 908
Englewood, NJ 07632
(201) 567-8952

Bavaria Yachtbau GmbH
Postfach 14
8701 Giebelstadt
Warzburg, Germany

Bayfield Boat Yard, Ltd.
P.O. Box 1076
Clinton, Ontario
N0M 1L0 Canada
(519) 482-3425

Bristol Yacht Co.
Bristol, RI 02809
(401) 253-5200

Caliber Yacht Corp.
3671 131st Ave. North
Clearwater, FL 33520
(813) 576-0627

Cape Dory
160 Middleboro Ave.
East Taunton, MA 02718
(617) 823-6776

Catalina Yachts
21200 Victory Blvd.
P.O. Box 989
Woodland Hills, CA 91367
(818) 884-7700

Cat Ketch Corp.
3830 Shipping Ave.
Miami, FL 33146
(305) 448-9898

C & C Yachts Ltd.
526 Regent Street
Niagara-on-the-Lake
Ontario, L0S 1J0, Canada
(416) 468-2101

Chantier Henri Wauquiez
174 Boulevard Carnot
59420 Mouvaux, France

Concordia Yacht Sales
South Wharf
South Dartmouth, MA 02748
(617) 999-1381

Cooper Yachts
2700 West Coast Highway
Suite 230
Newport Beach, CA 92663
(714) 642-0152

Cruise Away Yacht Sales
434 City Island Ave.
City Island, NY 10464
(212) 885-3300

CS Yachts Ltd.
79 Bramsteele Rd.
Brampton, Ontario
L6W 3K6 Canada
(416) 457-6713

David Walters Yachts, Ltd.
Lagoon Rd.   Melville
Newport, RI 02840
(401) 683-2700

Dickerson Boatbuilders, Inc.
R.D. 2, Box 92
Trappe, MD 21673
(301) 822-8556

Dodson Boat Yard
P.O. Box 272
Stonington, CT 06378
(203) 535-1507

Endeavour Yacht Corp.
11700 South Belcher Rd.
Largo, FL 33543
(813) 541-3553

Ericson Yachts
1931 Deere Ave.
Irvine, CA 92714
(714) 250-7000

Express Yachting
Div. of 523989 Ont. Ltd.
P.O. Box 697
Midland, Ontario
L4R 4P4 Canada

Formula Yachts
185 South Rd.
Groton, Ct 06340
(203) 445-4413

Freedom Yachts International, Inc.
49 America's Cup Ave.
Newport, RI 02840
(401) 847-7475

Ft. Myers Yacht & Shipbuilding
2909 Frierson St.
Ft. Myers, FL 33901

Gilbert Marine, SA
P.B. 32
17230 Marans, France

Gloucester Yachts, Inc.
P.O. Box 307
Rte. 623
Gloucester, VA 23061
(804) 693-3818

Gulfstar Yacht Sales
Gulfstar Mall
101 16th Ave. South
St. Petersburg, FL 33701
(800) 237-1107
(813) 821-3550 in Florida

Hans Christian Yachts, Inc.
6201 Bayshore Walk   Pier B
Long Beach, CA 90803
(213) 434-2076

Hartmann-Palmer Yachts, Inc.
17201 Biscayne Blvd.
North Miami Beach, FL 33160
(305) 940-6007

Henry R. Hinckley & Co.
Southwest Harbor, ME 04679
(207) 244-5531

Hinterhoeller Yachts
8 Keefer Rd.
St. Catharines, Ontario
L2M 7N9 Canada
(416) 937-4440

Hobie Cat
1925 East Oceanside Blvd.
P.O. Box 1008
Oceanside, CA 92056
(714) 758-9100

Hunter Marine
P.O. Box 1030
Rte. 441
Alachua, FL 32615
(904) 462-3077

Intrepid Yachts
160 Middleboro Ave.
East Taunton, MA 02718

Irwin Yacht & Marine Corp.
13055 49th St. North
Clearwater, FL 33520
(813) 577-4581

Islander Yachts
1922 Barranca Rd.
Irvine, CA 92714
(714) 549-8526

Island Packet Yachts
1979 Wild Acres Rd.
Largo, FL 33541
(813) 535-6431

J Boats
P.O. Box 90
24 Mill St.
Newport, RI 02840
(401) 846-8410

Kadey-Krogen Yachts, Inc.
P.O. Box 350519
Miami, FL 33135
(305) 326-0266

Kanter Yachts Corp.
Industrial Park
9 Barrie Blvd.
St. Thomas, Ontario
N5P 4B9 Canada
(519) 633-1058

La Fitte Yachts, Inc.
Grasonville, MD 21638
Newport Beach, CA 92627

Laguna Yachts, Inc.
10960 Boatman Ave.
Stanton, CA 90680
(714) 527-7262

Lear Siegler Marine
848 Airport Rd.
Fall River, MA 92720-4793
(617) 678-5291

Little Harbor Custom Yachts
Little Harbor Way
Marblehead, MA 01945
(617) 631-8840

MacGregor Yacht Corp.
1631 Placentia
Costa Mesa, CA 92627
(714) 642-6830

Marine Concepts
159 Oakwood St. East
Tarpon Springs, FL 33589
(813) 937-0166

Master Mariners Corp.
2616 Newport Blvd.
Newport Beach, CA 92663
(714) 673-3055

Marshall Marine Corp.
Shipyard Lane
P.O. Box P-266
South Dartmouth, MA 02748
(617) 994-0414

Mirage Manufacturing Co.
3009 N.E. 20th Way
Gainesville, FL 32601
(904) 377-4146

Mirage Yachts, Ltd.
887 Harwood Blvd.
Vaudreuil, Quebec
J7V 5V5 Canada
(514) 455-9177

Mistral Sailboats, Inc.
2187, de la Province
Longueuil, Quebec
J4G 1R2 Canada
(514) 679-6221

Morris Yachts
Clark Point Rd.
Box 58
Southwest Harbor, ME 04679
(207) 244-5866

Nassau Yacht Corp.
P.O. Box 58218
Houston, TX 77058
(713) 280-0070

Nautique International, Inc.
6100 North Keystone
Suite 318
Indianapolis, IN 46220
(317) 251-9199

Nautor East
55 America's Cup Ave.
Newport, RI 02840
(401) 846-8404

New Wave
56 Bridge St.
P.O. Box 478
Newport, RI 02840
(401) 849-2450

Nordic Yachts, Inc.
Box 964
Bellingham, WA 98227
(206) 398-1090

North Castle Marine, Ltd.
P.O. Box 373
Goderich, Ontario
N7A 4C6 Canada
(519) 524-2120

Offshore Yachts
128 Water St.
South Norwalk, CT 06854
(203) 853-0753

Pacific Asian Enterprises, Inc.
Box FA
Dana Point, CA 92629
(714) 496-4848

Pacific Boats, Inc.
1041 17th Ave.
Santa Cruz, CA 95062
(408) 475-8586

Pacific Seacraft Corp.
3301 South Susan St.
Santa Ana, CA 92704-6883
(714) 751-1343

Pearson Yachts
West Shore Rd.
Portsmouth, RI 02871
(401) 683-0100

Rival Yachts, Inc.
Port Annapolis
P.O. Box 4518
Annapolis, MD 21403-6518
(301) 268-2725

Sabre Yachts
Hawthorne Rd.
Box 10
South Casco, ME 04077
(207) 655-3831

Satellite Management, Inc.
P.O. Box 357
Larchmont, NY 10538
(914) 833-0043

Scandvik, Inc.
2190 S.E. 17th St.
Ft. Lauderdale, FL 33316
(305) 524-7666

Scanmar Boats
Varmdovagan 703
13200 Saltjo-Boo
Sweden

Seidelmann Yachts
Cushman Ave.
P.O. Box 2529
Berlin, NJ 08009
(609) 768-1707

Shannon Boat Co., Inc.
19 Broad Common Rd.
Bristol, RI 02809
(401) 253-2441

Southern Offshore Yachts, Inc.
P.O. Box 6
Tarpon Springs, FL 34286-0006
(813) 937-3188

Southwest Marine Sale, Inc.
Seabrook Marina
P.O. Box 447
Seabrook, TX 77586
(713) 474-2576

Sovereign Yacht Co., Inc.
233 Commerce Dr.
Largo, FL 33540
(813) 581-1382

Soverel Marine, Inc.
2225 Idlewilde Rd.
Palm Beach Gardens, FL 33410
(305) 622-9191

Stellar Technology, Inc.
P.O. Box 4612
Middletown, RI 02840
(401) 847-4723

Stevens Yachts of Annapolis, Inc.
P.O. Box 129
Stevensville, MD 21666
(301) 269-0810

S2 Yachts, Inc.
725 East 40th St.
Holland, MI 49423
(616) 392-7163

Ta Chiao, USA, Inc.
17 Lakewood La.
Seabrook, TX 77586
(713) 474-5967

Tanzer Industries, Inc.
P.O. Box 67
Dorion, Quebec
J7V 5V8 Canada
(514) 455-5681

Tartan Marine Co.
320 River St.
Grand River, OH 44045
(216) 354-5671

Ta-Shing Yacht Building Co., Ltd.
4 Shing Yih Rd.
An-Ping Industrial District
Tainan, Taiwan

Valiant Yachts
1325 North Northlake Way
Seattle, WA 98103
(206) 547-1552

Vandestadt & McGruer, Ltd.
Box 7
Owen Sound, Ontario
N4K 5P1 Canada

Vindo North America, Inc.
P.O. Box 1383
New London, NH 03257
(603) 526-9337

W. D. Schock Corp.
3502 South Greenville St.
P.O. Box 26709
Santa Ana, CA 92799-6709
(714) 549-2277

Westover Yachts
105 Rowayton Ave.
P.O. Box 156
Rowayton, CT 06853
(203) 838-3022

Whitby Boat Works, Ltd.
1710 Charles St.
Whitby, Ontario
L1N 1C2 Canada
(416) 668-7755

Windward Maritime Affiliates Corp.
48 Shore Rd.
Glen Cove, NY 11542
(516) 676-0006

Index of Boats

NOTES

NOTES

NOTES

NOTES